FURNITURE AND CABINET MAKING

FURNITURE AND CABINET MAKING

John L. Feirer

Bennett
Publishing
Company

Peoria, Illinois 61615

Distributed to the book trade by
Charles Scribner's Sons
New York

84 85 86 87 RRD 5 4 3 2

ISBN 0-02-664050-3
(Previously ISBN 0-87002-388-8)

Library of Congress Catalog Card Number: 82-72259

Printed in the United States of America

Cover art courtesy of Riviera Kitchens, an Evans Products Company

Preface

FURNITURE AND CABINET MAKING is designed for anyone interested in the fundamentals of materials, tools, machines, and processes used in the building of furniture and the production of cabinets. This book can be used in senior high school, in vocational and technical schools, and in colleges. It will be useful for studying not only cabinetmaking but also building construction and related activities. It includes coverage of which woods to use and tells why and how to use them. Fixed installations such as built-ins and cabinets are discussed, as well as furniture.

In our industrialized world, the cabinetmaker and finish carpenter require knowledge and skills that are very similar. Either of these can profit by using this book. So can people entering any business or profession which relates to furniture, building construction, or other wood industries. The prospective interior designer, the furniture designer, the industrial education teacher, the architect, and those who sell lumber and lumber products will all find valuable information in these pages. This book should also have great appeal to anyone who likes to work with woods as a hobby.

FURNITURE AND CABINET MAKING is divided into five sections, each dealing with a different aspect of woodworking.

Section I covers the history of cabinetmaking, the major furniture styles, and the elements and principles of design. It also discusses woodworking as a vocation and as a hobby, and it reviews important safety rules.

Section II, "Materials and Layouts," includes chapters on the nature and properties of wood and the common wood species used for furniture, as well as information on plywood, hardboard, particle board, and other manufactured wood products. Since most furniture includes hardware and has some parts made of plastic or other nonwood materials, these items are also covered. Section II also describes how to plan a woodworking project: estimating and ordering materials, reading prints, making a layout, and so on.

Section III, "Tools and Machines," gives detailed information for using hand and power tools and machinery. These chapters contain step-by-step instructions for dozens of woodworking operations, including surfacing and squaring up stock; ripping and crosscutting; cutting joints, curves, and tapers; shaping; routing; drilling; sanding; and woodturning. Safety and maintenance are emphasized; each chapter on power tools has a special section of tips for safe use and proper maintenance.

Construction techniques are covered in Section IV. This section includes chapters on joinery; gluing and clamping; frame-and-panel construction; doors; drawers; shelves; legs, posts, and feet; tabletops; and many others. Various levels of construction, from simple to complex, are presented.

"Finishing," Section V, describes the various techniques for finishing wood cabinets and furniture. This section discusses the equipment, supplies, and procedures needed to produce an attractive and durable finish for any project.

A special attempt has been made to design this book with visual appeal. It contains over 1500 drawings and photographs. Two-color printing has been used throughout to emphasize the important points of each process or procedure. The layout has been designed so that illustrations are placed as close as possible to their text references. Throughout this book, the importance of cabinetmaking to the woodworking field has been stressed.

Acknowledgments

Corporations

Adjustable Clamp Co.
Airco Ophthalmic Products
Ajax Hardware Corp.
American Chair Co.
American Forest Products Industries
American Hardboard Association
American of Martinsville
American Plywood Association
Amerock
Architectural Woodworking Institute
Arist O Kraft—Beatrice Foods Co.
Armstrong Cork Co.
Arvids Iraids Multipurpose Spring
    Clamps
Athens Home Decor
Auto-Nailer Co.
Avco Corp.
Baker Furniture Co.
Bara Industries Corp.
Barton Wood Products, Inc.
G. M. Basford Co.
Bassett Furniture Industries
Baumritter Corp.
Behr-Manning Division of Norton
    Co.
Robert Benjamin, Inc.
George B. Bent Co.
Better Homes and Gardens
The Black and Decker
    Manufacturing Co.
The Black Brothers' Co.
Bostitch, Inc.
The Brandt Cabinet Works, Inc.
Brett-Guard Corp.
British Columbia Industrial Design
    Committee
Broyhill Furniture Industries
Buck Brothers Co.
Burris Industries
California Redwood Association
Ronald C. Carriker Photography
Caterpillar Tractor Co.
Century Furniture Co.
Chaircraft, Inc.
Clamp Nail Co.
Clausing Corp.
Cleveland Twist Drill Co.
Thayer Coggin, Inc.
Columbia Fastener Co.

Comet Industries Corp.
Conant Ball Furniture Makers
Conap, Inc.
The Condé Nast Publications, Inc.
Congoleum Corp.
Crestwood Kitchens, Ltd.
H. T. Cushman Manufacturing Co.
Dansk Designs, Inc.
DelMar
The DeVilbiss Co.
Directional Industries, Inc.
Disston Saw Co.
DM Furniture, Inc.
Domore Office Furniture
Drexel Heritage Furnishings, Inc.
Drez Co.
Dunbar Furniture Corp.
E. I. duPont de Nemours & Co.,
    Inc.
Duro Metal Products Co.
Dux, Inc.
Era Industries, Inc.
Ethan Allen
Evans Products Co.
Filon Division of Vistron Corp.
Fine Hardwoods Association
Foley Saw Co.
Formica Corp.
Forms Surfaces Co.
Francher Furniture Co.
The Franklin Glue Co.
Furniture Design and Manufacturing
General Electric Co.
Georgia-Pacific Corp.
The Otto Gerdan Co.
Gizco
Gold Medal, Inc.
Greenlee Bros. and Co.
The Gunlocke Co.
Haas Cabinet Co.
Hamilton Manufacturing Co.
Handy Manufacturing Co.
Hardwood Plywood Institute
Hekman Furniture Co.
Imperial Furniture Co.
Independent Nail and Packing Co.
International Paper Co.
IXL Furniture
Jansen Furniture Co.
Jens Risom Design, Inc.

B. P. John Furniture Co.
Johnson Furniture Co.
Junior Achievement, Inc.
Keller
Kemper/Tappan
Kitchen Kompacts, Inc.
Kittinger Company, Inc.
Knape and Vogt Manufacturing Co.
Knoll Associated, Inc.
Koehring Corp.
The Lane Company, Inc.
Laskowski Enterprises, Inc.
Mahogany Association, Inc.
B. L. Marble Furniture, Inc.
Martin Senour Paints
Masonite Corp.
Medallion Kitchens, Inc.
Merit Abrasive Products, Inc.
Howard Miller Clock Co.
Millers Falls Co.
Minnesota Mining and
    Manufacturing Co.
Module Grille Co.
Mohawk Furniture Finishing
    Products, Inc.
Molly Corp.
Benjamin Moore and Co.
Mutschler Brothers Co.
Myrtle Desk Co.
National Association of Furniture
    Manufacturers
National Lock Co.
National Lumber Manufacturers
    Association
National of Mt. Airy, NC
National Particleboard Association
National Safety Council
National Woodwork Manufacturers
    Association
Neal Small Designs
Noblecraft Industries, Inc.
Northfield Foundry and Machine Co.
Oliver Machinery Co.
Owens Corning Fiberglas Corp.
Patroit Industries, Inc.
Frank Paxton Lumber Co.
Pennsylvania House
Perkins Glue Co.
Philippine Mahogany Association,
    Inc.

Phillips Petroleum Co.
Pittsburgh Plate Glass Co.
Powermatic, Inc.
Red Devil Tools
Riverside Furniture Corp.
Riviera Kitchens Division of Evans Products
Rockwell Manufacturing Co.
Rohm and Haas Co.
Ronthor Reiss Corp.
Saranac Machine Co.
Scandiline Furniture, Inc.
Scandinavian Design, Inc.
H. J. Scheirich Co.
Senco Products, Inc.
Seth Thomas, Inc.
Shakeproof—Division of Illinois Tool Works, Inc.
Sherwin-Williams Co.
Shopsmith, Inc.
Simonds Saw and Steel Co.
Simpson Magazine—Betty Johnson and Karen Johnson
Simpson Timber Co.
Singer Corp.
Skil Corp.
Slight Furniture Co.
Southern Hardwood Lumber Manufacturers Association
Southern Pine Association

Sperry and Hutchinson Furniture Co.
Stanley Tools
Star Chemical Company, Inc.
Statton Furniture Manufacturing Co.
John Stuart, Inc.
George Tanier, Inc.
Thomas Industries, Inc.
Thomasville Furniture Industries, Inc.
Thonet Industries, Inc.
Tomlinson Furniture Co.
Toolmark Co.
Triangle Pacific Corp.
UGL
Union City Chair Co.
Union-National, Inc.
USDA Forest Service, Forest Products Laboratory
United States Gypsum
U.S. Industries, Inc.
United States Plywood Corp.
Universal Furniture Industries, Inc.
Vecta Contract Co.
Victorian Furniture Corp.
Vistron Corp.
Vocational Industrial Clubs of America
Watco-Dennis Corp.
Weldotron Corp.

Wesley Pusey
West Coast Lumbermen's Association
Western Electric Co.
Western Wood Moulding and Millwork Producers
Western Wood Products Association
Westinghouse Electric Corp.
Weyerhaeuser Co.
John Widdicomb Co.
Winchendon Furniture Co.
Window Shade Manufacturers Association
Wisconsin Knife Co.
Wood-Mode Kitchens
Woodwork Institute of California
The Woodworker's Store
Woodworking Machinery Manufacturers of America
WorkRite Products Co.
Xacto Co.
Yorktowne Cabinets, Inc.

Individuals
Karen Jamison, NJ VICA
Keith Klobucar
Carlton Moe
Janet Rosenblum
Peter Strazdas
Jim Thomas

Table of Contents

Section I

INTRODUCTION

The Art and Craft of Cabinetmaking

1

Cabinetmaking is as old as civilization. Since the days when people began building shelters in which to live, they have made furniture in some form. Furniture is built to serve a function; it is used for seating, sleeping, eating, or storage. But it also serves as a medium for creative expression. Since early times, cabinetmakers have used carving, turned work, inlay, and ornamentation to enrich and beautify their furniture. Fig. 1-1.

HISTORY OF CABINETMAKING

While there is not a great deal of information on the first furniture that people used, it is known that tribes in Africa and Polynesia made stools and head rests. These were usually carved from solid pieces of wood.

Five thousand years ago, Egyptians made fine furniture that was artistically carved, inlaid with gold, ivory, and silver, and sometimes veneered and painted with designs. The wooden furniture was sometimes overlaid with gold foil. Fig. 1-2.

The people of ancient Greece also made beautiful furniture of oak, cedar, and olive wood. They adorned the pieces with precious metals and added cushions covered with fine fabrics. Greek furniture had great beauty and perfection of form. Greek principles of design are still applied to present-day standards of good design.

The Romans adapted the Greek standards and elaborated on them with greater use of curved lines and carvings. The Romans used bronze for tables and chairs, and they used marble for tabletops. Except for fancy carving and inlays, furniture in those years was not very different from furniture of today.

During the Middle Ages (A.D. 500 to 1500), little furniture was produced in Europe. The only people who could afford good furniture were the nobility, and even they did not own much. It was a common practice for visitors to bring their own beds with them.

The latter Middle Ages did bring some new developments in furniture. In the early 1400s framed paneling was introduced in the

1-2. *The Egyptians built folding stools like this one that were finely carved and inlaid.*

Netherlands. (Although framed paneling had been known by the Romans, this construction technique had been long forgotten.) The reintroduction of framed paneling was an important event in cabinetmaking. Before that time, much construction was done using wide boards (planks). These had several disadvantages. The front of a cupboard, for example, was limited to the size of the plank that could be obtained. The planks often warped and cracked. Framed paneling made it possible to construct furniture with larger surface areas, without as much danger of the wood warping or splitting. Other new developments in cabinetmaking were the invention of drawers for storage furniture and the use of better joints, such as the miter and the mortise and tenon.

1-1. *The cabinetmaker seeks to build furniture that is beautiful as well as functional.*

The Renaissance brought a renewed interest in the finer things in life. There were more wealthy people, and their desire for luxury and beauty encouraged a surge of creativity. Skilled woodworkers of this period labored continuously to increase the variety of designs. The Renaissance, beginning in Italy in the fifteenth century, gradually brought about a complete change in the furniture of Europe. The purpose of a piece of furniture became less important than its form.

During and shortly after the Renaissance, from the fifteenth to the seventeenth centuries, there was an increased interest in fine woodworking for both interiors and home furnishings. Custom furniture making reached the height of individual achievement during the eighteenth century. This period was known as the Golden Age of furniture design. Fig. 1-3. The English designers Thomas Chippendale, George Hepplewhite, Thomas Sheraton, and Robert and James Adam set the standards. Many of their apprentices came to America and established shops of their own. Then, as production machines began to produce furniture less expensively, most such furniture makers closed up shop.

Duncan Phyfe, an immigrant from Scotland, was the only American designer and furniture maker for whom a style of furniture was named. At one time he employed as many as one hundred cabinetmakers, turning out some of the finest furniture then available. He was forced to close his shop when the machine began to take over the manufacture of furniture.

Cabinetmakers for interior work did not become active again in the United States until the late nineteenth century. During that time, the popularity of circular stairways and decorative wood panels created great demand for skilled cabinetmakers.

HISTORY OF MILLWORK

In the early history of the United States, homes were built almost entirely by hand on the site. These early homes, some of which can still be seen, included excellent examples of cabinetmaking created by the early carpenters who made their own doors, shutters, moldings, and trim. In many cases, the skills and knowledge of early carpenter-cabinetmakers were acquired in the Old World. Some of these people excelled in fabricating more complicated wood items such as windows, doors, and cabinets. They emerged as the *millwrights* who set up wood shops to fill the needs of local communities. The millwright's counterpart is still found in custom shops, mills, and furniture plants.

THE KEY TO ALL WOODWORKING

Cabinetmaking is the key to all woodworking. Its basic skills and knowledge are needed by all those who work in wood, whether or not they carry the title of cabinetmaker. Fig. 1-4.

Look at the description of what

14

1-3. *The great cabinetmakers of eighteenth-century England achieved such stately, balanced beauty in furniture design that their creations have outlasted the fads of many succeeding generations.*

1-4. *The same basic skills are needed for all types of woodworking. The woodworker must know how to select, lay out, cut, shape, join, and finish wood.*

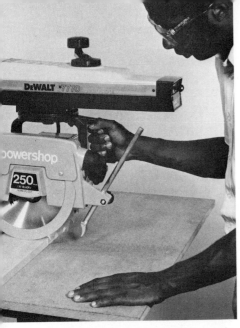

1-5. *Cabinetmakers operate a variety of power tools, such as the radial-arm saw.*

cabinetmakers must be able to do: They perform hand and machine operations to lay out, cut, shape, and assemble high-quality products for furniture, cabinets, store fixtures, office equipment, and home furniture. They study drawings of products and lay out an outline or dimension of the parts on the stock to certain specifications. They also operate such woodworking machines as the radial-arm saw, circular saw, band saw, jointer, mortiser, and others, to cut and shape parts. Fig. 1-5. They bore holes for installing screws or dowels by hand or machine. They add glue to parts and clamp them together. They insert nails, dowels, and screws through joints to reinforce them. They glue and fit sub-assemblies and other parts together to form completed units. They smooth surfaces with scrapers and sandpaper and also install hardware such as hinges, catches, and drawer pulls.

There are some who still think of the cabinetmaker as a specialized woodworker who laboriously builds a piece of furniture using hand tools and hand-controlled machine tools. Such cabinetmakers are rare, however. Today most furniture is mass produced. Yet the "know-how" of

cabinetmaking is becoming increasingly important to the finish carpenter, millwright, patternmaker, and even the boat builder. Today a little fewer than 100,000 persons are employed strictly as cabinetmakers. The closely associated field of carpentry, however, is the largest skilled trade in the United States. It employs over one million people.

In carpentry there are two types of work: rough carpentry and finish carpentry. Let's look at the work of the finish carpenters. They cut, fit, and install moldings, baseboards, door frames, doors, hardwood floors, windows, kitchen and bathroom cabinets and built-ins, and paneling. Fig. 1-6. They perform a wide variety of other work requiring the skillful use of many different tools and machines. Their work must be done accurately and carefully.

Note the similarity between the two occupational groups of finish carpenter and cabinetmaker. Many of the same skills and knowledge are required by both. The need for cabinetmaking skills is increasing. With more production-type homes being built, there is great need for woodworkers who can do the details of finish carpentry. Today more than ever the finish carpenter must know excellent cabinetmaking. In better-quality homes, a large part of the total cost is involved in the labor and materials that go into paneling, cabinetwork, and built-ins. Many of today's cabinets are equal in quality —as far as materials, work, and finish are concerned—to some of our finest furniture. Fig. 1-7. Many house plans include designs for special furniture that must be custom-built by the skilled carpenter or cabinetmaker.

1-6. *This finish carpenter is installing paneling in a home.*

SURVEY OF OCCUPATIONS

Following is a survey of some major occupational areas that either require skill in cabinetmaking or are associated with the trade:

Vocational and Skilled Occupations

The *cabinetmaker* may be an all-around woodworker or a specialist such as an assembler, a bench worker, a cabinet-frame assembler, a detailer, or a layout person.

The *finish carpenter* may be an all-around skilled carpenter or specialize in some particular area of work such as installing plastic laminates, building kitchen cabinets, or installing paneling and trim.

The *maintenance cabinetmaker* may repair furniture, sharpen and

1-7. *Building and installing cabinets of this quality can be done only by the skilled woodworker.*

15

1-8. *The interior designer must not only understand furniture design and construction but must also have artistic talent for selecting fabrics and wallcoverings.*

adjust equipment, or make jigs and fixtures. This person may be designated according to the product made, such as "piano-case maker."

Professional and Semi-Professional Occupations

The wood industry offers thousands of opportunities to enter one of the professional or semi-professional occupations in which a knowledge of cabinetmaking is required. While most of these careers do not demand that you actually use tools and machines to fabricate wood products, this "know-how" will make you much more successful in your field or specialty. For example, an interior designer who knows woods, finishing, and construction can be far more creative than one who knows only the aesthetics of decorating. The business executive in the building-construction industry or in furniture manufacturing can do a much better job with a background in cabinetmaking. For best advantage in one of the many professional careers, you must plan to complete a college degree in a program such as Industrial Education, General Forestry, Wood Technology, Furniture Manufacturing, Wood Products Engineering, or Architecture. Following are some of the major careers:

A *modelmaker* uses wood and clay to make models for production.

Some modelmakers work in the automotive and aircraft industries, while others specialize in making architectural models. Modelmakers also work in the theater, television, and motion-picture industries making set models.

Interior designers must know furnishings and woods in order to select correct styles of furniture, design custom furniture, and specify the specialized cabinetmaking necessary for interior decorating. Fig. 1-8.

The *industrial education teacher* is responsible for teaching students the fundamentals of tools, materials, and processes relating to the use of wood products. Fig. 1-9.

The *forester* is responsible for supervising the growth and harvest of timber crops and for other activities that supply raw materials to the forest-products industry. Fig. 1-10.

The *wood technologist*, *wood products engineer*, or *scientist* may work at any one of a wide variety of jobs in research and development, production, and sales. In the forest-

1-9. *This industrial education teacher has an interesting occupation. He works with people to show them the use of tools and materials.*

1-10. *This forester is checking the size of trees to determine their rate of growth.*

16

1-11. *These wood chemists are making laboratory tests of wood materials.*

products industry there are thousands of chemists, physicists, engineers, and technologists who continually search for new and better ways to use wood as well as its fibers and extractives. Fig. 1-11.

Thousands of others, working as professional managers and supervisors, are responsible for the technical operations in construction and wood-products manufacturing.

Many other professional people are needed for work in lumbering,

1-12. *Each structure that architects design must have a distinct character.*

plywood and furniture manufacture, and in other types of production plants. Those who work in product sales must have a first-hand knowledge of their products, from the raw lumber to finished items. Those who sell equipment and materials in the woodworking fields need to know everything they can learn about what they are selling.

The *architect* designs all kinds of homes and other structures. He or she must know materials. Fig. 1-12.

The *furniture designer* must have creative ability as well as drafting skills and knowledge of cabinetmaking.

Training Requirements for Cabinetmaking

Well over a million people are employed in the woodworking craft trades which require the skills and knowledge of cabinetmaking. The requirements for all of these occupations are very similar. If you wish to enter the woodworking field as a skilled worker, you must be able to use hand and machine tools for cutting, shaping, fitting, and assembling parts made of wood and related materials. You must also have a good general education which includes the ability to read technical literature and prints and do mathematics through algebra. After this general education, you must complete a specialized educational training program of at least two to four years. This may include vocational or technical education as well as an apprenticeship.

To do cabinetmaking, you must have the temperament to enjoy variety or change of work since jobs tend to be somewhat different from each other. You must be able to set limits, tolerances, and standards of accuracy. You should be interested in things and objects showing tangible results. You should find satisfaction from building and producing something with your own hands.

All woodworking crafts require

1-13. *Many people like to refinish furniture.*

only medium strength, but they also include a great deal of kneeling, stooping, reaching, and handling. Most jobs are inside, although there may be some outside work. You must be willing to work in an area that is relatively noisy and vibrant. Most jobs involve some hazard, since the work includes handling materials and working with sharp cutting tools, both hand- and power-operated.

CABINETMAKING AS A HOBBY

You may not want to enter one of the woodworking occupations as a lifework. There are few people, however, who do not enjoy working with wood. As a matter of fact, woodworking is the most popular creative hobby in this country. You may want to build a piece of furniture, install a cabinet, or design and build a wood model. There is genuine joy of accomplishment in working with woods as you cut, shape, fit, assemble, and finish something of your own design or selection. Knowing something about woodworking will also be useful when you want to repair and refinish old furniture. Fig. 1-13. Woodworking skills and knowledge will be of value to you all of your life, both on the job and as a hobby.

17

Furniture Styles

People live in many different places: in houses and condominiums, apartments and mobile homes, and in unusual places such as boats or motor homes. Regardless of its location, size, shape, or design, our home is an important part of our life. A home should be pleasant and comfortable. It should be suitable to the life style and tastes of the people who live there.

One thing that gives a home its character is the furniture. Today there are many styles from which to choose. In selecting or building furniture or cabinets, there are three major categories to consider: Traditional, Provincial, and Contemporary. Within these categories are many variations to suit different needs and tastes.

TRADITIONAL

Most of the Traditional styles had their beginning in the royal courts of eighteenth-century Europe. Furniture styles associated with monarchies include Queen Anne, Georgian, and Louis XV. Styles were also named for their designers. Prominent English furniture designers included Thomas Chippendale, George Hepplewhite, Thomas Sheraton, and the Brothers Adam (Robert and James). Figs. 2-1 through 2-3.

The American colonists adopted many of the English designs as their own. The people of eighteenth-century Williamsburg, for example, furnished their homes using both English imports and American pieces. The American designer Duncan Phyfe was influenced by the work of the English as well as the French designers. American interpretations of the European styles gave rise to the Federal style (about 1790 to 1820).

2-1.

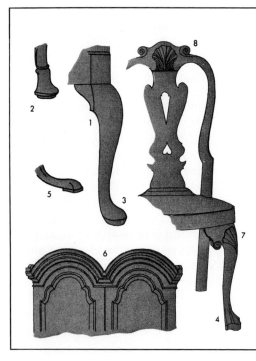

QUEEN ANNE

Queen Anne, second daughter of James II, ruled England from 1702 until 1714. The furniture style that bears her name, however, covers a period of forty years and includes the reign of George I and part of the reign of George II.

The style developed during this age of flourishing craftsmanship is considered one of the most graceful of the century. Its most distinctive feature is an undulating line based on the "S" or cyma curve—an unbroken line with a convex and concave curve. William Hogarth, the celebrated 18th-century English painter and engraver, called this curve the "line of beauty."

The most fashionable wood was walnut, but mahogany was introduced about 1720. With the use of this wood, furniture became lighter and more graceful. Elaborate carving, to which mahogany was especially suited, began to appear.

The Queen Anne chair is perhaps the most familiar design of the period. It has an extremely comfortable splat often shaped to fit the back. Card tables with turnover hinged tops, small tables, and lower chests of drawers were popular.

Characteristics of the Queen Anne style as interpreted in America were cabriole legs (1) with numerous forms of the foot: hoof (2), pad (3), trifid (4), and slipper (5). The claw-and-ball foot was also used during this time.

Other characteristics of this style are scroll tops on chests (6), and scalloped shells on knees of legs (7) and on crests of chairs (8).

CHIPPENDALE

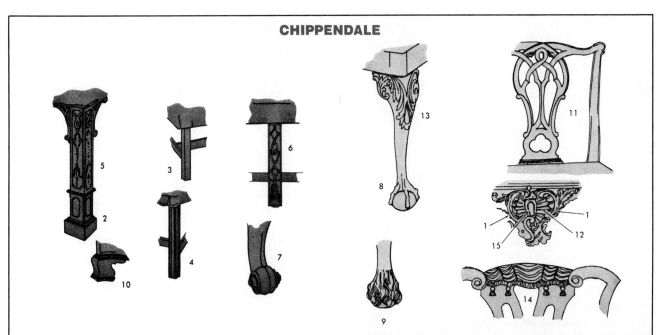

Thomas Chippendale, the best-known and best-advertised figure in the history of furniture-making, was born about 1705 and died in 1779. The first cabinetmaker to have his name associated with a furniture style, Chippendale was paradoxically a master of the derivative. Rarely inventive, he borrowed elements from Gothic, Chinese, and French designs and translated them into a new style.

Walnut and fruit woods, as well as mahogany, were widely used in America at this time, while English cabinetmakers preferred mahogany, an excellent wood for the crisp carving associated with Chippendale. Other popular Chippendale motifs included rococo or asymmetrical designs, simulated Chinese bamboo, the "C" scroll (1), and extensive use of fretwork.

The Chippendale straight leg, often terminating in a distinct Marlborough foot (2), was plain (3), fluted (4), carved (5), or decorated with applied frets (6). His cabriole leg was supported by the following types of feet: scroll or French toe (7), claw-and-ball (8), and hairy paw (9). The ogee bracket foot (10) was often used on case pieces. Characteristic carved forms were the pierced or interlaced splat (11), tattered shell (12), acanthus leaf (13), drapery (14), and cabochon (15).

2-2.

2-3.

FEDERAL

American furniture of the late 18th century and early 19th century was tremendously affected by the designs of Hepplewhite and Sheraton. Their books and examples inspired the Federal Period style, its beauty derived from a simplicity of line and form, embellished with contrasts of inlay and veneer.

Distinctive features of the Hepplewhite inspired designs were the shield-shape chair backs (1), carved drapery (2), bell flowers (3), and sheaves of wheat (4).

Sheraton used rectangular chair backs (5), rounded and tapered legs with reeding or fluting (6), spiral turnings (7), and brass terminals (8).

The celebrated Duncan Phyfe was one of many American cabinetmakers influenced by the Sheraton style. The scroll back chair (9) is attributed to him—1810-1820, in New York City. The use of the carved eagle is typical of the individuality of American cabinetmakers as the Federal Period style evolved from the English designs. The work table (10) top and legs were a favorite form crafted in the early 1800's in Salem, Massachusetts.

2-6. *Chippendale tea table, also known as a piecrust table because of its raised, carved edge. The top tilts up so that the table can be placed against a wall when not in use. Note the claw-and-ball feet on the cabriole legs.*

2-4. *The romanticism of Louis XV brought human scale, grace, and comfort to furniture. This modern adaptation features fine carving and delicate curves. Note the cabriole legs, which are thinner than those of the English furniture styles.*

These eighteenth-century styles were graceful and well-proportioned. They made use of fine woods such as walnut, mahogany, and satinwood. Delicate carvings, marquetry, and gilding decorated the furniture. Fabrics on upholstered pieces were rich and elegant, often employing elaborate needlework.

Modern Interpretations

Most of the Traditional furniture made today is an adaptation of eighteenth-century styles rather than an exact copy. Today's Traditional furniture is less ornate, and modern finishes are used. Many pieces are scaled down for today's smaller rooms. Quality Traditional furniture retains the grace and elegance of the eighteenth century while suiting the needs and tastes of today. Figs. 2-4 through 2-6.

PROVINCIAL

Many furniture makers in the rural areas and small towns of France, England, and the United

2-5. *Queen Anne. The cabriole legs on the chairs and table are characteristic of this style. The game table features an inlaid chess or checker board and is made of mahogany with veneers of mahogany, cherry burl, and maple. The center section can be turned over for a plain surface.*

2-7. *Dining room furniture made of antiqued oak in the English countryside manner. Much of the furniture of early England was imported from Italy, Spain, and France. It was ornate and massive. When the local craftspeople of England produced their versions, they simplified much of the design.*

CONTEMPORARY

Contemporary, sometimes called Modern, varies greatly in design. Some Contemporary furniture is very austere because of its heavy use of chrome, glass, plastic, and smooth-surfaced upholstery. Other Contemporary is made of traditional materials such as wood and natural textiles. In general, Contemporary furniture is functional, simple in form, and has a minimum of ornamentation. It makes wide use of manufactured products (plastics, foam, synthetic fabrics, etc.) and machine processes (such as laminating, wood bending, and molding). Fig. 2-9.

OTHER INFLUENCES

Traditional, Provincial, and Contemporary are the major categories of furniture styles today. As stated earlier, there are many variations within these styles. There are also styles which do not fit easily into any of the major categories.

Victorian furniture (about 1840 to

States did not have the material or equipment to produce the finely styled furniture associated with Traditional. Thus Provincial furniture developed. It was a country interpretation of the high styles found in the city. French Provincial, for example, has been influenced by the designs of Louis XV and Louis XVI. Mediterranean is a country style that combines the influence of France, Spain, and Italy. American Colonial and some Early American can also be classified as Provincial furniture.

Early Provincial furniture was usually made of solid wood because this material was readily available. The work of the country woodworker was informal, rugged, and durable —well suited to country life. Today's Provincial furniture is patterned after these styles. Figs. 2-7 and 2-8.

2-8. *Provincial furniture is practical and simpler in design than Traditional furniture. A good example is the trestle table in this dining room set. The first trestle tables were simply boards laid on top of supports. After the meal, they could be taken apart and put away. This was a useful feature in homes where one room had to serve as kitchen, dining room, living room, and bedroom.*

2-9. *Contemporary furniture finished with plastic and chrome. The simple rectangular forms, the smooth finish, and the absence of drawer pulls and knobs give this bedroom set its modern look.*

2-11. *Many cultures have influenced our furniture designs. This end table reveals an Oriental influence.*

1900) is an example. Victorian was actually a blend of numerous styles from the past: Sheraton, Empire, Louis XIV, Gothic, Renaissance, Oriental, and others. It was massive and elaborate. Although not widely used today, some Victorian furniture is still being made. Fig. 2-10.

Oriental furniture is another example. During the eighteenth century, increased trade with China brought Oriental influences to European furnishings. Chippendale, for example, used Chinese fretwork, bamboo forms, and lacquer on some of his furniture. Since that time, Oriental has periodically enjoyed popularity.

Currently there is renewed interest in Oriental furniture and accessories. The pure, simple lines of Oriental blend well with many Traditional and Contemporary pieces. Fig. 2-11.

ECLECTIC

Most people acquire their furniture over a period of years and from various sources. *Eclectic* decorating combines two or more styles of furniture to achieve a look that is lively and highly individual. Some pieces may be Traditional in design, while others are Provincial or Contemporary. All of these, with the correct accessories, rugs, wallcoverings, and drapes, can blend together into a very pleasing and livable room. Fig. 2-12.

2-10. *This Victorian chair is a copy of one that was made 100 years ago.*

2-12. *Here Traditional, Provincial, and Contemporary pieces are combined in a living room that is pleasant and comfortable.*

3 Designing Furniture and Cabinets

Good furniture and cabinet design should be determined by the need to live with things that are comfortable, convenient, pleasing in appearance, sturdy, and easy to maintain. Fig. 3-1. If a piece of furniture meets most of these requirements, the chances are that it is well designed.

It is almost impossible to make a list of specific rules that will produce a well-designed piece. Taste and a feeling for good design can be acquired by observing quality furniture in homes, stores, magazines, and books. Many of the designs that appear on the following pages are the work of the finest furniture designers in America today. All illustrate better than average design. While certain styles may not appeal to you or suit your needs, still they represent quality furniture and cabinets.

FUNDAMENTALS OF GOOD DESIGN

The fundamentals of good design include purpose or function, appearance, materials, and construction.

Function

A product is well designed only if it meets the need for which it is intended. For example, the function of a chair is to provide seating. To function *well*, a chair must be comfortable. Chairs are made in different heights and seat depths. The angle between the seat and chair back also varies. These and other

dimensions must be designed so that a person can sit in the chair comfortably.

Thus you see that furniture sizes are influenced by the sizes of human beings. The designer makes a careful study of the human body to determine furniture needs. Fig. 3-2.

Equally important, the designer must know the answer to the question, "For what will the piece be used?" A chest, for example, must be designed for storage, but what

will be stored: books, clothing, utensils, or other items? Only when this is known can many other points be decided, such as height of the chest and size of drawers.

Appearance

The furniture piece or cabinet must be "in tune" with the user's personality. Even though two chests may be equally efficient for storage, one may have greater appeal simply because of its appearance. Fig. 3-3(a).

3-1. *Furniture that is well designed is not only attractive now but will remain so in years to come.*

AVERAGE FURNITURE DIMENSIONS

Item	Length (Inches)	Depth-Width (Inches)	Height (Inches)
DINING TABLE	60	42	29
KITCHEN TABLE	42	30	30
CARD TABLE	36	36	30
COFFEE TABLE	36-60	18-24	15-18
COFFEE TABLE round	36 dia.		15-18
END TABLE	24	15	24
DRUM TABLE	36 dia.		30
LAMP TABLE	24 dia.		30
DESK	48	24	30
SECRETARY	36	24	84
LOWBOY	30	18	30
HIGHBOY	36	18	60-84
BREAKFRONT BOOKCASE	48-60	18	78-84
SOFA	72	30	36
LOVE SEAT	48	30	36
OCCASIONAL CHAIR	27	30	36
OCCASIONAL CHAIR armless	24	30	30
WING CHAIR	30	30	36
DINING, DESK, FOLDING CHAIR	18	18	30
TWIN BED	78	39	20-23
DOUBLE BED	78	54	20-23
DRESSER	42-60	22	32-36

3-2. *Average dimensions of common furniture pieces.*

People have strong preferences for different styles of furniture. That is why so many styles are on the market. For some, the informality of Contemporary seems best. To others, furniture in the classic Traditional fashion is more appealing. Still others prefer the elegance of French Provincial.

Furniture and cabinets that are true to their own particular style are attractive and, in most cases, represent the principles of good design. When established styles are disregarded, poor design usually results. In furniture that you construct, why not try to express your tastes by making your own development of some established style? You will find this a true test of originality. Fig. 3-3(b).

Materials

Materials selected for furniture must be right for both use and style. It is possible to imitate a more expensive hardwood with one

3-3(α). *These two chests are almost identical in size and usefulness. Which one would you choose?*

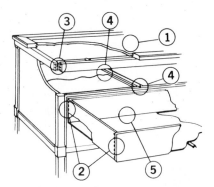

3-5. *Fine construction in a cabinet or chest: 1. Exposed panels are of five-ply veneer construction for maximum strength, durability, and uniformity of grain character and color. 2. Drawers are dovetailed and made of carefully finished, solid hardwood. 3. Double-dowel construction of case goods provides a close, strong joint. 4. Drawers are fitted with solid hardwood guides and wood, metal, or plastic runners to insure smooth operation. 5. All drawers are dustproofed.*

3-4. *This high-quality bookcase uses solid wood for the posts and other structural parts, but veneers are used on the door fronts and other large surfaces.*

3-3(b). *One of these piecrust tilt-top tables was designed and built by a student. The other is a commercial product. Can you tell which one was built in the school lab?*

of lesser quality. For example, gumwood is sometimes stained to imitate mahogany. However, this practice would never deceive anyone who knows fine furniture woods.

The fine hardwoods possess great beauty and durability, but it must be remembered that well-designed furniture also makes use of plywoods. Fine hardwood plywoods are ideal for the large, flat surfaces of

chests, tables, and cabinets. There are still people who consider the term *veneer* to mean something of inferior quality. Actually, good veneers, properly used, can enhance the value of a product. Fig. 3-4. Quality furniture today also makes use of many nonwood materials such as plastic laminates, ceramics, tile, metal, glass, cane, and textiles.

Construction

The construction of furniture and cabinets must be basically sound. Fig. 3-5. Good joinery should be the rule throughout the product. Flimsy construction in itself is poor design. A table that is wobbly or a chair that tips is useless. If the glue joints don't hold, the product is worthless.

Quality furniture construction means building to last a long time with minimum maintenance. It also means that if two construction

methods provide equal durability and sturdiness, the less expensive method should be followed. In chairs and tables, for example, modern adhesives with dowels and corner blocks on legs and rails are just as effective as mortise-and-tenon joints. Furniture intended for hard use, as in motels or in homes with small children, is often made with plastic laminates for the tops of chests, desks, and tables. Frequently these materials closely match the grain of fine wood veneer. The resulting product is just as attractive, lasts longer, and is easier to maintain than one made entirely of wood.

There are several basic ways in which furniture and cabinets are put together. The most important of these are:

One-member pieces. These are made from a single piece of wood. Most of these are small items, principally accessories. Fig. 3-6.

Duplicate parts. Most pieces of furniture have two or more duplicate

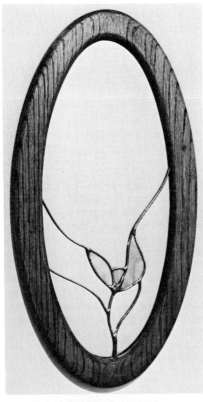

3-6. *A small one-piece oval mirror.*

3-7. *This wall cabinet has many duplicate parts.*

parts. In some of the smaller accessories, the duplicate parts are the dominant feature. Fig. 3-7.

Leg-and-rail. Leg-and-rail (sometimes called frame) construction is used for most standard chairs, tables, benches, and beds. In table designs this usually consists of four legs and four or more rails. The structural parts are usually of solid wood, while the top may be particle board or lumber-core plywood. The rails are usually joined to the legs with dowels and corner blocks, or with mortise-and-tenon joints. Fig. 3-8.

Box. A box consists of four sides, with the grains running in the same direction, and a bottom. The corners are joined with any kind of satisfactory joint, ranging from a simple butt joint to a fine finger or dovetail joint. The bottom is usually fastened to the sides by means of a rabbet. The box may or may not

have a cover. A drawer is an example of a simple box without a cover. Fig. 3-9.

Case. Case construction is usually a box turned on its side. This is typical of chest construction, bookcases, cabinets, and many built-ins. The back is often enclosed by cutting a rabbet around the inside and fastening in a panel. The front may be trimmed with molding or with some kind of edging. The shelves may be fixed or adjustable. Fig. 3-10.

Carcass. A carcass is an enclosed cabinet that usually has drawers and doors. Often this construction is called casework. A major difference between case and carcass construction, however, is that case construction involves fewer internal details. A more thorough discussion of carcass construction is included in the units on cabinets and fine furniture. Fig. 3-11.

ELEMENTS OF DESIGN

The elements of design include *line*, *shape*, *mass*, *color*, *tone*, and *texture*. These "building blocks" of

all design are found to varying degrees in all furniture and cabinets.

Line

Lines may be straight, curved, S-shaped, circular, or spiral. They reveal a great deal about a product. Much Contemporary or Modern furniture is largely made up of straight lines, whereas Traditional, Early American, and French Provincial styles have many curves. Lines can be used to give a certain feeling to an object. Graceful curves, such as those found in French Provincial, have a light, "soft" quality, while straight, geometric lines give furniture a bold, solid look. Fig. 3-12.

Shape

Lines make up the shape of a product. The most common shapes are square, rectangular, round, triangular, diamond, elliptical, hexagonal, and octagonal. Fig. 3-13. We see these shapes in all kinds of furniture. For example, tabletops can take almost any shape, from the common rectangle to the unusual hexagon. Many drawer pulls are circular, while a table leg commonly has a triangular shape. As you look through the illustrations of furniture and cabinetry in this book, see how many common shapes you can identify. Fig. 3-14.

Mass

Line and shape make up mass. (In this sense, *mass* means the three-dimensional appearance of an object.) All furniture has height, depth, and width or length. Basic construction materials come in many shapes. Some examples are the rectangular pieces of wood, round dowel rod, and oval or triangular drawer pulls. In planning the mass of a furniture piece, the designer thinks more in terms of form than of a solid shape. The form may be open, as for a table or chair, or closed, as for a chest, cabinet, or storage unit. Fig. 3-15.

3-8. *Most tables are made with four legs and rails.*

3-9. *These record cabinets are examples of box construction.*

3-10. *This bookcase is an example of case construction.*

3-11. *This hutch with doors and drawers plus shelves illustrates complex carcass construction.*

3-12. *Gently curved lines give French Provincial its light, graceful "feel." Compare this china cabinet with the one in Fig. 3-11.*

27

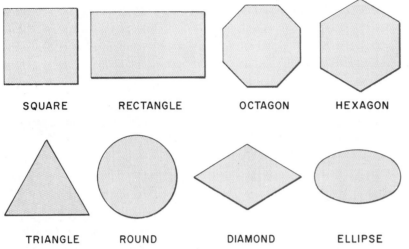

SQUARE   RECTANGLE   OCTAGON   HEXAGON

TRIANGLE   ROUND   DIAMOND   ELLIPSE

3-13. *Common shapes used as design elements in furniture.*

Color

Color is a most important element in furniture and interior design. The appearance of a room will not be pleasing unless there is a close relationship between the colors of the furniture and those of the background and accessories. Nature has given each species of wood a color all its own. Color can be enhanced or changed by using stains, fillers, and other finishing materials. Upholstering also adds color to furniture.

There are three primary colors: red, yellow, and blue. All other colors are mixtures of the primary colors. The secondary colors, for example, are obtained by mixing two primary colors. The tertiary colors are made by mixing a secondary color with a primary color. In Fig. 3-16 primaries are marked No. 1, secondaries No. 2, and tertiaries No. 3. Pairs of adjoining colors on the color wheel are known as *harmonious* hues. Those opposite each other are *complementaries*.

The furniture designer considers color as important as line or form. Sometimes it is added to furniture by using rich bright plastic laminates, ceramic tile, cane, or fabrics. Some interior designers like to relate all of the colors in a room to one major color. One-color interiors can be monotonous. Therefore, accent colors from another part of the wheel are effective. Other designers prefer lavish use of colors from all parts of the wheel.

3-15. *Note the difference between the open form of the table and the closed form of the storage unit.*

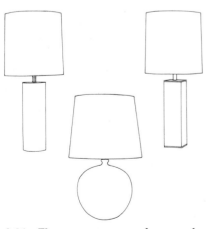

3-14. *Three common shapes for lamp bases.*

Tone and Texture

Tone is the degree of light or dark in a color. Adding black to a color yields a darker tone (a shade) of that color. Adding white yields a lighter tone (a tint).

Texture is the way a surface feels to the touch. Each wood has its own texture. Further variations in texture can be achieved by combining the wood with different kinds of materials, by cutting and finishing the wood in various ways, by machining, and by installing hardware.

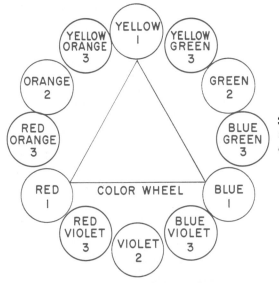

3-16. *Color wheel with three primary, three secondary, and six tertiary colors.*

with bulky ones has poor proportion. Slight variation in the sizes of parts will frequently influence proportion to a great extent. Often the "school-made" or "home-made" look in furniture is due to the use of parts that are either too bulky and heavy or too light and flimsy in appearance.

Balance

An object that appears stable or at rest is said to have balance. When a designer arranges the parts of an object symmetrically (so that both sides are the same), this produces *formal* balance. Fig. 3-19. Another kind of balance, called *informal*, results when dissimilar parts are arranged to make an object appear stable. Fig. 3-20. This, of course, is not symmetrical.

Harmony

Harmony is concerned with the way materials and parts of a product "get along" with one another. Even when many different materials are to be used, the combination must blend. Fig. 3-21. You do not have harmony, for example, if you combine a French Provincial leg with a Modern style tabletop, if you combine too many different materials, or if you use too many colors.

PRINCIPLES OF DESIGN

Proportion

Proportion is the relationship of the parts of an object to each other and to the total product. A rectangle often has better proportion than a square because the exact relationship between its height and width or width and depth is not easy to see. This creates interest. Many designers consider the *golden mean rectangle* to have perfect proportion. The ratio between its shorter and longer dimensions is 1 to 1.618, or approximately 5 to 8. Fig. 3-17. Many picture frames, chests, and cabinets show this proportion. Fig. 3-18. A relationship of 1 to 3 or 2 to 3 is also better than a perfect square in many instances.

However, much modern furniture of excellent design does make use of the perfect square and the cube, as you saw in Fig. 3-9. As stated, proportion is the relationship of one part to another. A large chair with spindly legs or a dainty coffee table

3-17. *Developing the golden mean rectangle. Start with the smallest square that measures 1 unit on each side. Find the center of the bottom edge and mark with an x. Open a compass to a distance equal to the distance from x to the upper right-hand corner of this square. With x as the center strike an arc (R.A) until it intersects with a continuation of the bottom edge. This will be line ab. Complete the rectangle. It will measure 1 unit by 1.618 units (the golden mean rectangle). To draw the next larger rectangle use "a" as the center and strike an arc (Radius B) equal in length to line ab until it intersects the vertical line formed by extending the left edge of the first small square. This second rectangle will have the same proportions. To draw the next larger rectangle strike an arc (Radius C) until it intersects the line formed by an extension of the upper edge of the first small square. Continue to enlarge the rectangle to obtain proportionate rectangles.*

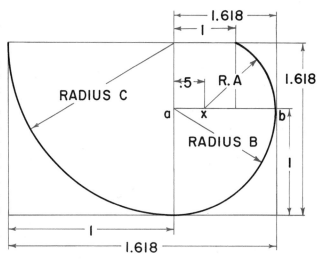

3-18. This beautiful cabinet is a "golden mean" rectangle in its overall width and height. Note also the repetition of rectangular shapes.

3-19. In formal balance, the design is symmetrical. For example, the left and right sides of this cabinet are the same.

3-20. In informal balance, the object seems balanced even though the two sides are really different in size, shape, color, or design details.

3-21. Here wood, metal, and glass are combined in a striking coffee table. Note, too, the different shapes that are used.

Rhythm

Rhythm in design is marked by the repetition of certain distinct features or elements at regular intervals. Rhythm can be achieved by repetition of shape, color, line, or design details. The repetition of rectangular shapes in Fig. 3-18 is an example of rhythm.

Emphasis

Emphasis means focusing attention on a point of special interest. Fig. 3-22. It might be obtained by skillful use of carving, by placement of hardware, or by choice of fabric.

COMMON ERRORS IN DESIGN

It is important to know the elements and principles of design, but this does not mean you must follow them rigidly. It is much better to work with materials in a creative and experimental fashion. As you develop a feeling for good design, you will instinctively know when the principles and elements have been successfully applied. The common mistakes in furniture and cabinet design which impart an undesirable appearance are these:

● A definite style of furniture has not evolved. As stated earlier, too often a piece represents no particular style but rather a combination of many, resulting in a complete *lack of style*.

● Basic principles of design have been ignored. The appearance of a school-made or home-made object is often too heavy and clumsy, rather than light and attractive.

● A poor selection of materials has been made. It is impossible to produce quality furniture from cheap woods. Likewise, it is usually faddish and garish to combine woods of highly contrasting color, texture, or quality.

● A product has been over decorated. Surface decoration should be applied sparingly and only as is fitting to the particular furniture style.

● Work is poor. The quality of work is extremely important in furniture construction. If there are large cracks in the joinery or rough edges, the final product certainly will not be attractive.

● The finish is bad. Poor finish will ruin an otherwise fine piece of furniture. Quality furniture has a smooth, even, attractive finish. Most furniture manufacturers use lacquer or a synthetic finish. Furniture made in the school lab or home workshop too often suffers from a varnish finish that dries too slowly, becomes tacky, and picks up dust, making the finish quite uneven.

STEPS IN DESIGNING FURNITURE

1. Determine your own need and the exact use of the piece. Do you need something for sitting, sleeping, storage, or other uses? How big should the product be? Remember, a sound product is attractive, fits into the space available, and has a distinctive style.

2. Develop several sketches of the product. When you have decided on a particular furniture style, become thoroughly familiar with its characteristics. Fig. 3-23.

3. Develop a model and do some experimenting. For example, if you are designing a stereo cabinet, you may want to study the sound-reproduction qualities of various woods. You may also want to investigate which kinds of construction in the speaker cabinet will produce the best sound. The sizes of the compo-

3-22. The "twisted" legs of this sideboard are certainly a point of emphasis.

3-23. The total effect of a product is greatly influenced by such details as surface decoration, hardware, and finish. Keep these in mind when preparing sketches.

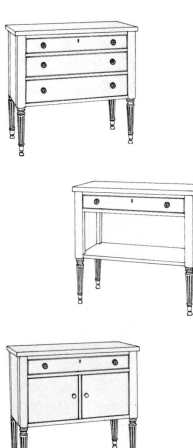

3-24. *The same basic unit can be used for a variety of purposes.*

EARLY AMERICAN
OR COLONIAL

MAPLE WITH
RUSSET BROWN COLOR
IN WIPE-ON FINISH

TRADITIONAL

MAHOGANY WITH
RED STAIN AND
LACQUER FINISH

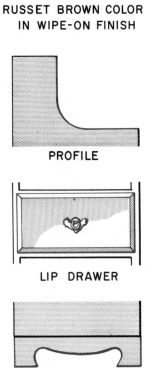

PROFILE

LIP DRAWER

CURVED FRONT

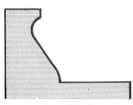

PROFILE

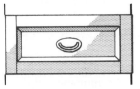

FRAME AND
PANEL DRAWER

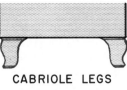

CABRIOLE LEGS

3-25. *A few external details can greatly influence the look of a product. The function and size of this nightstand are the same regardless of changes in outward appearance.*

nents will also affect your design. Balsa wood is often a good choice for building a small model of the product.

4. Develop the sketch and model into final drawings. These should be complete furniture drawings such as appear in this book.

5. Select the materials. Make a bill of materials and a plan of pro-cedure. This book will show you how.

6. Construct the piece, using appropriate woods and correct pro-cedures, as explained in this book.

7. Apply a good finish.

8. Finally, judge the product to see if it fits your needs and is satis-factory in every respect. Remember that good design involves sensitivity to beauty. As you learn more about design, you will become more sensi-tive to it and will reject products that reflect poor design.

Simplified Style Changes

Some automobile makers use only two or three basic body shells for all the models of cars they produce. Variety in appearance is achieved by changing the grills, fenders, trim, and other exterior parts. This keeps down the cost and simplifies pro-duction. To a limited extent the same technique is applied by some furniture manufacturers. The same basic unit may be used for several different types of furniture. Fig. 3-24. The kind of wood, the finish, the hardware, and certain other ex-terior items can be changed to give one chest Colonial and another Traditional style. Fig. 3-25.

When you build furniture, you too may want to start with a basic de-sign and make your own modifica-tions. Just remember the elements and principles of good design and avoid the errors that lead to poor design.

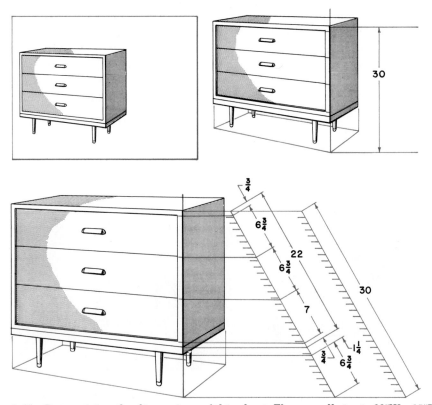

3-26. *Determining the dimensions of this chest. The overall size is 30″W x 15″D x 30″H.*

MAKING A WORKING DRAWING FROM A PICTURE OR SKETCH

You may see a picture or sketch of a furniture piece that you would like to make. In many cases the three major dimensions of height, depth, and width are given. With careful planning you can design a product that is very similar by following this procedure:

1. Fasten the picture or sketch to the left edge of a piece of paper. Fig. 3-26.

2. Use a T square or drafting machine to project straight lines from the edges of the furniture piece.

3. Suppose that the overall height is 30″. Select a scale in which 30 units equal in length will fit diagonally between the two horizontal lines. Place the first division point on the scale on the top line and the last on the bottom line.

4. Now project lines until they intersect the diagonal line for each dimension needed. It is then easy to count the number of units or inches for each part.

Another method is to scale a piece of furniture that has been photographed at an angle. If the overall dimensions are known, it is possible to determine the proportions for each of the parts. Fig. 3-27.

1. Fasten the photograph to a clean sheet of paper.

2. Extend lines from the photograph onto the paper.

3. Determine the scale to use. For example, if the piece is 35″ high, divide the distance between the bottom and top of the illustration into 35 parts. Each of these divisions will represent one inch.

4. Draw a verticle line with this scale and then pick off the dimensions, such as the drawer height. Normally, the depth and width of the piece are also available so that you can determine the size of each part.

Another method of determining sizes from an illustration is to use an opaque projector.

1. Place a large sheet of paper on a wall. The sheet must be large enough to equal the actual height of the product.

2. Draw two horizontal lines representing the height of the product.

3-27. *Scaling a piece of furniture from a photograph taken at an angle.*

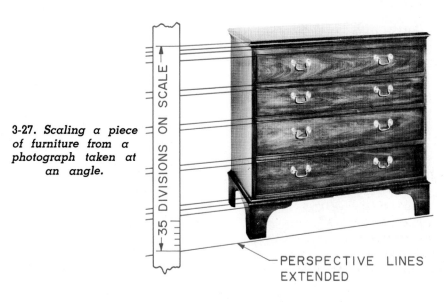

PERSPECTIVE LINES EXTENDED

3. Place the illustration in the machine. Move the machine back and forth until the height of the object fits the lines on the paper. Focus the projector and make dimensions directly on the paper.

This process can also be used to make a quarter- or half-size drawing. If the furniture has been photographed at an angle, part of it will be foreshortened and some adjustments must be made. One method of doing this is to try to determine the angle at which the photograph was made and adjust the projector to the same angle.

Often a sketch of a product will include the general information for building it. The skilled woodworker must make a detail drawing to determine the bill of materials and the actual construction details.

4 Safety

An accident can cause injury to you or other people. It can damage machinery or the product you are making. A serious accident could ruin your life. Though you are safer working with good woodworking machines and tools than in certain other activities, the wood shop does have its dangers. The accident rate for industrial woodworking is about twice as high as the national average for all industries. This must be expected since woodworking is done with sharp cutting tools and high-speed machines.

To avoid accidents, safety must be foremost in your mind at all times. Though damage to a piece of wood or a machine can be serious, it is not a tragedy like the loss of a finger. Remember at all times that you must guarantee safety for two: *the tool and you*. The machine can't think, *but you can*. Make safety a habit. Some people are "accident prone." If you are one of these, you probably shouldn't be working with power tools.

To achieve maximum safety in the wood shop, the equipment must be kept in top condition. Still more important, you—the operator of the machine—must know what you are doing and how to do it. You will find this information throughout the book. There are special safety suggestions for each machine.

You must realize that each woodworking machine and tool has its own special hazards. When working with the circular saw, keep your fingers away from the revolving blade, and make sure that the stock does not kick back and injure you. On the jointer, the problem is to keep your fingers away from the revolving cutter. The shaper is particularly dangerous because it operates at such extremely high speeds and because it is difficult to guard the cutters. The major hazard of the surfacer is the danger of kickback. Machines such as the band saw and the jigsaw are relatively safe to use.

Cabinetmakers work in various kinds of places. They may work with hand tools and stationary machines in a well-equipped shop; or they may work in a new house installing kitchen cabinets or built-ins. Perhaps they will remodel the interior of a store or office, which requires tearing out old fixtures as well as installing new ones. In each of these cases there are special things to remember.

OCCUPATIONAL SAFETY AND HEALTH ACT

The Congress of the United States in April, 1971, made the federal Occupational Safety and Health Act (OSHA) an official part of the national labor law. The purpose of this law is ". . . to assure so far as possible every working man and woman in the nation safe and healthful working conditions and to preserve our human resources."

The law contains standards on nineteen different categories concerned with safety of employees, from working standards and work surfaces to machinery and machine

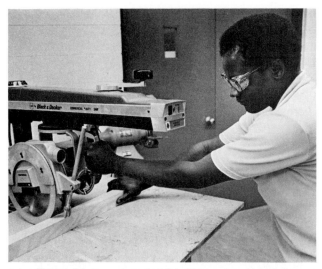

4-1. *Short sleeves are safer than long sleeves when you are working around machines.*

4-2. *Long sleeves that are tightly buttoned are also approved clothing for working around machines.*

guarding. For example, the law requires, "One or more methods of machine guarding shall be provided to protect the operator and other employees in the machine area from hazards such as those created by point of operations, ingoing nip points and rotating parts."

This law affects all employees in the woodworking trades where one or more workers are employed. For an individual employed in woodworking, it is just as important to develop the safe work attitudes and habits outlined by this law as it is to develop the skills of the trade. Employers are looking for people with these traits, for their benefit and welfare as well as yours. Thus it is important to know and follow safety rules.

DRESS

Wear clothing suitable to the activity. Safety experts recommend:

• Short sleeves are *safest* when working around machines. Fig. 4-1.

• If you wear long sleeves, be sure they're fitted and buttoned at the cuffs. Fig. 4-2. Whenever possible, roll long sleeves up above the elbows. (OSHA recommends long sleeves with tightly buttoned cuffs

and protective gloves when working around certain plastics, solvents, and other irritants.) Long sleeves are required when doing work out-of-doors during cold weather.

• Wear approved safety eye protection at all times except in areas and activities that have been designated safe. Fig. 4-3.

• Never wear loose clothing that can get caught in machinery. Torn clothing, loose pockets, ties, and

scarves are dangerous around machinery. If you can't remove it, keep loose clothing tucked in.

• Always wear gloves when using paint remover because the chemicals are very caustic. Fig. 4-4.

• When operating machines, avoid wearing jewelry such as rings, wristwatches, and similar items. Though it is not always convenient to remove such items, they do present a hazard.

4-3. *Always wear safety glasses when using power tools.*

4-4. *Always wear protective gloves when using caustic materials such as paint remover.*

• Wear a good, sturdy pair of shoes, especially when working outdoors.

HOUSEKEEPING

Many accidents are caused by poor housekeeping in regard to tools, machines, and materials. Make sure all materials are neatly stacked where they will not interfere with the use of tools and machines. Keep the areas around each machine and where you are working free of lumber scraps, workpieces, excessive sawdust, and oil. Always take nails and screws out of boards that have been removed for remodeling. Arrange tools neatly in a case or cabinet. Keep tables of machines and other work surfaces free of nails, tools, and materials.

COURTESY TO OTHER WORKERS

Do not try to move materials or equipment past a person who is using a power tool or machine. Also, do not come up behind a person who is doing such work. Startling him or her could easily cause a serious accident. Wait until a worker has finished using a machine before moving into the area.

When you are through using a machine, remove the special setups. Leave the machine in its normal operating condition for the next person. Clean up waste stock and place it in a scrap box. Never start or stop a machine for someone else. If you are working with someone else on a machine—for example, as the tail-off person on a circular saw or surfacer—always follow the operator's directions. Never try to pull stock through the machine.

HAND TOOLS

While hand tools are relatively safe, they are the cause of many small injuries. Make sure that all tools are sharp and in good condition. That way they will do their job better and will be safer to use. Always carry sharp-pointed tools away from your body. Never hold a small piece of wood in your fingers as you cut it. It is always better to clamp it in a vise. If it is necessary to hold the stock, make sure that the cutting edge moves away from your hand, not toward it.

PORTABLE POWER TOOLS

Portable power tools are widely used for on-the-job construction. In using these tools, the cutting edge is fed into the stock. For safe operation, make sure that the stock is fixed so that it will not move. Keep your hands away from the cutting edge and, whenever possible, keep both hands on the portable tool. Never use electrical equipment on a wet or damp floor. Make sure that the tool is properly grounded and that the extension cord wire is large enough. There are, of course, many cordless power tools that are relatively safe to use, especially on cabinetwork around water and in damp buildings. Also, some portable tools have a housing of fiberglass which eliminates much danger of shock.

WOODWORKING MACHINES

Detailed instructions for safe use of stationary machines are given in each unit. However, there are some general practices that should be observed. Make sure you know how to use the machine properly before you attempt to operate it. Keep guards in place for all cutting and shaping operations. Guards should always be used unless it makes cutting impossible. If a standard guard cannot be used, make use of holding and clamping devices, and push sticks.

ALWAYS PLAN YOUR WORK BEFORE STARTING

Planning your work before you begin can eliminate much potential danger.

• If large stock is to be cut, get help before you begin, not after you are in difficulty.

• Keep your mind on your work. Guard against becoming distracted by noise or anything that is going on around you.

• Make sure that all clamping devices are secured before turning on the power.

• Wait until the machine is at full speed before using it. Then feed the stock into the machine with a firm, even touch.

• Never hurry when working on a machine. Accidents often happen when someone tries to do things too fast or fails to follow instructions.

• Never attempt to stop the machine with a stick of wood or anything else after the power is off. Make sure that the machine has come to a dead stop before adjusting, oiling, or changing a blade.

• *Always wear goggles or a face mask when there is danger of flying chips.* This especially applies to wood turning, grinding, and most sanding operations. Fig. 4-5. Keep your fingers away from the path of the cutting tool.

FIRE CONTROL

There is special danger of fire in the cabinet shop due to sawdust and flammable materials. A good dust-collection system for stationary tools is necessary for fire control and health reasons. Store finishing materials in metal containers and cabinets. Keep oily rags in metal waste cans.

Fires must be extinguished differently, depending upon what is burning. Three classes of fires are a threat to the wood shop. Therefore three kinds of fire extinguishers should be available. Fig. 4-6.

A *class A* fire involves only ordinary combustible material such as wood chips, paper, or rubbish. The cooling and quenching effect of water or a watery solution works well against such fires.

4-5. *Wear eye protection when working around the tools and machines shown here.*

A *class B* fire involves flammable liquids such as alcohol, paint or lacquer thinner, or other chemicals. Use an extinguisher that will cover the burning area with a chemical blanket.

A *class C* fire is one involving electrical equipment. It is very important to use an extinguishing agent that will not conduct electricity.

All fire extinguishers should be clearly marked A, B, or C to indicate which type of fire they can be used on.

TREATMENT OF INJURIES

Most accidents can be avoided. However, there is always the possibility that one may happen. Make sure that you get first aid and medical treatment promptly for even the slightest scratch. Only a person with medical training should remove something from your eye. If you get a small sliver in the skin, remove it and then treat against infection.

FOR CLASS "A" FIRES   SODA-ACID   WATER PUMP   FOAM

FOR CLASS "B" FIRES   CARBON DIOXIDE   DRY CHEMICAL   FOAM   VAPORIZING LIQUID

FOR CLASS "C" FIRES   CARBON DIOXIDE   DRY CHEMICAL   VAPORIZING LIQUID

4-6. *These kinds of fire extinguishers are needed in the wood shop.*

Section I
QUESTIONS AND DISCUSSION TOPICS

Chapter 1

1. How did the technique of framed paneling improve furniture design during the Middle Ages?

2. Name four furniture designers of the eighteenth century.

3. Why is cabinetmaking the key to all woodworking?

4. Compare the work of the finish carpenter and the cabinetmaker.

5. Name four skilled occupations in which a knowledge of cabinetmaking is important.

6. In what professional and semi-professional occupations would a knowledge of cabinetmaking be valuable?

Chapter 2

1. Name the three major categories of furniture styles.

2. Who was Duncan Phyfe? What was his contribution to the development of furniture?

3. How does Traditional furniture made today differ from the furniture made in the eighteenth century?

4. How did Provincial furniture styles develop?

5. Describe the characteristics of Modern furniture.

6. What is eclectic decorating?

Chapter 3

1. Discuss how human dimensions influence furniture design.

2. Why is the appearance of a furniture piece important?

3. Is veneered furniture of inferior quality?

4. Name the elements of design.

5. What is the golden mean rectangle? Tell how it can be applied to furniture design.

6. Give examples of the two kinds of balance.

7. Discuss the common errors in furniture and cabinet design.

8. Describe the steps in designing furniture.

9. Describe one way to make a working drawing from a picture or sketch.

Chapter 4

1. Describe the correct way to dress in the woodworking shop.

2. What is meant by good housekeeping in a shop?

3. How does courtesy to other workers in the shop relate to safety?

4. What safety practices should be followed when using hand tools?

5. Discuss fire hazards found in wood shops.

6. List woodworking operations that require eye protection.

PROBLEMS AND ACTIVITIES

1. Make a detailed study of one occupation in which a knowledge of cabinetmaking is essential. Use the *Occupational Outlook Handbook* and other publications to get this information; also interview someone working in the occupation.

2. Study the life of a great cabinetmaker (Chippendale, Sheraton, Duncan Phyfe, or other). Pay special attention to his contributions to the field.

3. Review the life and work of a current designer of wood products.

4. Design and sketch a furniture piece or other wood product that you would like to build.

5. Visit a furniture store or showroom and evaluate a piece of furniture displayed. Discuss its design, construction, and finish.

6. As a group, develop a cleanup schedule for your shop.

7. Design safety posters to display in the shop.

Section II

MATERIALS AND LAYOUTS

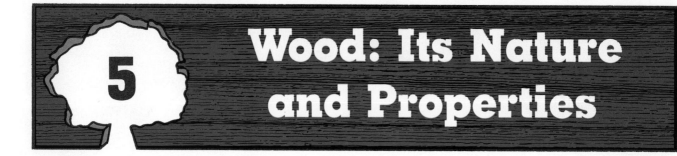

Wood: Its Nature and Properties

5

Wood is a remarkable raw material with thousands of uses, many of them in cabinetmaking. While wood may seem to be a simple substance, it is in some ways one of the most unusual and complicated natural materials. Fig. 5-1. The more you know about the characteristics of wood and its properties, the more valuable wood becomes to you.

Wood is made up of countless tiny, tubular cells. These are cemented solidly together by wood's own adhesive, *lignin*. These tubes or cells form a sort of plumbing system, supplying chemical materials which nourish the life processes of the tree. The walls of these tubes also provide strength for the tree trunk. In general, these tubes run up and down the trunk. They produce the grain that you see on cut surfaces and edges. Fig. 5-2.

PARTS OF A TREE

The tree is the largest plant found in nature. Roots anchor it to the ground and absorb water, minerals, and nitrogen. Roots also help to hold the soil against erosion. The tree trunk produces the bulk of useful wood by increasing in diameter each year. It supports the crown, the bushy part of the tree, which includes the twigs and leaves. The leaves use sunlight, carbon dioxide, and the nutrients absorbed by the roots to make the food used by the tree. This process is called photosynthesis.

A cross section of a log cut from a tree trunk is shown in Figs. 5-3 and 5-4. Its parts function as follows:

The *outer bark* is a shield that protects the tree from fire, insects, and disease. This dead, corky part varies in thickness with the kind of tree and its age. The inner bark, called *bast* or *phloem,* is living material. Its cells carry the food (sap) made in the leaves downward to feed the branches, trunk, and roots. The *cambium* is a living layer between the bark and the wood. This is where the tree grows in width. New wood forms on the inside of the cambium, and new bark on the outside.

The wood itself is the part of the tree used to make lumber. It is called *xylem* and consists of *sapwood* and *heartwood*. Sapwood is the newer, lighter-colored, growing part of the tree. It carries water and nutrients from the roots to the leaves. The heartwood, which at one time was sapwood, has become inactive. It is usually darker than sapwood and is dead as far as growth is concerned. The *pith,* at the center of the tree, is the first growth. It is formed when the woody stem or branch grows longer. Radiating out from the center of the tree are the *ray cells*. These struc-

5-1(α). *Forestry students learn about tree growth by working in a nursery which develops healthy seedlings for planting.*

5-1(b). *This tree has been marked for cutting.*

40

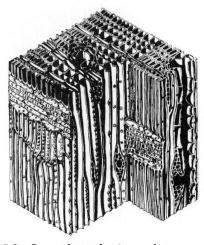

5-2. *An enlarged view of a very small piece of wood. The top represents end grain. As you can see, the cells are hollow.*

tures form horizontal passageways for the food which nourishes the tree. Energy in the form of sugar is carried through these cells and starts the tree growing in the spring, until the leaves are formed and the tree makes its own food.

CELL STRUCTURE

As stated earlier, wood is made of tiny units called cells. These cells are very narrow but may be rather long. The cells consist of a cell wall and a cell cavity (space) within the wall. In dead cells the cavity is empty; there is no protoplasm or nucleus. Most of the cells in a tree are dead. The exceptions, as stated earlier, are the recent growth produced by the cambium and certain cells in the sapwood.

Pores are cross sections of cells. When wood is sawed, the cavities in the cell walls are exposed. To give you some idea of how porous wood is, one cubic inch of wood, having an average specific gravity of 0.40, will have about 15 square feet of internal surface area at the first level of cells. Even more astonishing, if this internal surface area could all be laid out flat in its green condition, it would equal 21,780 square feet, approximately the size of a football field!

This interesting structure of open spaces and cell walls gives wood its tremendous strength and unique properties.

HARDWOODS AND SOFTWOODS

The terms *hardwood* and *softwood* as used to identify woods are botanical terms and do not indicate actual softness or hardness. Some hardwoods are actually softer than some of the softwoods. Softwoods are those that come from *conifers* (evergreens), which are cone-bearing or needle-bearing trees. Common examples are pine, fir, cedar, and redwood. Hardwoods are cut from the broadleaf, *deciduous* trees. A deciduous tree is one that sheds its leaves annually. Some common hardwoods are walnut, mahogany, maple, birch, cherry, and oak.

GROWTH RINGS

The term *growth ring* is often used in reference to the annual growth of a tree. However, the rings are not always as easy to see as in Fig. 5-5. In certain warm climates, as well as cold ones, there is no sharp division between seasons of growth and nongrowth. Therefore some tropical woods do not display definite annular (ringlike) indications of growth. Also, some species of woods have distinct growth rings, while others are quite indistinct.

Growth rings in trees are made up of springwood and summerwood. The portion formed early in the growing season is called springwood, or early wood. That which forms later is summerwood, or late wood. In general, springwood has larger cell cavities and thinner walls.

Hardwoods are classified in three groups, based on the pattern of growth rings:

ANNUAL RING

PITH

SUMMERWOOD

SPRINGWOOD

RAYS

HEARTWOOD

SAPWOOD (XYLEM)

RAYS

CAMBIUM

INNER BARK (BAST OR PHLOEM)

OUTER BARK

5-3. *Cross section of a tree trunk.*

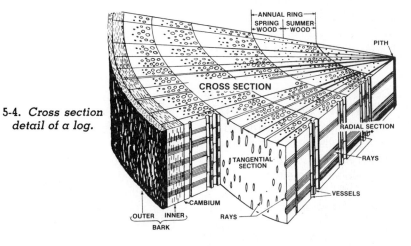

5-4. *Cross section detail of a log.*

ANNUAL RING
SPRING WOOD SUMMER WOOD
PITH
CROSS SECTION
RADIAL SECTION
TANGENTIAL SECTION
RAYS
VESSELS
CAMBIUM
OUTER INNER BARK
RAYS

5-5. *Growth rings. Each ring represents the growth of the tree during one year. If you counted the growth rings on this disk from a pine tree, you'd find that there are 43, which is the age of the tree. In counting growth rings, the end of the log towards the ground should be examined. The upper part of the tree shows fewer rings because it is more recent growth.*

Ring porous has springwood cells that are large and distinct, usually several tiers of cells wide. The summerwood cells are small, indistinct, and thick-walled. The growth rings are very distinct. Good examples are oak and ash.

Semi-ring porous has fairly distinct springwood cells but not as wide a band of them as in ring-porous wood. Summerwood is composed of indistinct, thick-walled cells. This is found in hickory and elm.

Diffuse porous has no distinct difference between springwood and summerwood. As a result, there is no distinct grain pattern. Examples are birch, poplar, walnut, maple, basswood, and cherry.

CHARACTERISTICS AND PROPERTIES OF WOOD

Color in lumber is determined by chemical substances that are part of the cell walls. Because heartwood contains these materials in greater amounts, it is the darker portion of most woods. Wood colors are often quite variable, particularly in highly pigmented woods such as walnut. Most woods darken with exposure as the coloring matter in the cell walls combines with oxygen. This process is called *oxidation*.

Texture is defined according to the relative porosity or uniformity of the wood tissues. Wood made up entirely of small cells has *fine* texture. When many of the cells are relatively large, the texture is *coarse*.

Grain is the arrangement of cells when the wood is cut longitudinally (from end to end). When most cells are parallel to the center of the tree, the result is called *straight grain*. Frequently, knots from tree limbs or the presence of other defects will cause wood tissues to be arranged in a nonparallel manner. This is called *irregular or localized steep grain. Curly grain* is found in wood in which the fibers of the cells are distorted, giving them a curly appearance. A good example is bird's-eye maple. *Spiral grain* results when wood cell fibers take a spiral course around the trunk of the tree instead of the normal vertical course. The spiral may extend in a right-handed or left-handed direction. *Interlocked grain* develops when the fibers of the growth ring twist in alternate directions as they go up the tree.

Figure is the pattern produced in the wood surface by growth rings, rays, knots, irregular colorations, and deviations from regular grain such as interlocked or curly grain. Fig. 5-6.

Density is the weight (mass) per unit volume of a substance. The density of wood is usually measured in grams per cubic centimetre. The higher the density, the stronger and harder the wood. Actually, the density of the *wood substance* is about the same in all species. Differences in density between various kinds of woods and between individual pieces of lumber are due mainly to the open spaces in the cells and the thickness of the cell walls.

Specific gravity is a scientific way to measure the relative density of a substance. This measurement is expressed as the ratio of the substance's density to the density of water. Thus, the weight of a piece of wood divided by the weight of an equal volume of water at 4 degrees Celsius determines the specific gravity of the wood. For instance, the specific gravity of ash is 0.50, which means that the wood substance weighs exactly half as much as an equal amount of water. Basswood, a lighter wood, has a specific gravity of about 0.35, while that of hickory, a relatively heavy wood, is about 0.61.

Because it is based upon the amount of actual wood substance in a piece of wood, specific gravity is an excellent indication of strength and hardness. In general, the higher the specific gravity, the stronger the wood.

Hardness is the ability of wood to resist indentation. It depends largely upon the thickness of the cell walls and the size of the cell cavities. Hardness is an important characteristic in selecting woods for furniture.

CUTTING METHODS

There are two common ways of cutting boards. One method is

5-6. *The wood used in this desk has a very distinct figure.*

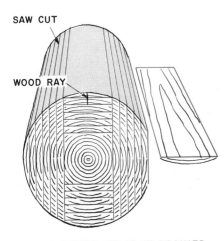

SAW CUT

WOOD RAY

PLAIN-SAWED OR FLAT-GRAINED
(CUT TANGENT TO GROWTH RINGS)

5-7(a). *This is the least expensive way to cut lumber because it involves less labor and waste. The surface of the lumber shows a U-shaped figure due primarily to the growth rings.*

5-7(b). *This flat-grained redwood shows how growth rings form the grain pattern.*

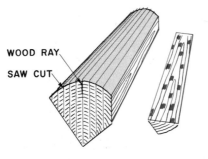

WOOD RAY

SAW CUT

QUARTER-SAWED OR EDGE-GRAINED

5-8(a). *Lumber cut like this is somewhat more expensive to produce but has the advantages of less shrinkage across grain and a better-wearing surface.*

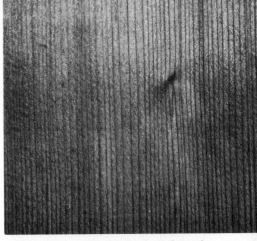

5-8(b). *This edge-grained redwood shows clearly how the growth rings appear as straight lines.*

called *plainsawed* when it is hardwood and *flat-grained* when softwood. The log is squared and sawed lengthwise (tangent to the annual growth rings). Fig. 5-7. The other method is called *quartersawed* when hardwood and *edge-grained* when softwood. Fig. 5-8. In this method the lumber is not cut parallel with the grain. The log is first quartered, and then it is sawed so that its rings

form angles of forty-five to ninety degrees with the surface.

Plainsawed lumber is usually cheaper. It is also easier to kiln dry and produces greater widths. However, it has a high tendency to shrink and warp. A knot will extend through more boards in plainsawed lumber than in quartersawed.

Quartersawed lumber has less tendency to warp, shrink, and swell. It provides a more durable surface, does not tend to twist or cup, and

holds paints and finishes better. Fig. 5-9.

DECORATIVE FEATURES OF COMMON WOODS

The decorative value of wood depends upon its color, figure, and luster; the way in which it bleaches or takes fillers, stains, and transparent finishes; and the way it is cut.

Because of the combinations of color and the many shades found in wood, it is impossible to give detailed descriptions of colors of the various kinds. Sapwood of most species, however, is light in color,

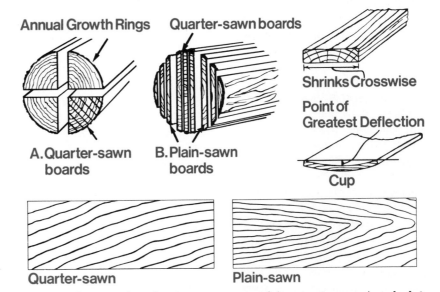

Annual Growth Rings   **Quarter-sawn boards**

Shrinks Crosswise

A. Quarter-sawn boards

B. Plain-sawn boards

Point of Greatest Deflection

Cup

Quarter-sawn   **Plain-sawn**

5-9(a). *Lumber is referred to as quartersawed (or quarter-sawn) and plainsawed (or plain-sawn). Note that some pieces of plainsawed lumber can be classified as quartersawed.*

ADVANTAGES OF PLAINSAWED AND QUARTERSAWED LUMBER

Plainsawed	Quartersawed
Figure patterns resulting from the annual rings and some other types of figure are brought out more conspicuously by plainsawing.	Types of figure due to pronounced rays, interlocked grain, and wavy grain are brought out more conspicuously.
Round or oval knots that may occur in plainsawed boards affect the surface appearance less than spiked knots that may occur in quartersawed boards. Also, a board with a round or oval knot is not as weak as a board with a spiked knot.	Raised grain caused by separation in the annual rings does not become so pronounced. It surface-checks and splits less in seasoning and in use.
Shakes and pitch pockets, when present, extend through fewer boards.	The sapwood appearing in boards is at the edges, and its width is limited according to the width of the sapwood in the log.
It is less susceptible to collapse in drying.	It shrinks and swells less in width.
It shrinks and swells less in thickness.	It twists and cups less. It wears more evenly.
It may cost less because it is easier to obtain.	It does not allow liquids to pass into or through it so readily in some species. It holds paint better in some species.

5-9(b). *This table compares the qualities of plainsawed and quartersawed lumber.*

and in some species it is practically white. White sapwood of certain species, such as maple, may be preferred to the heartwood for specific uses. In some species, such as the true firs and basswood, there is typically little or no difference in color between sapwood and heartwood, but in most species heartwood is darker and fairly uniform in color.

In plainsawed boards and rotary-cut veneer, the annual growth rings frequently form ellipses and parabolas that make striking figures, especially when the rings are irregular in width and outline on the cut surface. On quartersawed surfaces, these rings form stripes, which are not especially ornamental unless they are irregular in width and direction. The relatively large rays, sometimes referred to as flecks, form a conspicuous figure in quartersawed

oak. With interlocked grain, which slopes in alternate directions in successive layers from the center of the tree outward, quartersawed surfaces show a ribbon effect, either because of the difference in reflection of light from successive layers when the wood has a natural luster or because cross grain of varying degree absorbs stains unevenly. Much of this type of figure is lost in plainsawed lumber.

In open-grained hardwoods, the appearance of both plainsawed and quartersawed lumber can be varied greatly by the use of fillers of different colors. In softwoods, the annual growth layers can be made to stand out more by applying a stain.

SEASONING

When a tree is cut down, the wood may contain from 30 to 300 percent more moisture than it will after drying. For example, a piece of wood 2″ x 4″ x 8′ may contain as

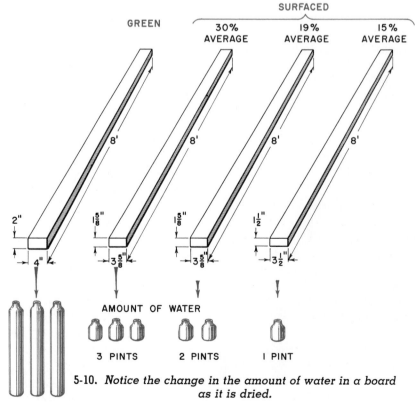

5-10. *Notice the change in the amount of water in a board as it is dried.*

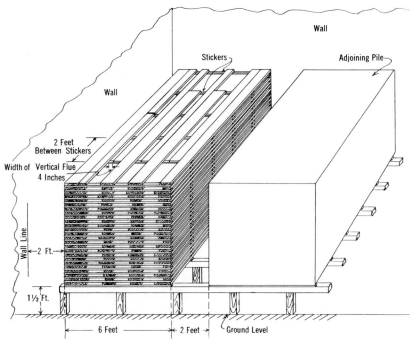

5-11. *Correct stacking of lumber for kiln drying.*

apparent effect upon the properties of wood except to reduce its weight. However, below the fiber saturation point, moisture is being removed from the cell walls. Therefore the wood begins to shrink.

Fiber saturation point for woods varies from about 23 to 30 percent moisture content. For practical purposes, it can be taken as approximately 28 percent for most woods. Reductions in moisture from the green condition down to roughly 28 percent therefore do not result in shrinkage. Fig. 5-12.

After the fiber saturation point has been passed and the cell walls begin to give up their moisture, they shrink in all directions but not uniformly. The cause of shrinkage is contraction of the cell walls. The

much as three gallons of water! Fig. 5-10.

There are two main methods of seasoning (drying) wood: *air drying* and *kiln drying*. Air drying is done out of doors. The rough lumber is stacked either on end at an angle or in layers separated by crosspieces called *stickers*. The wood is usually allowed to remain stacked from one to three months, sometimes longer. After correct air drying, the wood should have a minimum moisture content of about 12 to 15 percent, but no more than an average of 19 percent.

In kiln drying, the lumber is stacked in layers with stickers between the boards. Fig. 5-11. It is placed in a kiln (oven) in which moisture, air, and temperature are carefully controlled. A typical kiln schedule starts with low temperature and high relative humidity. As the wood dries, the temperature is increased and the relative humidity decreased. Properly kiln-dried lumber for interiors should have 8 to 10 percent moisture content. Moreover,

if it is intended for cabinet and furniture construction, it should have 7 to 8 percent, or even slightly less.

SHRINKAGE OF LUMBER

In the drying process, lumber tends to shrink, both in width and in thickness. Shrinkage in length, or along the grain, is normally so small that in almost all species it is not considered a problem. The United States Forest Products Laboratory has conducted many tests which bear this out. Following is an explanation of why wood shrinks.

Water or moisture in green (unseasoned) wood exists in two forms: as free or liquid water in the cell cavities and as bound moisture held within the cell walls. In a freshly cut tree or log, most of the cells contain some free water, and all the cell walls contain bound water. As wood dries, the free water is the first to be removed. When all the free water has been removed and the cell cavities are empty of liquid water, the wood is at the *fiber saturation point.* Removal of this free water has no

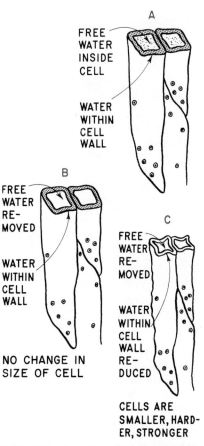

5-12. *This drawing shows how cells change in size as water is removed.*

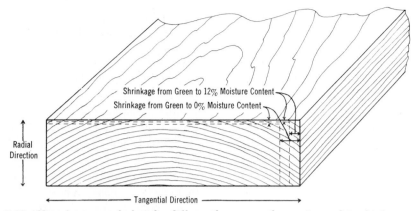

Shrinkage from Green to 12% Moisture Content
Shrinkage from Green to 0% Moisture Content

Radial Direction

Tangential Direction

5-13. *Note how wood shrinks differently across the grain and in thickness.*

es a certain amount of shrinkage across the face of wood that is edge-grained (vertical) or quarter-sawed, and about twice as much in plainsawed or flat-grained wood. Fig. 5-13.

Rays are groups of cells that radiate from the center of the tree, passing between cell bundles, through the cambium layer, to almost the outer part of the bark. The stiffening effect of these rays helps prevent edge-grained or quarter-sawed wood from shrinking as much as plainsawed or flat-grained wood. Fig. 5-14.

Another factor which influences the extent to which wood shrinks is its density; that is, the actual amount of wood substance in a unit of volume, as indicated by the dry weight of the wood. Denser woods shrink and swell more than lighter ones with a given change in moisture content.

In carefully dried wood there is little difference between sapwood and heartwood in respect to shrinking and swelling. Sapwood, however, may be more susceptible to changes in atmospheric humidity, and therefore its dimensions may change more quickly than those of heartwood.

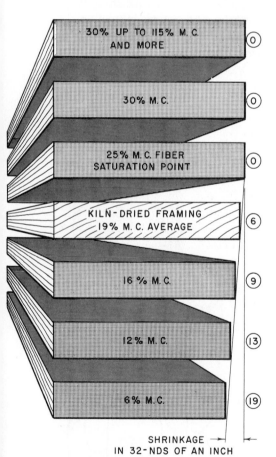

30% UP TO 115% M.C. AND MORE — 0

30% M.C. — 0

25% M.C. FIBER SATURATION POINT — 0

KILN-DRIED FRAMING 19% M.C. AVERAGE — 6

16% M.C. — 9

12% M.C. — 13

6% M.C. — 19

SHRINKAGE IN 32-NDS OF AN INCH

5-14. *Here you see how much shrinkage there is in the width of a plainsawed piece of 2" x 10" softwood lumber. The circled numbers show the shrinkage in 32nds of an inch. There is zero shrinkage in width until the wood is kiln dried to 19% moisture content. At this point the width shrinks by* 6/32".

cells are reduced in diameter and drawn closer together. This is traceable to the peculiar structure of the cell walls. The theory is that most vegetable-cell walls are composed of very small, elongated fibrils which have an attraction for water. The water is held around each fibril and holds the groups of fibrils apart. As the cell walls dry out, the space between the fibrils becomes narrower and the fibrils themselves draw together, causing shrinkage of the cell walls. Combined shrinkage of all cell walls decreases the size of the whole piece. This process caus-

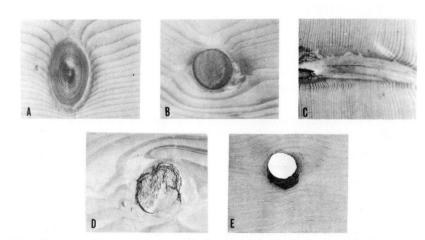

5-15. *Common kinds of knots: (A) Intergrown. (B) Encased. (C) Spiked. (D) Decayed. (E) Knot hole.*

5-16. *Check defect.*

LUMBER DEFECTS

Defects in lumber are faults that detract from its quality, either in appearance or utility. There is much technical information about defects that lumber graders must use in their work. The woodworker needs only to recognize the basic defects that will affect the selection of lumber for cabinets and furniture. There are four basic types of defects: natural defects, those that result from improper conditioning or storage of lumber, defects caused by the way the lumber is sawed, and defects caused by machining.

Natural Defects

Cross grain. Grain is not parallel with the axis of a piece. It may be diagonal or spiral grain or a combination of the two.

Knot. That portion of a branch or limb that occurs in a piece of lum-

5-17. *Decay.*

ber. Fig. 5-15. There are many kinds of knots. An *intergrown knot* is one partially or completely intergrown on one or two faces with the growth rings of the surrounding wood. An *encased knot* is one whose rings of annual growth are *not* intergrown with those of the surrounding wood. Other knots will be described under other types of defects.

Peck. The presence of areas of disintegrated wood caused by advanced stages of localized decay in the living tree. It is usually associated with cypress and incense cedar. There is no further development of peck once the tree is felled.

Pith. The small soft core occurring in the structural center of a log.

Pocket. A well-defined opening between the rings of annual growth, usually containing pitch or bark.

Spiral grain. A type of growth in which the fibers take a spiral course about the bole of a tree instead of the normal vertical course. The spiral may extend in a right-handed or left-handed direction around the tree trunk.

Defects Resulting from Improper Conditioning and Storage

Check. A separation of the wood normally occurring lengthwise across the rings of annual growth and usually as a result of seasoning. Fig. 5-16.

Decay. Disintegration of wood due to the action of wood-destroying fungi. The words *dote* and *rot* mean the same as decay. Fig. 5-17.

Decayed knot. A knot which, due to advanced decay, is not as hard as the surrounding wood.

Dry rot. A term loosely applied to many types of decay but especially to that which, when in an advanced stage, permits the wood to be easily crushed to a dry powder. The term is actually a misnomer, since all fungi require considerable moisture for growth.

5-18. *A heavy stain developed in this lumber when it was piled solid outdoors in wet, warm weather.*

Shake. A lengthwise separation of the wood. It occurs usually between the rings of annual growth.

Split. A lengthwise separation of the wood due to the tearing apart of the wood cells.

Stain. A marked variation from the natural color of the wood. Fig. 5-18.

Warp. Any variation from a true or plane surface. It includes bow, crook, twist, cup, or any combination of these. Fig. 5-19. *Bow* (rhymes with low) is a distortion in a board so that it is no longer flat lengthwise but has remained flat across the surface. *Crook* is a defect in which the edges do not form

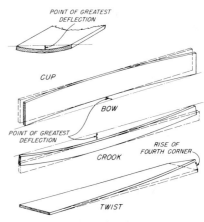

5-19. *Kinds of warp.*

a straight line from end to end. *Twist* is a defect characterized by a turning or winding of the edges of the board so that the four corners of any face are no longer in the same plane. *Cup* is the warping of a board so that it is no longer flat across its width.

Wormholes. Caused by beetles and other insects. May vary from very small to quite large. Fig. 5-20.

Defects Caused by Slicing or Sawing

Loosened or raised grain. A small portion of the wood is being loosened or raised but not displaced.

Spiked knot. A branch or limb which has been (a) cut across the rings of annual growth showing the end section on a surface or (b) cut lengthwise showing the lengthwise section on the adjacent surface, with the end section and the lengthwise section intersecting at the two adjacent faces.

Variation in sawing. An unintended deviation from line of cut, either outside or inside the line.

Wane. Bark or lack of wood from any cause on the edge or corner of a piece.

Defects Caused by Machining

Chipped grain. Consists of a part of the surface being chipped or broken out in particles below the line of cut. It should not be classed as torn grain.

Hit and miss. In surfaced lumber, a series of skips by planer knives with surfaced areas between skips.

Hit or miss. In surfaced lumber, *hit or miss* means completely surfaced, partly surfaced, or entirely rough.

Imperfect manufacture. Includes all defects or blemishes produced in manufacturing.

Machine burn. A darkening of the wood due to overheating by the machine knives or rolls when pieces are stopped in a machine.

Skip. An unsurfaced area.

Torn grain. A part of the wood is torn out in surfacing.

SELECTION OF LUMBER

Here are some suggestions for selecting and preparing lumber and using it in a finished product.

Before the lumber is machined, make sure moisture content of the pieces is uniform and correct. Lumber that is too wet will shrink. If it is too dry, it will swell.

Never store finish lumber in a house that has just been plastered. The lumber will pick up the moisture from the walls.

If shrinkage across the grain is likely to be serious, use edge-grained stock.

The moisture content of a finished article should be about the

5-20. *Insect damage. The upper piece has large grub holes probably caused by round-headed borers. The lower piece has small pin holes probably caused by beetles.*

same as that in the place where it is to be used. While many types of protective coatings help, they do not keep out all of the moisture. Protective coatings help to prevent a difference in moisture distribution between the surface and the interior.

After an article has been built, try to protect the wood from great extremes of humidity. It is very important for a woodworking shop or storeroom to be equipped with a ventilating system and with devices to control humidity.

6 Kinds of Woods

In the United States more than 100 woods are available to the prospective user, but it is very unlikely that all are available in any one locality. Commercially, there are about 60 native woods of major importance. Another 30 woods are commonly imported in the form of logs, lumber, and veneer for industrial uses, the building trades, and furniture.

Even among the more common woods there is great difference in demand, partly depending on the availability of the particular wood in various sections of the country. Except for the fine cabinet woods described in the next unit, cabinetmakers tend to use those woods that are readily available in the areas where they work.

Identifying most of the *common* wood species is relatively simple. However, identification of each kind of wood is more difficult because there are so many kinds and because pieces of the same kind vary in appearance and properties. Mahogany, for example, is sometimes light-colored and sometimes dark. One piece of mahogany can be twice as heavy as another of the same size. Sometimes there is also a superficial resemblance between entirely unrelated woods. Birch and maple or cherry and mahogany can, at times, look very much alike. For these reasons it is necessary to be precise when describing woods.

You can learn to recognize the more common woods by general ap-pearance. However, precise identification requires careful study of such details as pores, growth rings, rays, color, odor, weight, and hardness. If you ever have difficulty identifying a particular wood, the safest practice is to send a sample to the official wood identification agency of the United States Government. This is the Forest Products Laboratory at Madison, Wisconsin. This organization receives thousands of requests annually for identification.

Most woods for furniture must have good appearance, be comparatively free from warp, excessive shrinking, and swelling, and have sufficient hardness to resist indentation. For these reasons, most furniture woods are hardwoods.

CATEGORIES OF WOOD

There are two main categories of wood: hardwood and softwood. This is rather misleading as it has nothing to do with the hardness or softness of the wood.

Hardwood is cut from deciduous (broadleaf) trees. Both maple and basswood are considered to be hardwoods, although maple is hard and basswood is soft. The more common hardwoods include maple, birch, oak, yellow poplar, mahogany, cherry, and walnut.

Softwood comes from conifers (trees with needle-shaped leaves). Yellow pine is heavy and hard, while northern white pine is light and soft. Both are considered to be softwoods. White pine, Douglas fir, pon-derosa pine, and redwood are some of the most common softwoods.

SOME COMMON VARIETIES

The table in Fig. 6-1 (pages 50-53) lists and describes some of the common types of wood. Following is an explanation of the headings and abbreviations used in the table. Figure 6-2 show the distribution of common wood species in the United States.

"Common Name" is that by which the wood is presumed to be best known to most people.

"Other Common Name" is included as a cross reference because the same common name is often used to identify many entirely different species.

"Botanical Name" is the Latin name assigned by a recognized botanist. Common names are unreliable and misleading. Example: one lexicon lists 197 different common names for a single species. The Latin name affords positive identification because it is the same everywhere in the world.

Under "Botanical Name," the abbreviation *spp.* is the plural of *species.* It indicates that several closely related species of the genus shown are cut and marketed together.

"Color" refers to heartwood only. Color descriptions are unavoidably inexact. A personal sense of a wood's color can best be gained by personal examination.

(Text continued on page 52.)

COMMON TYPES OF WOOD

Common Name	Other Common Name	Botanical Name	Color	Density	Texture
1. AFRORMOSIA	kokrodua (African teak)	Pericopsis elata	lt. brown	med. hard	fine
2. ALDER, RED	(none in U.S.)	Alnus rubra	pale reddish brown	medium	fine
3. APITONG	keruing, yang	Dipterocarpus spp.	brownish red	hard	coarse
4 & 5. ASH	(none in U.S.)	Fraxinus spp.	white to light tan	medium	coarse
6. BALSA	corkwood	Ochroma pyramidale	pale tan	very soft	coarse
7. BANAK	mahban	Virola spp.	reddish brown	soft	medium
8. BASSWOOD	American linden	Tilia glabra & heterophylla	white to pale brown	soft	fine
9. BEECH (U.S. and Canada)	(none in U.S.)	Fagus grandifolia	pale reddish brown	med. hard	medium
10. BIRCH	boileau (Canada)	Betula spp.	pale brown	hard	fine to medium
11. BUTTERNUT	white walnut	Juglans cinerea	lt. brown	soft	medium
12. CANALETE	geiger tree, cordia	Cordia spp.	streaked brown	very hard	medium
13. CEDAR, AROMATIC RED	juniper	Juniperus virginiana	heart: red sap: white	medium	fine
14. CEDAR, SPANISH	cedrela	Cedrela odorata	pale brown to red	soft to medium	medium
15. CEDAR, WESTERN RED	shinglewood	Thuja plicata	reddish brown	soft	medium
16. CHERRY	fruitwood	Prunus serotina	med. reddish brown	medium	fine
17. CHESTNUT	(none in U.S.)	Castanea dentata	pale grayish brown	medium	coarse
18. COCOBOLO	Nicaragua rosewood	Dalbergia retusa	streaked dk. brown	hard	medium
19. COTTONWOOD	western poplar, Balm of Gilead	Populus spp.	pale brown	soft	medium
20. CYPRESS	bald cypress, swamp cypress	Taxodium distichum	orangey brown	soft	medium coarse
21. DAMAR MINYAK	almaciga (P.I.) kauri pine (Aus.)	Agathis alba	pale tan	soft	fine
22. EBONY	gabon ebony, macassar ebony	Diospyros spp.	(G) solid black (M) strkd. black	very hard	fine
23. ELM	gray elm, soft white elm, wahoo	Ulmus spp.	pale brown (grayish)	medium	coarse
24. GUM, BLACK	sour gum	Nyssa sylvatica and biflora	pale yel. brown	medium	fine
25. GUM, RED	sweet gum, hazel	Liquidambar styraciflua	reddish brown	medium	fine
26. HEMLOCK WESTERN	Alaska pine	Tsuga heterophylla	pale grayish brown	med. soft	coarse
27. IMBUIA	Brazilian walnut	Phoebe porosa	brown	med. hard	fine
28. KOA	(none in U.S.)	Acacia koa	golden brown	med. hard	fine
29. KORINA	limba, afara	Terminalia superba	very pale yel. white	medium	fine
30. MAGNOLIA	cucumber tree	Magnolia frandiflora and virginiana	lt. greenish brown	medium	fine
31. MAHOGANY, AFRICAN	acajou d'Afrique (French)	Khaya spp.	pale reddish brown	medium	medium
32. MAHOGANY, GENUINE	acajou (French)	Sweitenia macrophylla	med. reddish brown	medium	medium
33. MAHOGANY, PHILIPPINE (dk. red)	guijo, red lauan, tangile	Shorea spp.	med. to dark red	medium	med. to coarse
34. MAHOGANY, PHILIPPINE (lt. red)	almon, bagtican, mayapis, white lauan	Shorea and Parashorea spp.	light red	medium	coarse
35. MANSONIA	bete, ofun, aprono, African walnut	Mansonia altissima	medium to dk. cocoa	medium	medium
36. MAPLE, HARD	sugar maple, (bird's-eye, curly)	Acer saccharum	cream	hard	fine
37. MAPLE, SOFT	(none in U.S.) (usually includes box elder)	Acer spp.	pale tan	medium	medium
38 & 39. *OAK, RED	pin oak, black oak, etc.	Quercus spp.	salmon pink	hard	medium open-pored
40. OAK, WHITE	bur oak, post oak, chestnut oak, etc.	Quercus spp.	pale tan	hard	medium close-pored

6-1. *This table lists common types of wood and gives some of their characteristics. Categories and abbreviations are explained in the text.*

COMMON TYPES OF WOOD (Continued)

Grain	Ease of Working	Stability Rating	Durability	Availability	Source	Cost	Beauty Rating
straight to roey	2	1	1	1	West Africa	medium	1 to 2
straight	2	1	3	1	Western U.S.	medium	2
straight to roey	3	2	1	1	P.I., Malaysia, Thailand	medium	3
straight	2	1	2	1	Northern and Eastern U.S.	medium	2
straight	2	2	3	1	Ecuador and Latin America	medium	4
straight	1	2	3	1	Central and South America	low	2
straight	1	1	3	1	Eastern U.S.	medium	3
straight	2	1	2	1	Eastern U.S.	medium	2
straight	2	2	3	1	Eastern U.S. and Canada	med. high	2
straight to irregular	2	2	2	1	Eastern U.S.	high	1
straight to roey	3	2	1	3	Florida thru Brazil	high	2
irregular (knotty)	2	1	1	1	Southern & Eastern U.S.	medium	2
straight to roey	1	1	1	2	Latin America	medium	2 (excessive gum)
straight	1	1	1	1	N. California to Alaska	med. low	3
straight	2	1	2	1	Eastern U.S.	med. high	1
straight	1	1	1	1, but wormy only	Eastern U.S.	high	2
roey	2	2	1	2	Mex., C. Ameri., and Columbia	high	1
straight	1	3	3	1	Eastern U.S., California, Canada	low	3
straight	1	1	1	1	Southern U.S.	medium	2
straight	1	2	3	1	S.E. Asia, P.I. & Australia	medium	2
straight to irregular	3	2	1	1	Gabon: W. Africa, Macassar: P.I. & E. Indies	very high	1
straight to irregular	2	2	3	1	Eastern U.S., S.E. Canada	med. low	2
irregular	2	3	3	1-usually mixed w/tupelo	Southeastern U.S.	med. low	3
straight	2	2	3	1	Southeastern U.S.	med. high	2
straight to irregular	2	2	3	1	Western U.S.	med. low	3
straight to roey	2	2	3	3	Brazil	high	2
roey	2	2	2	1	Hawaii	med. high	1
straight	1	1	3	1	West Africa	med. high	1
straight	2	2	3	1	Eastern U.S.	medium	3
roey	2	1	2	1	West Africa	med. high	2
straight to roey	2	1	2	1	Mexico to Nor. S. America	med. high	1
straight to roey	2	2	2	1	Philippine Islands	medium	2
straight to roey	2	2	2	1	Philippine Islands	medium	2
straight	2	2	2	1	West Africa	med. high	2
straight (plain maple)	2	2	3	1	Eastern U.S. and Canada	med. high	2
straight	2	2	3	1	Eastern U.S., Canada & Pacific N.W.	med. low	3
straight	2	2	3	1	Eastern U.S.	medium	2
straight	2	2	2	1	Eastern U.S. and California	medium	2

(Continued on next page)

COMMON TYPES OF WOOD (Continued)

Common Name	Other Common Name	Botanical Name	Color	Density	Texture
41. OBECHE	ayous, samba, African whitewood	Triplochiton scleroxylon	off-white to yellow	soft	medium
42. PADAUK	vermillion, (narra in P.I.)	Pterocarpus spp.	red (some kinds golden)	hard	medium
43. PECAN	sweet pecan, bitternut hickory, etc.	Hicoria spp.	pale tan	hard	medium
44. PINE, PARANA	araucaria	Araucaria angustifolia and araucana	pale reddish brown	med. soft	fine
45. PINE, PONDEROSA	bull pine, black jack	Pinus ponderosa	lt. orangey brown	soft	medium
46. PINE, SUGAR WHITE	(none in U.S.)	Pinus lambertiana	lt. orangey brown	soft	fine
47. PINE, SOUTHERN YELLOW	longleaf pine, shortleaf pine, etc.	Pinus spp.	pale orangey yellow	medium to hard	coarse
48. POPLAR, YELLOW	tulip tree	Liriodendron tulipifera	lt. brn. with greenish cast	medium	medium
49. PRADU	(first cousin to Padauk)	Pterocarpus spp.	red	hard	medium
50. RAMIN	melawis	Gonystylus bancanus	white	med. hard	fine
51. REDWOOD	(none in U.S.)	Sequoia sempervirens	brownish red	soft	medium to fine
52 & 53. ROSEWOOD	palisander, marnut, jacaranda	Dalbergia spp.	striped dark brown	hard	fine to medium
54. SASSAFRAS	gumbo file	Sassafras albidum	pale orangey brown	medium	coarse
55. SATINWOOD, CEYLON	East Indian satinwood	Chloroxylon swietenia	pale to golden yellow	hard	very fine
56. SPRUCE, SITKA	tideland spruce	Picea sitchensis	pinkish white	soft	medium coarse
57. SYCAMORE	American plane tree, buttonwood	Platanus occidentalis	lt. pinkish brown	medium	medium
58. TEAK, GENUINE	(none in U.S.)	Tectona grandis	med. brown	hard	coarse
59. TULIPWOOD	pau rosa (rosewood group)	Dalbergia aff. frutescens	striped yellow & red	very hard	medium
60. WALNUT, NORTH AMERICAN	black walnut	Juglans nigra	dk. brown	med. hard	medium
61. WENGE	Panga panga, dikela	Milletia laurentii	striped dk. brown to black	hard	coarse
62. WILLOW	(none in U.S.)	Salix nigra	varied lt. tan to dk. brown	soft	coarse
63. ZEBRAWOOD	zebrano, zingana	Brachystegia spp.	striped pale brown	hard	medium
64. BIRD'S-EYE FIGURE	A decorative feature in hard maple due to small conical depressions in the outer annual ring. See 36.				
65. BURL FIGURE	Walnut from the part of the tree immediately surrounding a knot. See 60.				

*Rift red describes a method of cutting similar to quartersawing.

Under "Color," most of the abbreviations are self-explanatory; *lt.* means *light*, *r.* means *red* or *reddish*, *y.* means *yellow* or *yellowish*, *brn.* is *brown*, *wh.* is *white*, *dk.* is *dark, etc.*

"Density" ratings are assigned on the per-thousand-board-feet weight of thoroughly air-dried or kiln-dried lumber in the rough. Ratings are as follows:

2500 lbs. or less . . . . .Soft
over 2500 to 3600 lbs. . . . .Medium
over 3600 to 4800 lbs. . . . . .Hard
over 4800 lbs. . . . . .Very Hard

"Texture" refers to the general physical composition of the wood. The ratings "fine" and "coarse" are self-explanatory. Texture affects both superficial and finishing qualities.

"Grain" is a guide to the growth characteristics of the tree. The term *straight* in this context is self-explanatory. *Roey* is an industry term meaning that the grain is interlocked, irregular, or wavy. Woods with roey grain nearly always display ribbon stripe figure on quarter section.

"Ease of Working" is graded as:
1—Very easy to work.
2—Moderately easy to work.
3—Difficult to work.
4—Carbide-tipped tool edges recommended.

"Stability Rating" refers to the wood's tendency to stay in place, both before and after it is worked.

COMMON TYPES OF WOOD (Continued)

Grain	Ease of Working	Stability Rating	Durability	Availability	Source	Cost	Beauty Rating
straight	1	1	3	2	West Africa	medium	2
straight to interlocked	2	1	1	1	West Africa, S.E. Asia	high	1
straight	3	1	3	1	Eastern and Southern U.S.	medium	2
straight	1	3	3	1	Latin America	med. low	3
straight	1	1	3	1	Western U.S.	medium	2
straight	1	1	3	1	Western U.S.	medium	2
straight	2	2	3	1	Southern U.S.	med. low	3
straight	2	2	3	1	Southeastern U.S.	medium	2
straight to interlocked	2	1	1	2	Thailand	high	1
straight	2	2	3	1	S.E. Asia	medium	2
straight	1	1	1	1	N. California and Oregon	medium	2
straight to wavy	3	1	1	1	India and S. America	very high	1
straight	2	1	1	1	Eastern U.S. & S. Ontario	medium	2
roey	2	1	3	3	India & Ceylon	high	1
straight	2	2	3	2	Alaska to N. California	medium	3
irregular	2	3	3	1	Eastern U.S.	medium	2
straight to wavy	4	1	1	1	S.E. Asia, India, etc.	high	1
straight to roey	3	2	3	2	Brazil	high	1
straight to irregular	2	1	1	1	Eastern U.S.A.	high	1
straight	2	2	1	2	West African Congo	high	1
straight	2	2	1	1	Eastern U.S.	med. low	3
roey	2	2	2	1	West Africa	high	1

Ratings are:

1—Exceptionally stable.
2—Of satisfactory stability.
3—Below average in stability.
Woods rated below average in stability can nearly always be used successfully when the nature of this characteristic is understood.

"Durability" refers to rot resistance in situations favoring decay, such as direct contact with earth. It also refers to heartwood only, as no sapwood is durable in this sense.

Conversely, any wood not exposed to unfavorable conditions is "durable" in the sense of lasting so long as it remains dry . . . there is no such thing as "dry rot."

Durability ratings are as follows:

1—Exceptionally durable.
2—Moderately durable.
3—Not durable in this sense.

"Availability" needs no explanation except to say that this rating refers only to the United States market. Ratings are:

1—Normally found on U.S. market.
2—Usually obtainable on order.
3—Not commonly marketed in the U.S. but might be obtained through extra effort.
4—Generally unavailable because rare or because export forbidden by country of origin.

"Source" refers to geographical origin. Listings include only principal recorded sources, not necessarily all of them.

"Source" abbreviations are easily

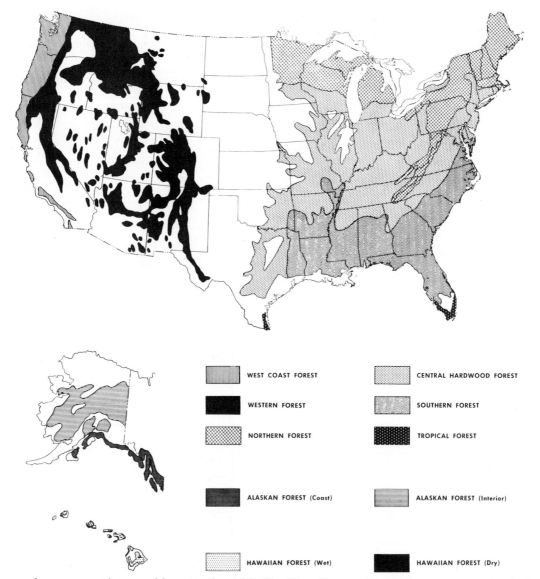

6-2. *This map shows areas of renewable natural wealth. The West Coast or Pacific forests are primarily Douglas fir. However, they also have western red cedar, spruce, and hemlock. The western forests include much of our softwood timber, primarily pine, although there are some hardwoods. The northern forests have such trees as hemlock, red spruce, white pine, and several kinds of hardwoods. The central hardwood forests include oak, cherry, birch, and many other kinds of hardwoods. In the southern forests are such softwoods as pine and cypress, and many kinds of hardwoods. The tropical forests have ebony and palm trees. The coast regions of Alaska have primarily western hemlock and spruce, while the interior forests are heavy with white spruce and white birch. The Hawaiian forests have many softwoods and some unusual trees such as monkey pod and koa. The forest areas of the United States comprise over three-quarters of a billion acres, or more land than in all the states east of the Mississippi.*

understood, a possible exception being *P.I.* for Philippine Islands.

"Cost" refers to no particular figure. It is an attempt to compare the wood's price with the price of other species from the same general area.

"Beauty Rating." Woods of pronounced color and figure, with desirable finishing characteristics, rate best and are generally most favored.

Fine Furniture Woods*

Most fine furniture is made from hardwoods, although a few softwoods, particularly pine, are also used. There are about 50 commercial varieties of hardwoods, but only about a half dozen are universally popular for furniture. Many of the better hardwoods, particularly fine walnut, are in rather limited supply. For this reason more plentiful woods are often substituted in furniture manufacturing. A good example is pecan, which is a member of the hickory family. Fig. 7-1. Following are the most popular and important hardwoods for fine furniture.

WALNUT

Furniture woods have their ups and downs in popularity, like the furniture styles for which they are used. However, one which seems to have kept its popularity is walnut. One reason for this is that walnut grain has an almost endless variety of figures.

Persian walnut, the original species, is quite rare today. It is reserved for fine detail work such as inlays because of its dramatic figuring. The walnut crotch produces the most remarkable patterns. Crotches are cut from the trunk of the tree just below the branches. Here the growing fibers swirl as they twist their way toward first one branch, then another.

Walnut burls are often interesting enough to hang on walls. The prized burl is actually cut from a wartlike growth, sometimes several feet in diameter. When the burl is cut crosswise, tiny circular mottled areas can be seen.

Stumpwood provides grain with another pattern. Walnut veneers sawed from the base or stump of the tree have a great variety of dark and light tones that provide a rich, dramatic appearance.

Walnut varies considerably in color, depending on where it is grown. The American variety is called *black walnut*, but only because of the color of the nut shells. Actually the wood ranges from light gray brown to darker, purplish

7-1(a). *Pecan is a southern hardwood whose hardness and strength have made its use for furniture widespread. While its availability is still limited in some areas, its use in woodwork is increasing. Its color can vary from the creamy white of its sapwood to the reddish brown (with some darker streaks) of its heartwood. Also common are small, dark "burls." If uniformity of color is desired, some stain must be applied and further toning anticipated. Its principal use is as a veneered product for interior cabinetry and paneling, where its rather strong but pleasing and warm grain is displayed.*

---

*Adapted from material by courtesy of Condé Nast Publications, Inc.

7-1(b). *This furniture is a good example of a pleasing combination of woods. The solid parts are pecan, and the front features a pattern of walnut veneers.*

7-2. This end table shows a typical use of walnut for Contemporary furniture.

brown. It is often treated to remove the purplish cast.

In addition to its beauty, walnut has many practical advantages. Though not as hard as oak, it is harder than mahogany. It shrinks less than most woods; so it can withstand varying climatic conditions.

Walnut has been given almost every known finish. No other wood so readily takes oil finishes.

The History of Walnut

Walnut has a long ancestry. Around 500 BC seeds of the great tree were carried from Persia to eastern Europe. By the time of the Renaissance, walnut had become a dominant wood for fine furniture and interior architecture. Early settlers in America found walnut trees in great supply, including some of great height and with diameters of eight or nine feet. The trees were cut down indiscriminately to make way for the first farms and roads and later for cities and highways. Only in the last 40 or 50 years has any attempt been made to restore this loss. These recent plantings comprise our present source for cabinet woods.

Walnut has always been popular for American furniture. It was com-

monly used in this country before mahogany, and it is still popular today. Fig. 7-2. It is used in much the same way that the Scandinavians use teak: in very simple designs that let the fine grain speak for itself.

Buying Walnut

The wise buyer looks for proof of authenticity when buying a piece of walnut furniture. Many trade names for walnut apply to cheaper woods or are actually plastic laminates printed with walnut grain and color. Sometimes walnut comprises only a small part of the wood used in a furniture piece. While this is not necessarily a disadvantage, you should know what you are buying. Walnut veneers are widely used on cabinets and tabletops to provide decorative interest, but the legs and structural parts should be solid walnut rather than veneered.

Care of Walnut Furniture

Walnut furniture takes about the same care and attention as other hardwood furniture. For conventional finishes, water and mild hand soap and a good paste wax will pre-

serve the original appearance. An oil finish needs only a light application of boiled linseed oil about twice a year. Buy the oil already boiled and warm it up in a double boiler. For regular care, wipe off an oil finish occasionally with a damp cloth and a little linseed oil soap.

MAHOGANY

The word *mahogany* has become almost synonymous with fine furniture. Its popularity results from many excellent qualities. It has a handsome grain, is adaptable to finishes, and has a texture that is firm, yet easy to cut and carve. It is softer than many hardwoods, yet has excellent strength compared to its weight. Fig. 7-3. Mahogany boards have fewer defects than most other hardwoods. This makes for economy in production. Also, some of the broadest boards come from the huge mahogany tree.

The great variety of distinctive mahogany figures lends itself to practically any design. This wood can be finished in red, yellow, or bleached tones, high-gloss or dull, and many others. Natural mahogany, when given only a protective

7-3. Mahogany is an excellent wood for turning, carving, fluting, and other machining. It also has great tensional strength.

covering of colorless beeswax, will mellow to light brown.

In the 18th century, Thomas Chippendale introduced and popularized the familiar red finishes also used by Sheraton, Hepplewhite, and the Adam Brothers. There was no major change until bleached mahogany became the favorite for the garish Modern of the 1920s. The "bleached look" remained popular until the trend to Contemporary design called for more natural finishes. It is to mahogany's credit that it takes flat, rubbed oil finishes as readily as it takes hard, glossy lacquer finishes.

Note that certain other woods are sometimes finished to look like mahogany. Also, some woods commonly called mahogany are not of the true variety. It should not be assumed that all products resembling mahogany, or even those advertised as mahogany, will have the excellent qualities of the true species.

Mahogany's Rise to Popularity

Mahogany grows only in the tropical regions of the West Indies, Central America, South America, and along the Gold Coast of Nigeria. No one in England knew of its existence until the 16th century era of exploration. Cortez is said to have built ships with mahogany planking during the first half of the 16th century. In America, early woodworkers were more interested in woods that were easy to obtain. They turned to native woods such as maple, cherry, birch, and walnut. However, colonial landowners and traders soon began to improve their homes, bringing delicate mahogany furniture into fashion. Since then mahogany has enjoyed continuing popularity.

Buying Mahogany

From true mahogany you can expect furniture and veneers of high quality. Mahogany furniture is available in every price bracket, but on the average it tends to cost a little less than other hardwood pieces. This is because the lumber has little waste and can be sawed into wide planks requiring fewer joints. For veneers, the fine quality and even grain of mahogany make thin slicing possible, and its open pores help glues to hold firm.

Care of Mahogany Furniture

Care of mahogany was once a problem. Early methods of finishing gave the wood surface little protection from scratches or discoloration. However, improved finishes now give mahogany the same resistance to stains, burns, water-ring marks, and scratches as any other fine hardwood. Periodic application of a furniture paste or spray wax will clean and preserve the wood.

CHERRY

Cherry furniture is an undeniable part of the American tradition. However, this wood was used in furniture making at least as early as 400 BC. Greek and Roman artisans, highly skilled in the decorative arts, used cherry wood for inlays. At that time furniture consisted mainly of benches, tables, and a few accessory pieces. By the 16th and 17th centuries, when oak and walnut were the most popular cabinet woods in Italy and France, cherry was still used widely for inlay. In 19th century Europe, cherry was one of the leading furniture woods.

Cherry was introduced into American furniture in the 17th century when it caught the fancy of colonial cabinetmakers because of its good qualities and abundance. White pine and maple were used for most of the practical household furniture we usually think of as Early American, while cherry was reserved for the more elegant adaptations of European designs. Fig. 7-4. By the 19th century, cherry was sharing favor with walnut and mahogany.

7-4. *A plentiful supply of cherry in the New England colonies made it a logical choice of early American cabinetmakers.*

Characteristics

Wild black cherry is the species that provides furniture hardwood. It is strong, stiff, and moderately hard. Though considered close-grained, there is enough character in the grain to interest many designers. The markings of cherry are less distinct than walnut and mahogany.

People often associate cherry with a reddish brown color seen most frequently in cherry furniture. However, cherry logs often have a distinct grayish cast, while others are light straw-colored. The freshly cut heartwood is usually of a light amber hue which darkens with age. Heartwood may eventually show alternate light and dark streaks. Sapwood is even lighter, varying from white to yellow brown.

Forests of cherry are found principally in the Appalachian region of Pennsylvania, West Virginia, and Ohio. There are also some growths in Michigan and upper New York State. In Europe this wood grows in

France, Italy, Germany, Spain, and Portugal.

The Range of Finishes

Cherry takes a variety of finishes. Many furniture manufacturers prefer to treat it with a clear, natural lacquer-and-wax finish. However, because of its close grain this wood may also be given a sleek, painted finish, and you may see very dark, almost black finishes on some of the more expensive cherry furniture.

The finish most often associated with cherry is the so-called "fruitwood." Originally the term referred to the delicate, natural color of furniture made of any of the fruitwoods, such as cherry, apple, or pear. Although many of these woods are no longer popular, a version of the original fruitwood finish is now commonly applied to maple and birch as well as to cherry. It features the distressed appearance popularized by early French Provincial furniture.

Buying Cherry

Cherry is not too difficult to identify. You can tell this wood by its strong annual growth rings and by numerous character markings such as pitch pockets and tiny pin knots.

Cherry is a relatively expensive wood. While the price of logs is not great, the percentage of waste is high. This means that the quality standards of the manufacturer are an important element in the price of the furniture. Manufacturers who insist on the finest wood and maintain the best quality of construction must put a higher price tag on their cherry furniture.

If a piece of furniture is advertised as wild black cherry, you can be reasonably certain that it is made of this wood. However, there is quite a bit of inexpensive furniture on the market in which cherry is combined with less expensive maple.

7-5. *This simple, sturdy chest of Early American design is made of maple.*

Care of Cherry Furniture

Black cherry furniture requires no special care beyond the usual fine treatment any hardwood deserves. An occasional washing with mild soap and water followed by a gentle rubdown with a soft cloth will maintain the original beauty of the wood. An application of furniture wax three or four times a year will highlight cherry's lovely color and grain.

MAPLE AND BIRCH

Maple trees that give us maple sugar and syrup for pancakes also supply us with fine hardwood for furniture. Birch trees that once gave bark for Indian canoes—as in the poem *Hiawatha*—now provide hardwood for chairs, tables, and chests. Maple and birch have been twin favorites of American furniture makers since early colonial days.

Both trees grow all across the northern part of our country. The ready supply of both woods has had much to do with their long popularity.

Characteristics

Two species of birch are used in furniture production: yellow birch and sweet birch. Yellow birch is far more abundant today. Sweet birch, which is found in the Appalachian region, was more popular in colonial days and was called "mountain mahogany" because of its dark reddish brown color. In its natural state yellow birch is actually a warm, light brown. It is dense and hard and ranges from a very straight, fine grain when the logs are quartersawed to a swirl figure when they are flat-sliced or rotary-cut. Stumps, crotches, and trees which have been subjected to unusual growing conditions produce intricate curls and swirl patterns that are used in furniture veneers and wall paneling.

The species of maple most commonly used in furniture is usually known as sugar maple. Fig. 7-5. It is a hard, heavy wood of fine and even texture. While the grain is normally straight, lumber with a bird's-eye figure or with wavy, curly grain is also available. Maple sapwood is white to pinkish white in color. There is an abrupt change from sapwood to the pinkish brown heartwood. The dark pink to reddish brown growth rings can be easily seen, but the pores are almost invisible. Maple is not as easily glued as some of the softer, more porous woods, but modern production techniques have overcome this problem to some extent. The fine, even texture of maple makes it highly suitable for painted and enameled finishes, since the surface needs no filling and paint adheres to it well.

Birch has a similar close, compact grain which makes it ideal for spool beds and turned posts and legs of tables, chairs, and desks. Birch is often used in combination with maple because of their similarity in color and grain. Fig. 7-6.

Range of Finishes

Maple is often used for Early American furniture pieces. At one time such pieces were stained or glazed to a red brown shade, but in recent years a more mellow yellow brown finish has become popular. The natural light tone of birch brought it to the attention of 18th and 19th century designers. In the present century birch again had a surge of popularity for Modern Scandinavian style pieces. These pieces are usually given a natural finish. For a short time maple had a similar popularity for Modern furniture. Today maple is generally found in Early American designs.

Multitude of Uses

In production volume of lumber and other wood products, maple ranks fourth among hardwoods. It is found in a remarkable range of everyday items. Because of its hardness, superior strength, and fine grain, it makes excellent flooring and is often used in combination with walnut for parquet floors (inlaid floors made up of geometric designs). Because of its acoustical properties, maple is used for making pianos and stringed instruments. Maple breadboards, meat servers, and similar kitchen woodenware are in countless American homes. For recreation we use croquet mallets and balls, Indian clubs and dumbbells, bowling pins, and billiard cues, all commonly of maple.

Birch in its many different tones and grain patterns is widely used for doors, floors, and wall paneling. Kitchen-cabinet manufacturers are very partial to both birch and maple. Both woods have the

strength to take daily wear, and both have a clear, smooth grain that takes natural or painted finishes well. Maple and birch furniture ranges from low-priced, painted pieces to quite expensive designs. As with other furniture, the cost is not affected as much by the wood itself as by the quality of work, the construction standards, and the finishing techniques.

Durability and Maintenance

Both maple and birch stand up well under ordinary household use. Because gluing maple and birch cabinetwork is more difficult than gluing softer, more porous woods, it may not survive high humidity. On the other hand, these solid woods can be relied upon to keep their shape in humid climates where solid doors and tabletops of softer woods are likely to warp.

Caring for birch and maple furniture presents no problems. Today's tough, sturdy finishes protect the wood from wear and tear. Periodic wiping with a damp, soaped cloth along with monthly treatments with a good paste or spray wax will keep the luster bright.

OAK

It would be difficult to name a wood with a longer and more illustrious history in furniture design than oak. Oak furniture has been found in excavations of Greek and Roman homes. History shows that oak has remained in constant use in many countries, and during the Middle Ages in England it took on singular importance. Lords and ladies sat around great oak tables in medieval halls while jesters squatted on oak stools. Bishops and cardinals mounted oak pulpits. English kings ruled from carved oak thrones. The "Golden Age of Oak" continued from the 14th through the 17th centuries when it merged with the "Age of Walnut."

The historical popularity of oak was not confined to England. This wood was also dominant in carved and ornamented Spanish furniture, and in our country it is most commonly associated with the furniture of the early Spanish missions. "Mission oak" or "ranch oak" furniture was a part of life in the Old West.

As more elegant, refined furniture styles came into fashion, oak was replaced by walnut and mahogany. The return of oak in the Victorian period was unfortunate in that the designs of that period—the late 19th century—were grotesque. Similarly, a great deal of the early Modern oak furniture of the 1920s showed remarkably poor design. Of course, these failures of design do not reflect discredit upon oak.

Kinds of Oak

Of the more than 200 species of oak distributed over the world, about 50 are native to the United States. Among the best-known is white oak, a stately tree which reaches heights of 70 to 100 feet.

7-6. *A dresser of maple and birch.*

7-7. *The durability of oak makes it a happy choice for a dining room that will get hard use.*

Red oak is perhaps the most beautiful of the American species. Its wood is an attractive amber color with a reddish tinge, and it is coarse-textured, hard, and durable.

Oak is extremely well adapted to woodworking. Depending upon the way the wood is sliced, the figures vary from a straight, pencil-striped, open-pored surface to a leaf-and-lacewood effect. Oak is often used today in furniture and paneling for which a bold texture is desired. Fig. 7-7. Oak is heavier than most cabinet woods, at least as strong as most, and exceptionally durable. It works well by machine. The woodcrafter can utilize its strong, interesting figure and open-pore grain without having to worry about the splintering or fuzzing of hickory, ash, and other similar woods.

Historically, oak was almost always used in its solid form; but since the advent of modern veneer and plywood, it has been used more for its decorative figures. Often it is combined with close-grained woods such as walnut, cherry, and ebony.

Oak Finishes

Oak takes many distinctive finishes. Because of its open grain, unique coloring effects can be obtained by varying the material used to fill the pores before applying lacquer or varnish finish. Water stains can also be used to achieve a variety of color effects ranging from dark brown to gray, amber, and red brown. With the use of bleach and a white filler, oak can be given a light platinum tint. Often a light gray filler is used, then a paint is applied and wiped off, revealing the wood's distinctive figure in flaky white outlines.

Care of Oak

Oak furniture, flooring, and paneling are highly resistant to changes in climate and to general use. White oak's close cell structure makes it practically impervious to liquids. Red oak cells are not so close, and the wood therefore is less resistant to stains.

Because of its sturdy character, oak furniture needs less care and

attention than most. Occasional wiping with a soft cloth or washing with mild soap and water will keep oak looking as good as new. If oak has not been properly dried, you may have a warpage problem.

THE EXOTICS

Most furniture hardwoods come from rather familiar trees, but there is one group—the exotics—that is unfamiliar to most North Americans. These woods and their names, such as paldao, teak, limba, zebrawood, ebony, and rosewood, suggest the jungles of Africa, the mountains of Japan and India, and other faraway, romantic lands from which they come. Teak has gained prominence for its use in Scandinavian design, and occasionally you will find a chest or table made of some other exotic wood. However, the vivid colors and dramatic textures of the exotics are used mostly for decorative accent.

Teak

Teak comes from the rugged regions of the Indian Peninsula, Burma, and Thailand. Because of its extraordinary weight and density, it will not float. The logs have to be hauled down from the mountains by elephant. A single log may weigh as much as seven tons and require seven elephants to move it!

East Indian teak is one of the most versatile and valuable foreign woods and has attained great prestige value. The figure variations are extensive, and it is available in both lumber and veneered products. Adding to its appeal is its color, which varies from tawny yellow to dark brown, often with light and dark accent streaks. It is perhaps most appealing in plainsawn or sliced cuts. It has unique stability and weathering properties that make it ideal for exterior applications. However, its high cost usually limits its use to decorative interior woodwork, most often in veneer form. Its great beauty and interest dictate its being finished in its near natural state.

Today teak is popular for furniture of Scandinavian, Oriental, and Contemporary styles. Fig. 7-8. The worldwide reputation of teak is based on its high resistance to decay, its ability to hold its shape under varying moisture conditions, and the relative ease with which it can be worked with carbide tools. The wood feels oily to the touch. It is hard and comparable in strength to our native white oak.

Satinwood

Satinwood comes from Sri Lanka and India. Furniture made of this wood has been uncovered in the ruins of Pompeii, buried by a volcano in 79 AD. A French nobleman, Count de Caylus, during the 18th century created the elegant, carved and gilded satinwood designs with which we are most familiar today. The wood has a deep luster and is often highly figured. It is extremely hard and brittle, which makes it subject to surface checking. Satinwood is so expensive that you will

7-8. This teak chest is typical of Contemporary furniture, which often features rare woods.

find it used in only the finest furniture, usually in the form of banding.

Myrtle

Southern Oregon and northern California have myrtle trees which are widely known for their interesting burls. Myrtle bowls, plates, and other accessories are popular tourist items. The wood varies from golden brown to yellow green, splotched with purple. Because of this unusual coloring, the wood is used in furniture as an accent.

Paldao

Paldao is often described as "the wood afire." While many woods appear somewhat flat when a finish is applied, paldao becomes even brighter. The wood varies in color from gray brown to red brown with sharp, black markings. Paldao trees grow in small clusters deep in the jungles of southeastern Asia and the Philippines. Logging is therefore difficult.

Paldao is a hard wood that is not too difficult to work with hand tools. It has good strength and high resistance to decay. Because of limited supply and high cost, this wood is used only in very high quality furniture, principally of Contemporary design.

Zebrawood

One of the most dramatic of the exotic woods, zebrawood comes from gigantic trees that grow on the west coast of Africa. It gets its name because of its basic markings, which consist of black or dark brown stripes on a light background. The wood can assume a variety of patterns, depending on the way it is cut. When cut on the bias, the stripes make a shell design. By matching several pieces, any num-

7-9. Limba comes from Africa.

ber of figures can be obtained. As a rule, zebrawood is used sparingly, principally in inlay. Too much of it would appear garish.

Limba

In this country, limba is sometimes known as korina. Fig. 7-9. It is an African wood distinguished by its naturally blond, pale yellow color. Its open grain structure is much like the true mahoganies, but is slightly softer. Unlike the mahoganies, it has little decay resistance and should be used only for interior woodwork.

Availability in both lumber and veneer form is subject to some regional limitations. In lumber, limba is usually plainsawn, and in veneer form it is quarter-sliced with resulting straight grained effect. Its light color affords extreme versatility in finishing, and its general usage is for paneling, cabinetwork, and store fixtures.

Elm

Though not strange or scarce, elm is used in ways that are similar to those of truly exotic woods. Elm makes a warm, elegant accent for other woods, although it is sometimes used alone. Fig. 7-10. Whether from France, England, or the

7-10. *Elm burl is used as an accent in the drawer fronts and top of this cherry chest.*

today for both inlay and cabinet-work. Fig. 7-11.

Yew

Yew wood from England often has a wild but graceful pattern which varies in color from pale red to cedar. Yew is popular for small, occasional furniture such as desks and commodes.

Ebony

Ebony from Africa and Asia is perhaps the best-known of the exotic woods. It is used for the black keys of a piano. Ebony used in furniture is not solid black but is striped with bands of dark brown or salmon pink. Ebony furniture has been traced as far back as the 17th century BC when the Egyptians and the Babylonians used it in combination with gold, silver, and ivory for court furniture. The wood was highly prized by the Greeks and Romans

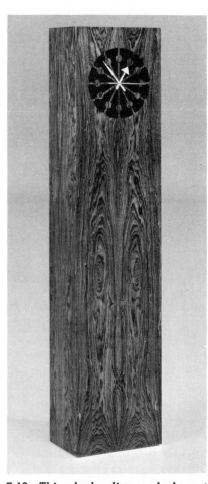

7-12. *This sleek, slim, and elegant clock of rosewood veneer has a face of ebony.*

United States, elm has a prized burl with a small-to-medium pattern. The color varies from light brown to tan or reddish brown tones.

Rosewood

Rosewood comes from Brazil and India. Its name derives from the fragrance given off when it is cut or burned. The wood is very hard, with dense open grain.

Rosewood has variegated and irregular grain patterns resulting from its growth characteristics. Color varies from rose to dull red, purple, cream, and even black. The lumber is in very limited supply and seldom available in squared planks. The true beauty of rosewood is best expressed in veneer form, where flitch selection of widely different patterns of color and grain is possible. A heavy residue of oil in the wood makes possible high-luster finishes. Rosewood is used in fine furniture

7-11. *This cabinet is made from oak with rosewood inserts.*

and was again popular in Europe in the 15th century. Ebony is exceptionally hard and heavy. At present it is used mostly for decorative inlay. Fig. 7-12.

Primavera

Primavera comes from Mexico and Central America. It is sometimes misnamed "white mahogany" because both woods have a medium-to-course texture and a straight or slightly wavy grain. The color of primavera is lighter than mahogany, varying from yellow white to yellow brown. The wood is most commonly used for cabinet-work, although highly figured boards are good for inlay.

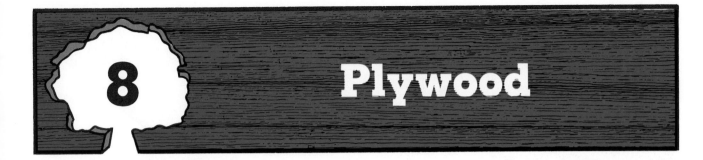

8

Plywood

Plywood is a manufactured wood product widely used in furniture, built-ins, kitchen cabinets, and paneling. There is a common, but mistaken, belief that quality furniture is made entirely of solid wood. The fact is that the greatest part of the wood used in fine furniture today, over 90 percent, is plywood.

Most furniture pieces are a combination of plywood and solid wood. Fig. 8-1. Large, flat areas, such as the tops of tables, cabinets, and desks, are usually of plywood construction, and this technique can also be used for simple and compound curves.

ADVANTAGES OF PLYWOOD

Plywood has many advantages over solid wood. Some of these include:

● Plywood has equal strength both along and across the panel. While solid wood is relatively strong with the grain, it is weaker across the grain. In plywood, the grain direction of adjoining plies is at right angles, giving strength in both directions.

● Checking, splitting, and warpage are greatly reduced.

● Dimensional stability is high. In plywood there is little change in dimensions due to moisture.

● The natural beauty of the wood (color, figure, grain, and texture) can be shown to best advantage because of the various methods of cutting the veneers.

● A wide range of sizes and thicknesses is possible. Special sizes and types of panels can be produced for specific purposes.

● Plywood conserves our wood supply by making maximum use of natural raw materials.

● Ease of construction and finishing with large plywood panels saves time and money.

KINDS OF PLYWOOD CONSTRUCTION

There are four methods of producing plywood. *Veneer-core* plywood is made by gluing together three, five, seven, or nine plies of thin veneer to make up a sort of "wood sandwich." Fig. 8-2.

Lumber-core plywood contains a core of narrow, sawed-lumber strips with crossbands and face veneer glued on both sides. Figs. 8-3 and 8-4. Generally, lumber-core plywood is five-ply, although some furniture manufacturers use a three-ply variety. Lumber-core plywood is commonly used in furniture, cabinetry, and other pieces that call for dowels, splines, dovetail joints, exposed edges, or butt hinges. *Particle-board* plywood has a core of particle board. Fig. 8-5.

Composite plywood has a rigid core of oriented-fiber flakes. The flakes are oriented in the opposite direction of the veneer face and back. Fig. 8-6.

8-1. *A piece of quality furniture with just the right combination of plywood and solid wood. The posts, frame parts, drawer sides, and back are made of solid wood. The remainder of the desk is lumber-core plywood made in the manufacturer's own plant. In this way, the consumer is assured of the best possible construction.*

Three-ply Veneer Core Construction

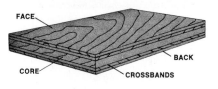

Five-ply Veneer Core Construction

Multiply Veneer Core Construction

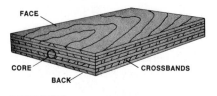

Five-ply Lumber Core Construction

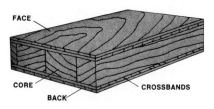

Five-ply Particleboard Core Construction

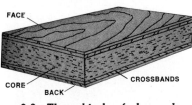

8-2. *Three kinds of plywood.*

Because of their balanced construction, plywood panels do not warp easily. *Balanced construction* means that all plies are arranged in pairs, one on either side of the core. For each ply on one side of the core, there is a similar, parallel ply on the other side. The matched plies should be of the same thickness and have similar properties with regard to shrinkage and densi-

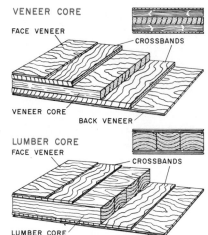

8-3. *Here you see the difference between veneer-core and lumber-core plywood. The standard face and back veneer thickness is 1/28" for hardwoods. For softwoods it is 1/10", although it can be cut in any thickness from 1/32" to 1/8". Crossband veneers are from 1/24" to 1/10" thick. Core veneers range from 1/32" to 7/32".*

ty. All plies should also have the same moisture content. However, it is not necessary that the matching plies be of the same kind of wood. In fact, the back ply of many hardwood plywoods is of less expensive wood than the exposed face.

MANUFACTURE OF PLYWOOD

Most plywood is produced in plants designed specifically for this purpose. Fig. 8-7. Smaller sizes of lumber-core plywood, for use in plywood furniture, are sometimes made in furniture plants.

Softwood (also called "construction and industrial") plywoods and hardwood plywoods are made in about the same way. Fig. 8-8. The first step is to cut the log sections, called *peeler blocks* or *flitches,* to a specific length. Next the bark is removed. The sections are then tenderized in a bath of hot water or steam. Temperatures are varied according to the species to obtain veneers with the smoothest possible

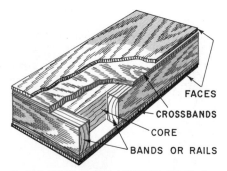

5-PLY WITH SAWN LUMBER CORE & BANDING OR RAILING

8-4. *Smaller pieces of lumber-core plywood are often made with a banding or railing of the same wood as the face veneer. Then machining can be done on the edges.*

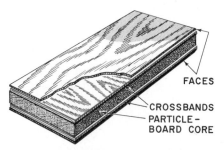

5-PLY WITH PARTICLE-BOARD CORE

8-5. *Plywood made with a particle-board core simplifies production problems and provides a very stable panel.*

8-6. *The core of composite plywood is made of large flakes of wood. These flakes are much larger than the wood chips in particle-board plywood.*

8-7. *Assembling veneer sheets in plywood production.*

surface. Veneers are then cut with one of two types of machines.

● A *rotary lathe* is used for most veneer cutting, perhaps 80 to 90 percent. The log is fastened in the lathe. The lathe spindle rotates the log against a sharp knife which peels off a continuous sheet of veneer, about the way paper is unwound from a roll.

● A *veneer slicer* is used for cutting face veneers for such woods as walnut, mahogany, cherry, and oak. The steamed flitch is held securely

in a viselike clamp and moved against a razor-sharp knife. This shears off the veneer sheets, which are kept in sequence for matching purposes. See Chapter 42 for more information about veneers.

Rotary-cut veneer then goes through an automatic clipper that cuts it to the best width and also eliminates most of the defects. Pieces that come from the clipper or directly from a veneer slicer go through driers. The driers are huge chambers equipped with heating coils and fans to reduce the wood to the desired moisture content.

While some of the veneer that has been rotary cut is large enough to be used as full-size sheets, most pieces must be edge glued. The narrower veneer sheets are put through an edge jointer and then permanently bonded together at the edges in a tapeless splicer to make sheets of the required width. After this the veneer sheets are repaired as necessary.

When panels are to have a solid lumber core, selected kiln-dried lumber is planed and trimmed so that the surfaces and edges are uniform and smooth. Then they are glued edge to edge, forming large sheets.

The veneers and the solid lumber core are now ready for the second gluing operation, in which the plies are bonded together to produce the panel. In assembling panels, the crossband veneers are put through a glue spreader that distributes the adhesive uniformly on both sides. The crossbands are then laid with their grain at right angles to the face, the back, and the core.

As stated earlier, almost all lumber-core plywood has five plies —that is, the core, two crossbands, and face and back veneers—while veneer-core plywood is made in panels of three, five, seven, or nine plies. The assembled wood sandwich is placed in a hot press. The controlled heat sets the adhesive, permanently bonding the layers together into a single, strong panel.

After the bonded panel leaves the press, it is carefully trimmed to size, and its face and back are sanded. The panel is now ready for inspection, grading, and shipping.

HARDWOOD PLYWOOD

Plywood of which the face ply is hardwood is called *hardwood plywood*. Of course, in some instances all plies are hardwood. Many species of wood and different kinds of adhesives are used in making the various grades of hardwood plywood. Fig. 8-9.

Grades

Grades designate the quality of the face, back, and interior plies. There are six grades of hardwood plywood:

Premium grade (A-1 or 1-2) has a face of some specified kind of hardwood, such as walnut or mahogany. The face must be made of tight and smoothly cut veneers which are carefully matched as to color and grain.

Good (cabinet) grade is for a natural finish and is similar to premium. However, the face veneers do not need to be matched as accurately.

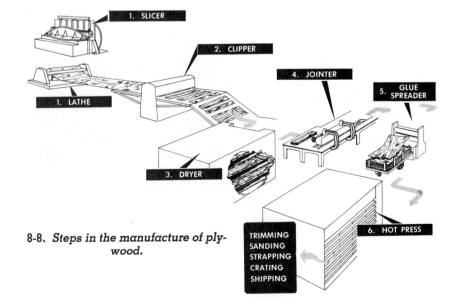

8-8. *Steps in the manufacture of plywood.*

1. SLICER
2. CLIPPER
4. JOINTER
5. GLUE SPREADER
1. LATHE
3. DRYER
6. HOT PRESS

TRIMMING
SANDING
STRAPPING
CRATING
SHIPPING

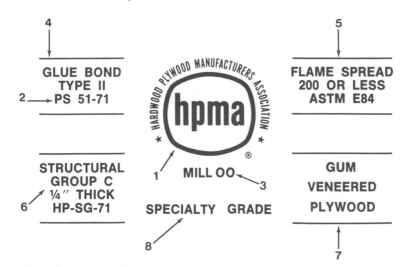

8-9. *Typical grade marks used on hardwood plywood include: (1) The trademark of the HPMA (Hardwood Plywood Manufacturers Association). (2) The
standard governing the manufacture. (3) The HPMA mill number. (4) The type
of adhesive bond: Type I (Exterior) or Type II (Interior). (5) The flamespread
rating. The lower the number, the slower the flamespread. Asbestos sheet is
0, and red oak is 100. Drapes, rugs, newspapers, clothing, etc., have a
flamespread of about 200. (6) Structural description. (7) Species of wood on
face. (8) Veneer grade of face. The grade of veneer on back is sometimes
shown following grade of face; this is optional.*

Sound (paint) grade is used as a
base for smooth, painted surfaces.
The face is free from open defects,
although it may show stains and
streaks. The veneer is not matched
for grain or color.

Utility grade can have some discoloration, knotholes up to ¾" in diameter, minor open joints, and
small areas of rough grain, but no
shake (crack between growth rings)
or similar defects.

Backing grade is unselected for
grain or color. There may be limited
knotholes and splits, as detailed in
the grading standards. Small defects are permitted, but none that
will impair panel strength.

Specialty grade is used for architectural plywood, matched-grain
panels for certain uses, and special
veneer selections.

Types of Bonds

Besides the grading system, plywood is also classified according to
its adhesive bond. There are four
types.

● The **technical fully waterproof
bond** will withstand full exposure to
water.

● Type I (exterior) is a **fully waterproof bond** which will withstand exposure to all weather.

● Type II (interior) is a **water-
resistant bond** that will keep its
strength through some wetting and
drying. This is the most common
type for hardwood plywood.

● Type III (interior) is a **moisture-
resistant bond** that will retain its
strength when subjected to occasional moisture.

Dimensions

Plywood panels are commonly
available in widths from 24" to 48"
in 6" increments, and in lengths
from 48" to 96" in 12" increments.
The most common size is 4' × 8'.

Veneer-core plywood is available
in three, five, seven, and nine plies
in the following thicknesses:

● 3 ply: ⅛", 3/16", ¼".
● 5 ply: 5/16", ⅜", ½" and ⅝".
● 7 ply: ⅝" and ¾".

● 9 ply: ¾".

Lumber-core or particle board-
core plywood is available in five
plies, ¾" thick.

Molded Plywood

Many types of hardwood plywood
are made in simple and compound
curves. Good examples of compound curves are seen in the chair
in Fig. 8-10. Curved and molded
plywood is produced either by bending and gluing in one operation or
by bending previously glued, flat
panels. See Chapter 41 for information about wood bending. Plywood
bent and glued in one operation is
usually more satisfactory because it
holds its shape better.

Appearance of Hardwood Veneers

Frequently the same kind of
wood, such as walnut or mahogany,
will appear to have different patterns
and figures. This raises the question
of how two pieces of veneer from
the same species of tree can look so
utterly different. In general, the type
of figure pattern in fine veneers depends on three things:

The **wood species**. Rosewood has
an entirely different appearance, for
example, from walnut or mahogany.

The **portion of the tree** from which
it is cut. Most veneers are cut from

8-10. *The seat and back of this chair
are molded plywood.*

the trunk, also called long wood. Other parts of the tree produce veneer that is different in appearance. See Chapter 42. The burl develops an unusual and exceptionally fine figure.

The **method of cutting**. See Chapter 42.

CONSTRUCTION AND INDUSTRIAL PLYWOOD

These plywoods are still commonly called *softwood plywoods*, even though some hardwoods are used in their manufacture. Construction and industrial plywood is made from 70 different wood species, including softwoods and native and imported hardwoods. These woods are divided into five groups. Group 1 is the strongest and stiffest; Group 5, the weakest.

These plywoods have veneer-core construction with the veneer cut by the rotary method. Plywood can be made of 3, 4, 5, 6, or 7 plies (sheets of veneer), but the number of layers is always odd—3, 5, or 7. If an even number of plies are used, two of the plies are glued with their grains parallel to form one layer. Fig. 8-11.

Plywoods are made in two basic types: exterior, made with 100 percent waterproof glue, and interior, made with highly moisture-resistant glue. The top quality veneer used is N. The quality of others ranges from A to D, with D having lowest quality. For most built-ins and paneling, interior grades ranging from A-D to B-D are used.

A-D is for interior applications where the appearance of only one side is important: paneling, built-ins, cabinet shelving.

B-D is a utility panel with one smooth, paintable side. It is used for backing, sides of built-ins, and utility shelving. *Decorative* B-D has rough sawn, brushed, grooved, or striated faces for paneling, accent walls, counter facing, and displays.

Softwood plywoods come in

(a) INTERIOR GRADES

Panel Grade Designations	Minimum Veneer Quality			Surface
	Face	Back	Inner Plies	
N-N	N	N	C	Sanded 2 sides
N-A	N	A	C	Sanded 2 sides
N-B	N	B	C	Sanded 2 sides
N-D	N	D	D	Sanded 2 sides
A-A	A	A	D	Sanded 2 sides
A-B	A	B	D	Sanded 2 sides
A-D	A	D	D	Sanded 2 sides
B-B	B	B	D	Sanded 2 sides
B-D	B	D	D	Sanded 2 sides

(b) VENEER QUALITY

N	Intended for natural finish. Selected all heartwood or all sapwood. Free of open defects. Allows some repairs.
A	Smooth and paintable. Neatly made repairs permissible. Also used for natural finish in less demanding applications.
B	Solid surface veneer. Repair plugs and tight knots permitted. Can be painted.
C	Sanding defects permitted that will not impair the strength or serviceability of the panel. Knotholes to 1½″ and splits to ½″ permitted under certain conditions.
C plugged	Improved C veneer with closer limits on knotholes and splits. C plugged face veneers are fully sanded.
D	Used only in Interior type for inner plies and backs. Permits knots and knotholes to 2½″ in maximum dimension and ½″ larger under certain specified limits. Limited splits permitted.

(c) TYPICAL WOOD SPECIES

Group 1	American Birch, Douglas Fir, Sugar Maple, and Southern Pine
Group 2	Cypress, White Fir, Western Hemlock, Philippine Mahogany, Black Maple, Red Pine, and Yellow Poplar
Group 3	Red Alder, Alaska Cedar, Eastern Hemlock, Jack Pine, Redwood, and Black Spruce
Group 4	Quaking Aspen, Western Red Cedar, Eastern Cottonwood, and Sugar Pine
Group 5	Basswood, Balsam Fir, and Balsam Poplar

(d) TYPICAL GRADE MARKING

(Also available in Groups 2, 3 and 4)

8-11(a-d). Construction and industrial plywood.

thicknesses from ¼″ to 1¼″; in widths of 36″, 48″, and 60″; and in lengths from 60″ to 144″ in 12″ increments. Plywood 48″ wide and 96″ long (4′ × 8′) is most commonly available. Plywood is ordered by width and length, type, wood species, grade, and thickness.

In furniture construction these plywoods are used primarily for interior details and for surfaces to be covered by veneer or plastic laminates.

Top quality plywood can also be used for fine finished built-ins, kitchen cabinets, and paneling.

PLYWOOD PRODUCTS WITH SPECIAL PROPERTIES

Plywood manufacturers are constantly improving both the quality and variety of their products. Many have developed some special procedure or product of their own. For instance, one manufacturer has a continuous process for making a hard-surfaced panel, called *fiberply*, which has a tough, smooth surface on both sides. A special type of hot press, the largest plywood press in the world, is used for manufacturing this product. A continuous sheet of veneer moves directly from the log, through driers, into the press. The plies are heat bonded with dry glue, and the outside layers are given a resin-impregnated surface. This process eliminates the need for a

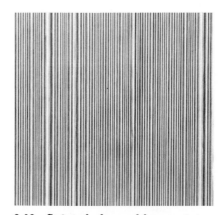

8-13. *Striated plywood has an interesting textured surface.*

8-14. *Ripplewood plywood.*

paint undercoating and reduces checking and grain raising. Fiberply comes in both interior and exterior grades and has two more plies than regular plywood—five plies in the ⅜″ thickness, seven plies in the ½″, ⅝″, and ¾″ thicknesses.

Another material is *prefinished hardwood plywood used for wall panels*, made with a permanent, factory finish. In manufacture, their surface is given a fine sanding and then a complete finishing so that the panels can be used as they are shipped. Fig. 8-12.

Prefinished plywood planks are available in pieces 16¼″ wide and 6′, 7′, or 8′ long. They can be obtained with tongue-and-groove edges so that they can be used for interior paneling.

Striated plywood has a combed surface that gives it an unusual texture. Fig. 8-13. The surface of *ripplewood plywood* has a grain pattern that is accentuated to produce a three-dimensional appearance. Fig. 8-14. Other panels may be embossed, antiqued, color-toned, or receive other woodgrain decoration.

WORKING WITH PLYWOOD

Selecting Plywood

Never attempt to use interior plywood for exteriors. This is especially

important when making furniture and in home construction. Excessive dampness or moisture will cause the plies to separate.

Storage

The best method of storing plywood is to lay the sheets flat. If this is not possible, they should be stored on edge and supported. Never lay plywood at an angle because it will warp. This is especially true of thinner panels.

Cutting

When hand sawing, always place the good face of the plywood up. Use a saw that has at least 10 points to the inch. Make sure that the panel is supported firmly so that it will not sag. Hold the saw at a low angle when cutting. If possible, place a piece of scrap stock underneath.

When using the circular saw, install a sharp combination blade or one with fine teeth. Adjust the blade so that the teeth just clear the top of the stock. Always place the plywood on the table saw with the good side up. However, when cutting with a portable power handsaw, place the good face down.

Planing Edges

It is seldom necessary to plane the edges of plywood, but when it

8-12. *This factory-finished plywood paneling requires only wiping after it is installed.*

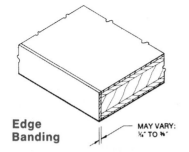

Edge Banding ⌐ MAY VARY: ¼" TO ¾"

8-15. *Edge veneer is used to cover the edges of plywood, particle board, and hardboard.*

1 *Sand the edge of the plywood or lumber you are working on. Remove sanding dust. Cut the edge veneer about ½" longer than the edge to be covered.*

2 *Preheat household iron to 300°F. On most irons, this is the setting halfway between Off and the highest setting. Increase temperature as needed to assure glue melt.*

must be done, always work from both ends toward the center. This prevents any tearing out of the plies at the end of the cut. Use a plane with a sharp blade and take shallow cuts. When using a jointer, adjust it to a very thin cut.

Treating the Edges

There are several ways to finish the edges of plywood. The most common is to use an edge-banding material of the same veneer as the face. Fig. 8-15. In some cases this material has an adhesive on it. Fig. 8-16. In other cases it is necessary to use contact cement since some edge bands have fabric backing but no adhesive. Also, laminated plastic materials may be applied with contact cement to the edges of tables. Some of the more common edge treatments are shown in Chapter 50. If plywood is to be painted, the edge-end grain can be filled with wood putty.

Using Nails and Screws

When nailing plywood, always choose nails that are the right size in relation to panel thickness. Select as follows:
- For ¾" plywood, 6d casing nails or 6d finishing nails.
- For ⅝" plywood, 6d or 8d finishing nails.
- For ½" plywood, 4d or 6d.
- For ⅜" plywood, 3d or 4d.
- For ¼" plywood, ¾" or 1" brads.

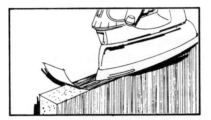

3 *Hold the veneer flush against top edge of the board. Press it on with the heated iron, allowing excess veneer to overlap. Be sure to apply even pressure and keep the iron moving. If you notice excess glue, use a strip of aluminum foil to protect the bottom of the iron. If iron gets soiled, clean before using again.*

4 *After using iron, immediately run a rolling pin or block of wood back and forth over surface of edge, applying pressure until the veneer has cooled to the touch. If you make a mistake, simply reheat the edge veneer and remove it. Then apply again.*

5 *To cut end flap, use a razor blade or sharp knife with a downward sawing motion—or —use a sandpaper block toward the face of exposed flap. Usually, only 3 or 4 strokes are necessary for a flush cut.*

6 *Since the edge veneer is square cut, it is necessary to trim only one side of the edging. This can be done with a razor blade or a sharp knife. Then sand entire edge with fine sandpaper and finish in the same manner as the panel surface.*

8-16. *This is one type of real wood veneer edging. One surface of the veneer is covered with adhesive. It is easy to apply with an ordinary household iron.*

For very careful installations, pre-drill to keep the nails from splitting the edge. The drill should be slightly smaller in diameter than the nail. Space nails about 6″ apart for most work. When nailing thin plywood, closer spacing may be necessary to avoid buckling between the joints. Nails and glue together produce a strong joint. Flathead wood screws are needed when nails will not provide adequate holding power. Glue should also be used whenever possible.

The following gives plywood thicknesses and the diameter and length of the *smallest* screws recommended. Use longer screws when the work permits:

- ¾″ plywood: No. 8, 1½″.
- ⅝″ plywood: No. 8, 1¼″.
- ½″ plywood: No. 6, 1¼″.
- ⅜″ plywood: No. 6, 1″.
- ¼″ plywood: No. 4, ¾″.

Screws or nails should be countersunk and the holes filled with wood dough, putty, or plugs. Apply filler until it is slightly higher than the plywood surface and then sand it level after it is dry.

Nails or screws do not hold well in the edge of plywood. It is important to remember this, especially when attaching hinges. Whenever possible, hinges for plywood doors should be attached to the face rather than to the edge.

Drilling

If the back side of plywood is going to show, chipped edges can be eliminated by placing a wood block under the back when drilling.

Selecting Corner Joints

When working with plywood, selecting the correct kind of corner joint is important for both strength and appearance. For simple construction in which the surfaces are to be painted, butt joints can be used. Frame construction with butt joints makes it possible to use thinner plywood.

Rabbet joints are simple to make and are excellent for many types of drawers, buffets, chests, or cupboards. The only problem is that the plies are exposed where the faces meet. One method of eliminating this is to cut the rabbet from one piece of the plywood and then cut the entire stock away from the other member, leaving only the face veneer which overlaps the first piece.

The best joint for plywood corners is the miter joint or some adaptation of it. The more difficult miter joints are the rabbet miter and lock miter. (See Chapter 39.)

Protecting the Face Veneer

In working plywood, it is important not to chip off the expensive face veneer, especially in hardwoods. This can happen at an exposed edge or corner. After stock is cut, the face corners can be protected by fastening tape to them during the construction process.

Sanding

Since most good face veneers are only 1/28″ thick, it is very important not to sand the surface too much. Good hardwood plywoods come with a super-fine sanded surface to which a finish can be applied directly. The greatest care in sanding must be taken when plywood is used in combination with solid lumber. It is easy to over-sand plywood surfaces, especially with a portable or stationary belt sander.

Removing Nails

Plywood resists splitting much more than ordinary woods. Therefore nails and screws can be fastened close to the edges. However, when removing nails from plywood, pull straight out rather than at an angle. You may splinter the outside ply if you pull out the nails at an angle.

Hardboard and Particle Board

9

Widely used for furniture and cabinets, hardboard and particle board are manufactured products of modern wood technology and research. Both combine the best characteristics of wood and adhesives, and reflect modern technology's ability to control the size, shape, and working qualities of raw materials.

HARDBOARD

Hardboard is available in boards or panels. Fig. 9-1. As the name implies, it is relatively hard. It is commonly known by the trade name Masonite.

Manufacture of Hardboard

Hardboard is manufactured from refined or partly refined wood fibers. Fig. 9-2. The first step is to chip the

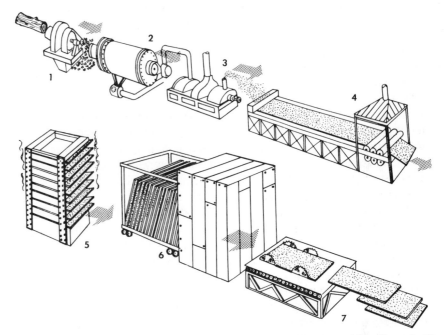

9-2. *A simplified diagram of the steps in the manufacture of hardboard. (1) Log handling. (2) Defibering. (3) Refining. (4) Forming the mat. (5) Hydraulic press. (6) Humidifying. (7) Shipment.*

9-1. *The walls of this room are paneled in hardboard. Note the pegboard above the counter.*

wood into thin pieces ⅝″ wide and 1″ long. The chips are then reduced to individual wood fibers either by steam or by a mechanical defibering process. Next, the fibers are further refined through mechanical processes which vary with the method of manufacture. Small amounts of chemicals may be added to improve the resulting board. In a machine called a felter, the fibers are interlocked into a continuous mat and compressed by heavy rollers. Lengths of this mat, called *wetlap*, are fed into multiple presses where

9-3 *Standard sheets of hardboard.*

heat and pressure produce the thin, hard, dry board sheets. After the boards leave the presses, moisture is added in a humidifier to stabilize them to atmospheric conditions. The boards are then trimmed to standard dimensions and wrapped in packages ready for shipment.

Types and Sizes of Hardboard

Hardboard is made in three basic types: standard, tempered, and service. *Standard hardboard* is given no additional treatment after manufacture. This board has high strength and good water resistance. It is commonly used in furniture and cabinetwork because it has a good sheen and finishes well. *Tempered hardboard* is standard board to which chemical and heat-treating processes have been applied to improve stiffness, hardness, and finishing properties. *Service hardboard* has somewhat less strength than standard. It is used where low weight is an advantage. It does not have quite as good sheening and finishing characteristics as standard.

Hardboard is manufactured with one or both sides smooth. One side smooth is known as S1S and two sides smooth is S2S. Hardboard is available in thicknesses from 1/16" to 3/4", the common thicknesses being 1/8", 3/16", and 1/4". The standard panel size is 4' × 8', but it is also available in widths up to 5' and in lengths to 16'. Fig. 9-3.

Specialty Hardboards

Because hardboard is manufactured, it can be made in shapes, sizes, and surfaces to meet varying needs of the furniture and cabinet-making industries. Here are a few of the many kinds available:

Perforated hardboard (pegboard) has very closely spaced holes punched or drilled in the surface. The holes may be round, square, or diamond-shaped and can be fitted with metal hooks, holders, supports, or similar fittings. Fig. 9-1. Such hardboard is in common use not only in homes but also in stores for display and storage.

Embossed pattens are available in simulated leather, wood grain, and other designs. Fig. 9-4.

Acoustical hardboard has perforations which improve its properties for controlling sound. It makes an excellent covering for ceilings and walls.

Wood-grained hardboard is printed with wood grain to match the color and texture of oak, walnut, mahogany, and many other woods. Fig. 9-5.

It is popular for interior paneling. Many other types of hardboard panels are designed for building construction.

Uses of Hardboard

Hardboard is used not only in wood products like furniture, cabinets, and homes but also in many basically metal products such as automobiles, refrigerators, and trailers. Furniture manufacturers use hardboard for such items as exteriors of television cases, drawer bottoms, and the backs of cases and cabinets. Some furniture manufacturers use hardboard in making their own lumber-core plywood. Strips of solid wood or particle board are used for the core; then hardboard is applied for the crossbands. Layers of veneer attached to the hardboard complete the panels.

Working with Hardboard

For ordinary interior installations, individual sheets of hardboard should stand on edge 24 hours or more. This allows them to adjust to the surrounding air. Hardboard that will be used in areas of high humid-

9-4. *Embossed hardboard paneling.*

9-5. *This wood-grained hardboard makes attractive wall paneling.*

ity (for bathrooms, utility rooms, or exterior use) should be "pre-expanded" by long exposure to damp air or by scrubbing water into the back of the panel with a broom. Scrubbed panels should then be stacked back-to-back under a tarpaulin for 24 hours if standard board, 48 hours if tempered.

SAWING

Hardboard may be sawed as any other wood product with hand or power tools. For best results, sharp high-speed power saws should be used. For high-production work, saws must be carbide-tipped, of a design recommended by the saw manufacturer.

MACHINING

Hardboard may be machined the same way as other wood products. Such operations as shaping, routing, and planing give best results if tools are kept sharp. Absence of grain in hardboard allows uniformly fine machining without splintering.

SANDING

The quality of hardboard is such that surface sanding is not normally required. However, sawed edges, machined surfaces, and surface scratches can be dressed up by normal wood-sanding procedures. Also, precision sanding to close tolerance can be done.

BENDING

Wide, dry bends may be made by fastening hardboard solidly to curved forms. For smaller-radius bends, wet the hardboard, then bend it over heated forms until dry. Tighter bends without rupturing may be made by slow, deliberate bending. The thinner the board, the sharper the curve that can be bent. Also, tempered hardboard will bend tighter than the same thickness of non-tempered varieties.

DRILLING

Hardboard may be drilled the same as other wood products. For best results, the face of the piece should be placed upward and a solid backing used to attain clean edges.

GLUING

For gluing hardboard, follow the directions of the glue supplier.

APPLYING HARDBOARD OVER STUDDING

If nails may show, good results are obtained by spreading adhesive with a knife or gun on the studs and panels and securing with a minimum of nails or staples. If no nails can be used, contact cement (the kind used for plastic laminates) is excellent. Follow manufacturer's instructions for proper application.

FASTENING

Hardboard may be fastened with any of the common wood fasteners, such as nails, staples, automatic nailers, screws, bolts, adhesives, or rivets.

To nail hardboard, start at the edge adjoining the previous panel and work across the board toward the free edge. Use 3d finishing nails (galvanized preferred) for interiors. As insurance against fiber puffing around nailheads and nail loosening, select annular-thread or ring-groove hardboard nails. These nails are designed to be set flush with the work. Allow some freedom of movement between the boards, taking care not to force them tightly together. Space nails 6″ on center. Make joints only where solid support is available. For exteriors, at least a 5d galvanized nail (casing or box), a shake nail, or a hardened siding nail should be chosen.

To staple hardboard, use staples with a narrow crown and divergent points (branching out in different directions). Apply them with a hammer-type stapler or air gun. Spacing of 4″ or 6″ is recommended. Length of staples should be at least ½″ plus the thickness of the board. The power required varies with the thickness and kind of board. For further advice, refer to the staple supplier's directions.

Any thickness of hardboard may be screwed or bolted to a frame or base after drilling holes large enough to accommodate the shank of the screws or bolts. Also, hardboard ¼″ or ⅜″ thick has excellent screw-holding strength for attaching hinges or other hardware. Drill holes smaller than the screw diameter, and use sheet metal screws.

HARDBOARD JOINTS AND EDGES

Joints and edges may be scored, routed, beveled, grooved, or otherwise treated as use requires. Some hardboards are patterned so that their edges will blend into the overall pattern of the board when butted together. If joints are to be hidden, leave space the thickness of a single nail, then apply tape and joint cement as in normal drywall construction. This may be painted or otherwise covered. Where joints are exposed, the edge may be beveled or routed. Wood, metal, or plastic battens or inserts may be used to accentuate the joints. Inside corners may be covered with cove molding or may be butted.

PAINTING HARDBOARD

Hardboard will take almost any type of finish. A brush, spray, or roller may be used according to the finish required. Interior wall panels require no special sealer. However, if sealer is to be applied, rubber or vinyl-base white is a good choice. Wall paints (oil-base flat) require no special sealer. Water-mix sealers may be used as well as standard oil-base primers. With enamel finishes, apply a pigmented primer-sealer as the base coat. Enamel undercoat may be applied and rubber or vinyl emulsions also. Clear finishes require a recommended non-pigmented sealer. Clear varnish or resin sealers should not be used as a first coat. Best results are obtained with transparent filler-sealer, natural paste-wood filler, or clear-drying white vinyl glue. Stain finishes may be obtained with pigmented resin sealers, oil wood stains, colored paste-wood fillers or stain waxes. These are wip-on finishes. Varnish stains are not recommended. Texture paints or wallpaper may be applied when joints are properly taped and filled.

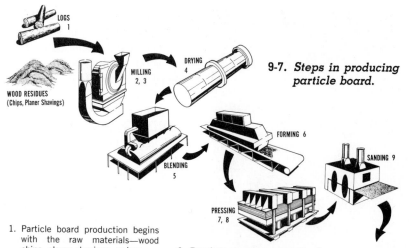

9-7. Steps in producing particle board.

1. Particle board production begins with the raw materials—wood chips, planer shavings, or logs.
2. Flakers, hammermills, or other types of milling equipment produce the desired types of tiny wood particles.
3. Screens classify the particles into the proper mixture of sizes.
4. Dryers remove excess moisture and uniformly control the moisture content to the desired level.
5. Resin binders and other chemicals are sprayed onto the wood particles at a controlled rate in a blending operation.
6. Forming machines deposit the treated particles onto belts or metal cauls forming mats.
7. Particle mats are consolidated and the binders are cured in heated hydraulic presses with temperatures up to 400 °F and pressures up to 1000 p.s.i.
8. After pressing, boards are trimmed to the desired length and width.
9. Sanding in high-speed belt sanders produces the smooth surfaces and accurate thickness tolerances characteristic of particle boards.

9-6. Precision-cut shavings are made into fiberboard.

PARTICLE BOARD

Particle board is made of wood particles such as chips, splinters, shavings, flakes, even sawdust. Many of the materials used to make particle board were once considered waste at the sawmill. These wood fragments are combined with an adhesive to form a medium-density board. There are about 19 basic kinds of particle board, not merely with different commercial names but of different composition or construction.

Medium-density fiberboard (MDF) is a high-quality particle board used for cabinets. To make it, flakes are carefully cut with the grain to precise thickness and length, then bonded together with a special adhesive. Fig. 9-6. As a result, fiberboard has better working qualities than most particle board.

Some manufacturers of particle board use only softwoods, while others use certain hardwoods, especially poplar. Properties of particle board can be changed by varying such things as the kind and shape of chips, kind and amount of adhesive, pressure, and methods of forming. The two basic methods of producing particle board are the *extrusion method* and the *mat-formed, flat-pressed method*. In extrusion, which is the less common method, the board is formed by forcing the wood particles and adhesive through a small opening. (The way you get toothpaste out of a tube is another example of extrusion.)

Most particle board is produced by forming the wood particles and adhesives into a mat, then pressing this in a hot press. Fig. 9-7.

Particle board is available in thicknesses from ¼" to 2", in panel widths from 2' to 5', and in lengths from 4' to 16'. The more common panel sizes are ½" to 1" thick and 4' × 8' and 5' × 8' sheets.

Particle board is available from the manufacturer as unfinished sheets or in various stages of finish-

9-8. *A counter top made of particle board covered with plastic laminate.*

works with great ease. Fig. 9-9. Mass production requires the use of carbide-tipped tools.

JOINERY

Particle board is often edge banded with solid wood for the tops of tables and cabinets and similar areas. Particle board can be glued directly to solid wood with a butt joint, using a gap-filling urea formaldehyde adhesive. However, it is much better to make some kind of joint such as a spline, tongue-and-groove, dowel, or dovetail. Adding an edge band of solid wood greatly increases the overall strength of the top. It also provides an edge that can be shaped and contoured. Fig. 9-10.

APPLYING VENEERS, VINYLS, AND PLASTIC LAMINATES

With the improved surface qualities of many particle boards, it is not necessary to add crossbands. This permits relatively simple three-ply construction. Veneers, vinyls, and plastic laminates are applied to

9-9. *Cutting a rabbet on the edge of particle board with a router. Note the smooth, clean cut. Since it has no grain, there is no splintering.*

ing with the surfaces and edges filled, colored, and sealed. Fig. 9-8. Particle board and fiber board are made by a large number of manufacturers under their own trade names. It is a good idea to check with your lumber supplier concerning commercial names, characteristics, and uses. There is one that is best for each kind of furniture or cabinet job. Some are well suited for doors, built-ins, and wall surfaces, others are meant to be painted, while still others are best for veneering and applying plastic laminates.

Working with Particle Board

Most of what has been said concerning the methods of working hardboard also applies to particle board. Both are manufactured products without grain. Particle board, however, is not as hard as hardboard. Here are some suggestions for working with it.

SAWING AND MACHINING

All standard woodworking tools and machines can be used. Because it has no grain, particle board

the core with contact cement. Both the veneer and the particle board should have approximately 6 to 8 percent moisture content. Wood veneers can be bonded either in a hot

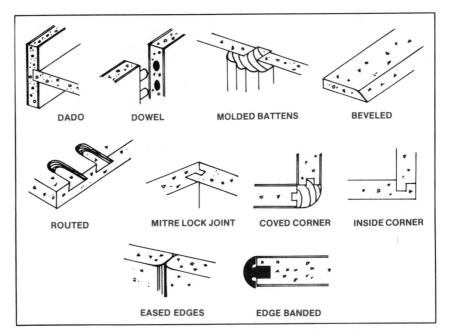

DADO   DOWEL   MOLDED BATTENS   BEVELED

ROUTED   MITRE LOCK JOINT   COVED CORNER   INSIDE CORNER

EASED EDGES   EDGE BANDED

9-10. *Common methods of joining particle board.*

LAMINATING RIGID FACE SHEETS

LAMINATING FLEXIBLE FILM

9-11. *Most particle board is covered with either rigid face sheets, such as plastic laminates, or flexible film, such as vinyl. The vinyls may look like fine hardwood or leather, or they may come in abstracts, solid colors, or metallic patterns.*

or cold press. For small projects and on-the-job construction, it is better to use contact cement when applying veneers, vinyls, and plastic laminates to particle board.

FASTENING WITH NAILS AND SCREWS

The nail-holding power of particle board is affected by the kind of board and the density. Its nail-holding power is generally less than that of solid wood. The best nail to choose is a finishing nail no larger than 4d. The use of annular-thread or cement-coated nails improves holding power. While standard wood screws are satisfactory, the same size sheet metal screws have 20 percent greater holding power in particle board. The pilot hole for all screws should be quite small since there is no cell structure of solid wood to hold the screw in place.

FINISHING

Most particle board is used as core stock. Some manufacturers apply a filler and sealer to cover the boards before applying veneer, vinyl, or plastic laminate. Fig. 9-11. Filler and sealer are necessary if the board is to be finished by painting, enameling, or some kind of transparent finish.

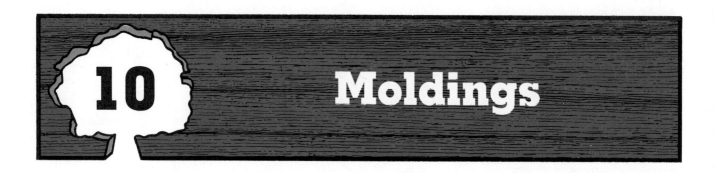

10 Moldings

Moldings are strips of wood shaped on a molder. They have many uses, both decorative and practical. In cabinetwork they help to achieve a finished appearance, and in homes they add decoration to interiors. Fig. 10-1. Moldings are also used for picture framing and for enriching furniture design, particularly on such casework as chests and cabinets. Moldings can be installed horizontally or vertically to serve as drawer or door pulls. They are important on all built-in furniture since they impart a solid finished appearance to cabinets, closets, desks, and shelving. Some of the common molding patterns are shown in Fig. 10-2. Their uses are as follows:

Crown moldings soften sharp lines where two planes meet, usually at the junction of wall and ceiling or under exterior eaves. Fig. 10-3.

Bed moldings are used for the same reason and generally the same places as crown moldings.

10-1. *Moldings add greatly to the character of this room.*

A **cove molding** has a concave face and is used for the same purpose as a bed or crown molding.

A **casing** is used as trim for doors and windows or as a baseboard where wall and floor meet.

Stools lie flat on the inside of sloping window sills, making a snug joint with the lower sash.

Rounds are used for many purposes. *Full rounds* make curtain rods, banisters, closet poles, and other similar items. *Half rounds* can be used as decorative trim to cover joints. *Quarter rounds* are installed on the inside of corner trim. Rounds can also be used as part of a room divider.

Balusters are used as uprights in railings of all types. These handy squares serve other purposes also.

Battens are decorative strips placed over breaks in flat surfaces such as the cracks between boards in paneling and siding.

Glass beads are used to hold glass or other materials in frames.

Stops make snug joints and hold window sash in place.

Mullions are decorative trim between windows in a series.

10-3(α). *This ceiling molding consists of a crown molding, a rectangular molding, and dentil molding. Dentils are the equally spaced rectangular pieces.*

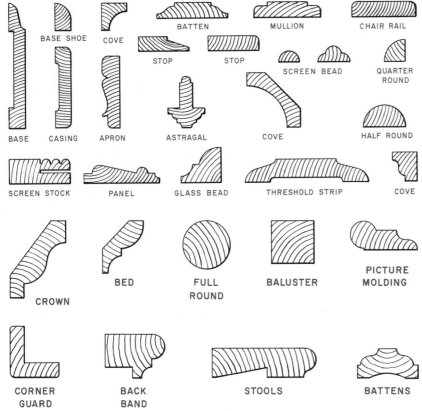

10-2. *Standard shapes of moldings.*

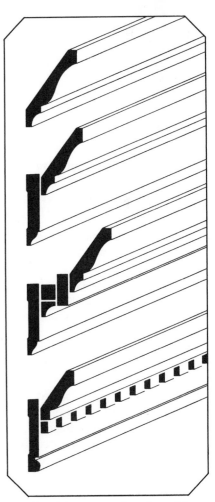

10-3(b). *A few examples of combinations for ceiling moldings.*

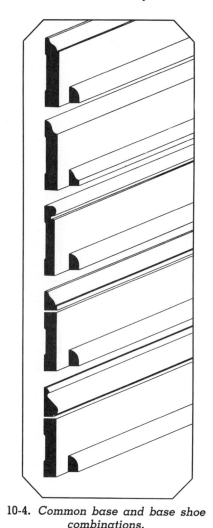

10-4. *Common base and base shoe combinations.*

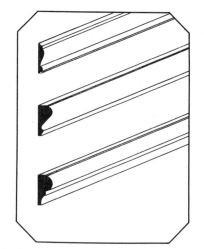

10-5. *Common types of panel moldings.*

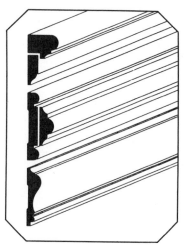

10-6. *Some types of chair rail moldings.*

10-7(a). *An inexpensive, unfinished chest.*

10-7(b). *By adding moldings, drawer pulls, and a finish, the chest becomes a distinctive piece of furniture.*

Base and **base shoe** are used where baseboard and floor meet. Fig. 10-4.

Corner guards are designed for interior and exterior "outside" corners. They neatly cover exposed corner construction.

Back band is used in place of corner guards when only one edge is exposed.

Picture moldings are installed where walls meet ceilings; the design allows for picture hanging.

Screen stock is material used for making window and door screen frames.

Screen beads are strips fastened over the edge of a screen to hold it neatly and firmly in place.

Panel moldings are used to give character to walls. Fig. 10-5.

Chair rails are installed along the wall to protect it from damage by chairs and other furniture. Fig. 10-6.

Furniture and cabinet manufacturers also make many other kinds of moldings that are machine-shaped and carved for the outside of furniture. These are nailed, stapled, and/or glued to the exterior of drawers, doors, and edges of casework for decoration. Frequently, moldings can change a simple piece of casework into furniture with a definite style. Fig. 10-7. Sometimes the same basic casework is used for several styles, with only the molding and hardware changed. This technique is popular with kitchen cabinet manufacturers.

11 Fasteners

Nails, screws, and similar fasteners are chiefly used for two purposes: to hold parts together and to hold a completed product to a wall, floor, or other part of a building. In furniture construction, metal fasteners are used mainly for holding structural parts and trim. A good example of this is a back panel attached to a case by nails or staples. Screws are used instead of nails in places that require great strength, such as corner blocks in leg-and-rail construction. There is limited use of exposed nails and screws in furniture. Usually, the heads are countersunk and covered. Some cabinets are held together with nails alone or nails and screws, but better-quality ones have screws only, or screws plus glue.

NAILS

Nails for wood construction come in almost endless variety. The right kind of nail must be carefully chosen for each job to avoid splitting the material or distorting the wood fibers, for desired holding power, and for the appearance of the finished work. For interior cabinetwork, general-purpose *casing* or *finishing* nails of mild steel are commonly selected. Fig. 11-1. (Nails are also made of aluminum, copper, brass, and other metals.) For most casework a casing nail holds better than a finishing nail. Casing nails are also excellent for window and door frames, cornices, corner boards, and similar construction. Some cab-

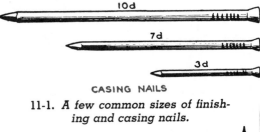

CASING NAILS

11-1. *A few common sizes of finishing and casing nails.*

FINISHING NAILS

inetmakers prefer them for all interior work. Finishing nails are used largely in cabinetwork trim and in other places where the nail head should not show.

The *penny system* is used to designate the size of a nail in terms of length from head to point. The letter *d* is used as a symbol for penny. Thus *two penny* is written *2d.* Lengths range from 2d, which is 1″ long, to 60d, which is 6″ long.

A wire gauge system is used to indicate the diameter of a nail. As the gauge number goes down, the diameter of the nail goes up. (Note that an opposite gauge system is used for wood screws, in which low numbers mean small diameters.) Figure 11-2 shows length, gauge, thickness, and number of nails per pound of casing and finishing nails. Nails are commonly purchased by the pound.

Other Types of Nails and Staples

Tacks are available in lengths from ³⁄₁₆″ to 1⅛″ and in size numbers from 1 to 24. Fig. 11-3.

Escutcheon pins are small brass (or stainless steel) nails with round heads. They are available in lengths from ³⁄₁₆″ to 2″, in gauge sizes from 24 to 10, smooth or with annular thread. Fig. 11-4.

Wire brads are small, flathead, mild steel nails with sharp points. They are available in lengths from ½″ to 1½″ and in gauge sizes from 20 to 14.

Staples are installed with hand-operated tools or with portable or stationary air-operated machines. Fig. 11-5. Staple size is indicated by width and length. Staples must be purchased to match the size of the stapling machine.

Nailing Tools

The *claw hammer* is made with a metal head and a wood or metal

FINISHING NAILS

FOR FINISHED CARPENTRY, TRIM AND CABINET WORK

SIZE	LENGTH	GAUGE	DIAMETER HEAD GAUGE	APPROX. NO. TO POUND
3d	1¼ inch	No. 15½	12½	850
4d	1½ inch	No. 15	12	575
6d	2 inch	No. 13	10	300
8d	2½ inch	No. 12½	9½	192
10d	3 inch	No. 11½	8½	122

CASING NAILS

FOR INTERIOR TRIM AND CABINET MAKING

SIZE	LENGTH	GAUGE	DIAMETER HEAD GAUGE	APPROX. NO. TO POUND
4d	1½ inch	No. 14	11	450
6d	2 inch	No. 12½	9½	240
8d	2½ inch	No. 11½	8½	145
10d	3 inch	No. 10½	7½	94
16d	3½ inch	No. 10	7	71

Note: The decimal equivalent of common gauge numbers is:

15 = .072	12 = .106	9 = .148	6 = .192
14 = .080	11 = .121	8 = .162	5 = .207
13 = .092	10 = .135	7 = .177	4 = .225

11-2. *Comparative sizes of nails. Note that finishing and casing nails of the same pennyweight are made from different-size wire and have different diameters.*

11-5. *Using a stapling machine to assemble a cabinet.*

handle. Hammers are designated by the weight of the head, which varies from 5 to 20 ounces. Most cabinetmakers like to have two hammers, a light one of perhaps 9 or 10 ounces for light work and one of medium weight, 14 to 16 ounces, for heavier work. The *nail set* is a small metal punch with a cupped end. Fig. 11-6. It is used to sink the heads of casing and finishing nails below the wood surface so that they can be covered. The *hand-operated stapling tool* or *gun* is commonly used by the cabinetmaker to install certain types of medium-density or thin panel material such as particle board. A *mallet* is used to strike the stapler. Fig. 11-7. *Ripping bars* and *ripping chisels* are sometimes needed to remove old cabinetwork and paneling before remodeling. Fig. 11-8.

Nailing Techniques

Nailing can be done in two ways: straight nailing and toenailing. *Straight nailing* is used for most cabinetwork. *Toenailing* is done when joining end grain to face grain. Nails should be driven at an angle of about 30 degrees for toenailing. Fig. 11-9.

For cabinetwork, the nailheads are driven flush with or slightly below the work surface. In the latter case, first drive the nail until just

11-6. *A nail set.*

11-7. *A hand-operated stapling tool requires a mallet as well as staples.*

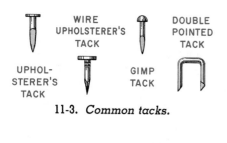

WIRE UPHOLSTERER'S TACK

DOUBLE POINTED TACK

UPHOLSTERER'S TACK

GIMP TACK

11-3. *Common tacks.*

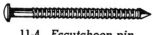

11-4. *Escutcheon pin.*

11-8. *Common shapes of ripping bars.*

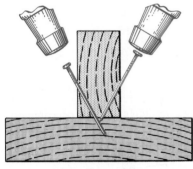

11-9. *Toenailing.*

the head is exposed, then finish driving with a nail set. To nail hardwood, it is a good idea to first drill a hole that is slightly smaller than the diameter of the nail shank and about two-thirds its length. In nailing solid lumber, a few staggered nails provide greater strength than more nails in a straight row. Nails for plywood should be selected in terms of thickness of the material. For ¾" plywood, use 6d casing or finishing nails. For ⅝" plywood, use 6d or 8d finishing nails. For ½", 4d or 6d finishing nails. For ⅜", 3d or 4d finishing nails. For ¼", use ¾" or 1" brads.

SCREWS

In furniture building and cabinet-making, screws are used far more than nails for assembly, reinforcing structural parts, and attaching fittings such as hinges, catches, and

handles. Screws have much better holding power than nails and also can be removed and replaced without damaging the wood. They are available in a wide variety of types, screw slots, sizes, and finishes. For this reason, it is impossible for a cabinet shop to stock all kinds. Fortunately, most metal items that require screw installations are packaged with the correct screws.

Common screws have flat, oval, or round heads. Fig. 11-10. They are made of mild steel, aluminum, copper, brass, or Monel Metal. Roundhead screws of mild steel have a blue finish; flathead screws, a bright finish. Ovalhead screws are usually plated with cadmium or chromium since they are used to install hinges, hooks, and other hardware.

FLAT HEAD   ROUND HEAD   OVAL HEAD

11-10. *Common head shapes of wood screws. Note that all of these have the recessed (Phillips) head. For an illustration of a slotted head, see Fig. 11-13.*

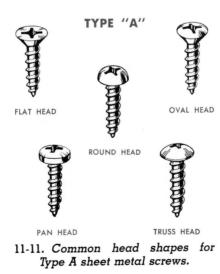

TYPE "A"

FLAT HEAD   OVAL HEAD
ROUND HEAD
PAN HEAD   TRUSS HEAD

11-11. *Common head shapes for Type A sheet metal screws.*

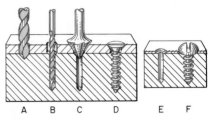

A   B   C   D   E   F

11-12. *Installing sheet metal screws in manufactured wood products: (A) Drilling the clearance hole. (B) Drilling the pilot or anchor hole. (C) Countersinking. (D) Screw installed. (E) Hole for roundhead sheet metal screw. (F) Screw installed.*

11-13. *A self-drilling screw with a straight shank and off-center slot.*

Screws are made with either slotted or recessed (Phillips) heads. The *recessed head* is used in most production work because it is easier to install and can be drawn up tighter. Such screws require a Phillips-head screwdriver. In buying screws for a small shop, it is a good idea to select flathead and roundhead screws in a limited number of lengths and gauge sizes, and with only one type of head slot.

Self-tapping sheet metal screws that are pointed are ideal for joining sheet metal to wood. These are Type A screws. Fig. 11-11. (Type B screws are not pointed and are not used in woodworking.) Type A is made in several head shapes and with either slotted or recessed heads. Sheet metal screws differ from wood screws in that they are threaded along their entire length. Sheet metal screws are also recommended for manufactured materials such as hardboard and particle board. Fig. 11-12.

Another type of wood screw, used primarily for production work, has an off-center slot. Fig. 11-13. No

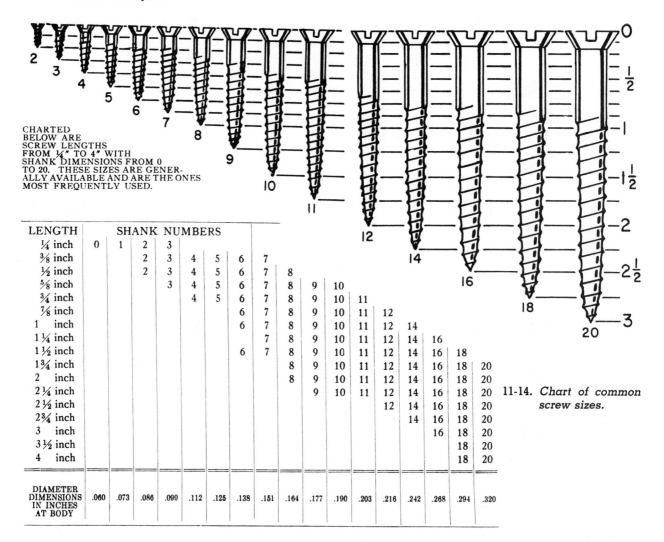

CHARTED BELOW ARE SCREW LENGTHS FROM ¼" TO 4" WITH SHANK DIMENSIONS FROM 0 TO 20. THESE SIZES ARE GENERALLY AVAILABLE AND ARE THE ONES MOST FREQUENTLY USED.

LENGTH	SHANK NUMBERS																
	0	1	2	3	4	5	6	7	8	9	10	11	12	14	16	18	20
¼ inch	0	1	2	3													
⅜ inch			2	3	4	5	6	7									
½ inch			2	3	4	5	6	7	8								
⅝ inch				3	4	5	6	7	8	9	10						
¾ inch					4	5	6	7	8	9	10	11					
⅞ inch							6	7	8	9	10	11	12				
1 inch							6	7	8	9	10	11	12	14			
1¼ inch								7	8	9	10	11	12	14	16		
1½ inch							6	7	8	9	10	11	12	14	16	18	
1¾ inch									8	9	10	11	12	14	16	18	20
2 inch									8	9	10	11	12	14	16	18	20
2¼ inch										9	10	11	12	14	16	18	20
2½ inch													12	14	16	18	20
2¾ inch														14	16	18	20
3 inch															16	18	20
3½ inch																18	20
4 inch																18	20
DIAMETER DIMENSIONS IN INCHES AT BODY	.060	.073	.086	.099	.112	.125	.138	.151	.164	.177	.190	.203	.216	.242	.268	.294	.320

11-14. *Chart of common screw sizes.*

pilot hole is needed with such a screw. (A pilot hole is ordinarily drilled to receive a wood screw, as explained later in this chapter.)

Screw Size

Screws come in lengths from 3/16" to 6" and in gauge sizes from 0 (smallest) to 24 (largest). Fig. 11-14. Note that the higher the number, the greater the diameter of the screw. (You will recall that the wire gauge used for *nail* diameters has higher numbers for small diameters.) Each screw length comes in 3 to 10 different gauge diameters. The smallest, 0, has a diameter of 0.060". The diameter of each succeeding number is 0.013" larger. For example, a No. 5 screw is

0.125", or ⅛" (5 × 0.013 added to 0.060). Generally, the lower gauge numbers are for thinner woods. Screws 4" and shorter are factory packed by the gross. Those over 4" come in packages of one-half gross.

Kinds of Screwdrivers

For slotted head screws a plain screwdriver is used. Fig. 11-15. Screwdriver size is designated by the bar length and tip width. The tip should be straight and the sides nearly parallel, with a slight taper. Several sizes should be available. The blade should just slip into the slot of the head and should be slightly less wide than the diameter of the screw head. A screwdriver that is too small will not provide

enough leverage and will mar the slot. One that is too large will damage the wood around the screw. Except when cramped conditions call for a stubby or offset driver, use the longest one possible.

The *Phillips* screwdriver comes in sizes 1 through 4. Fig. 11-16. Use size No. 1 for screws from 0 through 4 gauge; No. 2 for gauges 5 through 9; No. 3 for gauges 10 through 16; and No. 4 for screws 17 gauge and larger.

11-15. *Plain screwdriver for slotted head screws.*

11-16. *Phillips screwdriver.*

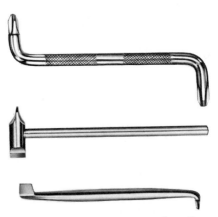

11-17. *Common types of offset screwdrivers for both slotted and recessed head screws.*

11-18. *Two types of countersinks: the one on the top is for a brace, and the one on the bottom is for a hand drill or drill press.*

11-19. *Spiral-type screwdriver.*

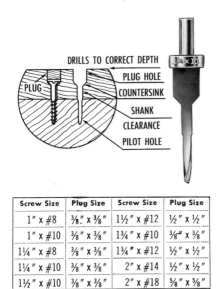

DRILLS TO CORRECT DEPTH ¼ x 10
COUNTERSINK
SHANK
CLEARANCE
PILOT HOLE

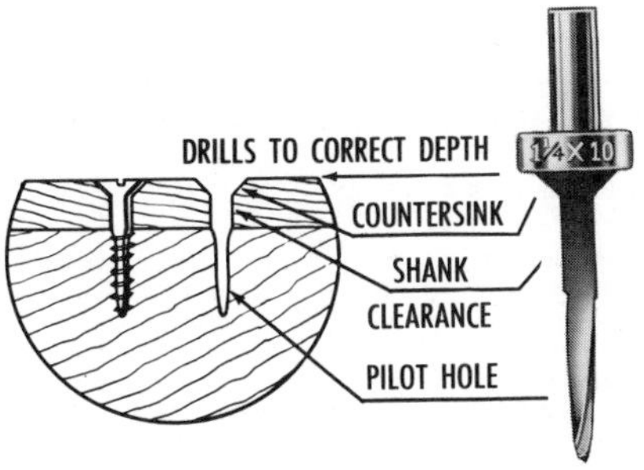

Screw Size	Screw Size	Screw Size
½″ x #5	1¼″ x #8	1½″ x #14
¾″ x #6	1¼″ x #9	1¾″ x #8
¾″ x #7	1¼″ x #10	1¾″ x #10
¾″ x #8	1¼″ x #12	1¾″ x #12
1″ x #6	1¼″ x #14	2″ x #10
1″ x #7	1½″ x #8	2″ x #12
1″ x #8	1½″ x #10	2″ x #14
1″ x #10	1½″ x #12	2½″ x #12

11-20. *Screw-mate drill and countersink. The chart shows common combinations of length and gauge number.*

DRILLS TO CORRECT DEPTH ¼ x 10
PLUG
PLUG HOLE
COUNTERSINK
SHANK
CLEARANCE
PILOT HOLE

Screw Size	Plug Size	Screw Size	Plug Size
1″ x #8	⅜″ x ⅜″	1½″ x #12	½″ x ½″
1″ x #10	⅜″ x ⅜″	1¾″ x #10	⅜″ x ⅜″
1¼″ x #8	⅜″ x ⅜″	1¾″ x #12	½″ x ½″
1¼″ x #10	⅜″ x ⅜″	2″ x #14	½″ x ½″
1½″ x #10	⅜″ x ⅜″	2″ x #18	⅝″ x ⅝″

11-21. *Screw-mate counterbore. The chart shows width and depth of plugs for use with common-size screws.*

Offset screwdrivers are made for use in close quarters. Fig. 11-17.

An *82-degree countersink* is needed for flathead screws that are to be flush with the surface. There are two types, one for a brace and the other for a hand drill or drill press. Fig. 11-18.

The *spiral-type* screwdriver is sold with four bits, three for plain screws and a No. 2 Phillips bit. Fig. 11-19. This tool provides a quick way of installing screws, but correct-size shank and pilot holes are important.

A *screwdriver bit* in a brace can be used for setting screws.

A *screw-mate drill and countersink* is a tool for installing flathead screws. Fig. 11-20. It will do the four necessary things at one time: drill to correct depth, countersink, make the correct shank clearance, and make the correct pilot hole. This tool is stamped with the length and gauge number. For example, a ¾″ × #6 is used for a flathead screw ¾″ long and No. 6 gauge size.

A *screw-mate counterbore* will do all the drill-countersink operations and also drill holes for wood plugs. Fig. 11-21. Use a *plug cutter* of the correct size to cut a wood plug for covering the hole. Fig. 11-22. An *auger bit* can be used to counterbore a hole if a screw-mate counterbore is not available. The counterbore hole should be ⅜″ deeper than an ordinary pilot hole. Cover the hole with plastic wood or a wood plug.

Screwdriver attachments for portable drills and *power-operated screwdrivers* are used for production work. A power screwdriver can be operated by air or by electricity.

Installing Screws

Wood screws have two diameters besides that of the head. Therefore

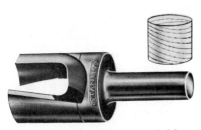

11-22. *Plug cutters are available in different sizes.*

HOW TO USE THIS CHART

The table of wood screw specifications simplifies the selection of the bit or drill size best suited to your requirements. The fractional equivalents and undersize and oversize decimals indicate how close a bit of given fractional size will bore to the actual screw dimension and whether the fit will be snug or loose. In selecting a tool size for the pilot hole (for threaded portion of screw), note that root diameters are average dimensions measured at the middle of the threaded portion. On some screws the root diameter tapers slightly from the end of the screw, increasing toward the head. It is usually good practice to bore the pilot hole the same size as the root diameter in hardwoods, such as oak, and about 15% smaller for soft woods, such as pine and Douglas fir. In some cases, allowances can be made to advantage for moisture content and other varying factors. This same rule can be used for shank holes. The SHANK DIAMETERS shown below are standard specifications subject to tolerances of $^{+.004}_{-.007}$. MAXIMUM HEAD DIAMETERS are also standard specifications which apply to flat and oval-head screws. Head sizes run from 5% to 10% smaller for round-head screws.

NO. OF SCREW	MAXIMUM HEAD DIAMETER	SHANK DIAMETER		ROOT DIAMETER		THREADS PER INCH	NO. OF SCREW
		BASIC DEC. SIZE	NEAREST FRACTIONAL EQUIVALENT	AVERAGE DEC. SIZE	NEAREST FRACTIONAL EQUIVALENT		
0	.119	.060	1/16 OVERSIZE .002	.040	3/64 OVERSIZE .007	32	0
1	.146	.073	5/64 OVERSIZE .005	.046	3/64 BASIC SIZE	28	1
2	.172	.086	3/32 OVERSIZE .007	.054	1/16 OVERSIZE .008	26	2
3	.199	.099	7/64 OVERSIZE .010	.065	1/16 UNDERSIZE .002	24	3
4	.225	.112	7/64 UNDERSIZE .003	.075	5/64 OVERSIZE .003	22	4
5	.252	.125	1/8 BASIC SIZE	.085	5/64 UNDERSIZE .007	20	5
6	.279	.138	9/64 OVERSIZE .002	.094	3/32 BASIC SIZE	18	6
7	.305	.151	5/32 OVERSIZE .005	.102	7/64 OVERSIZE .007	16	7
8	.332	.164	5/32 UNDERSIZE .007	.112	7/64 UNDERSIZE .003	15	8
9	.358	.177	11/64 UNDERSIZE .005	.122	1/8 OVERSIZE .003	14	9
10	.385	.190	3/16 UNDERSIZE .002	.130	1/8 UNDERSIZE .005	13	10
11	.411	.203	13/64 BASIC SIZE	.139	9/64 OVERSIZE .001	12	11
12	.438	.216	7/32 OVERSIZE .003	.148	9/64 UNDERSIZE .007	11	12
14	.491	.242	1/4 OVERSIZE .008	.165	5/32 UNDERSIZE .009	10	14
16	.544	.268	17/64 UNDERSIZE .002	.184	3/16 OVERSIZE .003	9	16
18	.597	.294	19/64 OVERSIZE .003	.204	13/64 UNDERSIZE .001	8	18
20	.650	.320	5/16 UNDERSIZE .007	.223	7/32 UNDERSIZE .004	8	20
24	.756	.372	3/8 OVERSIZE .003	.260	1/4 UNDERSIZE .010	7	24

11-23. *This chart shows the proper size bit or drill needed for drilling shank holes and pilot holes.*

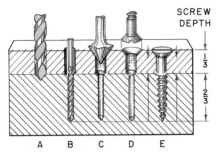

SCREW DEPTH

A B C D E

11-24. *Steps in installing a flathead screw: (A) Drill the shank hole. (B) Drill the pilot hole. (C) Countersink. (D) Check the amount of countersink with the screw. (E) Screw properly installed.*

two holes must be bored to install such screws: the *shank hole* for the threadless part of the screw and the *pilot hole* for the threaded portion. Also, if the screw has a flat head, it must be countersunk flush with or below the wood surface. When a screw head below the surface is to be concealed by a wood plug, a plug hole must be bored.

Select a screw long enough so that all of the threaded portion—or two-thirds of the screw's length—will go into the second member. Choose a smaller diameter for thinner woods, a larger diameter for heavier woods. Choose screws of

smaller diameters and greater lengths whenever practical. Use enough screws to make the joint as strong as the wood itself.

Drill the shank hole to a size *equal* to the diameter of the screw shank. The screw should slip into the hole with a free fit. Next, drill the pilot hole. For hardwoods, its diameter should be approximately the same as the root (or smallest) diameter. For softwoods, it should be about 15 percent less than root diameter and not quite as deep as the threaded portion is long. Fig. 11-23. If flathead screws are used, countersink until the surface diameter equals the largest diameter of the screw head. Fig. 11-24. Install with a screwdriver. *Never hammer the screw into the hole* as this destroys the contact between thread and wood.

If a wood plug is used to cover the head of the screw, it should be cut from the same kind of wood used in the furniture or cabinet piece so that the grains will match as much as possible. Plug cutters are available in various sizes. Bore the plug hole ⅜″ deep and drive the head of the screw to the bottom of the plug hole. Cut the plug, apply glue to it, and force it into the hole

with the grain direction matching the wood itself. After the glue dries, the excess can be trimmed off with a chisel. A piece of dowel rod can be used if the product is to be painted or if the plugs are to be part of the design, as in some Colonial furniture. The head of the screw can also be covered with crack filler or wood dough. Fig. 11-25.

Brass screws are always used with oak. If steel screws are used, acid in the oak will make stains. When installing a brass screw, which is relatively soft, be careful not to break it off as you tighten it in place. First lubricate the screw with paraffin. You can also install a steel screw of the same length and diameter first, then replace it with a brass screw.

It is especially important to select screws of the correct gauge and length for plywood. For ¾″ plywood, use 1½″ No. 8 screws; for ⅝″ plywood, 1¼″ No. 8 screws; for ½″ plywood, 1½″ No. 6 screws. For ⅜″ plywood, choose 1″ No. 6 screws, and for ¼″ plywood, use ¾″ No. 4 screws.

HOLLOW-WALL FASTENING DEVICES

Many devices can be used to fasten cabinets to walls. It is extremely important to select the correct kind. There are two basic types of walls with which the cabinetmaker must deal: *hollow walls* of drywall or lath-and-plaster construction found in most wood homes and *masonry walls* common in basements and commercial buildings. The two fastening devices most often used for hollow walls are toggle bolts and hollow-wall fasteners (molly screw anchors).

A *toggle bolt* is made with either a spring head or a solid head. Figs. 11-26 and 11-27. Such bolts are available in a wide range of sizes from ⅛″ × 2″ to ⅜″ × 6″. Holding power increases with size. A hole

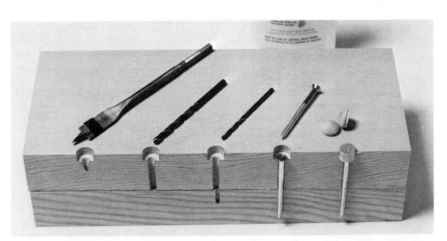

11-25. *A method for installing a flathead screw that will be covered with a wooden plug. First, cut the hole for the plug with a speed drill. Then drill the shank hole in the first piece and a pilot hole in the second piece. Install the screw and cover with a wooden plug.*

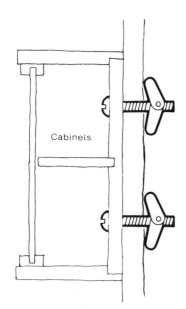

11-26. *Spring head toggle bolts.*

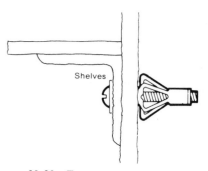

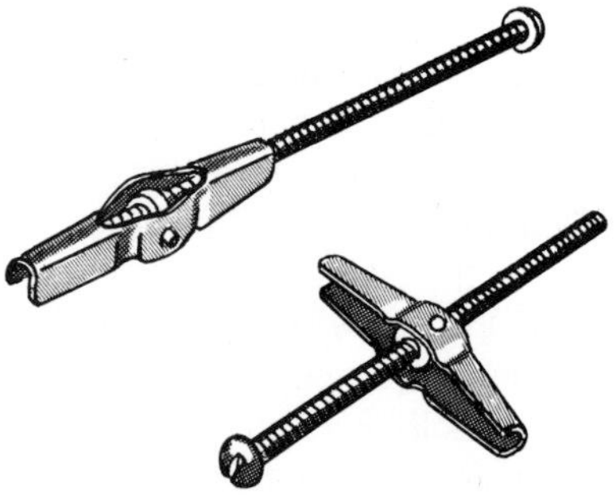

11-27. *Solid head toggle bolts.*

must be drilled large enough for the bolt to slip through. At one time there was a problem with toggle bolts. When the screw was removed to replace a fitting, the nut would fall off on the inside of the wall. Nuts are now made with serated metal along the edge to keep them in place.

Hollow-wall fasteners are available in several lengths and diameters. Fig. 11-28. This type of fastener

has several advantages. The anchor shank completely fills the hole, giving a more durable, secure anchoring. Fig. 11-29. The supporting material can be removed and replaced without loss of the anchor. To install, first drill a hole of the correct diameter. Then insert the unit and screw it tight until the interior sleeve squeezes in place. A fiber washer under the head of the screw protects the screw as it is tightened. When the screw is removed, the item can be fastened in place.

Also available is a *plastic screw anchor* for fastening parts to hollow walls. This screw anchor is designed especially for fastening brackets, cabinets, and shelving to hollow walls such as plasterboard, wall-

board, tile, or plywood. A ¼" hole must be drilled and a No. 6 through No. 10 sheet metal screw used. The plug is inserted. After the screw is driven in all the way, a few more turns cause the plug to bulge against the wall, providing a permanent mounting. Fig. 11-30.

FASTENERS FOR MASONRY WALLS

There are many types of fasteners for attaching cabinets to basement walls or to buildings of masonry construction. *Masonry nails* of hardened steel with a knurled body are the simplest to use. Fig. 11-31. These nails can be driven through wood into concrete block and other relatively soft concrete. Masonry nails provide a quick way of fastening shelves and similar items to basement walls.

An *anchor bolt* with a perforated plate can also be used on solid ma-

11-29. *Fastener secured.*

11-30. *A plastic screw anchor.*

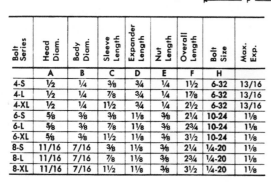

11-31. *Masonry nails are "fatter" and tougher than ordinary nails. They can be driven into concrete blocks to anchor furring strips of wood or accessories.*

HOW TO SELECT PROPER SIZE

4-S, 4-L, 4-XL are for light objects

6-S, 6-L, 6-XL are for medium objects

8-S, 8-L, 8-XL are for heavy objects

4-S, 6-S, 8-S are for walls ⅛" to ⅝" thick

4-L, 6-L, 8-L are for walls ⅝" to 1¼" thick

4-XL, 6-XL, 8-XL are for walls 1¼" to 1¾" thick

11-28. *Common sizes of hollow-wall anchors. Use a 5/16" drill for 4-S, 4-L, or 4-XL. Use a 7/16" drill for 6-S, 6-L, or 6-XL. Use a ½" drill for 8-S, 8-L, or 8-XL.*

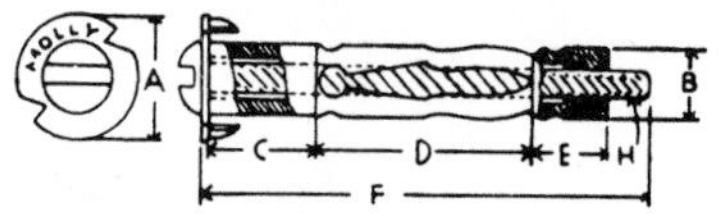

Bolt Series	Head Diam.	Body Diam.	Sleeve Length	Expander Length	Nut Length	Overall Length	Bolt Size	Max. Exp.
	A	B	C	D	E	F	H	
4-S	½	¼	⅜	¾	¼	1½	6-32	13/16
4-L	½	¼	⅞	¾	¼	1⅞	6-32	13/16
4-XL	½	¼	1½	¾	¼	2½	6-32	13/16
6-S	⅝	⅜	⅜	1⅛	⅜	2¼	10-24	1⅛
6-L	⅝	⅜	⅞	1⅛	⅜	2¾	10-24	1⅛
6-XL	⅝	⅜	1½	1⅛	⅜	3½	10-24	1⅛
8-S	11/16	7/16	⅜	1⅛	⅜	2¼	¼-20	1⅛
8-L	11/16	7/16	⅞	1⅛	⅜	2¾	¼-20	1⅛
8-XL	11/16	7/16	1½	1⅛	⅜	3½	¼-20	1⅛

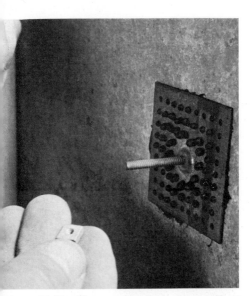

11-32. *The anchor bolt is excellent for fastening a kitchen cabinet or other heavy object to a masonry wall.*

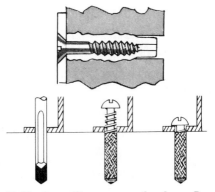

11-33. *Installing a rawl plug. Be sure to drill the hole the exact depth of the plug.*

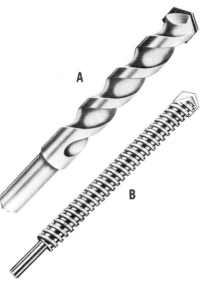

11-34. *Two kinds of carbide-tipped masonry drill bits: (A) Standard. (B) Fast spiral. This kind is faster-cutting, less likely to stall.*

11-35. *A lead expansion screw anchor with setting tool.*

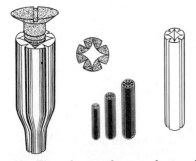

11-36. *This plastic plug can be used with any kind of screw or nail. Drill a hole the same diameter as the plug and about ⅛" deeper than its length. Drive the plug into the hole, then use a screw or nail to hold the part in place.*

11-37. *Chevrons (miter joint fasteners) are made of hardened steel and are designed to draw wood together, making a perfect joint. Just hammer them into the wood as shown here.*

sonry walls. The base is attached to the wall with a black mastic or epoxy cement which squeezes through holes in the base. After the adhesive dries, a shelf or similar item can be attached to the wall with relative ease. Fig. 11-32.

The *rawl plug* is made of fiber and is used with wood, sheet metal, or lag screws. Fig. 11-33. Rawl plug sizes, which range from No. 3 to No. 20, should match the gauge size of the wood screw to be used. For example, a No. 8 rawl plug will accept a No. 7 or No. 8 screw.

There are two ways of boring holes in masonry to install the plug. The quicker way is with a carbide-tipped masonry drill bit in an electric drill. Fig. 11-34. Or you can use a star drill and hammer. To install a rawl plug, first screw the plug onto the wood screw one or two turns, or just enough to hold it. Then push the plug into the hole the full depth. Turn the screw into the plug until the shank is about to enter, then withdraw the screw. You are now ready to attach a cabinet or fitting to the plug.

A *lead expansion screw anchor*

can be used with a lag or wood screw in masonry construction. The anchor is inserted in the hole. Then a setting tool is placed over it and given a sharp rap with a hammer to hold the anchor in place. The screw is slipped through the part to be held and is started in the anchor. As it is tightened, the anchor will expand and grip the wall. Fig. 11-35.

A *plastic plug* similar to a rawl plug can be installed in any solid wall. Then nails or screws are fastened into the plug. Fig. 11-36.

MITER-JOINT FASTENERS

Three common types of metal fasteners are used on miter corners. *Chevrons* are designed to draw wood together to make a tight joint. Fig. 11-37. *Clamp nails* are used in place of wood splines. They are made of high grade steel and have gripping flanges. They produce a clamping action as they are driven

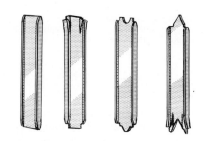

11-38. *Clamp nails are flat, with flanged edges. They can be used on any joint.*

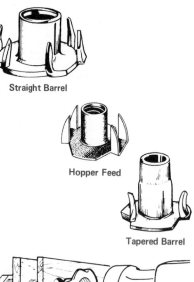

Straight Barrel

Hopper Feed

Tapered Barrel

into the wood, wide end first. To install a clamp nail, a saw kerf must be cut with a 22-gauge band or circular saw across the face of each piece of wood to be joined. The clamp nail is driven in with a few blows of a hammer. The joint produced equals the strength of the wood. Clamp nails are about ⅝″ wide and come in lengths from ½″ to 2″. Fig. 11-38. *Corrugated fasteners* (wiggle nails) are used for holding miter and other joints together. Fig. 11-39.

OTHER FASTENERS FOR FURNITURE

Tee nuts are made in many types and shapes. Fig. 11-40. The most

11-40. *This unique piece of hardware has unlimited uses for furniture and doors and for fixing worn screw holes.*

11-41. *A hanger screw.*

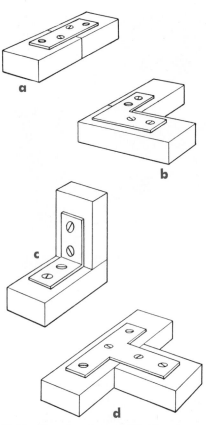

a

b

c

d

11-43. *Repair plates: (A) Mending. (B) Flat corner. (C) Bent corner. (D) T plate. When installing a plate, drill the holes for the screws slightly off center and away from the break or joint. This ensures a tight joint.*

11-39. *Corrugated fasteners can be used to hold a joint together where appearance is not important.*

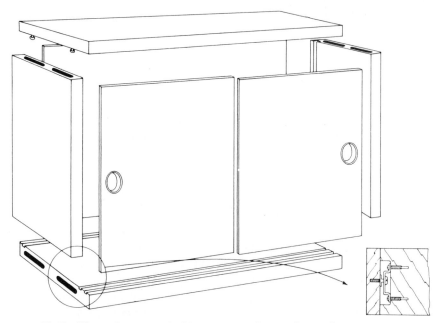

11-42. *These fasteners hold parts together without glue or screws.*

common has a round base with twisted prongs and a threaded hole in the center. A hole is bored into the wood just large enough for the center portion (the barrel). Then the nut is driven into the wood. A screw or bolt is inserted from the opposite side and tightened. Tee nuts are useful for holding legs or other parts. *Hanger screws* have a wood-screw thread on one end and a metal-screw thread on the other. The wood-screw end is installed in the end of a leg, then the metal-threaded end is fitted into a tee nut. Fig. 11-41.

Special commercial fasteners are available so that manufactured cabinets and other furniture can be shipped "knocked down" and then assembled on the job without glue, screws, or other traditional fasteners. Fig. 11-42.

REPAIR PLATES

Repair and mending plates come in many sizes and shapes and are used primarily for simple cabinetwork. Fig. 11-43. A *mending plate* can be used in a butt or lap joint. The *flat corner iron* is an excellent device for strengthening the corner of a frame such as a screen door or window. A *bent corner* can be applied to shelves and to inside corners of tables, chairs, and cabinets. It can also be used to hang cabinets and shelves. Fig. 11-44. The *T plate* is used to strengthen the center frame of a rail.

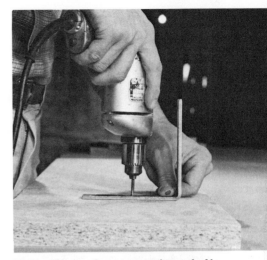

11-44. *Using a bent corner for a shelf support. Because the shelf is made of particle board, a sheet metal screw or special fastener should be used.*

12 **Hardware**

12-1. *The drawer and door pulls on this server are Traditional in style.*

Since there are so many different kinds and styles of hardware for furniture and cabinetwork, it is impossible to illustrate them all. However, there are certain basic facts about hardware which you must know and be able to apply to various woodworking products.

Hardware is manufactured in many qualities and styles. For example, hinges and pulls can be purchased in Early American, Traditional, Contemporary, French and Italian Provincial, or Spanish styles. Fig. 12-1. Different hardware items are needed for drawers, cases, closets, kitchen cabinets, folding screens, and doors.

It is a good idea to buy hardware for a product before building the product. For example, until you know the kind of drawer guides you will use, you cannot determine their location in the case or cabinet or provide proper clearances.

Hardware stores and building-supply companies handle many of the more common hardware pieces. A large number of catalogs are also available for specialized hardware items. For instance, some companies deal exclusively in drawer fix-

12-2. *A butt hinge. The doors of the server shown in Fig. 12-1 have butt hinges.*

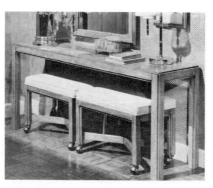

12-5. *These benches have metal casters.*

12-6. *Hardware for this revolving shelf is typical of many metal items needed in a kitchen.*

12-3. *Surface hinges have been installed on the lip doors of this Early American dry sink.*

12-4. *The diamond-shaped metal grilles on the doors of these wall units are strictly ornamental. How many other hardware items do you see in this illustration?*

tures, while others carry hardware for folding doors only.

In general, hardware requirements are as follows:

For **hinge doors** you need pulls, catches, and perhaps a lock, besides the hinges. For various doors, the following hinges are required: for a *flush door*, some type of surface hinge; for a *lip door*, an offset surface hinge or a butt, concealed, or semi-concealed hinge (Figs. 12-2 and 12-3); for *overlapping doors*, some kind of pivot hinge.

Sliding doors call for hardware for the slide, which may be metal, wood, or plastic.

Rolling doors require handles and a metal track for rolling the base guides.

Folding doors must have many special types of hardware, including tracks, locks, and ways for moving the door back and forth.

Drop doors often have a continuous or piano hinge for greater strength, along with some type of lid support, such as a chain or folding hinge, to hold the door open. Some drop doors make use of a special hinge that opens only 45 degrees.

Open-frame doors require metal grilles. Fig. 12-4.

Hardware for **drawers** includes slides, pulls, and locks. Slides can be shop-made. There are also metal or plastic slides which can be purchased.

Chairs and **tables** must have hardware such as tabletop supports, dropleaf hinges, dropleaf supports, and casters. Fig. 12-5.

Cabinet interiors need shelf hardware, as does open shelving. A wide variety of metal hardware is made for closets. To name only a few, there are shoe holders, tie racks,

12-7. *Several types of double-action hinges can be installed on a screen to make it fold in either direction.*

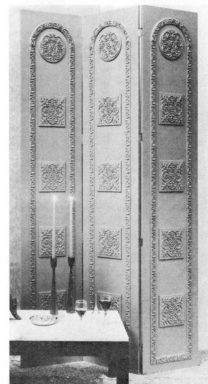

holders for trousers, and closet poles. *Kitchen cabinet* fittings also include many different pieces of hardware. There are pieces for holding pots, pans, dishes, garbage pails, and similar items. Fig. 12-6.

Screens take some type of double-action hinge. Fig. 12-7.

To learn all you can about hardware, follow these suggestions:

● Pay special attention to the most common hardware items. They are discussed throughout this book, wherever basic hardware is specified.

● Become familiar with catalogs that include less common hardware. Fig. 12-8.

12-8. *Some furniture requires special hardware.*

● Study the home and commercial hardware sections of Sweet's catalogs in the library.

● Learn how to order hardware as to size, type, style, and design.

● When installing hardware, carefully follow the instructions included in the package.

The major kinds of hardware used in making furniture and cabinets are as follows:

● Hinges.
● Catches.
● Casters and glides.
● Drawer guides.
● Lid supports.
● Shelf supports.
● Extension table hardware.
● Cabinet locks.

13 Plastics

Cabinetmaking and furniture construction are making increasing use of plastics. Some furniture is all plastic. Fig. 13-1. Even products that appear to be all wood actually contain a variety of plastic materials. The plastics described in this unit are the kinds found in such "all-wood" products.

Plastics are used to make particle board, hardboard, plywood, most adhesives, and finishing materials. Furniture such as tables and chests and almost all cabinets contain plastic laminates (urea and melamine) for parts that take hard wear. Parts made of nylon are used for

drawer guides and slides, shelf buttons, casters, dowels, and many other items not visible on the outside of the product. Many drawer units are made of molded plastics. Acrylics are used in place of glass in some furniture.

Plastics are synthetic materials. They are not found in nature, the way wood and metal are. Plastics are made by combining chemicals. The word *resin* is often used to mean the same thing as *plastic.*

In finished form plastics are solid. Even a can of plastic paint is solid in its finished form; that is, after it has dried on the wall. Usually plas-

13-1. *This door chest is made entirely of plastic. Note the molded handles.*

13-2. *An acrylic plastic is used as an insert to protect the top of this beautiful table.*

13-3. *The door on the left is an all-wood pattern that was used to produce the urethane door on the right. It is quite difficult to tell the real wood from the plastic.*

tics are liquid at some stage in their manufacture, and then they can be formed into various shapes. Heat and pressure, singly or together, are applied to do the forming.

Plastics are made with a wide variety of properties. For example, they may be tough or brittle, hard or soft, clear or opaque. By themselves, plastics lack color. Therefore dyes and pigments can be added to produce a wide range of colors.

The two basic types of plastics are thermoplastics and thermosets. *Thermoplastics* are melted by heat and later hardened by cooling. As with water and ice, the process can be repeated indefinitely by melting down and cooling again. *Thermoset* materials are also melted, formed, and hardened, but this can be done only once. As with a hardboiled egg, heating will not return the material to its liquid form for use again.

Of the many kinds of plastics, only a few are commonly used in "all-wood" furniture.

Polyvinyl chloride (PVC). This plastic is produced in several different forms. It is not affected by contact with water, oil, food, common chemicals, or cleaning fluids. Much of the particle board used in cabinets is covered with flexible vinyl, available in a wide variety of wood grains, solid colors, and patterns.

Nylon is a generic term for a wide variety of products. It is the basic material for most plastic hardware used on the internal parts of furniture, such as tracks and guides, shelf supports, nylon buttons and tapes that make doors and drawers slide easily, and parts of casters and glides.

Acrylonitrile-butadiene-styrene (ABS) is widely used for door handles and drawer pulls. This material can be chrome-plated to look like metal.

Acrylics are used on many furniture pieces instead of a glass insert or as a protective cover. Fig. 13-2.

Rigid plastic foam is made of a variety of plastics. The most common is polyurethane, commonly called urethane. This material is widely used for cabinet doors and decorative parts for furniture. It can be made to look like carved wood. Fig. 13-3.

High-pressure laminates. Decorative laminates are made of urea and melamine, along with other materials. They form a hard, scratch-resistant, strong—but not unbreakable—surface. Laminates are unaffected by common chemicals, acid, oil, and cleaning fluid. They will not burn but will discolor or char. Laminates are the most widely used material for the tops of cabinets, tables, chests, and desks. (See Chapter 43 for a detailed discussion of plastic laminates.)

Epoxies. Epoxy resins are widely used for adhesives and for a variety of finishing materials.

14 Glass, Cane, Metal, and Leather

In addition to wood and plastic, many other materials are used to make cabinets and furniture. Some of these materials are glass and mirrors, cane, metal, and leather.

GLASS AND MIRRORS

Glass and glass mirrors are used extensively in furniture, built-ins, and store fixtures. Fig. 14-1. Normally, the cabinetmaker does not install these items. However, he or she must be able to order and handle them.

Production of Glass

Glass consists of about 70 percent silica, 13 percent soda ash, and 13 percent limestone. The remaining 4 percent is made up of carbon in the form of coal, iron in the form of ferric oxide, and traces of other chemicals.

The making of glass today is a continuous, automated process. First step is mixing the raw materials which are fed into one end of a large tank. Here they are melted at 2,800 degrees Fahrenheit. At the other end of the tank, the molten glass flows through forming rolls. The forming rolls shape it into a continuous ribbon. From these rolls

the semi-molten ribbon goes through a series of steel rolls where it cools and solidifies into sheet glass or rough plate glass. After the glass has been formed in this manner, it is annealed (heated and then cooled to make it less brittle). For plate glass, the sheets next go through a grinding and polishing process. After it is ground, the glass is automatically cut into plates. It then goes to the polishing lines where it is given a beautiful, transparent finish and washed clean. After polishing, plate glass is cut to size, wrapped, and packaged for shipment. For sheet or window glass, the grinding and polishing steps are skipped.

Kinds of Glass

There are many different kinds of glass. The ones commonly used in

furniture and building construction are as follows:

Sheet or *window* glass has a fine finished surface which is produced as the sheet is drawn from the molten pool. This kind of glass is used for most cabinet doors and for windows. Fig. 14-2. It comes in single strength, which averages 0.091″ in thickness, and double strength, which averages 0.125″ thick. The quality of this glass is rated as: AA, the highest; A, which is select quality; and B, which is used in general work. Heavier sheet glass, also called *crystal* glass, is made in thicknesses of ³⁄₁₆″ and ¼″. It is sometimes used in furniture and built-ins as a substitute for plate glass. All sheet glass has some inherent wave or distortion. Usually it is more prominent in one direction than the other.

14-1. *A plate glass top with beveled edges gives this coffee table an appearance of lightness.*

14-2. *A wall system of wood with plastic laminate surfaces and chrome finished accents. Tempered glass is used for some shelves and doors.*

Plate glass is different from sheet or window glass because of the grinding and polishing mentioned earlier. These produce flat, parallel surfaces with little or no distortion. Standard plate glass is made in common thicknesses of ⅛″ and ¼″ and in several grades of quality. The highest quality is completely free from defects. The next best has little or no distortion but is not perfect. The lowest quality has a little more distortion and is used primarily for windows. Heavy commercial grades of plate glass are made in thicknesses of 5⁄16″ to ¾″.

Glass bent to various shapes is available in both sheet and plate varieties and in many thicknesses. These are used primarily in store and office fixtures. Bent glass is produced by causing flat glass to form in a mold by the action of heat and gravity only. It is not a machined product and is therefore subject to more distortion and wider tolerances than polished plate or sheet glass.

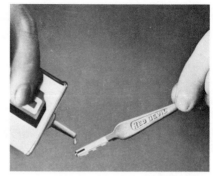

14-3. *Lubricate the wheel of the cutter so that it turns freely.*

Other kinds are colored, heat absorbing, and wire glass. Wire glass is glass with wire netting embedded in it.

Mirrors are made from highest-quality plate glass. The glass is first thoroughly cleaned, then given a double coat of silver on one side. A layer of copper is deposited over the silver by electrolysis (an electro-chemical process). The copper, in turn, is covered by a pigmented priming coat and, finally, by a special mirror-backing coat.

Cutting Glass

Both plate and sheet glass can be cut in the same manner, although more pressure is required for plate glass since it usually is heavier and thicker. Tools needed to make straight cuts include a straightedge, a measuring tape, and a glass cutter. Make sure the cutting wheel operates freely. Fig. 14-3. Necessary materials include lubricating oil, a rag, and kerosene or turpentine.

The glass to be cut should be placed on a large bench that has a smooth, even top. If necessary, pad the top with newspapers or an old rug. One simple method of determining where to cut the glass is to draw the full-size pattern on a piece of wrapping paper and place this under the glass.

Wipe the surface of the glass with a rag soaked with lubricating oil, turpentine, or kerosene. Be sure

14-4. *Wipe the surface of the glass with a cloth, especially along the layout line. The cloth should be dampened with oil, turpentine, or kerosene.*

14-5. *The correct way to hold a glass cutter.*

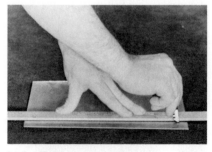

14-6. *Hold a straightedge on the glass, then draw the cutter along.*

to wipe along the area to be cut. Fig. 14-4. This will keep the cut edge from chipping.

The secret of successful cutting is to cut a sharp, even groove in the glass. This is called *scoring*. Figs. 14-5 to 14-7. Too-light pressure won't score a line; too-heavy pres-

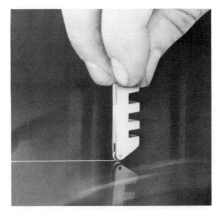

14-7. *Here you see a sharp, uniform score along the glass.*

14-8. *Apply quick downward pressure to break the glass. Do this immediately because glass tends to "heal" itself.*

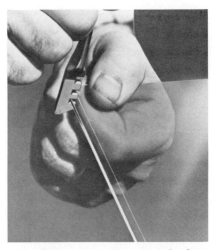

14-9. *If a narrow edge must be broken off, apply pressure with one of the cutterhead grooves.*

14-10. *Try to make a clean, sharp score with one swing of the cutterhead. Don't retrace the entire circle, but go over sections you may have missed.*

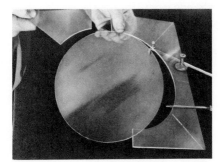

14-11. *Note that several straight lines have been cut in the waste glass so that it can be broken away a portion at a time.*

sure will cause chipping along the groove, resulting in a ragged edge and small cracks. As soon as the score is made, move the glass so that the scored edge is over the edge of the bench; if it is a small piece, raise the glass at an angle. Now snap the waste piece off with a quick downward pull. Fig. 14-8. Another method is to hold the glass at an angle on the bench and tap along the underside of the score with the handle of the cutter. If the waste strip is too narrow to be broken by these methods, use one of the grooves in the cutter head to apply pressure. Fig. 14-9. Pliers with masking tape on the jaws can be used to break off small pieces.

A circle-sweep glass cutter is used to cut circles from 2" to 24" in diameter. To cut out a circle, set

the tool to the correct diameter. Hold the center firmly with one hand as you apply pressure and swing the arm to score the glass. Fig. 14-10. Then use the straight glass cutter to score several lines from the circle to the edge of the glass. In this way the waste glass can be broken away in sections. Fig. 14-11.

Installing Glass

The cabinetmaker must know how to install glass in cabinets and furniture pieces. (It is usually not her or his responsibility to replace glass in broken windows.) Glass for interior cabinets does not have to be set in glazing compound as is necessary for exterior windows. Usually the glass is held in place with a wood or plastic stop or a patented glass holder. Fig. 14-12.

If plate or crystal glass is used for furniture, any edge that will be wholly or partly exposed must be

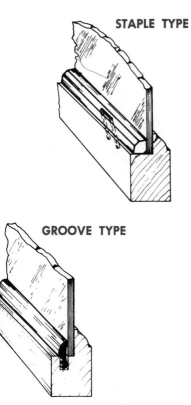

14-12(a). *Two kinds of plastic stops, or retainers. These can be used for installing glass, grilles, or screens.*

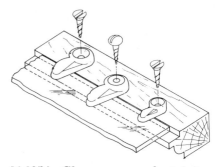

14-12(b). *Glass- or panel-retaining buttons can be used to hold glass firmly in place.*

ground and polished. Such edges may also be shaped square, round, or at an angle.

You can smooth the edges of cut glass yourself with a stationary belt sander or a portable finishing sander. Use waterproof silicon-carbide paper of a grit number from 80 to 180. Apply soapy water to the edge as a lubricant. Bring the edge and the abrasive into contact and move along slowly. Use plenty of lubricant (water and soap) so that not too much heat is generated. It is usually better to have this done by a glass company.

14-13. *The cane back of this chair is made with a traditional hexagonal weave.*

MACHINE-MADE CANE WEBBING

Cane is a common decorative feature of furniture, especially chair seats and backs. It is made from the stems of rattan palms. A characteristic of fine Chinese cabinetwork is the extensive use of cane webbing as accent and enrichment. In Modern or Contemporary furniture and cabinetwork, cane may be found in many places—on a door enclosure of a stereo cabinet, a table shelf, an insert for a screen, or a chair seat or back. In the past, caning was done by hand. The strands were laboriously woven into a design. Today machine-made webbing is almost universally used for both new construction and reupholstering.

Kinds of Weave

Cane weave may be either the traditional hexagonal chair-seat variety or one of the more modern basket weaves. Fig. 14-13. Modern weaves include the smaller square and rectangular weaves. Fig. 14-14. The more common weaves of cane are medium, fine, fine-fine, and superfine mesh. Cane is sold in rolls of common widths from 14″ to 24″, with the price quoted per square foot. The wedge-shaped hickory spline to hold the cane in place and the reed which covers the spline should be purchased with the cane.

Installing Machine-Woven Cane

Before cutting the cane, it is important to make a paper pattern, especially if the opening is of irregular shape. Place this pattern over the cane, with the front edge parallel to the design. Cut a piece about 1″ wider in all directions than the size of the pattern.

To install the cane in the frame, cut or rout out a groove about 3/16″ wide and 3/8″ deep around the opening to be covered, about 3/8″ to 1/2″ from the edge. The groove should

14-14. *This chair has a contoured back and gently angled walnut frame. Note that the tightly woven cane is used as an upholstery fabric. It is stretched up and over the top of the chair and down the back, providing a double thickness separated by the width of the frame.*

be cut so that the spline will fit in it loosely enough to be removed without prying. For a shelf, the inner edge of the cane can be undercut slightly so that it will be level with the frame.

Cut a dozen or more hardwood taper wedges with the small end slightly thinner than the width of the groove. Fig. 14-15.

Place the cane in a bucket of warm water for about two hours to make it completely pliable. Cane will expand about five percent. Let the cane drip-dry for three minutes.

Then place the cane over the frame so that it overlaps in all directions. Check it for size and make sure the strands run straight with the groove.

Drive the cane into the groove using the wedges and a small mallet. Place the wedges at equal distances around the frame to hold the cane firmly in place. It is best to do

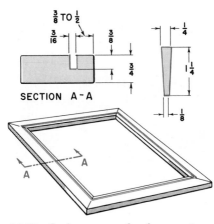

SECTION A-A

14-15. *A frame ready for caning. Wedges, as in the upper right-hand corner, hold the cane in place before the hickory spline is installed.*

the part farthest away from you first (usually the back), then the part nearest, and then the two sides.

The ends of the cane will stick out beyond the groove. Trim this excess cane by chiseling at the outer edge of the groove bottom.

Now cut the tapered splines to length with a mitered corner to fit the frame. Pour a small amount of liquid hide glue into the grooves. (White glue can be used, but it is not as good.) Drive the spline into the groove, starting from one corner and working toward the other. Fig. 14-16. Remove the wedges that held the cane in place as you install the spline. After the spline is installed, glue in the reed over it. Wipe off excess glue with a damp sponge. Allow the cane to dry for twenty-four hours at room temperature. As the cane dries, it will shrink and become taut.

Sometimes cane is stretched around the frame and held in place by a strip of wood nailed to the edge.

METALS

The metals used in all-wood furniture are primarily mild steel and brass, with some aluminum and chrome-plated steel for fasteners, hardware, and trim. Mild steel is used for:

● Fasteners such as staples, nails, and screws.
● Mending plates.
● Hinges, knobs, and drawer pulls.
● Drawer guides and slides.

Brass is used for:

● Fasteners, such as wood screws, for fine furniture.
● Fancy-head nails such as escutcheon pins.
● Upholstery nails.
● Trim on furniture.
● Hardware, such as the more expensive hinges, drawer knobs, drawer pulls, back plates, corner plates, and furniture locks.

LEATHERS

Natural cowhide is sometimes used in upholstery or for trim on furniture. This material is known as furniture-hide. Today real leather is rarely used. Most leatherlike materials are made of plastic. Polyvinyl chloride (PVC) or vinyl can be used separately or combined with natural materials to produce a wide variety of upholstery materials that look and feel like natural leather. Fig. 14-17.

CHISEL

CANE

TRIM CANE ENDS BY CHISELING AT OUTER EDGE OF GROOVE BOTTOM

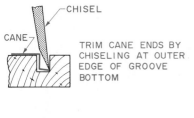

14-16. *Trim the cane ends. Use a wooden mallet to drive the spline into the groove.*

14-17. *The padded seat and back and the arms of this chair are vinyl suede, a plastic that looks and feels like real suede leather.*

15 Measurement and Measuring Devices

Two systems of measurement are used in constructing wood products. The *customary* (sometimes called English) system is based on the inch (in. or ″) as the unit of length. The *metric* system uses the *millimetre* (mm) as a unit of length. Since length is usually the only measurement unit needed, it is easy to build a product using either system. Different measuring tools are needed for working in inches and millimetres. Most woodworkers have "inch" measuring tools; so this system will be used for years to come.

RULES USED FOR MEASURING

Rules are marked in customary units, in metric units, or with a combination of customary and metric units. Most customary rules used in woodworking are divided into inches. The inches in turn are divided into halves, quarters, eighths, and sixteenths. Metric rules are divided into millimetres. On most metric rules, this is the smallest unit. A millimetre is very short (about ⅟₂₅″). Combination rules have inches along one edge and millimetres along the other. They are useful when converting from inches to millimetres or the reverse.

Common lengths of customary rules are one foot (12 inches), 18 inches, 2 feet, and 1 yard (36 inches). Tape measures come in lengths up to 100 feet.

Metric rules are available in lengths of 300 millimetres (about 1

foot), 0.5 metre (500 mm), and 1 metre (1000 mm). When selecting a metric rule, make sure that every tenth millimetre is marked (10, 20, 30, *etc.*). Ten millimetres equal one centimetre; so some rules mark every tenth millimetre as a centimetre (1, 2, 3, *etc.*). Such rules are harder to use.

CHANGING MEASURING SYSTEMS

Most drawings in this book are dimensioned in inches. To change to millimetres, multiply inches by 25.4 to get millimetres. For example, if the measurement is 3¼″, first change to the decimal size of 3.25 and then multiply by 25.4. This will give you the metric equivalent, slightly more than 82 millimetres. If you use a combination customary-metric rule, you can read this change directly on the rule. Fig. 15-1.

METRIC DESIGN

If the product is to be redesigned from customary to metric measurements, the dimensions should be rounded to at least the nearest millimetre. However, for best use of the metric system, the dimensions should be rounded to the nearest 5 to 10 millimetres. When this is

done, the total size of the project will change slightly. For example, if the dimension is 12 inches (which converts to 305 millimetres), it would be better to use 300 millimetres.

MEASURING DEVICES

If the finished product is to turn out as planned, measurements must be accurately made and then checked for errors. Use of the correct measuring device for the work to be done will be of great help in making accurate measurements.

Rules

Ordinary 12-inch (bench rule), 18-inch, or 2-foot rules are used for measuring small projects because they are more manageable than the longer rules. These shorter rules may be made of wood, plastic, or steel.

Folding or Zigzag Rule

This rule unfolds to 6 feet in length. It is made of wood or lightweight metal and folds so that it can be easily carried or stored. Fig. 15-2. This rule is used in measuring distances where slight variations in measurement are not important. It is easily bent or broken, particularly while it is being opened. When not

---

15-1. *You can read the change from inches to millimetres directly on this combination tape. For example, 2½″ is about 64 mm.*

15-2. *This 6-foot zigzag rule is useful, mostly to carpenters, for measuring long lengths.*

15-3. *This push-pull steel tape is handy as a shop rule. It will take inside and outside measurements accurately. Note that it is marked in both inches and millimetres.*

in use, it should be folded up and put away to prevent damage.

Steel Tape

The steel tape is a ribbon of steel ⅜ to ½ inch wide and marked in feet, inches, and fractions of an inch. Fig. 15-3. These tapes are available in 6-, 8-, 10-, 12-, 50-, and 100-foot lengths and are used for measuring longer distances than is convenient with a folding rule.

The tape is fixed to a reel and is housed in a case into which it retracts automatically. A small metal tab is attached to the end of the tape so that it can be easily held or attached to an object. This makes it unnecessary to have someone hold the end in position while a measurement is being taken.

The tape should be returned to its case immediately after use in order to prevent kinking. Care must also be taken to keep the tape from kinking when measuring around corners or when it becomes twisted. If the tape is of uncoated steel, care must be taken to prevent rust. (Tapes are available with a plastic coating.) If the tape is used in

damp or wet areas, it must be thoroughly dried and lightly oiled before reeling it back into its case.

Try Square

The try square is composed of a steel graduated blade set at a right angle in a thicker beam (handle) of steel or wood. Fig. 15-4. The beam butts against the stock that is being squared. The try square is used as a guide in marking lines at right angles to an edge or surface, to determine if a board is the same thickness throughout its length, and to test an edge or surface for squareness.

Both the steel and the wooden parts should be lightly oiled to prevent rusting and drying out. The try square is accurately machined so that the handle and the blade are at right angles to each other. Never use this tool as a pounding device.

The handle and blade may work loose from one another and thereby lose squareness. To test for this, place the handle against the edge of a straight board and make a mark along the blade. Turn the square over and see if the blade rests on the same mark. If it does not, the angle between the two marks made by the blade is twice the amount by which the try square is in error. To correct, loosen the screws by which the handle is fastened to the blade and adjust the blade until it tests correctly.

Sliding T Bevel

The sliding T bevel, or bevel square, as it is sometimes called, has a steel blade from 6 to 12 inches long with a 45-degree bevel point at one end. Fig. 15-5. The other end is fitted into a slotted wooden or metal beam or handle and is held in place with a thumbscrew. With this thumbscrew, it can be set at any desired angle. It can be used to transfer angles from one piece of lumber to another or to test bevels. Fig. 15-6.

The T bevel is cared for in the same way as the try square. When not in use, the blade should be fixed into the handle with the thumbscrew.

Steel or Carpenter's Square

Also called a framing square, this is an all-steel, L-shaped tool consisting of two arms. The longer one is called the blade and the shorter one the tongue. These meet at a right angle, called the heel. The blade and tongue are marked into inches and fractions thereof. Framing squares come in different sizes for marking on different sizes of stock.

To use the square, the blade is held along the edge of the board with the tongue across the face of the board. A line is marked along the tongue. If this is done correctly,

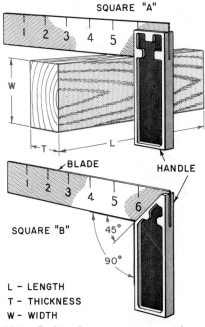

SQUARE "A"

W

T

L

BLADE

HANDLE

SQUARE "B"

45°

90°

L – LENGTH
T – THICKNESS
W – WIDTH

15-4. *A 6-inch try square with a metal blade and handle. The lower picture shows a try and miter square with one edge of the handle shaped at an angle of 45 degrees. For many layout jobs this kind of try square is better and more convenient to use.*

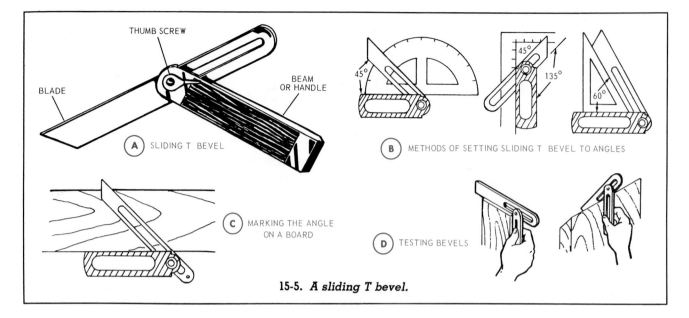

THUMB SCREW

BLADE

BEAM OR HANDLE

(A) SLIDING T BEVEL

(B) METHODS OF SETTING SLIDING T BEVEL TO ANGLES

45° 135° 60°

(C) MARKING THE ANGLE ON A BOARD

(D) TESTING BEVELS

15-5. *A sliding T bevel.*

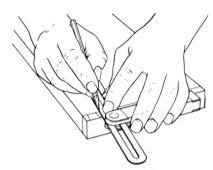

15-6. *Using a sliding T bevel to mark out a wood joint.*

the line will be at a right angle to the edge of the board. The square can be used to measure, to test for squareness, and to check for warping of the board. Fig. 15-7.

Squares are usually made of steel; so they must be kept lightly oiled to prevent rusting. However, they will sometimes rust from the humidity in the air. When this happens, the markings become hard to read. Squares may be cleaned by rubbing lightly with fine steel wool or emery cloth and applying a light coat of oil.

Combination Square

The combination square has a steel graduated blade from 6 to 24 inches long. It is grooved along one side. The blade is fitted to a metal head which can be clamped at any distance along the blade. This head has machined edges which are at 90-degree and at 45-degree angles to the blade. The head is fitted with a level, and a steel scriber is set into the end of the head opposite to the blade. The head can be clamped securely in any position along the blade with the clamping screw.

The combination square can be used as a try square, a depth gauge, or a marking gauge. It can also be

15-7. *Using a framing square to check for squareness.*

used to check 45-degree angles and to test for level. Fig. 15-8.

The combination square is cared for in the same way as the carpenter's square. However, it is a more precise instrument which must be handled with care.

Marking Gauge

The marking gauge is a wood or metal tool consisting of a beam, head, and a pin. Fig. 15-9. It is used to mark a line parallel to an edge or end of a piece of wood. (A light line is preferable to a deep one. If the line is not plain, a light pencil mark is put on the gauge line.) File the pin to a wedge shape. This will make a clean line instead of the fuzzy one made by a rounded point. The beam is graduated, but, for accurate marking, it is best to use a rule to measure the desired distance from the pin, or spur, to the head. Fig. 15-10. Then use the thumbscrew to set the head at the desired distance from the pin. When the marking gauge is used, the pin should project $\frac{1}{16}$ inch. Fig. 15-11.

Dividers

Dividers consist of a pair of pointed legs, joined together at or near

15-8(a). *Combination square and pencil used as a marking gauge.*

15-8(b). *Checking to make sure the end and edge are square with each other.*

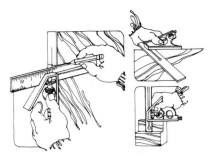

15-8(c). *Other uses for the combination square.*

the top. Wing dividers have an arc (called a wing) that holds the legs apart at any desired distance by means of a setscrew. At one end of the wing are an adjusting screw and

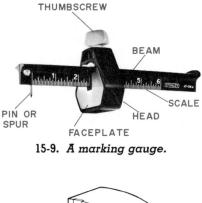

15-9. *A marking gauge.*

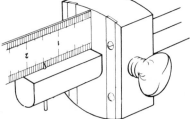

15-10. *Set distance with a rule as shown.*

spring that permit fine setting of the legs. Fig. 15-12.

Dividers are used to describe circles or arcs, to transfer measurements from the work to the rule or from the rule to the work, and to mark lengths into equal parts.

Dividers must be treated like any other sharp instrument. They must not be left lying around where they might be knocked to the floor or where someone might brush against the sharp points. They must not be carried in the pocket but should be placed flat in the toolbox or hung on a toolboard when not in use.

The points of dividers can be kept sharp by rotating them against an oilstone. If they are badly dulled or bent, they can be ground by rotating them against a grinding machine. If this is done, care must be taken to prevent loss of temper of the metal and to keep the legs even in length. Because they are made of steel, dividers should be kept lightly oiled. When not in use, the setscrew should be set lightly to prevent damage to the arc or to the legs of the dividers if they should fall.

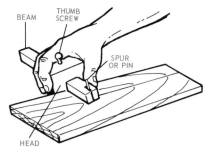

15-11. *Using a marking gauge. Note that the head of the gauge is tipped slightly as it is pushed along.*

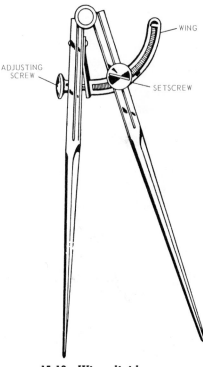

15-12. *Wing dividers.*

Level

The level is an 18- to 28-inch wood block or metal casting with true surface edges. It is used to determine whether a surface is level or if an upright is plumb. It has two bubble tubes. These tubes contain a liquid and an air bubble. The tube in the middle of one of the long edges indicates levelness of a surface. The surface is level if the bubble comes to rest exactly between the two scratch marks on the bubble tube. The other bubble tube is at right angles to the first one and indicates vertical level or "plumb." Fig. 15-13.

The level should be handled with care, as the bubble tubes break easily. It should also be rubbed with a light rubbing oil to prevent drying of the wood.

Contour Gauge

The contour gauge, or template former, outlines any shape. Fig. 15-14. To use it, press the steel teeth against an irregular surface, slip it away, and trace either the male or female template of the irregular contour onto paper, wood, or any surface. The gauge is 6 inches long, but two or three can be joined to make a 12- or 18-inch tool for wider areas.

MARKING TOOLS

An ordinary lead pencil is the most common marking tool. Its mark can be seen easily on both rough and finished lumber. The mark is easy to remove, and the pencil does not scratch or mar the wood surface. Use a pencil with a rather hard lead for laying out fine, accurate lines. Keep the pencil sharpened in the shape of a chisel so that the point can be held directly against the edge of the rule or square.

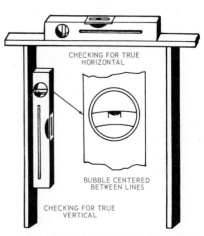

CHECKING FOR TRUE HORIZONTAL

BUBBLE CENTERED BETWEEN LINES

CHECKING FOR TRUE VERTICAL

HORIZONTAL AND VERTICAL USE OF LEVEL

15-13. *Uses for a level.*

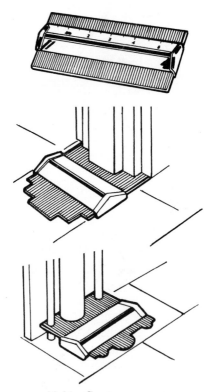

15-14. *Contour gauge.*

Utility Knife

A utility knife is a good tool for very accurate marking. Fig. 15-15. However, be careful to use it only when you know that the mark will disappear as the wood is cut, formed, or shaped.

Sloyd Knife

A sloyd knife is a very handy tool because it can be used for such jobs as trimming a fine edge, slicing a piece of thin veneer, and whittling a small peg. Fig. 15-16.

Scratch Awl

The scratch awl is a thin metal-pointed tool with a wooden handle. It is good for marking and punching the location of holes to be drilled or bored. Fig. 15-17.

HOLDING DEVICES

Bench Vise

For good work you must have a solid workbench with a sturdy bench

vise. Fig. 15-18. The woodworker's bench vise holds lumber to be worked. The vise is attached to the bench so that the two top edges of the vise are flush with the top of the bench. The movable jaws may be adjusted by turning the handle. Some vises have a more rapid method of adjustment. The handle is set, the movable jaw is pushed to approximately the correct position, and then it is firmed against the mark by turning the handle. These vises vary in size and weight and usually open from 9 to 12 inches.

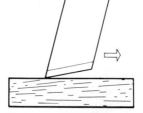

15-15. *Utility knife. Use only the point of the knife, drawing it towards yourself. Hold the knife like a pencil.*

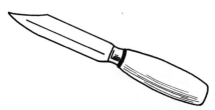

15-16. *The sloyd knife is excellent for layout work and also for many odd jobs such as cutting, trimming, and whittling.*

15-17. *The scratch awl is another layout tool that is very handy. It is used to lay out the positions for drilling and boring holes.*

15-18. *A sturdy bench with metal vises.*

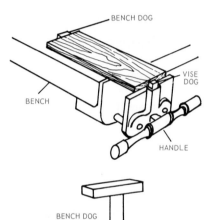

15-19. *Use a vise dog and bench dog to hold the workpiece.*

15-20. *This kind of sawhorse is most practical for layout and cutting. Because it is open down the center, the sawing can be done with the blade free to move down the center of the opening.*

Keep the work in the vise from being damaged by protecting it with pieces of scrap wood. Lumber too large to be held in the vise may be held between the vise dog (the part of the vise that can be pulled higher than the top of the bench) and the bench dog (the metal T-shaped piece that fits into holes in the bench). Fig. 15-19.

The screws of the bench vise must be kept clean, free from rust, and lightly oiled.

Sawhorse

When handling large pieces for layout, sawing, or assembling, one or two wood sawhorses are needed. They should be about 20 inches high. The best kind is open down the center, like that shown in Fig. 15-20.

MEASURING STOCK

Thickness

The lumber should be checked for thickness, width, and length. Measure the thickness of the lumber by holding the rule over the edge. The thickness is found by reading the two lines on the rule that just enclose the stock. Fig. 15-21.

Width

Measure the width by holding the left end of the rule (or the inch mark) on the edge of the stock. Slide your thumb from right to left along the rule until the width is shown. Fig. 15-22.

Length

To measure *short* lengths, select the end of the stock from which the measurement is to be taken. Check its squareness by holding a try square against the truest edge. Make sure that the end is not split or checked. If it is, the end of the wood should be squared off and cut and the measurement taken from the sawed end. Hold the rule on

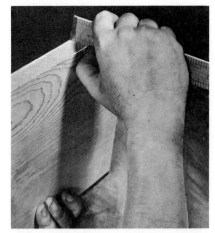

15-21. *Measuring the thickness of stock with a bench rule. Hold one end of the rule directly over one edge of the wood. Slide your thumb along until the thickness of the stock is indicated.*

15-22. *Measuring the width of stock. The rule is held on edge for more accurate measurement.*

edge and mark the length with a pencil or knife.

For measuring *long* stock, use a zigzag rule or a steel tape. This will eliminate measurement errors that come from moving a short rule several times. Make a small mark at the point to be squared.

MARKING STOCK FOR CUTTING TO LENGTH

Marking Lengths on Narrow Lumber

If rather narrow lumber must be marked for cutting, hold the handle

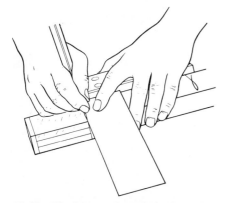

15-23. *Marking a length before cutting. Place the knife point on the pencil line, slide the try square up to the knife, hold firmly, and draw the knife toward yourself.*

of the try square firmly against the truest edge of the stock. Square off a line. Fig. 15-23.

Marking Lengths on Wide Lumber

Use a framing square on wide stock. The framing square is uniform in thickness. Therefore the

blade should be tipped slightly and then held firmly against the truest edge while the mark is made across the stock.

Marking Duplicate Parts

If a group of pieces must be measured and marked out to equal lengths, place them side by side. Make sure that the ends are lined up by holding a try square over the ends. Then move the try square to correct length to mark the pieces.

MARKING STOCK FOR CUTTING TO WIDTH

Decide on the width of stock you need. Hold the rule at right angles to the truest edge of the stock and measure the correct width. Fig. 15-24. This can also be done with a try square or combination square (Fig. 15-8a). Do this at several points along the stock. Then hold a straightedge over these points and connect them.

A framing square may be used to

15-24. *Measuring the correct width of stock with a zigzag rule. Place your left thumb on the correct width and hold this firmly against one edge of the stock while you mark the width with a sharp pencil.*

measure the width of stock needed. Another method for marking the width of rough stock is to hold a rule to the correct width between the thumb and forefinger. Then guide it along the truest edge of the stock with a pencil held against the end of the rule.

16 Ordering Lumber and Other Materials

Lumber and other materials are processed, manufactured, and sold according to long-established standards. It is important to know how to order these materials, whether they are for a built-in cabinet or a piece of furniture. Fig. 16-1.

People who write orders for building materials use abbreviations instead of writing out all the terms.

Figure 16-2 lists abbreviations that are commonly used to order lumber and other materials.

SOLID LUMBER

The standard customary unit of measurement for solid lumber is the *board foot* (Bd. Ft.). It is easy to remember that a board foot is a piece 1″ thick by 1′ square, or 144

cubic inches (1″ × 12″ × 12″). Fig. 16-3. Therefore a board that is 1″ thick, 12″ wide, and 10′ long would contain 10 board feet. Stock that is less than 1″ thick is figured as 1″. Lumber that is thicker than 1″ is figured as its actual thickness. Hardwood lumbers between 1″ and 2″ thick are figured by the nearest ¼″ thickness. For example, 1¼″ (which

16-1(a). *To build this loveseat, you need a variety of materials and tools.*

is often referred to as ⁵⁄₄, or five quarter) would be the thickness used in figuring board feet for lumber delivered as surfaced two sides (S2S). Such lumber actually measures 1¹⁄₁₆".

The three simple formulas used to figure board feet are:

● Board feet equals thickness in inches times width in feet times length in feet. Bd. Ft. = T (in inches) × W (in feet) × L (in feet).

16-1(b). *Here are all of the materials and portable power tools needed to complete the project.*

COMMON LUMBER ABBREVIATIONS

AD—Air dried	H&M—Hit and miss	SH D—Shipping dry
AL—All lengths	HDWD—Hardwood	SM—Surface measure
ALS—American Lumber Standards	HRT—Heart	SQ—Square
AV—Average	HRTWD—Heartwood	SQRS—Squares
B&B or B&Btr—B and better	IN—Inch or inches	STD—Standard
BD—Board	JTD—Jointed	STD M—Standard matched
BD FT—Board feet	KD—Kiln dried	STK—Stock
BDL—Bundle	LBR—Lumber	STRUCT—Structural
BEV—Bevel	LGTH—Length	SYMBOLS
BM—Board measure	LIN—Lineal	"—Inch or inches
BTR—Better	LIN FT—Lineal (or linear) foot	'—Foot or feet
C/L—Carload	M—Thousand	×—By, as 4 × 4
CLG—Ceiling	M BM—Thousand (ft.) board measure	⁴⁄₄, ⁵⁄₄, ⁶⁄₄, etc.— thickness expressed in fractions of an inch
CLR—Clear	MC—Moisture content	
COM—Common	MLDG—Moulding or molding	S&E—Side and edge
CSG—Casing	MR—Mill run	S1E—Surfaced one edge
CU FT—Cubic feet	N—Nosed	S2E—Surfaced 2 edges
DF—Douglas fir	OC—On center	S1S—Surfaced one side
DIM—Dimension	OG—Ogee	S2S—Surfaced two sides
DKG—Decking	P—Planed	S4S—Surfaced four sides
D/S, DS—Drop siding	PC—Piece	S1S&CM—Surfaced one side and center matched
D&M—Dressed and matched; center matched unless otherwise specified	QTD—Quartered, when referring to hardwoods	S2S&CM—Surfaced two sides and center matched
D&CM—Dressed and center matched	RDM—Random	S4S&CS—Surfaced four sides and caulking seam
D&SM—Dressed and standard matched	REG—Regular	S1S1E—Surfaced one side, one edge
	RGH—Rough	
E—Edge	RIP—Ripped	S1S2E—Surfaced one side, two edges
EBIS—Edge bead one side	R/L, RL—Random lengths	
EG—Edge (vertical) grain	RND—Round	S2S&SM—Surfaced two sides and standard matched
FAS—Firsts and seconds	R/W, RW—Random widths	
FG—Flat or slash grain	RWD—Redwood	T&G—Tongued and grooved, center matched unless otherwise specified
FCTY—Factory lumber	SAP—Sapwood	
FLG—Flooring	SD—Seasoned	
FT—Foot	SDG—Siding	VG—Vertical (edge) grain
FT BM or FBM—Feet board measure	SEL—Select	WDR—Wider
	SF—Surface foot; that is, an area of 1 square foot	WT—Weight
FT SM—Feet surface measure		WTH—Width
GR—Green	SG—Slash grain	

16-2. *Abbreviations used frequently to order lumber and other materials.*

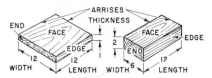

16-3. *Each of these pieces contains one board foot.*

Example: A piece 1″ × 8″ × 12′ contains 8 board feet.

$$\text{Bd. Ft.} = \frac{1}{1} \times \frac{2}{3} \times \frac{12}{1} = 8$$

• Board feet equals thickness in inches times width in inches times length in feet divided by twelve.

$$\text{Bd. Ft.} = \frac{T(\text{in.}) \times W(\text{in.}) \times L(\text{ft.})}{12}$$

Example: A piece 2″ × 6″ × 10′ contains 10 board feet.

$$\text{Bd. Ft.} = \frac{2 \times 6 \times 10}{12} = 10$$

• Board feet equals thickness in inches times width in inches times length in inches divided by 144.

$$\text{Bd. Ft.} = \frac{T \times W \times L \text{ (in inches)}}{144}$$

Example: A piece 1″ × 12″ × 24″ contains 2 board feet.

$$\text{Bd. Ft.} = \frac{1 \times 12 \times 24}{144} = 2$$

Lumber is priced at so much per thousand board feet. The Roman numeral *M* stands for one thousand. A lumber order of 1000 board feet at $800 per *M* would cost $800. At this price, one board foot would cost 80 cents.

OTHER MATERIALS

Plywood, hardboard, particle board, and other sheet materials are sold by the *square foot*. The most common sheet size is 4′ × 8′, or 32 square feet. If the price for a certain thickness of plywood, for example, is 75 cents per square foot, then the standard 4′ × 8′ sheet costs $24. Moldings, trim, dowel rod, and similar materials are sold by the *linear foot* (Lin. Ft.). For example, a 10′ piece of cove molding at 40 cents a foot would cost $4.00.

LUMBER SIZES

Some lumber is purchased just as it comes from the sawmill with the surface rough (rgh). Before it can be used, this lumber must be smoothed by running it through a planer or surfacer. Most lumber is dried and dimensioned (surfaced) at the mill. The dressed or surfaced (actual) size is smaller than the rough (nominal) size. Lumber sizes are based on the rough, green dimensions. American Lumber Standards for softwoods allow the nominal 2 × 4 to measure 1½″ × 3½″ if dried to 19 percent moisture content or less and 1⁹⁄₁₆″ × 3⁹⁄₁₆″ if the moisture content is over this amount. A 1″ hardwood piece, when surfaced, is reduced to ¹³⁄₁₆″, while the dressed 1″ pine becomes ²⁵⁄₃₂″ or ¾″.

In lumber dimensions, the first figure is always the thickness, the second the width, and the third the length. Softwoods are cut to standard thickness, width, and length. Figure 16-4 shows the standard thicknesses and widths of softwood lumber. The standard lengths range from 8′ to 20′ in increments of 2′. Hardwood lumber is generally available in standard thicknesses. Fig. 16-5. Because of its high cost, however, hardwood is cut to whatever widths and lengths are most economical and convenient. These are called *random* widths and lengths.

Metric Sizes

As cabinetmaking converts to the metric system, lumber and other wood products will be specified in metric measurements. A *hard* conversion would mean a change in the actual sizes of materials. A *soft* conversion would mean simply a change in the measurement language. For example, in softwood lumber the customary 2 × 4 (nominal size) is available in dressed, or actual, size at either 1½ × 3½ inches dry or 1⁹⁄₁₆ × 3⁹⁄₁₆ inches green. In the metric system, the 2 × 4 would have a nominal size of 50 × 100 millimetres and actually measure about 38 × 89 millimetres dry and 40 × 90 millimetres green. *This soft conversion is merely a change in the measuring language.* The wood is not cut differently than before. Where the metric system is in common use, such as in Canada, nominal sizes of lumber have been eliminated. The sizes are stated only in their actual metric dimensions.

In the metric system, large volumes of lumber are sold by the cubic metre. The cubic metre is a very large unit (about 424 board feet) and therefore is not suitable for individual orders for furniture and cabinets. Smaller orders are expressed in exact metric dimensions for thickness and width and in multiples of 300 mm for length. For example, a typical order might be 10 pieces of 14 × 44 × 2400 mm lumber.

Metric sizes of plywood and other panel stock will be 1200 × 2400 mm, which is slightly smaller than the customary sizes. The plywood is sold by the square metre, while molding and similar items are sold by the linear metre.

LUMBER GRADING

To know how to order lumber, you need to understand something about lumber grading. This is a rather complicated subject and especially difficult for softwoods since uniform standards are not accepted throughout the country. Lumber is divided into two major groups: softwoods and hardwoods. Softwoods are used mainly for paneling and interior cabinetwork. Hardwoods are used for the same purposes, and they are used for building fine furniture as well.

THICKNESS AND WIDTH OF SOFTWOOD

THICKNESS

Nominal			Minimum Dressed					
	Exact	Rounded	Dry			Green		
				Exact	Rounded		Exact	Rounded
inches	mm	mm	inches	mm	mm	inches	mm	mm
1	25.4	25	¾	19.1	19	25/32	19.8	20
1¼	31.8	32	1	25.4	25	1 1/32	26.2	26
1½	38.1	38	1¼	31.8	32	1 9/32	32.51	33
2	50.8	50	1½	38.1	38	1 9/16	39.7	40
2½	63.5	63	2	50.8	50	2 1/16	52.4	52
3	76.2	75	2½	63.5	63	2 9/16	65.1	65
3½	88.9	90	3	76.2	75	3 1/16	77.8	78
4	101.6	100	3½	88.9	89	3 9/16	90.5	90

WIDTH

Nominal			Minimum Dressed					
	Exact	Rounded	Dry			Green		
				Exact	Rounded		Exact	Rounded
inches	mm	mm	inches	mm	mm	inches	mm	mm
2	50.8	50	1½	38.1	38	1 9/16	39.7	40
3	76.2	75	2½	63.5	63	2 9/16	65.1	65
4	101.6	100	3½	88.9	89	3 9/16	90.5	90
5	127.0	125	4½	114.3	114	4 5/8	117.5	117
6	152.4	150	5½	139.7	140	5 5/8	142.9	143
7	177.8	175	6½	165.1	165	6 5/8	168.3	168
8	203.2	200	7¼	184.1	184	7 ½	190.5	190

16-4. *Standard thicknesses and widths of softwood lumber. Both nominal (rough) and dressed (surfaced) dimensions are given.*

THICKNESS OF HARDWOOD

Nominal (Rough)	Exact mm	Rounded mm	Surfaced 1 Side (S1S)	Exact mm	Rounded mm	Surfaced 2 Sides (S2S)	Exact mm	Rounded mm
⅜"	9.5	10	¼"	6.4	6	3/16"	4.8	5
½"	12.7	13	⅜"	9.5	9	5/16"	7.9	8
⅝"	15.9	16	½"	12.7	13	7/16"	11.1	11
¾"	19.1	19	⅝"	15.9	16	9/16"	14.3	14
1"	25.4	25	⅞"	22.2	22	13/16"	20.6	21
1¼"	31.8	32	1 ⅛"	28.6	29	1 1/16"	27.0	27
1½"	38.1	38	1 ⅜"	34.9	35	1 5/16"	33.3	33
2"	50.8	50	1 13/16"	46.0	46	1 ¾"	44.5	44
3"	76.2	75	2 13/16"	71.4	71	2 ¾"	69.9	70
4"	101.6	100	3 13/16"	96.8	97	3 ¾"	95.3	95

16-5. *Standard rough and surfaced thicknesses of hardwood. Widths vary with the grade.*

Softwood Grading

The National Bureau of Standards has established *American Softwood Lumber Standards* for softwood lumber. These standards are intended as guides for the different associations of lumber producers, each of which has its own grading rules and specifications. Most of the major associations, such as the Western Wood Products Association, Redwood Inspection Service, and many others participated in developing these grading rules. If you work with just a few kinds of lumber most of the time, you should obtain grading rules from the associations involved with that kind of lumber and become familiar with those rules. One of the main ideas of these standards is to divide all softwood lumber for *grading purposes* into two groups:

• Dry lumber is seasoned, or dried, to a moisture content of 19 percent or less.

• Green lumber has a moisture content in excess of 19 percent.

Grading rules for softwood lumber are outlined in the bulletin "PS 20-70, American Softwood Lumber Standards, American Lumber Standards Committee." This bulletin is available from the Superintendent of Documents, U.S. Government Printing Office, Washington, DC.

Softwood lumber is classified according to use and extent of manufacture as follows. See also Fig. 16-6.

USE CLASSIFICATIONS

Yard lumber. Lumber of those grades, sizes, and patterns which are intended for ordinary construction and general building purposes.

Structural lumber. Lumber that is 2 or more inches in nominal thickness and width for use where working stresses are involved. (NOTE: See Fig. 16-4 for comparison of nominal sizes with actual or dressed sizes.)

Factory and shop lumber. Lumber

GENERAL CLASSIFICATIONS OF SOFTWOOD LUMBER

				Grades
Softwood lumber (this classification applies to rough or dressed lumber; sizes given are nominal)	**Yard lumber** (lumber less than 5 inches thick, intended for general building purposes; grading based on use of the entire piece)	Finish (less than 3 inches thick and 12 inches and under in width)		A select B select C select D select
		Boards (less than 2 inches thick and 2 inches or over in width). Strips (under 8 inches in width).		No. 1 boards No. 2 boards No. 3 boards No. 4 boards No. 5 boards
	Structural material (lumber 2 inches or over in thickness and width, except joist and plank; grading based on strength and on use of entire piece)	Dimension (2 inches and under 5 inches thick and 2 or more inches in width)	Planks (2 inches and under 4 inches thick and 8 inches and over wide)	No. 1 dimension No. 2 dimension No. 3 dimension
			Scantling (2 inches and under 5 inches thick and under 8 inches wide)	No. 1 dimension No. 2 dimension No. 3 dimension
			Heavy joists (4 inches thick and 8 inches or over wide)	No. 1 dimension No. 2 dimension No. 3 dimension
		Joist and plank (2 inches to 4 inches thick and 4 inches and over wide)		
		Timbers classified as beams, stringers, posts, caps, sills, girders, purlins, etc., must be 5 or more inches nominally in least dimension		
	Factory and shop (grading based on area of piece suitable for cuttings of certain size and quality)	Factory plank graded for door, sash, and other cuttings 1 inch to 4 inches thick and 5 inches and over wide	Factory clears upper grades	Nos. 1 and 2 clear factory No. 3 clear factory
			Shop lower grades	No. 1 shop No. 2 shop No. 3 shop
		Shop lumber graded for general cut up purposes	1 inch thick (northern and western pine, and Pacific coast woods)	Select Shop
			All thicknesses (cypress, redwood, and North Carolina pine)	Tank and boat stock, firsts and seconds, selects No. 1 shop No. 2 shop, box

16-6. *Softwood lumber classifications.*

that is produced or selected primarily for remanufacturing purposes.

Yard lumbers are cut for a wide variety of uses. They are divided into two grade qualities—finish (select) and common grades.

Finish (select) grades are further classified. Grade A is practically clear wood and is used for such items as finish flooring, ceilings, partitions, and siding. Grade B has very few imperfections, though it may include small checks or stain marks. Grades C and D have increasingly more imperfections, but are still suitable for a good paint finish.

The common grades of boards are suited for general utility and construction purposes. The major differences between the grades are in the number of knots and amount of pitch. The grades range from Nos. 1 and 2, which can be used without waste, to Nos. 3, 4, and 5, which involve a limited amount of waste. (In some grading rules, No. 1 is considered *construction grade;* No. 2, *standard;* No. 3, *utility;* and Nos. 4 and 5, *economy.*) Fig. 16-7.

MANUFACTURING CLASSIFICATIONS

Rough lumber. Lumber which has not been dressed (surfaced) but which has been sawed, edged, and trimmed at least to the extent of showing saw marks on the four longitudinal surfaces of each piece for its overall length.

Dressed (surfaced) lumber. Lumber that has been dressed by a planing machine for smoothness of surface and uniformity of size. Lumber may be surfaced on one side (S1S), two sides (S2S), one edge (S1E), two edges (S2E), or a combination of sides and edges (S1S1E, S1S2E, S2S1E, S4S).

Worked lumber. Lumber which, in addition to being dressed, has been matched, shiplapped, or patterned. *Matched lumber* has been worked with a tongue on one edge of each piece and a groove on the opposite edge. This provides a close tongue-and-groove joint by fitting two pieces together. When end-matched, the tongue and groove are worked in the ends also. *Shiplapped lumber* has been worked or rabbeted on both edges of each piece to provide a closelapped joint by fitting two pieces together. *Patterned lumber* is shaped to a pattern or to a molded form, in addition to being dressed, matched, or shiplapped, or any combination of these workings.

Hardwood Grading

With some exceptions, hardwood lumber is graded on the basis of the size and number of cuttings (pieces) which can be obtained from a board

16-7. *Grade stamp: (a) The official Western Wood Products Association mark on a piece of lumber is assurance of its assigned grade. Grading practices of Western Wood Products Association member mills are supervised to assure uniformity. (b) Each mill is assigned a permanent number for grade stamp purposes. (c) An example of an official grade name abbreviation. The official grade name, as defined by the Association, gives positive identification to graded lumber. (d) This mark identifies the wood species. (e) This symbol denotes moisture content of lumber when manufactured. S-Dry indicates seasoned lumber. S-Green would indicate unseasoned or "green" lumber. It is recommended that S-Dry lumber be used for all interior construction.*

when it is cut up and used in the manufacture of a hardwood product such as furniture, flooring, or interior house trim. Usually the buyer is interested only in the clear material in a board. Therefore the best grade would have the largest area of usable material. When cut up for remanufacture, nearly all of this best grade could be used in a small number of large-sized cuttings, while lower grade boards would produce several smaller-sized cuttings.

In rough lumber, the grade is determined from the poorer side of the board. In surfaced lumber, the grade is determined from the better face. The reverse side must be sound.

The standard grades of hardwood lumber are Firsts, Seconds, Selects, No. 1 Common, No. 2 Common, Sound Wormy, No. 3A Common, and No. 3B Common. Lumber may be sold separately by each grade or in a combination of grades. These combinations are:

FAS. Firsts and Seconds are usually combined as one grade. This is the best grade for most furniture construction.

No. 1 Common and better. The full run of the logs with all grades below No. 1 Common excluded.

No. 2 Common and better (log run). The full run of the logs, excluding all grades below No. 2 Common.

No. 3B Common and better (mill run). The full run of the logs; below-grade lumber excluded.

Nos. 3A Common and 3B Common may be combined as No. 3 Common. When so combined and specified, they are understood to include all the No. 3A Common that the logs produce.

Lumber grading cannot be understood or practiced until you know and understand the terms. The following are basic definitions.

Surface measure (S.M.)—The surface area of a board in square feet. To determine surface measure, multiply the width of the board in inches and fractions by the length in feet and divide the product by 12.

$$S.M. = \frac{W \text{ (in.)} \times L \text{ (ft.)}}{12}$$

Examples: A piece of lumber 6″ × 8′ has a 4 sq. ft. surface measure.

$$S.M. = \frac{6 \times 8}{12} = 4$$

A piece 6″ × 12′ has a surface measure of 6 sq. ft.

$$S.M. = \frac{6 \times 12}{12} = 6$$

Clear face cutting—A cutting having one clear face (ordinary season checks are admitted) and with the reverse side sound as defined in *Sound cutting.* The *clear face of the cutting shall be on the poor side of the board* except when otherwise specified.

Sound cutting—A cutting free from rot, pitch, shake, and wane. Texture is not considered. Sound knots, stains, streaks, or their equivalent are allowed. Season checks not materially impairing the strength of a cutting are also acceptable.

Hardwood grading is a complicated subject that can be understood only by studying a complete set of grading rules. These are obtained from the association responsible for that species of wood. For example, the National Hardwood Lumber Association produces standards for hardwood and cypress lumber. The National Oak Flooring Manufacturers Association has standards for oak and maple flooring. Other associations, such as the Northeastern Lumber Manufacturers Association, have standards for both hardwoods and softwoods.

To get an idea of how Firsts are graded, look at Fig. 16-8. Study the line that shows: *4 to 9' 91⅔ 1*. This is explained as follows:

The first step in grading a board for Firsts is to determine the surface measure. Remember, this is the number of square feet in the board. For a board containing *4 to 9* square feet, *91⅔* percent of the board must be clear (without defects) by taking only *1* cut. For example, suppose a board 6 inches wide and 8 feet long has a small defect at one end. This board has the minimum surface measure of 4'. If the defect could be cut off and 91⅔ percent of the material retained, the board meets the grade standard.

If the board is larger and contains from 10 to 14 feet, then *2* cuts can be made to retain 91⅔ percent of the board.

ORDERING FROM A LUMBERYARD

If you know exactly what you want to do, your building materials dealer will usually be able to help you choose the right materials for your project. Consult the dealer also about how to use the lumber you buy, what tools are needed, and how to cut, fasten, and finish for best results. Softwood lumber is available in well over a dozen species. Douglas fir and southern pine, the most plentiful, are also the strongest. Other softwoods include cedar and redwood, both popular for their workability and natural beauty. Some local dealers stock a limited selection of hardwoods. Many regional lumber dealers specialize in these woods. As you plan your project, remember the best ways to prevent overspending for lumber are:

● Buy the lowest grade of lumber that will do the job.

● Buy the smallest quantity possible.

WRITING LUMBER SPECIFICATIONS

Lumber is ordered either for a specific product to be built or for general stock to meet a variety of needs. For a specific product, it is fairly simple to determine exactly what and how much is needed.

CUTTING REQUIREMENTS FOR STANDARD GRADES OF HARDWOOD LUMBER

Firsts	Seconds	Selects	No. 1 Common	No. 2 Common
Widths: 6" and wider Lengths: 8 to 16 feet *S.M. % Cl. Face Cuts	Widths: 6" and wider Lengths: 8 to 16 feet *S.M. % Cl. Face Cuts	Widths: 4" and wider Lengths: 6 to 16 feet *S.M. % Cl. Face Cuts	Widths: 3" and wider Lengths: 4 to 16 feet *S.M. % Cl. Face Cuts	Widths: 3" and wider Lengths: 4 to 16 feet *S.M. % Cl. Face Cuts
4 to 9' 91-⅔ 1 10 to 14' " 2 15' & up " 3	4' & 5' 83-⅓ 1 6' & 7' " 1 8' to 11' " 2 12' to 15' " 3 16' & up " 4 6' to 15' S.M. will admit 1 additional cut to yield 91-⅔% Cl. Face. **	2' & 3' 91-⅔ 1 Reverse side of cutting sound or reverse side of board not below No. 1 Common. 4' and over shall grade on one face as required in Seconds with reverse side of board not below No. 1 Common or reverse side of cuttings sound.	1' Clear 2' 75 1 3' & 4' 66-⅔ 1 5' to 7' " 2 8' to 10' " 3 11' to 13' " 4 14' & up " 5 3' to 7' S.M. will admit 1 additional cut to yield 75% Cl. Face.	1' 66-⅔ 1 2' & 3' 50 1 4' & 5' " 2 6' & 7' " 3 8' & 9' " 4 10' & 11' " 5 12' & 13' " 6 14' & up " 7 2' to 7' S.M. will admit 1 additional cut to yield 66-⅔% Cl. Face.
Minimum cutting 4" × 5' or 3" × 7'			Minimum cutting 4" × 2' or 3" × 3'	Minimum cutting 3" × 2'

*Surface measure.
**Admits also, pieces 6" to 9" wide of 6' to 12' surface measure that will yield 97% in two clear-face cuttings of any length, full width of the board.

16-8. *Description of standard grades for hardwood lumber.*

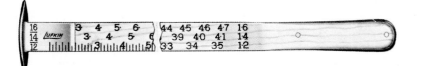

16-9. *Board measure rule. Note that the head acts as the starting mark.*

When ordering general stock, the usual practice is to base estimates of future needs on the amounts used in the past. In either case it is important that the lumber order be clear, concise, and complete in every detail. This is equally true whether the order is for a few pieces from a local lumberyard or for a large amount from a supplier in some distant city. The following are suggestions for making your written lumber specifications accurate and complete:

1. *Use standard terms in describing the quality.* These should be the terms developed by the appropriate national associations. For example, when ordering hardwood lumber, always follow the rules of the National Hardwood Lumber Association (NHLA). If you wish to order the best grade of hardwood, specify FAS (firsts and seconds). Not all lumber dealers follow these standards. Therefore it is good practice to write the following on each order: "NHLA rules to apply. Measurement and inspection to be in accordance with the rules. Vendor must indicate lumber grade alongside each item appearing on quotation or invoice."

2. *Make your order of hardwood sizes realistic.* Fine cabinet hardwoods are in limited supply. Large logs of woods such as walnut are not readily available. For this reason, these woods are cut in random widths and lengths. Generally, most hardwoods are cut in multiples of 2' lengths (8', 10', 12', etc.) with some pieces in odd lengths. It would be poor practice to ask for all walnut in 12" widths and 16' lengths. The usual practice is to specify random widths and lengths (RW & L). Remember that the grade of hardwood specified will limit the minimum sizes included in the delivery.

3. *Always specify rough thickness of the wood, then add such information as S2S (surfaced two sides) if you wish the lumber to be surfaced.* As you know, 1" S2S hardwood measures $^{13}/_{16}$". If you wish a different thickness, such as ¾", then specify as such. For example: 100' 1" FAS white oak S2S to ¾".

4. *Make your specifications as complete as possible.* This should include:

   a. *Quantity.* The number of board feet needed.

   b. *Thickness.* The standard thickness in the rough. This can be stated in inches (for example, 1" or 2") or in fractions of an inch (for example, ⁴⁄₄, or four quarters, is 1" thick. Other thicknesses are ⁵⁄₄, ⁶⁄₄, etc.).

   c. *Grade.* As indicated by the national grading rules.

   d. *Species.* Indicate the exact kind of wood, not just the name of a broad group such as oak or pine. Instead, specify white oak or ponderosa pine.

   e. *Surfacing.* Specify the kind of surface, such as rough (Rgh), surfaced two sides (S2S), or surfaced four sides (S4S).

   f. *Condition of seasoning.* Indicate if it is to be air dried (AD) or kiln dried (KD) and to what percentage. The percentage is especially important for kiln-dried lumber.

   g. *Widths and lengths.* In softwoods, the specific widths and lengths can be ordered. For hardwoods, unless otherwise specified, you should accept random widths and lengths of lumber for that particular grade as it comes from the sawmill.

A typical order might read: "100' 1" FAS Light Red Philippine Mahog-
any, Rgh, KD to 5% to 8%, RW & L." This order would be interpreted as meaning that you want 100 board feet of nominal 1-inch lumber of light red Philippine mahogany of firsts-and-seconds grade, in the rough, kiln dried to a moisture content from 5 to 8 percent, in random widths and lengths.

MEASURING THE AMOUNT OF LUMBER

After the lumber has been delivered, you should check to make sure you have received the correct species, grade (this may be difficult), and amount.

Surface or board measure is used to determine the amount of board feet in a piece or a pile of lumber. Sometimes you will be able to calculate this easily. You know, for example, that for any board 1" thick and 12" wide, the number of board feet is the same as the length of the board in feet. If a piece is 1" thick, 12" wide, and 8' long, you know immediately that it contains 8 board feet. For harder problems, use a measuring device called a *board rule,* also known as a *lumberman's board stick.* Fig. 16-9. Follow these directions:

1. Determine the length of the board.

2. Place the rule across the width of the board, with the "start" mark exactly even with the left edge of the board.

3. On the rule find the row of figures based on the length of the board.

4. Follow this row to the extreme right edge of the board. The number which appears there indicates board feet.

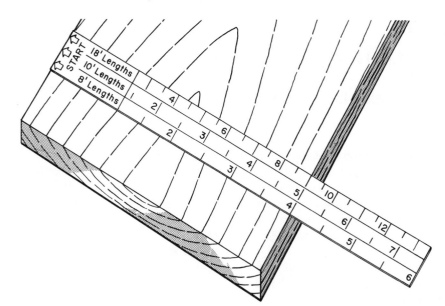

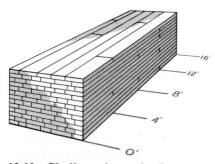

16-10. *Using a board rule to find the surface measure of a piece. If this board is 8' long, it contains 4 square feet; this would be 4 board feet if it is 1" thick, or 6 board feet if it is 1½" thick. How many square feet are there in the board if it is 10' long? How wide is this board in inches?*

16-12. *Chalk marks on the floor near the lumber rack simplify the job of determining length. Just slip a board off the pile and place it on the marks. In native hardwoods, fractional lengths are measured at the next lower foot length. For example, a 10'6" board would be figured as 10'. In true mahogany, the fractions over 6" are measured as the next higher length.*

For instance, suppose a board 1" thick is 8' long and 6" wide. Place the rule across the stock with the "start" mark lined up with the left edge. Find the row of figures marked *8' Lengths* and follow it across to the right edge of the board, where the number 4 appears. Of course you already know that a board this size contains 4 board feet. Fig. 16-10.

The *Essex board-measure table* on the framing or rafter square can also be used to determine board feet quickly. Fig. 16-11. In a board 12" wide and 1" thick, the number of board feet will equal the number of linear feet. The figure 12, therefore, on the outer edge, represents a board 1" thick and 12" wide. To use a simple example, suppose you are checking a board that is 1" thick,

12" wide, and 8' long. Look at the column of figures under the 12 on the square until you reach the figure representing the length of the board in feet. This gives you the answer, 8 board feet.

Let's take another example. Suppose the board is 8" wide and 14' long. You again look under the 12 and move your eye down the column until you reach the figure 14 (the length). Then follow along this line to the left until you reach a point directly under the figure 8 (width in inches) on the edge graduations. Here you will find 9 to the left of the cross line and 4 to the right of the same line. This tells you there are 9$\frac{4}{12}$ (or 9$\frac{1}{3}$) board feet in a 1" thick board. If the board were 2" thick, the total would be twice this amount. If the board is wider than

12", the answer will be found to the right of the 12" mark.

Remember, the board rule and the Essex board-measure table give the *surface measure* of a board. Surface measure is the square feet in the surface of a board of any thickness. In the examples just given, the board thickness was 1". Thus surface measure and board feet were the same. If the thickness had been 2", the board feet would be twice the surface measure.

Follow these simple suggestions in measuring the amount of lumber delivered:

1. Use chalk to mark lengths of 4, 8, 12, and 16 feet on the floor. Pile the lumber of one species next to these marks so that the length can be immediately determined. Fig. 16-12.

2. Use a board rule or the Essex board-measure table to determine the surface measure in each piece.

16-11. *Essex board-measure table on a framing square.*

Measure lumber as though all pieces were 1″ thick and then add for thickness later (see Step 3).

3. Use several tally-sheet forms, one for each thickness, to keep track of individual pieces as they are measured. Fig. 16-13. Then total the board feet on each sheet. Now add a percentage for all lumber over 1″. For example, add ¼, or 25 percent, for 1¼″; add ½, or 50 percent, for 1½″; double the amount, or add 100 percent, for 2″ lumber. If only one tally sheet is used for all thicknesses, then it is necessary to convert each thickness to the total board feet after each piece is measured and before it is tallied. For example, if a piece measures 8

square feet and is 1½″ thick, add 50 percent, make it 12 board feet, and record it as such.

4. Add the totals for each grade of lumber to determine how much was delivered. Then check this amount against the order and invoice to see if they agree. The amount should not deviate more than 1 to 2 percent. If it does, you should check with your supplier.

16-13. *Simple tally-sheet form. Use a separate one for each thickness of stock. Mark a slanting line through the first four pieces of the same square footage to show a tally of five pieces.*

TALLY SHEET FORM

DATE _____

FROM _____

ORDER NO. _____

THICKNESS _____ KIND _____

GRADE _____

FOOTAGE PER BD.	PIECES	TOTAL PIECES	TOTAL FEET
1			
2			
3			
4			
5			
6			
ETC.			
TOTAL			

17 Reading Prints and Making Sketches

A woodworker usually works from a print. A print is a copy of a drawing giving dimensions and other information needed to construct an object. Print reading is a basic source of information to the builder. It must be mastered by every woodworker, but especially by the cabinetmaker and the finish carpenter.

Blueprints are very common in the building trades because they do not fade when exposed to direct sunlight as some kinds of prints do. They are made on chemically treated paper which shows the drawing in white against a blue background. In furniture making and interior cab-

inetwork, white-background prints are used on which black, blue, or brown lines appear. It is easier to add penciled corrections to these *whiteprints* than to blueprints.

From prints, woodworkers make a materials list and layout and build the product. They must also decide whether additional information is needed. Often they must use their own "know-how." For instance, a print may give only the overall size of a certain part. The woodworker then must use his or her own judgment about what kind and size of materials to use and what method of joinery to employ.

An architect, designer, or drafter usually has the responsibility for making the original drawing. However, many cabinetmakers and finish carpenters also have the ability to make a good sketch. Such skilled workers must often take measurements "on the job" and then make sketches. Sometimes these sketches are used to build the product. At other times the sketches are reviewed, refined, and then made into a set of drawings and prints.

ELEMENTS OF DRAWING

A drawing consists of lines, dimensions, symbols, and notes.

Sample	Name	Pencil	Use	Example
	Construction	3H to 5H	Very light line used to "block in" an object. These lines are made so light that little or no erasing is needed. Serve as base for darkening in the permanent lines.	
	Border	H or HB	Heavy, solid line used to frame in the drawing.	
	Visible or Object	H or 2H	A heavy line used to outline the exterior shape of a part. Shows outstanding features.	
	Hidden or Invisible	H or 2H	A light line used to show edges and contours not visible to the eye.	
	Center	H or 2H	A light line used as axis of symmetry. Used for center of circle and arcs. Sometimes the symbol ₵ is shown.	
	Dimension and Extension	2H or 3H	Light, thin lines used to show the sizes of the object. Extension lines start about $\frac{1}{16}$" from visible or object line. The dimension line is broken near the center for the dimension.	
	Long Break	H or 2H	Light, ruled line with freehand zigzags. To break an object when it is too big for paper.	
	Short Break	H or 2H	Wavy line drawn freehand. For same purpose as long break.	

Other important lines are shown in later units when they are first used.

17-1. Kinds of lines and their uses.

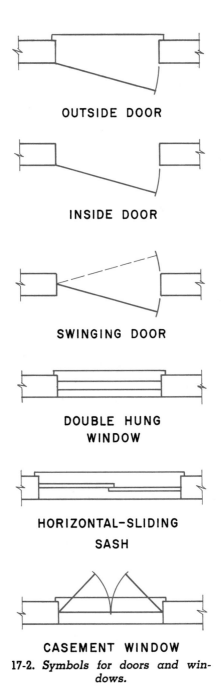

OUTSIDE DOOR

INSIDE DOOR

SWINGING DOOR

DOUBLE HUNG
WINDOW

HORIZONTAL-SLIDING
SASH

CASEMENT WINDOW

17-2. Symbols for doors and windows.

COMMON ABBREVIATIONS USED ON DRAWINGS

AP—Access panel	DRW (DRWS)—	MLDG—Molding
B&C—Bead and cove	Drawer(s)	MULL—Mullion
BT—Bathtub	EL—Elevation	MUNT—Muntin
BASMT—Basement	ENT—Entrance	NWL—Newel
BEV STKG—Bevel	EST—Estimate	NO. (#)—Number
sticking	EXT—Exterior	OA—Over-all
BR—Bedroom	FAB—Fabricate	OC—On center
BC—Between centers	FIN—Finish	OG—Ogee (sticking)
B/M—Bill of materials	FL—Floor	OVO—Ovolo
BLDG—Building	FD—Floor drain	PLAS (PL)—Plaster
BL—Building line	FRA—Frame	QUAL—Quality
BDY—Boundary	FDN—Foundation	QTY—Quantity
BRK—Brick	FTG—Footing	RAB (RABT)—Rabbet
CAB—Cabinet	GR—Gas range	RAD—Radiator
CASWK—Casework	GL—Grade line	REQD—Required
CLG—Ceiling	GRV—Groove	¼RD—Quarter-round
CL—Center line	½RD—Half-round	RF—Refrigerator
C TO C—Center to center	INSTL—Install	RFG—Roofing
CS—Cut stone	INSUL—Insulation	SC—Scale
CUP—Cupboard	INT—Interior	SK—Sink
DSGN—Design	KD—Knocked down	SB—Standard bead
DET—Detail	LAV—Lavatory	S—Stile
DIN RM—Dining room	LIV RM—Living room	STKG—Sticking
DVTL—Dovetail	LOC—Locate	SYM—Symbol
DWL—Dowel	MATL—Material	T—Truss
DS—Downspout	MILWK (MLWK)—	VARN—Varnish
DWG—Drawing	Millwork	WD—Windows
DR—Door (or doors)	ML—Material list	WC—Water closet

17-3. These are some of the abbreviations used on drawings.

Lines show the shape of a product and include many details of construction. Fig. 17-1. *Dimensions* are numbers that tell the sizes of each part as well as overall sizes. The woodworker must follow these dimensions in making the materials list and the layout. On most furniture and cabinet drawings the dimensions are given in inches, but on architectural drawings they are in feet and inches. *Symbols* are used to represent things that would be impossible to show by drawing—such as materials—or things that would be very hard to draw exactly—doors and windows, electrical circuits, plumbing, and heating. Fig. 17-2. Some drawings also contain *notes*—written information to explain something not otherwise shown. Frequently, abbreviations are used for common words in these notes. Fig. 17-3.

SCALE

Drawings must often be reduced from actual size so that they will fit on a piece of paper. Care is taken to make such drawings according to *scale;* that is, exactly in proportion to full size. For example, an architect can represent any size of building on a single piece of paper by drawing it to the right scale. The scale is not a unit of measurement but represents the ratio between the size of the object as drawn and its actual size. If the drawing is exactly the same size as the object itself, it is called a full-size or full-scale drawing. If it is reduced, as most scale drawings are, it will probably be drawn to one of the following common customary scales:

$$6'' = 1'$$
or $\Big\}$ half size
$$½'' = 1''$$
3″ = 1′ : one-fourth size
1½″ = 1′ : one-eighth size
1″ = 1′ : one-twelfth size
¾″ = 1′ : one-sixteenth size
½″ = 1′ : one twenty-fourth size
⅜″ = 1′ : one thirty-second size
¼″ = 1′ : one forty-eighth size
³⁄₁₆″ = 1′ : one sixty-fourth size
⅛″ = 1′ : one ninety-sixth size

A scale of ¼″ equals 1′ is often used for drawing buildings and rooms. Detail drawings, which show

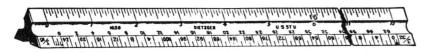

17-4(a). *An architect's scale makes it easier to measure lines for a scale drawing.*

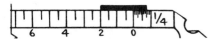

17-4(b). *This shows a measurement of 2'9", or 33". On this edge of the architect's scale, ¼" = 1'.*

how parts of a product are made, are prepared to scales of ⅜", ½", ¾", or 1½" equals 1'. Special measuring tools called scales can be used to make the drawings. Fig. 17-4.

Metric scales are used for making metric drawings. A comparison of the common metric and customary scales is shown in Fig. 17-5.

KINDS OF DRAWINGS

In woodworking, four basic kinds of drawings are commonly used: the *perspective* drawing, the *cabinet* drawing, the *isometric* drawing, and the *multiview working* drawing. The first three have a picturelike quality and are called *pictorial.*

Pictorial Drawings

The pictorial drawing that looks most like a photograph is the *perspective* drawing, sometimes also called a *rendering.* It shows the finished appearance of an object. Fig.

17-6. All house plans include such a drawing.

The *cabinet* drawing is used for rectangular objects such as chests, cases, tables, and of course cabinets. Fig. 17-7. It is a simple drawing in which the shape of the front surface is shown in exact scale. The sides and top may slant back at any angle between 30 and 60 degrees, but usually it is 45 degrees. These slanted lines are made just half as long as if they were drawn to scale. This gives the drawing a more natural appearance. However, in dimensioning these lines, the actual sizes are always specified.

Isometric means "having equal measure." An *isometric* drawing is constructed around three lines that are exactly 120 degrees apart. Fig. 17-8. One line is vertical and the other two lines are 30 degrees to the horizontal. In isometric drawings, one corner of the object appears closest.

All lines parallel to the isometric lines are drawn to scale. For this reason the isometric is best for rectangular objects. All lines not parallel to the isometric lines are called nonisometric and are not true to scale. Nonisometric lines must be drawn by locating the ends of the

isometric lines and connecting the points with a straightedge.

Multiview Drawings

The *multiview working* drawing, also called an *orthographic projection,* is the most common type of drawing in industry. It shows an object from more than one viewpoint. For example, a six-sided object, such as a chest, would be shown from the front, top, and right side (end). Fig. 17-9. For some objects only two views are needed. For instance, if the front and top of a bookcase have the same dimensions, drawings of only the front and right side are necessary. Fig. 17-10. Because such drawings involve more than one view of an object, you can see why they are called "multiview."

"Orthographic" refers basically to straight lines. The term "projection" also is fairly easy to understand. Assume you have the drawing of the front of a chest, just as you would see it from the front. Directly beside this you want to draw the right end of the chest as it would appear if you stood facing that end. The line which forms the right side of the front view represents the height of the chest. Since the front and the end come together at a corner, the

17-6. *This is a rendering of a wall system.*

CUSTOMARY AND METRIC SCALES

Metric Scale	Customary Equivalent
1:1 (Full Size)	1" = 1" or 12" = 12" (Full Size)
1:2 (Half Size)	½" = 1" or 6" = 12" (Half Size)
1:3 (Third Size)	⅜" = 1" (Three-eighth Size)*
1:5 (Fifth Size)	¼" = 1" or 3" = 12" (Quarter Size)*
1:10 (Tenth Size)	⅛" = 1" (Eighth Size)*

* Approximate equivalent.

17-5. *Comparison of typical customary and metric scales.*

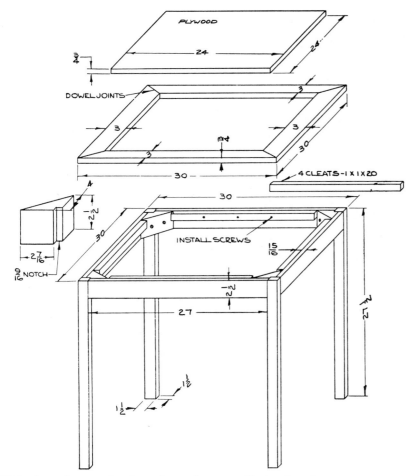

17-7. *A good example of a cabinet drawing. Notice that the top was removed to show the construction better.*

height of the front can be *projected* to form the height of the end. In the same way, the width of the front could be projected to form the width of a top view. If two views are given—for instance, front and side —still more projections to top and bottom views can be made rather simply.

It is important to remember that the views of an orthographic projection are shown *all in the same plane,* not at angles to each other. When there is a slanted surface that does not show in true shape on the front, top, or right-side view, an *auxiliary view* is needed. A *section view* shows the interior of an object as if the surface had been cut away. Fig. 17-11 (Page 120).

A complete set of drawings includes not only *detail* drawings that show each part but also *assembly* drawings which give information for building the object.

Cabinetmakers and finish carpenters must be acquainted with the drawings that are commonly used in the furniture industry, the millroom, and the building industry. A furni-

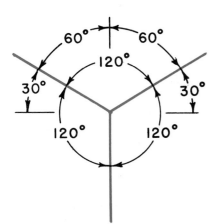

17-8(a). *The three lines used as a base for constructing an isometric drawing. Notice that they are 120 degrees apart. Two lines are drawn at an angle of 30 degrees to the horizontal.*

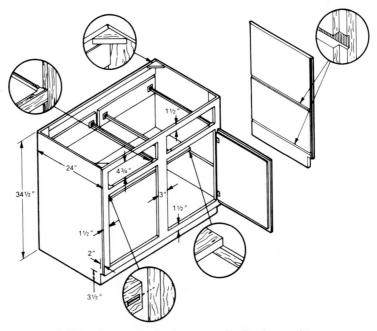

17-8(b). *An isometric drawing of a kitchen cabinet.*

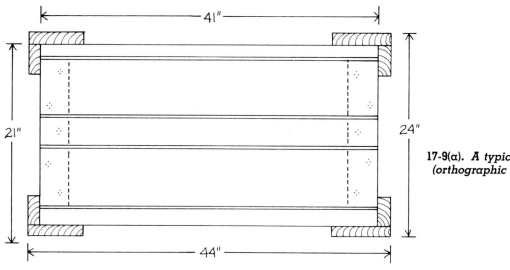

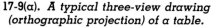

Top View

17-9(a). *A typical three-view drawing (orthographic projection) of a table.*

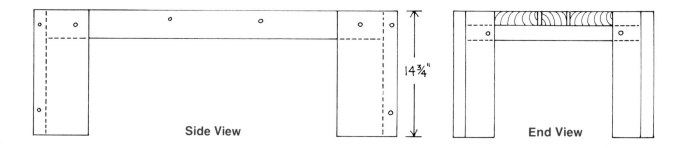

Side View

14¾"

End View

Material list

A. Legs	4—2x4x14¾"	
	4—2x8x14¾"	
B. Apron	2—2x4x41"	
C. Top	2—2x8x41"	**17-9(b).** *Material list for the table.*
	1—2x4x41"	
D. Top brace	2—2x4x18"	
E. Screws	34—2½" #9 wood screws	
F. Plugs	20—½x⅜" Birch dowel	
G. Glue	1—Pt. White glue	

17-9(c). *These tools and materials are needed to build the table.*

ture drawing is first made full size with three basic views: the front (or *elevation view*), the top (or *plan view*), and the right-side view. From these, detail drawings to scale are made for each part to be manufactured. The detail drawing, along with the matching route sheet, follows each piece through the factory as it is processed. A full-size engineering drawing or an assembly drawing is used to put the parts together into the finished product.

Furniture drawings in popular magazines are often either cabinet or isometric drawings because of their pictorial quality. Cabinet and isometric drawings can be made as *exploded* drawings with the individual parts separated so that the construction can be seen more clearly. Fig. 17-12.

Furniture and cabinet drawings do

118

17-9(d). *The finished project. The design highlights the natural wood grain. Screw plugs may protrude slightly or be sanded flush.*

not always follow standard drafting practices. Some of the differences include:

● Several types of drawings may be combined. For example, there may be a front view of the object along with a perspective or isometric view of the product.

● In multiview drawings, the views are not always in their proper location. For example, the top view may not be directly above the front view as it should be. This is often done to save space on the paper.

● Many drawings do not contain details of construction for joints, drawers, doors, and similar items. The woodworker must then decide on these details which, of course, may be extremely important to the overall design of the product. A finish carpenter who would build the cheapest kind of drawers in a high-quality home would not be considered a reputable worker.

● Many woodworking drawings contain inch marks on all dimensions.

In furniture making and cabinetwork, a woodworker should have a drawing or print of the product, a bill of materials or materials list, and a plan of procedure.

In home building, a finish carpenter needs a set of prints including all the individual drawings, a de-

tailed materials list or bill of materials, and a complete set of specifications. *Specifications* are written descriptive material that accompanies the plans. They cover items such as general condition of construction, excavation and grading, masonry, framing, carpentry, sheetmetal, lath, plaster, electrical wiring, plumbing, heating, painting, and finishing. The specifications also set forth the standards of work, the

responsibilities of the people involved in the construction, time limits, and other matters that could cause disagreement as the building progresses.

MAKING A SKETCH

A *shop sketch* is a simple drawing made with basic equipment. Actually a sketch can be made with a scratch pad of paper and a pencil. All that is necessary is knowledge of the elements of drawing and how to apply them. The important thing about a sketch is accuracy of dimensions. Usual practice is to make measurements on the job, then develop a sketch. For most work you should use drawing paper that is cross-sectioned into squares, eight to the inch. Fig. 17-13. With this paper, it is easier to make the sketch to the correct size, shape, and scale.

To make a sketch, proceed as follows:

1. Decide on the views needed. For example, in planning a new kitchen, a floor-plan sketch is absolutely essential. The floor plan

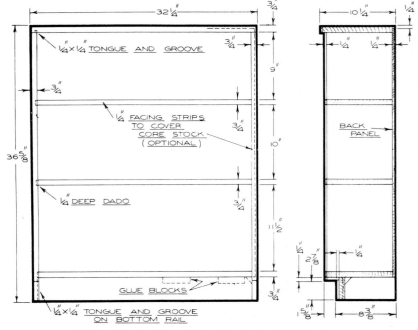

17-10. *This bookcase drawing has only two views.*

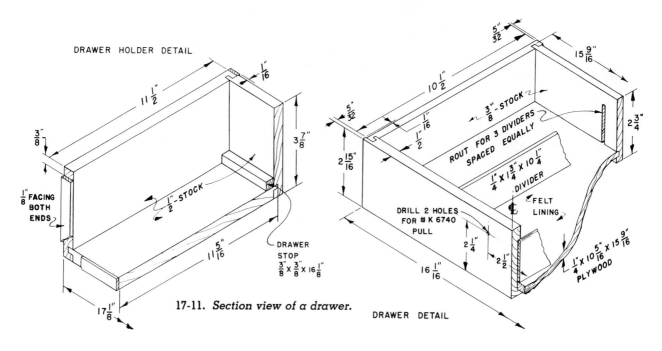

DRAWER HOLDER DETAIL

17-11. *Section view of a drawer.*

DRAWER DETAIL

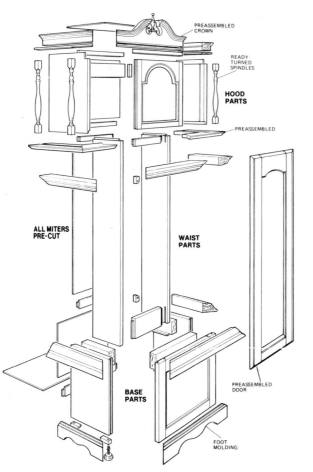

PREASSEMBLED CROWN

READY TURNED SPINDLES

HOOD PARTS

PREASSEMBLED

ALL MITERS PRE-CUT

WAIST PARTS

BASE PARTS

PREASSEMBLED DOOR

FOOT MOLDING

17-12. *An exploded pictorial drawing of a clock case.*

shows the shape of the room and the arrangement of cabinets and appliances. You may also need several elevation sketches for different sides of the kitchen.

2. Decide on the scale. Some common scales used on squared paper are:

● Full size, with each square representing 1/8″.

● Half size, with each square representing 1/4″.

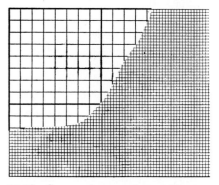

17-13. *Squared paper for making a sketch.*

- Quarter (or one-fourth) size, with each square representing ½″.
- Eighth (or one-eighth) size, with each square representing 1″.

3. Take measurements careful-ly. Fig. 17-14. Show the location and measurement of all windows and doors (including trim) as well as all obstructions, such as pipes, radi-ators, chimneys, offsets, and stair-ways. Indicate where the doors lead and also show which direction is north. Show the location of plumb-ing, gas, electrical, and other wall outlets that will affect the design of the new kitchen.

HOW TO MEASURE YOUR KITCHEN

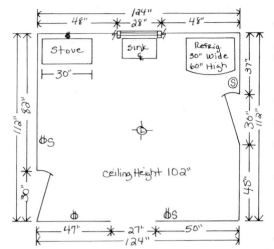

- Draw a free hand sketch of the entire room.
- Measure everything in inches.
- Start measuring from a corner and work in sequence around the room until you have returned to starting point.
- Measure major appliances and their location against the wall.
- Measure at approximately countertop height.
- Always measure outside of window and door casings. Be sure to make note of casing width.
- Note ceiling height.

NOTE: HEAT REGISTERS RADIATORS - AIR CONDITIONING VENTS - COLD AIR RETURN AND ELECT. OUTLETS AND SWITCHES

TYPICAL CONSTRUCTION SYMBOLS

17-14. *This kind of sketch must be made before remodeling a kitchen.*

Planning and Estimating

18

BILL OF MATERIALS

After a final drawing or print is ready, several additional steps must be taken before construction can begin. You must first make a list called a *bill of materials, materials list,* or *stock bill.* Fig. 18-1. The procedure for making the list is known as *stock billing.* Fig. 18-2. The list includes the following (not always in this order):

- Number of pieces.
- Name of part.

- Materials. (This may not be necessary if only one kind of lum-ber, plywood, or other material is involved.)
- Finish size in thickness, width, and length.
- Rough or cutout size, also called the *stock-cutting* list. (Some-times a separate form is used for the stock-cutting list. If this is done, the number of pieces, name of part, and materials information should be repeated.)

It is standard practice to list the pieces in order of thickness, width, and length, but in the furniture in-dustry this is sometimes reversed. Lumber *thickness* depends on whether the boards are purchased rough or surfaced two sides (S2S). Generally, if the material called for has ¾″ or $^{13}/_{16}$″ finish thickness, then the rough stock should be 1″, or 4/4 (four-quarter). From $^{1}/_{16}$″ to ⅛″ must be allowed for surfacing. For such materials as plywood, hard-

BILL OF MATERIALS

No. of Pieces	Part Name	Material	Finish Size			Rough Size		
			T	W	L	T	W	L

18-1. *Form for a bill of materials, materials list, or stock bill.*

LUMBER AND MATERIAL ORDER

No. of Pieces	Dimensions			Kind of Material	Number of: Bd. Ft. Sq. Ft. or Lin. Ft.	Cost per: Bd. Ft. Sq. Ft. or Lin. Ft.	Total Cost
	T	W	L				

18-2. *Form for a lumber and materials order.*

SUPPLIES, FASTENERS AND HARDWARE LIST

Item	Quantity	Size	Unit Cost	Total Cost

18-3. *Form for supplies, fasteners, and hardware.*

18-4(a). *The next four illustrations show plans for this table.*

board, or particle board, the finish cut and the cutout or rough thickness are the same. For solid lumber, the *width* of the cutout or rough size is usually ⅛″ to ¼″ greater than the finish cut. From ½″ to 1″ is normally added to the *length*.

Points to Remember in Stock Billing

• The *net size* is the actual or *finish size* of the part. It is given in thickness, width, and length, usually in that order. Additional length is needed for tenons. When reading a drawing in leg-and-rail construction where only shoulder length is shown, you must add the necessary finish length for the tenons.

• Rough or cutout size is the size that must be cut from the standard piece of lumber. This size includes the amount that will be removed in machining.

• In the lumber order, always list plywood, particle board, hardboard, softwood, and hardwood separately.

• Always write sizes in inches and fractions of an inch, not in feet.

MAKING ORDERS FOR LUMBER AND OTHER MATERIALS

Lumber and similar materials are purchased in standard sizes. Once you know the rough or cutout sizes you will need, you must decide which standard sizes of materials to buy. Fig. 18-2. First, look down the bill of materials to find items of the same kind and thickness. For example, if the list calls for five pieces to be made of the same hardwood, all ½″ in thickness, you will want to buy this material in a size that will produce these five pieces with the least amount of waste. Jobs vary greatly, so there are no fixed rules for selecting these sizes.

The lumber and materials order should list the number of pieces; sizes in thickness, width, and length; and kind of wood. The list

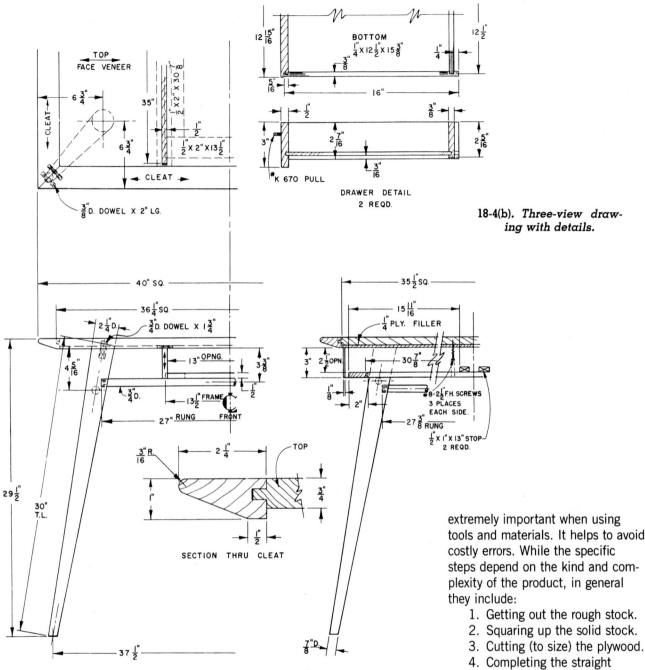

18-4(b). *Three-view drawing with details.*

should also mention the number of board, square, or linear feet for each size. You must figure this according to one of the formulas given in Chapter 16. You must also determine the cost per board, square, or linear foot. This information can be obtained from any lumber dealer. Then the total cost should also be figured.

In addition to the lumber order, make a list of other standard supplies needed, such as fittings and finishing materials. Fig. 18-3.

DEVELOPING A PLAN OF PROCEDURE (PROCEDURE LIST)

This list details the steps needed to complete the product. Planning is extremely important when using tools and materials. It helps to avoid costly errors. While the specific steps depend on the kind and complexity of the product, in general they include:

1. Getting out the rough stock.
2. Squaring up the solid stock.
3. Cutting (to size) the plywood.
4. Completing the straight parts.
5. Completing the curved and irregularly shaped parts.
6. Making the joints.
7. Sanding the parts.
8. Assembling.
9. Finishing.
10. Installing hardware.

Good plans for a table are shown in Fig. 18-4. Included are a drawing, bill of materials, and a plan of procedure.

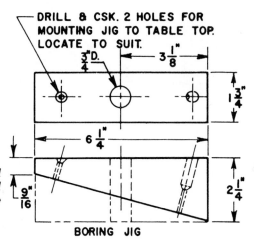

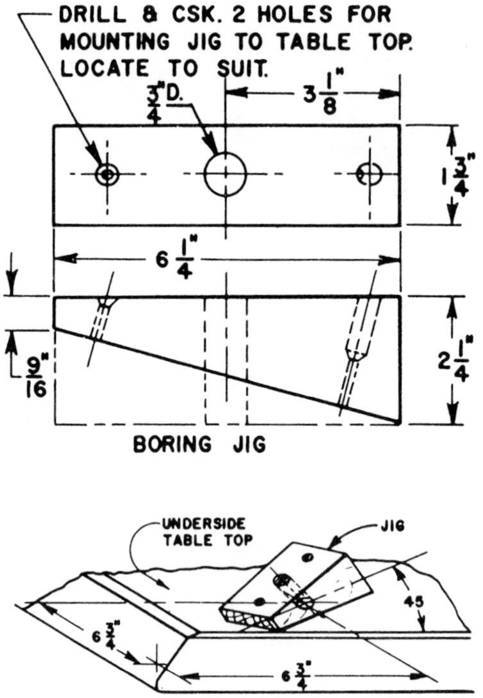

18-4(c). *Boring jig. This is used as a guide when boring dowel holes in the tabletop for the legs.*

ESTIMATING

Often the self-employed cabinetmaker or finish carpenter must estimate the total cost of producing a piece of furniture or cabinetwork. Larger cabinet shops and fixture manufacturers have full-time employees called *estimators* who specialize in this work. These people make accurate estimates of any job, based on known costs, standard formulas, and expert judgments.

Three main factors must be considered when making an estimate: *materials, labor,* and combined *overhead and profit.* If you are building a product in school, it would be good experience for you to include all of these items in the cost. Too often the student considers only the cost of materials.

Materials

The materials estimate must allow for the cost of materials actually used in the product, plus an added amount for waste, spoilage, pieces built or machined wrong, and similar cost-increasing factors. This estimate is usually made in one of two ways. One method is based on actual cost of materials from the supplier. To this total is added a fixed percentage—usually about 35 percent—for waste and similar items. The other method is simply to use a much higher figure than actual cost per board, square, or linear foot. This higher unit price takes into account such things as waste and spoilage.

Labor

Labor cost must include not only the actual amount per hour paid to the worker but also such items as social security tax, pension fund allotment, and supervisory labor. Usually, total cost per hour ranges from 15 to 25 percent more than the worker's wages. Even the self-employed worker must not forget about such "hidden" labor costs when making estimates.

BILL OF MATERIALS

IMPORTANT: All dimensions listed below are FINISHED size.

Pieces No. of	Part Name	Thickness	Width	Length	Material
1	Top	¾″	36¼″	36¼″	Comb Grain White Oak Plywood
4	Top Cleats	1″	2¼″	40″	White Oak
4	Legs	2¼″ dia.		30″	White Oak
2	Rungs	¾″ dia.		27″	White Oak
2	Rungs	¾″ dia.		27⅜″	White Oak
2	Drawer Case Sides	½″	3″	35″	Comb Grain White Oak Plywood
2	Drawer Frame Fronts	½″	2″	13½″	Hardwood
2	Drawer Frame Sides	½″	2″	30⅞″	Hardwood
2	Drawer Stops	½″	1″	13″	Hardwood
2	Drawer Fronts	½″	3″	12¹⁵⁄₁₆″	Comb Grain White Oak Plywood
4	Drawer Sides	⅜″	2⁷⁄₁₆″	16″	Solid Oak
2	Drawer Backs	⅜″	2⁵⁄₁₆″	12½″	Solid Oak
2	Drawer Bottoms	¼″	12½″	15⅜″	Birch Plywood
4	Facings	⅛″	½″	3″	White Oak
2	Top Filler Strips	¼″	1½″	35½″	Plywood
4	Dowels	¾″ dia.		1¾″	Hardwood
8	Dowels	⅛″ dia.		2″	Hardwood
6	No. 8 x 2½″ F. H. Wood Screws				
2	Drawer Pulls No. K670				

18-4(d). *Bill of materials for the table.*

PROCEDURE

1. Cut all pieces to size on circular saw.
2. Turn legs to shape on wood lathe. Bore dowel hole in top of each leg.
3. Set circular saw arbor to 1¼°, miter gauge to 16½°. Cut angle on top of each leg using miter gauge on left side of saw. Then put gauge on right side of saw and cut bottom of leg to length keeping angle parallel to top.
4. Set drill press table to angle of 16° and bore rung holes. Caution: Be sure angle of top of leg is in right position. Use a jig.
5. Cut tongue on all sides of top panel.
6. Groove top cleats with dado head or molding head on circular saw. Miter corners. Bore dowel holes. Set saw arbor to angle of 22° and cut bevel on cleats. Round edges on drill press or shaper.
7. Assemble top.
8. Make boring jig:
   a. Accurately cut out block 1¾″ × 2¼″ × 6¼″.
   b. Locate and bore ¾″ hole through center of block.
   c. Lay out diagonal cutting line. Set miter gauge to 69° 50′ and cut out on circular saw.
   d. Locate and drill screw holes for fastening jig to tabletop. Diagonally-cut face of block should be against drill press table.
   e. Fasten jig into place and bore dowel holes for mounting legs.
9. Glue plywood filler strips into place.
10. Assemble top, legs, and rungs.
11. Make up drawer case and fasten into place with flathead wood screws.
12. Make up drawers.
13. Finish-sand entire table and apply modern oak finish.
14. Install drawer pulls.

18-4(e). *This is the plan of procedure for building the table.*

Overhead and Profit

Overhead refers to the more or less fixed costs of running a business. It includes buildings, machines, utilities, and office expenses, among other things. Profit must also be added so that there will be a return to the investor, whether he or she runs the business or is one of many stockholders. Usually the cost of labor and materials for one year is computed. Then a fixed percentage—up to 50 percent—is added to cover overhead and profit. Even though labor, overhead, and profit are usually not considered in determining the cost of a school-shop project, you will understand industry better if you keep these factors in mind. When figuring the costs of your projects, estimate what an industrial firm would charge for the same products.

19 Making a Layout

19-1(a). *The furniture designer must be a skilled drafter.*

The ability to lay out work accurately is one of the distinguishing characteristics of a skilled woodworker. Fig. 19-1. The old adage "Measure twice and cut once" is good advice since once material is cut there is no way to make it longer. The popular suggestion "Get a board stretcher" indicates that too often an incorrect layout has been made and the stock cut too short.

There are many methods of using drawings (or their equivalent) for making layouts. When working

19-1(b). *The carpenter must be able to make on-the-job calculations.*

125

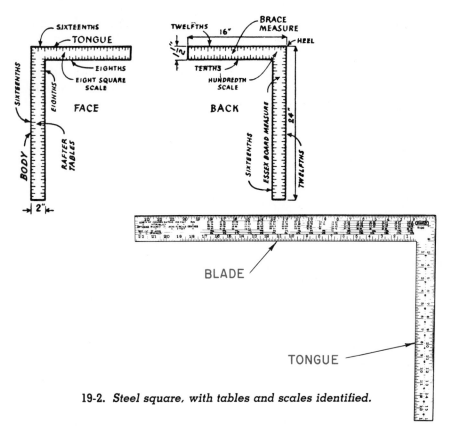

19-2. *Steel square, with tables and scales identified.*

scales are the divisions in inches and fractions of an inch found along the outer and inner edges of the square. The following scales are on the square.

• Face of body, outside edge: inches and sixteenths of an inch.

• Face of body, inside edge: inches and eighths.

• Face of tongue, outside edge: inches and sixteenths.

• Face of tongue, inside edge: inches and eighths.

• Back of body, outside edge: inches and twelfths.

• Back of body, inside edge: inches and sixteenths.

• Back of tongue, outside edge: inches and twelfths.

• Back of tongue, inside edge: inches and tenths.

There is also a scale on the back of the tongue in the corner near the brace measure. This scale is one inch divided into one hundred parts. The longer lines represent twenty-five hundredths and the shorter lines five hundredths.

The scales on the square can be used for measurement and layout work that is done on stock. The square can also be used for marking out stock for cutting and for hundreds of other uses.

Tables

Besides the rafter tables, which are found on the face, the square has several other important tables and measures.

The *octagon scale,* or eight-square scale, is found along the center of the tongue face. Fig. 19-3. It is used for laying out lines to cut an octagonal (eight-sided) piece from a square one. For example, suppose it is necessary to cut

alone, the usual practice is to follow a drawing or sketch and the plan of procedure. The dimensions from the drawing are transferred to the stock. Then the cutting, shaping, and assembling are done. Other common methods are (1) the use of route sheets with accompanying detail drawings of each part and (2) layout on the rod. Route sheets are used mainly in industry. Layout on the rod is explained later in this chapter.

STEEL SQUARE

For all types of layout, no tool is used more often by the cabinetmaker and finish carpenter than the steel square. This tool is also called the carpenter's square, framing square, or rafter square. It is used extensively to determine rafter length. However, this use will not be discussed here because it is a part of rough carpentry and building construction.

The steel square has two arms which make an angle of 90 degrees (a right angle). The arms are called the *body,* or *blade,* and the *tongue.* The body, which is longer and wider than the tongue, is normally 2″ × 24″. The tongue is usually 1¼″ × 16″. The *heel* is the point where the body and the tongue meet on the outer edge. The *face* is the side that is visible when the square is held so that the heel is at the upper left and the body points towards you. The *back* is the opposite of the face. Fig. 19-2.

Scales

There are two types of markings on a square: *scales* and *tables.* The

19-3. *Octagon scale on the face of the tongue.*

Octagon or "Eight-Square" Scale

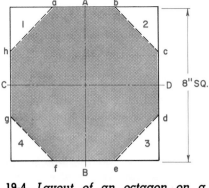

19-4. *Layout of an octagon on a square piece of stock.*

an octagon from an 8″ square piece. Through the center of the stock, draw lines *AB* and *CD* parallel to the sides and at right angles to each other. Fig. 19-4. With dividers, take as many squares from the scale as there are inches in the width of the stock (8) and lay off this space on both sides of points *A, B, C,* and *D.* When these points are connected, as by lines *Ab, bc,* and *cD,* you will have a perfect octagon.

The *brace measure* is found along the center of the tongue back and is used to find the exact length of common braces. For example, suppose the length on both the vertical and horizontal equals 39″. To find the length of a brace, you would first find number 39 on the brace measure. Immediately behind it you would find the number 55.1, which is about 55⅛″. Fig. 19-5. For braces in which the vertical and horizontal measurements are different, make use of the rafter tables to find the exact length, since the brace is actually a rafter. (A complete discussion of rafter tables is given in

the book *Carpentry and Building Construction,* by John L. Feirer and Gilbert R. Hutchings, Bennett Publishing Company.)

The *Essex board measure,* which is used to find the board or surface measure of lumber, is discussed in detail in Chapter 16.

GEOMETRIC CONSTRUCTION

Many layouts contain geometric shapes. Some of these, such as a circle, square, triangle, or rectangle, are very simple. Many other constructions are used by designers. A few of the more common ones include:

Bisecting a line or an arc (dividing it into two equal parts). Fig. 19-6.

1. To bisect the line or arc *AB,* adjust a compass to a radius greater than one-half *AB.*

2. With *A* and *B* as centers, draw arcs that intersect at *C* and *D.*

3. Draw line *CD.* This will divide the line or arc *AB* into two equal parts.

Dividing a line into several equal parts. This procedure is used frequently with material of odd width. Suppose you want to divide a board 3⅝″ wide into four equal parts. Fig. 19-7. Hold the rule at an angle across the board with one end of the rule on one edge and the 4″ mark on the other. Mark a point at 1″, 2″, and at 3″. To divide a line on a drawing, do the following:

1. Draw a line of any length, *AB.* Fig. 19-8.

2. Draw another line at any acute angle to *AB.* (An acute angle is less than 90 degrees.)

3. Starting at point *A,* lay off

several equal divisions on this second line with a dividers, compass, or rule. The number of divisions should equal the number of parts into which you wish to divide line *AB.*

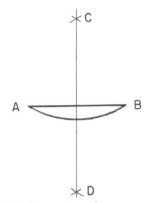

19-6. *Bisecting a line or arc.*

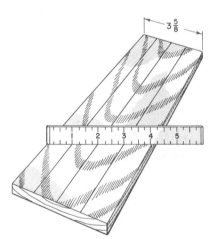

19-7. *Dividing a board into equal parts.*

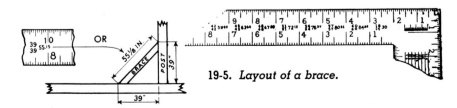

19-5. *Layout of a brace.*

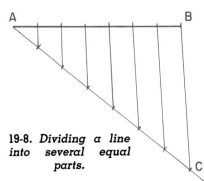

19-8. *Dividing a line into several equal parts.*

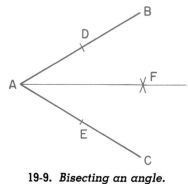

19-9. *Bisecting an angle.*

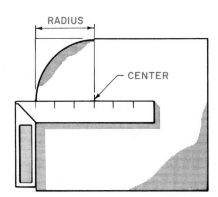

19-11. *The shop method of drawing an arc at a square corner.*

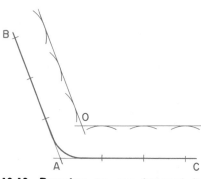

19-12. *Drawing an arc tangent to two lines that are not at right angles.*

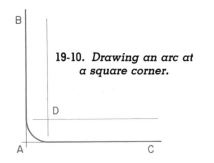

19-10. *Drawing an arc at a square corner.*

2. Determine the desired radius of the arc.

3. Measure in from lines *AC* and *AB* this distance and draw parallel lines to these lines that intersect at *D.*

4. Set a compass to the radius of the arc.

5. Use *D* as the center and draw the arc.

This procedure may be followed in the shop as shown in Fig. 19-11. Determine the radius of the arc. Mark this distance from the corner on the adjacent side and end. Hold a try square against the edge and end, and draw two lines to locate the center. Use dividers to draw the arc.

Drawing an arc tangent to two lines that are not at right angles. Fig. 19-12. Sometimes an irregularly shaped object has a rounded corner. This can be shown as follows:

1. Draw two lines to represent the edges of the materials, *AB* and *AC.*

2. Determine the desired radius of the arc.

3. Adjust the compass or dividers to this amount.

4. At several points along both lines, draw small arcs.

5. Draw straight lines tangent to these arcs until the lines intersect at *O.*

6. Using *O* as center, strike the arc.

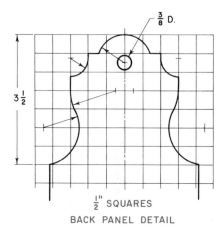

19-13. *Note the tangent arcs on this detail drawing of a back panel.*

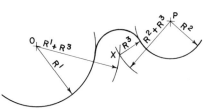

19-14. *Drawing a series of tangent arcs that join.*

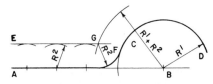

19-15. *Drawing an arc with a given radius tangent to a straight line and a circle or arc.*

4. Draw a line from the last division mark (point *C*) to point *B.*

5. Draw lines parallel to *BC* at the divisions on *AC.* These lines will intersect *AB* and divide it into equal parts.

Bisecting an angle. Fig. 19-9.

1. Draw the given angle *BAC.*

2. Adjust the compass to any convenient radius.

3. With *A* as the center, strike an arc intersecting *AB* at *D* and *AC* at *E.*

4. Adjust the compass to a radius of more than half *ED.*

5. With *D* and *E* as centers, strike two arcs that intersect at *F.*

6. Draw the line *AF* to divide the angle into two equal parts.

Drawing an arc at a square corner. Many projects have rounded corners to improve their appearance and utility. In geometry this would be called drawing an arc tangent to lines at 90 degrees. Fig. 19-10.

1. Draw the two lines, *AB* and *AC,* that intersect at *A.*

Drawing tangent arcs. Many irregularly shaped objects, such as Early American furniture pieces, have arcs or circles that are tangent. Fig. 19-13. Arcs or circles are tangent when they touch at only one point and do not intersect. To join a series of arcs, proceed as follows. Fig. 19-14.

1. With *O* as center and *R1* as radius, draw the first arc.

2. With *P* as center and *R2* as radius, draw the second arc.

3. With *O* as center and *R1* plus *R3* as radius, strike a small arc at the approximate center location for the third arc.

4. With *P* as center and with *R2* plus *R3* as radius, strike a second small arc that intersects the first at *X*.

5. With *X* as center and *R3* as radius, strike the last arc.

Drawing an arc with a given radius tangent to a straight line and a circle or arc. Fig. 19-15. This procedure is used often in drawing wood parts.

1. Draw line *AB* to the desired length.

2. With *B* as center and with a compass adjusted to radius *R1*, draw arc *CD*.

3. Draw line *EF* the given radius (*R2*) above and parallel to line *AB*.

4. With *B* as center and with *R1* plus *R2* as radius, strike an arc that intersects the parallel line at *G*.

5. With *G* as center and the compass set at *R2*, draw the arc joining the straight line and arc *CD*.

Drawing an octagon. An octagon has eight equal sides and angles. Fig. 19-16. This shape is often used for wood products such as wastepaper baskets and small tables.

1. Draw a square the size of the octagon.

2. Draw diagonal lines *AB* and *CD*.

3. Adjust the compass to half the length of one of the diagonal lines.

4. Using points *A*, *B*, *C*, and *D*

as centers, strike arcs intersecting the sides.

5. Connect the points where the arcs intersect the square.

Drawing a hexagon. A hexagon has six equal sides and angles. Fig. 19-17. It is another shape used often in woodworking.

1. Draw a circle with a radius equal to one side of the hexagon.

2. Keep the compass equal to the radius of the circle.

3. Start at any point on the circle and draw an arc that intersects the circle.

4. Move the point of the compass to this point and strike another arc. Divide the circle into six equal parts.

5. Connect these points.

Drawing an ellipse. An ellipse is a regular curve that has two different diameters. It is a flattened circle. You find this shape often in the tops of tables. Wherever anything round is shown in isometric, draw an ellipse. Fig. 19-18.

1. Draw the major and minor axes, *AB* and *CD*, at right angles to each other.

2. Lay out *OE* and *OF*, which are equal to *AB* minus *CD*.

3. Make *OH* and *OG* equal to three-fourths of *OE* or *OF*.

4. Draw and extend lines *EG*, *EH*, *FG*, and *FH*.

5. Using *E* and *F* as centers

and *ED* as radius, strike arcs *IJ* and *KL*.

6. Using *G* and *H* as centers and *GA* as radius, strike arcs *IK* and *JL*.

There is another method of drawing the ellipse that is very simple. You will want to use it in the shop. Fig. 19-19.

1. Draw tbe major and minor axes *AB* and *CD*.

2. Set the dividers equal to half the longest diameter (AB ÷ 2).

3. Using *C* as center, strike an arc intersecting *AB* at *X* and *Y*.

4. Place a pin at *X*, *Y*, and *C*. Tie a string around these three pins.

5. Take the pin at *C* away and put a pencil point in its place.

6. Hold the point of the pencil

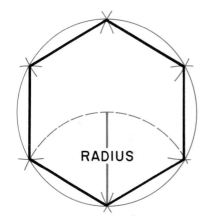

19-17. *Drawing a hexagon.*

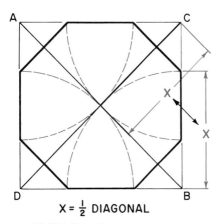

X = ½ DIAGONAL

19-16. *Drawing an octagon.*

19-18. *Drawing an ellipse. This method can be used only if CD is at least two-thirds of AB.*

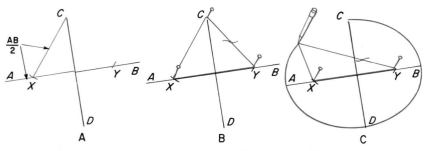

19-19. *A shop method of drawing an ellipse.*

ENLARGING AND TRANSFERRING AN IRREGULAR DESIGN

tight against the string. Carefully draw the ellipse.

Projects found in books and magazines are seldom drawn to full size. If the product contains irregular parts, it is necessary first to enlarge these to full size. Usually the design is drawn on grid squares, with the size of the full-scale squares indicated. For example, in Fig. 19-20 the note tells you that the squares must be 1″ in size for the enlarged drawing.

On a large piece of wrapping paper or cardboard, carefully lay out 1″ squares to equal the number in the smaller drawing. It is a good idea to letter the horizontal lines and number the vertical lines. Using these letters and numbers, locate a position on the original drawing, then transfer this point to its proper place on the full-size pattern. Continue to locate and transfer points until enough are marked for the pattern. Sketch the curves lightly freehand. Then use a French curve to darken the lines and to produce a smooth, evenly curved line.

If the piece is symmetrical (the same on both sides of a center line) you need to lay out only half of the design. Then fold the sheet of paper down the center and cut the full pattern. Place the pattern on the stock and trace around it. If the paper is thin, it may be better not to cut out the pattern but rather to

transfer it to the stock by placing carbon paper between the pattern and the stock.

If many parts of the same design are to be made, it is a good idea to make a template (pattern) of thin plywood or sheet metal from the paper pattern.

LAYOUT ON THE ROD

While a set of drawings or prints is highly desirable for most cabinetwork, it is not absolutely essential, especially for simpler projects. Instead, you can use a rod or stick on

which the full-size measurements are placed. This is called *layout on the rod.* Sometimes, in finish carpentry, the rod is called a *story pole* (measuring stick) and is used when cutting, installing, and checking. The rod or pole is a straight, smooth piece of stock at least 1″ × 2″ or 1″ × 4″, surfaced all four sides. Its length must be slightly greater than the largest dimension of the piece being built.

In the planning and layout room of some furniture and cabinet shops, there are many pieces of wood (rods) with a series of marks on three or four sides. These are usually hanging over the desk or drafting table of the person responsible for making the rod layouts. If an item must be produced again, its dimensions are quickly available on the rod. This layout method is used for the following reasons:

● To provide a full-scale or full-

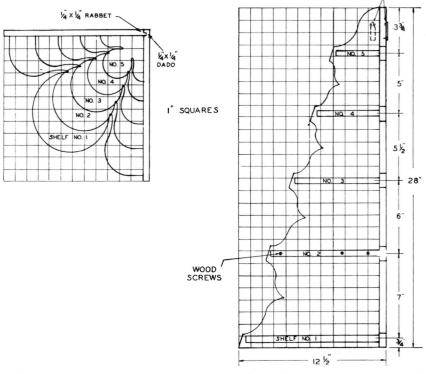

19-20. *The original drawing for a corner shelf. To enlarge this, make 1″ squares and transfer the design to them.*

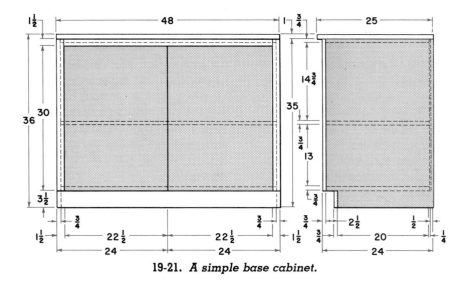

19-21. *A simple base cabinet.*

size layout for each part of a cabinet or other structural assembly.

- To provide a quick and easy way of making a stock list, or bill of materials.
- To check the material as it is being machined and assembled, to make sure it is the right size.
- To store the information for further use.

Making a Rod Layout for a Base Cabinet

The example for explaining this procedure is a simple base cabinet that might be used for kitchen or other storage. Case size is 24″ × 36″ × 48″, with a 1″ finish top overhang on the front only. To simplify the explanation, only butt joints are used. Fig. 19-21. The case materials consist of the following:

- A 1″ finish top.
- Plywood ¾″ thick for sides, top, doors, bottom, and shelf.
- Plywood ¼″ thick for the back.
- Solid stock ¾″ × 1½″ for face frame and toe board.

Let's proceed to make the rod layout. Fig. 19-22. Note that the edges of the rod are marked *A* and *C* and the surfaces *B* and *D*. Generally, only three sides—*A*, *B*, and *C*—are needed. Side *A* is used for depth measurements, *B* for height,

and *C* for width. The fourth side, *D*, could be used if a matching cabinet were to be made with a different depth, but with all other dimensions the same.

1. Place the rod in front of you with the *A* edge up. Start from one end and mark a line 1″ away from the end to represent the overhang. Mark the next line ¾″ away from this to represent the face frame. Measure in another 2½″ to represent the toe-space cut. Then measure back ¾″ to represent the thickness of the toe board. Now measure and mark the overall depth of 25″. Starting from the opposite end, measure in ½″ to represent the scribing line. Measure in from the scribing line ¼″ to represent the thickness of the back.

2. Turn the rod so that side *B* is up, ready to use for the height layout. Measure in from the end 1″ to represent the finish top. Measure in ¾″ from this line to represent the case top. Measure from the finish top line 1½″ to represent the face frame. Now measure 36″ and mark a line for the overall height. Measure back 3½″ to represent the toe-space cut. Measure back another ¾″

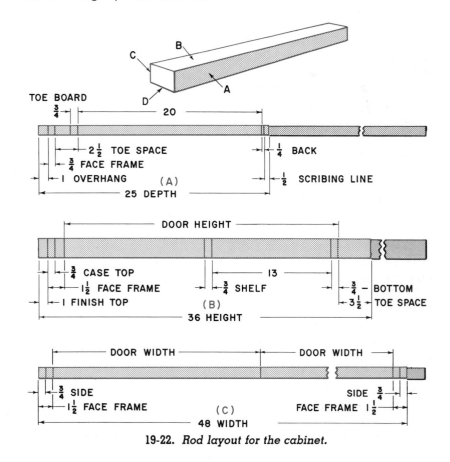

19-22. *Rod layout for the cabinet.*

for the bottom. Measure up 13″ to represent one face of the shelf, then another ¾″ for the other face. Note that there is no face frame across the bottom of the cabinet so that the door height is from the face-frame line to the top of the toe-space cut.

3. Turn the rod to side *C,* ready to use for marking the width dimensions. From the end, measure in ¾″ to represent the thickness of the side. Measure in from the same end

1½″ to represent the face frame. Measure 48″ and mark the overall width. Then measure back ¾″ from the other end for the thickness of the sides and 1½″ to represent the width of the face frame. Now divide the 48″ width in the middle. Note then that the door width is the distance from the inside face-frame line to the middle of the rod. Also note that this cabinet is designed with flush doors. If lip doors were used, this would have to be taken

into consideration in making the rod layout.

Now drill a hole about 2″ in from the end of the rod for hanging it up for storage. If the rod is to be kept for a long time and there is danger that the ends may become damaged, it is a good idea to scribe a line completely around the rod, 1″ in from the end, and use this as the starting line.

Section II
QUESTIONS AND DISCUSSION TOPICS

Chapter 5

1. The outer bark of a tree is dead tissue. What useful function does it perform for the tree?

2. What does the phloem do?

3. Describe the differences between sapwood and heartwood.

4. What is the function of the ray cells?

5. Hardwoods are not always harder than softwoods. Explain.

6. What are growth rings?

7. Name the three growth-ring classifications for hardwoods.

8. What is grain?

9. What is specific gravity?

10. Does hickory or basswood have higher specific gravity?

11. Describe the two common methods of cutting lumber. Discuss the advantages and disadvantages of each method.

12. Name the two methods of seasoning lumber.

13. Describe how lumber shrinks when seasoned.

14. What is meant by fiber-saturation point?

15. Name four natural defects that occur in lumber.

16. Name five defects that can result from improper conditioning and storage of lumber.

17. Name two defects caused by slicing or sawing.

18. Name four defects that are caused by improper machining of lumber.

Chapter 6

1. What governmental agency can supply detailed information about any kind of wood?

2. Define the two major classifications of woods.

3. Name four woods that have a high density.

4. What is roey grain?

5. Name five woods that are very easy or moderately easy to work *and* are readily available in the United States.

Chapter 7

1. Name five furniture woods.

2. Why has walnut always been a popular American furniture wood?

3. What kind of finish did Thomas Chippendale use on mahogany?

4. Why was cherry a popular choice with cabinetmakers in colonial America?

5. What do maple and birch have in common with regard to their use in furniture?

6. What are the two main kinds of oak?

7. List five exotic woods.

Chapter 8

1. List four advantages of using plywood instead of solid lumber.

2. Define the four major methods of producing plywood.

3. Describe the two common methods of cutting veneer.

4. What is hardwood plywood?

5. What is another name for construction and industrial plywood?

6. Why should plywood not be stored at an angle?

7. When cutting plywood with a table saw, which face should be up?

8. How can the face veneer of plywood be protected?

Chapter 9

1. Briefly describe how hardboard is manufactured.

2. Discuss the uses of hardboard.

3. What types of nails should be used to fasten hardboard?

4. What is particle board?

5. Describe the two basic methods of manufacturing particle board.

Chapter 10

1. Name five common types of moldings.

2. What is the purpose of chair rail molding?

Chapter 11

1. What are the two major purposes of fasteners?

2. Name three metals from which nails are made.

3. What does *penny* mean as applied to nails?

4. As the gauge number goes down, the diameter of the nail goes up. True or False?

5. What is the purpose of a nail set?

6. Describe the two major methods of nailing.

7. What are the advantages of screws as compared with nails?

8. Why are recessed (Phillips) head screws preferred to the type with slotted heads?

9. How are sheet metal screws used in woodworking?

10. Name three types of screwdrivers.

11. What is the purpose of the shank hole and pilot hole?

12. Describe two hollow-wall fastening devices.

13. What kinds of fasteners can be used in masonry construction?

14. What types of metal fasteners are used on miter corners?

15. What are hanger screws?

Chapter 12

1. Why is it important to select hardware before construction is completed?

2. What kinds of hinges can be used on a lip door?

3. From what materials can slides for drawers be made?

Chapter 13

1. How might plastics be used in "all-wood" furniture?

2. What are the two basic types of plastics?

3. Name one use for polyvinyl chloride in furniture.

4. Which plastics are used as a substitute for glass?

5. For what are plastic laminates used?

Chapter 14

1. What is glass made of?

2. Name the two major kinds of glass used in furniture making and cabinetwork.

3. Describe how to cut glass.

4. How is glass held in place in cabinets?

5. Why is cane used in furniture construction?

6. Describe the way to install machine-woven cane.

Chapter 15

1. Name the two measuring systems used in constructing wood products.

2. How long (in inches) is a millimetre?

3. How many millimetres in a centimetre?

4. Name five types of measuring devices.

5. What is the purpose of a scratch awl?

6. Describe how to measure stock for length.

Chapter 16

1. What is a board foot?

2. Lumber is sold by the board foot. How are sheet materials such as plywood sold?

3. Explain the following terms: S2S, FAS, and AD.

4. In lumber dimensions, what does the first figure represent?

5. Why is it difficult to explain the softwood grades?

6. What is yard lumber?

7. What is the highest grade of hardwood lumber?

8. What is dressed lumber?

9. What four things should be considered in writing lumber specifications?

10. What is the Essex board-measure table, and how is it used?

Chapter 17

1. What is a print?

2. Why is it important for a woodworker to know how to read prints?

3. What are the four elements of a drawing?
4. Describe *scale* as it relates to drawing.
5. Name three kinds of pictorial drawings.
6. What is a multiview drawing?
7. What is the purpose of a section view?

Chapter 18

1. What information is included in a bill of materials?
2. What is a procedure list?

3. What factors must be included when estimating the cost of an item?

Chapter 19

1. Why is the steel square an important tool for the cabinetmaker?
2. What is meant by geometric construction?
3. Describe briefly how to make a layout on the rod.

PROBLEMS AND ACTIVITIES

1. Obtain a section of a log and identify the parts by lettering in their names on the trunk itself or by using identification numbers and a code.
2. Using the oven-dry method, determine the moisture content of a piece of wood.
3. Get samples of four or five different woods from a lumber dealer or warehouse and identify them.
4. Describe in detail why maple and birch are the most common selections for Early American furniture.
5. Select one of the exotic woods. Study the geography of the country from which it comes and the significance of the wood to the economy of that country.
6. Make a model of a plywood manufacturing plant.

7. Compare the working properties of several different particle boards.
8. Study the production of particle board. Gather some chips from the planer and try to make a small piece of particle board.
9. Using wood screws, study the holding power of various woods.
10. Write a report on the use of glass in the furniture industry.
11. Make a full-scale drawing of a furniture piece that you would like to build.
12. Make a rod layout for a cabinet.

Section III

TOOLS AND MACHINES

20 Handsaws

A saw is a wood-cutting tool that has a thin steel blade with small sharp teeth along the edge. Fig. 20-1. Woodworker's saws include the crosscut saw, ripsaw, backsaw, veneer, miter, keyhole, compass, and coping saws. While each type has a specific use, all the saws have certain similarities. The cutting edge of each saw is a line of sharp teeth. These teeth act as two rows of cutting tools, running close together in parallel grooves. The teeth of most woodworking saws are designed to cut as the saw is being pushed away.

To prevent a saw from binding as it is pushed through the wood, the teeth are set. This means that the saw teeth bend alternately to right and left. In this way the saw cuts a groove (called a *kerf*) wider than the thickness of the saw. The amount of set given a saw is important because it determines the ease of cutting. It also insures accuracy of cutting and helps keep the saw sharp for a longer time.

Points to the inch is a term used to designate the size of teeth in a

saw. There is always one more point per inch than there are teeth. Fig. 20-2. The fewer points to the inch, the rougher and faster the cut. Saws with ten or more points to the inch make smooth, even cuts but do not cut as fast as the coarse tooth saw.

SAFETY PRECAUTIONS
● Position yourself in such a way that the saw will not cut your hands or legs if it slips from the work.
● Always lay the saw down carefully in such a position that no one can brush against the teeth and be cut.
● Keep saws sharp. A sharp, well-cared for tool is safer than a poorly maintained, dull one.
● Make sure both rows of teeth are the same length. If they are not, the saw will curve as it cuts.

CROSSCUT SAW
The crosscut saw is used for cutting wood *across* the grain. The teeth cut like sharp-pointed knives. The front face of a crosscut saw tooth has an angle of 15°; the back of the tooth has an angle of 45°. A

crosscut saw cuts on both the forward and the back strokes.

The nature and character of the wood to be cut must be considered when choosing a saw. Green or wet wood requires a saw with coarse teeth and wide set, 7 points to the inch. A 10- or 11-point saw with light set will work better on dry, well-seasoned lumber. For ordinary crosscutting, the 8- or 10-point saw is best.

The length of the crosscut saw is measured from toe to heel along the cutting edge. Crosscut saws commonly have blades 16, 20, 22, 24, or 26 inches long. Saws 24 inches and shorter are often called panel saws. The 20-inch, 10-point crosscut saw is most popular.

Using a Crosscut Saw
● Lay out the cutoff line across the board.
● Place the board in a vise or over one or more sawhorses. The cut-

20-2. *Tooth points per inch on a crosscut saw (A) and on a ripsaw (B).*

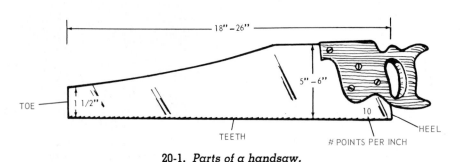

20-1. *Parts of a handsaw.*

off line must be outside the supports, never between.

• Hold the handle of the crosscut saw in your right hand with the index finger extended to support it. If left-handed, reverse the procedure.

• Place your free hand on the board, using your thumb as a guide for the saw blade. Keep in mind that the kerf should be in the waste stock. To start the cut, place the saw at the side of the line to assure proper length. Start the cut near the handle of the saw, using a short draw stroke. Repeat slowly a few times until a slight groove is started, then cut straight with a full, easy stroke. Use light pressure on the push stroke. Fig. 20-3. *Be careful that the saw doesn't jump and cut your thumb.*

• After the kerf is started, hold

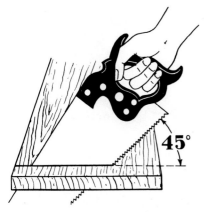

20-3. *Starting a cut. Hold the thumb of one hand against the smooth surface of the blade to guide the saw as you draw it towards yourself.*

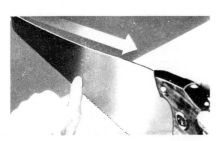

20-4. *Hold the crosscut saw at an angle of about 45 degrees to the stock.*

the saw at an angle of 45 to 60 degrees to the surface. Move your hand away from the blade. Fig. 20-4. Take long, even strokes.

• Sight along the saw or check with the try square to make sure you are making a square cut.

• As you cut, watch the layout line, not the saw. Blow the sawdust away.

• If the saw is moving into or away from the line, twist the handle slightly to bring it back.

• As the final strokes are made, hold the end to be cut off. If you don't, the corner will split out as the piece drops. Never twist off thin strips of wood with the saw blade.

Cutting Plywood

The crosscut saw is good for cutting plywood. Place the plywood with the finished face up. Use a saw having ten to fifteen points per inch. Support the panel firmly so that it won't sag. You can reduce splitting out of the underside by putting a length of scrap lumber under the saw line. Use a sharp saw and hold it at a low angle, about 30 degrees, to do the cutting.

When cutting a large sheet of plywood, place it on edge with guide boards securely clamped at top and bottom. The distance between the guides should equal the width of the saw teeth. Saw with the blade between the clamped boards. Your cut will be straight and true. Fig. 20-5.

RIPSAW

The ripsaw is used to cut *with* the grain. It has a different cutting action from the crosscut saw. The ripsaw has chisel-like teeth that form the saw kerf by cutting the ends of the fibers. Most ripping is done on the forward stroke. Fig. 20-6.

A ripsaw has fewer points to the inch than a crosscut saw. A ripsaw used for ordinary woodworking ought to be 24 to 26 inches long, with 5½ points per inch.

20-5. *Using guide boards for cutting panel stock.*

Cutting with a Ripsaw

• **Short pieces.** If a short board is to be ripped, place it in the vise as in Fig. 20-7. Do the sawing close to the vise jaws so that the board will not vibrate. Begin with the board near the top of the vise and move it up a little at a time as you continue your work.

• **Long pieces.** Place the board at about knee height. This enables you to get well above your work, to saw with comfort, and to cut a straight kerf.

20-6. *A ripsaw is used to cut with the grain. It has chisel-shaped teeth.*

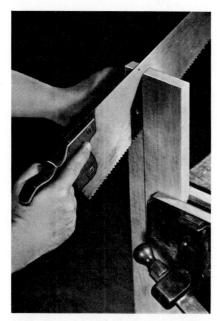

20-7. *Ripping short pieces of stock can sometimes be done more conveniently in a bench vise than on a sawhorse. Notice that the saw is held at an angle of about 60 degrees to the work. Make sure that the saw does not strike any other tools on the bench or cut the bench.*

If you are right-handed, put your right knee on the board and your left hand a few inches to the left of the cutting line. Do the opposite if you are left-handed. In this way the weight of your body is comfortably balanced.

Start the cut by taking a draw stroke with the teeth at the end of the blade. Put very little pressure on the saw until the kerf is well started. Then take long, easy strokes. If only the middle section of the saw

20-8. *A wedge of wood or a commercial unit is inserted into the kerf to keep it open.*

blade is used, the saw will dull more rapidly and wear unevenly.

Hold the saw at an angle of 60 degrees. If the board is thin, lessen this angle to about 45 degrees. Do not force the blade at any time. This makes the work tiring and also makes following the line more difficult. Get well above your work so that your eye is in line with the saw blade and your markings.

As you cut a long piece of stock to width, the saw kerf may close in behind the saw and cause binding. Placing a little wedge at the beginning of the saw kerf will help keep it open. Move the wedge along as you proceed. Fig. 20-8.

BACKSAW

The teeth of a backsaw are similar to those of a crosscut saw; but since there are about fourteen per inch, they are smaller and finer. Fig. 20-9. The average length of a blade is about 12 inches. The blade is thin, but it is stiffened with a heavy metal back. Because of its construction, the backsaw makes a finer cut than the crosscut saw. Figs. 20-10 and 20-11. It is often used with a small wood, plastic, or metal miter box for making angle cuts. Fig. 20-12.

DOVETAIL SAW

The dovetail saw is very similar to the backsaw except that it has a narrower blade and finer teeth. It cuts a true, smooth, and narrow kerf. Fig. 20-13.

MITER SAW

The miter saw looks like a backsaw. However, it is longer and is

BACK HANDLE

BLADE

20-9. *Parts of a backsaw.*

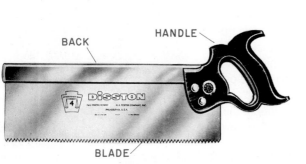

USE THIS CLEAT, AS SHOWN, WHEN SAWING WITH RIGHT HAND

BENCH HOOK

WHEN SAWING WITH LEFT HAND, TURN BENCH HOOK OVER, AND HOLD WOOD AGAINST THIS CLEAT

BOTH CLEATS ARE SHORTER THAN WIDTH OF THE HOOK, & ARE SET TO RIGHT OR LEFT OF CENTER

20-10. *Using a backsaw with the work held on a bench hook.*

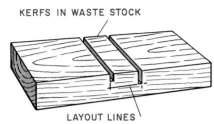

KERFS IN WASTE STOCK

LAYOUT LINES

20-11. *Always make the cuts in the waste stock.*

20-12(b). *Cutting a miter joint with a homemade miter box and backsaw. Be certain that the line to be cut is directly under the saw teeth. Hold the work tightly against the back of the box. Start the cut with a careful backstroke.*

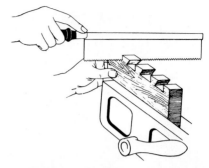

20-13. *Dovetail saws are designed for cutting dovetails, for tenoning, and for precision work such as ship-model building, toy making, and patternmaking.*

20-12(a). *A simple miter box you could make for cutting 45- and 90-degree angles. The front side extends below the base so that it can be clamped in a vise or held against the corner of the bench.*

used with a miter box. With this saw, lumber can be cut precisely to almost any angle. This is helpful in making accurate joints. Fig. 20-14.

KEYHOLE SAW

This saw is used for making small cuts, such as those needed for key-holes and for fitting locks in doors. It is narrow enough to enter a ¼-inch hole. It cuts a wide kerf so that the blade can turn to make curved cuts. It often comes in a set that includes a keyhole saw blade, a compass saw blade, and an easily removable pistol-grip handle that fits both. Fig. 20-15.

COMPASS SAW

The blade of the compass saw is also designed to cut a wide kerf for

sawing curves. It is used for cutting curves and inside openings. The compass saw may be used for either crosscutting or for ripping. Fig. 20-16.

COPING SAW

The coping saw is a versatile saw for cutting thin wood and plastics. It consists of a steel frame, a handle, and a replaceable blade. Fig. 20-17. The blade is held under tension by a spring in the frame. In some saws the frame is bent together to insert the blade. In others the handle or the adjustment screw is turned until the right amount of tension is obtained.

In most frames, the blade is adjustable so that it can be used at any angle. For example, the blade can be inserted with the teeth pointing away from the handle. In this case the saw is used in a manner similar to the way a ripsaw or crosscut saw is used. Fig. 20-18. If the teeth point toward the handle,

20-14. *The commercial miter box can be set to almost any angle. (It is better not to wear a watch when using tools.)*

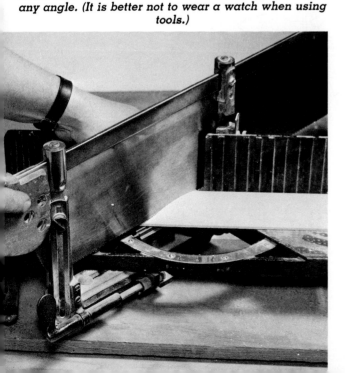

KEYHOLE SAW

COMPASS SAW

HANDLE

20-15. *A keyhole and a compass saw with an interchangeable handle.*

20-16. *Cutting an inside curve with the compass saw. Note that a hole has been bored in the waste stock close to the layout line.*

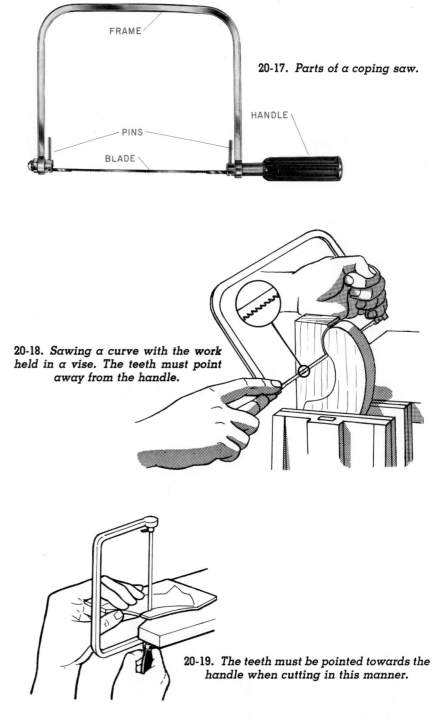

20-17. *Parts of a coping saw.*

FRAME

HANDLE

PINS

BLADE

20-18. *Sawing a curve with the work held in a vise. The teeth must point away from the handle.*

20-19. *The teeth must be pointed towards the handle when cutting in this manner.*

the saw is used as a jeweler's saw. Fig. 20-19. In that case, the thin material being cut should be supported on a "V" board which is held in a vise.

Some coping saw frames are made to hold blades with a pin in each end, while others hold only blades bent into loops or a kink. Blades for cutting either wood or metal are available in different widths and lengths and in various points per inch.

Planes

The plane gets its name from the fact that its basic purpose is to produce a smooth, perfectly flat, "plane" surface; that is, a surface having no elevations or depressions. The present-day plane evolved from a chisel. It actually is a chisel placed in a block of wood or metal so that it may be more easily controlled in taking an even cut. Fig. 21-1.

Most planes are made of metal, although some wood planes are still used by skilled woodworkers. Metal planes are made with either a smooth or corrugated bottom. There are three broad classifications of planes:

21-1. *The chisel and plane are very similar in their cutting action.*

- **Bench planes** are called "smooth," "jack," "fore," or "jointer" planes, depending upon their length.
- **Block planes** are small planes which have low-angle cutters. They are designed to cut the end grain of wood.
- **Special planes** include rabbet, router, modelmaker, combination, and other special-purpose types.

The most generally useful plane is the smooth plane. It will do a good job on most planing operations. Block planes, designed to cut end grain, will do that job better than a smooth plane.

BENCH PLANES

The *jack plane* ("Jack of all trades") is the most common one. It is 14 inches long with a 2-inch blade. It is ideal for rough surfaces that require a heavier chip. It is also good for obtaining a smooth, flat surface. Fig. 21-2.

A *smooth plane* is 9¼ to 9¾ inches long and is used for smaller

work. It is a good plane for general use around the home. Fig. 21-3.

A *fore plane* is longer (18 inches) and has a 2¾-inch cutter. It is used to plane long surfaces and edges. Fig. 21-4.

The largest plane is called a *jointer plane*. It is 22 inches long with a 2¾-inch cutter. Carpenters use it for planing long boards such as the edges of doors.

Parts of the Plane

Let's look at the hand plane in Fig. 21-5. The main part is called the body, or bed, and the wide flat

21-4. *The fore plane is needed for planing long and straight edges.*

21-2. *The jack plane is the most useful, all-around plane for both rough surfaces and smooth, flat surfaces.*

21-3. *The smooth plane is best for small jobs.*

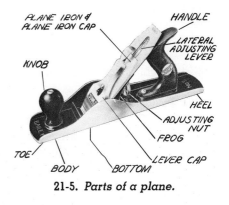

21-5. *Parts of a plane.*

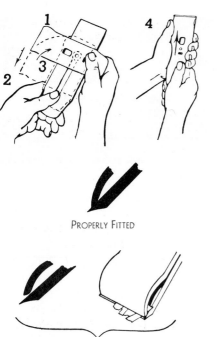

PROPERLY FITTED

POORLY FITTED

21-6. *Assembling a double plane iron. The plane iron cap must fit the plane iron tightly. If it doesn't, chips get between the two parts and cause poor planing action.*

part is called the bottom. The back of the bottom is the heel, and the front is the toe. The opening across the bottom is called the mouth or throat. The knob (in front) is held in one hand and the handle (in back) in the other hand. Lift up on the cam lever to release the lever cap. Then slide the lever cap up and it will come off over the lever cap screw. Now carefully lift the double plane cutter (or plane irons) out of the plane. The double plane cutter is made in two parts. The top one, called the plane cutter (or plane iron) cap, breaks the chips and forces the chips or shavings up and out. The lower part of the cutter cap is called the chip break. The blade that does the actual cutting is called a single plane cutter (or plane iron). The part that supports the double plane cutter (or plane irons) is called the frog. There is an adjusting nut for changing the depth of the cut. A lateral adjusting

lever can be moved to the right or left so that the cutting edge will be parallel to the bottom.

Assembling the Double Plane Cutter

To put the plane cutter and the plane cutter cap together:

1. Lay the plane cutter cap on the flat side of the plane cutter and at right angles to it with the screw in the slot.

2. Draw the plane cutter cap back.

3. Turn it straight with the plane cutter.

4. Slide the plane cutter cap back until its edge is just back of the plane cutter's edge. The plane cap should be set 1/16" back of the cutting edge for most work, closer for cross or curly grained wood. Fig. 21-6.

5. The plane cutter cap must not be dragged across the cutting edge. Hold the plane cutter and the plane cutter cap firmly and tighten the screw to hold the two parts together.

Assembling the Plane

1. Lay the double plane cutter, bevel side down, on the frog. As shown in Fig. 21-5, the frog is the sloping part of the plane which sup-

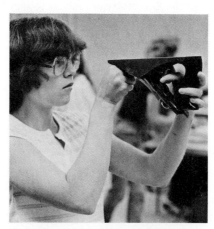

21-7. *Adjusting the plane. Sight along the bottom of the plane to make sure the cutting edge is parallel with the bottom.*

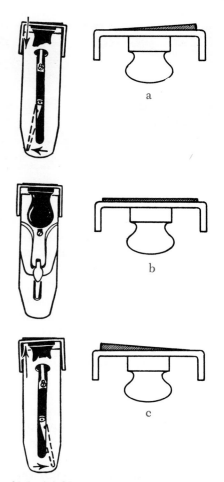

a

b

c

21-8. *(a) Moving the lateral adjustment lever to the left raises the right side of the plane iron. (b) The plane iron is parallel with the bottom. (c) Moving the lateral adjustment lever to the right raises the left side of the plane iron.*

ports the double plane cutter. It is adjustable to widen or narrow the mouth. Be sure the roller on the lateral adjusting lever, the upper end of the "Y" adjusting lever, and the head of the plane cutter cap screw are correctly seated.

2. Slip the lever cap over the lever cap screw and press down the cam. If the plane cutter is in the correct position, the cam will easily clamp into place. If the cam will not clamp in place easily, slightly loosen the lever cap screw. If the plane cutter is not firmly held when the cam is in place, slightly tighten the lever cap screw.

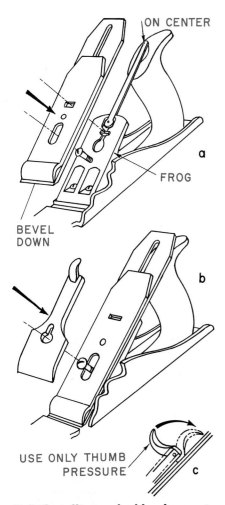

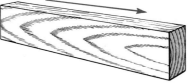

DIRECTION TO PLANE

21-10. *Plane with the grain.*

21-9. *Installing a double plane cutter in the plane: (a) The double plane cutter is assembled and placed over the frog. (b) The double plane cutter is in place and the lever cap is inserted. (c) The lever cap holds the double plane cutter firmly in place. If the cap will not close with thumb pressure, loosen the lever screw a little bit.*

Adjusting the Plane

To adjust for the thickness of the shaving, sight along the bottom of the plane and turn the adjusting nut until the cutting edge projects about the thickness of a hair. The plane cutter moves out when the adjusting nut is rotated clockwise (the nut moves toward the handle). The plane cutter moves in when the adjusting nut is rotated counter-clockwise (nut moves toward the frog).

To adjust for the evenness of the shaving, sight along the bottom of the plane and move the lateral adjusting lever toward the right or left as required. Fig. 21-7. The cutter will move in on the side toward which the lateral adjusting lever is moved. Fig. 21-8. When all adjustments have been made, fasten the double plane cutter in the plane. Fig. 21-9.

Points to Remember

• Determine the grain direction of any piece of wood to be planed. Planing against the grain roughens the wood, while planing with the grain produces a smooth surface. Fig. 21-10.

• A good vise or a bench stop is required for surface planing in order to hold the board securely. The board should be held with the grain running in the direction in which you will be planing.

• If you have a choice, it is better to avoid planing a side containing knots. Old or used pieces of wood should be examined to discover possible nails or other defects which might damage the cutter.

• Your plane is no better than its cutter. For this reason, frequent inspection of the cutting edge should be made. A blade which is sharp

will not reflect light, while a dull blade will appear shiny. When not in use, the plane should be placed on its side to protect the cutting edge.

• Each time the cutter is ground or honed, the edge should be checked with a try square. The edge should be square with one side of the cutter.

• The cutting edge should be adjusted to take a thin shaving, not thicker on one edge than on the other. If the blade is set too far out, it will gouge the work or clog the throat of the plane with the thick shavings.

BLOCK PLANES

The block plane has a single plane cutter set at a low angle to cut end grain. Because of the low angle, the cutter is set bevel up. It is a handy plane for light trimming. Fig. 21-11.

Adjusting the Block Plane

To adjust the cutter vertically for thickness of the shavings, sight along the plane bottom and turn the adjusting screw, either to push the cutter out or to pull it in.

To adjust the cutter laterally for evenness of the shavings, sight along the plane bottom and move the lateral adjusting lever to the right or left as necessary. On planes without a lateral adjusting lever, the cutter may be tapped lightly at either side to make this adjustment.

Using the Block Plane

The block plane is used to plane small pieces of wood and the ends of moldings, trim, and siding. It is especially useful on end grain. The

21-11. *Parts of a block plane.*

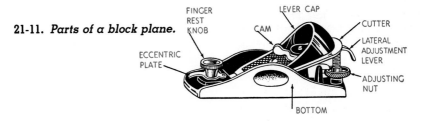

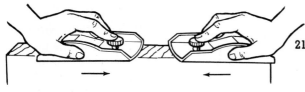

21-12. *Planing end grain. Note that the cutting should be done from the edges toward the center.*

block plane is operated with one hand. This makes it easy to use when the work cannot be taken to a vise. The block plane is also the handiest tool for planing corners

21-13(a). *Router plane with cutters.*

21-13(b). *Using a router plane to trim out the bottom of a dado joint.*

21-14. *This small bullnose rabbet plane can be held in one hand for fine trimming small amounts of material when fitting parts (such as joints) together.*

and chamfers on small pieces of wood. To avoid breaking the corners when planing end grain, plane from the ends or corners toward the center. Fig. 21-12.

SPECIAL-PURPOSE PLANES

There are many kinds of special-purpose planes designed to do one or more specific jobs. Some of these are described here.

The **router plane** comes with several widths of cutters. The cutter can be adjusted to different depths. The common cutters are one-quarter inch, one-half inch, and a V-cutter. The router plane is used to surface the bottom of grooves and dadoes and for trimming dovetail joints. Fig. 21-13.

The **bullnose rabbet plane** is a small plane that can be held in one hand. The sides and bottom are square with each other, and the blade is the full width of the base. This plane is used for trimming a rabbet and for cutting close to corners and other hard-to-reach places. Fig. 21-14.

The **duplex rabbet plane** is a larger plane made with a one-piece casting. It has two seats for the cutter: one for regular work and another for bullnose work; that is, work which requires planing to a corner. The plane has a depth stop and an adjustable fence. When the cutter is used in the rear seat, it is adjustable for depth of cut. The fence controls the width of the rabbet. Fig. 21-15.

The **modelmaker's plane** is a small plane with the bottom curved in both directions. It is commonly used to plane concave surfaces, particularly when doing model work. This plane is equipped with a curved handle similar to that of a cabinet scraper. It is designed to be held in one hand for use in shaping scale models. Fig. 21-16.

The **combination plane** is available with a variety of cutter blades, each of which is a different shape. It can be used for dadoing, grooving, rabbeting, and for shaping the edge of stock. It is a good tool to have if a router or shaper is not available.

21-15. *Duplex rabbet plane.*

21-16. *The modelmaker's plane has a bottom curved in both directions.*

22 Other Edge-Cutting Tools

In addition to planes, the woodworker uses many other edge-cutting tools, such as chisels, gouges, scrapers, drawknives, and spokeshaves. Each of these has a single blade and cutting edge that is used to remove small amounts of wood, often from very hard-to-reach places. Other edge-cutting tools, such as files, rasps, and forming tools (also called Surforms) have a great number of cutting edges.

CHISELS

Wood chisels are used for accurate cutting and for fitting and shaping, as in making wood joints. They are also used for surface decorating. The chisel consists of a single beveled steel blade fitted with a wooden or plastic handle. Chisels are di-

BEVEL EDGE BLADE

CUTTING EDGE   HANDLE   HEAD

22-1(a). *A tang chisel. The tang, or shank, extends all the way through the handle and is attached to a steel head.*

22-1(b). *A socket chisel. The handle fits into the socket (the cup-shaped part of the blade).*

22-2. *Always cut with the grain or across it. Avoid cutting against the grain.*

vided into two types—tang and socket—according to the way in which the handle is attached. Fig. 22-1.

The upper end of the *tang chisel* blade is shaped into a tapering point which is driven into the handle. A ring, called a ferrule, is fitted around the lower end of the handle to prevent it from splitting. The tang chisel will not withstand heavy blows.

The upper part of a *socket chisel* blade is shaped like a hollow cone. The handle of the tool is fitted into it. The construction is strong, and the chisel will withstand the blow of a mallet. The chisel blades range in width from ¼ to 2 inches.

Using a Chisel

Cutting against the grain tends to split the wood and make the tool more difficult to control. To obtain a cut that is well controlled and smooth, cut with the wood grain. Fig. 22-2.

A chisel blade has a beveled side and a flat side. When the blade goes vertically into the wood, it leaves a straight cut on the flat side of the blade and an angular cut on the beveled side. The bevel should al-

ways face the area to be removed. Fig. 22-3.

When making heavy cuts, the work must be planned so that if the wood splits, it will split in only the part to be removed. Make a stop cut by tapping the chisel vertically into the wood at the point where the cut should stop.

Holding the chisel with the bevel up gives a planing action. Holding the bevel down gives a lifting or gouging action. Fig. 22-4.

For smoothing cuts, the chisel should be held with the left hand close to the cutting edge in order to

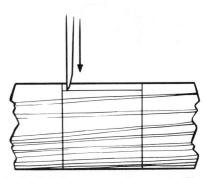

22-3. *Starting a mortise cut. The beveled side of the chisel blade faces the waste stock.*

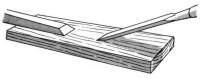

22-4. *For light chiseling (trimming), hold the beveled side up, as shown at left. For heavier cutting, place the bevel side down (right).*

22-5. *Cutting a convex curve. Raise the handle a little at a time to follow the curve.*

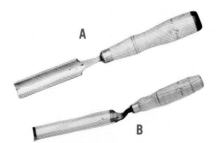

22-6. *Types of gouges: (A) Gouge with a bevel on the outside. (B) Gouge with a bevel on the inside.*

22-7. *A drawknife is especially useful for removing large amounts of stock rapidly.*

22-8. *Using a drawknife to shape the hull of a model boat.*

22-9. *A spokeshave is used to cut concave and convex surfaces and for molding and forming work. The type shown has two narrow nuts on the top for adjusting the depth of the cutter. The cutter is held in place with a cap which is fastened by a thumbscrew.*

22-10. *Cutting with a spokeshave by drawing it toward you. The blade should be set just deep enough to form a thin shaving.*

guide the chisel accurately. The right hand furnishes the power to make the cut. If the smoothing or planing stroke is done sideways, the shearing action will give a smoother cut. In smoothing an outside curve with a chisel, the chisel is held with the bevel up while making a series of short strokes. Fig. 22-5.

GOUGES

These tools are similar to chisels except that the cutting end has a different shape. The shapes vary from a wide arc to a V. There are two kinds of gouges: *outside ground,* with the bevel on the convex surface (outside) of the blade, and *inside ground,* with the bevel on the concave surface (inside) of the blade. Fig. 22-6. Some gouges are made with an offset shank. This makes room for the worker's hand when the bevel is being held parallel to the cutting surface.

Using Gouges

Gouges are used for wood carving, decorating, and shaping wood, as in modeling. Gouges are handled in the same manner as chisels. Their care and maintenance are the same except for sharpening.

DRAWKNIFE

The drawknife is a U-shaped tool. It has a blade 8 or 10 inches long

with a handle at each end. This tool is very good for removing large amounts of stock rapidly and for doing molding work such as shaping a Queen Anne leg. Be very careful in using this tool because the long, exposed blade can be dangerous. Fig. 22-7.

Cutting With the Drawknife

Clamp the work in a vise in such a way that the cutting will take place with the wood grain. Hold the tool in both hands, with the blade firmly against the wood and the bevel side down. Fig. 22-8. Turn the blade at a slight angle to the work. Carefully draw it into the wood until a thin chip forms; then draw the knife steadily towards you.

SPOKESHAVE

The spokeshave is a small plane-like tool that is used to form irregularly shaped objects. It has a frame with two handles which hold a small cutting blade. It is used to plane convex (dome-shaped) and concave (cup-shaped) edges. Depth of cut can be regulated with one or two small thumbscrews. Fig. 22-9.

Cutting with a Spokeshave

Place the work in a vise with the edge to be smoothed near the top of the vise. Hold the tool with both hands. You can either draw the spokeshave toward you or put your thumbs behind the frame and push it as you would a small plane. Fig. 22-10.

Place the cutting edge on the wood and apply even pressure. Work with the grain of the wood. Your experience in using a plane will tell you if the proper chip is being formed.

MITER TRIMMER

A miter trimmer is used to make very accurate joints. This tool cuts with a razor-sharp knife to shear off

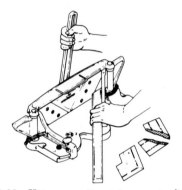

22-11. *Using a miter trimmer to finish a miter cut.*

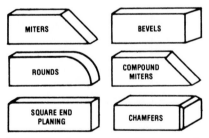

22-12. *Kinds of cuts that can be made with a miter trimmer.*

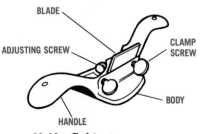

22-13. *Cabinet scraper.*

wood for a smooth finish cut. It is equipped with a gauge on the left and right that can be adjusted and locked to any angle from 45 to 90 degrees. All cuts should be rough-sawn, slightly over length. Rough-cut close to the line by taking two or three chops, depending on the size and hardness of the stock. Then finish with a thin shaving cut. Generally, the harder the wood, the thinner the cut. Figs. 22-11 and 22-12.

SCRAPERS

The *cabinet scraper* consists of a metal frame with two handles which hold a scraper blade. Fig. 22-13. Adjust the blade for depth by means of the thumbscrew. The cabinet scraper should produce a fine, thin, even shaving as it is pushed with the grain. Use long, even strokes along the surface of the wood. The scraper will remove irregularities in the wood left by the plane. It works well in the final dressings of woods with irregular grain or burl.

The cabinet scraper has many other uses. It can remove old finishes without the use of solvents. It is excellent for removing paper after veneering. It also removes excess glue. If sharpened correctly, it will put a fine finish on burl woods or delicate veneers.

The *hand scraper* is a rectangular piece of steel. Fig. 22-14. The working edge of the scraping tool is the burr which does the actual cutting. The scraper can be used for rough and fine work, to scrape glue or to produce a high-gloss finish with lacquer or shellac. Fig. 22-15. It is better than steel wool between coats of finish since it doesn't leave tiny shreds of metal embedded in the wood pores.

To use, hold the scraper firmly in both hands and angle it toward the wood in the direction it is being pushed or pulled. When removing the wavy mill marks left from a power plane, hold the scraper at

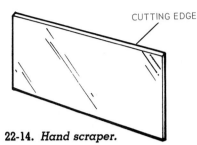

22-14. *Hand scraper.*

22-15. *Using a hand scraper. It can be pushed or pulled across the surface.*

about a 30-degree angle to the edge of the wood.

FILES AND RASPS

Files and rasps are used for shaping wood when other edge-cutting tools won't do the job as well.

There are many shapes of files, but the most common ones for woodworking are half-round cabinet and flat wood files in lengths of 8, 10, or 12 inches. Fig. 22-16. Wood files usually have double-cut teeth. This means there are two rows of teeth diagonally across the face. Files are not as rough as wood rasps.

The rasp is a tool with individual cutting teeth. It removes material faster than a file but leaves a rougher surface.

Using a File or Rasp

Files or rasps are never to be used without handles. The tang can puncture your hand and cause a serious injury. Always fit a handle to

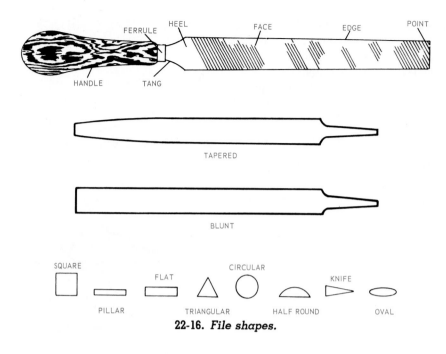

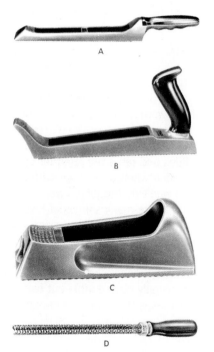

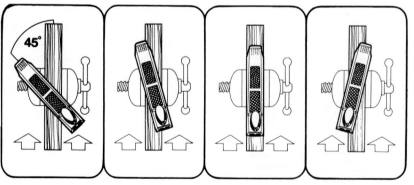

22-16. *File shapes.*

slight angle. Lift the file slightly on the return stroke.

To shape a curved edge, use the round side of the file. Twist the tool slightly as you push.

Always keep the teeth clean with a file card or cleaner.

FORMING TOOLS

There are several different kinds of commercial forming tools. The most common is the Surform, a forming tool with a hardened and tempered tool-steel cutting blade. It is available in many shapes and styles, including file-like tools as well as rotary tools that can be used in a drill. Fig. 22-17. The blade has 45-degree cutting edges that easily cut wood, plastic, or soft metals. The teeth of this tool never become clogged because the waste material goes through small holes in the blade. The replaceable blade fits into a holder. This tool is used in much the same way as a file. Fig. 22-18.

the tool before using it. Hold the handle of the tool in your right hand and the point in your left. Apply medium pressure on the forward stroke. Make a shearing cut at a

22-17. *Common types of Surform tools: (A) File. (B) Plane. (C) Block plane. (D) File type.*

To remove a maximum amount of material, simply hold the tool at 45° to the direction of the stroke.

To remove less material and obtain a smoother surface, reduce angle.

To finely smooth the work surface, simply direct the tool parallel to it.

And you can achieve an almost polishing effect by directing the tool at a slightly reversed angle.

22-18. *Using a Surform tool.*

Working with wood often requires drilling or boring holes. The process is usually called *drilling* when the holes are ¼" or smaller and *boring* when the holes are larger than ¼". There are several kinds of drills and bits, each designed for a certain type of job. This chapter discusses hand tools for drilling and boring. Power tools are discussed in Chapter 34.

DRILLING DEVICES

The *hand drill* is a relatively small drill used to make holes with a di-ameter of ¼ inch or less in either wood or metal. Fig. 23-1. It consists of a shaft with a handle at one end and a chuck for holding twist drills at the other. (The twist drills are replaceable bits that do the actual cutting.) Near the middle of the shaft is a ratchet wheel with a crank handle. Turning this handle causes the shaft and the chuck to turn. Straight shank twist bits from $\frac{1}{32}$ to ¼ inch may be used in this drill.

The chuck has several V-grooved fingers, or jaws, that hold the bit. To insert the bit, open the chuck by grasping the shell and turning it to the left. When the jaws are open wide enough, insert the shank of the bit. Close the chuck by turning it to the right until the bit is held firmly.

It is often necessary to cut a hole to a measured depth or to make several holes of the same depth. This can be done by making a depth gauge from a piece of scrap wood. The piece should be exactly as long as that section of the drill which should *not* bore into the lumber. Fig. 23-2. Several kinds of commercial depth gauges are available also. Figs. 23-2 and 23-4.

The *brace* is used for holes that are larger than can be drilled with the hand drill. Fig. 23-5. It is made to take bits with round or square shanks up to ½ inch in diameter, including a screwdriver bit, twist drill, expansive bit, auger bit, and countersink bit. The brace consists of a head that is fastened to a crank by a bearing that permits the crank to turn while the head remains still. The crank consists of a wood handle and a U-shaped steel shaft that provides leverage. A ratchet determines whether or not the chuck turns

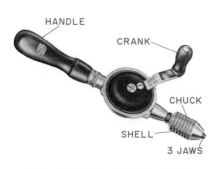

HANDLE
CRANK
CHUCK
SHELL
3 JAWS

(FOR STRAIGHT SHANK DRILLS)

23-1. *Parts of a hand drill.*

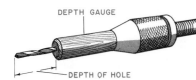

DEPTH GAUGE

DEPTH OF HOLE

23-2. *A depth gauge made from a piece of dowel rod. It covers a part of the drill like a sleeve. Cut the piece until the drill sticks out the right amount.*

23-3. *Commercial depth gauges: (left) solid type; (right) spring type.*

23-4. *A ring-type depth gauge.*

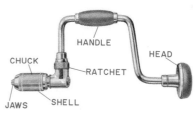

HANDLE
HEAD
CHUCK
RATCHET
JAWS
SHELL

23-5. *Parts of a brace.*

23-6. *The automatic drill is very efficient when drilling many small holes, such as for installing hardware.*

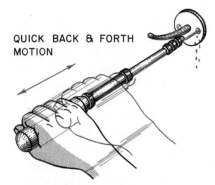

QUICK BACK & FORTH MOTION

23-7. *Using an automatic drill to install a coat hook.*

when the crank is turned. The ratchet may be set to permit the chuck to turn either forward or backward and then remain stationary as the crank is turned in the other direction. This allows holes to be bored or screws to be driven in places where complete turns of the crank cannot be made. It is possible to drill either vertically or horizontally with this brace.

The *automatic drill* provides an easy and quick way to drill small holes. Fig. 23-6. Pushing down on the handle makes the chuck turn.

23-9. *The bit-stock drill must be used in a brace because of the shank design.*

The drill can be used with one hand. Fig. 23-7. It takes special bits which are inserted in the chuck. These bits range in size from ¹⁄₁₆ to ¹¹⁄₆₄ inch. Usually these special bits are stored in the handle of the drill.

DRILLS AND BITS

A small set of *twist drills* ranging in size from ¹⁄₁₆ to ½ inch, in intervals of ¹⁄₆₄ inch, is used for drilling both metal and wood. Twist drills are used in hand drills as well as in portable electric drills and drill presses. Fig. 23-8. *Bit-stock drills*, Fig. 23-9, are designed for use in a brace. For boring holes that are ¼ to 1¼ inches, an *auger bit* is used. Fig. 23-10. The size of the auger bit is stamped on the tang, always in a single number such as 4, 5, 6, *etc.* This means that it will bore a hole with a diameter of ⁴⁄₁₆″, ⁵⁄₁₆″, ⁶⁄₁₆″, *etc. Brad point bits*, especially designed for wood, are similar to twist drills but have a center point. Fig. 23-11. For holes larger than 1 inch, you need an *expansion (expansive) bit.* Fig. 23-12. When you want to enlarge an existing hole or bore a hole partway into a thin board, a *Foerstner (Forstner) bit* is the tool to choose. Fig. 23-13. *Speed (flat or spade) bits* are also

useful for boring holes, especially angle holes in wood. Fig. 23-14. The *countersink bit* has a conical cutting head and a square shank. Use it in a brace to form the top of the hole for a screw. In this way the flat head of the screw will be flush with the surface of the wood. Fig. 23-15.

Using Twist Drills

To use, first insert the shank of the bit into the chuck of the drill. Make sure that it is exactly straight by watching for any "wobble" when the crank of the drill is turned.

Before starting to drill, it is sometimes helpful to make a small guide hole in the wood or metal with an awl or center punch. The hole should be just deep enough to keep the bit on the right spot. With the point of the bit where the hole is to be drilled, turn the crank of the ratchet in a clockwise direction.

A

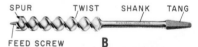

SPUR TWIST SHANK TANG

FEED SCREW B

23-10. *(A) A single-twist auger bit. (B) A double-twist auger bit with parts labeled.*

23-11. *Brad point wood bit.*

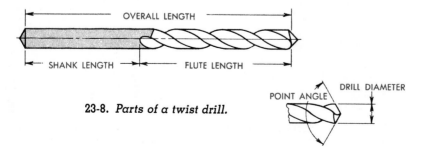

OVERALL LENGTH

SHANK LENGTH FLUTE LENGTH

23-8. *Parts of a twist drill.*

DRILL DIAMETER

POINT ANGLE

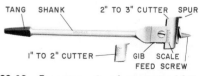

TANG SHANK 2″ TO 3″ CUTTER SPUR

1″ TO 2″ CUTTER GIB SCALE
FEED SCREW

23-12. *An expansion (expansive) bit. There are usually two cutters, a small one for holes 1 to 2 inches in diameter and a larger one for holes 2 inches and more in diameter.*

23-13. *A Foerstner bit is used to enlarge existing holes or to cut a hole partway through thin stock. Both hand and machine types are shown.*

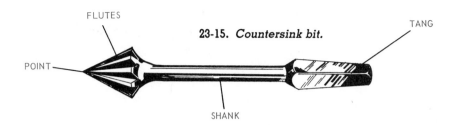

FLUTES

23-15. *Countersink bit.*

TANG

POINT

SHANK

Apply light pressure to the handle of the drill, as this pressure is what keeps the bit going through the wood or metal. When the hole is deep enough, pull out the drill while continuing to turn the ratchet wheel in a clockwise direction. This will clear the hole of shavings. When drilling completely through the wood, it is a good idea to use a backup board of scrap stock.

Using Auger Bits

Insert the tang of the bit into the chuck of the brace as far as possible. Put the point of the screw at the exact center of the spot where the hole is to be bored. Turn the crank of the brace. Be sure that you

23-14. *A speed bit is a good tool for counterboring holes for wood screws that will be covered with wood plugs.*

apply only enough pressure to assist the screw in drawing the bit into the wood. (As the screw draws the bit down, the spurs first cut the fibers of wood at the side of the hole; then the lips chip the wood out to make a hole.)

When the hole is the right depth, back the bit out by turning the crank or handle in the opposite direction until the spur is free from the bottom of the hole. Withdraw the bit the rest of the way, turning it clockwise in order to remove the shavings from the hole.

When a hole is bored completely through a board with an auger bit, the board will split on the underside as the bit goes through. There are two ways to prevent splitting:

1. Pull the bit out of the wood when the tip of the screw begins to show through the board. Insert the screw on the opposite side at the spot where it began to come through. Finish boring the hole.

2. Clamp a piece of scrap wood very tightly to the underside of the board. Take care to prevent the good lumber from being marked by the clamps.

Using a Foerstner (Forstner) Bit

The Foerstner bit is used to bore holes nearly all the way through a piece of wood without splitting the other side. It can be used to clean out the rough bottom of a hole made by an auger bit or to bore a large hole where a small one was. It cuts end grain in thin stock. The average set of Foerstner bits ranges from $\frac{1}{4}$ to 1 inch in diameter. The Foerstner is similar to the auger bit

in several ways. It may have a square shank so that it can be held in a brace.

Using an Expansion Bit

This is an auger-type bit. Because of the adjustable cutting blades, it takes the place of several large auger bits. There are usually two interchangeable cutting blades.

To set the expansion bit with a screwdriver, loosen the setscrew, slide the cutter to the right size, and then tighten the screw. Read the diameter of the hole from the scale marked on the blade. Fig. 23-16. By moving the cutter $\frac{1}{32}$ inch, the diameter of the hole is changed $\frac{1}{16}$ inch. Make sure the size is right by boring a test hole in scrap wood.

Splitting the wood with this bit can be prevented in the same way as when using the auger bit.

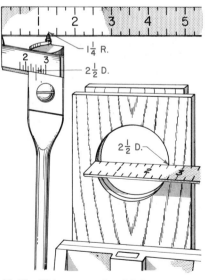

23-16. *This expansion bit is set to bore a hole $2\frac{1}{2}$ inches in diameter.*

151

24 Tool and Machine Maintenance

The experienced woodworker knows the value of sharp tools. Time used for sharpening tools and adjusting machines will be regained many times over in greater speed and better work.

Most tool and knife sharpening can be done by the person who uses the equipment. However, certain types of cutting tools, particularly hand saws and the blades of circular saws and band saws, should be sharpened by a well-equipped professional. Though saw filing and setting can be done by hand, generally this is too time-consuming. Also, some school and home shops are not equipped with saw filing machines and sharpeners.

Grinding means reshaping the cutting edge of a tool. It should be done when a tool needs a new bevel or when its edge has been nicked. *Honing* (sharpening the tip of the cutting edge) is enough when the edge is only slightly dull.

EQUIPMENT FOR SHARPENING

Several types of power-driven grinders can be used to sharpen tools. *A standard two-wheel grinder*, Fig. 24-1, should have a motor speed of 1425 or 1725 RPM. For general grinding purposes, the motor usually has a speed of 2850 or 3450 RPM. However, at the higher speeds care must be taken because tool edges tend to burn very easily. Accessories are available for grinding drills and plane blades. Fig. 24-2.

The *tool grinder* is designed for grinding all types and shapes of edged tools. It is well suited for sharpening single-point tool bits that are either carbide-tipped or of high-speed steel. The tool grinder has a water pot over one abrasive wheel. This keeps the wheel lubricated for wet grinding. It also has

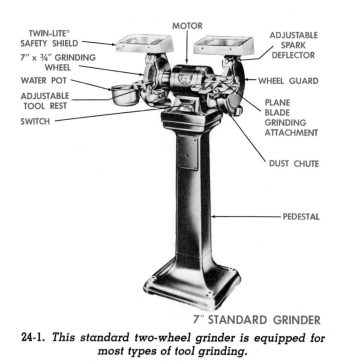

TWIN-LITE® SAFETY SHIELD — MOTOR — ADJUSTABLE SPARK DEFLECTOR

7" x ¾" GRINDING WHEEL

WATER POT — WHEEL GUARD

ADJUSTABLE TOOL REST — PLANE BLADE GRINDING ATTACHMENT

SWITCH

DUST CHUTE

PEDESTAL

7" STANDARD GRINDER

24-1. *This standard two-wheel grinder is equipped for most types of tool grinding.*

24-2. *This plane-blade grinding attachment is ideal for sharpening plane irons, wood chisels, and other single-edge tools. The blade is securely held in place and the attachment adjusted for correct angle. The tool is moved back and forth across the abrasive wheel. Also, the tool can be lifted off to inspect the cutting edge or cool it in water.*

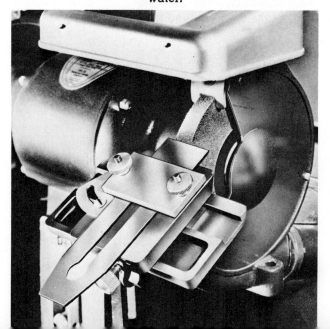

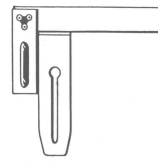

24-3. *Checking the cutting edge of a plane blade with a try square.*

tables on both sides that can be tilted 30 degrees in and 45 degrees out to allow for various grinding angles. A tilting angle jig that swings 45 degrees to the left and right can also be used for angle cutting. A reversing switch allows either right or left cutting tools to be ground while the wheel turns down towards the cutting edge.

Grinding wheels of the correct *size*, *kind of abrasive*, and *grit* must be selected.

The size of the wheel is determined by the machine on which it is to be used. The thickness and diameter of the wheel and also the arbor-hole size must be specified.

The abrasive may be a natural material such as fine white Arkansas stone, or it may be silicon carbide or aluminum oxide.

Silicon carbide wheels and stones are used primarily for sharpening high-carbon tools and for knives. The harder and tougher grains of aluminum oxide wheels and stones make them ideal for sharpening hard tool steels. For grinding carbide-tipped tools, a diamond abrasive wheel designed especially for this purpose is recommended. (See Chapter 35 for more information about abrasives.)

The grit number indicates whether the abrasive is coarse, medium, or fine. A 36-grit is a coarse wheel, 60-grit is medium, and 120 is fine. A good selection for a standard two-wheel grinder, for example, would be an aluminum oxide wheel, ¾″ x

7″, with ¾″ arbor hole, either 60-grit or 120-grit. For general-purpose grinding, use a 36-grit wheel.

After considerable use, grinding wheels become clogged with metal and wear down unevenly. They must be cleaned and straightened. While there are several tools for this, the best and simplest is a diamond-pointed wheel dresser. This is a long, thin metal rod with an industrial diamond on one end and a wood handle on the other. The tool is held firmly against the face of the revolving wheel with the rod on the tool rest. Then the face is trued by moving the dresser back and forth across it.

For hand sharpening, there are abrasive stones of all sizes and shapes. Again, these may be natural stones, such as the Arkansas or Washita, but more often they are artificial. If the stone is artificial, half can be coarse and the other half fine. Artificial stones are oil-soaked at the factory for general sharpening of such edged tools as plane irons and chisels.

A cutting oil is needed in many sharpening and honing operations for faster work, a finer edge, and to keep the stone free of chips. A good lubricant can be made of equal parts of oil and kerosene.

An 8″ taper file and a 10″ mill file are needed to sharpen some tools such as hand saws.

SHARPENING HAND TOOLS

Plane Iron Blade

Remove the double plane iron from the plane and loosen the screw that holds the cap on the plane iron. Separate the two parts. Look at the cutting edge under a good light to see if there are any nicks or if the bevel is rounded off a good deal. If so, both grinding and honing must be done. If the cutting edge is in good condition, only honing will be necessary.

24-4. *Grinding a plane-iron blade without a guide. With this method, hold the blade at the desired angle to the wheel and move it back and forth as it is being ground. This requires considerable skill to keep the bevel even.*

For grinding, hold a try square against the cutting edge of the plane iron to see if it is square. Fig. 24-3. Grind off the old edge at right angles to the sides until the nicks are removed and the edge is straightened. Move the tool from left to right across the face of the wheel. Dip the tool frequently in water, if using a high-speed grinder. Friction heats the tool, and the cutting edge will lose its hardness if it is allowed to get too hot and turn blue. If a grinding attachment is available, fasten the blade to it with the bevel side down. If you don't have a grinding attachment, the blade must be held freehand against the wheel. Fig. 24-4. Use the adjustable tool rest to support the blade. The bevel should be 2 to 2½ times the thickness of the blade to give a 20- to 30-degree angle. Fig. 24-5. Continue to grind the blade until a wire edge (a very thin burr) appears.

Now hone the blade. Apply a few drops of oil or lubricant to the face of an oilstone. Place the blade at a very low angle to the surface, bevel side down. Raise the end slowly until the blade makes an angle of

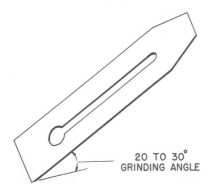

24-5. *A plane-iron blade should be ground at an angle of 20 to 30 degrees.*

about 30 to 35 degrees with the stone. Note that honing puts a second bevel on the tool. When this honed bevel becomes too long, it is necessary to regrind the tool.

Move the blade back and forth in a straight line or a figure eight. Fig. 24-6. Be sure to hold the blade so that the angle will remain the same throughout the stroke. Then turn the blade over and place it flat on the stone. Move it back and forth to remove the burr. Make sure the blade is held perfectly flat. The slightest bevel on the back side will prevent the cap from fitting properly. Wood chips will get between the cap and the blade, making it impossible to do a good job of planing.

The plane iron can be checked for sharpness in several ways. One method is to hold it with the cutting edge down and allow the edge to rest lightly on your thumbnail. As the tool is moved, it tends to "bite" into the nail if it is sharp. If dull, it will slide across easily. Another method is to look closely at the edge. If it is sharp, the edge can't be seen. If it is dull, a thin, white line can be seen. A third method is to cut paper with the plane iron.

Wood Chisel

The chisel is ground and honed in exactly the same way as the plane iron. The angle of the chisel should be from 20 degrees for softwoods

to 27 degrees for hardwoods. An angle of about 25 degrees is best for general-purpose work. Notice that plane-iron blades and hand chisels are *hollow-ground*; that is, the major bevel is ground with a slight curve, then a secondary bevel is formed to produce the actual cutting edge.

Hand Scraper

A hand scraper must be sharpened frequently. Place the tool in a vise with the cutting edge showing. To remove the old cutting edge, hold a file flat against the side of the scraper and take a few strokes. Then use a fine file to drawfile the edge until it is square with the sides of the scraper. Fig. 24-7.

Whet (hone) the cutting edge by moving it back and forth across an oilstone. Hold the blade at right angles to the surface. Then hold the sides of the blade flat against the stone, again working it back and forth, to remove the wire edge.

Place the scraper flat on the bench with the cutting edge extending slightly over the edge of the bench. Hold a burnisher flat on the side of the scraper and take a few firm strokes toward you to draw the edge.

Then hold the scraper on edge as shown in Fig. 24-8. Use the burnishing tool held at an angle of about 85 degrees to turn the edge

of the scraper. This is done by drawing the burnisher up with a firm, brisk stroke. The edge is sharp when it will catch your thumbnail as the scraper is drawn across it.

Auger Bit and Spade Bit

Choose a small flat or triangular auger bit file or a small auger bit stone. Clamp the auger bit in a vise with the cutting end up, or hold the tool over the edge of a bench. File across the inside of the spurs. Fig. 24-9. Never touch the outside of the spurs as this will change the size of the bit. Also file the lips on the underside or the side toward the shank. Be careful to retain the original angle of the bevel. Fig. 24-10. Keep the bit in good condition by cleaning off pitch with a solvent.

File the spade bit on the two cutting edges to sharpen it. Fig. 24-11.

24-7. *Drawfiling the hand scraper. Use a fine file in this manner until the edge is square with the sides of the scraper. To prevent excess vibration, lower the scraper in the vise.*

24-6. *One method of honing the edge is to move the tool in a figure-eight pattern.*

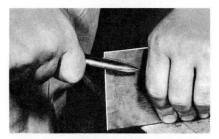

24-8. *Use a burnisher to turn the edge of the scraper. Hold the scraper as shown.*

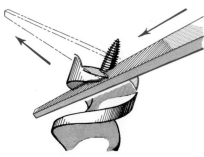

24-9. *Sharpening a spur. Hold the bit with the feed screw uppermost. Place the twist against the bench. File the inside of the spur only—never the outside.*

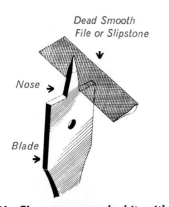

24-10. *Sharpening the underside of the lip on an auger bit. The phantom lines show the file sharpening the spur.*

24-11. *Sharpen a spade bit with a small slipstone or dead-smooth file. Make sure that the original angles are maintained and that each side of the nose is sharpened equally. Do not file the sides of the blade.*

24-12. *Honing the cutting edge of a drawknife.*

Drawknife

If grinding is necessary, the drawknife can be sharpened on a power grinder in the same general manner as a plane iron. The honing can be done in one of two ways. One method is to place a larger stone on the table or bench. Hold the drawknife by its handles at the correct angle to the surface of the stone. Draw it across diagonally so that all parts are equally honed. Fig. 24-12. Another method is to hold the tool with one handle against the top of the bench and the other handle in your hand. Then hold a small oilstone in the other hand and move it back and forth along the bevel at a slightly higher angle to hone a keen edge.

Screwdriver

The screwdriver should be ground with a very slight taper on the sides and edges and with the end perfectly flat. Fig. 24-13. A rounded end or sides that are too sharp will cause slipping and burring. The screwdriver can be sharpened on a grinding wheel or with a coarse abrasive stone.

Countersink

Sharpen the faces of the cutting edges. Don't change the shape or angle of the tool by grinding the outside bevel.

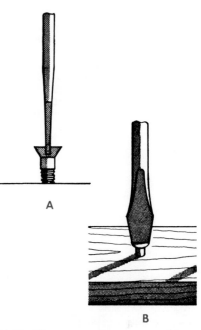

24-13. *The tip of a screwdriver should look like this: (A) Edge. (B) Side.*

Woodturning Tools

The correct shapes and grinding angles for each of the woodturning tools are shown in Fig. 24-14. If the tools are to be used for cutting (in contrast to scraping), they must be ground and honed with a flat bevel. Any secondary bevel on the skew, for example, will keep it from cutting. This is not important if the tools are used for scraping.

The skew can be ground on the side of a straight or recessed grinding wheel. While the grinding can be done freehand, it is better to use a wood jig, as shown in Fig. 24-15. Hold the chisel against one of the beveled guide blocks first and then against the other side. When honing the skew, maintain the same angle. Don't hone a secondary bevel, especially if the tool is used for cutting. A fine wheel can also be used for honing.

A gouge can be ground in one of several ways. The best method is to use a cup wheel mounted on a wood or metal lathe. The curved interior surface of the wheel helps to

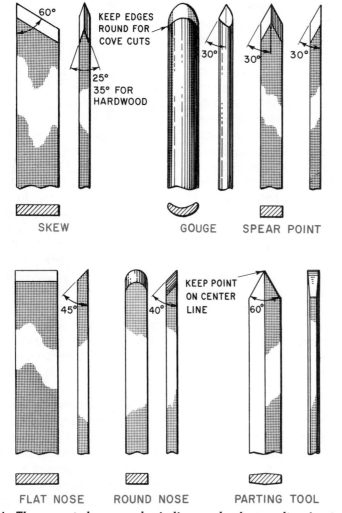

SKEW GOUGE SPEAR POINT

FLAT NOSE ROUND NOSE PARTING TOOL

24-14. *The correct shapes and grinding angles for woodturning tools.*

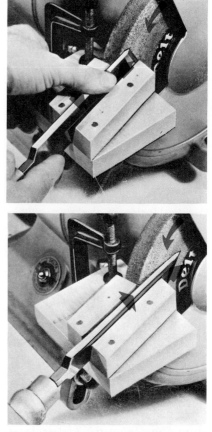

24-15. *The bevels on the skew should be ground flat. This simple wood jig will make the work easier.*

shape the cutting edge, and less rolling of the tool is required. Fig. 24-16. The gouge can also be shaped by rolling the tool against the face or side of a standard grinding wheel.

The honing is done on a gouge slipstone. Hold the stone in one hand and place the convex side of the tool in the concave side of the stone. Hone by pushing the gouge forward and rotating at the same time. Keep the stone flat so that the back edge is not beveled. Fig. 24-17.

Spear-point, flat-nose, and parting tools all require flat-angle grinding and honing that can be done freehand or with a simple jig. The round nose is sharpened in a similar manner to the gouge.

Handsaw

Jointing means bringing all the teeth of a saw to the same height. This needs to be done only when the teeth are uneven and incorrectly shaped. To joint a saw, place it in a clamp, with the handle to the right. Lay a mill file lengthwise, flat upon the teeth. Pass it lightly back and forth along the length of the blade on the tops of the teeth until the file touches the top of every tooth. Do not allow the file to tip to one side or the other. Fig. 24-18.

Examine the tooth edge of the saw to see if the teeth are uniform in size and shape and if they are properly set. It is not necessary to reset the teeth of a well-tempered handsaw every time it needs sharpening. If the teeth are touched up with a file from time to time as the saw is used, the saw will cut better

24-16. *Grinding a gouge on a cup wheel.*

24-17. *Honing a gouge.*

and longer, and sufficient set will remain to enable the saw to clear itself. Study the shape of the teeth. Teeth of saws for crosscutting should be shaped as shown in Fig. 24-19. Teeth of the ripsaw should be shaped like those in Fig. 24-20. A saw cannot give good service unless the teeth are even and uniform in size and properly shaped.

After jointing, all teeth must be filed to the correct shape. The gullets (low parts between the teeth) must be equal in depth. Fronts and backs of the teeth must have proper shape and angle. The teeth must be uniform in size. (Note that merely shaping the teeth does not sharpen them.)

Place the file well down in the gullet, then file straight across the saw, at right angles to the blade. If the teeth are unequal in size, press the file against the teeth that have the largest tops until you reach the center of the flat top made by jointing. Then move the file to the next gullet and file until the remainder of the top disappears and the tooth has been brought up to a point.

The purpose of *setting* the teeth of saws (springing over the upper part of each tooth, one to the right and the next to the left) is to make the saw cut a kerf (groove) that is slightly wider than the blade. Fig. 24-21 (Page 160). This prevents friction which would cause the saw to bind in the cut and make it hard to push. Start the setting from the

small end (toe) of the saw. Bend to the left and right alternately. It is important that the depth of the set go no lower than half the tooth. If deeper, it is likely to spring, crimp, or crack the blade. It could even break out a tooth. Particular care must be taken to keep the set regular. It must be the same width from one end of the blade to the other, and the same width on both sides of the blade. Otherwise the saw will not cut true. If not properly set, the saw line and the cut will be "snaky."

FILING A HANDSAW FOR CROSSCUTTING

Place the saw in a filing clamp with the handle at the right. The bottom of the tooth gullets should be ⅛" above the clamp jaws. If more of the blade projects, the file will chatter or screech. This dulls the file quickly.

Select the correct size taper file, as follows:
4½, 5½, 6 points—7" slim taper
7, 8 points—6" slim taper
9, 10 points—5" or 6" slim taper
11, 12, 13, 14, 15 points—4½" slim taper

Stand at first position, shown in Fig. 24-22. Start at the point. Pick

out the first tooth that is set toward you. Place the file in the gullet to the left of this tooth. Hold the file directly across the blade. Then swing the file handle toward the left to the same angle as the bevel. Keep the file at this angle and level. Fig. 24-23. Be sure the file sets down well into the gullet. The file should cut on the push stroke. It files the back of the tooth to the left and the front of the tooth to the right at the same time. Skip the next gullet to the right and place the file in the *second* gullet from the one you just filed. Repeat the operation, being careful to file at the same angle as before. Continue this way, placing the file in every second gullet until you reach the handle end of the saw.

Study the second position shown in Fig. 24-24. Turn the saw around in the clamp, with the saw handle to the left. Take the second position. Place the file in the gullet to the right of the first set toward you. This is the first of the gullets you skipped when filing the other side of the saw. Turn the file handle to the correct angle toward the right. Now file until the teeth are sharpened to a point. Continue this, placing the

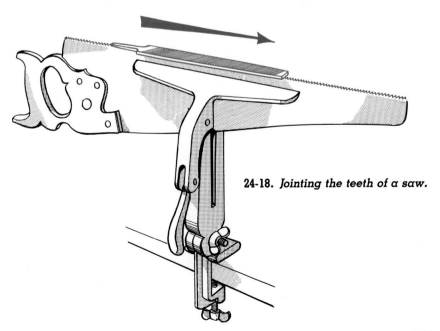

24-18. *Jointing the teeth of a saw.*

CROSSCUT HAND SAW

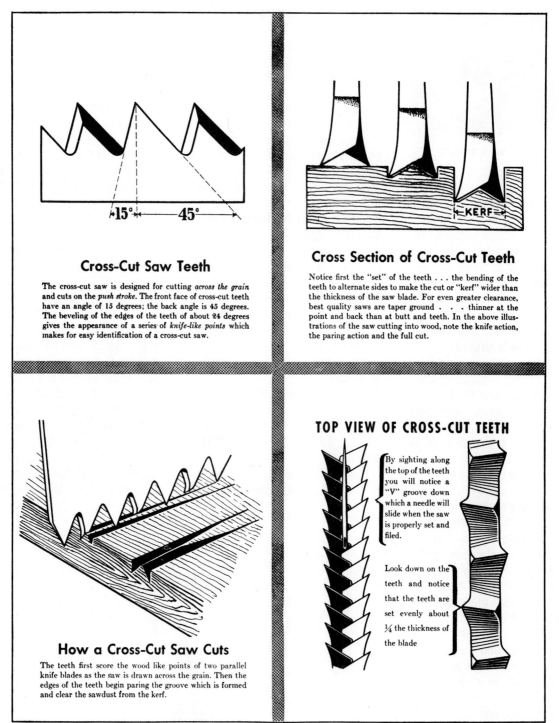

Cross-Cut Saw Teeth

The cross-cut saw is designed for cutting *across the grain* and cuts on the *push stroke*. The front face of cross-cut teeth have an angle of 15 degrees; the back angle is 45 degrees. The beveling of the edges of the teeth of about 24 degrees gives the appearance of a series of *knife-like points* which makes for easy identification of a cross-cut saw.

Cross Section of Cross-Cut Teeth

Notice first the "set" of the teeth . . . the bending of the teeth to alternate sides to make the cut or "kerf" wider than the thickness of the saw blade. For even greater clearance, best quality saws are taper ground . . . thinner at the point and back than at butt and teeth. In the above illustrations of the saw cutting into wood, note the knife action, the paring action and the full cut.

How a Cross-Cut Saw Cuts

The teeth first score the wood like points of two parallel knife blades as the saw is drawn across the grain. Then the edges of the teeth begin paring the groove which is formed and clear the sawdust from the kerf.

TOP VIEW OF CROSS-CUT TEETH

By sighting along the top of the teeth you will notice a "V" groove down which a needle will slide when the saw is properly set and filed.

Look down on the teeth and notice that the teeth are set evenly about ¼ the thickness of the blade

24-19. *An understanding of the cutting edges of the crosscut handsaw will help you in sharpening the tool.*

RIP HAND SAW

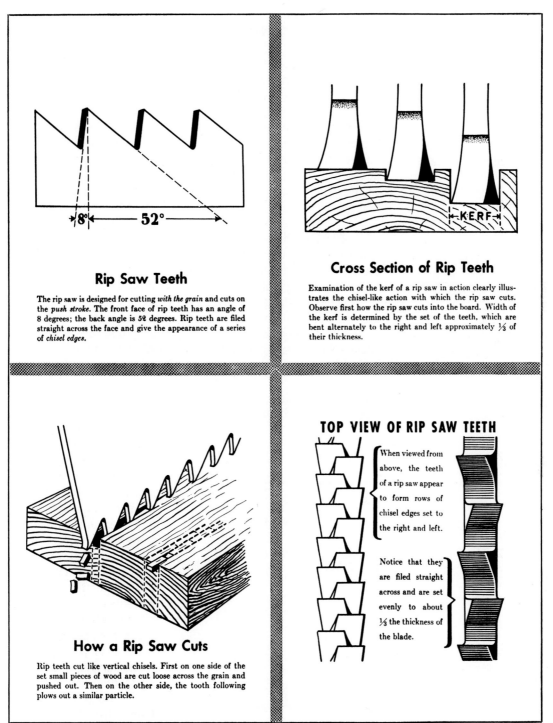

Rip Saw Teeth

The rip saw is designed for cutting *with the grain* and cuts on the *push stroke*. The front face of rip teeth has an angle of 8 degrees; the back angle is 52 degrees. Rip teeth are filed straight across the face and give the appearance of a series of *chisel edges*.

Cross Section of Rip Teeth

Examination of the kerf of a rip saw in action clearly illustrates the chisel-like action with which the rip saw cuts. Observe first how the rip saw cuts into the board. Width of the kerf is determined by the set of the teeth, which are bent alternately to the right and left approximately ⅓ of their thickness.

How a Rip Saw Cuts

Rip teeth cut like vertical chisels. First on one side of the set small pieces of wood are cut loose across the grain and pushed out. Then on the other side, the tooth following plows out a similar particle.

TOP VIEW OF RIP SAW TEETH

When viewed from above, the teeth of a rip saw appear to form rows of chisel edges set to the right and left.

Notice that they are filed straight across and are set evenly to about ⅓ the thickness of the blade.

24-20. *Note how the rip handsaw differs from the crosscut handsaw.*

24-21. *Saw set. This tool is used to bend the upper half of each tooth to one side or the other to form the set.*

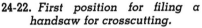

24-22. *First position for filing a handsaw for crosscutting.*

file in every second gullet until you reach the handle of the saw.

FILING HANDSAWS FOR RIPPING

With one exception, this operation is exactly the same as for crosscut saws. This exception is that *the file is held straight across the saw*, at a right angle to the blade. The teeth should be filed to an angle of 8 degrees at the front and 52 degrees at the back. Check this angle with the protractor head of a combination set.

MACHINE TOOLS

Machines for cutting wood operate at maximum efficiency only when the cutting tools are sharp. Frequently, a little touch-up with an oilstone will help if the tool is basically in good condition. However, when a knife or saw has become dull, it is necessary to have it reground. To avoid excessive sharpening costs and delays, the best practice is to buy high-quality cutting

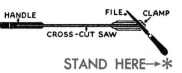

24-24. *Second position for filing a crosscut saw.*

tools in the first place. Whenever possible, make use of carbide-tipped tools so that grinding will be needed less often.

More important, however, is using the machines properly. This will prolong the life of cutting edges more than any other single factor. It takes only one board with a nail in it to ruin a set of planer or jointer knives. If power equipment isn't available for sharpening, saws and knives should be sent out periodically to a shop that specializes in this work. While hand methods of sharpening saws are covered in this unit, they are not recommended except for emergencies.

Refitting Narrow Band Saws by Hand

When an automatic filing machine is not available, narrow band saws may be sharpened by hand. Place the saw on a long bench so that its entire length is supported on the same level. Make sure the teeth point to the left. The clamp will hold a section of approximately 50 teeth at one time. The saw is then moved as often as necessary until all the teeth have been sharpened.

However, before filing the teeth, it is the usual practice to joint the section slightly. This is done by lightly running a mill file over the tops of the teeth to make them uniform in height. Jointing will also assist as a guide in filing, and it will help keep the saw teeth as much like new as possible.

Choose taper files for sharpening narrow band saws as follows: for saws with 3, 3½, 4, 5, or 6 points use a 6″ band file; for 7, 8, 9, or

24-23(a). *Hold the file at approximately the angle shown here.*

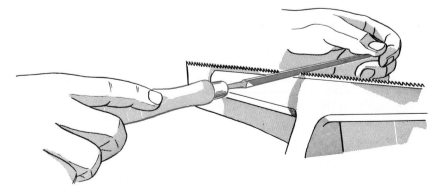

24-23(b). *Make sure the file is level as the stroke is made.*

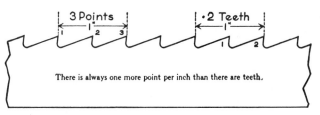

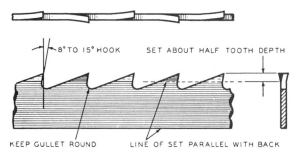

24-25. *A standard band saw blade has teeth shaped like a ripsaw. The teeth should be filed straight across with a hook from 8 to 15 degrees.*

10 points use a 7" extra slim taper file.

Hold the file in a horizontal position. File each tooth straight across the saw at right angles to the blade, raising the file on the back stroke. Fig. 24-25. If the point of any tooth is not brought up sharp after the stroke of the file, do not immediately file it again. Instead, continue until you have filed the section you are working on. By this method, each section may require two or three repetitions.

Teeth may be set with a pistol-grip saw set, as handsaw teeth are set. When setting is necessary, it should be done before the teeth are filed. Remember that if the saw is to do only straight-line cutting, best results are obtained with the least set possible. Greater set is necessary when cutting curved lines.

Repairing a Broken Band Saw Blade

When a band saw blade breaks, it must be hard soldered or welded back into a continuous piece. If only a small section must be removed during repair, the upper wheel can be adjusted to compensate for this. However, if a bigger section must be removed, it is necessary to add a piece of the same kind and size.

If the blade is to be hard (silver) soldered by brazing, a scarf joint that is one or two teeth long should be filed. Apply brazing flux and a small amount of silver solder. Place

the ends together on the brazer and clamp in position. Turn on the electricity until the joint becomes red hot and the solder melts. Then turn off the electricity and press the handle down firmly to hold the joint together for three or four seconds. Remember that this should be done immediately after the current has been switched off.

Some large band saws have a built-in electric butt welder for repairing blades. This device squares off the ends of the blade and butt welds them together. Then a small grinding wheel smoothes the sides to the same thickness as the blade itself.

Sharpening Circular Saw Blades by Hand

As with the band saw, the best way to keep circular saw blades sharp is with automatic saw-filing equipment. However, if it is necessary, hand sharpening can be done to a blade that is basically in good condition. Four basic steps must be followed to put a dull blade back into shape: *jointing or rounding, gumming, setting,* and *filing.* Fig. 24-26.

Jointing makes the saw as round as possible so that all teeth are of equal height. Gumming is necessary when the teeth have become shallow after repeated filing and must be ground deeper. Setting bends the teeth to the right and left to provide clearance. Filing or grinding sharpens the teeth. This last step is

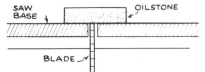

1-JOINTING : REVERSE SAW ON ARBOR. RAISE BASE . PLACE STONE IN PLACE AND LOWER BASE UNTIL TEETH STRIKE . DO NOT JOINT ANY MORE THAN IS NECESSARY TO LEVEL TEETH.

2-GUMMING: MAKE PENCIL MARK TO SHOW BOTTOM OF GULLET (¹¹/₃₂" FROM EDGE OF BLADE). FILE OR GRIND GULLETS TO LINE . FOLLOW SHAPE AS SHOWN IN PLAN.

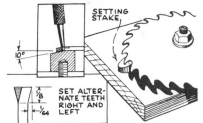

3-SETTING: USE SUITABLE SETTING STAKE OR HAND SET. DO NOT EXCEED AMOUNT OF SET AS SPECIFIED. KEEP SET UNIFORM.

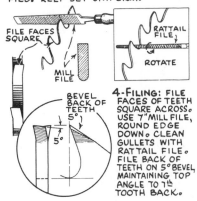

4-FILING: FILE FACES OF TEETH SQUARE ACROSS. USE 7" MILL FILE, ROUND EDGE DOWN. CLEAN GULLETS WITH RATTAIL FILE. FILE BACK OF TEETH ON 5° BEVEL MAINTAINING TOP ANGLE TO 7ᵗʰ TOOTH BACK.

24-26. *Steps in sharpening a circular saw blade.*

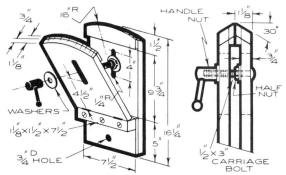

24-27. *This circular saw blade vise is made of hardwood. A standard ½" hexagon nut or a wing nut can be used with the carriage bolt instead of the handle nut shown.*

generally the only one that should be attempted by the hand method. In filing, do not reduce the size, shape, or length of the teeth; simply bring them up to a sharp point. Have all the teeth the same shape, with gullets of even depth. Filing should be done with the blade held in a blade vise. Fig. 24-27. Use a taper or saw file. Carbide-tipped blades must, of course, be ground with an abrasive wheel.

Do not file sharp corners or nicks in the bottom of the gullets. This usually results in cracks in the gullets. Bevel the teeth of cutoff saws on both the face and back edges—more on the face than on the back. File ripsaw teeth straight across to a chisel-like edge. Then give a very slight bevel to the back of the teeth. In filing any saw, take care that the bevel does not run down into the gullets. The bevel on both face and back should be about one-third the length of the teeth.

In filing a flat-ground combination saw which crosscuts, rips, and miters, follow the same method used in sharpening a crosscut saw. In sharpening a hollow-ground combination saw, also follow this method, but do not set the teeth because the hollow grinding provides ample clearance.

Some combination saws have rakers, or "cleaner" teeth. These remove material left in the cut by the

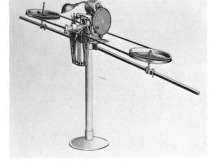

24-28. *Complete instructions on how to sharpen saws come with the automatic saw-filing equipment. The same machine can be used for sharpening all types of blades. Here, an attachment has been added to hold a band saw blade for sharpening.*

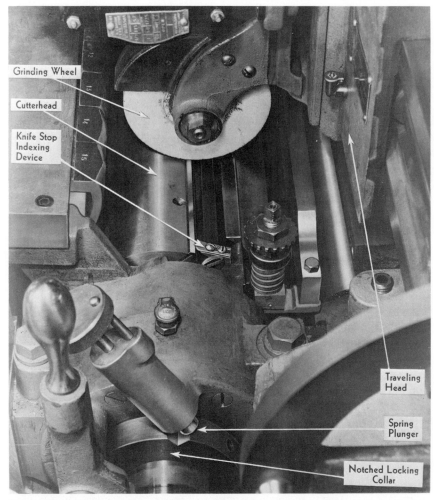

24-29. *A close-up view of knife grinding. Note that the knife stop indexing device holds the knife in the correct position.*

beveled cutting teeth. The points of these rakers should be filed shorter than the points of the beveled teeth —1/64″ shorter for cutting hardwood, 1/32″ for softwood. After filing these raker teeth, square the face of each and bring it to a chisel-like edge by filing on the back of the tooth only.

Saw-Filing Equipment

Automatic saw-filing equipment not only provides greater accuracy than can be achieved by hand but also adds mechanical precision to the sharpening. A single machine can be used to sharpen blades for circular, band, and hand saws. Fig. 24-28. The basic principles of sharpening must be followed. Each type of saw tooth (crosscut, rip, or combination) requires a different adjustment of the machine. Also, different attachments must be used to hold and move the various saws.

Automatic saw sharpening is a highly specialized part of the cabinetmaker's trade. Some people, especially those working in the tool rooms of furniture factories or operating their own business, do saw and knife sharpening on a full-time basis. The skilled all-around cabinetmaker and finish carpenter send their cutting tools to a specialist for sharpening. Even more highly specialized equipment is needed for sharpening carbide-tipped tools.

Grinding and Jointing Planer Blades

Before these blades can be sharpened, the exhaust pipe must be disconnected and the dust hood removed from the surfacer or planer. Modern planers, except for the smallest sizes, are usually equipped with attachments for grinding the knives without removing them from the cutterhead. This equipment consists of a small abrasive wheel with its motor. These devices are attached to a grinding and jointing bar above the cutterhead and are moved back and forth along the knife

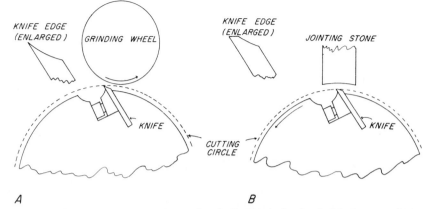

24-30. *(A) Note how the grinding wheel sharpens the knife blade to a sharp edge with the bevel in an arc shape. (B) Jointing produces a land or joint (secondary bevel) on the knife. The enlarged edge shows a land that is too wide. When this happens, the knives must be reground.*

edges. Knives are ground one by one while the cutterhead is stationary. Fig. 24-29. The bevel that is ground in this way is not a straight line but conforms to the circumference of the grinding wheel. Fig. 24-30.

Knives on a cutterhead often project unequally and therefore do not cut evenly. With a four-knife cutterhead, for instance, one knife that projects a little too far may wipe out the marks of the other three knives. As stated earlier, the purpose of jointing is to even up the projection of the knives. In jointing, a carrier which holds an abrasive stone is attached to the grinding and jointing bar, and the cutterhead is then set in motion. The stone is lowered until it barely touches a knife edge and is then traversed along that edge. Fig. 24-31. This is continued until a fine line, called a *joint* or *land*, appears on the full length of each knife edge. The knives should not project evenly. As they gradually become dull, jointing may have to be repeated several times for sharpening. However, repeated jointing finally causes a pronounced heel. (Part B of Fig. 24-30.) The jointed portion of the bevel is part of the cutting circle and therefore has no clearance. The wider it becomes beyond certain

limits, the more pounding and rubbing take place, resulting in poor work. Knives should therefore be reground as soon as the joint reaches a width of about 1/32″.

Most manufacturers supply tools for this, replacing the knives when necessary. One such device is a knife puller to remove the knife from the slot after the bolts or setscrews in the knife bar or throat piece are loosened. Another device is available for setting all the knives in the cutterhead to the same height. The knife and knife bar are inserted in the slot and the setscrews lightly tightened with the knife extended a little more than necessary. Put the block in place and strike with a hammer all along the knife. Then tighten the setscrews securely. Fig. 24-32.

Grinding Jointer Knives

Jointer knives should be ground when:

• The knives are so dull that honing will not put a good cutting edge on them.

• The joint or land becomes too wide (over 1/16″).

• Nicks develop or the knives become uneven.

Some jointers have a knife-grinding attachment. Fig. 24-33. The knives can be ground without

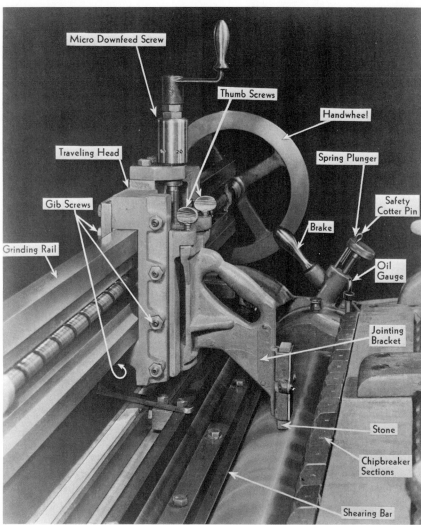

24-31. *Jointing the knives in a cutterhead. The power is on so the cutterhead is revolving at high speed. Great care must be taken when doing this. The stone must just touch each of the blades. The downfeed screw can be moved only a few thousandths of an inch at a time.*

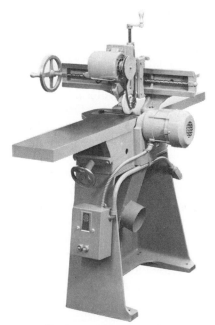

24-33. *Knife-grinding attachment on a jointer.*

24-34. *Grinding jointer knives on a drill press. A stop block controls the grinding. This one is clamped to the table.*

24-32. *Cross section of a cylinder showing the details of a four-knife cutterhead and the method of using the knife puller and knife setting block.*

removing them from the machine. On other machines the entire cutterhead must be removed to do the grinding. If a surfacer or planer that has a grinding attachment is available, this machine can be used for grinding jointer knives. However, this method should be used only when the planer knives themselves are also to be sharpened. Otherwise, resetting the planer knives may cause difficulties. To sharpen, remove one planer knife, place all jointer knives in a line, and grind as a single knife.

Several different machines can be used to grind jointer knives that have been removed from the cutterhead. In each case a wood jig must be constructed to hold the knives. If a two-wheel grinder is to be used, cut a groove at 35 to 36 degrees in the edge of a hardwood piece. Install a wood screw at either end that can hold the knives firmly in place. Dress the grinding wheel. Adjust the tool rest so that the bevel of the knives will be ground at approximately 35 degrees. Clamp a guide block to the tool rest to make sure the grinding is straight along the length of the knife.

Make a single light cut by moving the knife slowly from one side to the other. Check the edge to make sure it is ground to a single bevel. When this is done, grind the other knives. Make sure that each knife is ground the same amount so that all will weigh the same. Otherwise there will be excessive vibration when the cutterhead is revolving at high speeds. After grinding, light honing on the back edge will remove the burr.

If the grinding is to be done on a

drill press with a cup wheel, the groove should be cut in one corner of the wood jig. The knife is mounted with the bevel up. Fig. 24-34.

The same jig can be used to grind the knives on a circular saw that has an abrasive wheel mounted on the arbor. With this method the bevel is turned toward the edge of the jig.

Changing or Resetting Jointer Knives

Removing and replacing jointer knives must be done with great care. If not, the jointer will not operate smoothly or produce a good surface. Before working on the machine, remember to turn off the power both at the machine and at the master switch. Remove the fence and guard, and move the infeed table as far away as possible so that you can work at the cutterhead freely. To remove the knives, loosen the setscrews or bolts that are part of the knife bar or throat piece (the clamp that holds the knives tightly in the cutterhead). Lift out the knife first and then the throat piece. Turn the head to the next position and repeat this process.

To replace and reset the knives, reverse the process. Insert the throat piece first and then the knife, with the bevel toward the outfeed table. Use a straightedge on the outfeed table as a guide to set all knives to the same height. One of the best methods of doing this is to use a U-shaped or straight magnet as a straightedge. Place a stop block across the front table and then slide the magnet against it. It is a good idea to have an index mark on the magnet. This mark should be in line with the cutting edge of the knife at its highest point. With the knife in the slot and the throat piece loosened, allow the magnet to hold the knife up to the required level. Then tighten one setscrew or bolt just enough to hold. Move the magnet to the other end

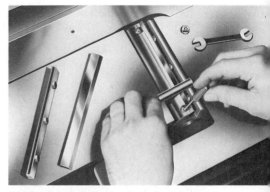

24-36. *Adjusting the height of the knives by turning a setscrew. Another knife and throat piece are shown ready to be installed in the next position on the cutterhead.*

of the knife and repeat. Reset the other knives in a similar manner. Make sure you move the magnet from one side to the other so that the knives are the same height along the entire cutterhead. Fig. 24-35.

On some machines the knives can be moved up or down with setscrews that are part of the cutterhead itself. With this type of machine a steel bar is used as a positive setting stop. By using screw lifters, raise the knife ends to the correct height and lock them in place. Fig. 24-36. After all knives are in place, tighten the remaining screws or bolts lightly. Then rotate the cutterhead by hand to check the knives. Tighten all screws or bolts again to be sure the knives are held firmly in place. Recheck with a straightedge to make sure all knives are the same height. Move the infeed table back to the correct position.

After the jointer knives have been sharpened and reset, it is wise to joint the knives so that they are exactly the same height. Cover all but about one-fourth the length of a large abrasive stone with wax paper. Place the stone on the rear table with the exposed section over the knives. Clamp a wooden stop block

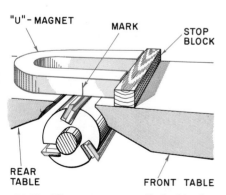

24-35. *The magnet will hold the jointer knife at exactly the same height as the rear table. The back of the bevel should clear the cutterhead itself by about ¹⁄₁₆″.*

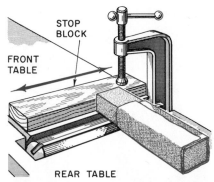

24-37. *Place the stone on the rear table as shown. Remember that the cutterhead is revolving at high speed. KEEP YOUR FINGERS AWAY FROM THE KNIVES AND HOLD THE ABRASIVE STONE FIRMLY. DON'T LET IT SLIP OUT OF YOUR HAND.*

24-38. *Honing the face of a shaper cutter.*

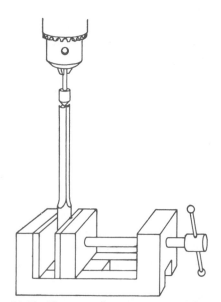

24-39. *How to sharpen a mortising chisel.*

to the front table to help guide the stone. Lower the table until the stone barely touched the knives. Fig. 24-37. Turn on the power. When the cutterhead is revolving, move the stone slowly from one side to the other. A true cutting circle will result. Be sure to joint the entire length of the knives. The joint or land (sometimes called the *heel*) should not be wider than ⅓₂″. After jointing, replace the fence and guard.

Router Bits and Shaper Cutters

In sharpening these tools, it is important not to change the shape of the cutting edge. Therefore most grinding and honing should be done on the face of the tool. To sharpen bits for a portable router you need an accessory for holding the bits. Fasten a small cup-shaped abrasive wheel to the collet of the router to do the grinding.

The face of a shaper bit can be ground on a small grinding wheel. Honing is done as shown in Fig. 24-38. A slipstone can be used to touch up the beveled cutting edge but take care not to change its shape.

Molding-Head Cutter Blades

The individual blades of a molding head can be honed on their front face. The beveled edge can be touched up with a slipstone.

Mortising Chisel

To sharpen a mortising chisel, install a conical-shaped wheel in the chuck of the drill press or lathe. Grind the inside bevel. Fig. 24-39. Then hone the outside, holding the abrasive stone flat against the sides to remove any burr.

Sharpening a Twist Drill

A correctly sharpened twist drill must have a point angle of 59 degrees on each side of the axis. The lips must be the same length, and there must be enough lip clearance (or relief behind the cutting edge) so that the tool can cut into the material. A lip clearance of 8 to 12 degrees is considered right for ordinary work. To grind a drill, hold the shank in one hand and the point between the thumb and forefinger of the other hand. Hold the drill in a horizontal position at an angle of 59 degrees to the grinding wheel. Grind the cutting edge on the face of the wheel. Then rotate the drill clockwise, at the same time swing-

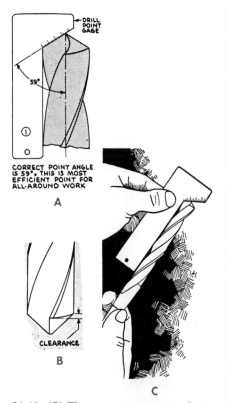

24-40. *(A) The correct point angle is 59 degrees on either side of the axis, or an included angle of 118 degrees. (B) Notice the clearance behind the cutting edge. (C) Check the angle and length of the cutting edge with a drill gauge.*

ing the shank down in an arc of about 20 degrees. Grind a little off both sides. Continue to grind and test the point until the cutting edges are sharp and both are the same length. Fig. 24-40. Usually one or two light twists on both lips will bring the drill to a sharp point.

A drill-grinding attachment is available on some grinders. With this anyone can do an excellent job of sharpening a drill. The grinding is done on the face of the wheel. The drill is clamped in a V groove, and the grinder is turned on. Then an adjustment is made so that the cut-

ting edge of the tool touches the wheel. The handle is rotated to grind one lip. The drill is then reversed in the holder and the other lip is ground. The micrometer setting insures evenly ground lips.

25 Planer or Surfacer

The purpose of the planer or surfacer is to smooth stock and to cut it to uniform thickness. *The planer will not straighten warped stock.* The pressure of the infeed roll will momentarily flatten a warped board as it moves under the cutterhead, but the board will resume its warped shape as soon as it leaves the outfeed rolls. Therefore one face of a warped piece should be planed true on the jointer.

Planers are made with either single or double surfacing knives. The single planer cuts only the top surface. The double planer cuts both top and bottom at the same time. Most small to medium planers have only one cutting head. Fig. 25-1.

PARTS AND CONTROLS

The planer is ruggedly built to take the shock and stress of cutting wide lumber surfaces. The size of a planer is determined by the length of the knives, or the widest stock that can be surfaced. Planers range in size from 12" to 52". The 18" to

30" sizes are the most common. Fig. 25-2. The table moves up and down on two screws or by sliding on a wedge-shaped casting. A cross section of the planer head in Fig. 25-3 shows its major parts.

The upper and lower infeed rolls move the stock into the cutterhead. The *upper infeed roll* is corrugated and usually made in sections. Fig. 25-4. With the sectional infeed roll, several pieces of slightly different

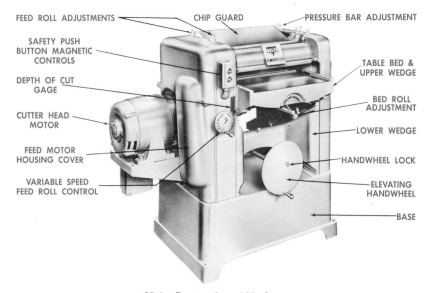

25-1. *Parts of an 18" planer.*

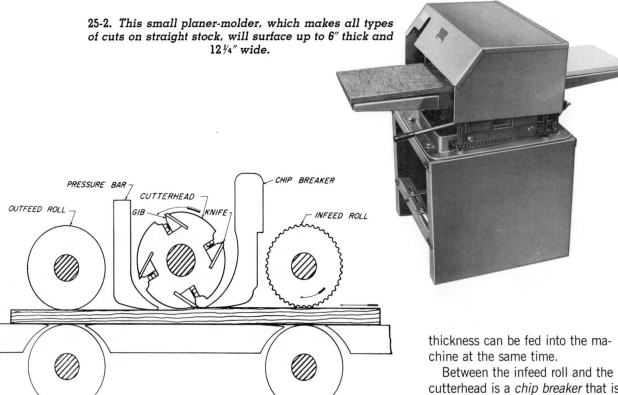

25-2. This small planer-molder, which makes all types of cuts on straight stock, will surface up to 6" thick and 12¼" wide.

25-3. Parts of a two-roll planer head. Most medium-size planers have two infeed rolls.

thickness can be fed into the machine at the same time.

Between the infeed roll and the cutterhead is a *chip breaker* that is also usually made in sections. Fig. 25-5. The edge of the chip breaker is set fairly close to the knives and

SURFACER-PLANER

MAINTENANCE
• Make sure the planer knives are sharp. Grind and joint as necessary (See Chapter 24).
• Check to see that the bed moves up and down easily. If there is too much wear and "play," the *gibs* must be tightened. (A gib is shown in Fig. 25-4.)
• Make sure the feed rolls are clean. If they are coated with pitch, clean them off with a rag soaked in benzine.
• Adjust the knives, chip breaker, and pressure bar to the manufacturer's specifications.
• Make sure the dust-collection system is not overloaded and is working properly.

LUBRICATION
• Use S.A.E. No. 40 lubricating oil on the infeed- and outfeed-roll bearings.
• Use S.A.E. No. 10 lubricating oil on the table gibs.

SAFETY
• Wear proper clothing and eye protection. (See Chapter 4.)
• Know the location of the stop switch, elevating handwheel, and brake (if any) so you can stop the machine quickly.
• Check the wood for defects such as large knots that might cause the board to split under pressure.

• Never surface painted or varnished stock. In fact, used lumber of any kind should not be surfaced.
• Make sure that the board to be surfaced has one true surface.
• The shortest board that should be run through the machine should be 2" longer than the distance between the infeed and outfeed rolls.
• Always stand to one side of the table, never directly in line with the stock.
• Try to determine grain direction and feed the stock into the machine so that the cutting will be done with the grain.
• As the feed rolls take hold of the stock, allow the machine to do the work. Take your hands off the board.
• If a board gets stuck in the machine, turn off the machine. Then lower the bed.
• Never stoop down to watch a board being surfaced.
• Be especially careful of your fingers when surfacing a short board. Sometimes the infeed rolls will tip the board up and then down quickly so that the fingers get pinched between the tabletop and the stock.
• If the stock is long, get someone to help you take the stock off as it leaves the machine.

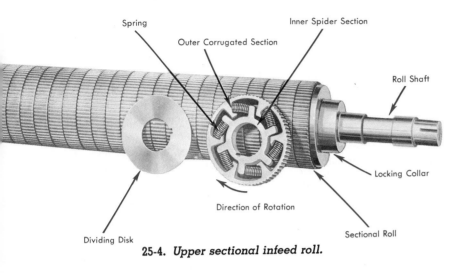

Spring
Outer Corrugated Section
Inner Spider Section
Roll Shaft
Locking Collar
Direction of Rotation
Dividing Disk
Sectional Roll

25-4. *Upper sectional infeed roll.*

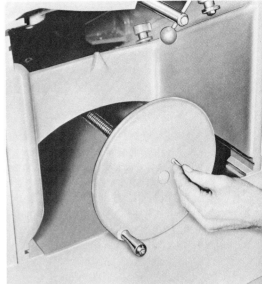

25-6. *To adjust for the correct depth of cut, loosen the handwheel lock and turn the elevating handwheel up or down. The finish thickness will register on the depth-of-cut gauge.*

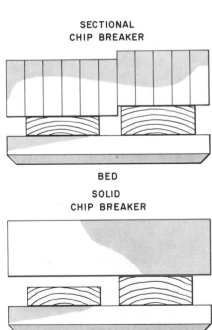

SECTIONAL
CHIP BREAKER

BED

SOLID
CHIP BREAKER

BED

25-5. *Note the advantage of a sectional chip breaker when surfacing two or more pieces of slightly different thickness. If a solid chip breaker is used, there is no pressure on the thinner stock. As a result, the cutterhead tears the grain.*

can be adjusted up and down slightly. This device keeps the stock firmly pressed to the bed and prevents torn grain. If there were no chip breaker, the stock would tend to tear or split off in long slivers.

The *cutterhead* itself is cylindrical. It has three or more knives which smooth the upper surface of the board and cut it to uniform thickness. As the shavings fly off, they are drawn into the exhaust system which is fitted over the top of the planer.

Just beyond the cutterhead is the *pressure bar* which holds the stock firmly to the bed after the cut is made.

Finally, the board passes between the smooth *upper* and *lower outfeed rolls*. These help to move the stock out of the machine.

The kind and number of controls on a planer vary somewhat with its size. There is a switch to turn the power on and off. All machines have an elevating handwheel that moves the bed up and down to control the depth of cut. Fig. 25-6. Additionally, some types have a quick control for changing from rough to finish surfacing. There is usually a feed control that determines the rate at which the stock moves into the cutters. Fig. 25-7. On some larger machines a speed control is available for changing the RPM of the cutterhead. The two most common adjustments, however, are to raise and

lower the bed and to adjust the feed. The cutterhead normally operates at a fixed speed of about 3600 RPM. The feed rate should be var-

25-7. *The feed control changes the rate at which the stock moves through the planer. Usually a fast feed is used for softwoods, slower for hardwoods.*

ied with the width of stock, the kind of wood, and the desired quality of the surfaces. Fairly wide, hard pieces of wood should be fed at relatively slow speed, and narrower pieces of softer wood at a higher feed rate.

OPERATING PROCEDURE

1. If long stock is to be surfaced, it is a good idea to get someone to help at the other end. If no one can help, place a roller ("dead man") at the "out" end of the planer to support the stock.

2. Before planing a warped board, true one face on the jointer.

3. If possible, determine the grain direction of each piece and feed *with* the grain. Place the pieces conveniently near the infeed table with the grain in the proper direction.

4. Measure the thickness of the stock and adjust the machine to remove about 1⁄16″ to 1⁄8″. Generally a piece is surfaced in one to three cuts. For example, if stock measures 1″ and you wish to reduce it to 13⁄16″, adjust the planer so that the first cut will be 1⁄8″ (2⁄16″). Then the second cut should be 1⁄16″.

5. Turn on the power and allow the planer to come to full speed. To avoid injury from kickback, stand to one side, *never directly behind the stock.* Fig. 25-8. Feed the stock into the infeed rolls and, as soon as it takes hold, remove your hands

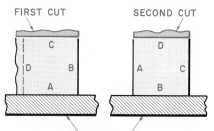

25-9. *Squaring up furniture legs on a planer.*

from the stock. Never let your fingers get under the edges.

6. If the wood starts into the machine slightly crooked, a tap on the edge will straighten it. If the stock sticks, turn off the machine immediately and lower the bed.

7. If large amounts of stock must be removed, always take some off both faces. If this is not done, the board will tend to cup because it has slightly more moisture toward the center than it does at the outside. (When a board warps so that its edges are higher than its center, this is called "cup.")

8. When stock has been glued up to make a larger surface, it is impossible to true or face it on the jointer. To do it on the planer, first remove all the glue from the surface. Then adjust the machine to a slow feed and a light cut. Place the best face on the bed of the planer and true one side. Then reverse the stock, readjust for thickness, and plane.

SQUARING LEGS

A common use for the planer is to square up stock to be used for legs, especially for Contemporary furniture.

Begin the squaring operation by cutting the stock to rough size. Joint one face and then one edge 90 degrees to the jointed face. (This face and edge are shown as sides A and B in Fig. 25-9.) Mark these surfaces for identification. Place the stock with jointed surface

on the planer table and the jointed edge to the right. Set the planer for the necessary cut. Fig. 25-9, side C. Make the cut.

As the stock comes from the outfeed table of the planer, special care should be taken not to alter the position of the pieces. Place the stock on the infeed table in the same position as for the first cut, then turn each piece one-quarter turn clockwise. Don't change the thickness setting.

Feed the stock through the planer for the second cut. Fig. 25-9, side D. Measure the stock and, if necessary, repeat the two cuts on sides A and B. It may also be necessary to make additional cuts on sides C and D. Continue until the stock is the correct size. Remember, try to plan your cuts so that an equal amount of material is removed from all sides.

PLANING THIN STOCK

If very thin stock must be planed, it is a good idea to use a backing board. This is true for all stock 3⁄8″ or less in thickness. Make sure that the backing board is true, smooth, and at least 3⁄4″ thick. Place the backing board on the bed and then put the thin stock on it. Adjust for the correct depth of cut, taking into consideration the thickness of the backing board. Then run the two

25-8. *Feeding stock into a planer.*

25-10. *Surfacing thin stock. Use a backing board so that the piece will not split.*

boards together through the surfacer. Fig. 25-10.

SURFACING SEVERAL SHORT PIECES

If several short pieces of the same thickness (such as four rails for a table) are to be surfaced at the same time, butt the ends together as they are fed through the planer. This helps keep the wood moving and eliminates the possibility of a clip or snipe dip. A *clip* or

snipe is a small, concave cut at the end of the stock.

The last board should always be a longer board, equal to at least 2″ more than the distance between the feed rolls. Feed the pieces at a slight angle to improve the quality of the surface. Fig. 25-11.

25-11. *Surface short stock by feeding one board behind the other at a slight angle.*

26 Circular or Variety Saw

The circular saw, also called a variety or table saw, is a most versatile machine. Fig. 26-1. It is used more than any other tool in the cabinet shop because a great deal of the basic cutting for construction can be done on it. Fig. 26-2. The saw consists of a heavy frame with a *table* and an *arbor*. The arbor holds the saw and revolves. The shaft in the arbor is connected to the motor by belts and pulleys. The table of the saw remains in a fixed, horizontal position, and the arbor tilts.

The size of the saw is determined by the diameter of the blade recommended for use. Sizes range from 8″ bench models to 16″ production machines. Most common for schools and cabinet shops is the 10″ size.

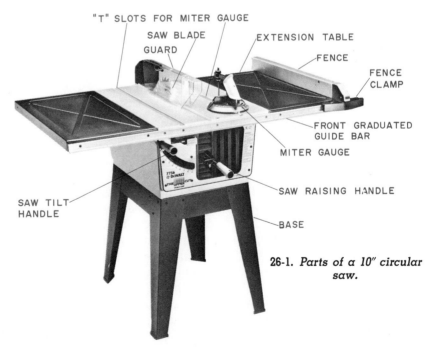

26-1. *Parts of a 10″ circular saw.*

CIRCULAR SAW

MAINTENANCE

- Keep all working parts free from sawdust and other substances that might wear down the parts.
- Clean out the sawdust from the base at regular intervals.
- Check the V belts to make sure they are in good condition. Avoid oil, grease, and other substances that would ruin the rubber.
- Keep the belts just snug enough to operate smoothly without slipping.
- Make sure the pulleys are aligned and tight on the shafts. If necessary to align them, use a narrow board with a double bevel on one edge as a guide.
- Make sure all safety devices operate easily, especially the guard.
- Make sure the fence is parallel to the saw blade. This can be checked by aligning the fence with the miter-gauge slot. If the fence isn't parallel, check the manufacturer's instructions for correcting it.
- Raise the saw blade to the highest position and check the angle between the tabletop and the blade with a combination square. Make sure the combination square is against the blade and between the teeth. If the blade is not perpendicular when set on zero, reset following manufacturer's instructions.
- Keep all machine surfaces, such as the tabletop, free of rust or corrosion.
- Set the miter gauge at the 90-degree position and check with a combination square against the blade to make sure that gauge and blade are at right angles. If not, readjust the miter gauge. Also check the 45-degree positions right and left to make sure they are accurate.
- Make sure the insert plate is in good condition. Replace it if necessary.

LUBRICATION

- Clean out all moving parts with a whisk broom or brush, then lubricate with oil or a good grade of ball-bearing grease. Don't over-lubricate since that would just collect dust. Wipe off excess oil or grease, being careful not to get any on the belt.
- Lubricate sliding ways of trunnion brackets with powdered graphite.
- Motor bearings are sealed and require no further lubrication.

SAFETY

- Wear proper clothing and eye protection. (See Chapter 4.)
- Use the saw guard as much as possible. Only a few operations can't be done with the guard in place. This is especially true of flexible guards. If a standard guard can't be used, use other safety devices such as a push stick, feather board, holding jig, fixture, and saw cover.
- Adjust the saw so that it clears the top of the stock by about ⅛" to ¼". The only exception to this is when using a hollow-ground blade. Then it is better if the blade projects above the stock enough to keep the cutting edge from overheating and burning the teeth.
- Make sure the blade is sharp and properly mounted.
- Make all adjustments with the saw at a "dead" stop. Never try to stop the rotating blade by holding a stick against it.
- Never attempt freehand cuts on the circular saw.
- Always stand to one side, never directly behind the saw blade.
- Make sure the miter gauge works freely in the slots and that it will clear both sides of the blade when tilted. On some saws the miter gauge can be used on only one side when the blade is tilted.
- Hold the work firmly against the miter gauge when crosscutting. Keep your fingers away from the line of cut.
- Never reach over the saw to pick up a piece of stock, even with the guard in place. Walk around.
- Never clear scraps away with your fingers. Have a stick at least 2' long for removing them.
- Always fasten a clearance block to the fence when cutting off duplicate parts.
- When ripping long stock, have someone assist you to "tail off" the work. However, never allow the person to pull or tilt the board as it is being ripped. The operator must always be in full charge.
- If a helper is not available, use a roller support to help hold up long stock as it is being ripped.
- When the piece is narrow, use a push stick to complete the cut.
- Before ripping make sure the fence is locked. During the operation use the splitter and anti-kickback fingers as well as the guard.
- Be sure the guard will not strike the saw when the blade is tilted for bevel and angle cuts.
- Allow the saw to come to full speed before starting to cut.
- Turn off the power immediately if the saw doesn't sound right.
- Watch carefully what you are doing. Avoid distractions and never look around while operating the saw.
- When the cutting is complete, turn off the power. Stay next to the machine until it comes to a dead stop.
- Always remove special setups and any waste stock, and leave the machine in normal operating condition.

The *rip fence* is a metal guide clamped on the table parallel to the saw blade. It is used for all ripping operations. Fig. 26-3. A clamp handle fastens it securely in place after it is adjusted. There is usually a knob for fine adjustments as well. The fence is predrilled with holes so that an auxiliary wood fence can be fastened to it. In many kinds of cutting this is necessary to eliminate danger of the saw blade striking metal fence. The fence usually is to the right of the saw. It is important that the fence be absolutely parallel with the blade.

The *miter gauge* is used for all crosscutting operations. Fig. 26-4. It slides into slots milled in the tabletop. There is one slot to the left and one to the right of the saw blade. On most saws, the miter gauge can be put into either slot, even when the blade is tilted. It is well to check this, however, because there are certain models in which it must be used only on one side when the blade is tilted. A *stop rod* can be clamped to the miter gauge to control the length of cut.

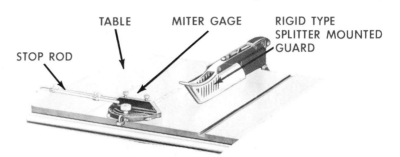

26-4. *A miter gauge is used for crosscutting. It slides into slots in the table. A stop rod can be fastened to the gauge to control length of cut.*

26-2. *A great deal of cutting must be done on the circular saw to produce this table.*

COMMON ADJUSTMENTS

The *saw-raising handwheel* raises or lowers the blade. The distance the saw projects above the work is very important. For safety, allow the blade to project only about ⅛" to ¼" above the stock. A high blade is more dangerous. Its greater area of contact with the stock is more likely to cause kickback. However, this does not apply to a hollow-ground blade, which should project well above the stock to keep the edge from overheating. A high blade is actually better mechanically because it cuts with less power and produces a cleaner edge. (Safety measures against kickback are discussed on this page and on page 172.) Be sure to loosen the locknut before making the height adjustment. Retighten it afterward.

The *tilt handwheel* is used to adjust the blade for angle cutting. It also has a locknut. A *tilt scale* with a *pointer* shows the exact angle of the tilt. This should be checked frequently by adjusting the saw to a 45-degree angle and holding a protractor or the head of a combination square between the blade and the tabletop. It is also a good idea to check the setting at 90 degrees to make sure the blade is at right angles to the tabletop. Then check the miter gauge with the side of the blade to make sure it is square.

GUARDS AND OTHER SAFETY DEVICES

Several protective devices are standard equipment. A *guard* should cover the saw whenever possible. Because protection has always been a problem, many different kinds of guards have been developed. With some guards, certain operations can't be performed. When it is necessary to remove the guard, always use a jig, fixture, or holding device.

The *basket guard*, made of metal or plastic, is the least satisfactory. Fig. 26-4. There are also several types of metal or plastic twin-action guards. Fig. 26-5. The sides of these move independently of one another. Such guards can be used when the blade is at an angle. Another type, all plastic, can be used when performing practically any standard operation. Fig. 26-6. It is fitted to the side of the tabletop.

A *splitter*, a piece of metal directly behind the blade, is used to keep the saw kerf open. This prevents the

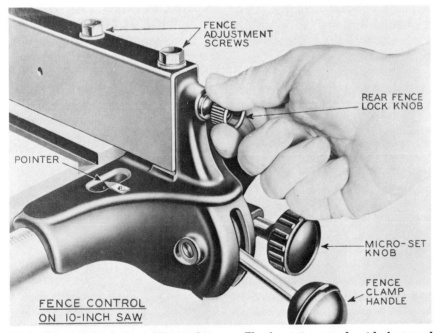

26-3. *Fence controls for a 10" circular saw. The fence is a steel guide fastened to the table, parallel with and usually to the right of the blade. The fence clamp handle is released and the fence moved sideways to adjust for width of cut. For final, precise adjustment, the micro-set knob is pushed in and turned. When the exact setting is obtained, the clamp handle is pushed down.*

173

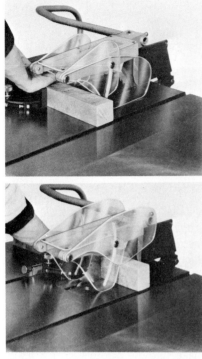

26-5. *This twin-action plastic guard gives excellent protection throughout the cut. The front shield rises as the work enters, then returns to place as the work moves on to raise the second shield.*

26-7. *The most common dado head consists of two blades and several different thicknesses of chippers. An assembled dado head is shown at left.*

wood from binding on the blade and causing kickback. It is especially important to use the splitter for all ripping operations. Many splitters are equipped with metal fingers or hold-downs that provide added anti-kickback protection.

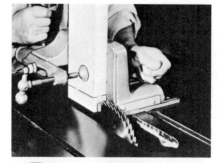

26-6. *Using a plastic guard while cutting a dado. This transparent guard can be used for all standard cutting operations.*

COMMERCIAL ACCESSORIES

There are five common accessories for the circular saw:

• A *dado head* for cutting wide grooves and dadoes. There are several types, but the most common is a set of blades and chippers. Fig. 26-7.

• A *tenoner* for making tenons and other end-grain cuts. The stock is clamped to it, and the device slides along the slot in the table. Fig. 26-8.

• A *clamp attachment* for the miter gauge. It holds the work se-

26-8. *The commercial tenoner can be used to make all kinds of cuts on end grain. NOTE: For some photos the guard was removed so that details could be seen. The guard symbol in the caption indicates you should use the guard when performing this operation.*

curely for accurate miter and cutoff operations. Fig. 26-9.

• A *molding cutterhead* with many different sets of knives for molding and shaping operations. Fig. 26-10.

• A *sliding table attachment*, used when cutting large panel stock. Fig. 26-11.

SELECTING THE SAW BLADES

Some saw blades are designed for special-purpose cutting. The more common ones include the following:

• The *crosscut* or *cutoff* saw blade has fine crosscut teeth designed primarily for cutting across grain. It is flat-ground, with the teeth set for clearance. Fig. 26-12.

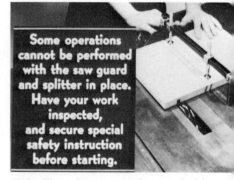

Some operations cannot be performed with the saw guard and splitter in place. Have your work inspected, and secure special safety instruction before starting.

26-9. *The clamp attachment holds stock in place for crosscutting.*

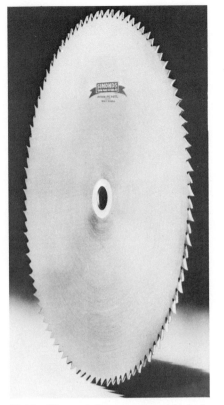

26-12. *The cutoff or crosscut blade is for cutting across grain.*

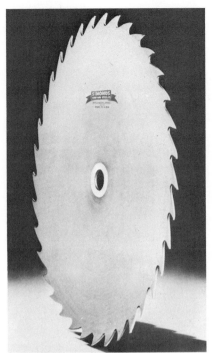

26-13. *A ripsaw blade is designed for cutting with the grain.*

26-10. *There are many different designs of molding heads. Matched cutters are needed to fit each type.*

- The *ripsaw* blade has larger teeth and is designed for cutting with the grain on all varieties of woods. Fig. 26-13.
- The *combination* saw blade is designed for general ripping and crosscut work. It is flat-ground and is good for the faster cutting required for ripping, crosscutting, and mitering. There are several designs. Fig. 26-14. Sometimes the combi-

nation saw is hollow-ground. This makes added clearance possible so that the saw will not tend to overheat. A *planer* saw blade is a

smooth-cutting hollow-ground combination saw. It is thinner toward the center than near the teeth. The *plywood combination* blade trims and cuts plywood smoothly, reducing splinters and slivers. Fig. 26-15.

- *Carbide-tipped blades* are extremely useful for high-production work and for cutting hardboard, plastic laminates, and other composition materials. Carbide is the name given to several different alloys of carbon and such metals as tungsten, titanium, and tantalum. It is extremely hard, almost as hard as diamond. It maintains a sharp cutting edge under conditions that would cause other tools to burn. Small carbide tips are brazed onto the blade. Such blades are made in all standard designs. Fig. 26-16.

REPLACING A BLADE

A soft metal *insert plate* surrounds the blade. Press the rear of this and lift it out of place. Then select a wrench that exactly fits the arbor nut. Check the direction for

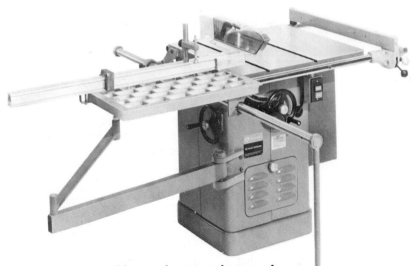

26-11. *A sliding table attachment makes panel cutting easy and accurate.*

175

A

B

26-14. *Two styles of combination saws: (A) This has teeth of the most common shape. (B) This will do a good job of cutting wood in several directions.*

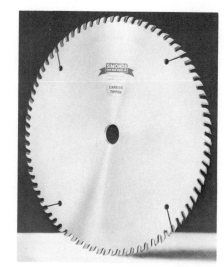

A

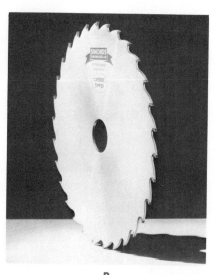

B

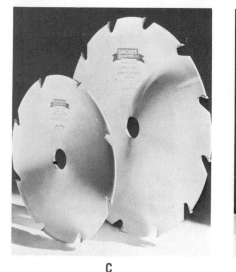

C

D

26-16. *Common carbide-tipped blades: (A) Crosscut. (B) Rip. (C) Easy cut. This one has only a few teeth and is considered very safe since it practically eliminates kickback. (D) Combination.*

26-15. *A plywood saw. This is one of many special-purpose saws. Another is designed specifically for cutting flooring to length, and still others for miter cuts and similar production work.*

loosening the nut before you start. Most arbor shafts have a lefthand thread that is loosened by turning it to the right, or clockwise. However, some are just the opposite. Force a piece of softwood against the blade and loosen the nut. Fig. 26-17. Remove the collar and the blade. Slide the new blade over the shaft threads, making sure that the tips point toward the operator and that the manufacturer's name is uppermost. Then replace the arbor washer and the nut. Tighten the nut securely and replace the insert plate. Rotate the blade by hand to make sure it is running free and clear.

CROSSCUTTING OPERATIONS

Simple Crosscutting

For all crosscutting operations the miter gauge should be used. Before starting, check the 90-degree angle of the miter gauge with a square.

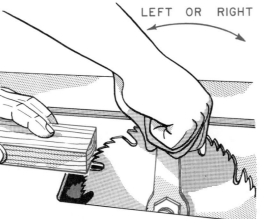

LEFT OR RIGHT

26-17. *Replacing a blade.*

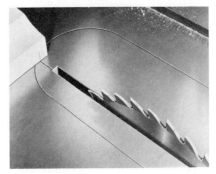

26-20. *A scribed line on the table insert makes it easy to line up the cut.*

26-18. *An auxiliary wood fence attached to a miter gauge.*

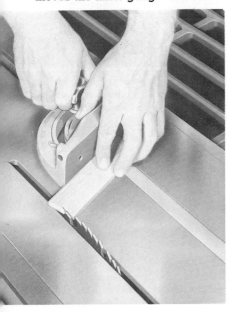

26-19. *It is good practice to use both hands for crosscutting. One hand should hold the work against the miter gauge while the other hand moves the miter gauge forward.*

Adjust the pointer when necessary. Frequently an auxiliary fence or facing strip is attached to the miter gauge to add support and for making special cuts. An auxiliary fence made of wood can be screwed or bolted to the miter gauge; this adds support for all types of work. Fig. 26-18. A scale (rule) can be fitted into the wood fence, and a piece of abrasive cloth can be glued to this fence to help hold the work securely. Normally the miter gauge is used in the left slot with the slide in front. The work is then held firmly against the miter gauge with the left hand while the right hand pushes the gauge along. Fig. 26-19.

The usual method is to mark the cutting line across the face or front edge of the stock. Sometimes a fine line is filed in the insert plate directly in line with one side of the saw blade. Because most of the cutting is done with the miter gauge located in the left slot, the line should extend back from the left side of the blade. Align this line with the cutting line on the stock. Fig. 26-20.

When cutting stock to length, especially for production work, it is often a good idea to use two miter gauges. The one on the right side is used to cut the left end square. The one on the left side has a stop block attached to the auxiliary

fence, for cutting the second end to exact length. The miter gauge can also be reversed in the slot for cutting wide stock. Fig. 26-21.

Cutting Duplicate Parts

There are several common ways of cutting parts to exact length. These methods are especially helpful when more than one piece must be cut to the same length.

● One way is to attach a stop block to the fence to control the length of cut. Make sure that the block is just in front of the blade itself so that once the cut is made the pieces will be free and clear and will not bind. Thus there will be no kickback. *Never attempt to use the fence itself as a stop block.* The

26-21. *A wider board can be cut with ease by reversing the miter gauge in the slot.*

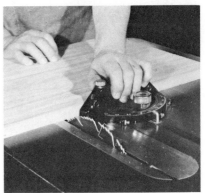

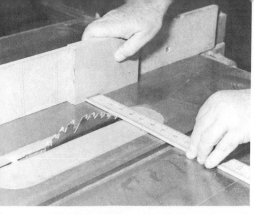

26-22(a). Measuring the length needed to cut duplicate parts.

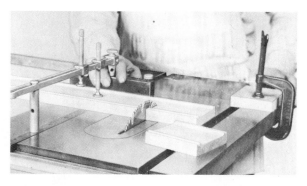

26-23. This is another good method of cutting shorter pieces to length. The miter-gauge clamp is excellent for holding the stock very accurately in the location established by the stop block.

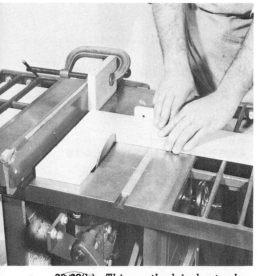

26-22(b). This method is best when cutting several shorter pieces from a long piece of stock. Note space between the fence and the pieces that have been cut off. This reduces danger of kickback.

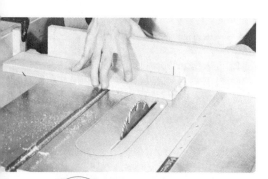

26-22(c). This method is best when cutting individual pieces to length after the first end has been cut square. Note that both ends can be cut off with one setup. The first end is cut with the stock to the left of the saw. Then the stock is cut to length by shifting it over to the right until it strikes the stop block.

block *must not* make contact with the work during the cutting. Fig. 26-22.

Place the stop block against the fence opposite the saw blade. Move the fence and block until the distance between the block and the right side of the blade is equal to the desired length. Lock the fence. Then move the block to about 4" from the front of the table. Clamp the block to the fence and do the cutting.

• Another way is to clamp a stop block directly to the tabletop at the front corner, on the side opposite the miter gauge. Fig. 26-23.

• A third way is to use a stop rod on the miter gauge. The rod can be set to any position so that all pieces are exactly the same length. Fig. 26-24.

• A fourth method is to attach a stop block to the auxiliary fence. Fig. 26-25.

Cutting Flat Miters

Flat miters are diagonal cuts made at an angle to the edge of the work. A 45-degree miter is the most common one for making square or rectangular frames. However, it is often necessary to cut miters at other angles.

The gauge can be set and used in either the open or closed position. Fig. 26-26. Closed is usually better because the work is then easier to control. However, unless the stock is held very tightly, it will creep while the cut is being made. This

26-24. Using the stop rod on the miter gauge is a quick, accurate way of cutting several pieces to the same length. Remember to square one end of each piece first.

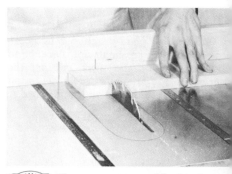

26-25(a). Here a stop block is clamped to the auxiliary fence or facing strip to control the length.

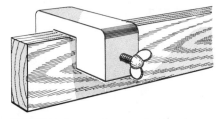

26-25(b). A simple wood clamp can be made that will eliminate the need for a block.

OPEN POSITION

CLOSED POSITION

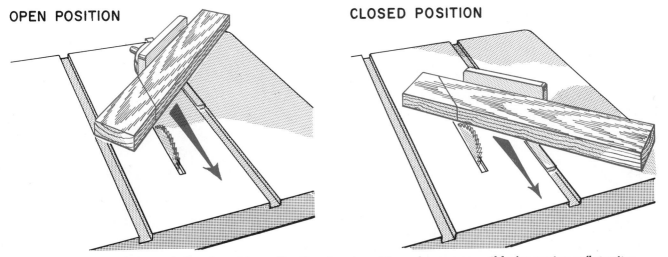

26-26. *Gauge in open and closed positions. Use the closed position whenever possible for cutting a flat miter.*

results in a less than perfect fitting angle. This can be corrected by having the saw blade very sharp, clamping the work to the miter gauge, and feeding the stock slowly. The open position can be used if the work is clamped to the miter gauge.

Several types of jigs can be used for accurate mitering. Either of the jigs shown in Fig. 26-27 and 26-28 will produce a perfect 45-degree right- and left-hand miter. Both types will hold the stock securely.

Cutting a Bevel across Grain

A bevel or edge miter is made by tilting the blade to the correct angle, usually 45 degrees, and using the miter gauge set at right angles. Fig. 26-29. Check the angle of tilt on the tilt gauge or, for more accurate work, use a sliding T bevel. Adjust the height of the blade for the thickness of stock. Also decide on whether to make the cut from the right or left side of the blade. Before turning on the power, slide the gauge along the slot to make sure the blade will not hit the gauge. It may be necessary to move the gauge to the opposite side. Hold the stock firmly against the gauge. Make the cut like any crosscut.

Cutting Sheet Materials

Because of its size, panel stock is hard to cut. Always adjust the blade so that it just clears the top. Place the stock with the good side up. There are several ways of doing the cutting:

• When the cut is started, reverse the miter gauge in the groove to guide the stock along as far as possible. Then the gauge can be removed and slipped into the regular position to complete the cut. Fig. 26-30.

• Panel stock can be cut with the fence acting as a guide. Fig. 26-31.

• A board with a straight edge can be clamped to the underside of the plywood. Fig. 26-32. This will act as a guide against the edge of the table. This method is especially

26-27(a). *Using a mitering jig to cut a 45-degree corner.*

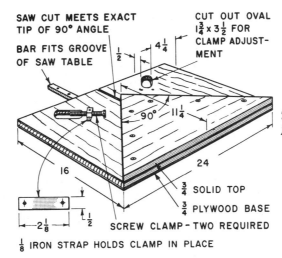

SAW CUT MEETS EXACT TIP OF 90° ANGLE

BAR FITS GROOVE OF SAW TABLE

CUT OUT OVAL $1\frac{3}{4} \times 3\frac{1}{2}$ FOR CLAMP ADJUSTMENT

$\frac{1}{2}$ $4\frac{1}{4}$

90° $11\frac{1}{4}$

16

24

$\frac{3}{4}$ SOLID TOP

$\frac{3}{4}$ PLYWOOD BASE

$2\frac{1}{8}$ $1\frac{1}{2}$

SCREW CLAMP - TWO REQUIRED

$\frac{1}{8}$ IRON STRAP HOLDS CLAMP IN PLACE

26-27(b). *One type of mitering jig, having a plywood base and a solid top.*

179

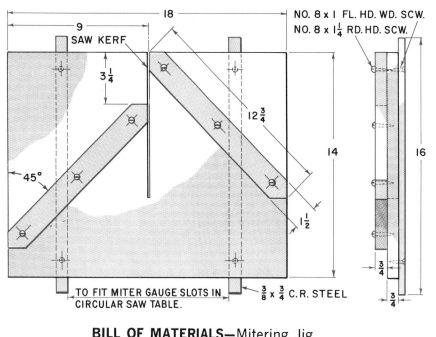

BILL OF MATERIALS—Mitering Jig

No. of Pieces	Name	Size
1	Mounting Board	¾ x 14 x 18
2	Guide Strips	¾ x 1½ x 12¾
2	Metal Guide Bars (C.R.S.)	⅜ x ¾ x 16
4	Round Head Wood Screws	No. 8 x 1¼
4	Flat Head Wood Screws	No. 8 x 1

26-28. *This mitering jig is made from ¾" plywood, fitted with metal guidebars that ride in the slots. For precision miter cuts, make the screw holes in the two guide strips about ¹⁄₁₆" larger than the screw shank to allow for adjustments.*

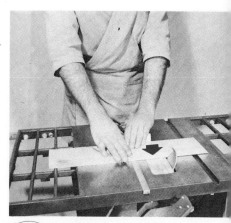

26-29. *Cutting a bevel across grain by tilting the saw blade to 45 degrees.*

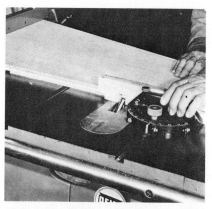

26-30. *The miter gauge is reversed in the slot and the fence used as a guide when cutting dadoes on a large plywood piece. If cutting through the stock, the fence should not be used.*

26-31. *Wide panel stock can be cut with the fence acting as a guide. An extension table will make it easier to handle the stock.*

good if one edge of the plywood is uneven.

● If a sliding table attachment is available, the panel can be held against the fence to do the cutting. Fig. 26-33.

Making a Compound Miter Cut

A compound miter cut, sometimes called a hopper or bevel miter, is a combination of a miter and a bevel. To make this cut, adjust the blade to the correct tilt and the miter gauge to the correct angle. Figs. 26-34 and 26-35.

RIPPING OPERATIONS

Ripping is cutting a board lengthwise with the grain. Use either a ripsaw or a combination saw blade. The fence is normally used as a guide to position and maintain the stock for the correct width of cut. It is usually placed to the right of the blade, although you can rip on either side of the blade. In all ripping operations, the stock should make solid contact with the top of the table and the fence so that it will not wobble or get out of line. Before ripping, make sure one edge is straight. The major hazard is kickback. If the kerf that is already formed binds on the saw, the stock is likely to shoot back with great force and injure anyone in its path. Several things can be done to minimize this danger.

● Never stand directly in back of

180

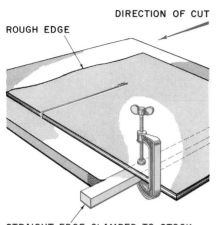

DIRECTION OF CUT

ROUGH EDGE

STRAIGHT EDGE CLAMPED TO STOCK

26-32. *A board that has a straight edge can be clamped to the underside of the stock and used as a guide against the edge of the saw table. If there is danger that the surface may be damaged, place a piece of scrap stock over as well as under the panel stock.*

26-33. *Cutting a 4 × 8 foot panel. The panel is held against the fence.*

the saw or in line with the revolving blade. Always stand behind and to the side of the saw, reaching over with the right hand to push the stock through. Fig. 26-36.

• Use a splitter to keep the kerf open. Fig. 26-37. Often there are

anti-kickback fingers on the splitter's top. These bear on the wood and keep it from moving backwards.

• Always make use of a guard when ripping. There are a few ripping operations that can't be done with the guard. If these must be done, use other protective devices.

• Never rip stock with loose or large, unsound knots. If a knot becomes loose just after it is cut in two, it can fly out with terrific force. Always knock out loose knots with a hammer before starting to saw.

Accessories for Ripping

There are several accessories for ripping. When sawing long lumber,

TABLE OF COMPOUND ANGLES

Tilt of Work	Equivalent taper per Inch	Four-Sided Butt		Four-Sided Miter		Six-Sided Miter		Eight Sided Miter	
		Bevel Degrees	Miter Degrees	Bevel Degrees	Miter Degrees	Bevel Degrees	Miter Degrees	Bevel Degrees	Miter Degrees
5°	0.087	½	85	44¾	85	29¾	87½	22¼	88
10°	0.176	1½	80¼	44¼	80¼	29½	84½	22	86
15°	0.268	3¾	75½	43¼	75½	29	81¾	21½	84
20°	0.364	6¼	71¼	41¾	71¼	28¼	79	21	82
25°	0.466	10	67	40	67	27¼	76½	20¼	80
30°	0.577	14½	63½	37¾	63½	26	74	19½	78¼
35°	0.700	19½	60¼	35½	60¼	24½	71¾	18¼	76¾
40°	0.839	24½	57¼	32½	57¼	22¾	69¾	17	75
45°	1.000	30	54¾	30	54¾	21	67¾	15¾	73¾
50°	1.19	36	52½	27	52½	19	66¼	14½	72½
55°	1.43	42	50¾	24	50¾	16¾	64¾	12½	71¼
60°	1.73	48	49	21	49	14½	63½	11	70¼

26-34. *This table of compound angles must be consulted before making a compound miter cut. For example, suppose you wish to cut a four-sided mitered frame with the sides tilted to 20 degrees. Look across the column to the 4-sided miter. Note that the tilt of the blade must be 41¾ degrees and that the miter gauge must be adjusted to 71¼ degrees.*

26-35. *Making a compound miter cut with the blade tilted and the miter gauge set at an angle.*

26-37. *The splitter helps to hold the kerf open. A push stick is good for final ripping.*

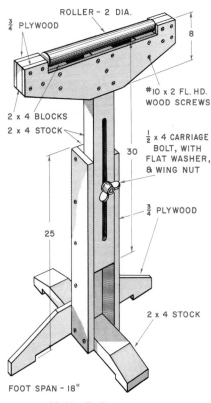

26-38. *Roller support.*

a *roller support* is needed at the outfeed end of the cutting. This device is especially useful if a helper is not available. Fig. 26-38. For ripping narrow stock, a *push stick* or *push block* is needed. There are many types of these. Fig. 26-39. It is good to have several different types and thicknesses ready. In every case, the *thickness* of the push stick should be *less than the distance between the saw and the fence.*

26-36. *Ripping on the circular saw.*

Another device that is extremely useful is a *feather board* or *spring board.* Fig. 26-40. This is a piece of wood cut on one end at an angle of about 45 degrees, with slots cut in the same end to make it somewhat flexible. The feather board, which is used to apply side pressure for ripping, should always be just in front of the saw blade. Fig. 26-41. Side pressure should never be applied to the blade as stock is being cut. A second feather board can be used to hold the stock firmly against the table. Fig. 26-42. Such an arrangement is good for resawing stock.

Many operators like to add an *auxiliary wood fence* to the metal one. While it isn't necessary for straight ripping, it is essential for work that involves the dado or molding head. It is also a good idea when thin stock is being ripped or whenever there is danger that the revolving saw will touch the fence. A piece of wood can be fastened to the inside of the metal fence. However, a wooden fence that fits completely over the metal one, with a recess cut out for the blade, is better. Fig. 26-43.

Ripping Wide Stock

Stock is considered wide when it measures at least 6" between the blade and the fence. Adjust the blade to the correct height by using the stock as a guide. Fig. 26-44. In the correct setting, the blade extends only slightly above the stock. Although the blade cuts less efficiently this way than if it protrudes 2" or 3", this method is safer, and that of course is most important.

The fence may be adjusted for width by holding a rule at right angles to it, Fig. 26-45, or by holding a large square against it, and measuring the desired width. A still more simple method is to place the marked stock against the fence and then move the fence until the cutting line on the stock is directly in back of the saw blade.

Turn on the power. With your left hand, hold the stock against the fence with a slight amount of side pressure. Push the stock forward with the thumb of your right hand. Fig. 26-46. Move the stock as fast as the saw will cut. As you near the end of the cut, continue to press forward with the right hand alone (between the blade and the fence).

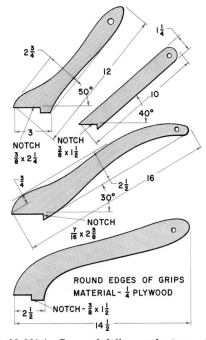

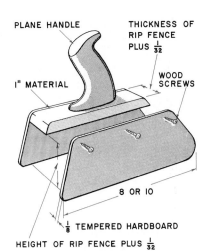

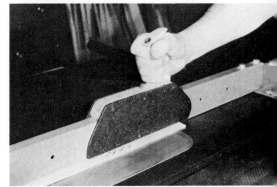

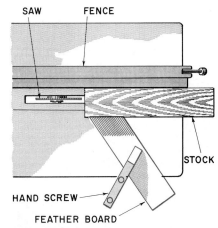

26-39(c). *Using the push block.*

26-39(a). *Several different designs of push sticks. Make sure the stick is always thinner than the width of stock to be cut. If the push stick is too wide, it will not clear between the guard and fence. Even more dangerous, if the saw cuts into the end of the stick, it may flip out of your hand, causing your hand to drop into the saw or making the stock kick back.*

Fig. 26-47. Allow the sawed-off stock to fall to the floor or have a helper (tail-off person) at the rear of

26-39(b). *This push block fits over the fence. It is excellent for cutting thin pieces of panel stock such as hardboard or particle board.*

the saw remove it. In ripping long stock, it is necessary to have a helper or a roller stand to hold the stock level and against the fence. The helper should never pull the stock.

Ripping Narrow Stock

If stock is less than 6″ in width, your hand will not pass safely between the saw and the fence. However, there are safe ways to rip narrow stock. The best method is to use a push stick. This stick should be thinner than the distance between the blade and the fence so

that it never comes in contact with the revolving blade. Apply forward pressure with your right hand and use the left hand to hold the stock firmly against the fence as the cut is started. When the end of the stock is over the front of the table, pick up the push stick. Continue applying pressure with the push stick to complete the cut and to move the stock beyond the revolving blade. Never reach over the saw itself,

26-41. *Note that the feather board is clamped to the table with a hand screw so that the pressure is just ahead of the saw blade. Apply just enough pressure to hold the stock lightly but firmly against the fence. If side pressure is applied next to the saw, it will cause binding which results in kickback.*

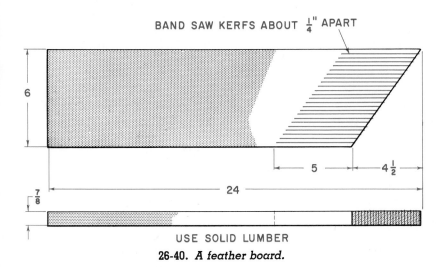

26-40. *A feather board.*

183

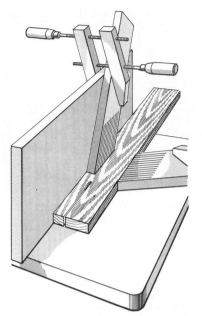

26-42. *This setup is good for ripping long, thin stock. A high auxiliary wood fence should be attached to the metal fence.*

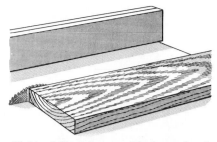

26-44. *Adjust the saw blade so that it extends about ⅛″ to ¼″ above the stock.*

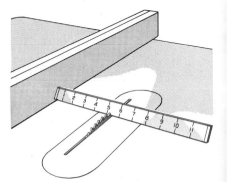

26-45. *Using a rule or square to adjust the fence for width of cut.*

Cutting a Bevel with the Grain

Tilt the blade to the desired angle and adjust for height. On most saws the blade tilts to the right. In such cases the fence should be placed on the left side (operator's view). (If the blade tilts left, the fence goes on the right.) Adjust for width and complete the cut as you would for straight ripping. Fig. 26-50.

Resawing

Resawing involves ripping a board to make one or more thin pieces. The sawing is done in the edges of the stock. While this can be done on the circular saw, the band saw is better for it since the blade is narrower and less stock is wasted. Also, a large band saw can make a wider

even with a guard on it, to pick up the stock. Fig. 26-48.

A second method of ripping narrow stock is to saw slightly more than half the length. Then draw the stock back out of the saw, turn it over end for end, and complete the cut from the other end. Fig. 26-49.

A third method is to use a push block to move the stock forward. Fig. 26-39(b & c).

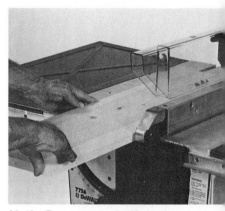

26-46. *Ripping stock. Note the position of the hands. Both hands are needed to start the cut.*

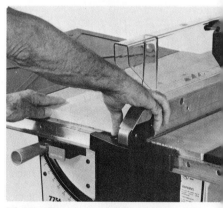

26-47. *When about 12″ are left to be ripped, press forward with the right hand alone. Push the workpiece with your thumb. Use your index and second fingers to hold the stock down, and hook the other two fingers over the fence. Always keep your thumb next to the fence. This procedure can be used only when the distance between the blade and fence is more than 6″.*

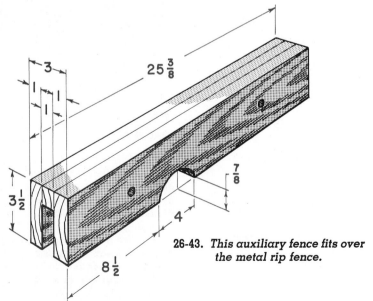

26-43. *This auxiliary fence fits over the metal rip fence.*

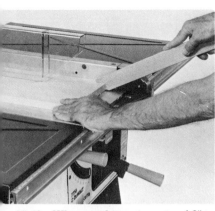

26-48. *When making rip cuts of 2" to 6", always use a push stick. Start the cut in the same way as described in Fig. 26-46. When your hands are within 12" of the blade, complete the cut with a push stick.*

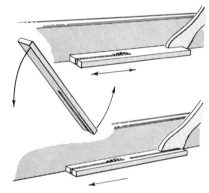

26-49. *Another method of ripping narrow stock. Saw halfway through the stock and then move the stock back out of the saw. Turn the stock end for end and complete the cut.*

26-50. *Cutting a bevel with the grain. Here the blade is set too high.*

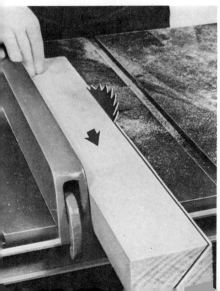

cut to complete the resawing in one step. On the circular saw, the stock is cut first from one edge; then it is turned and cut from the other edge.

The guard on most saws must be removed for resawing. Therefore a setup should be made that will provide plenty of support for the work and protection for the operator. One method is to attach a high auxiliary fence to the metal fence. Then use two feather boards, one to apply pressure from the top and the other to hold the stock against the fence. Adjust the saw to slightly more than half the width of the stock. When resawing hardwood, it is a good idea to make a shallow cut first and then raise the blade so that it extends above the stock about ¼" more than half the stock width. Make a cut from each edge to complete the operation. Another method of resawing is shown in Fig. 26-51. If the cut is still not complete, finish on the band saw.

Ripping Very Thin Stock

Install a hollow-ground blade. Clamp a plywood auxiliary table over the regular table and saw. Turn on the power and raise the blade slowly, cutting through the plywood table. Place the thin stock on the table; hold and feed it with a thick piece. The auxiliary table can be re-used.

Edge Cutting at an Angle

It is frequently necessary to make edge ripping cuts at an angle—for example, when cutting a raised panel. Whenever such cutting must be done, a wide auxiliary board should be fastened to the metal fence to give plenty of support for the cut. Also, make sure the metal insert is in good condition so there is no danger that the thin edge may slip into the opening. With both hands, hold the stock firmly against the auxiliary fence as the cut is made. Fig. 26-52.

26-51. *An L-shaped support is clamped to the back of the fence to support a hold-down clamp. The hold-down clamp will keep the stock on the table. The first cut has been made. Note the setup for completing the second cut. Side pressure is applied to the stock. The work must slide under the parallel hold-down clamp and therefore is held firmly to the table. The stock is moved with a push stick.*

26-52. *For better control when cutting a bevel on a raised panel, clamp a piece of wood to the panel to act as a support over the fence.*

CUTTING WEDGES OR TRIANGULAR PIECES

To cut wedges or triangular pieces, it is necessary to make a wood jig. For example, one should be used for cutting corner blocks. Several sizes and shapes should be available for cutting other common items. Fig. 26-53. A handle can be added to push the jig along. The jig can be made even safer by constructing it in two parts, with a hinge on one end so that the jig can actually close over the stock.

Cut the wedge opening in the jig. Place the stock in the notch. Adjust the jig while it is held firmly against the rip fence. Cut one wedge, then reverse the stock end for end to cut the second wedge.

TAPER CUTTING WITH A FIXED JIG

If only one angle of a taper is to be cut, a simple fixed jig is best. The jig consists of a guide board and a stop block with two notches in it. The distance from the first notch to the end of the guide board must equal the length of taper, and the notches themselves are each equal to the amount of taper on one side of the stock. Fig. 26-54. The jig is placed against the fence, and the fence is adjusted so that the work just touches the blade. Now place the work against the first notch and make one taper cut.

If a four-sided taper is to be cut, saw the adjacent side with the same

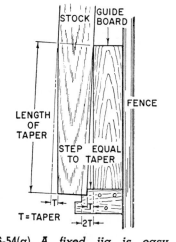

26-54(a). *A fixed jig is easy to make.*

setting. Then use the next notch to make the taper cuts on the opposite sides. Use a sharp, hollow-ground combination saw blade. Another type of fixed jig can be used when cutting a taper on only one side. Fig. 26-55.

TAPER CUTTING WITH AN ADJUSTABLE JIG

If several different tapers must be cut, it would be wise to make an adjustable tapering jig. Make the jig of two pieces of hardwood about $\frac{3}{4}'' \times 4'' \times 34''$. Join these pieces with a hinge on one end. Add a stop block and slotted adjustment strap. Lay off and make a permanent line 12" from the hinged end. Figure the amount of taper and then adjust the jig to the correct taper per foot. Fig. 26-56.

Another method is to lay out the taper line on the stock. Then place the jig and stock against the fence and open the jig until the layout line is parallel to the fence. Fig. 26-57. Make the first cut. Readjust the jig and make the second cut.

PATTERN SAWING

It is often necessary to cut several irregularly shaped pieces that have straight sides. This can best be done by using a pattern of the desired shape. The pattern must be

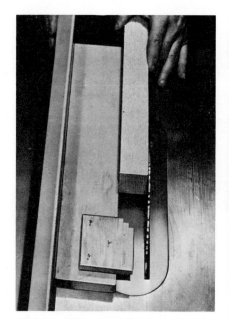

26-54(b). *Adjusting the fence before cutting the taper.*

fitted with anchor pins that will hold the work to it during cutting.

Clamp an auxiliary wood fence to the saw fence so that the work will slip underneath. Adjust the fence so that the front edge of the auxiliary wood fence is aligned with the left edge of the saw blade. Adjust the height of the blade so that it just touches the auxiliary fence.

Fasten the pattern to the work and then guide each edge of the pattern along the fence to do the cutting. Fig. 26-58.

USING THE DADO HEAD

The dado head is a most useful accessory for cutting grooves, da-

26-53. *This type of jig can be used to cut glue or corner blocks.*

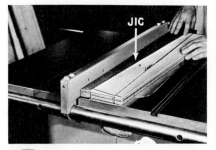

26-53. *This type of jig is good for cutting tapered plywood legs.*

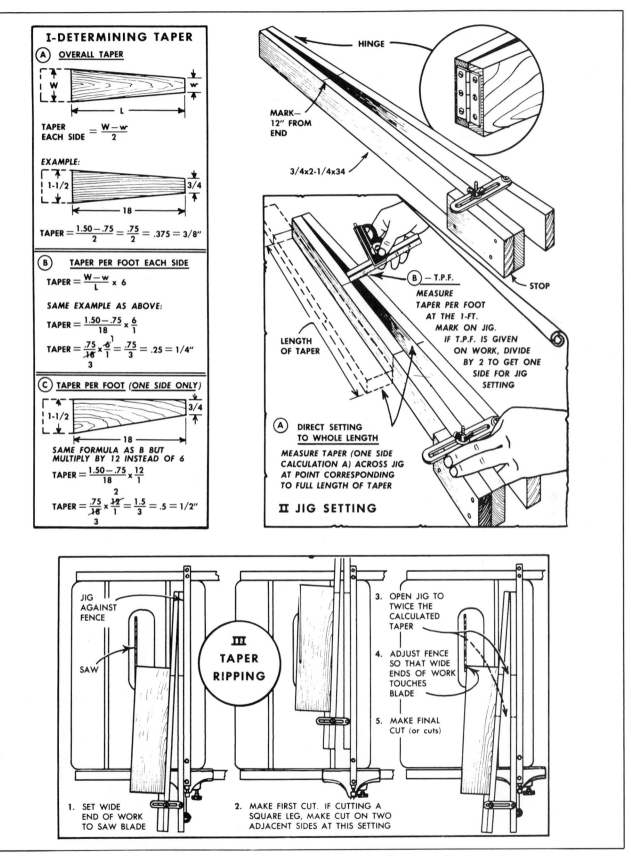

26-56. *Follow these steps in determining the taper, setting the jig, and ripping the taper.*

26-57. *Cutting a taper with an adjustable jig.*

26-59. *The typical dado head consists of two outside cutters and several inside chippers.*

does, rabbets, tenons, and lap joints. There are several kinds of dado heads. The most common one consists of several chippers of various thicknesses sandwiched between two ⅛" thick cutters. Fig. 26-59. Using various cutters and chippers, it is possible to cut grooves from ⅛" to ¹³⁄₁₆", in increments of ¹⁄₁₆". To cut a ⁷⁄₁₆" groove, for example, use two cutters of ⅛" each and two chippers, one ⅛" and one ¹⁄₁₆". If it is necessary to enlarge the groove slightly, paper washers can be placed between the chippers.

To install this kind of dado head, remove the insert plate and the saw blade. Place the inside blade on the arbor, then the chippers, then the outside blade, the collar, and the nut. When two or more chippers are

used, distribute them equally around the saw. Place the two cutting edges of the chippers in line with the bottom of the gullets (the spaces between the groups of blade teeth). This is necessary because the chippers are swaged (bent) thicker near their cutting edges. This swaged part must be allowed to enter the gullet. If this isn't done, oversized grooves and dadoes will be cut. Fig. 26-60. After the dado head assembly is attached to the arbor, use the large opening in the insert plate that is designed for this purpose.

There are several kinds of one-

unit, adjustable dado heads in which the desired width of cut can be obtained by setting a dial. Fig. 26-61.

Cutting Grooves

A *groove* is a slot cut with the grain of the wood. Fig. 26-62. The fence is used as a guide for this operation. Adjust the dado head for height and move the fence to the correct position. It is a good idea to clamp a feather board to the fence directly above the work, in order to hold the stock firmly against the table. The dado head takes a big "bite" out of the wood. Therefore there is a strong tendency toward

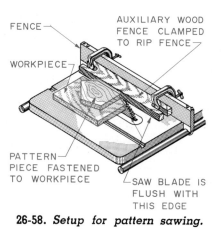

FENCE

AUXILIARY WOOD
FENCE CLAMPED
TO RIP FENCE

WORKPIECE

PATTERN
PIECE FASTENED
TO WORKPIECE

SAW BLADE IS
FLUSH WITH
THIS EDGE

26-58. *Setup for pattern sawing.*

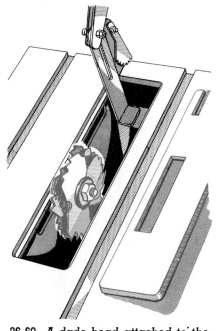

26-60. *A dado head attached to the saw arbor ready for use. The insert plate is ready to be replaced.*

26-61. *A one-piece, quick-set adjustable dado head.*

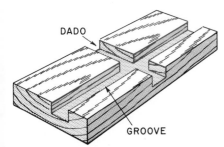

26-62. *A groove, sometimes called a plough, is a slot cut with the grain. A dado is a slot cut across grain.*

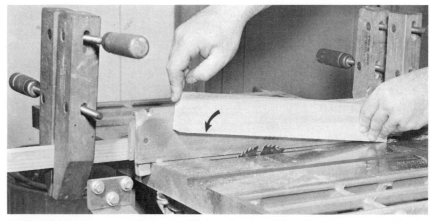

26-84. *Cutting a stopped groove. Notice the use of hand screws as stop blocks to control the length of cut. Use the guard shown in Fig. 26-84.*

kickback. Feed the stock into the dado head, applying side pressure to the fence to keep it in line. Fig. 26-63.

A *stopped groove* is one that stops short at one or both ends of the stock. This is made for a blind spline joint. To make this cut, one wood stop must be clamped to an auxiliary wood fence at the beginning of the cut, and another at the end. Turn on the power. Hold one end of the stock against the first stop and lower it into the saw. Push the stock along until it strikes the second stop, then carefully raise the stock. The first stop helps to prevent kickback, which takes place most often as the cut is started. Fig. 26-64.

Cutting a Dado

A *dado* is a slot cut at right angles to the edge grain. Remove the

fence and use the miter gauge with an auxiliary board to support the work. Mark the location of the dado on the edge of the stock and make the cuts. Fig. 26-65. The fence can be used as a stop block and guide to control the location of the dadoes. Fig. 26-66. This is especially useful when cutting matching dadoes for a chest or cabinet. To cut regularly spaced dadoes, the miter gauge can be used with the stop rod as a stop. To position the next dado, the stop rod can fit into the last dado that has been cut.

CUTTING JOINTS

The circular saw can be used for making most joint cuts. For many

kinds of joints, two or more methods can be followed. All joint cuts should be made with a standard combination blade, a carbide-tipped combination blade, or a dado head. There are also special-purpose blades like the miter saw for joint work. For many joint cuts it is difficult to use a standard guard. However, jigs, fixtures, and protective devices should be used whenever possible. Also, follow all safety rules with great care.

Butt Joints

All basic butt joints can be cut by simple crosscutting operations. A carbide-tipped blade will produce a better surface for gluing. Boring op-

26-63. *Cutting a groove with a dado head.*

26-65. *Cutting a dado with the stock held against the miter gauge.*

26-66. *Here the fence acts as both guide and stop block to cut several dadoes in a wide board.*

erations for dowel holes should be done on a drill press or boring machine when one is available.

Edge Joints

Edge joints involve ripping. The *plain edge* is a simple ripping operation that can be followed by smoothing the edge on a jointer. However, a carbide saw normally produces a satisfactory edge for gluing. The *rabbet edge* can be cut as described under the next heading. The *spline edge* is cut by using a single saw blade to form a groove on the adjoining edges. Two or more passes may be necessary to produce the correct width. Fig. 26-67. A better method is to use a dado head of the correct width. The *tongue-and-groove* joint is best cut with a dado head. The groove is cut in a single pass with a head of correct thickness. The matching tongue is cut by placing a spacer collar between the blades of the dado head, with a chipper on the outside of each blade to remove waste stock. The *dowel edge* is a plain edge with dowels installed.

Rabbet Joints

An *end rabbet joint* is a crosscutting operation that can be done with a single blade, though using a dado head is far better. If a single blade

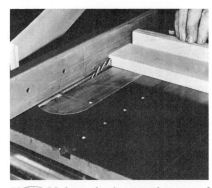

26-68. Making the first cut for an end rabbet.

is used, first mark the width and depth of the rabbet on one edge of the stock. For the first cut, have the end grain against the fence and the face surface against the table. Fig. 26-68. Make the second cut with the end of the stock held against the table and the face against a high fence.

To make this cut with a dado head, always use an auxiliary wood fence so that the dado head can cut into the fence slightly. Then hold the face of the stock against the table and the edge against the miter gauge to cut the rabbet in one or more passes.

To cut an *edge rabbet* with a single blade, mark the shape of the

26-70. Cutting a series of dadoes at an angle. This could be used to make shutters, for example.

rabbet on the end grain. Make the first cut with the face against the fence and the edge against the table. Make the second cut with the opposite edge against the fence and the face against the table. Fig. 26-69.

The dado head can also be used to cut a rabbet with or across end grain. This is ideal for production work since only one setup is needed.

Dado Joints

All standard dadoes are best cut with a dado head, set to exact width. They can also be cut by making several passes with a single blade, then cleaning out the waste with a chisel. The dado can be

26-67. Cutting a narrow groove for a spline.

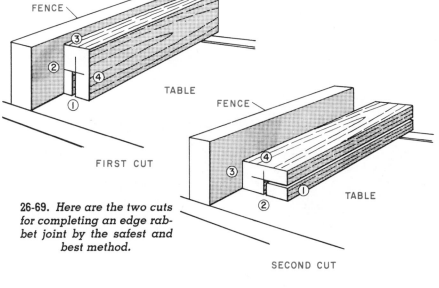

26-69. Here are the two cuts for completing an edge rabbet joint by the safest and best method.

FENCE

TABLE

FIRST CUT

FENCE

TABLE

SECOND CUT

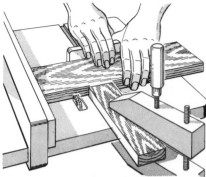

26-71. *Cutting a blind or stop dado with a stop block clamped to the table to control the length of cut.*

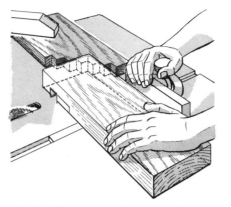

26-73. *Using a notched stop block to control the width of cut for a lap joint.*

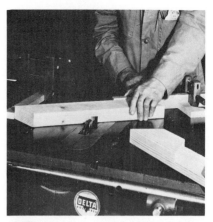

26-74. *Here's another method of cutting a cross-lap joint at an angle. One stop block is attached to the fence to locate one side of the lap, and a second stop block is fitted to the auxiliary fence to locate the other. Start with the stock against the first block, then make several passes until it is firmly against the second. Short sleeves are safer.*

cut at any angle to the edge. Fig. 26-70.

The *blind* or *stop dado* can be cut by clamping a stop block to the fence or the saw table to control the length of cut. Fig. 26-71. The corner will have to be squared with a chisel. However, it is easier to make this joint on a radial-arm saw. The *corner dado* is cut by holding the stock in a V block against the miter gauge. Fig. 26-72. The *full-dovetail dado* is made by first cutting a mortise or slot. Cut a dado to the narrowest width, as indicated on the drawing. Then replace the dado head with a single blade and adjust to an angle of 15 degrees. Make the angle cut on each side to clean out the mortise. (Using a dovetail bit in a router is a more accurate but harder way to make these angle

26-72. *Cutting a corner dado with a V block held against the miter gauge.*

cuts.) The tenon is cut in two steps with a single blade. First cut the kerfs in the faces. Then adjust the blade to a 15-degree angle and make the two shoulder cuts. (Again, a better method is to use the router.) The *half-dovetail dado* is cut the same way except that the angle cuts are made on only one side of the joint.

Lap Joints

All lap joints are best cut with a dado head. To cut the wide dado that is needed, clamp a notched stop block to the top of the table, far enough ahead of the saw blade so that it won't interfere. Use this stop block as a guide before starting each cut. Fig. 26-73. Several passes will be needed to cut the wide dado (for a cross lap) or wide rabbet (for an end lap). Fig. 26-74. Whenever possible, cut both pieces of stock at the same time to make a single joint.

Miter Joints

All *flat miter* joints are cut by a method similar to that shown in Fig. 26-75. A spline can be added to a flat miter by first making a jig of scrap wood to hold the stock at an angle of 45 degrees. Adjust the height of the blade to equal the depth of the spline cut. Adjust the fence so that the cut will be in the

26-75. *Cutting a flat miter to length, with one end held against a stop block clamped to the auxiliary wood fence. Short sleeves are safer.*

correct position from right to left. Hold the stock firmly against the jig and cut the groove for the spline. Fig. 26-76. If the spline is thicker than the width of the blade, a second pass may be necessary. A special thin blade may be needed if a groove is cut for clamp nails.

There are several methods of cutting the groove for a *spline miter on edge*. The simplest is to tilt the saw blade to an angle of 45 degrees, set the miter gauge at 90 degrees, and use the fence as a stop block. Note that an auxiliary wood fence is used so that there is no danger that the

26-76. *Cutting a groove for a spline in a flat miter joint.*

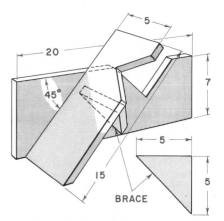

26-77(b). *A jig like this makes it possible to cut the groove for the spline with the saw blade at right angles to the table. The jig is held against the miter gauge.*

blade will strike the metal fence. Adjust the height of the blade and cut the groove. Fig. 26-77. To cut a groove for a *blind spline*, it is necessary to cut a recess from the same side of both pieces, about three-fourths the distance across the end grain. Fig. 26-78.

To install a *feather across a miter corner*, make a wood jig to hold the joint at an angle of 45 degrees. Set the blade to the correct height and adjust the fence so that the cut is in the center across the corners. Fig. 26-79. A *miter with rabbet* can be cut by following the steps on page 330. Lay out and cut the two rabbets, one of which is twice as wide as the other. Then make a miter cut on each piece to complete the joint. A *lock miter* can be cut on a circular saw by first cutting the

grooves and then the miter. However, it is much better to cut this joint on a shaper. To cut a *compound miter* or *hopper joint*, adjust the blade and the miter gauge to the correct settings. For a *miter with end lap*, the best method is to make the rabbet cuts with a dado head—a square cut on one piece, an angle cut on the other. Then cut the end of one piece at a 45-degree angle.

Mortise-and-Tenon Joints

All enclosed mortises (those with stock on four sides) should be cut with a mortiser, with a mortising attachment on a drill press, or with a router. Fig. 26-80. An open mortise can be cut on a saw by using a dado head of the correct thickness and holding the stock in a home-made or commercial tenoning jig. Figs. 26-81 and 26-8.

Several methods of cutting a tenon are described here:

● Adjust a dado head to a height equal to the thickness of the stock to be removed on one side of the tenon. Then make one or more passes to cut half the tenon. Reverse the stock and cut the other side. The work is held against the miter gauge, and a stop rod controls the length of the tenon. Fig. 26-82.

● Set the fence so that the dis-

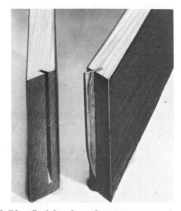

26-78. *A blind spline is cut about three-fourths of the way across the end, from matching edges on both pieces.*

26-79. *Making a saw kerf across the corner of a frame for installing a key or feather. Note the jig for holding the stock.*

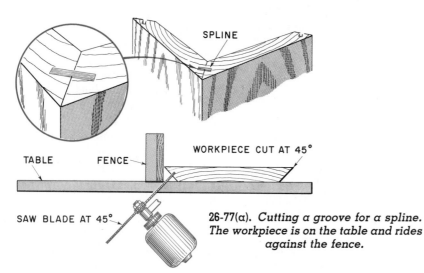

SPLINE

TABLE FENCE WORKPIECE CUT AT 45°

SAW BLADE AT 45°

26-77(a). *Cutting a groove for a spline. The workpiece is on the table and rides against the fence.*

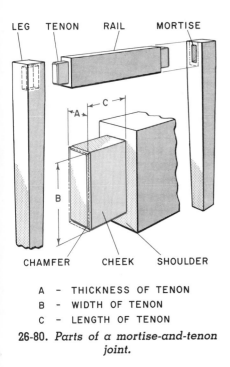

26-80. *Parts of a mortise-and-tenon joint.*

A – THICKNESS OF TENON
B – WIDTH OF TENON
C – LENGTH OF TENON

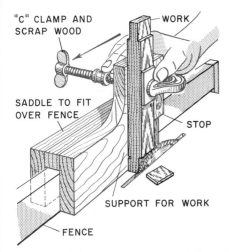

26-81. *A handmade tenoning jig.*

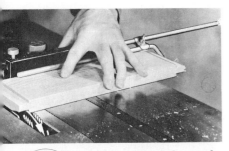

26-82. *Using the stop rod on the miter gauge to control the length of the tenon being cut with a dado head.*

tance from the outside of the saw to the fence is equal to the length of the tenon. Adjust the saw height for correct depth of shoulder cut. Use a miter gauge. Hold the end of the tenon against the fence and make the two shoulder cuts from each face. Fig. 26-83. Using the same fence setting, adjust the saw height to the correct depth and complete the shoulder cuts from the edges. Now adjust the fence and the height of the saw to make the cheek cuts from the end. Be sure that the waste stock is outside the saw. Use a guard when making these cuts. Fig. 26-84.

● In production work, an excellent method of cutting tenons is with a dado head which has a spacer between the blades, and chippers on the outside to remove the extra stock. A tenoning jig or a special bracket holds the stock. Fig. 26-85.

Miscellaneous Joints

To cut a *box* or *finger joint*, first fasten an auxiliary wood fence to

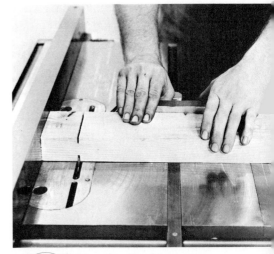

26-83. *Making the shoulder cuts.*

the miter gauge. Use a dado head of exactly the same thickness as the desired width of the fingers and grooves. Adjust the dado head for the correct depth of cut (equal to the thickness of the material). Then cut two dadoes in the auxiliary wood fence with a distance between them equal to the width of the

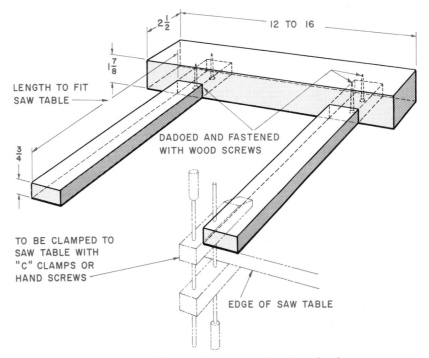

26-84(a). *This guard should be used when making the cheek cut on a tenon freehand if the conventional guard will not function.*

193

26-84(b). *The guard in use.*

dado. Mount a guide pin, equal in height and width to the dado cut, into the first dado. The guide pin is fastened to the auxiliary fence with a wood screw driven through the bottom of the pin and countersunk. Fig. 26-86.

Now butt one piece of stock against the guide pin and cut a

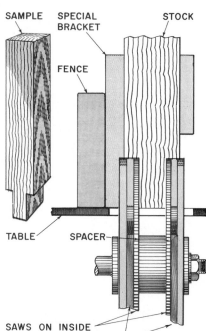

SAMPLE SPECIAL STOCK
BRACKET

FENCE

TABLE SPACER

SAWS ON INSIDE
CHIPPERS ON OUTSIDE

26-85. *Cutting a tenon, using a dado head with a spacer collar. In this setup, a homemade tenoning jig holds the stock. A commercial tenoning jig could also be used.*

dado. Reposition the piece against the guide pin as before. Place the second piece of stock over the cut on the first piece. Cut the dado. For succeeding cuts, shift the two pieces to the right so that the preceding cut fits over the guide pin. Fig. 26-87. Cutting both pieces at the same time in this offset position will result in a perfectly fitted joint. Fig. 26-88.

The *lock joint* can be cut on the saw with a dado head, although it is better to cut it on a shaper. If a saw is used, make cuts *a*, *b*, *c*, and *e* with a single blade and cut *d* with a dado head. See Fig. 39-58.

A *coped joint* is one which joins two molded pieces, such as window sash or frames. It is a fitted joint in which part of one piece is cut away or shaped to fit over the molded surface of the second piece. The joint is also found in interior trim work where the corners of moldings meet. A coped joint for a corner can be made by cutting one piece square and the other at a 45-degree miter. Then cut on the miter line of the second piece, using a jigsaw with the blade at right angles to the back surface.

CUTTING COVES

A *cove* is a rounded groove that can be made by feeding stock across the saw at a slight angle. It is necessary to take light cuts since there is a considerable amount of

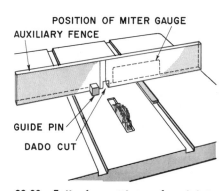

POSITION OF MITER GAUGE
AUXILIARY FENCE

GUIDE PIN
DADO CUT

26-86. *A jig for cutting a box joint. Note the location of the guide pin.*

side stress against the saw. Coves are especially popular in decorative designs such as Early American furniture.

As a first step, draw a pencil outline on the end grain of each piece. With a dado head, remove as much waste material as possible by making a series of grooving cuts. Now

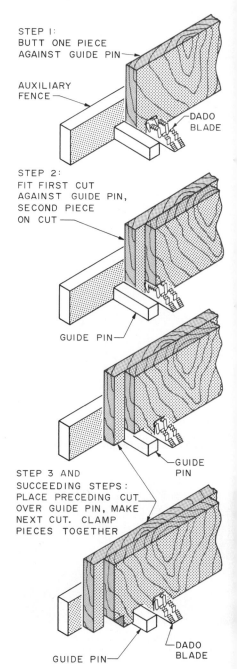

STEP 1:
BUTT ONE PIECE
AGAINST GUIDE PIN

AUXILIARY
FENCE

DADO
BLADE

STEP 2:
FIT FIRST CUT
AGAINST GUIDE PIN,
SECOND PIECE
ON CUT

GUIDE PIN

STEP 3 AND
SUCCEEDING STEPS:
PLACE PRECEDING CUT
OVER GUIDE PIN, MAKE
NEXT CUT. CLAMP
PIECES TOGETHER

GUIDE
PIN

GUIDE PIN

DADO
BLADE

26-87. *Steps in cutting a box joint.*

194

26-88. *The completed box, or finger, joint.*

adjust the saw blade to a height equal to the depth of the cove. The proper angle of the temporary fence for cutting the cove is determined by using a jig such as that shown in

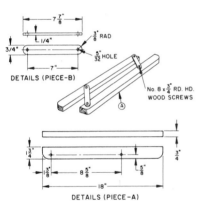

26-89(a). *A handy device for making concave cuts on moldings and picture frames is the cove-setting jig.*

26-89(b). *The proper angle of the wood fence is determined by using this set of parallel rules.*

Fig. 26-89. Open the jig an amount equal to the width of the cove. Place the jig over the saw and turn it until it just touches the front and rear teeth of the blade. This setting determines the proper angle for the fence. The fence itself is located so that the center line of the work will intersect the center line of the saw blade. Now turn the blade down so it projects about 1/8" to 1/4" above the table; make the first cut. Continue to raise the saw and make cuts until the desired depth is reached. Fig. 26-90.

SAW-CUT MOLDINGS

Attractive saw-cut moldings can be made by cutting a series of kerfs across grain on a piece of stock. The kerfs should be cut to about one-half the thickness of the stock. Then reverse the stock and cut another series equally spaced in between the first cuts. The stock then can be ripped to narrow widths. Several procedures for saw-cut moldings are shown in the chapter on the radial-arm saw (Chapter 27). These can also be carried out on the circular saw.

MOLDING HEAD

A molding head is used on a circular saw to make many kinds of fancy moldings and joint cuts. There are several types of molding heads, but the best for the circular saw is the cylindrical one in which three blades are securely locked. Fig. 26-91. A wide variety of molding cutter blades can be used. Fig. 26-92. They can be sharpened by rubbing the flat cutting-edge sides on an oilstone. Before using any molding head, attach an auxiliary wood fence to the metal fence. This can be a single piece of wood fastened to one or both sides of the metal fence.

To make a molding, first lay out the design on a piece of paper. The design should be identical in size to the end grain of the stock. Then

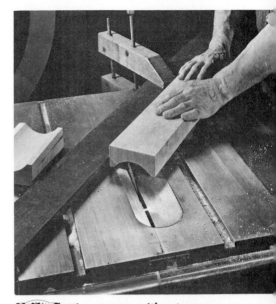

26-90. *Cutting a cove with a temporary wood fence attached to the table at an angle.*

choose the correct set of cutters and lock them firmly in the molding head. Remove the saw blade and attach the molding-cutter saw head. An insert plate with a wider opening, similar to that for the dado head, is required.

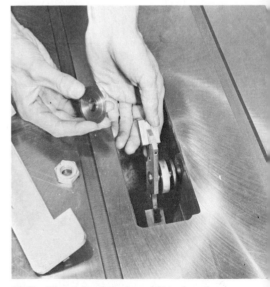

26-91. *The cylindrical molding head is the best type for the circular saw.*

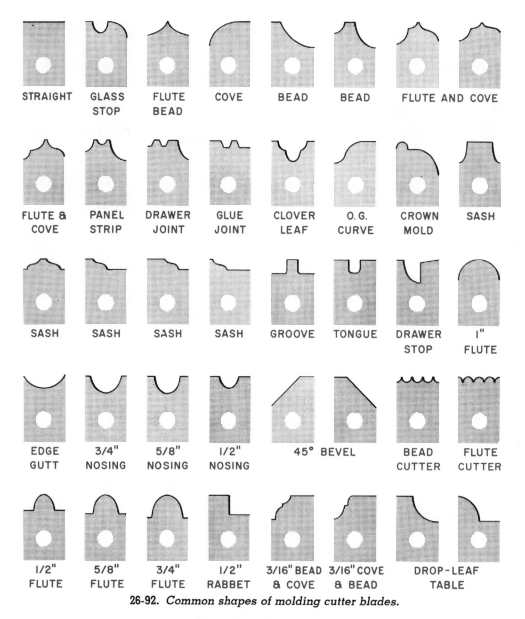

| STRAIGHT | GLASS STOP | FLUTE BEAD | COVE | BEAD | BEAD | FLUTE AND COVE |

| FLUTE & COVE | PANEL STRIP | DRAWER JOINT | GLUE JOINT | CLOVER LEAF | O. G. CURVE | CROWN MOLD | SASH |

| SASH | SASH | SASH | SASH | GROOVE | TONGUE | DRAWER STOP | I" FLUTE |

| EDGE GUTT | 3/4" NOSING | 5/8" NOSING | I/2" NOSING | 45° BEVEL | BEAD CUTTER | FLUTE CUTTER |

| I/2" FLUTE | 5/8" FLUTE | 3/4" FLUTE | I/2" RABBET | 3/16" BEAD & COVE | 3/16" COVE & BEAD | DROP-LEAF TABLE |

26-92. *Common shapes of molding cutter blades.*

26-93. *Using the molding head to cut a decorative edge. Note the use of a feather board to help guide the stock.*

Edge Molding of Straight Stock

Most moldings are cut on the edge or side of large stock. When the cut is made along the side, the operation is much the same as sawing. Fig. 26-93. First use a piece of scrap stock of the same size or thickness as the finished piece to check the operation of the molding head. When the stock must stand on edge, it is good to use a higher wood fence or to provide extra support as shown in Fig. 26-94. If both end grain and edge grain are to

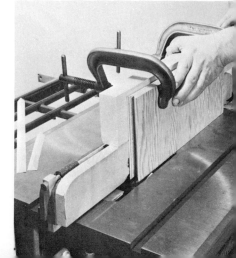

26-94. *Here's a good way to shape the edge of stock with a molding head. Note the extra piece of stock clamped to the work for support.*

26-95. Cutting moldings with the molding head. Note that the molding itself (dark wood) is fastened on top of a guide board (light wood) which has equally spaced cuts or slots. The pin located in the auxiliary fence controls the spacing.

be cut, cut end grain first since it may splinter a little. If the stock is held flat on the table, the miter gauge can be used to help guide the work.

Molding with the Miter Gauge

When molding edge grain or across face grain, the miter gauge with an auxiliary wood fence is used to hold the stock. Note that in Fig. 26-95 the auxiliary fence has a metal or wood pin attached to it. Then a guide board with equally spaced slots is attached to the stock. The pin can be located in any position since the guide board determines the spacing of the cuts. A series of crosscuts forms the molding. The shape of the molding is determined by the shape of the cutters used, by the spacing of the cuts, and by the height of the cutterhead.

Molding on Circular Stock

Circular stock is best shaped by cutting a reverse jig to the same

26-96. Press the work into the cutter and rotate it slowly.

radius as the stock. This jig is clamped or fastened to the fence so that the centerline of the work and that of the jig are in line. Push the work gradually into the cutter, then rotate it slowly. Fig. 26-96.

27 Radial-Arm Saw

The radial-arm saw, or radial saw as it is sometimes called, is an excellent sawing machine. In addition it can also be used as a shaper, drill, boring tool, sander, and router. With attachments (as for a combination machine), it can be used as a jointer or wood lathe. It is particularly good for fast, convenient, and accurate crosscutting (whereas the circular saw is better for ripping). It is also very useful for making many

kinds of joint cuts such as a dado or stop dado. The advantage of this saw is that all cutting is done from the top, making layout lines clearly visible. The saw is never hidden beneath the wood.

The radial-arm saw is almost always used to rough cut lumber to length if a special-purpose cutoff saw is not available. For all types of crosscutting, including straight cutting, cutting miters, bevels, dadoes,

and rabbets, the stock is held on the table in a fixed position and the saw is moved in the same direction as its rotation. Fig. 27-1. For ripping operations, the saw is held in a locked position and the stock is moved into the revolving blade. Fig. 27-2.

There are several designs of radial-arm saws. On one type, the motor unit containing the saw blade moves back and forth directly under

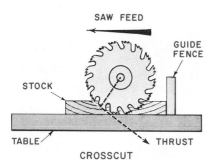

27-1. *In crosscutting, the saw blade moves in the same direction it is rotating. The saw's thrust is downward and to the rear, thus holding the stock firmly against the guide fence.*

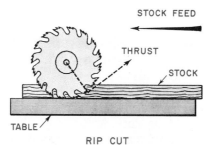

27-2. *When ripping stock, always feed it into the rotation of the blade.*

27-3. *On this machine the sawing unit moves back and forth directly under the radial arm.*

an *overarm*. Fig. 27-3. On another, an *arm track* that rotates for making certain cuts is fastened to the center of the overarm. Fig. 27-4.

The size of the radial-arm saw is determined by the diameter of the blade commonly used and the horsepower rating. A third factor sometimes involved is the length of the overarm or arm track. Machines are available with extra length overarms or tracks for cutting wide stock, particularly panel stock such as plywood, hardboard, or particle board. Common sizes of radial-arm saws are 10″, 12″, and 14″.

ACCESSORIES
Accessories and cutting tools for the radial-arm saw are available in wide variety so that this machine can be used for many specialized operations.

SAW BLADES
Radial-arm saw blades are similar to those for the circular saw. The basic ones are combination, hollow-ground, rip, and plywood. The combination blade is most commonly used since it can make many kinds of cuts effectively. Blades are made in diameters from 9″ to 18″ to fit the various sizes of saws. These saws also use dado heads, similar to those used on the circular saw, for cutting rabbets, dadoes, and other kinds of slots. Many other types of winged and straight cutters can be used, such as the panel raising tool. Fig. 27-5.

Replacing a Saw Blade
Remove the nut that holds the guard in place. Then remove the

---

RADIAL-ARM SAW

MAINTENANCE
• Clean the tracks inside the arm with a cloth dampened with lacquer thinner. This will remove grease and dirt. Do not lubricate the tracks.
• Make sure the wood table is in good condition. Replace it and the guide fence when they are warped or have too many saw kerfs.
• Check with a square to make sure the saw blade is square with the guide fence and tabletop when the arm and motor are in the zero position.
• Make sure all clamps and adjustments work easily.

LUBRICATION
• Apply a good grade of lubricating oil to the elevating screw or shaft, miter latch, swivel latch, and bevel lathe.
• Motor bearings are sealed and require no further lubrication.

SAFETY
• Wear proper clothing and eye protection. (See Chapter 4.)
• For all crosscutting operations the stock is held against the table and guide fence. This eliminates kickback, a major cause of saw accidents.
• Make sure the blade is sharp and properly mounted. It should be held securely with an arbor collar and nut.

• Keep the safety guard in position when operating the machine.
• Make sure all clamps and locking handles are tight.
• Always return the saw to the rear of the table after completing a cut.
• Shut off the power and wait until the saw comes to a dead stop before making any adjustments.
• Extension tables on the sides of the saw are helpful when working with long stock.
• Never remove stock from the table until the saw has been returned to the rear.
• Use a stick to remove small wood scraps from the table.
• Keep the table clean. Brush off sawdust after the saw has been used.
• Always keep your hands away from the saw's path.
• Use the guard and anti-kickback fingers when ripping.
• When ripping, make sure the blade rotates toward you.
• Also when ripping, feed the stock under the safety guard from the side opposite the anti-kickback fingers. Never stand directly behind or in line with the saw.
• When ripping narrow stock, always use a push stick to complete the cut.
• When properly used, the radial-arm saw is one of the safest power tools ever made.

guard assembly. Move the overarm up so that the blade will slide off the shaft easily and clear the table-top. Lock or hold the shaft and remove the nut and collar from the arbor. Fig. 27-6. Remove the blade. Insert the new blade with the teeth pointing in the direction of rotation. Replace the arbor collar and nut, and tighten securely. Then replace the guard. Fig. 27-7.

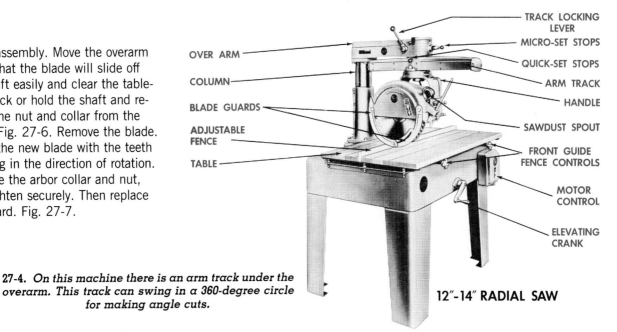

TRACK LOCKING LEVER
MICRO-SET STOPS
QUICK-SET STOPS
ARM TRACK
HANDLE
SAWDUST SPOUT
FRONT GUIDE FENCE CONTROLS
MOTOR CONTROL
ELEVATING CRANK

OVER ARM
COLUMN
BLADE GUARDS
ADJUSTABLE FENCE
TABLE

27-4. On this machine there is an arm track under the overarm. This track can swing in a 360-degree circle for making angle cuts.

12″-14″ RADIAL SAW

SAW BLADE REFERENCE CHART

	COMBINATION SET TOOTH	RIP	CROSS CUT PLY	HOLLOW-GROUND PLANER	CARBIDE 8-12 TEETH	CARBIDE MULTI-TOOTH	TOOL STEEL H.G. CROSS-CUT	CUT-OFF WHEEL
Wood— Natural	Fast Rough	Fast Rough	Slower Smooth Can't Rip	Slower Very Smooth	Fast Rough	Fast Smooth	Smooth Slow Cross-Cut Won't Rip	Will Not Cut
Wood— Artificial (Plywood) Masonite Novaply, etc.	Fast Rough Dulls Blade Quickly	Fast Splinters Dulls Fast	Slower Smooth Dulls Slowly	Fast Smooth Dulls Instantly	Fast Splinters Stays Sharp	Fast Smooth Stays Sharp Best	Fast Smooth Holds Edge Quite Long	Will Not Cut
Metals— Non-Ferrous Alum. Copper, etc.	O.K. On Soft Aluminum Dulls	Will Destroy Blade	Better O.K. on Aluminum Brass, Copper	Will Destroy Blade	Will Pull Out Teeth If Cut Too Fast	Very Good If Used Slowly	Very Good If Used w/Tallow or Spray	Slow Used With Spray
Metals— Ferrous Iron and Steel	Will Not Cut	Will Not Cut	Will Burn Through After Teeth Are Dull	Will Not Cut	Will Destroy Blade	Will Destroy Blade	Will Burn Through	Will Cut Slowly Use Coolant
Plastics— Soft	Will Chip	Will Shatter	Better May Melt Material Use Spray	Will Not Cut	Will Chip	Very Good	Good But May Bind or Melt Material	Slow May Clog, Bind and Melt Material
Plastics— Hard	Will Chip and Dull Fast	Will Shatter	Cuts Well Dulls Fast	Will Bind	Will Chip	Very Good Smooth	Good Smooth	Good Slow Use Lube
Paper Cardboard	Will Dull Very Fast	Will Tear and Dull Blade	Good Will Dull Very Fast	Will Bind and Dull Blade	Rough Cut Use Slowly	Good Will Dull Very Fast	Good Sometimes Binds	Will Burn
Bone Ivory etc.	Will Shatter	Will Shatter	Good Cut Slowly	Good Will Dull Fast	Will Shatter	Good	Good	Some Are Good Must Try

27-5. Use this chart when selecting a saw blade.

27-6. *The arbor can be held with a hex wrench. On some machines it can be locked. Use the correct size wrench to loosen the arbor nut.*

COMMON ADJUSTMENTS

Three common adjustments are necessary for making setups for all types of sawing. Figs. 27-8 and 27-9. The overarm or track can be rotated in a complete circle, although it is normally moved only 180 degrees. The yoke that holds the motor can be turned 360 degrees. The blade and motor unit in the yoke can be tilted 90 degrees to the right or to the left. The adjustments are made as follows:

• Adjustment for depth of cut is made by turning the elevating crank or handle, located directly above the

27-7. *Replacing the saw blade. On many machines an arrow on the motor housing shows the direction of rotation.*

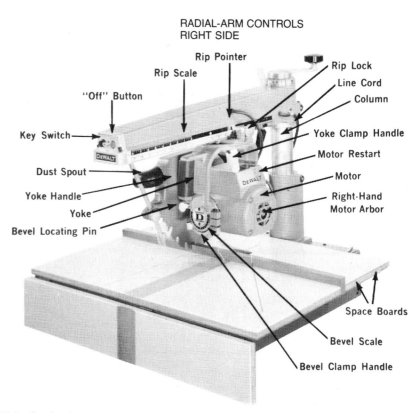

RADIAL-ARM CONTROLS
RIGHT SIDE

Rip Pointer
Rip Scale
Rip Lock
Line Cord
"Off" Button
Column
Key Switch
Yoke Clamp Handle
Motor Restart
Dust Spout
Motor
Yoke Handle
Right-Hand Motor Arbor
Yoke
Bevel Locating Pin
Space Boards
Bevel Scale
Bevel Clamp Handle

27-8. *Study the names of the parts and controls so you can follow directions for making adjustments and cuts. Another model with the elevating handle in a different location is shown in Fig. 27-10. See also Fig. 27-9.*

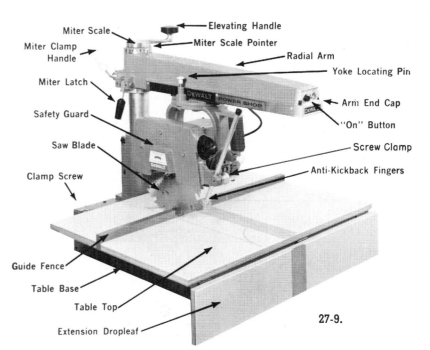

RADIAL-ARM CONTROLS
LEFT SIDE

Miter Scale
Elevating Handle
Miter Clamp Handle
Miter Scale Pointer
Radial Arm
Miter Latch
Yoke Locating Pin
Safety Guard
Arm End Cap
"On" Button
Saw Blade
Screw Clamp
Clamp Screw
Anti-Kickback Fingers
Guide Fence
Table Base
Table Top
27-9.
Extension Dropleaf

27-10. *Adjusting the depth of cut. On most machines each full turn of the elevating handle raises or lowers the arm ⅛". Only slight pressure is needed to keep the saw from moving.*

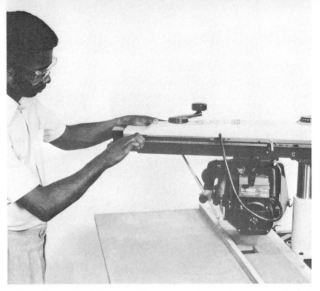

27-11. *To adjust for a miter cut, release the arm clamp handle and swing the arm to the angle you want.*

column or in front of the table. For normal cutting, the saw blade is adjusted so that it is ¹⁄₁₆" below the tabletop. Fig. 27-10.

● The angle of cut is adjusted by releasing the miter clamp handle or the track-locking lever and turning the radial arm or track to the correct angle. Most machines have an automatic stop for the 45-degree position both right and left. Fig. 27-11.

● Bevel cuts are made by releasing the bevel clamp handle and tilting the motor and saw unit to right or left to the correct degree. Fig. 27-12.

● For ripping operations, pull up on the yoke locating pin or the quick-set pin, then turn the motor and yoke one-fourth turn for ripping. There are also stops on the radial arm or track for limiting the outward movement of the saw. Fig. 27-13 shows settings being made.

CROSSCUTTING OPERATIONS

Simple Crosscuts

For straight crosscuts make sure that the radial arm or track is at right angles to the fence. This position is indicated by zero on the miter scale. Adjust the depth of cut so that the teeth of the blade are about ¹⁄₁₆" below the surface of the wood in the saw kerf. This extra clearance is needed to cut completely through the board. Adjust the guard so that it parallels the bottom of the motor. Set the anti-kickback fingers about ⅛" above the surface of the wood to keep your fingers away from the blade. Push the saw all the way back to the column, and mark a line on the stock where the cut is to be made. Slide the work on the table and against the fence until the layout line is in line with the saw blade.

201

27-12. *To tilt the motor, pull out the bevel clamp and locating pin, and move it to the desired angle. The locating pin automatically stops at 0, 45, and 90 degrees.*

27-13. *Release the yoke clamp and lift the locating pin. Then swing the yoke right or left to the correct position.*

27-14. *It is easy to crosscut stock with a straight-line movement of the saw.*

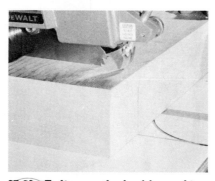

27-16. *To line up the kerf for making the second cut on heavy stock, use the kerf on the tabletop as a guide. NOTE: For some photos the guard was removed so that details could be seen. The guard symbol in the caption indicates you should use the guard when performing this operation.*

Turn on the power and allow the saw to come to full speed. Hold the stock firmly as you slowly draw the revolving blade into the work. Fig. 27-14. Little or no effort is required since the cutting action tends to feed the blade into the stock. As a matter of fact, never allow the blade to move too quickly through the work. When the cut is complete, return the saw blade behind the fence and turn off the power.

In holding the stock for crosscutting, it is possible to use either the right or left hand. Likewise, either hand can pull the saw to do the cutting. Fig. 27-15. Actually, the righthand method, with the longer part of the stock to the left of the blade, is easier. This method is shown in Fig. 27-14.

To cut stock that is thicker than the capacity of the machine, cut through half the thickness, then turn it over and cut from the other side. Fig. 27-16.

Cutting Identical Lengths

When several pieces of the same length are needed, a stop block can be clamped to the table. A rabbet cut at the end of the block will prevent sawdust from catching in the corner and interfering with the accuracy of the cuts. Another method of cutting several pieces to the same length is to clamp or hold them together and cut across all at the same time. Fig. 27-17.

To cut a board that is wider than the capacity of the saw, the stop-block arrangement can also be used. Cut from one side as far as possible, then turn the board over. Hold it against the stop block again to complete the cut. Figs. 27-18 and 27-19. Extra-length radial arms or tracks are available when a great deal of panel cutting needs to be done. This type of equipment is needed by finish carpenters who do interior paneling.

Bevel Cutting

To make a bevel cut, keep the track or radial arm at right angles to the fence, as for straight cutting, but tilt the motor unit to the correct angle. Before making the adjustment, raise the saw so that the blade will clear the tabletop when you swivel the motor and yoke. Then

202

27-15. *In the left-hand method most of the stock is to the right of the saw. Note the additional free-floating guard. The safety rings are free to adjust automatically for depth and angle of cut.*

27-17. *Trimming several pieces to the same length at one time.*

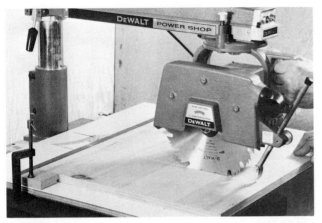

27-18. Hold the stock against a stop block and cut as far as possible on a wide board.

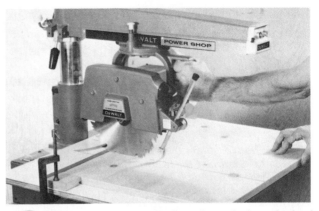

27-19. Reverse the board side for side and align the kerf by holding the end against the stop block. Complete the cut.

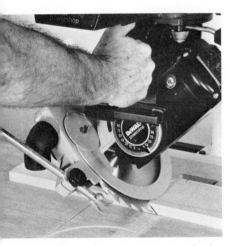

27-20. *To make a bevel cut, tilt the motor unit to the correct angle.*

27-21. *Hold the stock with your left hand and pull the saw with your right to cut a miter.*

lower the blade again until it just cuts into the wood tabletop about $\frac{1}{16}$″. If a 45-degree bevel is to be cut, there is a locking pin which will automatically stop at this position. The cutting is done exactly as straight cutting. Fig. 27-20.

Mitering

To cut a miter, the radial arm or the arm track is rotated to the right or left to the correct angle. The cutting itself is done the same as straight crosscutting. To make this adjustment, raise the blade slightly, then release the arm clamp handle or the track-locking lever and lift the miter latch. Swing the arm or track to the correct angle. For the 45-degree miter there is an automatic stop. After the angle has been set, readjust the blade for correct depth of cut. Adjust the anti-kickback fingers to clear the top of the work. Hold the stock with one hand and pull the saw through with the other. Fig. 27-21. Most miter cuts require a cut on both ends of the stock. This is true in making any kind of frame. Of course, the arm or track can be moved from one side to the other to make the cut, but there are simpler ways:

Method A. Adjust the arm to the right at 45 degrees, then clamp a straight guide board at right angles

to the guide fence. Make sure there is enough space between the extra guide board and the fence for the work to slip in between. Now place the stock against the guide board and also firmly against the fence. Cut one end of the stock. Fig. 27-22(a). Then hold the stock against the regular guide fence and cut the other end. Fig. 27-22(b).

Method B. Another method of mitering both ends is to use a large V block clamped to the tabletop. The saw is kept in straight crosscutting position. Hold the stock against the

27-22(a). *Note that the first end is cut with the stock held firmly against the auxiliary guide board. It's a good idea to check with a square to make sure this is at 90 degrees to the table guide board.*

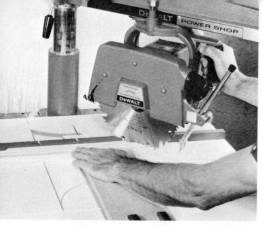

left side of the block for cutting one end and against the right side for cutting the other. Fig. 27-23.

Compound Miter Cuts

The compound miter, sometimes called a hopper or bevel-miter, is a combination of a miter and a bevel. It is used for making a frame or box with sloping sides and for certain roof framing cuts. Fig. 27-24. To make this cut, the arm or track is adjusted to the correct angle and the motor unit tilted the correct amount. Fig. 27-25. The cutting is done as any crosscutting operation.

RIPPING

For ripping, the radial arm or track must be at right angles to the

27-22(b). Notice that the beveled edge is held against the table guide board when cutting the second miter. A stop block could be used to control length. The matching pieces would not have to be of identical length when following the method shown here.

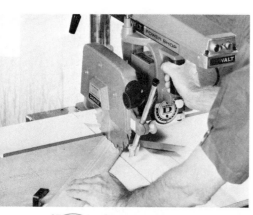

27-23(a). Cutting the miter on the first end. Stock is held against the left side of the V block.

27-24. A shadow box picture frame has a compound miter cut.

fence and the saw blade parallel to it. The saw can be adjusted to in-rip or out-rip positions. For the *in-rip* position, pull the swivel latch and turn the motor and yoke one-fourth turn, placing the motor toward the outside and the saw blade toward the column. Lock in position. Rip-

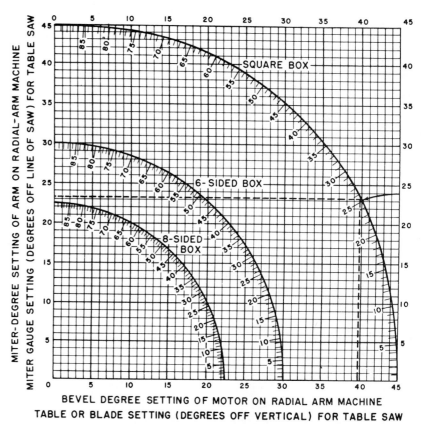

27-25(a). Chart for adjusting the machine to make compound miter cuts. As an example for using the chart, suppose you need a four-sided picture frame with the sides sloping out at 25 degrees. Follow the circular line marked "square box" and find 25 degrees. Follow the horizontal line across to right or left. It reads 23 degrees. This is your miter setting. Then, from 25 on the curve again, follow the vertical line down and you will find it reads 40. This is the bevel setting.

27-23(b). Cutting the second end. Stock is held against the right side of the V block. With this method, matching pieces must be of identical length before mitering. Note also that the hands must shift to do the cutting. The right hand is on the saw on the first cut, the left hand on the second cut.

COMPOUND ANGLES

The figures in the table below are degrees to nearest quarter-degree, and are for direct setting of track-arm and blade tilt. Taper per inch given in second column applies only to front elevation and only to a 4-side figure.

Tilt of Work	Equivalent Taper per Inch	4-Side Butt		4-Side Miter		6-Side Miter		8-Side Miter	
		Blade Tilt	Track Arm	Blade Tilt	Track Arm	Blade Tilt	Track Arm	Blade Tilt	Track Arm
5°	0.087	½	5°	44¾	5°	29¾	2½	22¼	2
10°	0.176	1½	9¾	44¼	9¾	29½	5½	22	4
15°	0.268	3¾	14½	43¼	14½	29	8¼	21½	6
20°	0.364	6¼	18¾	41¾	18¾	28¼	11	21	8
25°	0.466	10	23	40	23	27¼	13½	20¼	10
30°	0.577	14½	26½	37¾	26½	26	16	19½	11¾
35°	0.700	19½	29¾	35¼	29¾	24½	18¼	18¼	13¼
40°	0.839	24½	32¾	32½	32¾	22¾	20¼	17	15
45°	1.000	30	35¼	30	35¼	21	22¼	15¾	16¼
50°	1.19	36	37½	27	37½	19	23¾	14¼	17½
55°	1.43	42	39¼	24	39¼	16¾	25¼	12½	18¾
60°	1.73	48	41	21	41	14½	26½	11	19¾

27-25(b). *Table of compound angles for use on the radial-arm saw. Note that angles are given for both butt and miter joints.*

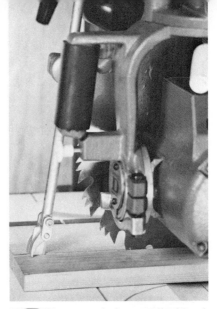

27-27. *Fingers of the anti-kickback device should rest firmly on the wood surface.*

2" beyond the saw; then pull the stick directly back.

For extremely wide cuts, the saw can be adjusted to the *out-rip* position, with the motor toward the column. Fig. 27-28. When the machine is set in this position, the stock must be fed from the left side.

Bevel ripping is done by tilting the blade to the correct angle and cutting as for straight ripping. Fig. 27-29.

Cutting Tapers

There are several common methods of cutting a taper on a radial-arm saw. The simplest is to use a step jig exactly like that for the circular saw. Fig. 27-30. The second method is to use an adjustable jig like that used on a circular saw. Fig. 27-31.

The third way involves clamping a piece of narrow stock to the lower edge of the stock, thus making the front edge of the table into a second guide fence. Taper ripping can be done at the correct angle with this method. Just decide the degree of taper and clamp the lower guide board to the piece to be ripped. Turn the saw to the out-rip position. This allows the blade to be positioned directly over the front edge of the work table. The completed cut

ping is then done from the right side of the table. Fig. 27-26.

Move the saw in or out for the correct width of cut, then lock it in position. Now lower the overarm or track until the saw blade just touches the table and is slightly below it. Adjust the guard so that it clears the top of the stock by about ⅛". Set the anti-kickback fingers so that the prongs rest firmly on the wood surface and hold it against the table. Fig. 27-27. The saw must rotate up and toward you. The dust spout on top of the guard should be adjusted to carry the dust away from you.

Turn on the power and allow the saw to come to full speed. Feed the stock from the right side of the machine. Place one edge of the stock against the guide fence. Place your left hand about 6" behind the safety guard and use it to hold the stock down and against the guide fence. Feed stock with your right hand. Let the stock slide under your left hand. When the right hand comes up even with the left, that is the time to use a push stick. Push the stock about

27-26. *Ripping stock with the blade in the in-rip position. Note the use of a push stick to complete the cut.*

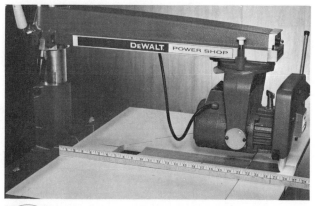

27-28//The maximum width of cut can be made with the saw in the out-rip position. The stock must then be fed from the left side. Note that the guide fence has been moved as far toward the column as possible.

27-29//Cutting a bevel with the grain by tilting the motor unit to the correct angle.

will be at the same angle as the guide board.

HORIZONTAL CUTTING

In horizontal cutting the motor unit is set to a vertical position so that the saw blade is actually parallel with the tabletop. Usually an 8" blade is used with a special guard. An auxiliary wood table is needed for cutting thin stock since the blade can't be lowered more than 1¼" above the tabletop. Fig. 27-32.

Horizontal Crosscutting

This is cutting across the end of stock. To position the saw for this, raise the radial arm approximately 3" above the tabletop. With the saw in the crosscut position, pull it to the front of the arm. Hold the top of the saw guard in your left hand, then release the bevel clamp handle and bevel latch. Swing the motor into a 90-degree horizontal position and lock the bevel clamp handle by pushing it back. Depth of cut depends upon position of the stock in relation to the saw blade. Turn on the motor and pull the saw through the stock as in crosscutting. Fig. 27-33.

Horizontal Ripping

Horizontal ripping is exactly the same as horizontal crosscutting except that the cut is made on the side of stock instead of on the end. To place the blade in the horizontal rip position, set the saw in the in-rip position and tilt it 90 degrees.

Place the stock against a regular or auxiliary table guide fence, depending on the stock's thickness, and locate the height and depth of the cut. A piece of ¾" plywood can be used as an auxiliary table. Fig. 27-34.

USING A DADO HEAD

As mentioned earlier, the same types of dado heads used on the circular saw are also used for radial-arm work. These are used for such operations as cutting grooves, rabbets, dadoes, and tenons, in widths

27-30//The step or fixed jig is made to cut a specific taper. See Fig. 26-54(a). One end of the stock is placed in the correct notch, while the other end rides against the far end of the jig. Place the stock in the first notch and cut one side of the taper. Turn the stock one-quarter turn and use the same notch to make the second cut. Then use the second notch to cut the adjoining tapers.

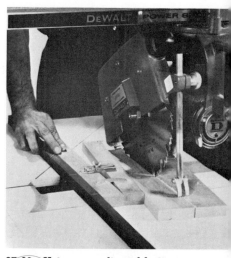

27-31//Using an adjustable jig to cut a taper.

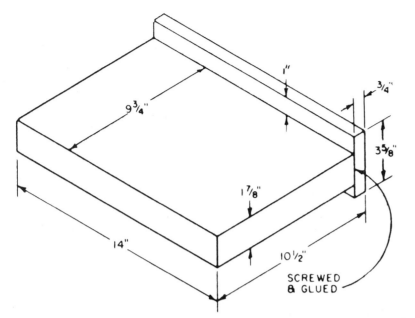

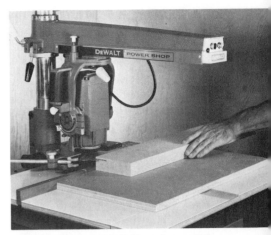

27-34. *Horizontal ripping along the edge of stock.*

27-32. *Auxiliary wood table for horizontal cutting. This table is installed in place of the standard guide fence. To do this, release the clamp screws, lift out the guide fence, slide in the auxiliary table, and retighten the clamp screws.*

from ⅛" to ¹³⁄₁₆" in a single cut. The most common type of dado head consists of two outside saws, or cutters, which are ⅛" thick, combined with inside chippers of different thicknesses. Teeth on the outside cutters do not have any set. The combinations of chipper thicknesses vary somewhat. Some manufacturers include one ¹⁄₁₆" chipper and four ⅛" chippers. Others include one ¼" and two ⅛". The inside chippers are swaged or bent thicker toward the cutting edges to overlap the adjacent chipper or saw. Without this there would not be a clean cut. The bent portion of the chippers must always be placed in the gullets of the outside cutters, never against the teeth. Also, the inside chippers should be staggered. For example, if four inside chippers are to be used, they should be set 45 degrees apart. The chippers must never be used alone, but always in combination with the outside cutters.

If the dado or groove is to be wider than the dado head, two or more passes must be made. Three or four paper or cardboard washers can be put between the blades and chippers to control the width.

Several other types of dado heads are available that are single, adjustable units. The width of the dado can be set on the unit itself before it is fastened securely to the arbor of the saw. (See Chapter 26.)

Mounting a Standard Dado Head

A dado head is installed on the shaft or arbor in the same way as a saw blade. For example, if a ½" dado is to be cut, it would be necessary to have two ⅛" chippers with the two cutters. Place one cutter against the arbor collar, then place the two chippers so that they are 90 degrees apart and fit into the gullets of the cutter. Place the other cutter in the arbor. Fig. 27-35. Then place the arbor collar with the recessed side against the dado head and tighten the arbor nut. If the dado head is more than ½", one of the arbor collars must be eliminated. If a ¹³⁄₁₆" dado must be cut, neither of the arbor collars can be used.

27-33. *Horizontal crosscutting across the end of stock.*

27-35. *Mounting the dado head. Note how the chippers are equally spaced.*

207

Cutting a Plain Dado

A dado is a groove cut across the grain. The procedure followed is very similar to crosscutting. Adjust the arm or track at right angles to the fence and lower the blade to the correct height. Radial-arm saws are lowered by turning the elevating crank; on most saws one complete turn lowers the blades ⅛". This feature makes it possible to set the depth of the dado with great accuracy. A piece of scrap stock the same thickness as the piece to be cut can be placed under the dado head. The blade is lowered until it just touches the surface. Then the piece is removed, and the crank is given the correct number of turns for the desired depth. For example, if a dado is to be ⅜" deep, three complete turns should be made (assuming the usual ⅛" per turn ratio).

In making a chest or cabinet, it is usually necessary to cut several matching dadoes on both of the sides. One method of doing this is with a stop block clamped to the table. In this way a dado can be cut first on one piece, and then a matching one can be cut on the other. Fig. 27-36. If parallel dadoes are needed, a series of marks can be made or a series of stops fastened to the guide fence.

In cutting a dado, always allow the motor to come to full speed. Then make the cut slowly and smoothly. If extremely deep cuts are required, it is usually best to make them in two steps.

A *blind dado* can be cut by using a stop clamp on the radial arm to control the distance the saw will move. Fig. 27-37. A *corner dado* is often necessary when installing a shelf in a table. This can be made by placing the stock at 45 degrees in a V block that is clamped to the guide fence. Raise or lower the radial arm to the correct depth. Fig. 27-38. An *angle dado* is cut exactly like a plain dado except that the radial arm is set at the desired angle. Fig. 27-39.

With the dado head in the ripping position, many types of grooves can be cut with the grain. In using the dado head for grooving, adjust the guard so that the spring clip on the infeed touches the stock. Lock the wing nut and lower the anti-kickback fingers ⅛" below the surface of the stock. The stock should be held against the fence guide and pushed past the blade. Fig. 27-40. *Feed the wood into the rotation of the blade.* Never feed it from the anti-kickback end of the guard. A V can be cut by tilting the motor to the 45-degree position. Fig. 27-41.

Blind Grooving

Sometimes it is necessary to cut a groove partway along the center of a board. This can easily be done with the dado head in the rip position. The best method of controlling length of cut is to fasten two stop blocks on the guide fence for the start and stop of the groove. Adjust the motor unit for the correct location of the groove, then raise the dado head. Place the stock underneath the head and against one of the stop blocks at the start position. Then hold the stock firmly and turn on the power. Lower the head to the correct depth of cut. Push the stock

27-37. *Cutting a blind, or stop, dado. Note the stop clamp on the radial arm.*

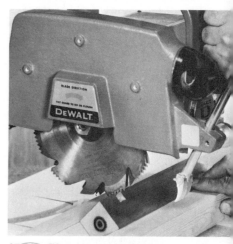

27-38. *Cutting a corner dado. Note the use of the V block.*

27-36. *Using a stop block to control the position of the dado.*

27-39. *Cutting dadoes at an angle.*

27-40 *Using the dado head for grooving (sometimes called ploughing). Note that a push stick is being used to complete the cut.*

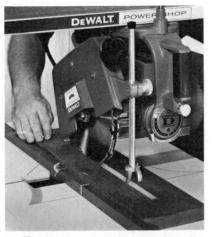

27-42 *Cutting a blind groove. Extreme care must be taken, especially when raising and lowering the saw.*

27-43 *Cutting stock to length with a rabbet on the end.*

along to complete the groove, then raise the dado head and turn off the power. Fig. 27-42.

Cutting and Dadoing

By combining a larger combination saw blade with a dado head, it is possible to do both cutting and dadoing or cutting and grooving at the same time. This operation would be useful primarily in production work when many pieces of the same kind are needed. With the extra blade on and with the machine in crosscut position, stock can be cut to length with a rabbet across grain. Fig. 27-43. With the machine in ripping position, stock can be cut to width with a rabbet along the edge. Fig. 27-44. For such operations an 8″ dado head with a 10″ saw blade is commonly used. If thinner stock is to be cut, use an auxiliary wood table to protect the regular table.

JOINERY

The radial-arm saw is an ideal tool for making many joint cuts. It is particularly useful with the dado head since it allows you to see the cut being made. Also, the length of crosscuts can be easily controlled by putting a stop clamp directly on the arm or track of the machine.

Anytime the dado head is used in a horizontal position, a special tool guard should be substituted for the standard one. After the dado head is installed, place this tool guard on the motor exactly like the standard one. Lock it in place with a wing

nut. This guard can be raised high enough to check the position of the cutting tool by loosening the thumbscrews on either side of the center nut. Fig. 27-45.

With various attachments the radial-arm saw can cut almost all joints used in cabinetmaking. Following are helpful suggestions.

Butt Joints

All basic butt joints, including a butt joint on edge, a butt joint flat,

27-41 *Cutting a V groove (bevel ploughing) is done with the radial arm and yoke in the straight ripping position but with the motor tilted 45 degrees. This is a good method of cutting the V block that is often needed as a jig for other machining operations.*

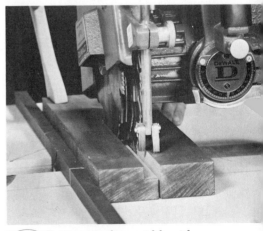

27-44 *Cutting stock to width with a rabbet on the edge.*

209

27-45. Raising the special guard to check the setting of the blades.

leg-and-rail joints, corner butt, and middle-rail butt, can be cut by simple crosscutting operations. All boring operations for the dowel holes can be done with the boring bit and adapter unit as described in Chapter 34.

Edge Joints

Most common edge joints involve ripping operations. The *plain edge* is a simple ripping procedure. For a better glue joint, use a carbide-tipped blade.

Cuts for the *rabbet edge* joint can be made in two ways. One is to make a simple vertical and horizontal ripping cut on each piece. Fig. 27-46. A ¼" piece of plywood should be used as an auxiliary table to clear the guide fence when doing this kind of cutting. The other method is to cut the rabbet in each piece with a dado head. Fig. 27-47.

A *spline edge* involves cutting a groove along the middle of the edges of two pieces. This is done with a dado head in a horizontal position, set to the correct depth. Using the dado head for a wide groove eliminates making several passes, as would be necessary when grooving with a single saw blade. Fig. 27-48.

The *tongue and groove*, commonly used in wood paneling, consists of a tongue, or tenon, on one edge and a groove on the other. The best method of cutting these is to have the saw in a horizontal rip position and to use a dado head to cut all the grooves. The tongues can be cut by placing a spacer collar between the saw blades. Cut tongues on all pieces first, then reverse the stock to cut all of the grooves.

The *dowel edge* joint is a simple ripping operation. Holes must be

27-47. Cutting an L-shaped notch along the end of stock is simple with a dado head in the horizontal position.

bored for the dowels. The glue joint is cut with the shaper attachment.

Rabbet Joints

A simple end rabbet joint is a crosscutting operation that can be done with either a single blade or a

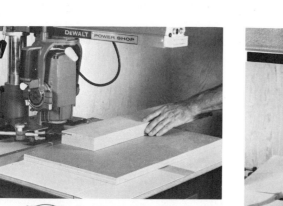

27-46(a). To cut a rabbet along edge grain, first make the layout on the end of the stock. Place the stock on an auxiliary table (a piece of plywood) and against the guide fence. Make the first cut with the saw in the horizontal rip position.

27-46(b). The second cut, which completes the rabbet, is made with the saw in the in-rip position.

27-48. Cutting a groove with a dado head. Note the plywood placed over the table so that the groove just clears the guide fence.

27-49(a). *To make an end rabbet, place the stock flat against the auxiliary table and fence (see Fig. 27-32) and then make the first cut with the saw in horizontal position.*

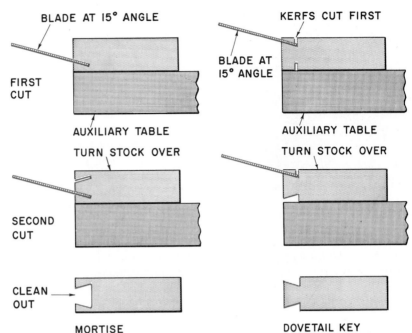

27-50. *This shows the correct method of cutting a dovetail dado across grain. Note the use of the auxiliary table. The dovetail cut can also be made with the grain.*

dado head. If a single blade is used, horizontal and vertical cross-cuts are required. Fig. 27-49. The rabbet can be cut very simply with a dado head in crosscutting position. One or more passes are needed, depending on the rabbet width.

Dado Joints

These joints are best cut with a dado head of correct width. Howev-

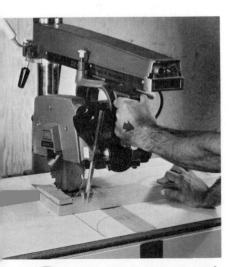

27-49(b). *The second cut is a simple crosscut with the blade set for correct depth.*

er, they can also be cut by making several passes with a single blade, then cleaning out the waste with a chisel. A *simple dado* is a crosscutting operation. The *stop, housed,* or *blind dado* is very easily cut using the dado head and a stop clamp attached to the arm to control the length of the dado. If a square cut is needed at the blind end, this can be done with a wood chisel, with a mortiser, or with a mortising attachment on a drill press. The *dovetail dado* is easy to cut. The mortise, or dovetail slot, is cut first. Tilt the saw blade to 15 degrees and make two angle cuts as shown in Fig. 27-50. Then clean out the mortise. The bottoms of the slots will not be perfect, but this is not essential to a good joint. The tenon, or dovetail key, is made by first cutting the straight kerfs, then tilting the blade to 15 degrees to complete the key.

Lap Joints

Lap joints are best cut by using a dado head. Both pieces of stock to

form the joint can be cut at one time. Fig. 27-51.

Miter Joints

All *flat miter* joints are simple to cut by the methods described in Chapter 39. Fig. 27-52. A spline can be added to the flat miter joint by placing the motor in a horizontal crosscutting position with the arm moved right or left 45 degrees. A slot for a key can also be cut by adjusting the motor to horizontal crosscutting position with the arm set at zero. Dowel holes can be made with the boring attachment.

The *miter with end lap* can easily be made by first cutting one piece to a 45-degree miter, then cutting the rabbet on that piece. The other piece should be cut at a 90-degree angle and then the angle rabbet cut.

All *edge miter* joints are made as bevel crosscuts with the motor locked in a 45-degree bevel position. To make the slot for the spline, reverse the stock. Leave the motor in the bevel position but ele-

211

27-51(a). *Making the cuts for an end-lap joint. The half-lap joint is cut in the same manner except that the pieces are joined end to end.*

27-51(b). *Cutting a cross-lap joint. The dado is cut the same width as the stock and half as deep as the thickness of the stock.*

vate the blade to the correct height, or approximately ⅜". Now the saw blade will not cut completely through. Pull the saw across the bevel cut, leaving a shallow slot. Fig. 27-53. A *blind spline* is very easily cut by using a stop clamp on the radial arm to cut only partway through the beveled edge.

A *miter joint with rabbet* can be cut by following the layout shown in Fig. 27-54.

The *compound miter joint* is commonly used for frame or open con-

struction such as a shadow box picture frame or a molding for a cabinet front. The angle of slant (pitch of the sides) is important in making this cut. For example, if you wish to make a four-sided shadow box picture frame with the sides sloping at 45 degrees, this means that the pitch is 45. In Fig. 27-25(a), look at the curved line labeled "square box" and find the 45-degree mark. Find the horizontal line that intersects the curved line at 45 and follow it to the left or right. It reads 35 degrees. This is the miter setting. Then follow the vertical line intersecting at 45 to the top or bottom of the chart. You will find it reads 30 degrees. This is the bevel setting. With the machine set at these two positions, the cut can be made. For six- or eight-sided boxes, use the correct curve and follow the same procedure.

Mortise-and-Tenon Joints

To make a blind mortise-and-tenon joint, cut the angular opening on a mortiser or with the mortising attachment of a drill press. The mortise can also be cut by using the router attachment. The tenon is cut by placing the motor in a vertical position and a dado head in a horizontal position. A spacer collar is inserted into the dado head so that stock is left to form the tenon. Use an auxiliary table. Place the stock against the fence and mark the stock for the correct depth. With the dado head at proper height, pull the motor forward to cut the tenon. Fig. 27-55.

The *bare-face tenon* is made with a rabbet cut. For an *open mortise-and-tenon*, first cut the tenon. Then reverse the stock and cut the mortise by cutting a groove the same width as the tenon. Fig. 27-56.

Dovetail Joints

This joint is relatively simple to make with a router attachment and a dovetail jig.

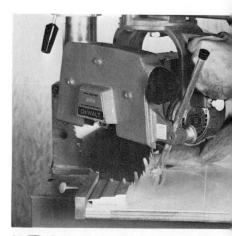

27-52. *A simple method of cutting a flat miter is to move the arm or track first to the right at 45 degrees, then left to the same setting to cut the ends.*

27-53(a). *Cut the edge miter by making a bevel crosscut with the motor in the 45-degree position.*

27-53(b). *To make the slot for the spline, reverse the stock on the table and, with the motor in the same bevel position, raise it so that the blade will cut only the depth of the slot. The slot width is usually ⅛" or ¼".*

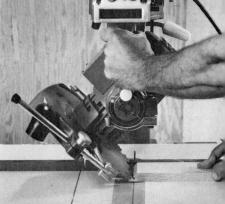

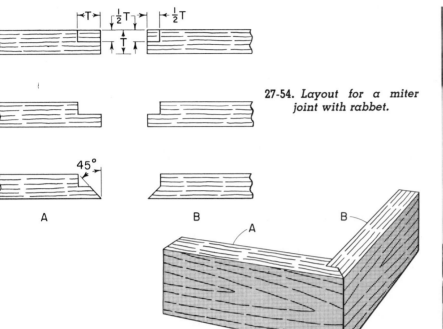

27-54. Layout for a miter joint with rabbet.

27-55. Cutting a tenon by using a spacer collar between the dado head blades.

27-56. Cutting a mortise for an open mortise-and-tenon joint. Make sure the length of the tenon is the same as the width of the mortise stock and the depth of the mortise is the same as the width of the tenon stock.

1. To make a dovetail jig, refer to Figs. 27-57 and 27-58. Dado cut the frame support, D, ¼" deep to receive part E. Use three wood screws and glue to hold these parts together.

2. Dado cut the base, A, ¼" deep to receive the frame support assembly. Fasten B to base A with four wood screws.

3. Mount the frame support (D and E) into the dado grooves in base A, and glue and nail in place. Riser R can now be nailed in place in front of D.

4. Mount hinge K on the base A with three wood screws. Attach pressure clamp G to hinge K with a countersink bolt 1½" long, a washer, and a winged nut.

5. Drill holes in E to line up with upper slots in G in the position shown in Fig. 27-57.

6. Nail cleats C to base A.

7. On thin cardboard, draw a template like the one in Fig. 27-58, but make it 8¾" wide. Cut this out.

8. Using this template as a pattern, carefully trace the exact outline for the dado slots on pressure clamp F.

9. Fasten hinge H to pressure clamp F with three wood screws and to the base A with a 3" bolt, washer, and winged nut.

10. Drill a hole in D to line up with the upper washer slot in F for a 3" bolt, washer, and winged nut.

If you prefer, a simple jig can be made by eliminating the pressure clamps, hinges, and winged nut, substituting pairs of C-clamps to hold the drawer front and sides in position.

To use a dovetail jig for drawer construction, fasten it to the table-top as shown in Fig. 27-59 (Page 216). Turn the motor 180 degrees from the crosscut position. Attach the dovetail router to the arbor. Slide the jig assembly right or left until the router extends exactly ⅜" deep in F, according to the template lines you have traced. Place a piece of stock ¾" × 5¾" × 10" behind clamp G. It should be tilted evenly against a second piece of stock that is ½" × 5¾" and as long as needed for the drawer side behind clamp F. These pieces of stock are the front and one side of the

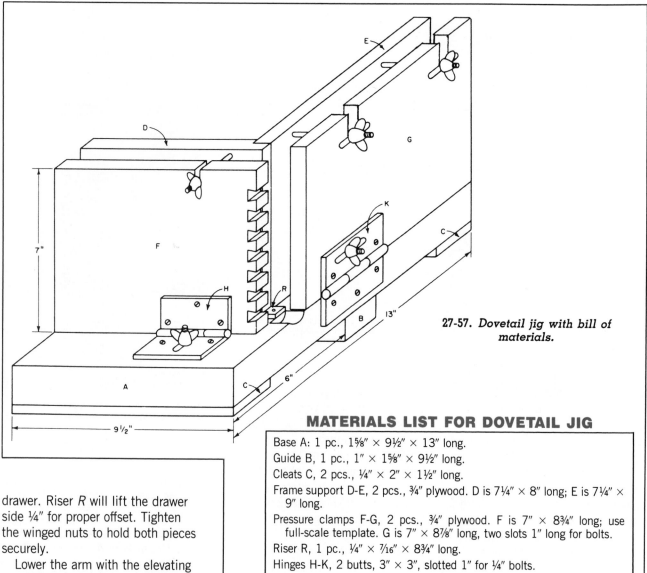

27-57. *Dovetail jig with bill of materials.*

MATERIALS LIST FOR DOVETAIL JIG

Base A: 1 pc., 1⅝" × 9½" × 13" long.
Guide B, 1 pc., 1" × 1⅝" × 9½" long.
Cleats C, 2 pcs., ¼" × 2" × 1½" long.
Frame support D-E, 2 pcs., ¾" plywood. D is 7¼" × 8" long; E is 7¼" × 9" long.
Pressure clamps F-G, 2 pcs., ¾" plywood. F is 7" × 8¾" long; use full-scale template. G is 7" × 8⅞" long, two slots 1" long for bolts.
Riser R, 1 pc., ¼" × ⁷⁄₁₆" × 8¾" long.
Hinges H-K, 2 butts, 3" × 3", slotted 1" for ¼" bolts.
Bolts, 4, each ¼" × 3" long; 1 other, ¼" × 1½".
Wing nuts, 5, each ¼", with washers.
Screws, Nails, Glue, etc., as needed.

drawer. Riser *R* will lift the drawer side ¼" for proper offset. Tighten the winged nuts to hold both pieces securely.

Lower the arm with the elevating handle until the router is directly in front of the top dovetail slot. Start the motor and push it slowly forward, moving it back and forth to clear the chips. Continue until the shoulder of the router passes through clamp *F*, through the ½" stock, into the ¾" stock, and comes to rest against the front edge of clamp *G*. After the first dovetail slot is cut, move the router to the next position, approximately seven turns down, and repeat this operation. Continue until all seven slots have been cut.

To undercut the back of the drawer side, remove the drawer front from behind *G* and turn the elevat-

ing handle to raise the router slightly above the top edge of the drawer side. With the edge of the router extended over the stock about ¹⁄₁₆", set the rip clamp firmly. Now turn the elevating handle slowly downward so that the lip of the router will remove the required undercut from the back edge of the drawer side. Then remove the side from behind *F*. The side and the front should now fit together.

The dovetail jig will cut matching drawer sides and fronts in stock of the following width: 1⅜", 2¼", 3⅛", 4⅞", and 5¾".

Finger or Box Joints

To make this joint it is necessary to use a saw blade or dado head that will cut a slot of precise width. Place the saw motor in horizontal crosscutting position. Use an auxiliary table to hold the stock the cor-

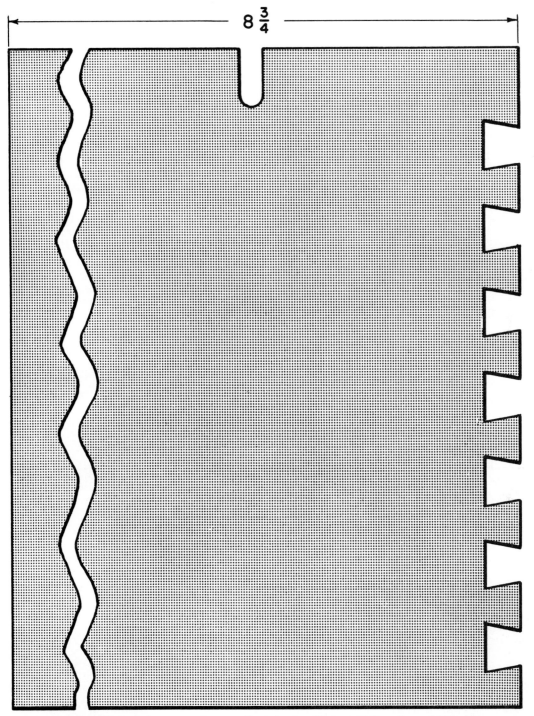

27-58. *Full-length pattern for part F of the jig. Make it 8¾″ wide and 7″ long.*

rect distance above the regular table. Also raise one stock piece the width of a groove above the other and clamp them together. Fig. 27-60. Mark the finger joint on the front piece so that the width of the fingers is exactly the same as that of the grooves. Lower the saw to the first groove and make the cut. Then lower it to the second groove and cut again. Fig. 27-61. Continue until all of the grooves have been cut. If the width of the groove is the same as the thickness of the fin-gers, they will match exactly and form a box, or finger, joint.

SPECIAL CUTTING OPERATIONS

Many special cutting operations can also be done on the radial-arm

27-59. *Cutting a dovetail joint.*

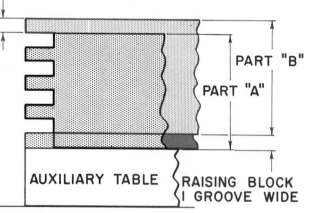

27-60. *The matching pieces are clamped together against the fence of an auxiliary table. One piece must be exactly the width of a groove above the other. The thickness of the fingers must match the width of the grooves.*

saw with a variety of setups. Following are some of the more common ones.

Making Saw Moldings

Several types of attractive moldings can be produced by making kerfing cuts in the wood. To do this, have a spacer mark on a guide fence and make a series of crosscuts along the entire length of the

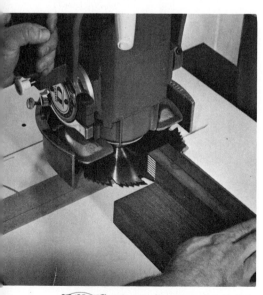

27-61. *Cutting a finger or box joint.*

board. Turn the stock over and repeat the operation so that the kerfs on the second side are equally spaced between the first saw kerfs. Then rip the molding into narrow strips. Fig. 27-62. It can be used for many decorative purposes.

Contour Cutting

Cutting coves on a piece of wood for trim is relatively simple with a standard blade on a radial-arm saw. First set the saw at a 45-degree bevel position. Locate the motor so that the lowest part of the blade is on the centerline of the stock, and tighten the rip clamp. Now lower the arm or track to about ⅛″ below the top of the stock. Feed the stock as you would for ripping. After each cut, lower the arm another ⅛″ until the desired depth is cut. The final cut should be very light, to assure a smooth finish. Fig. 27-63.

By changing the angle of the motor, various cove cuts can be made. For example, if the motor is set at an angle of 45 degrees and the yoke turned slightly off center, the radius of the cut will change, giving the cove a different appearance. This kind of sawing is excel-

27-62(a). *Making a series of crosscuts from both sides, about halfway through the thickness of the stock.*

27-62(b). *Ripping the stock into thin strips for decorative purposes.*

27-63. Cutting a contour surface with a single saw blade. The dado head can also be used for this operation, often with greater success.

27-64. Saucer cutting. Make sure the saw is lowered a little at a time to make this cut.

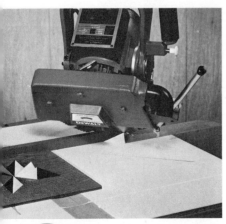

27-65. The second cut is being made with the V strip to the right of the saw blade.

lent for making certain kinds of picture frames.

Saucer Cutting

A slightly dish-shaped cut is sometimes made in the front of a cabinet door to add an interesting surface design. This can be done as follows. Remove the guide fence and back table board, and clamp the stock as shown in Fig. 27-64. Raise the column so that the motor can be tilted at a 45-degree bevel position. Locate the blade over the centerline of the stock. Tighten the rip clamp. Turn the machine on and lower the motor until it strikes the stock. Hold the anti-kickback rod in your left hand. With your right hand pull out the bevel latch and then swing the blade back and forth in an arc past the stock. Lower the saw blade one-half turn of the elevating handle and continue cutting until the proper depth is reached.

Rosette Cutting

A rosette for overlaying on a door can be formed by combining diamond-shaped pieces which are made as follows. First bevel rip the stock into V strips. Then set the motor at the 45-degree righthand miter position and the 45-degree bevel position. Make the first cut with the V strips to the left of the blade, then the second with the strips to the right of it. This forms the pieces that are used to make the rosette. Fig. 27-65.

MOLDING OPERATIONS

Many molding and shaping operations are possible on the radial-arm saw. The same kinds of molding heads used on the circular saw can be used on the radial-arm saw. These have knives mounted in a holder. Fig. 27-66. Solid one-piece molding heads can also be used.

For molding operations it is necessary to install a different kind of fence than is used for sawing. Between the two parts of the fence

27-66(a). This round molding head holds three identical knives by means of socket-head screws. Complete sets of knives for all different types of cuts are available. Since the spindle moves clockwise, all cutters must point in the same direction. In attaching the tool, use one arbor collar, the cutterhead, and the arbor nut.

27-66(b). This solid, one-piece cutter is made of tool steel and ground to shape. To install, add both arbor collars, then the cutter, and the nut last. Always place a guard over the molding head.

there must be an opening for the cutter. The standard fence can be replaced by two pieces of wood that are separated at the center to clear the cutters. However, if the complete edge is to be shaped, then it is necessary to have a special shaper-jointer fence. In this way the infeed side of the fence can be adjusted up to its full capacity of ½" while the outfeed side remains in a fixed position to support the work after the total edge has been cut. Fig. 27-67.

The proper cutter must be mounted on the motor shaft and a special guard attached. Then the arm is raised or lowered to the correct height. The work must be held firmly against the table and fence. If the complete edge is to be shaped, the infeed fence must be moved back just enough for the outfeed fence to support the machined

27-67. A shaper-jointer fence is made in two parts. The outfeed side is adjusted to the same relative position as the outside of the cutterhead. If only part of the edge is to be shaped, use a straightedge to align the infeed and outfeed sides. If the entire edge is to be shaped, the infeed side must be set back an amount equal to the depth of cut.

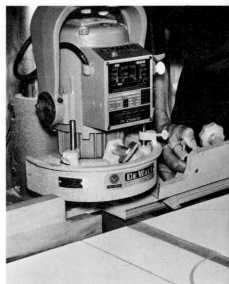

edge. When extremely deep edges are to be shaped, it is better to make two passes, resetting the fence after the first cut. For making narrow moldings, use a feather board and a push stick. Shaping on the radial-arm saw is discussed in Chapter 32.

28 Band Saw

The band saw is designed primarily for cutting curved or irregular shapes, although it can also do all kinds of straight cutting. Fig. 28-1. This saw gets its name from its narrow steel blade, the ends of which are welded together to form a continuous band. The sawing action of this machine is continuous and, if properly adjusted, the saw will do very true and accurate work.

SIZES AND PARTS

The size of the band saw is indicated by the diameter of the wheels. Typical sizes for the cabinet shop are from 14" to 36". Fig. 28-2. The maximum work thickness that can be cut is limited to the

distance between the tabletop and the blade guide in its uppermost position.

The band saw consists of a heavy frame to which are attached two wheels, a table, guides, guards, and a guide post. The lower wheel axle is held in a fixed position and the wheel is rotated by power delivered from the motor through belts. The upper wheel is free-running, having no power delivered to it. It is adjustable in two ways. The wheel moves up and down to accommodate slightly different lengths of blades. It also can be tilted forward and back to make the blades stay on the wheels. If the upper wheel were clamped in a rigid position, it would

28-1. The vertical curved parts for this magazine table can be cut on the band saw.

BAND SAW

MAINTENANCE

- Clean the band saw tires periodically to remove dust, pitch, and gum. Use a rag soaked in benzine.
- Replace the tires when they become worn.
- Make sure the belts are in good condition.
- Check the blade for sharpness and to see if it has sufficient set to prevent binding.
- Make sure the guide blocks and rollers are in good condition and properly adjusted.
- Replace the throat plate, if worn.
- Make sure the table tilts easily and that the pointer on the tilt gauge is accurate.

LUBRICATION

- Use S.A.E. 20 oil on slide ways of the upper wheel bracket trunnions and adjusting screw.
- Oil the following points each month if the saw is used frequently or every 6 months if it is used infrequently:
  - Upper and lower wheel bearings.
  - Table tilt supports or guide.
  - Upper wheel tilt and tension screws.
  - Blade guide blocks.
- Keep oil and grease away from the band saw tires as this would soon ruin them.

SAFETY

- Wear proper clothing and eye protection. (See Chapter 4.)
- Check the stock to make sure it is free of nails before cutting.
- Adjust the sliding bar or post so that the upper guide is about ¼" above the work. If the guide is too high, the blade will not have the proper support.
- Never allow anyone to stand to the right of the saw. If the blade breaks, it could fly out in that direction.
- Make sure the saw blade has proper tension and that the teeth are pointing down.
- Avoid backing out of a cut as this could pull the blade off the wheels.
- Never attempt to cut round stock without a holding jig. It will roll out of your hands as the saw starts the cut.
- Hold the stock firmly on the table to do the cutting.
- Never cut a curve of small radius with a wide blade unless you first make relief cuts.
- If you hear a rhythmic click as the wood is being cut, this usually indicates a cracked blade. Stop the machine and inspect.
- If the blade breaks, shut off the power and stay away from the machine until it comes to a complete stop. Never try to free the blade while the wheels are still turning.
- Never have your fingers or arms in line with the blade.
- Use a helper to handle long stock. Remember that the operator should do all the pushing.
- Keep a well-balanced stance as you do the cutting.
- Never try to pick pieces of wood out of the table slot while the saw is operating.

cause the blade to break. Therefore there is a tension spring that gives the upper wheel a little play. The tilt adjustment moves the upper wheel forward or back so that the blade will run on the center of the wheel. By tilting the wheel slightly,

the saw can be made to run on the front of the wheel rim or farther back. Fig. 28-3. To protect the teeth, a thin rubber tire covers both the upper and lower wheels. Fig. 28-4.

Because the blade is a continu-

ous piece of metal, the table has a slot so that blades can be removed and replaced. A larger opening in the center of the table is covered with a table insert or throat plate of soft metal. On most saws the table can be tilted about 45 degrees to the right and 5 degrees to the left.

The saw or blade guides consist of two pairs of guide pins, blocks, or small wheels, one above and one below the table. These hold the blade in line. Fig. 28-5. There is also a small ball-bearing guide wheel made of hardened steel, behind the guide pins. This wheel should run free except when cutting is being done. The back of the blade should not quite touch this wheel. The wheel should not turn unless it must absorb pressure against its face. The upper guides are attached to a guide post that can be raised or lowered when cutting different thicknesses of wood. Both the upper and lower wheels

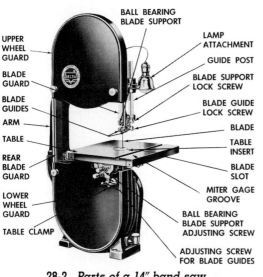

28-2. Parts of a 14″ band saw.

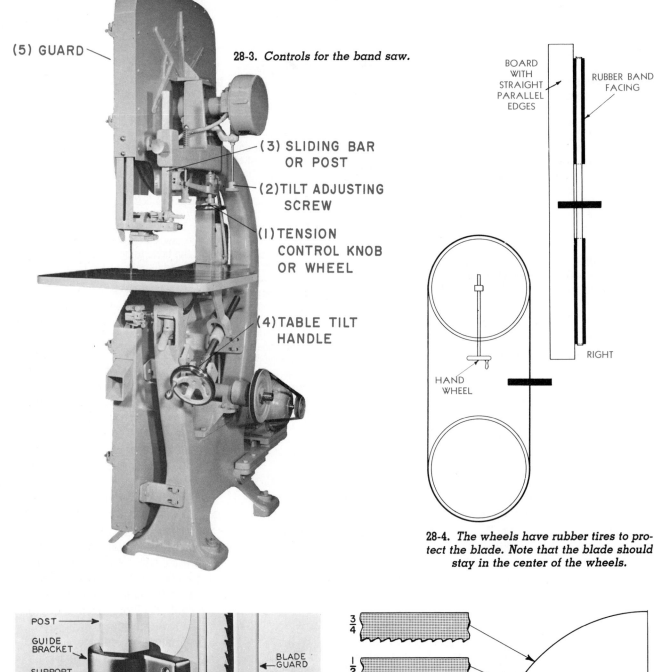

28-3. *Controls for the band saw.*

(5) GUARD

(3) SLIDING BAR OR POST

(2) TILT ADJUSTING SCREW

(1) TENSION CONTROL KNOB OR WHEEL

(4) TABLE TILT HANDLE

BOARD WITH STRAIGHT PARALLEL EDGES

RUBBER BAND FACING

RIGHT

HAND WHEEL

28-4. *The wheels have rubber tires to protect the blade. Note that the blade should stay in the center of the wheels.*

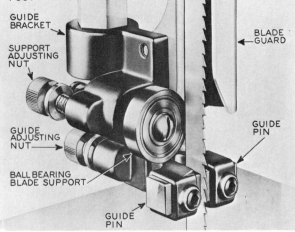

POST

GUIDE BRACKET

SUPPORT ADJUSTING NUT

GUIDE ADJUSTING NUT

BALL BEARING BLADE SUPPORT

GUIDE PIN

BLADE GUARD

GUIDE PIN

28-5. *Guides on a 14″ band saw. On large machines the guide pins or blocks may be replaced with guide wheels for easier action.*

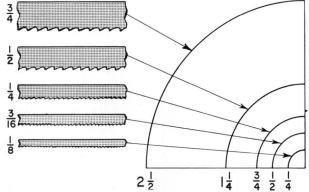

$\frac{3}{4}$

$\frac{1}{2}$

$\frac{1}{4}$

$\frac{3}{16}$

$\frac{1}{8}$

$2\frac{1}{2}$ $1\frac{1}{4}$ $\frac{3}{4}$ $\frac{1}{2}$ $\frac{1}{4}$

28-6. *This chart shows how to select the correct width of blade for a 24″ saw. The minimum radius that can be cut depends not only on the width of the blade but also on such factors as the thickness of the blade, the number of teeth per inch, the kind of teeth, and the set. Generally, a smaller band saw (14″) using the same width of blade will cut a smaller radius than a larger (24″) band saw.*

and the blade are covered with guards. It is important to keep these guards in place because if the blade breaks, it may fly out. Some band saws have a telescoping guard which encloses the blade from the guide to the upper wheel guard for maximum protection.

BAND SAW BLADES

Blades are made in widths from 1/8" to 1 1/2". In general, the number of teeth per inch is directly related to blade width—the narrower the blade, the finer the teeth. A narrow blade is needed to cut sharp curves. A wider one is better for larger curves and for resawing. Fig. 28-6. All standard band saw blades for cutting wood have teeth alternately set in opposite directions.

Replacing a Blade

Remove or open the guards that cover the upper and lower wheels. Take out the table insert or throat plate and remove the pin or set-screw at the end of the blade slot. Now release the tension on the upper wheel and remove the blade. If the blade is to be stored, wipe it with an oily rag to prevent rusting.

28-8. This blade will be ready for storing after it is fastened with string or masking tape.

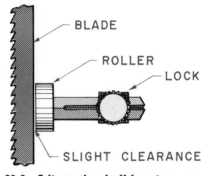

28-9. Adjust the ball-bearing support rollers to just clear the back of the blade.

To fold the blade, grip it with the back toward you and the teeth away from you. Place your right hand on the blade with the thumb up and the left hand with the thumb down. Hold the blade firmly. Now rotate your right wrist to turn the thumb down and the left wrist to turn the thumb up. As you twist, the blade will coil into three loops. Fig. 28-7. Tie the blade with a string or fasten it with masking tape. Fig. 28-8.

If a wider blade is to be placed on the band saw, loosen the blade guides. Release the ball-bearing blade support and move it back. Slip the new blade through the table slot and over the wheels, with the teeth pointing toward the table. Turn the tension handle to apply a small amount of tension to the blade. Now rotate the lower wheel by hand to see if the blade stays in the approximate center of the wheels. As necessary, tilt the upper

wheel slightly in one direction or another until the blade stays in the center of the wheel (tracks properly). If the blade does not track properly, it may ride against the guides and ruin them in a hurry. Now tighten the upper wheel until the blade is taut. For a 1/8" to 1/4" blade, the tension is correct when some pressure at the center of the unsupported area will move the blade about 1/8". Blades should always "give" slightly when pressed.

Replace the table insert or throat plate and the alignment pin. Move both the upper and lower ball-bearing blade support rollers until they just clear the back of the blade about 1/64". Fig. 28-9. Next, move the blade guides or wheels forward or back until the front of the guides is just back of the teeth. Fig. 28-10. Now place a heavy piece of paper around the blade and apply pressure to the blade guides or wheels. Fig. 28-11. Tighten them. When the paper is removed, blade clearance will be just right.

It is also important to make sure that the openings in the upper and lower guides are in the same plane. A wrong adjustment, such as that shown in Fig. 28-12 will soon break the blade or ruin the guides. Before starting to cut, check to see that the table is perfectly level, with the pointer on zero position.

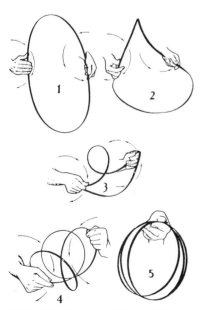

28-7. Folding or coiling a blade.

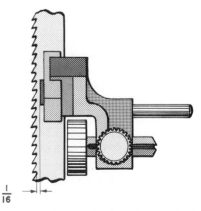

1/16

28-10. Make sure the guides are just back of the teeth.

221

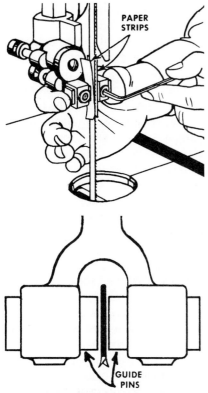

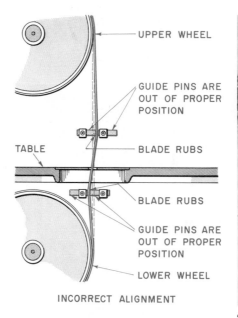

INCORRECT ALIGNMENT

28-11. *The strips of paper give just the right clearance between the blade and the pins or blocks.*

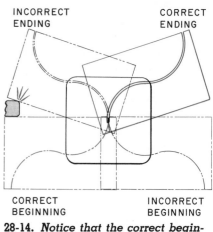

28-13. *This is the correct position when cutting.*

BASIC OPERATING TECHNIQUES

The correct cutting position for operators is facing the blade, standing slightly to the left of it. Fig. 28-13. The key to successful band saw work is the operator's skill. You must be able to follow just outside the layout line, allowing extra stock for smoothing the edges later. In cutting, guide the stock with your left hand and apply forward pressure with your right. Move the stock into the blade as rapidly as it will cut. Moving it too slowly will tend to burn the blade. Change the position of the upper guide before each cutting so that it just clears the upper surface of the stock by about ¼". After turning on the power, do not feed the work into the blade until the machine is operating at full speed.

Watch the feed direction. Before making a cut, think through the

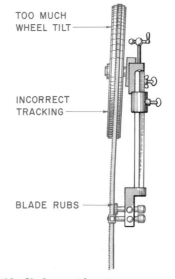

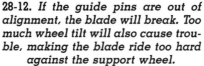

28-12. *If the guide pins are out of alignment, the blade will break. Too much wheel tilt will also cause trouble, making the blade ride too hard against the support wheel.*

path of the cut. Some pieces will swing in such a way as to hit the upper arm. You must have a plan or you will soon find yourself in difficulty and have to backtrack along the cut. Fig. 28-14.

Always make short straight cuts before long ones. When stock is cut from two sides, cut the short side first so that there will be a minimum

28-14. *Notice that the correct beginning for this cut is with the stock to the left of the blade.*

of backing out. Whenever possible, cut out through waste stock rather than backing out. It is easier to back out of a short cut than a long one. However, if the cutting includes both straight and curved lines, make the straight cut first, even though it may be a little longer. It is more difficult to back out of a curved cut. Fig. 28-15. It is a good idea to number each cut. Numbering helps you remember which cut to make next.

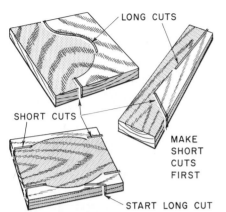

28-15. *If you make short cuts first, little backing out is necessary. Note that when the long cut is completed the waste piece will fall away.*

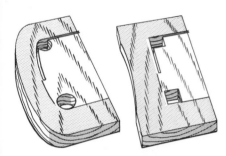

AN AUGER AND MORTISING CHISEL USED TO MAKE TURNING HOLES

28-16. *Use the auger bit or mortising chisel to cut turning holes.*

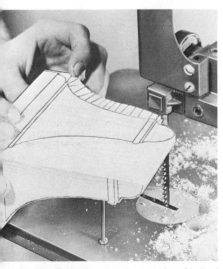

28-17. *Relief cuts up to within 1/32" of the layout line eliminate the twisting strain. The waste stock will fall away as the cut is made.*

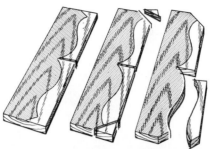

28-18. *Combination curves should be broken up into a series of smaller, simple cuts.*

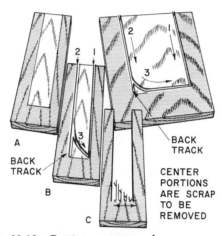

28-19. *Cutting rectangular openings. The numbers indicate the order of cuts. It is necessary to backtrack slightly on cut 2 before the curve is cut to the other corner.*

Make use of turning holes in the design. These are round or square holes in waste stock, drilled or bored on the drill press or mortising machine to help in the cutting. Fig. 28-16.

Break up short curves. Use a series of relief cuts when it is necessary to cut around a short curve with a fairly wide blade. Fig. 28-17. Break up complicated curves. Look at each layout and see if a combination of cuts can be made to divide the complicated curve into simpler cuts. Fig. 28-18.

On large rectangular openings, cut to one corner, then backtrack slightly before cutting to another corner. Narrow grooves can be cut in the same way except that the ends can be "nibbled" out. Fig. 28-19.

Sometimes beeswax applied to the blade sides will help in cutting hardwood or wood that has a great deal of pitch.

Sometimes the blade tends to run to one side, making it necessary to feed the work at an angle in order to cut a straight line. This condition, called "leading," should be corrected. It is caused by one or more of the following: slight wear on one side of the blade; more set on one side of the teeth than the other; guide too loose or out of line; or too narrow a blade. To correct the first two conditions, hold an abrasive stone lightly against the side on which the blade leads. For the other conditions, readjust the guide blocks or change the blade.

Straight Cutting

While the band saw is designed primarily for cutting curves, circles, and irregular shapes, it has many advantages for straight cutting jobs. It will handle any length of stock and will cut a width equal to the distance from the blade to the arm. The band saw will cut thicker material than the circular saw, and the narrow saw kerf results in less waste.

Freehand Cutting

Mark a straight line on the stock. Hold the stock in both hands, at least 2" away from the saw blade. Guide the stock with the left hand and move it along with the right. Fig. 28-20.

Ripping can be done in a freehand manner by using the thumb of your left hand as a guide and moving the stock along with your right hand. This is most satisfactory for short boards.

Using a Ripping Fence

A ripping fence can be fastened to either the right or left of the saw

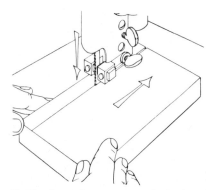

28-20. *Straight cutting with the band saw.*

blade. Stock can then be fed into the blade, applying slight pressure to the table and against the fence. A straightedge can be clamped to the table to replace the fence.

Cutting with a Miter Gauge

A miter gauge can be used on the band saw to cut any angle. It can be placed in standard or reverse position. Use your right hand to push the gauge and your left hand to hold the stock against the gauge.

Cutting Duplicate Parts

A number of identical parts can be cut by clamping a stop block to

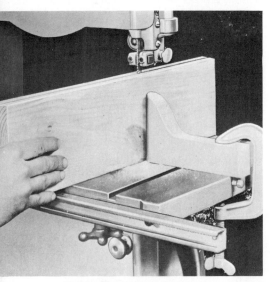

28-21. *Resawing stock using a pivot block.*

28-22. *Bevel ripping. Here stock is being cut to an octagonal shape in preparation for turning on a lathe.*

the table. Hold the stock against the miter gauge and the stop block, then move it into the saw to cut it off.

Resawing

Resawing is cutting stock into thinner pieces. The band saw has a distinct advantage for this kind of work since it does not waste as much material as a circular saw. *Always use the widest possible blade.* It is sometimes a good idea to cut a shallow kerf in each edge with the circular saw. The kerf will serve as a guide. Then do the resawing on the band saw.

The best method for resawing is to clamp a pivot pin to the table as a guide. This is especially good if the saw tends to lead to one side or the other. With the pivot pin, you can shift the board slightly to compensate for this. Fig. 28-21. The ripping fence can also be used as a guide for resawing. In resawing long work, have someone hold the other end of the board or use a roller support. Hold the stock against the guide block or fence and push it steadily forward.

Bevel Ripping

Tilt the table to an angle of 45 degrees and fasten the fence to it so that it just clears the blade. The clearance between the underside of

the fence and the saw table will make it possible to cut bevels up to 45 degrees without the blade hitting the metal fence. Fig. 28-22. A simple V jig can also be used to perform the same operations with the table in a level position. Fig. 28-23.

CUTTING CURVES

Shallow Curves

Most shallow curves can be cut freehand. Cut just outside the layout line so that a small amount of material remains for sanding.

Sharp Curves

A narrow blade is best for cutting sharp curves. If a wide blade is on the machine, a sharp curve can be cut by first making relief cuts to within 1/32" of the layout line. Then,

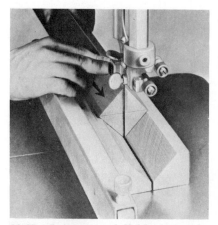

28-23. *A fence and V block can be used for diagonal ripping. This is also a good method of cutting a kerf across the corners to insert the spurs of the live center for wood turning.*

FIRST CUT

28-24. *Rough cut the curve through the waste stock before completing the final cuts.*

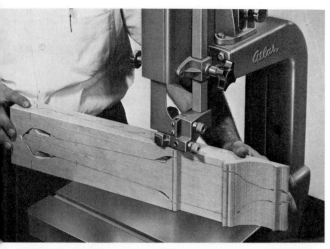

28-25. *Compound cutting is necessary to produce this sculptured letter holder. Notice how the saw cuts have been made from one side before the stock is turned on edge to complete the part. A thin nail or pin, placed so that it will not be struck by the blade, holds the parts together as the final cut is made.*

28-26. *Using an extension guide bar circle jig for cutting a true circle.*

during cutting, the wedges drop off one by one to give added clearance to the blade. Another method of making sharp cuts is to make several tangent cuts until the final curve is obtained. Rough cut complex curves before finishing the cut. Fig. 28-24.

COMPOUND SAWING

Compound sawing is done in making bookends, bases for lamps, and other decorative shapes cut from two adjoining surfaces of a square or rectangular piece of stock. A simple way to do such cutting is to make a pattern and trace it on two adjoining faces. Then cut the waste stock from two sides of the wood. Fasten this waste stock back in place in the waste portion of the main work. Turn the stock a quarter turn and saw from the other side.

Another method of doing this is to make the first cuts *almost* to the end of stock so that the waste material will stay in place. Fig. 28-25. Then turn the stock over a quarter turn and make the other two cuts. The cabriole leg is cut in this manner.

CUTTING CIRCLES

The simplest method of cutting a single circular piece is to do it freehand, carefully guiding the stock to follow the layout line.

Using Jigs for Circle Cutting

Several kinds of jigs can be used to cut circles. These are particularly useful in mass production. The commercial circle jig is fastened to the upper saw guide bar. It has an adjustable pivot pin which is set to the correct radius from the cutting edge. Fig. 28-26.

It is relatively simple to make a plywood circle jig. Cut a piece of ¾" plywood that is slightly wider than the distance from the blade to the table edge. Fasten two cleats to the underside. Cut a groove or a dovetail dado at right angles to the blade, with the center of the groove at the front of the teeth. Cut a small hardwood stick or bar (pivot slide) that will slip into the groove and be flush with the tabletop. Place a sharp pin or screw at the end of the pivot slide. Remember that the pin must be at right angles to the blade and

in line with the front of the blade. Adjust the pin to the correct radius and turn the board slowly as the circle is cut. Fig. 28-27.

Cutting Curved Rails or Segments

Pieces or segments of a circle can be cut with a simple jig. Lay

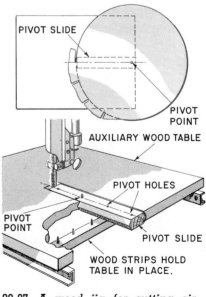

28-27. *A wood jig for cutting circles.*

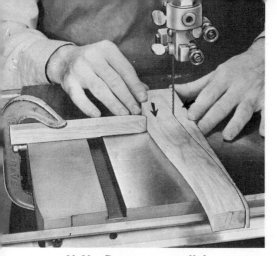

28-28. *Cutting parallel curves, using a pivot block or pin. (Short sleeves are safer.)*

out the curve on thick stock and make the first cut freehand. Then fasten a pivot block or ripping fence to the table a distance from the blade equal to the thickness of the segments you want. Hold the stock against the fence or pin to make this cut.

Curved work can be ripped to equal width in a similar manner with the use of a pivot block. Cut the first edge to the curved shape. Then hold the cut edge against the pivot block to cut the second edge. Fig. 28-28.

Cutting Segments of a Circle

Install a temporary wood table and attach an arm to it at right angles to the saw blade. Cut a pattern of the required circle segment. Attach another arm to this. Put two

28-29. *Cutting a rounded corner, using a jig.*

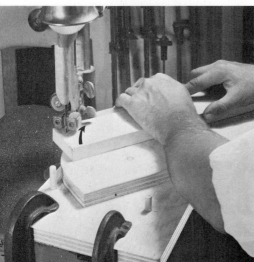

wood screws through the pattern from the underside, with the sharp points exposed. Now fasten the end of the pattern arm to the arm of the table with a single screw located at a point equal to the radius of the arc. Cut the stock, holding it over the pattern. The same technique can be followed for cutting the arc of a circle. Fig. 28-29.

SAWING WITH A PATTERN GUIDE

Another method of cutting duplicate parts is to use a simple wood pattern guide. However, this will work only for cutting broad, shallow curves. The guide arm is clamped to the inner side of the saw table so that the end of the arm is located at the saw blade. A recess is cut on the underside of the arm to permit the passage of waste stock. The end of the arm is curved to match the broadest curve of the pattern. A small slot in the end of the arm permits the recessing of the blade so that the outer side of the blade is flush with the guide arm. The stock is fastened securely to the underside of the wood pattern with sharp anchor points. To do the cutting, saw through the waste stock to locate the edge of the pattern firmly against the edge of the guide arm. Always keep the pattern squarely against the arm and feed the work around to complete the cut. Fig. 28-30.

MULTIPLE SAWING

There are various methods of cutting several identical pieces. One of

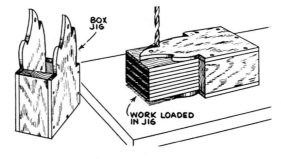

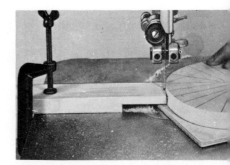

28-30. *Sawing with a pattern is an accurate method of cutting duplicate parts.*

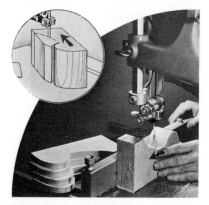

28-31. *Cutting duplicate parts by first cutting thicker stock to shape, then resawing to the correct thickness.*

the simplest is to cut the shape from thicker stock and then resaw to the thinner pieces. Fig. 28-31. Another method is to make a box into which the identical pieces will fit. On top of the box, nail the pattern to be cut, then follow the pattern to obtain the shape. Fig. 28-32. Still another good method is to clamp or nail the pieces together in the waste stock and then cut them.

28-32. *Cutting stock that has been loaded into a box jig.*

29 Scroll Saw

The scroll (jig) saw is used primarily for cutting curved or irregular work. Its main advantage over other curve-cutting saws is that it can be used to make inside cuts without cutting through the stock itself. The machine is particularly useful for cutting small parts of wood, metal, and plastic. Fig. 29-1.

PARTS AND SIZES

The major parts consist of a worktable, cast-iron base, curved removable overarm, upper and lower chucks, and the driving mechanism. Fig. 29-2. The standard scroll saw blade is attached to the lower chuck, then passed through the center hole and connected to the upper chuck at the end of the tension sleeve.

The crank shaft converts the circular motion of the motor pulley to the up-and-down motion of the lower chuck. This part of the scroll saw must be precision-balanced to avoid excessive vibration at high speeds. Most saws are equipped with a four-step cone pulley on the

motor and saw, with a V belt between them. The usual four speeds are 610, 910, 1255, and 1725 cutting strokes per minute (CSM). However, for jobs that require a wide variety of speeds, a saw with a variable-speed attachment is useful. This attachment is good for light metals, plastic, and delicate inlay work. With the variable-speed attachment and a 1725 RPM motor, speeds from 650 to 1700 CSM can be obtained. In general, high speeds are used for fast, fine work and slow speeds for heavy woods, metal, and other hard materials.

The size of the scroll saw is indicated by the distance from the

29-1. *The detailed internal and external cutting on the top of this mirror can best be done on a scroll saw.*

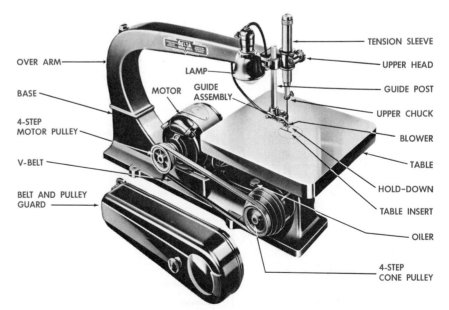

OVER ARM — LAMP — TENSION SLEEVE — UPPER HEAD — GUIDE POST — UPPER CHUCK — BLOWER — TABLE — HOLD-DOWN — TABLE INSERT — OILER — 4-STEP CONE PULLEY — BASE — MOTOR — GUIDE ASSEMBLY — 4-STEP MOTOR PULLEY — V-BELT — BELT AND PULLEY GUARD

29-2. *Parts of a 24″ scroll saw. This machine will cut to the center of a circle 48″ in diameter. It will cut stock up to 2″ thick.*

SCROLL SAW

MAINTENANCE
- Make sure the chuck jaws operate freely and that the thumb- or setscrew is in good condition.
- Make a careful check of the blade guides and hold-down to see that they are adjusted correctly.
- Replace the throat plate (table insert) if it is worn.
- See that the belts are in good condition and not too tight.
- Make sure the tilt action of the table is easy.

LUBRICATION
- The crankcase should be filled to the correct level with S.A.E. 10, 20, or 30 depending on the manufacturer's recommendation.

- Lubricate the moving parts of the table and adjusting screws with S.A.E. 20.

SAFETY
- Wear proper clothing and eye protection. (See Chapter 4.)
- Install the blade with the teeth pointing down.
- Adjust for tension by raising the tension sleeve the correct amount.
- Turn the pulley over by hand to be sure the blade operates properly before turning on the power.
- Make sure the blade guide and hold-down are adjusted properly.

---

blade to the overarm measured *horizontally*. The thickness of material that can be cut is also considered in the size of the saw. The table on the saw tilts to permit double-edge cutting, both straight and curved.

BLADE SELECTION

The three main types of blades are the power scroll saw blade (also called the fret saw), the saber blade, and the jeweler's piercing blade. In general, the kind of blade

as well as the thickness, width, and number of teeth per inch should be determined by the kind of material to be cut and the desired accuracy and smoothness of the cut surface. Choose extremely fine-tooth blades for delicate scroll and jewelry work. Thin, fine-tooth blades are needed for sawing thin woods, metal, veneer, plastic, and similar materials. Use medium-tooth blades for sawing wood and metal of medium thickness. Coarse, heavier blades

are selected for sawing thick materials. Stiff saber blades, fastened only in the lower chuck, are used for ripping and heavy sawing of large inside curves. The blade selected should have at least three teeth in contact with the stock at all times. Fig. 29-3.

Installing a Blade

Since all scroll saws are designed to cut on the downstroke, *teeth must point down*. To install the

Material Cut	Thick In.	Width In.	Teeth Per Inch	Blade Full Size	Material Cut	Thick In.	Width In.	Teeth Per Inch	Blade Full Size
Steel • Iron Lead • Copper Aluminum Pewter • Asbestos Paper • Felt	.020 .020	.070 .070	32 20		Wood Veneer Plus Plastics Celluloid • Hard Rubber Bakelite • Ivory Extremely Thin Materials	.008	.035	20	
Steel • Iron • Lead Copper • Brass Aluminum Pewter • Asbestos Wood	.020 .020 .020	.070 .085 .110	15 15 20		Plastics • Celluloid Hard Rubber Bakelite • Ivory Wood	.019 .019 .020 .020	.050 .055 .070 .110	15 12 7 7	
Asbestos • Brake Lining • Mica Steel • Iron • Lead Copper • Brass Aluminum Pewter	.028	.250	20		Wall Board • Pressed Wood Wood • Lead Bone • Felt • Paper Copper • Ivory • Aluminum	.020	.110	15	
Wood Panels and Veneers	.010	.048	18		Hard and Soft Wood	.020 .028 .028	.110 .187 .250	10 10 7	
Plastics • Celluloid Hard Rubber Bakelite • Ivory Wood	.010 .010 .010	.070 .055 .045	14 16 18		Pearl • Pewter Mica Pressed Wood Sea Shells Jewelry • Metals Hard Leather	.016 .016 .020 .020	.054 .054 .070 .085	30 20 15 12	

29-3. *Chart for selecting the correct blade.*

29-4. *Most blades are held in both upper and lower chucks. Note that the ends of the blade are held between the flat jaws.*

blade, first remove the table insert. Tilt the table to one side so that you can easily reach the lower chuck. Slip the blade between the flat jaws of the lower chuck. Tighten securely, making sure the blade is straight. The chuck is usually tightened with a thumbscrew. An allen wrench is needed if there is a setscrew. Now loosen the upper tension sleeve and lower it. Fasten the other end of the blade in the flat jaws of the upper chuck. Fig. 29-4.

Raise the tension sleeve to provide the right amount of tension on the blade. Correct tension is difficult to specify, but it should be sufficient to hold the blade straight against the cut, though not enough to cause the blade to break easily. Thicker and wider blades do not require as much tension as finer blades.

As part of the guide assembly, most scroll saws have a blade guide that prevents the blade from twisting. This guide is a simple slot cut in metal against which the back of the blade rides during cutting. Most saws also have a circular universal

guide disk which can be readily turned to accommodate blades of varying thicknesses. If a blade is replaced with one of the same thickness and width, this guide disk does not need to be turned. However, when larger or smaller blades are installed, the disk should be changed to give the blade good support. The guide should be adjusted so that the back of the blade, not the teeth, rides in the guide. On some machines there is a small guide roller or support wheel at the back of the guide. The back of the blade should just touch this roller. Fig. 29-5.

Replace the table insert and move the table back to a level position. Before turning on the power, rotate the pulley by hand to make sure the blade operates smoothly.

Since there is a tendency for the work to pull away from the table on the upstroke, a hold-down is needed. Adjust the hold-down so that it just lightly contacts the top of the stock. On some machines the hold-

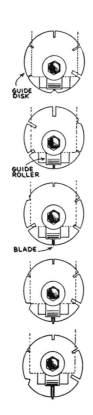

29-5. *Different settings of the universal guide can be used to fit different blades. The guide disk can be rotated and the guide roller moved back and forth. The forward edge of the guide disk should be just behind the bottom of the blade teeth.*

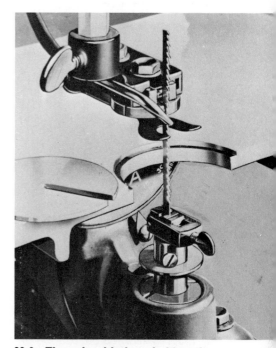

29-6. *The saber blade is held in the V jaws of the lower chuck and is supported above the table by the blade guide.*

down can be turned to the same angle as the table for making bevel cuts.

On some saws the lower chuck can be rotated 90 degrees and the tension sleeve turned the same amount. With this adjustment the cutting can be done from the side instead of the front of the machine. This is particularly useful for cutting a curve on a long piece.

Saber blades have a sharpened upper end and are fastened only in the lower chuck. They are very good for inside cutting if little or no curvature is involved. Though it isn't necessary for most work, the overarm can be completely removed when using a saber blade to cut an opening in a large surface. The saber blade should be clamped in the V jaws of the lower chuck. To do this, loosen the setscrew and turn the lower chuck one-quarter turn. Fig. 29-6. A special guide can be fitted below the saw table to give extra support to the saber blade.

29-7. *A special guide can be installed below the table to give added support to the saber blade. This guide is essential if there is no support for the blade above the table.*

Fig. 29-7. Of course, the upper guide is also used to support the blade except when the overarm is removed.

CUTTING EXTERNAL CURVES

Since the major use of the scroll saw is to cut curves, it is important to follow these suggestions carefully:

• The real value of this saw is for accurately cutting parts that will require little or no sanding. Before starting the cut, examine the design on the surface to determine how the cutting ought to be done. (For external cutting, much of the waste stock can sometimes be removed first on a band saw.)

• Hold the stock with the thumb and forefinger of each hand. Fig. 29-8. Apply slight side pressure to get the blade started in the waste stock, then cut up to the layout line. Apply even, slow forward pres-

sure but do not force stock into the blade.

• Turn the stock slowly when cutting a curve. If you turn too sharply, the blade may break.

• Break complicated cuts up into simpler curves. Fig. 29-9.

• When cutting a curve, always feed straight against the teeth, even when turning a shallow corner. Never apply side pressure against the blade.

• In a tight spot it is sometimes good to backtrack slightly and recut up to the line.

CUTTING INTERNAL CURVES (PIERCING)

To make an internal cut (to do piercing), drill one or more holes large enough for the blade to start in the waste stock. It is generally a good idea not to drill the holes close to the layout line. To insert the blade into the hole, release the upper chuck and loosen the clamp on the guide post so that it can be raised. Then the stock can be slipped over the blade. Fasten the blade in the upper chuck and lower the guide post again. Sometimes it is necessary to remove the table insert since the blade must be bent slightly to one side as the stock is slipped over it. Now cut from the waste hole up to the layout line at an angle so that you can watch the cutting action and correct the line of cut before it reaches the layout line.

STRAIGHT CUTTING

Straight cutting is usually done on small pieces, such as the letters for a raised name plate shown in Fig. 29-10. It is quite difficult to cut a long straight line on the scroll saw. However, the saw can be used on thin stock. The best way to do this is to clamp a guide board to the table the correct distance from the blade. Choose the widest blade possible to reduce the blade's tendency to stray off the straight line.

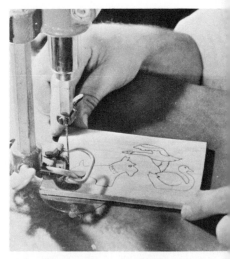

29-8. *The scroll saw is ideal for intricate external cutting. Note how the stock is held.*

There are at least three common ways of cutting a square corner on the scroll saw. Never come right up to the corner and attempt to turn 90 degrees since this will twist the blade and usually break it. For an outside corner, follow one of the methods shown in Fig. 29-11. An inside corner should be cut slightly rounded first; then complete the sharp corner from two directions. To cut a sharp angle, cut to the end along one side. Then cut a curve to reach the other side. After most of the waste stock is removed, cut

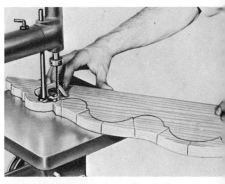

29-9. *Break up a complicated curve into several simpler cuts. Make relief cuts to the design so that small pieces of scrap wood will drop away as the curve is cut.*

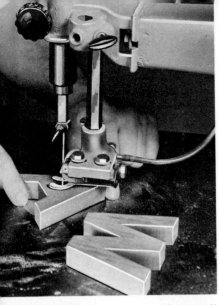

29-10. *Cutting letters on the scroll saw. Usually it is a better idea to make the external cuts on a band saw and then do the internal cuts on the scroll saw.*

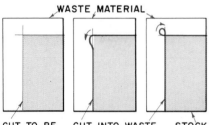

29-11. *Two methods of cutting an outside corner. One way is to make a slightly curved cut at the corner, then trim this off with a second cut. Another method is to make a complete circle in the waste area of the stock.*

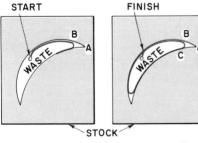

29-12. *Cutting a sharp angle. Start from a hole drilled in waste stock. Cut to point B, then make a curve as shown. Follow the layout line from point C to the opposite end, cut another curve, then follow the layout line again until the waste stock drops out. Finally, make the sharp corner by cutting from both B and C to A.*

from both sides to the point. Fig. 29-12.

BEVEL CUTS OR ANGLE SAWING

The table can be tilted up to 45 degrees to cut a bevel on straight, circular, or irregular designs. However, when cutting an angle or bevel, the work must always remain on the same side of the blade. For example, in cutting parts for a wood pattern to make a metal casting, a slight bevel (draft) must be cut. If the stock is swung completely around the blade, the bevel will change direction. Fig. 29-13. Other examples are shown in Fig. 29-14. A wide, coarse blade is recommended.

MAKING IDENTICAL PARTS

If two or more identical parts must be cut, one of the best methods is to make a "sandwich" of the material. Fasten the pieces together with small nails or brads in the waste stock.

CUTTING THIN METAL

Cutting metal is very much like cutting wood, except that slower speeds are recommended and finer teeth blades should be used. Aluminum can be cut at fairly high speed

and with coarse teeth, but harder metals require finer teeth and slower speeds. *When sawing metals, always lubricate the blade with beeswax or paraffin.* This will greatly prolong the life of the blade and result in much more efficient sawing.

It is often difficult to cut thin metal without excessive blade breakage. One method of overcoming this is to clamp the metal between two thin pieces of plywood. A piece of waxed paper included in the sandwich will help lubricate the blade and prevent chipping. Draw the design on the wood and cut as for making identical parts. This technique can also be used for cutting veneers.

MAKING A SIMPLE INLAY

A simple inlay can be made to form a design of two or more kinds

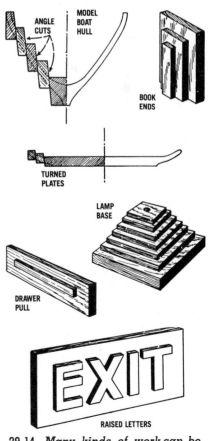

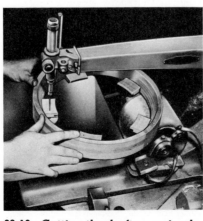

29-13. *Cutting the draft on a circular wood pattern.*

29-14. *Many kinds of work can be done by angle sawing.*

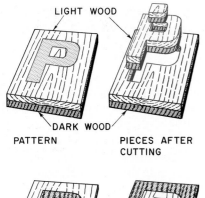

PATTERN | PIECES AFTER CUTTING

DARK WOOD INLAID ON LIGHT WOOD | LIGHT WOOD INLAID ON DARK WOOD

29-15(a). *Steps in making a simple inlay.*

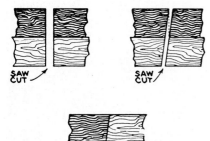

29-15(b). *Note that when cut at an angle, the pieces fit together with no visible saw kerf.*

of wood. Fasten two pieces of wood together in a pad and nail them with small brads in each corner. Drill a small hole at the inside corner of the design, to start the blade. Now

29-16. *Cutting a coped joint.*

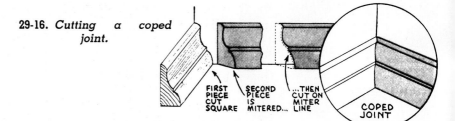

tilt the table about 1 or 2 degrees. Make the necessary cuts, keeping the work on the same side of the blade. Take the pad apart and assemble the design. When pieces with beveled edges are fitted together, the saw kerf will not be visible. Sanding the surfaces will tend to bind them even better. Fig. 29-15.

MAKING A COPED JOINT

Cut one piece square at the end. Miter the other piece at 45 degrees. On the scroll saw, cut the end at 90 degrees, following the contour created on the face by the beveled cut. Fig. 29-16.

FILING AND SANDING ATTACHMENTS

Small files of different shapes can be used on the scroll saw. These are particularly valuable in finishing metal edges for hardware and other special pieces of metal or plastic. The files have either ¼" or ⅛" shanks and come in a wide variety of shapes. Fig. 29-17. The file is held in the V jaws of the lower chuck. The work is usually fed to the tool from the pulley side. The saw can also be used for sanding. Fig. 29-18.

MACHINE FILES
With ¼" shank—Overall length 3¼"
Description

■	Square	●	Round
▮	Crochet	◀	Triangle
◀	Half Round	▮	Oblong

29-17. *Common shapes of files.*

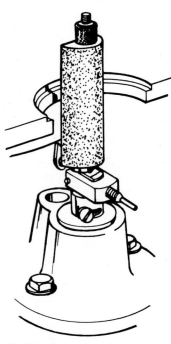

29-18. *Sanding attachment for the scroll saw.*

Portable Saws and Planes

Portable power tools help the cabinetmaker and finish carpenter do the job faster. Although portable saws and planes have only limited use in a well-equipped cabinet shop, they are ideal for on-the-job construction.

PORTABLE POWER SAW

The portable power saw (also called electric, hand, or cutoff saw) can be used for many types of cutting, particularly on large panel stock. Figs. 30-1 and 30-2. The size is determined by the diameter of the blade and ranges from 6″ to 10″. The most common sizes, 7″ and 8″, will easily cut through a 2 × 4. Blades are much the same as those for circular and radial-arm saws. A combination blade, for both crosscutting and ripping, is most commonly used.

One great advantage of the portable power saw is that sawing can be done on boards that have already been installed. It can, for example, trim off boards that extend beyond the edge of an adjoining surface. When cutting in a horizontal position over sawhorses, always tack an extra strip of stock over the sawhorses to protect them from the blade.

This saw cuts from the bottom up. Fig. 30-3. Therefore, when cutting plywood, *always place the good surface down.* This should be done because the top of the cut will not be as smooth as the bottom, and there is more tearing of the upper surface.

Parts

In addition to enclosing the motor, electrical parts, and gears, the *housing* incorporates blade guards, a base, and cutting-depth

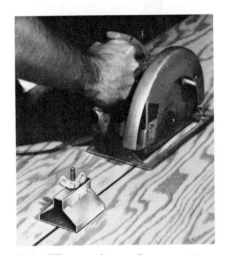

30-2. *When making a long, continuous cut, insert a wedge of wood or a commercial unit into the kerf to keep it open. Without this the kerf may close, causing the blade to bind.*

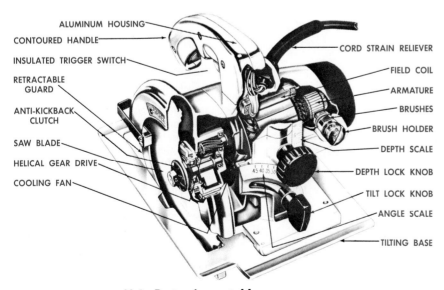

ALUMINUM HOUSING
CONTOURED HANDLE
INSULATED TRIGGER SWITCH
RETRACTABLE GUARD
ANTI-KICKBACK CLUTCH
SAW BLADE
HELICAL GEAR DRIVE
COOLING FAN

CORD STRAIN RELIEVER
FIELD COIL
ARMATURE
BRUSHES
BRUSH HOLDER
DEPTH SCALE
DEPTH LOCK KNOB
TILT LOCK KNOB
ANGLE SCALE
TILTING BASE

30-1. *Parts of a portable power saw.*

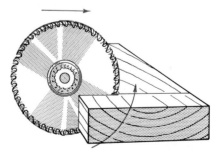

30-3. *The cutting action of the portable power saw is exactly opposite that of the circular saw. The portable saw cuts from the bottom up.*

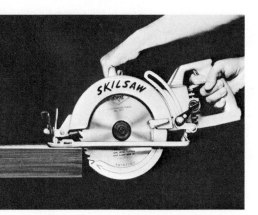

30-4. *Starting the saw. Hold it firmly on the work.*

and cutting-angle adjustments. Some models have a rip guide.

One of the *blade guards* is a stationary upper guard that covers the front, top, and back of the saw blade. There is also a retractable guard that covers the blade bottom when the saw is not in use. As you push a running saw into work, this retractable guard moves backwards and upwards into or outside the upper guard.

The *base* consists of one or more skids that rest on the workpiece and hold the saw upright when it is operating.

The *rip guide* and adjustment is a scale side extension to the base that keeps the saw blade parallel with the edge of the work. Some saw models include a built-in rip guide. For others it is an accessory.

The *cutting-depth* and *cutting-angle adjustments* enable movements of the base in relation to the blade. The depth adjustment moves the base up and down. The angle adjustment tilts the base as much as 45 degrees. The scale numbers should be easy to read, and the adjustment tilt lock knob should be easy to grasp and turn. It should tighten securely.

The portable power saw has a contoured handle for the right hand and, in some models, a front auxiliary handle for the left. There are also saws made for left-handed people. The tool should be comfortable to hold and provide a clear view of the blade front when the saw is in operating position.

Some saws have a *slip clutch*, or special washers, where the blade fastens to the drive shaft. It is designed to prevent motor burnout if the saw blade sticks. It can also reduce the likelihood of kickback and loss of control.

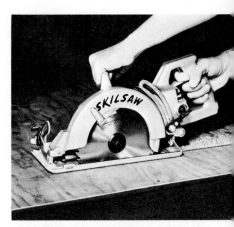

30-5. *Crosscutting. Whenever possible, place both hands on the saw.*

Crosscutting

Lay out a guideline across the stock. Before you begin, adjust for depth of cut so that the saw blade will penetrate the lower surface by about ⅛". (The saw will cut quicker and require less power when the blade clears the bottom of the stock by ½". However, this is more dangerous and is not recommended except for work fastened in place.) Place the base of the saw on the stock, with the blade in line with the guideline. Fig. 30-4. Turn on the saw and let it come up to full

---

PORTABLE SAWS AND PLANES

MAINTENANCE
- Check the sharpness of the blade or knives.
- Check the condition of the belt, if any.
- See that the guards operate easily.
- Check the tool for a broken plug or switch, bad connector, or poor insulation on the core.
- Keep the air passages clear.

LUBRICATION
- Motors on most portable tools have sealed bearings that require no further lubrication.
- Use S.A.E. 20 bearing oil or the best grade of nondetergent motor oil for any places that need oiling. Be sure to clean out the oil holes before adding the oil. Add no more than four or five drops.

SAFETY
- MAKE SURE THE SWITCH IS IN THE "OFF" POSITION

BEFORE CONNECTING ANY POWER TOOL TO THE POWER SUPPLY.
- Never run a tool where there is any chance of explosion or fire due to the presence of naphtha, gasoline, benzine, or any other explosive or flammable substance.
- Never wear loose clothing that might become tangled in the fast-turning parts. Wear eye protection. (See Chapter 4.)
- Keep your fingers away from blades and cutters.
- Turn off the motor immediately after finishing the cut.
- Disconnect the cord plug from the power outlet before making adjustments or replacing a blade or cutter.
- Make sure your hands and feet are dry when using a portable tool.
- Be sure the tool is properly grounded. It should have a three-pronged plug and/or be double-insulated.
- If an extension cord must be used, make sure it is 12-gauge wire or heavier for lengths up to 100′ and 10-gauge or heavier for lengths up to 150′. Use only approved heavy-duty extension cords.

30-6. *Making a compound miter cut using a protractor guide. (Short sleeves are safer.)*

speed before starting the cut. Guide it into the line gently but firmly, letting the blade and weight of the saw do the cutting. Fig. 30-5. If the saw sticks, pull it back slightly and allow it to come to full speed again before continuing the cut. Although it is not always convenient, use both hands on the saw whenever you can.

The saw can also be used for bevel cuts. However, remember to offset your guideline by the distance needed to follow the layout line on the underside. The long side of the bevel must be at the top of the cut

30-7. *Ripping stock with a portable power saw, using a rip guide. Make sure the right edge is true for guiding the saw.*

since the blade tilts under the saw. Make a practice of cutting just beyond the waste side of your guideline. A miter cut can also be made. This is a crosscut made at an angle. It can be done freehand or with a protractor guide. Fig. 30-6.

Ripping

Ripping can be done freehand in the same way as crosscutting. When making extremely long cuts, it is a good idea to walk the tool along slowly to complete the cut. Another method is to push the tool as far as you can, then hold it firmly in place while you move ahead far enough to make the next cut. To make a really accurate cut in ripping, install a rip guide or fence. This attachment can be fastened to the base. Fig. 30-7. If a rip guide is not available, a board can be clamped on the stock to guide the cutting.

Pocket Cuts

Internal, or pocket, cuts can be made in a panel. Swing the saw guard out of the way and keep it there. Place the front edge of the base on the work. Start the saw and let it come to full speed. Then slowly lower the blade into the work at the guideline. Fig. 30-8.

PANEL SAW

The panel saw is a portable power saw mounted in a large rack. It is used for cutting panels of plywood, hardboard, and other sheet materials. To locate the position of the cut, either mark a line across the back of the panel or use the scale that is attached to the base of the rack. Place the panel so that the good surface is toward the rack. Turn the saw on and pull it down to do the cutting. Fig. 30-9. A spring tape attached to the saw will help raise it after the cut.

BAYONET (SABER) SAW

The bayonet saw (saber or hand jigsaw) is most useful for cutting

30-8. *Starting a pocket cut. Notice that the guard must be held out of the way. Be sure to release the switch and let the blade come to rest before lifting the saw out. Clean out the corners with a handsaw.*

internal and external curves on-the-job. Fig. 30-10. The saw, which operates like a jigsaw but has the advantage of being portable, is relatively easy to use. It is particu-

30-9. *A panel saw is ideal for cutting large sheets of plywood to smaller sizes.*

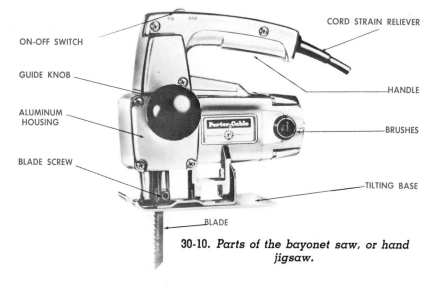

ON-OFF SWITCH

GUIDE KNOB

ALUMINUM HOUSING

BLADE SCREW

CORD STRAIN RELIEVER

HANDLE

BRUSHES

TILTING BASE

BLADE

30-10. *Parts of the bayonet saw, or hand jigsaw.*

larly useful for internal keyholing or cutting an enclosed opening in a product that has already been assembled. Design varies with the manufacturer, but most of these saws have a tilting base.

The blade, which resembles a saber, is installed with the cutting edges pointing *up.* The correct kinds of blades are shown in Fig. 30-11.

It is most important to hold the saw *firmly* on the work surface and guide it slowly. If these things are not done, the blade will break. To do internal cutting, drill a small hole in the waste stock, then start

METAL-CUTTING BLADES—for ferrous metals including mild steel, galvanized sheet; nonferrous metals including aluminum, brass and copper.

	recommended use	teeth per inch	length
	¼″ to ½″ ferrous; ³⁄₁₆″ to ¾″ nonferrous.	10	3⅝″
	³⁄₁₆″ to ¼″ ferrous; less than ¼″ nonferrous.	14	3⅝″
	⅛″ to ³⁄₁₆″ ferrous.	18	3¼″
	Less than ⅛″ ferrous.	32	3¼″

WOOD, PLASTIC AND COMPOSITION CUTTING BLADES—coarse tooth design for fastest cutting in ⅜″ or thicker material.

	blade type—recommended use	teeth per inch	length
	Fast scroll cutting, or "roughing-in" work.	6	4¼″
	Extra wide blade for straight cutting.	6	4¼″
	Hollow ground blade for extra-smooth finish.	6	4¼″
	Hollow ground, extra-wide for smooth finish, straight cutting.	6	4¼″
	Flush cutting blade ¾″ wide, extends to front of jigsaw foot, permits cutting up to corners, vertical surfaces.	6	4¼″

WOOD, PLYWOOD, PLASTIC AND COMPOSITION CUTTING BLADES—fine tooth design for fast smooth finish cutting in ½″ or thinner material.

	blade type—recommended use	teeth per inch	length
	Fast scroll cutting blade hardened for long life in hard compositions (Masonite, etc.) and hard plastics (Formica, etc.)	10	3⅝″
	Hollow ground for smooth finish cutting in plywood, plastics, veneers and hard compositions. Best blade for Formica, other plastic laminates.	10	3⅝″
	Extremely narrow blade for tight, intricate scroll cutting.	10	4¼″

30-11. *Blades for the saber saw.*

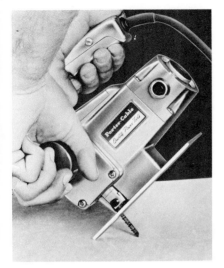

35-12. *Starting an inside cut without a clearance hole.*

the saw. It is possible to start an inside cut without drilling a clearance hole. This is called plunge cutting. To do this, rest the saw on the shoe at an angle of about 45 degrees. Turn on the power and slowly rock the saw back and forth until the blade cuts through. Fig. 30-12.

Move the saw fast enough to keep the blade cutting all the time. Turn

30-13. *Ripping stock with a bayonet saw, using a guide fence. A long, straight cut can also be made by clamping a straightedge to the stock to use as a guide.*

corners slowly and not too sharply. Cut curves freehand. Tilt saw base for accurate bevel cutting.

For straight cutting, a guide or fence should be used. Fig. 30-13. This can be a straight piece of wood clamped over the stock, or it may be a metal guide or fence attached to the machine. Circles can be cut freehand or by using the rip guide or fence as a jig. Fig. 30-14.

RECIPROCATING SAW

This all-purpose saw operates with back-and-forth movement like a keyhole saw or a hacksaw without a frame. Fig. 30-15. Blades are available for cutting wood, plastic, metal, ceramics, and other materials. Fig. 30-16. Most models have a speed adjustment. Use high speeds for fastest cutting in wood, composition board, and plastic. Use medium speed for plastic laminate. Low speeds are best for maximum control in finish wood cutting and for most metal-cutting jobs.

A multi-position foot at the end of the saw can be moved in or out and adjusted to different angles for obtaining variable cutting depths and positions. The saw is held like a drill but cuts like a jigsaw. It is extremely useful for finish carpenters, builders, and maintenance workers who do building and remodeling work. The saw can start its own hole, but is is better to drill a clearance hole for internal cutting.

PORTABLE PLANES

Electric Hand Plane

Also called the portable electric plane, this tool eliminates difficult

30-15. *The reciprocating saw is also known by many other names. It is basically a portable power hacksaw or keyhole saw, depending on the kind of blade installed.*

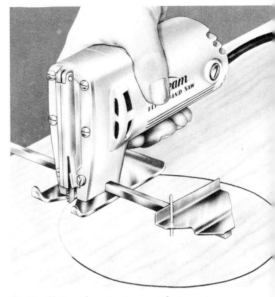

30-14. *Using the ripping guide to cut a true circle.*

and time-consuming hand planing. Fig. 30-17. It is particularly useful when installing large doors and paneling because it will make a smooth, accurate cut. The actual cutting tool is either a spindle and plane cutter combination or a one-piece plane cutter with a threaded shank. For most jobs the one-piece plane cutter is used.

The cutter must be set at zero before setting for depth of cut. Move the depth-adjustment lever (located at the front of the plane) to the zero position and turn the plane over. To the left of the handle and directly behind the motor bracket is a cutter-adjusting lever. Turn this lever toward the rear of the plane and lay a straightedge across the

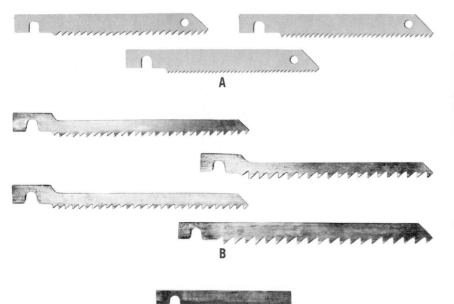

30-18. *Using a portable electric plane to surface the edge of a door. (Short sleeves are safer.)*

30-16. *Common kinds of saw blades. Choose the blade that will have at least three teeth in contact with the stock at all times. (A) Metal-cutting blades have from 10 to 24 teeth per inch. Choose a high number of teeth for relatively thin and hard materials. (B) Wood-cutting blades have from 3½ to 10 teeth per inch. Choose a blade with few teeth per inch for rough, fast cutting and a blade with relatively more teeth for cutting hardwood, plastic, and hard composition board. (C) A knife blade used for cutting cardboard and leather.*

cutter so that it rests on both the front and rear shoes. Turn the cutter by hand until it lifts the straightedge. Then adjust the lever until the tip of the cutting edge just touches the straightedge when it (the straightedge) rests evenly on both shoes. Now the desired depth of cut can be set by rotating the depth-adjustment lever.

To use, place the plane on the work, with the front shoe and fence held firmly against it. Fig. 30-18. Turn on the power. Then apply steady, even pressure as you do the planing. Never overload or push the plane too hard. When working on thick plywood or hardwoods, do not attempt to cut as fast as for softer woods.

The plane can also be set for outside bevel cuts from 0 to 45 degrees. In planing the edges of plywood, there is danger of breaking out the crossgrain plies at a corner. The best way to prevent this is to clamp a piece of scrap wood at the end of the plywood before the cut is made. As you near the edge, move the plane very slowly.

Power Block Plane

The power block plane is a small tool with a spiral cutter similar to that of the electric hand plane. Fig. 30-19. It can be used for many procedures, such as surface planing, edge planing, making and cleaning up rabbet cuts, planing cupboard doors to size, and beveling the edges of plastic laminates that have been bonded to a wood base. Fig. 30-20. Just under the handle is a knob for adjusting depth of cut. A small fence clamps to the bottom of the plane but can be removed for face planing. This lightweight tool can be controlled with one hand.

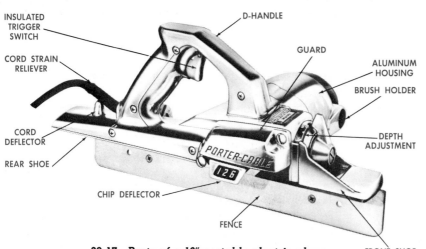

INSULATED TRIGGER SWITCH

CORD STRAIN RELIEVER

CORD DEFLECTOR

REAR SHOE

CHIP DEFLECTOR

FENCE

D-HANDLE

GUARD

ALUMINUM HOUSING

BRUSH HOLDER

DEPTH ADJUSTMENT

FRONT SHOE

30-17. *Parts of a 16" portable electric plane.*

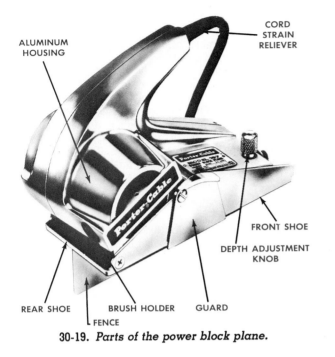

ALUMINUM HOUSING

CORD STRAIN RELIEVER

FRONT SHOE

DEPTH ADJUSTMENT KNOB

REAR SHOE

BRUSH HOLDER

GUARD

FENCE

30-19. *Parts of the power block plane.*

30-20. *Beveling the edge of plastic laminate.*

31 Jointer

The jointer is used primarily for planing the surfaces and edges of stock that has been cut on a saw. It does the same job as the hand plane but operates in an entirely different way. It has a solid steel circular cutterhead into which three or more knife blades are fastened. These knives revolve, cutting the wood. The smoothness of the cut depends on the number of knives, the speed of rotation, and the feed.

For most cabinetwork built on the job, lumber is purchased S2S (surfaced on two sides) so that only the edges need to be surfaced. In furniture manufacturing or in shops that have a surfacer, wood is purchased in the rough and must be surfaced on all four sides. With such wood it is important to remove any warp by first cutting *one face flat* on the *jointer*. This is the only sure way to get an accurate, rectangular piece

of stock. While both surfaces can be planed by running the stock through a planer, first with one side up and then the other, this will not remove the warp.

PARTS AND SIZES

The major parts of a jointer are a heavy base, a front infeed table, a rear outfeed table, fence, guards, and cutterhead. Fig. 31-1. On most jointers, both the front and rear ta-

JOINTER

MAINTENANCE
- Hone jointer knives frequently.
- Grind and reset knives when necessary. (See Chapter 24.)
- Make sure the guard is used and that it operates freely.
- Check the alignment of the tables to make sure they are level and not twisted.
- See that the fence operates properly.
- Adjust the outfeed table or cutterhead so that both are the same height (except for special operations).
- Check the pointer of the depth scale on the infeed table to make sure it indicates the correct depth of cut.

LUBRICATION
- Sliding members and table control screws should be oiled with lubricating oil.
- Most jointers have sealed bearings on the cutterhead and motor.

SAFETY
- Wear proper clothing and eye protection. (See Chapter 4.)

- Check the stock carefully before surfacing to make sure it is free of knots and other defects.
- Trying to surface short pieces (less than 12″) is a trap that is sure to lead to injury. Avoid it. Use hand tools for small wood parts. What happens when you attempt to surface short pieces? As the stock starts over the cutterhead, the corner is very likely to catch, throwing the wood out of your hand and allowing your fingers to drop into the revolving cutter.
- Use the safety guard at all possible times. (On some jointers the guard can't be used when cutting a rabbet.)
- Check to see that all parts of the machine are locked securely.
- Use a push block when jointing a thin piece or when face planing.
- Hold the board firmly against the fence and the table.
- The maximum depth of cut should be ⅛″.
- Always stand to the left of the machine.
- Never plane the end grain of narrow stock (less than 10″).
- Plane with the grain.
- Keep your fingers away from the revolving cutterhead.

---

bles can be moved up and down on inclined ways by turning a hand wheel. The cutterhead has three or more knives mounted in a cylindrical head. The knives revolve at a speed of 3500 to 4500 RPM. A fence similar to the one on a circular saw is used to guide the stock. The guard covers the cutterhead except for the portion that is actually doing the cutting.

Size of the jointer is indicated by the length of the knives or the maximum width of board that can be surfaced. For cabinet or school

shops a 6″ or 8″ jointer is a good size. Fig. 31-2.

ADJUSTMENTS

Rear Table and Cutterhead

For accurate cutting, the rear table must be exactly the same height as the knives at their highest point. Fig. 31-3. If the table is too high, it will cut a taper. If too low, it will cut a snipe (a small concave cut at the end of the stock).

Disconnect the jointer from the power source. Rotate the cutterhead

until one knife is at the top position. If the rear table is adjustable, first release the lock handle on the back of the jointer. Then lower the rear table so that the top is well below the top of the cutting circle. This is done to remove any slack in the screw when the final adjustment is made. Place a straightedge over the rear table and carefully raise the table until it is at exactly the same height as one knife. Fig. 31-4.

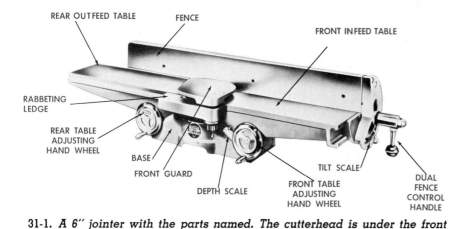

31-1. *A 6″ jointer with the parts named. The cutterhead is under the front guard.*

31-2. *This ruggedly constructed 8″ jointer is ideal for school and cabinet shops. It has a rear outfeed table that moves up and down.*

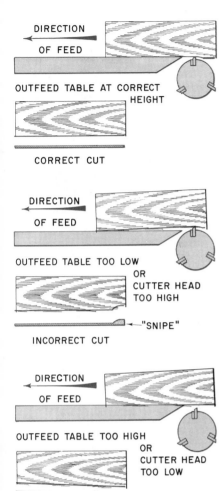

DIRECTION OF FEED

OUTFEED TABLE AT CORRECT HEIGHT

CORRECT CUT

DIRECTION OF FEED

OUTFEED TABLE TOO LOW OR CUTTER HEAD TOO HIGH

"SNIPE"

INCORRECT CUT

DIRECTION OF FEED

OUTFEED TABLE TOO HIGH OR CUTTER HEAD TOO LOW

INCORRECT CUT

31-3. *The jointer must be adjusted so that the outfeed table is at exactly the same height as the cutterhead knives at their highest point. Otherwise a taper or a snipe will be cut.*

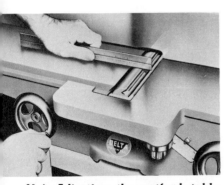

31-4. *Adjusting the outfeed table. Raise the table slowly until the straightedge rests evenly on the table and the knife. Always replace the guard after making this adjustment.*

Check at the middle and at both ends of this knife. Repeat this check for all other knives to make sure they project the same distance.

Once the rear table is adjusted, lock it in position. If the knives are out of alignment or need sharpening, see Chapter 24. There is usually no need to change the table adjustment unless the knives need resharpening or you want to do a special cutting job.

Infeed Table

The distance the infeed table is below the knives determines the depth of cut. The depth of cut to be taken will depend on:

● The width of the surface being jointed.

● The kind of wood and grain pattern.

● Whether you are making a rough or finish cut.

Loosen the lock on the side of the infeed table. Turn the handle beneath the table to raise or lower it. There are a pointer and scale which indicate the depth of cut. These must be checked periodically for accuracy. One way to do this is to adjust the front of the table to a ⅛" cut, as shown on the depth scale, then joint the edge for a short distance. Check to see whether this is exactly ⅛". Never make a cut deeper than ⅛". The average depth of cut is about 1⁄16". If you are making a finish cut, only 1⁄32" should be removed.

Fence

For most operations the fence should be at an exact right angle to the table. There is a tilt scale for making this adjustment, but it is a good idea to check with a square. The fence can be tilted in or out to cut a bevel or chamfer. This also can be set with the tilt scale; but again, for greater accuracy, it is good to check the angle with a sliding T bevel or the protractor head of a combination square. If a great

deal of edge jointing is done, move the fence to different positions (in and out) to equalize the wear on the knives.

HOLDING STOCK FOR FEEDING

Stand to the left of the front table with your feet turned slightly towards the machine. There are two common ways of feeding stock across the cutterhead. In the first method the hands are kept away from the danger zone above the cutterhead at all times. Start the cut by holding the stock with both hands, firmly pressing it against the front table and fence. After a portion of the stock is over the rear table, move the left hand onto that part of the stock. Then, when most of the stock is over the rear table, place the right hand also on that portion of the stock and finish the cut. With this method the hands are never over the danger zone of the cutterhead. Fig. 31-5.

The second and more common method is to use the left hand to guide the stock and hold it firmly against the table and fence. Use the right hand to move the stock forward. The stock slides under the left hand for most of the distance, and then it moves along with the right hand to complete the cut. Enough side pressure must be applied to keep the stock pressed firmly against the fence. Fig. 31-6.

OPERATIONS

Facing or Surfacing

As stated earlier, the only accurate method of producing rectangular shapes is to make sure that one face is cut flat and true. Most boards have some type of warp, usually cup or twist. (See Fig. 5-19.) *Cup* in wood is a dished-out portion from side to side across the board. In *twist* the edges of a board turn or wind so that the four corners of any face are not in the

241

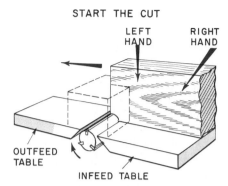

START THE CUT

LEFT HAND — RIGHT HAND

OUTFEED TABLE

INFEED TABLE

CONTINUE THE CUT

LEFT HAND — RIGHT HAND

OUTFEED TABLE

INFEED TABLE

31-5. *Correct method of feeding when the hands are moved as stock passes across the cutterhead. The danger area is in red.*

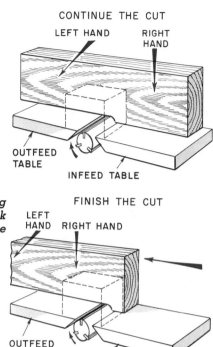

FINISH THE CUT

LEFT HAND — RIGHT HAND

OUTFEED TABLE

INFEED TABLE

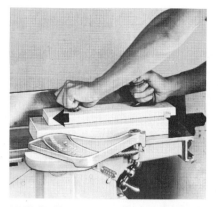

31-7(a). *Using a push block to do facing. The knob of the push block is held in the left hand and the handle in the right.*

same plane. When a board that has twist is placed on a flat surface, it rocks back and forth on the diagonal corners.

To surface a board that is cupped, place the concave side down and take several light cuts until it is flat. Twist is more difficult to remove. The best method is to mark the high corners and support the work so that stock at only these points is removed. Always use a

31-6. *Jointing an edge. The hand over the front table exerts no downward pressure but simply advances the work to the knives. Both hands exert side pressure to keep the work in contact with the guide fence.*

push block for these operations. Fig. 31-7.

To plane a surface, hold the board firmly on the infeed table with the left hand toward the front of the board and the right hand toward the rear. Move the stock along until the back end is over the front table. Then pick up the push block and use it to move the piece across the cutterhead. When surfacing thin stock, it is a good idea to fasten an auxiliary wood fence to the metal one to keep the stock from creeping under the fence. Another method is to use a hold-down push block with a foam rubber base in your right hand and move the stock with your left hand until it is over the outfeed table. Then take your hand away and complete the cut, holding the stock with the push block only. Fig. 31-8.

Edge Jointing

Edge jointing is the simplest and most common job performed on the jointer. Fig. 31-6. If the board is bowed (if the edges are concave on

one side and convex on the other), it is a good idea to cut one edge straight on the saw before cutting it on the jointer. Set the fence on the jointer at 90 degrees and lower the front table for a cut of about ¹⁄₁₆". The best surface of the stock should be placed against the fence. As the workpiece is pushed over the cutterhead, pressure is exerted so that it stays flat on the rear table. The right hand over the front table exerts no downward pressure but simply pushes the workpiece along to the knives. When the workpiece is over the outfeed table, both hands should exert downward and sideward pressure to keep the work in contact with the table and fence.

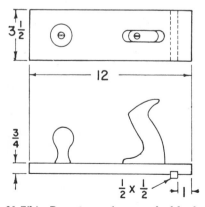

31-7(b). *Drawing of a push block. This one has a knob and handle from a hand plane.*

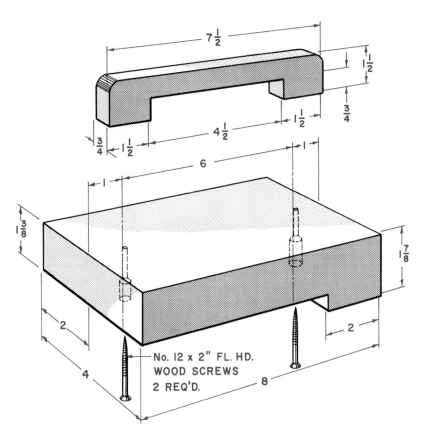

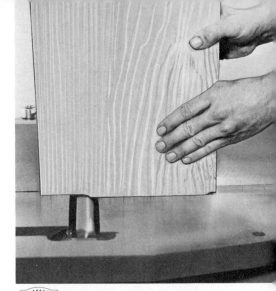

31-7(c). Another drawing of a push block. This one can be used with one hand.

surface against the fence and joint the first edge. Next cut to width plus ¹⁄₁₆″ and joint the second edge. Fig. 31-10(a). Now, from the working face, mark the thickness along the edges and ends. If the piece is not uniform in thickness, it will be necessary to take several lighter cuts on the thicker portion before making the final cut. Of course, if a surfacer or planer is available, surface to thickness on this machine. If only the edges and ends are to be surfaced, follow the steps shown in Fig. 31-10(b).

End Jointing

Most wood parts for furniture do not require that the end grain be

planed. Usually an end that has been sawed is accurate enough. End planing is quite difficult because you are actually cutting off the ends of the wood fibers. Therefore very light cuts should be made. In end jointing there is always a tendency for the wood to split out at the end of the cut. For this reason it is a good idea to make a short, light cut along the end grain for about 1″ and then reverse the board to complete the cut. Fig. 31-9. If the board is quite long, use an auxiliary wood fence for extra support.

Squaring Up Stock

If a board must be squared up on all six surfaces, the first step is to surface one face just enough to clean it up. Next, hold this face surface against the fence and joint the end grain. Cut to length (plus ¹⁄₁₆″). Reverse the stock and joint the second end. Then hold the face

Rabbeting

CAUTION: Rabbeting requires the removal of the cutter guard. Use extreme caution when the cutter guard is off. Note the safety decal on top of the fence warning to keep hands clear of the cutterhead.

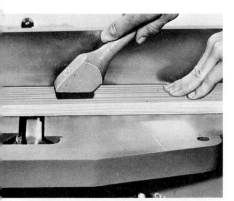

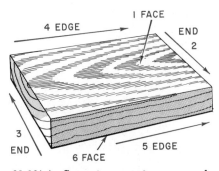

31-10(a). Steps in squaring up stock using a jointer only.

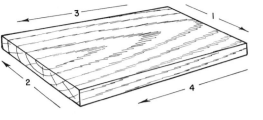

31-10(b). *Steps in squaring up stock if only the edges and ends need surfacing.*

Set the fence for the desired width of the rabbet. Check the width of the rabbet by measuring the distance from the end of the knife in the cutterhead to the fence. (Make certain power is off before making this check.) Make a trial cut using a piece of scrap material. Lower the infeed table 1/32″ at a time and make successive cuts until the desired depth of rabbet has been obtained. It is easier and safer to take a series of shallow cuts.

The width and thickness of the wood that can be rabbeted depend on the length and width of the rabbet. Fig. 31-11. However, never rabbet a piece of wood less than 12 inches long. When rabbeting long pieces, follow the same procedure as for surfacing or edging long pieces. Use push blocks when completing the rabbeting. Always replace the guard immediately after the rabbeting operation is completed.

Beveling

A bevel is cut by tilting the fence in or out. Generally it is safer to do

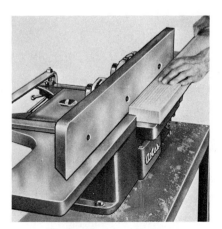

31-11. *Cutting a rabbet.*

the cutting with the fence tilted in. Fig. 31-12.

When the angle is small, there is little difference whether the fence is tilted in or out. However, at angles approaching 45 degrees, it is increasingly difficult to hold the work properly when the fence is tilted out. When tilted in, the fence forms a V shape with the tables, and the work is easily pressed into the pocket while passing it across the knives.

If the bevel is laid out on the piece in such direction that this involves cutting against the grain, it will be better to tilt the fence out.

The correct angle can be set on the tilt gauge. However, it is more accurate to check the fence angle with a sliding T bevel. Make several passes until the bevel is complete.

Chamfering

A chamfer is a sharp edge cut at a slight bevel. The cutting is done the same way as for the bevel except that only a small part of the edge is removed. Since the fence can be tilted both in and out, it is possible to chamfer both edges of a single face without cutting against the grain. Fig. 31-13.

Stop chamfering requires that both the front and rear tables be lowered an equal amount or that the cutterhead be raised. Clamp a stop block on the front table so that the stop chamfer will start at the correct spot. Clamp blocks on the front and rear tables so that the chamfer will be cut to the right length. Tilt the fence in to the angle you want. Remove the guard, hold one end of the stock against the stop block of the front table, and carefully lower

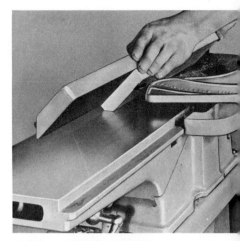

31-12(a). *Cutting a chamfer or bevel with the fence tilted in.*

the stock into the revolving cutter. Push it along until it hits the stop block on the outfeed table. Then raise the rear of the stock to remove it.

Cutting a Long Taper

There are several methods of cutting straight tapers, depending on the length of the stock.

• *If the stock is shorter in length than the front table,* lower that table to a depth equal to the taper. The stock is then placed so that the far end of the board rests on the rear table at the start of the taper. From

31-12(b). *Cutting a bevel or chamfer with the fence tilted out.*

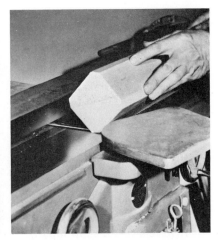

31-13. *The fence can be adjusted to cut an octagonal leg.*

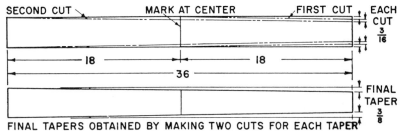

31-14(a). *Dividing the taper into two or more equal sections.*

this position the board can be moved forward to cut the taper.

● *For tapers longer than the front table,* divide the taper into two or more parts. Make sure that each section is shorter than the length of the front table. For example, if the taper is 22″ long, divide it into two 11″ sections. If the amount of the taper is ¼″, adjust the machine for a cut ⅛″ deep.

Lower the forward end of the workpiece onto the rear table. Do this very carefully, as the piece will span the knives, and they will take a "bite" from the wood. There is a tendency to kick back unless the piece is firmly held. Now push the work forward as in ordinary jointing. The effect is to plane off all the stock in front of the knives and to increase depth, leaving a tapered surface.

The ridge left by the knives when starting the taper may be removed by taking a very light cut according to the regular method for jointing, with the front table raised to its usual position. Practice is required in this operation, and the beginner is advised to make trial cuts on waste material.

Taper cuts over part of the length and a number of other special operations can easily be done by the

experienced woodworker. Make the first cut from the halfway point. A stop block can be clamped to the fence to control the start of the cut. Start the second cut at the beginning of the taper. Use a push block to complete the cut. Fig. 31-14.

Cutting a Stop Taper

The stop taper is often found on the legs of Traditional furniture designs. First mark the beginning and end of the tapered area. Draw a line completely around the stock at these two limits. Determine the amount of stock to be removed from the leg at the point where the cut will be deepest. Lower the front table this amount. Remove the guard and move the fence as close to the front of the jointer as you can without making the cut impossible.

Lay the leg on the jointer at a slight angle, with the top on the rear table and with the beginning of the tapered area directly over the front

edge of this table. Turn on the power. Now carefully lower the leg until it touches the front table. Move the stock along until the other end of the taper is reached. Then carefully raise the end away from the knives. Turn off the power. Stop blocks can be clamped to the fence to control the beginning and end of the cut. Fig. 31-15.

Cutting a Short Taper

Mark the length of the taper. Draw a line around the stock at this point. Clamp a stop block on the front table so that the distance from the edge of the rear table to the stop block is equal to the taper. Lower the front table to the depth of cut you want. Cut a small piece of scrap stock. Drive two thin nails or brads through it so that the points are exposed. Remove the guard. Now stand directly in front of the rear table and hold the end of the stock against the stop block.

31-14(b). *Cutting the first half of a longer taper. Note the stop block clamped to the fence to control start of cut. Use a push block to complete the cut.*

31-14(c). *Completing the taper cut. When the end of stock is over the front table, use a push block to complete the cut. Don't push the stock across the revolving cutterhead with your hand in this position.*

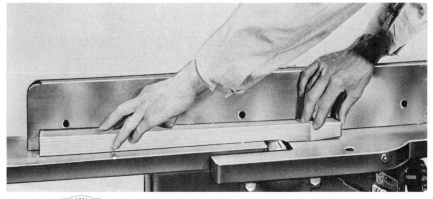

31-15. Cutting a stop taper. Short sleeves would be safer.

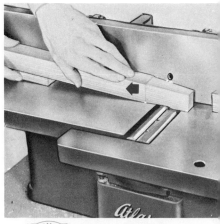

31-16. Cutting a short taper.

31-17. Making the cheek cut on a tenon.

Lower the stock and then slip the scrap block under the free end to maintain the correct position. Now pull the stock toward you to cut the taper. The block with the nails or brads will slide along the rear table as the taper is cut. Fig. 31-16.

Cutting a Tenon

Lay out the tenon. Make the shoulder cut on the circular saw. (See Ch. 26.) Then follow these steps:

1. Adjust the fence to equal the length of the tenon.

2. Lower the infeed table to equal the amount of stock to be removed from each side of the tenon.

3. Hold the end of the tenon firmly against the fence and move the stock past the cutter. Fig. 31-17.

A wide piece of scrap stock placed behind the workpiece and used as a miter gauge will help to hold the workpiece at right angles to the fence. It will also serve as a back-up board to prevent the end grain from tearing out.

32 Shaper

The shaper is used primarily for edge cutting on straight and curved pieces, for making decorative edges and moldings, for producing joints, and for grooving, fluting, and reed-ing. While most of its work is done on the edge of stock, the shaper can also be used for face shaping. This relatively simple machine can do a wide variety of operations de-pending on the kind of cutters available. However, it is a rather danger-ous machine because it must operate at a high speed and its cut-ters are difficult to guard completely.

SHAPER

MAINTENANCE

- Keep cutters clean and properly sharpened. Sharpen on the front face only, never on the contour shape.
- Check the belt for condition and tension. Keep the belt just tight enough to prevent it from slipping.
- Clean out the sawdust from the operating mechanism at regular intervals.
- Make sure the fence adjustments operate easily.

LUBRICATION

- Use S.A.E. No. 20 machine oil to lubricate elevating shaft, bevel gears, and column.

SAFETY

- Whenever possible, install the cutter so that the bottom of the stock is shaped. In this way the stock will cover most of the cutter and act as a guard.
- Make sure the cutter is locked securely to the spindle.
- Always position the left fence so that it will support the work that has passed the cutters.
- Adjust the spindle for correct height and then lock in position. Rotate the spindle by hand to make sure it clears all guards, fences, *etc.*

- Check the direction of rotation by snapping the switch on and off; watch as the cutters come to rest. ALWAYS FEED AGAINST THE CUTTING EDGE; THAT IS, FEED THE WORK INTO THE CUTTERS IN THE DIRECTION OPPOSITE TO CUTTER ROTATION. Some shapers have a reversing switch so that the spindle can be rotated either clockwise or counterclockwise.
- Examine the stock carefully before cutting to make sure it is free of defects. Never cut through a loose knot or stock that is cracked or split.
- Hold the stock down and against the fence with the hands on top of the material, yet out of range of the cutters.
- Use guards, jigs, and clamping devices whenever possible.
- Always use a depth collar when shaping irregular work. Put a guide pin in the table to start the cutting.
- Do not set spring hold-down clips too tightly against the work. Use just enough tension to hold the work against the fence.
- For contour work, when depth collars and a guide pin are used, you must swing the work into the cutters. It is a good idea to keep the stock in motion in the direction of feed.
- Never shape a piece shorter than 10″.

PARTS

The shaper consists of a heavy base to which a table is permanently attached. Fig. 32-1. The top of the table has a miter-gauge groove and also threaded holes for fastening the fence in place and for installing guide pins. The spindle, located in the center of the table, can be moved up and down to accommodate different thicknesses of cuts at various locations on the edge of the stock. Once it is adjusted to the correct height, the spindle is locked in place.

Many shapers are equipped with a reversing switch which allows the spindle to operate in either direction. In normal use the spindle moves counterclockwise, with the work moving from right to left. However, for many jobs it is better to reverse the work and feed it from left to right with the spindle rotating clockwise. The spindle speed of a shaper is between 5000 and 10,000 RPM. The standard spindle is ¾″ in diameter, but on many machines a spindle with a diameter of ½″ or ⁵⁄₁₆″ can be installed. Fig. 32-2.

The machine comes equipped with a fully adjustable fence. The fence is held firmly to the table by means of two threaded studs and wing nuts. Adjustment of either half of the fence can be done when necessary. For most shaping, the two halves of the fence should be in line. A punch mark across the two parts is a useful index in resetting

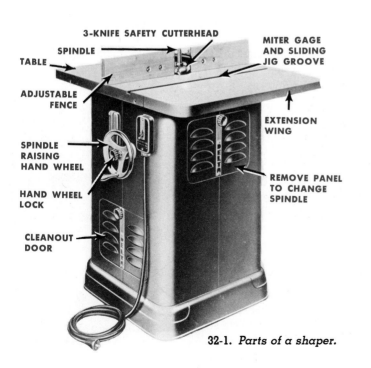

3-KNIFE SAFETY CUTTERHEAD
SPINDLE
TABLE
MITER GAGE AND SLIDING JIG GROOVE
ADJUSTABLE FENCE
EXTENSION WING
SPINDLE RAISING HAND WHEEL
REMOVE PANEL TO CHANGE SPINDLE
HAND WHEEL LOCK
CLEANOUT DOOR

32-1. Parts of a shaper.

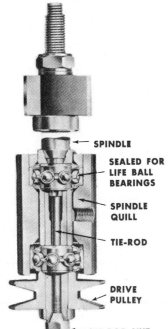

32-4. *With the sliding shaper jig, the ends of narrow stock can be shaped with safety.*

32-2. *The spindle assembly. A spindle of different diameter or length can be substituted by removing the tie-rod nut at the bottom of the spindle assembly. There are also removable table inserts with three sizes of openings.*

the fence. The wood face pieces of the fence can be adjusted to accommodate various sizes of cutters and the safety guard. Fig. 32-3. Changes in the wood facings are made by loosening the bolts, pushing the wood facings to the required position, and retightening.

Several accessories are also available to add to the convenience and safety of the machine. Spring holddowns hold work firmly against the fence and table. A sliding shaper jig is ideal for many horizontal shaping operations such as cutting tenons and grooves. This attachment holds short, narrow pieces tightly and prevents them from slipping. Fig. 32-4. The tenoner can be used for vertical shaping. A safety-ring guard that acts as a hold-down can also be used on the machine. Some machines have an exhaust or shaving chute that can be connected to a dust-collection system for clearing away sawdust and chips as the shaping is done.

KINDS OF CUTTERS

Three basic kinds of cutters are used on the shaper:

Three-lip cutters are considered safest. Fig. 32-5. These cutters are ground to shape on the back side so that honing the face doesn't change the shape. They are made of high-speed tool steel or are carbide tipped. They come in a wide variety of shapes to do many kinds of cutting. The versatility of a shaper is greatly increased by a complete set of these cutters. Fig. 32-6. Collars

are available for use with them. Some cutters are made with carbide inserts for better wear resistance.

Small grooving saws can be used on the shaper for making many kinds of joint cuts. For example, two or more saws with proper spacing collars can be used for making tongue-and-groove joints.

The *three-knife safety cutterhead* is very similar to a molding head used on the circular saw or radial-arm saw, except it is smaller in diameter. With this cutterhead, the same molding knives used on the saw can be used on the shaper.

As you can see in Fig. 32-6, cutting tools can be selected by name. Sometimes a complicated shape is produced by using two or more cutters. It is good practice to sketch the exact design of the desired cut on the end of a piece of scrap stock. The scrap stock should have the same thickness as the piece to be machined. Then check the cutter against this piece to make sure they match. Make a trial cut on a piece of scrap before machining the workpiece.

INSTALLING THE CUTTERS

On some shapers there is a flat portion on the upper end of the spindle which can be held with a

32-5. *Close-up of a three-lip cutter in use.*

32-3. *The wood facings of the fence can be moved to make the opening larger or smaller. Here the fence has been adjusted to accommodate the circular safety guard, which is mounted to the spindle.*

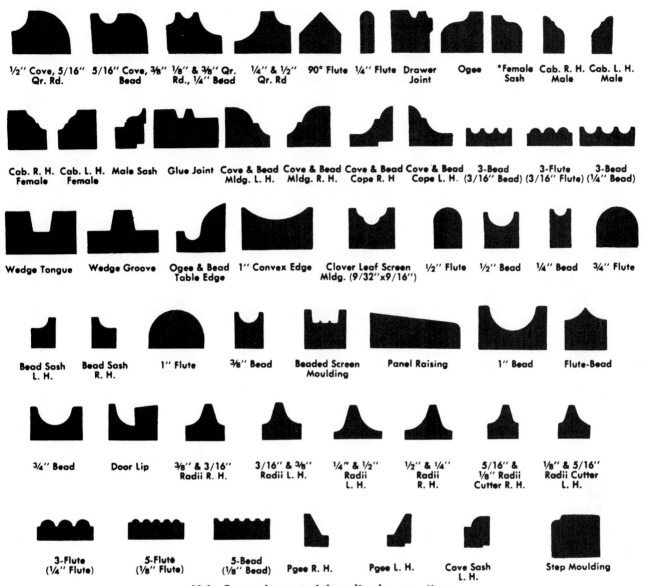

32-6. *A complete set of three-lip shaper cutters.*

wrench to keep the spindle from turning. Other shapers have a pin that slips in place to lock the spindle. If necessary, remove the fence or other setups. Remove the nut collars and cutter.

Install the correct kind of cutter. It should usually be installed with the larger diameter towards the table so that most of the cutting is done on the lower side of the work. Fig. 32-7. If the cutting is to be done without a fence, one or more depth collars must be placed above, below, or between the cutters to regulate the depth of cut. Sometimes spacer collars are put between two cutters, as when shaping a rather complicated edge or making moldings. Other spacer collars can be added above the cutter so that the nut will hold the assembly firmly to the spindle shaft. Tighten the assembly before unlocking the spindle.

ADJUSTING THE SHAPER

On the tabletop, place a piece of scrap stock with the design on the

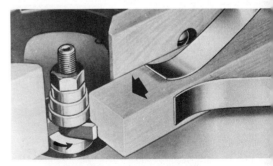

32-7. *Note that the cutter is installed so that the rabbet is formed at the lower edge of the stock. This is the safe method of shaping by undercutting. (Spring hold-downs are keeping the stock in place.)*

end grain. Loosen the hand-wheel lock and raise the spindle until it matches the design. Then lock the spindle.

The two-part adjustable fence can be moved in several ways. The opening between the two faces of the fence can be made wider or narrower. It should never be larger than is required for the cutter. To adjust the opening, loosen the setscrews that hold each wood face to the fence, and slide the wood pieces in or out. The entire fence can be adjusted forward and back with the faces in line with one another. It is also possible to move one half of the fence back slightly. This is done when it is necessary to support a cut that has been made, as when cutting the complete edge of stock. Fig. 32-8. The fence should be adjusted parallel with the miter-gauge groove by measuring the distance with a ruler at right angles to the slot.

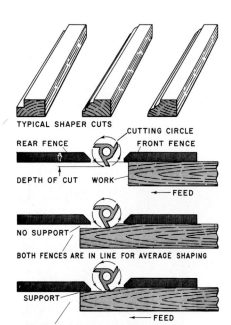

TYPICAL SHAPER CUTS

BOTH FENCES ARE IN LINE FOR AVERAGE SHAPING

WHERE THE ENTIRE EDGE OF THE WORK IS REMOVED, THE REAR FENCE MUST BE ADJUSTED TO FORM A SUPPORT

32-8. The offset between the two fences must be exactly equal to the depth of cut so that the rear fence will support the edge after it is shaped.

32-9. Cutters must rotate so that the flat side (not the beveled side) of the cutter hits the workpiece first. Cutters are designed to rotate counterclockwise, with the work fed from right to left. This is called the regular method. However, the cutter should also be mounted to do the majority of the cutting on the lower side of the board. This may necessitate turning the cutter over and reversing the direction of spindle rotation and the feed direction. This is called the inverted method of shaping.

METHODS OF SHAPING

There are four basic methods:

● Shaping with a fence or other guides. This method is used for shaping all straight edges in which the cut edge may be partially or completely machined.

● Shaping with depth collars. This method is used for irregularly shaped material. The depth of cut is controlled by putting depth collars on the spindle.

● Shaping with patterns. When a large number of irregularly shaped pieces are needed, an exact pattern of the desired shape is made. The stock is clamped to the pattern, and the unit is held against the shaper cutter.

● Shaping with forms. This method is used primarily for production jobs. Special jigs, fixtures, and other devices are used to hold and guide the work.

Shaping with the Fence or Other Guides

Select the correct cutter, as explained earlier in this unit. It is frequently necessary to select matching cutters; for example, in making a rule joint for a drop-leaf table.

Mount the cutter so that the major part of the cutting will be done at the bottom edge of the

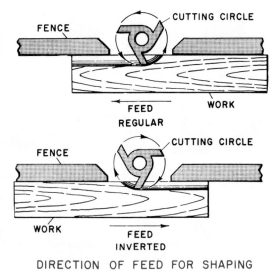

DIRECTION OF FEED FOR SHAPING

stock. This is not always possible when the complete edge will be machined. Make sure the direction of rotation and feed are correct. Fig. 32-9.

Adjust the fence. If only a partial edge is to be cut, the fence faces should be in line with each other and parallel with the groove in the tabletop. If the complete edge is to be shaped, half of the fence should support the work before cutting, the other half after cutting.

Whenever possible, cover the spindle with a guard. Turn on the machine and check the cutting action. It is a good idea to run through a piece of scrap stock of the same thickness to check the cut. If the cut is very deep, it is sometimes better to make two passes. Adjust the fence for one light cut and then readjust for the second cut.

For making many kinds of joint cuts when a small-diameter saw is used, a plywood fence can be made for clamping to the tabletop. The saw can then actually protrude through the fence to do the cutting. This method is very safe.

When face shaping wide or long stock, it is good to use a high wood fence that can be held in place with C-clamps. Fig. 32-10. This fence will give added support.

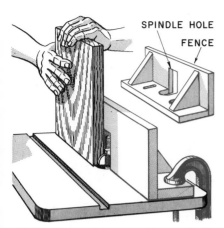

32-10. *A wood fence with a spindle hole is excellent for face shaping. Adjust the fence so that the knives extend the correct distance through the opening. A feather board or spring hold-down can be used to hold the stock against the fence and the tabletop.*

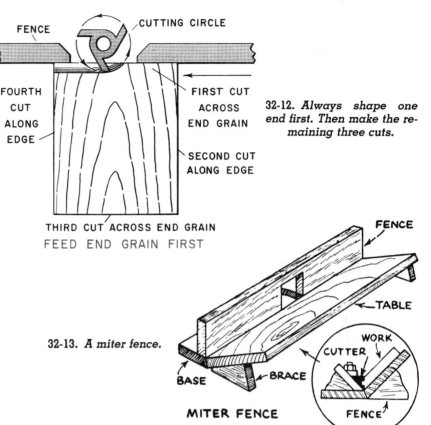

32-12. *Always shape one end first. Then make the remaining three cuts.*

FEED END GRAIN FIRST

32-13. *A miter fence.*

When end grain is to be shaped, a miter gauge or wide board can be used to help support the work. Fig. 32-11. The stock can also be clamped to the sliding shaper jig before cutting, to keep it from flying out of your hands.

In shaping all edges of stock, there are two methods that can be followed. One is to start on one edge and work completely around in a continuous cut. Depth collars are used in this method. The other is "start-and-stop" cutting, following the plan shown in Fig. 32-12.

32-11. *When shaping end grain, hold the work against a wide board to help steady it as the cut is made.*

A miter fence is a useful device. It can be made of plywood. With such a fence, the shaper can cut on a beveled edge or do molding on an angle cut. Fig. 32-13. Circular fences are useful in shaping the inside and outside edges of circular pieces. For outside cutting on curved pieces, the fence face must have exactly the opposite curvature of the workpiece. Fig. 32-14. A guide with a large V notch cut into it can be used on many different sizes of circular pieces by adjusting its location on the top of the shaper table.

Shaping with Depth Collars

One of the best methods of shaping an irregular edge is to use a depth collar. The diameter of the depth collar in relation to the diameter of the cutter determines the depth of cut. The collar may be used below, above, or between the cutters. Fig. 32-15. Because the

collar rotates with the spindle, it may slightly burn or darken the edge of the workpiece if held too firmly against it. For industrial use, therefore, a ball-bearing collar that ro-

32-14. *Shaping the outer edge of a circular piece using a two-part inside circle fence clamped to the standard fence.*

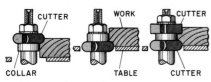

32-15. *Limiting the depth of cut by using a depth collar. If at all possible, place the depth collar on top of the cutter so that the safer, undercutting method is used.*

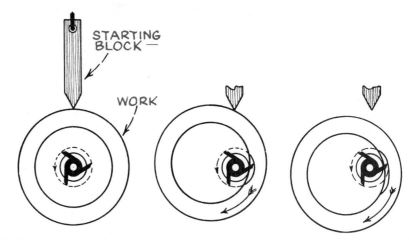

32-17. *A starting block serves the same purpose as a starting pin. It can be clamped to the table in any convenient position. Here it is used for shaping the inside edge of a circular piece.*

tates freely is used to prevent friction between the collar and the work. When using depth collars, only part of the edge of stock can be machined since it is always necessary to have the other part riding against the collar. This limits the use of collars to some extent.

The setup for collar work is about the same as for fence work except that no fence is used. To support the work at the start of the cut, a guide or starting pin is fastened in the tabletop. Place the pin in the left-hand hole if the cutter is rotating clockwise and in the right-hand hole if it is rotating counterclockwise.

When using depth collars, it is important that the edge of the stock be smooth and without irregulari-

ties. The stock must have the exact shape of the finished piece, and must be held firmly as the cut is started. This is extremely important.

Turn on the machine and allow it to come to full speed. Then hold the work against the guide pin and move it into the rotating cutter. When the uncut edge is moved against the knife, it will strike the cutter and bite into the edge. At this time there is a great danger of kickback. As soon as the cut is started, swing the work away from the guide pin and press it against the collar to do the cutting. Fig. 32-16. A starting block, which is a pointed piece of wood, can be used in place of the guide pin. It is clamped to the tabletop in a convenient position. Fig. 32-17.

Shaping with Patterns

Another common method for shaping large numbers of pieces which have irregular designs is to use a pattern. The pattern can be made of plywood, hardboard, metal, or plastic. The workpiece is attached to it so that the pattern will follow a guide or collar. Patterns should usually be made of material from ½″ to ¾″ thick. It is important to cut the pattern accurately and to make sure that the edges are smooth. Anchor pins (sharp-pointed

nails or screws) must be installed to hold the work on the pattern. The pattern, not the work, rides against the collar, making it possible to shape the edge of the stock completely. The work may be either above or below the pattern. Fig. 32-18. Another distinct advantage is that there can be slight variations in the stock since the entire edge will be cut accurately to the same size as the pattern every time.

When the complete edge of a piece is to be machined, it is some-

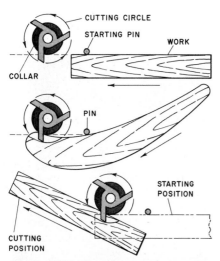

32-16. *Hold the stock against the starting pin until the edge is started. Then swing the work away from the pin and hold it firmly against the depth collar.*

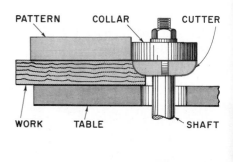

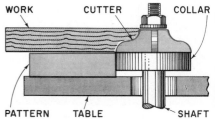

32-18. *The edge of the pattern rides against a collar. The pattern may be either above or below the work.*

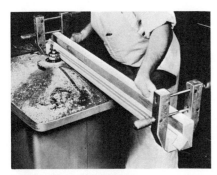

32-19. *Shaping the corner of a square leg. The work is held in a fixture, and depth collars are used to control the amount of cut.*

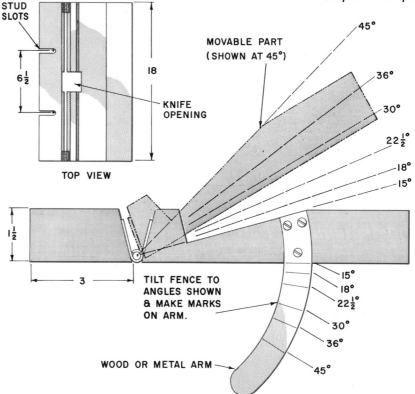

32-20. *An adjustable bevel jig. This can be used for edge cuts at any angle.*

times helpful to use a double pattern, one on top and the other below the workpiece. The work is then sandwiched between the two patterns. The advantage of this method is that it allows the work to be turned over at any time in order to cut with the grain.

Shaping with Forms

This means holding the stock securely by means of clamps, wedges, fixtures, jigs, or similar devices. Fig. 32-19. In this type of shaping, many special forms are used, primarily for production work. They can be used with a special fence, jig, or depth collars. Special jigs are needed for certain operations—fluting and reeding, for example, Fig. 32-20. Many of the same jigs and fixtures described for the circular saw can also be used on the shaper.

SHAPING ON THE RADIAL-ARM SAW

Many shaping operations can be done on the radial-arm saw by using a molding head or a three-knife safety cutterhead. A two-piece adjustable fence may be used instead of the standard guide fence. This fence is designed so that either the infeed or outfeed side can be independently moved closer to the center of the table or towards the ends. For shaping a complete edge, the

infeed side of the fence must be recessed (moved back) a distance equal to the exact amount of stock being removed. A special guard must be used to cover the cutter. Fig. 32-21.

Straight Shaping

In shaping a molded edge, the pattern is cut on the edge of the stock. Mount the proper cutter on the motor shaft. Place the motor in a vertical position and adjust for correct height. Move the motor unit in or out and lock it in position. Adjust the fence so that the work will be properly supported during cutting. Always feed from the right side into and against the revolving cutters. Hold the work firmly on the table. If the cut is very deep, it may be a good idea to make several passes.

End Shaping

End shaping can be done by holding the work firmly against the

standard guide fence and a stop block. Then feed the motor unit slowly forward.

Pattern Shaping

To do shaping with patterns, remove the standard guide fence and

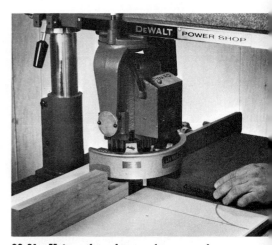

32-21. *Using the shaper fence and special guard for shaping the complete edge of the stock on the radial-arm saw.*

253

32-22. *Shaping with a pattern. Note that the pattern rides against the wood shaper ring mounted to the table just below the cutter.*

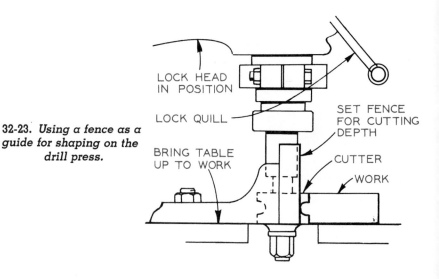

32-23. *Using a fence as a guide for shaping on the drill press.*

LOCK HEAD IN POSITION

LOCK QUILL

BRING TABLE UP TO WORK

SET FENCE FOR CUTTING DEPTH

CUTTER

WORK

make a circular guide ring with the same diameter as the cutting circle of the head. This guide ring must have the inner circle of wood removed so that the motor shaft can project below the surface. Then nail this ring to a scrap piece of 1" thick wood and use this to replace the standard guide fence. The ring must be directly under the revolving cutterhead. Now a pattern can be made to any size and shape. Rub a little paraffin on the edge of the pattern to make it slide easily. Place two or three anchor pins through the pattern to hold the stock firmly in

place. Adjust the collar and pattern for the correct depth of cut. The pattern then rests against the shaper ring as the cutting is done. Fig. 32-22.

SHAPING ON THE DRILL PRESS

Shaping can be done on the drill press if the spindle speed is 5000 RPM or higher. It is necessary to replace the chuck with a shaper

adapter to hold the cutters. Never attempt to fasten the cutters in a chuck used for drilling. The three-lip cutters used on the shaper can also be used on the drill press. Shaping can be done by using a guide fence or depth collars. The quill must be located in position. Fig. 32-23. Remember to check the setup before turning on the power. (Operation of the drill press is covered in Chapter 34.)

33 Router

The router, an overhead cutting tool, does work that is similar to that done by the shaper. (On the shaper, the cutting tool comes from underneath the table.) The router

has the advantage of entering the wood like a drill and then being able to move around to cut a recess in the wood surface. Fig. 33-1.

Routers are widely used for shap-

ing the surfaces and edges of stock and for joinery. The drill press and radial-arm saw can also be used for routing. With a floor router or drill press, the cutting tool is stationary

ROUTER

MAINTENANCE
• Keep all bits sharp. Grinding can be done by hand or with a grinding fixture that attaches to the router. Grind the underside of the lip of the bit.
• Keep the air vents free from sawdust.
• Check the brushes periodically and replace them immediately if worn away.

LUBRICATION
• Ball bearings on the motor shaft are grease-sealed to last the lifetime of the bearings. No further lubrication is required.

SAFETY
• Wear proper clothing and eye protection. (See Chapter 4.)

• Make sure the router is properly grounded. Most come equipped with a three-wire cord that will fit directly into corresponding grounding receptacles. An adapter for grounding a two-wire receptacle is usually furnished with the tool.
• Turn off the motor when the router is not in use.
• Disconnect the plug from the power circuit when changing bits.
• Hold the portable tool firmly but lightly in your hands.
• Never turn on the power until you are in a working position.
• Make sure the bit is properly installed before turning on the power.
• Never put anything into the ventilating holes of the router.

---

and the work moves. With a portable router or radial-arm saw, the work is held stationary while the tool is moved.

PORTABLE ROUTER

The portable router consists of a motor that is adjustable up and down in a base. Fig. 33-2. It operates at high speeds: 20,000 to 28,000 RPM. A collet (or split) chuck, attached to the end of the motor, holds the cutting tools (bits). The kind of work that can be done with the router depends on the cutters, fixtures, and attachments used.

Router Bits

Most router bits are made of selected tool steel. These are adequate for most cutting on hard and soft woods with the portable router. Carbide-tipped bits are normally used in production work and also for trimming the edges of plastic laminates.

Router bits are of two major types. The most common is the one-piece bit with a shank built into the cutting head. Some of these bits have a pilot or cylindrical tip built into the lower cutting edge. The shank fits into the collet of the router motor. The other type of router bit has a hole threaded completely through the center of the cutting head. When this bit is used with the router, a separate shank or arbor is screwed into the top of the cutting head. Also, if a separate pilot is needed, it is screwed into the bottom of the cutting head. When routing the edge of a board, the pilot controls the horizontal depth of cut by riding along the edge of the work.

Following are some common shapes of cutter bits and their uses. Fig. 33-3a.

• *Straight bits* are used for general stock removal, for cutting grooves and dadoes, inlay work, rabbeting,

33-1. *The shaped edges on this clock were cut on the router.*

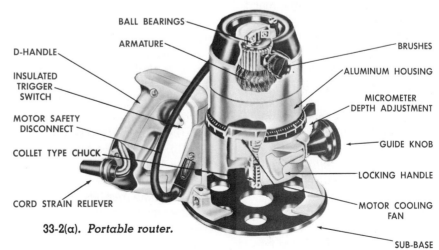

33-2(a). *Portable router.*

BALL BEARINGS
ARMATURE
D-HANDLE
INSULATED TRIGGER SWITCH
MOTOR SAFETY DISCONNECT
COLLET TYPE CHUCK
CORD STRAIN RELIEVER
BRUSHES
ALUMINUM HOUSING
MICROMETER DEPTH ADJUSTMENT
GUIDE KNOB
LOCKING HANDLE
MOTOR COOLING FAN
SUB-BASE

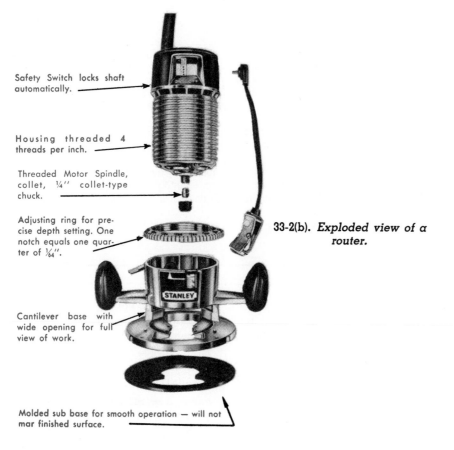

Safety Switch locks shaft automatically.

Housing threaded 4 threads per inch.

Threaded Motor Spindle, collet, ¼″ collet-type chuck.

Adjusting ring for precise depth setting. One notch equals one quarter of ¹⁄₆₄″.

Cantilever base with wide opening for full view of work.

Molded sub base for smooth operation — will not mar finished surface.

33-2(b). *Exploded view of a router.*

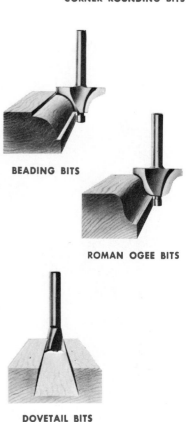

STRAIGHT BITS   ONE PIECE

RABBETING BITS

CORNER–ROUNDING BITS

BEADING BITS

ROMAN OGEE BITS

DOVETAIL BITS

and background routing. These are available in diameters from ⅛″ to ¾″.

• *Rabbeting bits* cut a rabbet or a step at the edge of wood.

• *Corner-rounding bits* round the corners of flat surfaces such as tables, desk tops, or cupboard doors.

• *Beading bits* are similar to corner-rounding bits except that they leave a sharp break or decorative bead at each end of the round.

• *Roman ogee bits* cut the decorative edge frequently found on the inside of paneled doors and frames.

• *Dovetail bits* cut a dovetail dado or a straight dovetail on the ends of stock to form a right-angle joint, as in drawer construction.

• *Chamfer bits* cut a 45-degree bevel on the edge of stock.

• *Sash beading bits* are used to cut beads or decorative edges on the inner surface of a window frame.

• *Sash coping bits* are used to cut copings in window-frame rails to match beads cut by a sash beading bit.

• *Cove bits* cut a concave radius in the edge of a warped piece. The cove bit is used for making a drop-leaf table joint.

• *"V" grooving bits* make V-shaped cuts to imitate plank construction on panels of plywood or boards.

• *Core-box bits* are similar to veining bits but larger in diameter. They get their name because of wide use in patternmaking.

• *Veining or round-end bits* are similar to straight bits except that they cut a radius in the wood. They are used for ornamental or decorative figure routing.

• *Hinge mortising bits,* Fig. 33-3(b), cut a groove that the knuckle (enlarged part) of a butt hinge fits into.

• *Rounding over bits* are similar to corner-rounding bits except that they leave a sharp break at one end of the round.

Controlling the Cutting

There are five basic ways of controlling the sidewise movement of a portable router:

Using a straightedge clamped to the top of the wood. To make straight cuts on flat surfaces, build a simple wood T square or other guide as shown in Fig. 33-4. This can be used for cutting rabbets, dadoes, grooves, and splines.

Using a straight or circular guide (also called edge guide). Fig. 33-5. This is the most practical and economical accessory for the router. It guides the router in a straight line along the edge of a board and is particularly useful in cutting grooves on long pieces. The edge of the guide can be adjusted the correct distance from the cutter so that it will ride along the edge or surface of the stock. Some guides can also be reversed so that the machine will make a two-point contact when used on circular work. Fig. 33-6.

Using a bit with a pilot end. Many router bits have a pilot end which limits the depth of cut. When the bit reaches the right amount of sidewise movement, the pilot contacts the stock and prevents a deeper cut. Pilot ends are common on

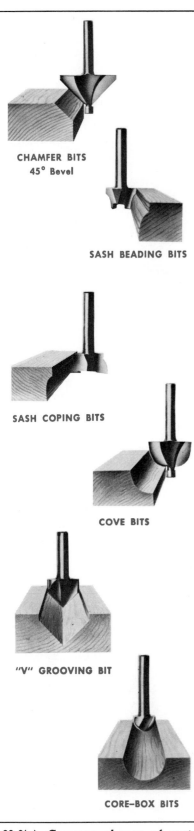

CHAMFER BITS
45° Bevel

SASH BEADING BITS

SASH COPING BITS

COVE BITS

"V" GROOVING BIT

CORE–BOX BITS

33-3(a). *Common shapes of router bits. Special shapes for any kind of routing can be ordered.*

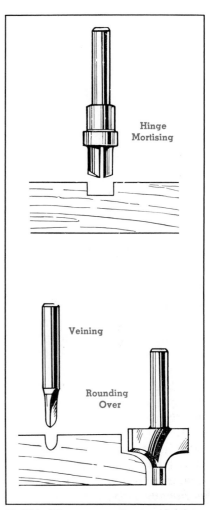

Hinge Mortising

Veining

Rounding Over

33-3(b). *Three more shapes of router bits.*

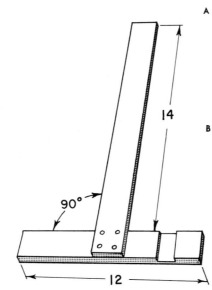

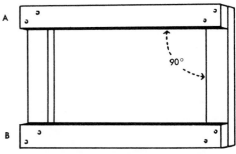

33-4. *Guides like this T square and box are useful for controlling the router when making straight cuts on flat surfaces. When making the box guide, be sure the distance between boards A and B is exactly the same as the width of the router base. To use, clamp the box guide to the work and feed the router between boards A and B.*

33-5. *An edge guide can be used to control the sidewise movement of the router.*

beading, rounding-over, cove, and molding bits. Fig. 33-7.

Using a template. A template (pattern) of the correct shape can be made of ¼″ plywood or hardboard. Fig. 33-8. With small brads, attach it to the stock where the work will not show or where it will be removed if the routing must go completely through the stock. If the cut is to go completely through, clamp scrap wood underneath. Use a straight or a rounding-over bit for corners, as needed. Several commercial templates are also available. The principal ones are for cutting a dovetail and for hinge-butt routing.

Freehand routing. This kind of cutting is done without any guide devices. The quality of the work is determined by the operator's skill. Freehand routing may be used, for example, to route out a background on stock, leaving raised letters. The letters or pattern can also be cut directly into the wood. Fig. 33-9.

33-6. *Most router guides can be reversed in order to make cuts that are parallel to curved or circular edges.*

33-7. *The pilot on the end of the cutter controls the amount of cut. It rides on the edge and does no cutting.*

The pattern is penciled directly on the workpiece. Usually, veining bits are used. It is suggested that the routing be not more than ⅜″ deep. Deeper cuts make it difficult to follow the pattern. For wood carving, some operators use the router to remove much of the background stock before doing the final shaping with a gouge and chisel.

Assembling and Adjusting the Router

Select the correct bit for the kind of work to be done. Remove the motor unit from the base by turning; or, if it is a clamp-on type, slip it off. Insert the bit shank into the collet chuck to a distance of about ½″. Lock the motor so that it will not turn. Then tighten the nut on the collet to hold it in place. Next, slip the motor into the base and place it over a piece of scrap stock. Move the motor down until the end of the bit touches the work surface. Fig. 33-10.

There are several kinds of routers that are adjusted in different ways. If the motor screws into the base, screw it in until the router bit is exposed an amount equal to the

33-8. *Using a hardboard template as a guide in routing out a scroll design.*

depth of the cut. If the motor moves up and down by a ratchet arrangement, slip the motor down into the base the correct distance. Lock the base to the motor securely.

Try cutting a scrap piece of the same thickness as the stock. Always make sure that the work is rigidly held in position. Since the cutter rotates clockwise, cutting is more efficient if the router is moved from left to right as you stand facing the

33-9. *Freehand routing can be done to shape recessed or raised letters. Here, recessed letters are formed by removing the wood to make the letter.*

33-11. *The router bit revolves clockwise. Therefore, when cutting straight edges, move the router from left to right. When making circular cuts, move the router in a counterclockwise direction.*

33-10. *Assembling a router: (A) The motor is readily removed from the base by loosening the clamping lever and disconnecting the light wire. (B) Select the correct bit and insert it all the way into the collet chuck. With the safety switch in the locked position, the shaft is held firmly. The chuck can be tightened with only one wrench. Return the motor to the base. (C) Loosen the clamping lever about one-quarter of a turn when raising or lowering the motor for exact depth setting. (D) For extremely accurate setting, use the micrometer depth adjustment. Each notch on the depth ring is equal to one-quarter of 1/64".*

dado. For example, if you are using ¾" material, it is best to use a ¾" bit. If a bit this size is not available, use a narrower one and make two or more passes. Either a straightedge or a commercial guide can be used to control the router when cutting. To locate the position of the straightedge, measure from the cutting edge of the bit to the outside edge of the router base. This will give you the distance from the straightedge to the point at which the cut is to be made. A stop dado can also be cut by limiting the distance that the router is moved across the stock.

work. Fig. 33-11. Also, in working on the inside of a template, work from left to right. Don't feed the router too slowly because this will make the bit grind the wood. Feeding too fast will produce excessive wear on the bits. For extremely heavy cuts, it is sometimes better to take a lighter cut at first, then make a second cut to the correct depth. The sound and feel of the motor will help you decide when to do this.

Cutting a Rabbet

A rabbet is an L-shaped groove along the edge or end of stock. It can be cut either with or across the grain. Use a straight bit and a gauge to control the width of the cut. Try the width and depth of the cut on a piece of scrap stock. When it is correct, proceed with cutting the rabbet. Figs. 33-12 and 33-13. Cutting two wide rabbets will produce a tongue.

Cutting a Dado

While there are many ways of cutting a dado, one of the simplest is with the router. Use a straight cutter of the same diameter as the thickness of the piece to fit into the

33-12. *Cutting a rabbet across grain using a straight bit and a straight guide. The diameter of the bit should be slightly larger than the width of cut you want.*

259

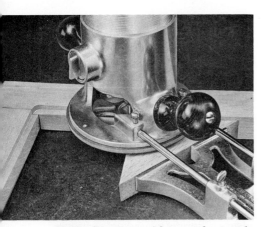

33-13. *To cut a rabbet on the inside of an opening such as a picture frame, it is necessary to use the straight router guide with an auxiliary wood block. A triangular wood block that has a 90-degree angle is fastened exactly in the center of the straightedge plate of the router guide. There are two holes in this guide to hold the wood block in place so that the rabbet can be cut right up to the corner with only a slight radius. This can be cleaned out by hand, using a chisel.*

Cutting a Groove

Grooves are cut in the direction of the grain. Grooves are found on the sides, backs, and fronts of drawers, boxes, and many other boxlike structures. They are also used on the inside edges of frames to make

33-14. *Cutting a groove in the edge of a board. Note the extra piece of wood about 2" high attached to the commercial guide for added stability.*

raised or recessed panels for door construction.

An edge guide that is in a straight line and parallel with the edge of the stock is used on the router. The simplest method of cutting a groove is to use a commercial guide with a straight cutter bit of correct diameter. Fig. 33-14. A circular groove can be cut by using a trammel point attached to the guide rods of the router guide. The trammel point has a needlelike projection that acts as a center. Circular parts can also be cut by placing the stock over a scrap piece so that the router bit can cut completely through the first piece.

Cutting a Blind Mortise and Tenon

The mortise-and-tenon joint is used in frame construction, for doors, fronts of drawers, and for leg-and-rail construction. The blind mortise, when cut with a router, has rounded ends which must be squared off with a hand chisel, or else the tenon must be made narrower to fill the opening.

Usually the mortise is cut in the exact center of the edge or surface. Use a straight bit and the router guide. When cutting in the edge of stock, it is a good idea to clamp a piece of wood on each side to give the base more support. The tenon can be formed by making rabbet cuts on all four sides. By clamping stock together, several tenons can be cut at the same time.

Spline Joint

The spline joint is used to reinforce the joining edges of two pieces of wood. To cut the groove for this joint, first select a straight bit of the correct width. Normally, splines are made of ⅛" or ¼" plywood or hardboard so a ⅛" or ¼" straight bit can be used. Use a gauge to control the location of the groove. In many cases a blind-spline cut is required. This is made by

33-15. *A blind spline has a good appearance. Note that both pieces of material are clamped between scrap pieces. The spline has been installed in one part of the miter joint.*

dropping the router into the work and moving it along the required distance. Fig. 33-15.

Cutting a Dovetail Dado Joint

The dovetail dado joint is relatively easy to cut with a router, dovetail bit, and router guide. First cut the slot or mortise portion. Take the board on which the mortise is to be cut and place it endwise in a vise. Place a scrap piece of wood on each side so that the router base has ample surface on which to ride. Adjust the bit for depth of cut. Position the guide so that the cut is

33-16. *Cutting the mortise or slot.*

exactly centered on the stock. Cut the slot. Fig. 33-16. It is possible to cut a wider dovetail by making two or more passes. However, it is important that the location and width of the dovetail be accurately marked.

To cut the tenon or stub portion of the joint, keep the depth setting the same as for the slot. Adjust the guide so that one cut is made on each side to form the tenon. Fig. 33-17. It is essential that the tenon be a few thousandths of an inch narrower than the slot. Before cutting the joint, it is good to make trial cuts on scrap stock of the same thickness.

The width of dovetail joints need not be limited by the size of bit available. With careful measuring, several cuts may be made with a single bit to form the mortise and tenon to the width desired. A little practice will enable you to get the cut equally distant from both sides of the piece being worked.

Naturally it is important to use wood that is not warped. Before starting the job, check the piece on a flat surface for uniformity.

Cutting a Dovetail Joint

The dovetail joint is used extensively in commercial furniture, espe-

33-17. *Cutting the tenon or stub. Note that two dovetails are actually cut to form this part.*

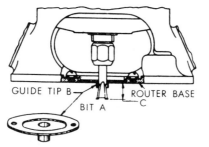

33-18. *Attach a template guide tip to the base of the router.*

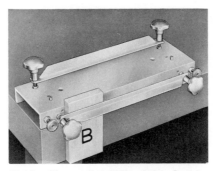

33-19. *Clamp the side of the drawer (Part B) in place.*

cially for fine drawer construction. Furniture factories use large, expensive dovetailing machines. However, the joint can also be cut with a dovetail attachment and a portable router. Both parts of the joint are cut at the same time.

1. Clamp the dovetail attachment to a bench or table so that the base projects slightly beyond the front. Attach a template guide tip to the base of the router. Fig. 33-18. Insert a dovetail bit through the template guide and tighten it in the chuck. Adjust the dovetail bit so that it is exactly $^{19}/_{32}$" below the base.

2. Square up the stock to form the joint. Cut two extra pieces of scrap stock of the same thickness and width to make a trial joint before final cutting. Clamp board *B*, which will be one side of the drawer or box, with the inner side out against the front of the base, about ½" above the top surface of the

base. This is a temporary setting to locate board *A*. Fig. 33-19.

3. Clamp board *A*, which will be the front or back of the drawer or box, with the inner side up. Make sure that board *B* is firmly against the locating pin. Then loosen the front clamp slightly and move *B* until the end grain is flush with the top of *A*. Fig. 33-20.

4. Place the template over the two pieces and clamp it in place. Make sure the template rests evenly on the material. Fig. 33-21.

5. Cut a trial dovetail joint, making sure that the guide tip of the router follows the template prongs. Always hold the router in the same position as it is moved around the template. Fig. 33-22.

6. Check the dovetail for fit. If it is too loose, lower the bit about $^{1}/_{64}$"; if too tight, raise the bit about $^{1}/_{64}$". If the fit is too shallow, set the template adjusting nuts a little more

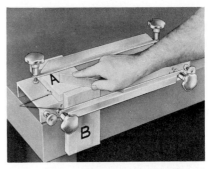

33-20. *Clamp front or back (Part A) in place.*

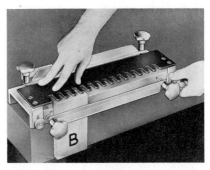

33-21. *Place the template over the pieces.*

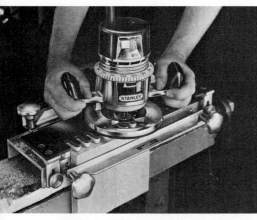

33-22(a). *Cut the dovetail with the router.*

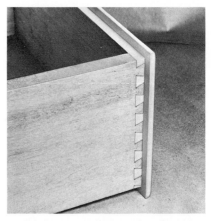

GAUGE BLOCK REMOVED AFTER CLAMP-ING DRAWER FRONT.

ALIGNMENT WITH VERTICAL SURFACE OF BASE

DRAWER FRONT

FIXTURE BASE

LOCATING PIN

33-23. *Position of the lip end of the drawer for cutting one part of the dovetail.*

33-24. *The completed dovetail joint that joins the side to the front of a lip drawer.*

33-22(b). *Here you see how the two parts of the joint are cut at the same time.*

toward the base. If it is too deep, set the template adjusting nuts away from the base. The accuracy of the joint depends on very fine adjustments. Trial cuts will help you make these adjustments.

7. The left end of the fixture is used for cutting the right front of the drawer and the left rear corner. The left front and right rear corners are cut at the right end of the fixture.

8. To cut a dovetail on a lip drawer front that has a rabbet cut on the back surface, the rabbet and the dovetail must be cut separately. Mount the rabbet piece of the draw-er front in a horizontal position, firmly against the locating pin. Make a gauge block by cutting a groove in a piece of scrap wood to hold the lip end of the drawer front. Use the gauge block, as shown in Fig. 33-23, to locate the rabbet sur-face and align it with the vertical surface of the fixture's base. When the stock is clamped, remove the gauge block and place the template in position. Cut the dovetail. To cut the side of the drawer, first cut a scrap piece the same thickness as the drawer front. Place this piece on top of the fixture and put the side piece in its correct position, as shown in Fig. 33-23. Then cut the dovetail. The two parts should fit accurately as shown in Fig. 33-24.

Hinge Butt Routing

A special template is available for hinge butt routing. Because the bits leave a slight curve at the corner of the cut, it is necessary to chisel the corner square for the hinges. Figure 33-25(a) shows a metal tem-plate in position on a door. This guides the router so that the hinge mortises are cut to uniform size and depth, easily and quickly.

If a door and jamb butt template is not practical for you, a tem-plate can be improvised as in

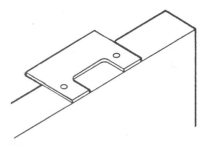

33-25(a). *Cutting a hinge mortise on a door. If a square corner hinge is used, the corners of the cut must be squared with a chisel. However, many hinges have round corners so that they fit directly into the open-ing. After gains or mortises are cut on the door, the template guide can be transferred to the door frame for cutting hinge mortises on the jamb.*

33-25(b). *Template for cutting a gain for a butt hinge.*

Fig. 33-25(b) from plywood or hardboard and tacked to the edge of the door or jamb. Here you must make all the measurements yourself to suit your particular hinge butt, template guide, and router bit.

Decorative Cutting

The router can be used to make all types of decorative cuts in wood. In many cases a template is needed for curved or irregularly shaped wood. The template should be made of ¼" plywood or tempered hardboard. Trace the pattern on the plywood or hardboard. Fig. 33-26. Cut out the template design on a jigsaw

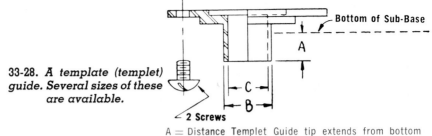

33-28. *A template (templet) guide. Several sizes of these are available.*

A = Distance Templet Guide tip extends from bottom of base.
B = Outside diameter Templet Guide tip.
C = Inside diameter Templet Guide tip.

33-26. *A template traced on a piece of plywood.*

33-27. *Place the template over scrap stock. Cut through the waste stock; then cut the stock ¹⁄₁₆" from the layout line. This must be done freehand. Remove the template; then file and sand up to the layout line.*

or with the router. Fig. 33-27. The template can then be fastened over the stock. You can use a bit with a smooth edge that will ride against the template. Or, use a template guide that fastens to the base of the router. This guide rides against the template. Fig. 33-28. For best results, make the first cut a little distance from the line. Then, on the second pass, cut up to the template. Fig. 33-29. Decorative work can also be done freehand. Veining

33-29. *Clamp the finished template to the work. Place a piece of scrap stock underneath. Make sure the sub-base and template guide are in place. Use a straight bit that is adjusted to the correct depth. Lower the bit into the waste stock; then guide the router along the edge of the template. Make sure the template guide is in contact with the edge of the template.*

and grooving can be done by using the gauge to control the location of the cut.

FLOOR-TYPE ROUTER OR DRILL PRESS

As stated earlier, on a floor-type router or drill press the bit rotates in a fixed position and the work is fed into it. Methods of controlling the cutter and the work are similar to those used with the portable router. Fig. 33-30.

The five basic methods of floor-type routing can also be used for shaping. They are described in the following:

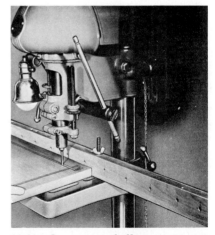

33-30. *On most drill presses an adapter must be used in place of the chuck when routing. Never attempt to hold a router bit in a drill-press chuck unless you are absolutely sure that the chuck is part of the spindle assembly. Note that the fence is used as a guide.*

● When the cut doesn't remove the stock from the entire edge of the material, a guide pin that extends up from the underside of the table can be used. Straight or circular stock is pressed against this pin to control the depth of cut. Fig. 33-31.

● If the entire edge must be shaped, make a fixture that has the same shape as the finished part. Put sharp spur points through the fixture to hold the stock in place. Then place the work over the fixture and on the table. The fixture rides against the guide pin so that the entire edge of the work can be routed. Fig. 33-32.

● For straight-line cutting, a fence or guide rail can be used. The stock is held against the fence. The position of the fence in relation to the router bit or cutter determines the amount of material removed. If the total edge is shaped, it is necessary to have a two-part, adjustable fence so that half of it can be moved forward to support the work after shaping. The same practice was described with regard to the jointer. Fig. 33-33.

● When only a part of the edge is to be shaped, a router bit with a pilot on the end can be used to control the sidewise movement of the work. However, this is not rec- ommended because the high speeds of floor routers tend to make the pilot burn the edge of the stock as the cut is made. Fig. 33-34.

● For internal routing and flat carving, a pattern is needed. On plywood or hardboard, make a pattern which represents the exact design to be duplicated. Cut out these areas on a jigsaw. Place small pins or spurs through the pattern to hold the work to be shaped. Use a guide pin in the table. Place the pattern over the guide pin. Then, with the power on, adjust the machine for depth of cut. Press the work firmly against the guide pin to do the routing. This technique is sometimes called *pin routing*. Fig. 33-35.

Fixtures for routing should be made of maple, birch, plywood, or hardboard. The edge of the template must be smooth, since any imperfection will show up on the work itself. Wax the bottom of the fixture so that it slides smoothly over the table.

ACCESSORIES

The router can become a small shaper by making or buying a special table for mounting it. Fig. 33-36. Use a fence for straight shaping or a fulcrum pin for free-hand shaping of edges.

Various attachments can be bought to increase the usefulness of the router. If a large number of cabinet doors need to be decorated with straight, arced, or shaped grooves, attachments are available that will perform these operations on many duplicate parts. Any number of doors can be decorated so that they will have identical designs. Fig. 33-37. Another useful attachment makes it possible for the router to do decorative work on all kinds of turned parts. For example, fluting or beading a set of legs is very simple with this attachment. A spindle carving attachment can be used to do all kinds of very intricate carving. With this attachment, any

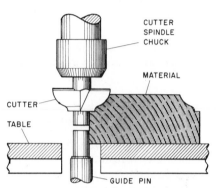
33-31. Using a guide pin to control the depth of cut.

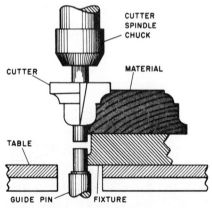
33-32. Using a fixture and a guide pin to shape the entire edge of stock.

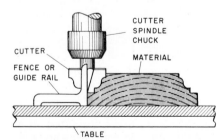
33-33. Using a fence or guide rail to control the depth of cut.

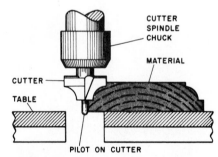
33-34. Using a pilot on the end of the cutter to control the depth of cut.

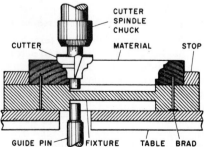
33-35. Using a fixture to do internal routing.

33-36. *Using a router as a shaper. Note the simple shop-built stand.*

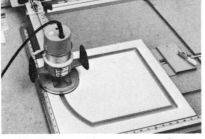

33-37. *A variable arc attachment can be used for routing arc designs in cabinet doors.*

33-38. *Using a V block as a guide for routing the edge of a round piece of wood. Notice that the block is clamped to the table with a C-clamp. The motor can be moved in or out and up or down to adjust for the correct cut.*

wood, metal, or plastic part can be used as the original.

ROUTING ON THE RADIAL-ARM SAW

The radial-arm saw can be converted into a router by first removing the guard, the arbor nut, the collars, and the saw. Then an adapter to hold the router bits is attached to the right end of the motor or the end opposite that used for sawing. The machine is then used as a floor-type router. In other words, the motor is locked in a fixed position and the work is moved under the revolving cutter.

For straight routing, the guide fence can be used. For curved or round work, a large wooden guide block is clamped to the table. Fig. 33-38. Freehand routing is done by moving the work under the cutter bit. The work will move more easily if placed on a piece of cardboard. For cross routing at any angle, the work is held against the guide fence and the bit is moved across the stock as for crosscutting. Several passes may be necessary to get the correct width or depth of cut.

34 Drilling, Boring, and Mortising Machines

Many drilling and boring operations must be performed in cabinetmaking. Sometimes the term *drilling* is used primarily for metalworking and *boring* for woodworking. At other times, *drilling* is used to mean cutting holes that are ¼" or smaller and *boring* refers to holes that are larger than ¼".

There are two kinds of drilling and boring operations: *precision boring* and *semi-precision drilling.* Precision boring is necessary in installing dowels. The holes must be in the correct location, accurately spaced, and of the right size and depth. Semi-precision drilling is done when installing screws and making openings that require less exacting standards. Drilling and boring are extremely important operations in woodworking since dowels have largely replaced the mortise-and-tenon joint in cabinet and furniture making.

STATIONARY EQUIPMENT

Two kinds of stationary drilling equipment are commonly used in school and cabinet shops: the drill press and the horizontal boring machine.

Drill Press

Drill presses are of either the bench or floor type. Fig. 34-1. Their size is determined by the diameter of the largest workpiece that can be drilled on center. For example, a 15″ drill press will bore a hole through the center of a round piece 15″ in diameter. Generally, a key-type chuck is used for holding the cutting tool. The speed is set either by changing a V belt on step pulleys or by the use of a variable-speed pulley arrangement. Fig. 34-2. The variable-speed-pulley drill press is extremely valuable in the wood shop since it provides a wide range of speeds from 500 to 4700 RPM. High speeds are necessary for such operations as shaping, routing, and planing. Speeds between 1200 and 3000 RPM are for drilling and boring wood. If the drill press is to be used as a boring machine, it is necessary to attach an auxiliary fence to the table against which the stock can be held.

Horizontal Boring Machine

The small horizontal boring machine with one, two, or three spindles is found in many shops. In smaller shops a single-spindle machine is usually used. Larger shops

34-2. *Controls for a variable-speed drill press. Never change the speed unless the motor is running.*

have machines with two or three spindles.

PORTABLE EQUIPMENT

Portable electric drills vary in capacity and horsepower rating. The capacity of a drill depends on its chuck size and rated revolutions per minute (RPM). The chuck size is the diameter of the largest bit shank the drill chuck can hold. Common sizes are ¼″, ⅜″, and ½″. Usually, the larger the chuck, the wider and deeper the holes the drill can bore.

Two types of chucks are available. Most are of the *geared type* that requires a special key for opening and closing. The other type, called a *hex key chuck*, requires an allen wrench to open and close it.

For most jobs, a single-speed drill is adequate. However, a two-speed or variable-speed model will be more suitable if you intend to drill material that requires a slow speed or if you want to use many accessories. A drill with both variable speed and reverse is useful for driving and removing screws. To protect the

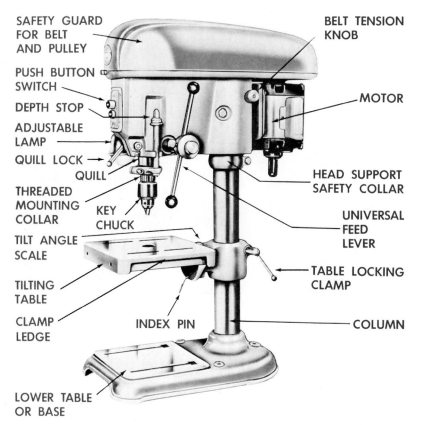

SAFETY GUARD FOR BELT AND PULLEY

PUSH BUTTON SWITCH

DEPTH STOP

ADJUSTABLE LAMP

QUILL LOCK

QUILL

THREADED MOUNTING COLLAR

KEY CHUCK

TILT ANGLE SCALE

TILTING TABLE

CLAMP LEDGE

INDEX PIN

LOWER TABLE OR BASE

BELT TENSION KNOB

MOTOR

HEAD SUPPORT SAFETY COLLAR

UNIVERSAL FEED LEVER

TABLE LOCKING CLAMP

COLUMN

34-1. *Parts of a 15″ bench-type drill press. Four speeds can be obtained by changing the position of the belt.*

DRILLING AND BORING MACHINES

MAINTENANCE
- On machines with step pulleys, check the belt tension. The belt should be just tight enough to prevent it from slipping, no tighter.
- Make sure the correct chuck key is available.
- Check the quill-return spring. It should have light tension.
- Excessive tension prevents sensitive drilling and causes pinion-gear breakage.
- Keep drills and auger bits properly sharpened.
- Keep motor and spindle pulley setscrews tight to prevent scoring the motor shaft and spindle.

LUBRICATION
- Cover the outside surface of the quill with powdered graphite.
- Light ball-bearing grease applied to the spindle spline maintains spindle lubrication and eliminates noise.

SAFETY
- Wear proper clothing and eye protection. (See Chapter 4.)
- Make sure the stock is clamped before drilling or boring.
- Never attempt to use a hand auger bit. Use only drills and bits designed for machine use.
- Always position the hole in the center of the table beneath the drill and place a piece of wood beneath the work to keep from drilling holes in the table.
- Use a brush to keep the table free of sawdust.
- Never try to stop the machine by taking hold of the chuck after the power is off.
- On deep cuts, back out often to clean out the hole.

---

motor, allow the drill to come to a full stop before reversing.

Most portable drills have a pistol-grip handle. It should be comfortable and well balanced. Some models include side handles so that the drill can be held with both hands for heavy work or for drilling in an unusual position. The trigger switch that starts the drill is on the pistol-grip handle. Many models include a switch lock for continuous operation. The lock instantly releases when the trigger switch is squeezed.

One problem in using a portable drill with a *metal* housing is the danger of shock, especially when working around damp areas. Many portable drills are now made with a heavy-duty, *plastic* housing to prevent this.

CUTTING TOOLS

Many kinds of cutting tools are used for making holes in wood and also for cutting out circular parts. The two most common are the *twist drill* and the *spur machine bit*. It was once thought that the twist drill could not do accurate dowel boring. However, experimentation has shown that the twist drill cutter will do almost as good a job as the spur machine bit. The advantage, of course, is that it is much easier to sharpen the twist drill.

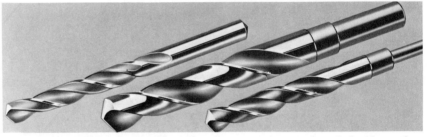

34-3. *Twist drills of several sizes. Note that some have reduced shanks so that holes larger than the portable drill's normal capacity can be drilled.*

Twist Drills
Carbon-steel twist drills for wood are available in diameters from $\frac{1}{32}''$ to $\frac{3}{4}''$ at intervals of $\frac{1}{64}''$. High-speed steel drills which may be used on both metal and wood are available in diameters from $\frac{1}{64}''$ to $\frac{1}{2}''$ at intervals of $\frac{1}{64}''$. Fig. 34-3. For general-purpose work, the high-speed steel drill point should have an included angle of 118 degrees. However, if the drills are to be used only for woodworking, an included angle between 60 and 82 degrees is better.

Spur Machine Bits
The spur machine bit has a brad and lip point and is one of the cleanest, fastest-cutting bits for dowel holes. Fig. 34-4. These bits come in standard sizes that are marked in 32nds of an inch.

Multispur Bit
The multispur bit is excellent for power cutting of larger holes. Fig. 34-5.

34-4. *Spur machine bit.*

34-5. *Multispur bit. This bit will bore plywood without tearing. It will also bore at an angle. It comes in diameters from $\frac{1}{2}''$ to $\frac{3}{4}''$, increasing by sixteenths.*

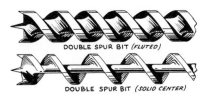

34-6. *Power auger bits have straight shanks and brad points.*

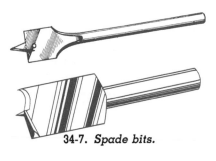

34-7. *Spade bits.*

34-8. *Masonry drill.*

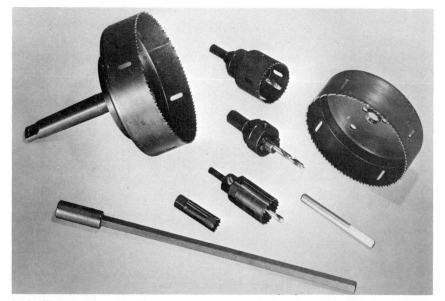

34-9. *Various sizes of hole saws. They are made in diameters from ⅝″ to 3½″. The saws fit on mandrels and have ¼″ or larger drills at their centers.*

Auger Bit

An auger bit for a power drill should have a straight shank and a brad point. Never try to use a bit with a tang in the power drill. The common auger bits are made either with a solid center or fluted. Fig. 34-6. Common sizes are from No. 4 (¼″) to No. 16 (1″).

Spade Bit

These bits, also called flat power or speed bits, are made in several types and shapes. Fig. 34-7. Typical sizes are from ¼″ to 1″, increasing by ¹⁄₁₆″, with ¼″ shanks. Some are made with changeable cutter-heads.

Masonry Bit

The cabinetmaker frequently must install cabinets in a masonry wall and therefore needs a number of masonry bits. Fig. 34-8. These carbide-tipped bits must be used at slow speeds and heavy pressure. Sizes vary. For ¼″ chucks, the bits

range from ⅛″ to ½″. For ½″ chucks the range is from ½″ to 1″.

Rotary Hole Saw

Rotary hole cutters vary as to type, diameter, and depth of cut. They are used to make holes of large diameters in wood, metal, and plastic. Fig. 34-9.

Plug Cutter

In fine cabinet work, screw heads are covered with plugs. These plugs are made of the same wood as the cabinet. Two types of plug cutters are shown in Fig. 34-10.

Circle Cutter

Circle cutters are made in a wide variety of styles and sizes to cut holes from ⅝″ to 8″ in diameter.

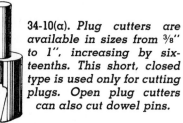

34-10(a). *Plug cutters are available in sizes from ⅜″ to 1″, increasing by sixteenths. This short, closed type is used only for cutting plugs. Open plug cutters can also cut dowel pins.*

These single-point tools are fastened to the end of a crossbar with a small drill in the center. It is extremely important to clamp the wood securely to the table before any cutting is done. Fig. 34-11.

Foerstner Bit

The Foerstner (Forstner) bit is used for intricate woodcutting. The

34-10(b). *This plug cutter is being used in an adapter, but such a cutter can be used in the drill press chuck.*

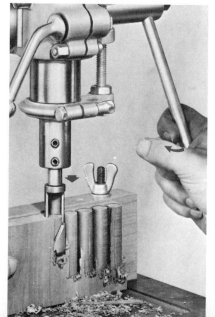

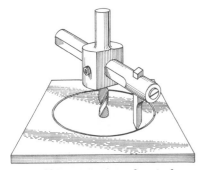

34-11. *Always operate the circle cutter at a slow speed and clamp the workpiece to the table.*

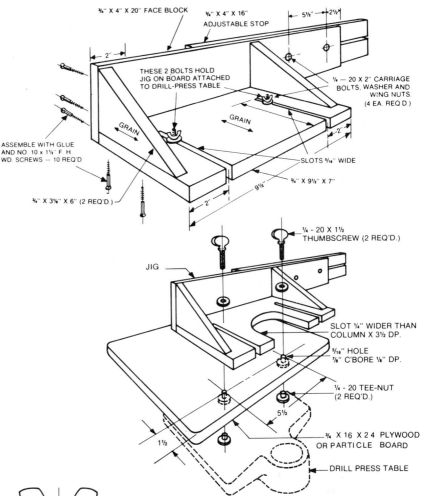

bit is guided by the edge of the tool, not by the center. This permits boring an arc in any direction, regardless of grain, to cut oval and curved openings, rounded corners, or holes with flat bottoms. It is available in sizes from ½″ to 2″. Fig. 34-12.

USING THE DRILL PRESS

General Procedures

1. Select the correct kind of bit or drill and fasten it securely in the chuck. CAUTION: Always remove the key before turning on the power.

2. Make sure the proper layout has been made and that the position of the hole is well marked.

3. Make sure the drill or bit is free to go through the table opening in the drill-press table. *Also, place a piece of scrap wood under the material. This will help prevent splintering when the drill goes through the underside of the work.*

4. Adjust the drill press for the correct cutting speed. The speed should vary with the type of bit, the size, the kind of wood, and the depth of the hole. In general, the smaller the cutting tool and the softer the wood, the higher the speed. Cutting tools up to ¾″ in diameter should operate at speeds

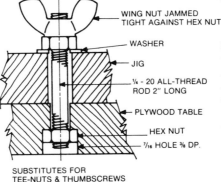

SUBSTITUTES FOR
TEE-NUTS & THUMBSCREWS

34-13. *This drill press jig can be used for many drilling operations. Note the adjustable stop. Using the stop will assure you that all holes are in exactly the same location when mass-producing parts. It is also very useful when drilling holes for dowels.*

from 3000 down to 1800 RPM. Bits above this diameter should maintain slower speeds down to 600 RPM. Select the approximate speed and then use good judgment when feeding the tool into the material. If the tool smokes, reduce the speed and the feed.

5. Clamp the work securely when necessary, especially when using larger drilling and boring tools, hole cutters, and similar cutting devices. Clamping is a must if the tool has only one cutting edge, such as a hole cutter. Fig. 34-13.

34-12. *A Foerstner bit.*

Drilling Small Holes in Flat Stock

To drill or bore a hole that is ¼" or smaller in size, use a twist drill. Locate the center of the hole and mark it with a center punch or scratch awl. Place it on the table over a piece of scrap wood. Turn on the power and slowly move the point of the bit into the stock. Hold the stock firmly and apply even pressure to the handle. If the stock is hardwood or the hole is deep, back up the bit once or twice to remove the chips before finishing the hole. Always bore through the hole and into the scrap wood.

Cutting Medium-Sized Holes in Flat Stock

Holes from ¼" to 1¼" can be cut with a variety of drilling and boring tools. For example, a twist drill, auger bit, Foerstner bit, or spade bit could be used. In boring a through hole, there are two methods. The simplest is to place a piece of scrap wood under the hole so that the tool will cut through the stock and into the scrap piece. This keeps the underside from splintering. The second method is to cut until

the point of the bit shows through the stock, then drill from the other side. To bore a hole to a specific depth, adjust the depth stop *with the power off*. Bring the cutting tool down to the side of the work where the depth is marked. Then set the depth stop. Fig. 34-14.

Boring Large Holes in Flat Stock

Holes larger than 1¼" are best cut with a hole saw or a circle cutter. Make sure that the work is firmly clamped, especially when using a hole cutter, since any tool with a single point has a tendency to rotate the work.

Boring Deep Holes

On most drill presses the spindle will move only four or five inches. Other methods must be found for deeper holes. If the hole is less than twice the quill stroke (the maximum distance the drill will move), one of the following methods can be used:

• Clamp a piece of scrap stock to the table. Install a bit of the correct size and bore a small hole. Fig. 34-15(a). Lower the table to

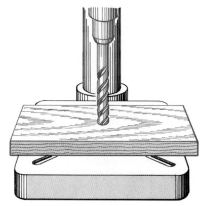

34-15(a). *Boring a hole in the scrap stock.*

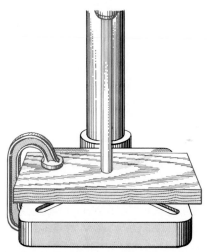

34-15(b). *Aligning the hole in the scrap stock with the chuck.*

accommodate the workpiece. To align the hole in the scrap stock with the chuck, it may be necessary to remove the bit and replace it with a long piece of dowel rod. Fig. 34-15(b). Reinsert the auger bit, position the workpiece, and bore the hole to maximum depth. Then cut a short piece of dowel rod and place it in the hole in the scrap stock. Turn the workpiece over the dowel rod and then bore from the other side. Fig. 34-15(c).

• The second method is to turn the table to a vertical position. Fasten an auxiliary fence to the table. The location for the hole must be aligned with the bit. Bore from both ends. If a hole longer than 8" is to

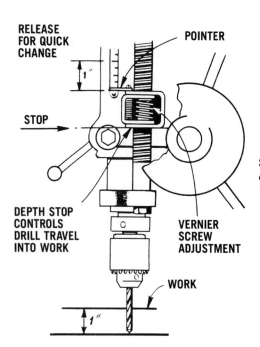

34-14. *Use the depth stop to control the depth of a hole. This one is set to drill a hole 1" into the work.*

RELEASE FOR QUICK CHANGE

POINTER

1"

STOP

DEPTH STOP CONTROLS DRILL TRAVEL INTO WORK

VERNIER SCREW ADJUSTMENT

WORK

1"

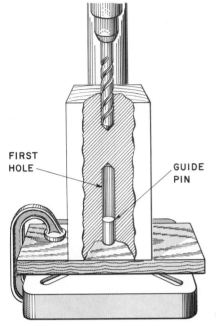

FIRST HOLE

GUIDE PIN

34-15(c). *Boring the workpiece from the second end.*

34-17. *Another method of boring holes in series. The stop pin goes through a block and is set in the previously drilled hole to locate the next hole. The distance between the first two holes must be accurately marked.*

34-18. *Using a drilling jig. Note that the jig and stock are moved from one position to the next to do the drilling.*

be bored, an extension auger bit can be made by brazing a rod to the shank of the bit; or a commercial bit extension can be used.

Boring Equally Spaced Holes along a Surface or Edge

To the table, clamp a temporary wood fence in which a series of equally spaced holes has been drilled. Hold the work against a dowel rod fastened in one of the holes in the fence. The "matching" hole will be correctly drilled in the workpiece. Move the dowel rod to

34-16. *Boring equally spaced holes using a fence as a jig.*

each of the other holes to complete the drilling. Fig. 34-16.

Another method of doing this is to have a stop block clamped to the auxiliary fence. Cut several identical wood pieces equal in length to the distance between the holes. Place these wood pieces against the stop block and then place the end of the work against these blocks. After the first hole has been bored, remove one block, push the work along, and bore the next hole.

Still another method is to use a stop pin clamped to an auxiliary wood fence. Fig. 34-17. And still one more excellent method of boring a series of holes, especially for production work, is to make a large drilling jig into which the material will fit. The guide piece of the jig is made of hardboard. Fig. 34-18.

Boring Holes at an Angle

There are many methods of boring a hole at an angle. The choice depends on the kind of cutting tool and the degree of the angle. In Fig. 34-19, a Foerstner bit is used to cut a hole at a very slight angle. This cutter will start easily, even at

an angle. If an auger bit is used, then another method is better. Tilt the table to the correct angle and check with a sliding T bevel or with the protractor head of a combination set. Clamp the work to the table with a wedge-shaped block over it so that the tool can start in a flat surface. Fig. 34-20. If a larger size twist drill is used, the drilling may be done without a guide block.

34-19. *Using a Foerstner bit to bore a hole in the side of a tapered leg.*

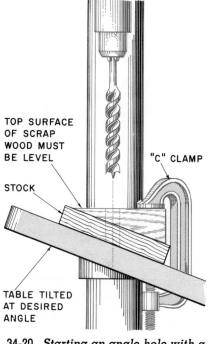

TOP SURFACE
OF SCRAP
WOOD MUST
BE LEVEL

"C" CLAMP

STOCK

TABLE TILTED
AT DESIRED
ANGLE

34-20. *Starting an angle hole with a scrap block.*

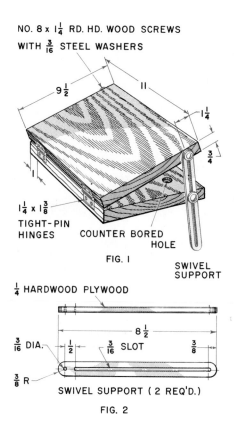

NO. 8 x 1¼ RD. HD. WOOD SCREWS
WITH 3/16 STEEL WASHERS

9½

11

1¼

¾

1

1¼ x 1⅜
TIGHT-PIN
HINGES

COUNTER BORED
HOLE

SWIVEL
SUPPORT

FIG. 1

¼ HARDWOOD PLYWOOD

8½

3/16 DIA.

½

3/16 SLOT

⅜

⅜ R

SWIVEL SUPPORT (2 REQ'D.)

FIG. 2

COUNTER BORE FOR ¼" CARRIAGE BOLT

JIG BASE-BOARD

DRILL PRESS
TABLE

FLAT WASHER
& WING NUT

FIG. 3

34-21. *Drill-press tilting table.*

34-22. *Drilling a hole on the tilting table. Note that the work is clamped to the tilting table with a hand screw to keep it from sliding.*

34-23. *Drilling holes in dowel rod.*

34-24. *Boring holes around the edge of a disk.*

Clamp the work securely to the table with a C-clamp.

An excellent device for boring at an angle is an auxiliary wood table, fastened to the table of the drill press. Fig. 34-21. The material to be drilled is then held or clamped to the auxiliary table, which is adjusted to the correct angle. Fig. 34-22.

Boring Holes in Round Work

For small round stock such as dowel rods, place a V block on the table. Make sure the center of the V is directly under the center of the drill. Fig. 34-23. To bore holes in the edge of a circular piece, turn the table to a vertical position and clamp a large V block to it. Again, make sure the center of the V is directly under the drill. Fig. 34-24. To drill holes around a circle from one surface, locate and drill two of the holes, leaving the drill in the second hole. Drive a nail through the center of the work to act as a pivot. Place a pin in the first drilled hole. The other holes are then locat-

ed by using the spacing pin. Fig. 34-25.

Enlarging Smaller Holes and Counterboring

A good method of enlarging a small hole is with a Foerstner bit. This can be done since the outer cutting edge guides the bit. A second method is to use a large auger bit which has a piece of dowel rod fastened to its point. The rod should be equal in diameter to the hole already bored.

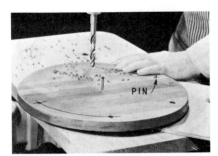

34-25. *Drilling a series of equally spaced holes around a circle. (Short sleeves are safer.)*

Counterboring is a process of enlarging only part of the outer end of an existing hole. This is often done so that the head of a screw or bolt may be sunk below the surface of the wood and then covered. The best method of doing this is to bore the larger hole first, then the smaller one.

Pocket Holes

The pocket hole is a simple method of attaching rails to tops, or legs to shelves. Fig. 34-26. Use a guide board that is beveled to about 15 degrees, and bore with a machine spur bit. This is actually a counterboring operation, since a larger hole is needed for the head of the screw and a smaller one for its body. Always drill the larger hole first. The same setup can be used for a corner pocket hole except that the work must be supported on edge at the corner.

Dowel Joints

In the school or cabinet shop that is not equipped with a boring machine, dowel holes are usually cut on the drill press. This is precision boring since the holes must be of correct diameter, depth, and location in order to match holes on the corresponding part of the joint. Methods of marking the dowel-hole location are described in Chapter 39. Remember that the dowels should be from one-third to one-half the thickness of the stock, and that

the holes for the dowels must be drilled with at least 1/16" clearance at each end.

EDGE BUTT

Lay out the location of the dowel holes on one stock piece. Mark all pieces with an "X" on the back surface (opposite the face surface). Fasten a fence to the table, using a wood jig such as is shown in Fig. 34-16. In this way all holes can be bored in the same location. Adjust the fence and jig so that the holes are centered. Always place the face surface against the fence so that, if there is any slight variation in thickness, that surface will be even. By using a jig, only one piece needs to be marked. The others will be bored accurately.

CORNER BUTT

Bore the holes in the edge grain as you would for a butt joint. Then turn the table to vertical position and bore in the end grain. When corner joints are to be rabbeted or grooved, always bore the dowel holes first.

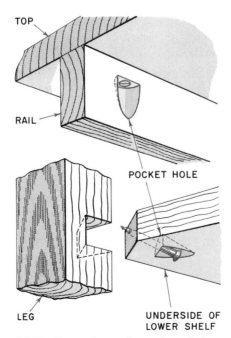

34-26. *Examples of pocket holes used in furniture construction.*

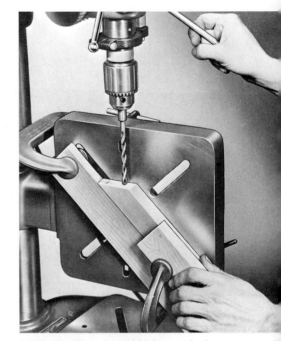

34-27. *Drilling dowel holes with the table turned to a vertical position.*

MITER JOINT

There are two common methods of boring dowel holes for a miter joint. The first is to tilt the table (or the auxiliary wood table) to an angle of 45 degrees to do the boring. The other method is to turn the table to a vertical position and use an auxiliary wood fence fastened to the table at 45 degrees. Fig. 34-27. A good method of spacing the two holes is shown in Fig. 34-28. A stop block is clamped to the auxiliary fence for the first hole; then a wooden spacer block is used for the second hole. With this method any number of pieces can be bored without an additional setup. Sometimes dowel holes must be installed in the end grain of a piece that is cut at an angle. To do this, adjust the table to this angle so that the hole is at right angles to the end grain.

USING A PORTABLE ELECTRIC DRILL

The portable electric drill is fairly simple to operate. It is commonly

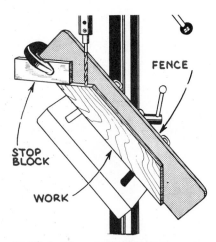

34-28(a). *The stop block automatically locates the position for the first dowel hole.*

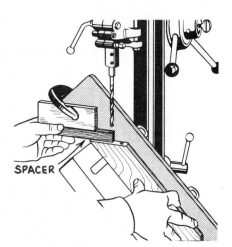

34-28(b). *A wood spacer between the stop block and the work locates the position for the second hole.*

34-29. *Using a portable drill.*

used to drill holes for installing all kinds of metal fasteners and hardware to wood products. Follow these suggestions:

1. Open the chuck far enough to allow the shank to slip in easily. Tighten it securely so that all three jaws hold the bit or drill.

2. Make sure that thin work is backed up with a solid piece of wood.

3. Grasp the control handle firmly and point the drill as you would a pistol. Use your other hand to control the feed as necessary. Press the trigger and guide the tool into the work. Fig. 34-29. For drilling pilot holes for screws, it may be necessary to use a small block of wood as a depth gauge to control the depth of drilling.

USING A SINGLE-SPINDLE BORING MACHINE

The single-spindle horizontal boring machine is found in many school and cabinet shops. Fig. 34-30. It can be used for boring holes for all types of dowel joints. The machine consists of a heavy base to which is mounted a table and motor unit. The table is raised or lowered by turning a handle just below it, and it can be locked in position. The hold-down is a hand lever that is adjusted to secure the stock. The bit is moved in by depressing the foot lever. To use the boring machine:

1. Mark the location of the dowel across the edge and back surface of the stock. If stop blocks are used to control the pieces, then only one piece needs to be marked.

2. Select the correct-size bit and install it in the machine.

3. Adjust for the correct depth of bore by depressing the foot level and adjusting the movement-control rod at the back of the stand.

4. Check the bit for elevation by moving the table up or down.

5. Complete the setup for bor-

ing. A wood fence can be attached to the table for boring at any angle. For example, if a miter joint with dowels is being made, fasten the guide fence at 45 degrees. Stop blocks can be attached to the fence to locate the holes. Usually at least two holes must be bored in each piece to match corresponding holes in the second piece. Use the lines on the back of the marked pieces for making the setup. Once the setup is made, bore all identical pieces before making any change.

6. Adjust the hold-down so that it will clamp the piece securely to the table. If there is danger of marring the surface, a piece of scrap stock can be placed under the hold-down. However, when boring with the face surface against the table, the clamp can be placed directly on the stock. It is good practice to do all boring with the face surface down. Then, if there is any slight variation in the thickness of the stock, the front surfaces will always be level. Mark all stock with an *X* on the back surface so that the pieces will be fed into the machine in the correct way. This mark can also be used for assembly.

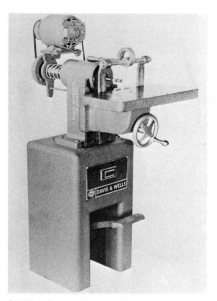

34-30. *A single-spindle boring machine.*

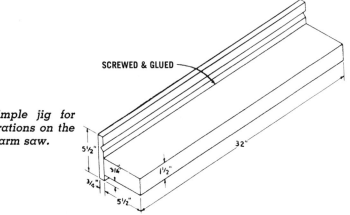

34-31. *A simple jig for boring operations on the radial-arm saw.*

SCREWED & GLUED

32"

5½"

¾"

1½"

¾"

5½"

34-33. *Edge boring. Use slow, even pressure.*

7. Check the setup by trying it on a piece of scrap stock. Turn on the power. Then feed the bit slowly into the wood. If the hole is unusually deep, release the bit to clear the hole after part of it is bored. Some boring machines can be converted for mortising by adding a holder for a mortising bit and by changing the fence arrangement.

DRILLING AND BORING ON A RADIAL-ARM SAW

For drilling and boring operations on a radial-arm saw, a simple jig is needed to raise the stock above the tabletop and to provide a higher guide fence. Fig. 34-31. Place a wedge between the jig and the column for support when boring. A flat board about 6″ high can also be

34-32. *Face boring. Always use a backing piece of scrap wood to prevent splintering as the bit goes through the wood.*

employed as a boring jig. To assemble the boring bit and adapter unit, remove the safety guard, the arbor nut, the cutting tool, and the arbor collars from the motor arbor. Place the boring bit in the adapter and tighten it in place with the ¼″ screw located on the motor opposite the arbor end. Insert the allen wrench into the front of the arbor, holding it securely while using the flat wrench to turn the right-hand-threaded adapter on the back of the motor shaft.

For all face-boring operations, be sure to mount the safety guard on the motor to cover the front end of the arbor. First mark the location of the holes on the stock. Then adjust the motor so that the boring tool is in the correct location, with the motor in the out-rip position. The bit will face the column of the machine. Adjust the arm so that the bit touches the stock at the correct location. A stop clamp can also be fastened to control the depth of the boring. If the hole is to be bored all the way through the stock, a piece of scrap wood should be clamped behind it. Fig. 34-32.

Here is a good method for boring a series of equally spaced holes. Bore the first hole in its correct location, entirely through the material and into the backup piece. Slip a dowel rod into this hole so it enters the backup. Move both the stock and the backup the correct distance and bore the second hole. After this point you no longer need to measure

the spacing. Remove the dowel rod; move only the stock. When the second hole in the stock is over the first hole in the backup, insert the dowel rod again, and drill. Continue in this fashion until all the holes are drilled.

Edge boring is done with the material flat on the jig and against the fence. Fig. 34-33.

Angular boring can be done two ways. One method is to position the stock and then move the radial arm right or left so that the bit will enter the stock at the correct angle. Fig. 34-34. Another method is to use a V block so that the material tilts toward the column. Fig. 34-35. End boring and miter boring can also be done on a radial-arm saw.

34-34. *Boring at an angle after adjusting the arm. The calibrated miter scale on the column will show the exact angle.*

34-35. *Boring at an angle with the work tilted.*

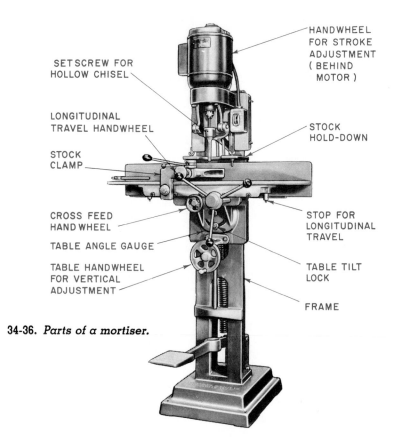

SETSCREW FOR HOLLOW CHISEL

LONGITUDINAL TRAVEL HANDWHEEL

STOCK CLAMP

CROSS FEED HANDWHEEL

TABLE ANGLE GAUGE

TABLE HANDWHEEL FOR VERTICAL ADJUSTMENT

HANDWHEEL FOR STROKE ADJUSTMENT (BEHIND MOTOR)

STOCK HOLD-DOWN

STOP FOR LONGITUDINAL TRAVEL

TABLE TILT LOCK

FRAME

34-36. *Parts of a mortiser.*

MORTISER

A mortiser cuts the rectangular opening for a mortise-and-tenon joint. An upright or vertical hollow-chisel mortiser is used in most shops. Popularly known as "the machine that bores square holes," it has a square, hollow chisel that clamps to the motor housing. There is a revolving wood bit in the center of the chisel. When the combination of bit and chisel is forced into the wood, the bit bores a hole almost as large as the chisel. The sharp edge of the chisel itself cuts a square opening.

Because the mortise chisel is of a fixed size, the mortise is always cut first and then the tenon is cut to fit it. In cabinet shops, the tenon is cut on a circular saw, shaper, or router.

Parts

The mortiser consists of a heavy, cast-iron column, a horizontal table, and a chisel ram attached to a motor. Fig. 34-36. The table itself can be moved vertically (up and down), transversely (in and out), and longitudinally (back and forth). On some mortisers, the table does not move back and forth; therefore you must move the work. On others the table can be tilted 45 degrees to the right or left. The head is moved up and down on the column by depressing a foot lever. At the lower end is a chuck for holding the bit and the chisel.

Mortising Chisels and Bits

The heart of the hollow-chisel mortiser consists of the hollow chisels and boring bits. Such chisels are

---

MORTISER

MAINTENANCE
- Check to see that the chisels and bits are properly ground.
- Check the gib adjustments on the head and table to make sure there is no excessive wear.
- Replace the auxiliary wood fence and table as necessary.
- Make sure all screw threads operate freely.

LUBRICATION
- Use S.A.E. No. 20 oil on all adjusting screws.
- Use light grease or No. 20 oil on ways or slides.

SAFETY
- Wear proper clothing and eye protection. (See Chapter 4.)
- Check the bit clearance at the end of the chisel before starting the machine.
- Make sure the stock is clamped securely whenever possible.
- Make all adjustments with the power off.
- Never apply too much foot pressure when cutting hardwoods.
- Keep your hands away from the revolving bit.
- Clean off the chips with a brush.
- On deep cuts, back out often to clean out the hole.

available in standard sizes from ¼″ to 1¼″, at intervals of ¹⁄₁₆″. Common sizes are ¼″, ½″, and ¾″. The chisel has openings on two sides so that the chips can escape freely. The shank end of the chisel fits into the frame of the motor. The chisel itself does not move. The cutting end of the chisel has a bevel on the inside to make a sheer cut into the wood. Boring bits are made to match the chisels. These are similar to auger bits but without a feed screw. Fig. 34-37. The end of the bit is flared so that its largest diameter is almost equal to the outside of the chisel itself. It is designed in this way so that the bit will remove

34-37. Mortising chisels and bits.

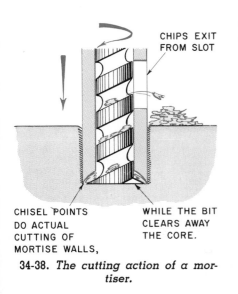

CHIPS EXIT FROM SLOT

CHISEL POINTS DO ACTUAL CUTTING OF MORTISE WALLS,

WHILE THE BIT CLEARS AWAY THE CORE.

34-38. The cutting action of a mortiser.

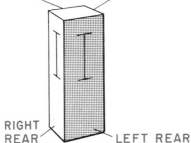

RIGHT FRONT   LEFT FRONT

RIGHT REAR   LEFT REAR

34-39. Right front indicates that the top of the leg is against the right stop when cutting the right-rear mortise. Place the leg against the left stop when cutting the left-rear mortise.

as much of the material as possible. All the chisel has to do is square up the hole. Fig. 34-38. Because of this flared end, it is extremely important that the cone tip of the bit does not rub against the chisel. If it does, both the end of the chisel and the bit will overheat and lose hardness. There must be from ¹⁄₃₂″ to 1″ clearance between the end of the bit and the chisel (depending on the size of the chisel and bit).

Using the Mortiser

Any product which features the mortise-and-tenon joint requires several identical mortises. For example, a simple table with four legs and rails requires eight mortises, two in each leg. When all pieces are identical, it is necessary to lay out the mortises on one leg only.

1. Square up the stock to size and lay out the location for one mortise on each of two sides of one leg. Also mark the depth of the mortise on the end of the leg. Then mark all other legs as shown in Fig. 34-39. (You can use abbreviations; LF for "left front," RF for "right front," etc.) The mortises on the other parts will be in the correct location if all pieces are placed on the table in the same way. When cutting mortises on two sides of each piece, always cut all mortises

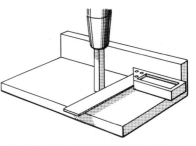

34-40. Use a try square to check the chisel with the fence. Usually the chisel openings are on the right and left so that the chips will come out the sides. However, when using the mortising attachment on the drill press, the openings are placed at front and back because of the table fence.

on one side first. Then reset the machine and cut all the mortises on the second side.

2. Select the correct-size chisel and bit. For example, use a ½″ bit and chisel for a ½″ mortise. Also, select the correct-size bushing for the chisel. These split bushings all have the same diameter on the outside, with varying inside dimensions to hold chisels of different sizes.

3. Insert the bushing for the chisel and then install the chisel itself. Place the chisel in the socket, with a slight clearance between its shoulder and the face of the socket. This clearance should be ¹⁄₃₂″ for chisels up to ¾″, and it should be ¹⁄₁₆″ for larger ones.

4. To align the chisel, hold a square against the side of it and also against the fence. Fig. 34-40. Then tighten the setscrews that hold the chisel in place. Next, insert the bit until the lips are flush with the cutting edge of the chisel. Fasten the bit securely. Loosen the socket and push the chisel up so that the shoulder rests against the face of the chisel socket. This will give proper clearance for the bit to run free. Fig. 34-41. Another method is to install the chisel so that it is firmly fixed against the shoulder and square with the fence. Then carefully install the bit so that the clearance is correct.

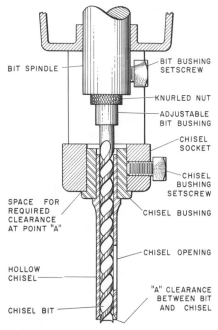

BIT SPINDLE

BIT BUSHING SETSCREW

KNURLED NUT

ADJUSTABLE BIT BUSHING

CHISEL SOCKET

CHISEL BUSHING SETSCREW

SPACE FOR REQUIRED CLEARANCE AT POINT "A"

CHISEL BUSHING

CHISEL OPENING

HOLLOW CHISEL

"A" CLEARANCE BETWEEN BIT AND CHISEL

CHISEL BIT

34-41. *Note that the bit must extend beyond the chisel a little to keep it from rubbing the chisel.*

CUTTING A MORTISE

1. Place the stock on the table with a mark on the end indicating the depth of the mortise. Depress the foot pedal as far as you can. Turn the screw adjustment on the table until the chisel, at the end of its stroke, is in line with the bottom of the mortise. Release the foot pedal.

2. Place the end of the stock under the chisel and move the table in or out until the chisel is directly over the layout. Move the work until

34-42. *Cutting the mortise.*

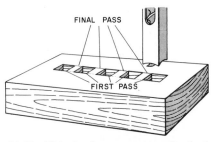

FINAL PASS

FIRST PASS

34-43. *This is the correct method of making rectangular mortises up to ½" in width. Note that cuts are not consecutive. Sometimes, however, consecutive cuts must be made when using a mortising attachment. This is simply because it is often difficult to force the chisel into hardwood when all sides are cutting.*

the mortising chisel is over the extreme right end of the mortise. Place a stop against the end of the stock so that other identical pieces will be located automatically. Also adjust the stop on the table. Now move the table until the chisel is at the left end of the mortise; adjust the stop. There are two hold-down clamps that can be used to keep the work in place.

3. Move the table back to the starting position, with the chisel at the left end of the mortise. Turn on the machine, depress the pedal, and cut to full depth. Fig. 34-42. Move the table to the right and

again cut to full depth. Then move along the layout, skipping a space slightly less than the size of the chisel after each cut. These alternate strokes are used to equalize pressure by bringing the bit into contact with the stock on four sides when making first passes and on two sides during final passes. If cutting is done continuously, the bit tends to bend since cutting is done only on three sides. Be sure to center the chisel over the waste stock on the final passes. Fig. 34-43. If a turned leg or a cabriole leg must have mortises, it is necessary to make a holding jig to keep the leg in proper position.

4. Cut all identical mortises before resetting for cuts in different locations. The cutting of matched mortises, as on table legs, requires that the entire setup be reversed before the second mortise of the pair is cut. The right-hand stop block should be placed on the left, and vice versa. Check each setup carefully with a sample piece.

Mortising Attachments

Attachments are available to convert most drill presses into mortising machines. These devices consist of a fence to guide the work, a hold-down—hold-in that keeps the work against the fence and table, a chisel

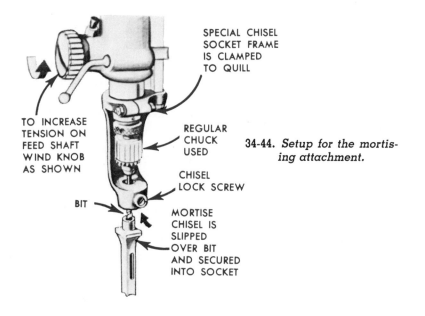

TO INCREASE TENSION ON FEED SHAFT WIND KNOB AS SHOWN

SPECIAL CHISEL SOCKET FRAME IS CLAMPED TO QUILL

REGULAR CHUCK USED

CHISEL LOCK SCREW

BIT

MORTISE CHISEL IS SLIPPED OVER BIT AND SECURED INTO SOCKET

34-44. *Setup for the mortising attachment.*

holder that is clamped to the quill of the drill press, and a bit that is fastened to the chuck. Fig. 34-44. In some cases an adapter is used instead of the regular chuck to hold the bit.

To use the mortising attachment, follow these steps:

1. Remove the chuck and the feed-stop bracket from the quill.

2. Replace the feed-stop bracket with the mortise-chisel socket and clamp it in place. Use a depth-stop stud in the chisel socket to keep the quill from turning and to regulate the depth of cut.

3. Replace the drill chuck or install an adapter.

4. Fasten the fence to the table so that it clears the chisel and is in about the final position. It can still be moved in and out to locate the mortise. Now adjust the fence back and forth until it is exactly over the mortise layout. Also fasten the hold-downs to keep the wood firmly on the table.

5. Install the correct chisel and bit in the socket.

6. Revolve the chuck by hand to see that the bit does not scrape.

7. Adjust the drill press to a speed of about 1000 RPM.

8. Cut the mortise. Stop blocks can be clamped to the tabletop to regulate the length of movement.

35 Sanding Machines & Coated Abrasives

An *abrasive* is any substance rubbed against a surface for the purpose of smoothing it. In woodworking this is commonly done before, between, or after applications of finish coats. Abrasives are also used for machining. Actually, each grain of abrasive is a cutting tool, just like a saw or chisel.

Some people still refer to coated abrasives as "sandpaper" even though there is no sand whatsoever on them. Coated abrasives consist of three materials: the *abrasive* itself, the *backing* on which it is fastened, and the *adhesive* that fastens the grains to the backing. The backing may be paper, cloth, fiber, or a combination of these materials. Various types of hide and resin glues are used as adhesives. Using a coated abrasive on a power-driven tool is commonly referred to as *machine sanding*.

TYPES OF ABRASIVES

The four major abrasives used in the woodworking industry are flint, garnet, aluminum oxide, and silicon carbide. The first two are natural abrasives, while the last two are synthetic.

● *Flint* is quartz (silicon dioxide). It is the material found on common "sandpaper" used for hand sanding. It is grayish white or eggshell in color. Flint has only limited use in the woodworking industry because it lacks toughness and durability.

● *Garnet* is another natural, mined material that makes a good abrasive both for hand and machine sanding. It is a good deal harder than flint, and the grains are narrow wedge shapes. Garnet, which is reddish brown, is widely used in woodworking, mainly for finish sanding.

● *Aluminum Oxide* is much harder than garnet. It has a grain shape of wide wedges. It is a product of the electric furnace and is made by purifying bauxite (an ore of aluminum) to a crystal form, then adding small amounts of other materials for toughness. When aluminum oxide comes out of the furnace, it is in large chunk form. If it is to be used for the woodworking trades, the crushing technique is varied to produce a sharper grain than that generally used for metalworking. Aluminum oxide is brown and is considered an excellent abrasive for sanding harder woods.

● *Silicon Carbide*, another product of the electric furnace, has grains that are sharp wedge shapes. It is greenish black and iridescent. Silicon carbide is not only the hardest but also the sharpest of the synthetic abrasives. It is the ideal abrasive for fibrous woods, plastic, enamel, and other relatively soft

SANDING MACHINES

MAINTENANCE
- Make sure the operating controls turn easily.
- Check the belt, disk, or sleeve to make sure the abrasive cloth or paper is not worn. Replace as necessary.
- Make sure the cloth or paper is attached properly. On belt sanders, the arrow on the belt indicates the direction of rotation.
- Maintain proper motor-belt tension.
- Keep the sander clean. When necessary, take it apart and remove all sawdust from operating parts. Make sure air vents are not plugged.

LUBRICATION
- Use S.A.E. No. 20 machine oil for lubricating.
- For the stationary abrasive belt sander, lubricate the idler drum bearing, belt-tension knob screw, and tracking-handle screw.
- For the stationary disk sander, lubricate the spindle bearing when needed.
- Check portable machines for any oil holes. Lubricate, if necessary.

SAFETY
- Use only light pressure—just enough to hold the work against the abrasive.
- Wear goggles and a filter mask.
- Remove sawdust from around the machine to prevent a fire hazard.
- Sand parallel with the grain whenever possible, to obtain a smooth finish.
- Sand only dry wood.
- Use a fixture to hold small pieces of wood when machine sanding.

materials. Commonly it is used in the finishing process. Though harder, it is not as tough and durable as aluminum oxide.

Crushing and Grading

All abrasives are crushed and graded by the same method. The crushed particles are separated into grade sizes by passing them through a series of very accurately woven screens. The mesh of these screens (the number of openings per linear inch) ranges from very fine to very coarse. Mesh numbers are used to designate the grade size. For example, particles that pass through a screen with 12 openings per linear inch are called grit size 12. The more openings per inch in the mesh, the finer the grit. Therefore abrasives get finer as the number goes up. The screen method is used for grading up to 240. Because it is impossible to make a screen of more than 240 openings per inch, finer grains are graded by an elaborate water flotation system.

An older system based on arbitrary symbols is still used to some extent for garnet paper. For example, garnet marked 30 under the new system is the same as that which is marked 2½ under the old. A mark of 280 in the new system

corresponds to 8/0 in the old. Fig. 35-1 gives a complete listing of the two systems.

KINDS OF BACKINGS

Letters after the grit number designate the weight of the backing. Four common kinds of backings are used for coated abrasives:

- A *high-quality paper* made especially for the abrasive industry. It

comes in four different weights: *A*, which is light paper stock, used primarily for light hand-sanding operations; *C* and *D*, intermediate papers with more strength and stiffness, commonly known as cabinet papers; and *E*, which is strong and durable, used especially for drum or belt sanding. *A* is 40-pound paper. This means that 480 sheets measuring 24" × 36" weigh 40 pounds.

35-1. *This table shows the uses for various abrasive grit sizes.*

GRIT SIZES

	Mesh or Grit No.	Symbols or O Grade	General Uses
VERY FINE	400 360 320 280 240 220	10/0 — 9/0 8/0 7/0 6/0	For polishing and finishing after stain, varnish, etc., has been applied.
FINE	180 150 120	5/0 4/0 3/0	For finish sanding just before staining or sealing.
MEDIUM	100 80 60	2/0 1/0 ½	For sanding to remove final rough texture.
COARSE	50 40 36	1 1½ 2	For sanding after very rough texture is removed.
VERY COARSE	30 24 20 16	2½ 3 3½ 4	For very rough, unfinished wood surfaces.

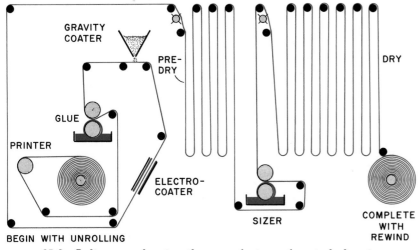

35-2. *A diagram showing the manufacture of coated abrasives.*

- *Cloth*, which comes in two weights. *J* is lightweight and more flexible, for use in contour work; *X* is heavier and stronger, best suited for flat work.
- *Fiber*, a very strong, stiff backing, made from ragstock paper. It is used mostly for disk and drum sanding.
- *Combination backings*. There are two of these: paper and cloth laminated together and fiber and cloth laminated together. The paper-and-cloth combination is used mainly on high-speed drum sanders, while the fiber-and-cloth type is used for disk sanders.

ADHESIVES OR BONDS

Several types of bonds or adhesives are used in the manufacture of coated abrasives. These are applied in two layers. The first is called the *bond coat*, the second the *size coat*. Five different types of adhesives or bonds are used:

- *Animal hide glue* is good for both the bond and the size coat.
- *Glue and filler*, a hide glue with filler added, produces a bond that is durable and strong. This is used both for the bond and size coats.
- *Resin over glue* is a combination of pure hide glue for the bond coat and a synthetic resin for the

size coat, making an abrasive that is extremely resistant to heat.

- *Resin over resin* — one layer of synthetic resin is used for the bond and another for the size coat. This is not only heat-resistant but also withstands moisture and humidity.
- *Waterproof* is a synthetic resin used for the bond and the size coat on a waterproof backing. With this it is possible to use water and other liquids with coated abrasives.

MANUFACTURING

The general procedure for manufacturing coated abrasives is about as follows. Fig. 35-2. The abrasive-making machine consists of three units: the printer, the adhesive coater, and the abrasive-grain dispenser. First, the backing is started through a press which prints on one side the trademark, brand name, manufacturer's name, mineral, grade number, name of the backing, and other necessary information. The backing next receives the bond coat of adhesive on its other side. The abrasive grains are then applied either by mechanical or electrostatic method. The mechanical method is sometimes called *gravity coating* since the abrasive grains are merely dropped onto the adhesive. In the

other method, called *electrocoating*, the grains are made to stand up on end as they are dropped onto the adhesive. Electrocoating has these advantages: the abrasive is longer-lasting because the grains are firmly imbedded in the coating; there is more uniform distribution of the grains; and more grain area is exposed for cutting.

There are two kinds of abrasive-grain coating: *closed coat* and *open coat*. In closed coat, abrasive grains completely cover the adhesive. In open coat, there is space between the grains. Closed coat is used primarily for semi-finish and finish sanding, whereas open coat is best for rough sanding and for removing paint, varnish, or other relatively soft materials. In the open-coated method, about 50 to 70 percent of the coated surface is covered with abrasive. Open-coated materials have greater flexibility and resist filling and clogging.

After the abrasive-grain coating, the size coat is applied. The coated abrasive is then dried and cured.

Next, the coated abrasives are made more flexible by controlled bending. The term *flexing* describes the actual controlled break of the bond at 45- or 90-degree angles. The direction and spacing of the breaks are the two most important items to be controlled in the flexing of abrasive-coated cloth.

There are four basic flexing patterns: single, double, triple, and Q-flex. Fig. 35-3. The *single flex* is done along the width of the sandpaper, at 90 degrees to the length, leaving the sandpaper stiff in one direction and flexible in the other. It is used for sanding moldings. In *double flex* the sheets are bent lengthwise at two 45-degree angles. The old-time craftspeople did this themselves, holding one corner of the sheet in one hand and the diagonally opposite corner in the other hand. They would then draw the back of the sheet over a bench, first

281

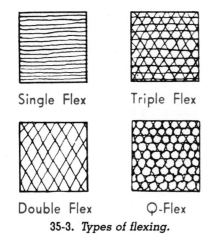

Single Flex   Triple Flex

Double Flex   Q-Flex

35-3. *Types of flexing.*

in one direction and then the other. Now this is done automatically in the factory. Double-flex paper is needed for sanding intricate contours, such as some moldings. The *triple flex* is a combination of single and double flex for sanding sharp or irregular contours. In *Q-flex*, the bending is done in all directions. This gives excellent self-cleaning

qualities to the paper and makes it ideal for edge sanding.

The last step in manufacture is to roll the coated abrasives into jumbo-sized rolls for later cutting into various shapes and forms.

Forms of Coated Abrasives

There are many forms of coated abrasives, but the most common are sheets, rolls, disks, and belts. Of course, abrasives are also used to make abrasive stones, grinding wheels, and similar items. Abrasives are also combined with fiberglass to form a soft abrasive wheel that is extremely useful for wood finishing. Another form is a belt which has a cloth back with a flexible nylon fiber coating impregnated with abrasive grains.

Sheets used for hand sanding and finishing sanders are available in many sizes. The common hand-sheet size is 9″ × 11″. Rolls are used for drum sanding and spindle

sanding. Disks are made for both portable and stationary disk sanders. They come in almost every diameter, although the common sizes are 7″ and 9½″. Sander belts come in many widths and lengths to fit the full range of sanders from small portable ones to large industrial equipment.

KINDS OF SANDING

Coated abrasives should be selected according to the work to be done. To obtain the same finish on two pieces, one hardwood and the other softwood, choose a slightly coarser grit for the hardwood. Fig. 35-1. For best results it is important that both the kind of abrasive and the grit number be chosen correctly. Fig. 35-4. The relationship between the kind of sanding and the grit size is summarized here:

● *Roughing or material removal* is a heavy sanding operation in which the maximum amount of material is removed with a coarse grit abrasive.

TYPES OF ABRASIVES

SANDPAPERS FOR WOOD

NAME	GRIT SIZES					AVAILABLE IN	USES
FLINT Paper	Extra Coarse	Coarse	Medium	Fine	Extra Fine	9″ × 10″ Sheets (See Note)	For hand sanding common woodwork, removing paint, varnish, *etc.* Also for small miscellaneous jobs.
GARNET Paper	Very Coarse 30-D(2½)	Coarse 50-D(1)	Medium 80-D(0)	Fine 120-C(3/0)	Very Fine 220-A(6/0)	9″ × 11″ Sheets	Good all-around paper for hand sanding good woodwork, furniture, *etc.*, dry.
NOTE: Flint paper is also available in packs containing an assortment of coarse, medium, and fine grits in 4½″ × 5″ sheets.							

SANDPAPERS FOR WOOD AND METAL

NAME	GRIT SIZES					AVAILABLE IN	USES
Paper (Aluminum Oxide)	Very Coarse 30-D(2½)	Coarse 50-D(1)	Medium 80-D(0)	Fine 120-C (3/0)	Very Fine 220-A(6/0)	9″ × 11″ Sheets	For hand or machine sanding of hardwoods, metals, plastics, and other materials.
Cloth (Aluminum Oxide)	Very Coarse 30-X(2½)	Coarse 50-X(1)	Medium 80-X(0)	Fine 120-X (3/0)		Belts for all popular belt sanders. X-weight	Strong cloth-backed belts for sanding wood, metal, plastic, and other materials with stationary or portable belt sanders.
Paper-Waterproof (Silicon Carbide)			Very Fine 220-A	Extra Fine 320-A	Super Fine 400-A	9″ × 11″ Sheets	Best paper for wet sanding by hand or machine, primers and between coats on wood, metal, or other materials. Can be used with water, oil, or other lubricants.

35-4. *Uses for common types of abrasives.*

- *Blending*, with some material removed and a fairly smooth finish, calls for medium grits. Less material is removed than in roughing, and a better surface is obtained.

- *Fine finishing* is done to remove scratch patterns formed by coarser grits. Fine grits are used.

- *Polishing and rubbing* are burnishing operations which remove or blend the fine scratch patterns left by earlier finishing steps. Extremely fine grits are needed, generally with some kind of lubricant such as oil or water.

When a series of abrasives is to be used, start with one just coarse enough to make the surface level and to eliminate excessive roughness. Then follow with a second, medium grit to improve the surface. Continue with a finer grit until the desired finish is obtained. *Never go from a very coarse to a very fine grit in one step.*

SANDING MACHINES

There are sanding machines for every type of cutting and finishing.

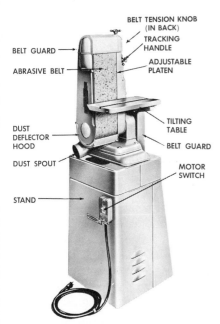

35-5. Parts of a belt sander. This is sometimes called an abrasive-belt finishing machine since it can be used for many kinds of finishing.

Labels: BELT TENSION KNOB (IN BACK), TRACKING HANDLE, BELT GUARD, ABRASIVE BELT, ADJUSTABLE PLATEN, DUST DEFLECTOR HOOD, DUST SPOUT, STAND, TILTING TABLE, BELT GUARD, MOTOR SWITCH

35-6. *Sanding a bevel or chamfer, using the miter gauge and table as guides.*

In the school and cabinet shop there are seven common pieces of equipment.

Floor-Type Belt Sander

The belt sander can be used in vertical, horizontal, or slant positions. Fig. 35-5. It is set in the desired position by loosening the hand lock and moving the entire unit. The table will tilt 20 degrees toward the belt and 40 degrees away from the belt. A miter gauge can also be used on the machine. With the machine in the horizontal position, a fence can be attached to guide the work for surface sanding.

To change a belt, first remove the guards. Then release the tension by turning the belt-tension knob. Remove the old belt and slip on a new one. Apply a slight amount of tension. Then center the belt on the drums by adjusting the idler pulley with the tracking handle. Next increase the tension and replace the guards. Check the centering adjustment again by moving the belt by hand. Readjust when necessary. If the sander is to be used in a tilted position, the centering should be done after this adjustment.

To do surface sanding, place the machine in a horizontal position. The work can be fed freehand across the belt by applying a very light, firm pressure. However, for more accurate edge sanding, use a fence to guide the work. Beveling and angle sanding can be done by tilting the fence.

For end-grain sanding, the unit should be in a vertical position and the table used as a guide. Bevels and chamfers can also be sanded in this manner by using a miter gauge as a guide. Fig. 35-6.

Many types of simple wood jigs can be used for mass production work. To do form sanding, make a wood form that is exactly opposite the shape of the piece to be sanded. Cover the form with a piece of sheet metal. Fasten this to the sanding table so that the belt runs over the form. Fig. 35-7.

Stationary-Type Disk Sander

The disk sander is a simple machine that can be used for some types of rough, end-grain sanding and for simple shaping. Fig. 35-8. It has limited use in cabinetmaking, however, because its circular motion causes crossgrain sanding scratches.

It is important that the abrasive cloth disk be firmly fastened to the metal disk. If the abrasive disk is

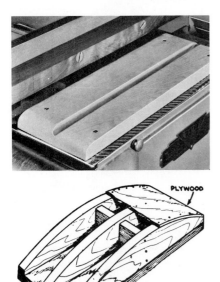

35-9. *Applying an adhesive to the metal disk. The adhesive is also applied to the back of the abrasive sheet by laying the sheet on a flat surface and rubbing the adhesive on the back.*

forth to loosen the old adhesive. Be sure the metal disk is dry before mounting the new abrasive.

To apply the new abrasive, hold the adhesive stick against the metal plate and move it back and forth. Make sure that there is a uniform coat of adhesive on the metal. Fig. 35-9. Then turn off the power and carefully apply the abrasive. Let dry a short time. Clamp on a flat piece of wood to prevent wrinkles.

The abrasive cloth can also be glued to the metal disk with water glass or a heavy grade of rubber cement.

Abrasive disks can be purchased already cut to exact size and with an adhesive coating on the back. All that is necessary is to make sure the metal disk is clean. Strip the cover paper off the abrasive disk, and install. Such disks make it easy to change grades.

The table on the disk sander can be used for end-grain sanding. It can be tilted and used in combination with a miter gauge to sand a chamfer or bevel. The disk sander can also sand the edge of a circular piece. Always sand on the "down" side of the disk. Also, move the stock back and forth on this side. Holding it in one position tends to burn the wood.

Most disk sanding is done free-hand. Remember that the edge of

the disk is moving much faster than the center, and allow for this. To sand circles or arcs, hold the work firmly on the table and revolve it slowly.

Spindle Sander

This sander is designed primarily for use on edges and irregular curves. It has a revolving, oscillating (moving up and down) spindle on which the abrasive paper or cloth is fastened. Fig. 35-10. The slow up-and-down movement spreads the wear and also prevents the wood from burning. The spindles come in various diameters and are made of metal, wood, soft rubber, or rubber tubing.

To replace the abrasive paper or cloth, remove the worn paper and cut a new one to size. On some sanders, a wedge on one side holds the paper to the spindle. Other spindles are made in two half-segments that can be separated for replacing the paper. Still others have a tube that slips into the drum, with a key that turns to lock it. Fig. 35-11.

Hand-Stroke Belt Sander

The hand-stroke belt sander is commonly used for flat-sanding,

35-7. *Form sanding. The form shown in the photograph is used to round the corners of stock. The form in the drawing is used for sanding a concave, circular part.*

worn, the first step is to remove it. If the abrasive disk is attached with glue, soak it in hot water until loose, then remove with a putty knife. If rubber cement or stick cement was used, turn on the sander and hold the end of a hardwood stick or screwdriver against it. Move the stick or screwdriver back and

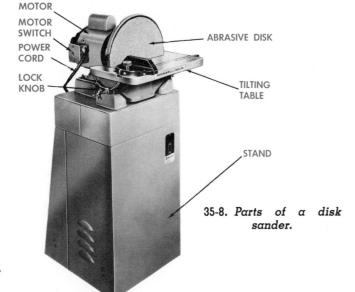

35-8. *Parts of a disk sander.*

35-10. *The spindle sander is constructed like a shaper. It has a cast-iron base and a horizontal table. The spindle projects through the center of the table. The table can be tilted 45 degrees to one side and 15 degrees to the other.*

when it is important to produce an even surface with a minimum of raised fibers. It has a long, continuous belt that moves around two drums or pulleys. A movable table rolls back and forth under the belt. The sanding block is held freehand to the back of the belt to apply pressure for sanding. Fig. 35-12.

The kind of sanding determines the grade and kind of abrasive belt. Use aluminum oxide for hardwoods and garnet for softwoods. If stock removal is necessary, cloth-backed abrasives having greater resistance to breakage should be chosen. For lighter operations, such as sanding furniture tops, a belt made of paper might be satisfactory. If a piece of hardwood furniture is to be sanded to a very high-quality finish, it may be necessary to use two grades of paper. Sanding on softer hardwoods

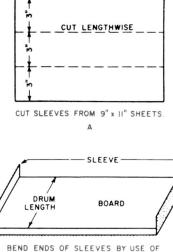

CUT LENGTHWISE

3"

3"

3"

CUT SLEEVES FROM 9" x 11" SHEETS.

A

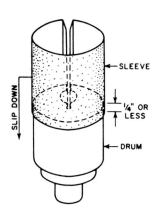

SLEEVE

DRUM LENGTH   BOARD

BEND ENDS OF SLEEVES BY USE OF BOARD AS SHOWN. BOARD MUST BE MEASURED ACCURATELY AND CUT <u>SQUARE</u>.

B

SLEEVE

SLIP DOWN

¼" OR LESS

DRUM

WRAP ABOUT ¼" OF DRUM OR LESS. THEN SLIP ON DOWN OVER DRUM. USE TALCUM POWDER IF NECESSARY TO MAKE SLEEVE SLIP EASILY.

C

SQUEEZE HARD TO GET SLACK OUT OF SLEEVE AND ENDS DOWN INTO SLOT. THEN INSERT TUBE AND TURN WITH KEY. OVAL TUBE SHOULD FIT SNUGLY. <u>DO NOT FORCE</u>. IF TOO TIGHT PUT IN VISE AND SQUEEZE EDGE. IF TOO LOOSE SQUEEZE FLAT SIDE OF TUBE.

D

35-11. *Replacing an abrasive sleeve.*

should be done first with No. 120 grit, then with 180 grit. A sequence of 100 and 150 should be chosen for harder hardwoods. For some woods, such as maple or birch, a single grade of 100 or 120 is satisfactory. For sanding veneers, the final grit should be about 220. The most common problem in stroke sanding is a streaked or nonuniform burnish finish. A worn belt often causes this.

In using the hand-stroke sander, place the pieces on the movable table and do the sanding in one of two ways. In the first method, the sanding block is moved back and forth along the total length of the material. Then the work is moved to a new position and the sanding repeated. The second method is to do the sanding in cross sections. Sand all the way across the end of the material, moving the table a little at a time. Then move the sanding block to a new position and sand slowly across in the other direction. There will be no excessive abrasive line if the cross movement is slow.

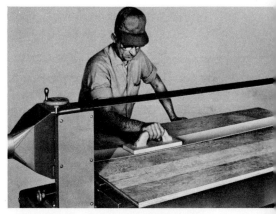

35-12. *Using the hand-stroke belt sander to sand a wide tabletop. The operator is using a flat-bottom block with round edges. Concave or convex surfaces can be sanded with a sanding block of proper shape. Stroke sanding should be the last machine sanding of the wood before finishing. Therefore it is important to obtain a very smooth surface.*

285

With an extra table attached, the top of the belt can be used for sanding assembled parts such as the sides of a drawer. Fig. 35-13. If one end of the sander has no guard, curved parts can be sanded over the drum.

Portable Belt Sander

Portable belt sanders are excellent for sanding assembled cabinetwork and furniture pieces. Fig. 35-14. The size of the machine is determined by the width and length of the belt. The most common sizes are 2″ × 21″, 3″ × 24″, 3″ × 27″, 4″ × 22″, and 4½″ × 26″. The belt should be so installed that the splice runs off the work. An arrow stamped on the back of each belt indicates the direction the belt should run. It is a simple job to replace a belt on most machines. Usually a clamp opens to release the tension on the belt. After a new belt is installed, it can be centered on the pulleys by turning the belt-tracking adjustment. The belt should never rub against the side of the machine. If the belt is a thick,

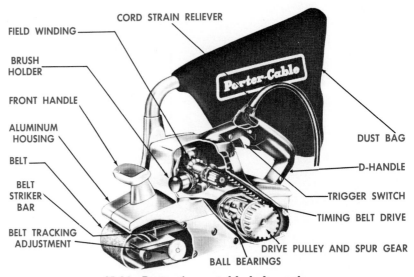

35-14. *Parts of a portable belt sander.*

soft one made of nylon impregnated with abrasive, then there must be extra clearance between the pulleys and the housing.

The portable belt sander should be used as follows. Place the cord over your right shoulder out of the way. Hold the machine firmly with both hands. Turn on the power. Lower the sander so that the heel touches the work first. Then move the sander back and forth in a straight line. Sanding is actually done *on the pull stroke*. Fig. 35-15. Never allow the sander to stand still for any length of time as this would cut deep grooves in the wood. It is particularly important to watch this when sanding plywood. Always machine slowly and evenly. Cross sanding is sometimes done first to obtain a level surface. On woods such as

fir, with both hard and soft grain, cross sanding should be done as much as possible. To sand the edges of boards, allow the belt to extend beyond the edge a little. Be careful that the sander doesn't tilt. For a panel door, sand the panels before assembly. Then sand the rails and, finally, the stiles. Fig. 35-16.

Finishing Sander

The finishing sander is used primarily for final sanding on the assembled product and for sanding between finish coats. Fig. 35-17. There are many sizes and styles. All finishing sanders, however, operate with orbital, straight-line, or multi-motion action. Fig. 35-18.

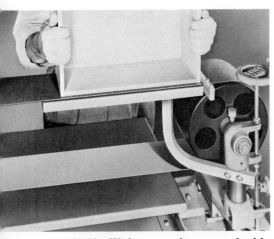

35-13. *With an auxiliary metal table clamped to the machine, the hand-stroke belt sander can be used for sanding drawers and other assembled parts. The work is held lightly but firmly against the belt. Notice the stop which keeps the work from moving with the belt.*

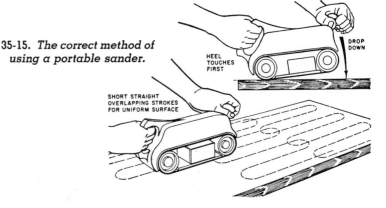

35-15. *The correct method of using a portable sander.*

SAND WITH GRAIN

SAND PANELS BEFORE ASSEMBLY

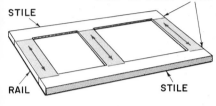

SAND RAILS BEFORE STILES

SAND STILES LAST

35-16. *Steps in sanding a panel door.*

Orbital action is best for rapid sanding and fast stock removal. However, it leaves swirl marks that show up under a finish. Straight-line sanding is best for transparent wood

finishes such as lacquer or varnish. Some sanders have two kinds of action and can be changed by flicking a switch.

Finishing sanders are relatively easy to use. Clip a sheet of abrasive paper or cloth to the pad. (Choose the correct grade for the work to be done. Fig. 35-19.) Lower the pad to the surface and move it back and forth slowly. Some school and cabinet shops have air-operated orbital or reciprocating sanders. These are similar to the finishing sander but are more powerful and therefore more efficient. These sanders are highly effective for final sanding before applying a finish and also between finish coats.

Rotary-Action Portable Sander

This sander is good for fast, rough sanding, but it has little use in cabinetmaking since, like the disk sander, it sands cross-grain. Fig. 35-20. If this tool is used to remove an old finish, hold it so that about the outer third of the sanding sheet is on the surface. Never try to use the entire abrasive surface at one time, as this will cause the sander to bounce and gouge the wood.

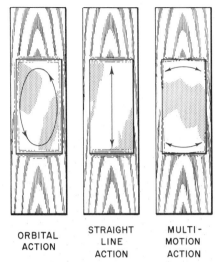

ORBITAL ACTION   STRAIGHT LINE ACTION   MULTI-MOTION ACTION

35-18. *Three kinds of sanding action found in finishing sanders. Orbital and multimotion action causes some cross-grain scratches. Straight-line action is like hand sanding and results in the best surface.*

RADIAL-ARM SAW AS A SANDER

The radial-arm saw can be quickly converted to a disk, spindle, or small drum sander to perform many power-sanding operations. To use the machine as a disk sander, first remove the safety guard, arbor nut, cutting tool, and the arbor collars from the motor shaft. Then replace one arbor collar and the disk plate on the shaft. Tighten this counter-clockwise with your hand. Sanding can be done by moving the work against the disk which rotates in a fixed position. Fig. 35-21. Another method is to fasten the work securely, then move the disk across the work as you would for sawing. Fig. 35-22. For surface sanding, the disk can be used vertically, like a disk sander, or horizontally. Fig. 35-23.

The disk can be removed and replaced with either a 1″ or 2½″ drum sander. Remove the sanding disk. Place the drum sander on the rear end (opposite the spindle end) of the motor shaft. Turn the drum by hand until it is tight. Unlike a spin-

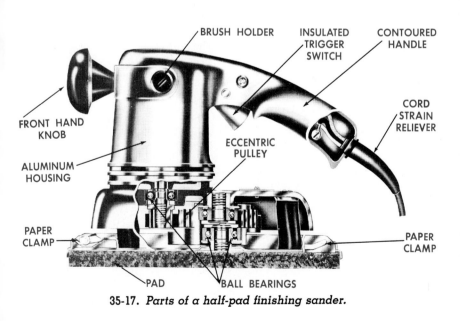

BRUSH HOLDER   INSULATED TRIGGER SWITCH   CONTOURED HANDLE

FRONT HAND KNOB

CORD STRAIN RELIEVER

ALUMINUM HOUSING

ECCENTRIC PULLEY

PAPER CLAMP

PAPER CLAMP

PAD   BALL BEARINGS

35-17. *Parts of a half-pad finishing sander.*

ABRASIVES FOR THE FINISHING SANDER

Kind of Material	Material Removal		Fair Finish		Fine Finish	
	Grit	Size	Grit	Size	Grit	Size
Soft Wood Soft Wallboard	Cabinet Paper (Garnet)	2-1	Cabinet Paper (Garnet)	½-2/0	Finishing Paper (Garnet)	3/0-5/0
Plastics	Cabinet Paper (Aluminum Oxide)	60-100	Wet Paper "C" Weight (Silicon Carbide)	120-220	Wet Paper "A" Weight (Silicon Carbide)	240-600
Hard Wood Hard Compositions Wallboards	Cabinet Paper (Aluminum Oxide)	36-50	Cabinet Paper (Aluminum Oxide)	60-100	Finishing Paper (Aluminum Oxide)	120-180
Hard Brittle Minerals and Compositions	Cabinet Paper (Aluminum Oxide)	50-80	Finishing Paper (Aluminum Oxide)	100-180	Wet Paper "A" Weight (Silicon Carbide)	220-320
Hard Tough Minerals and Compositions	Metalworking Cloth (Aluminum Oxide)		Metalworking Cloth (Aluminum Oxide)	80-120	Finishing Paper (Aluminum Oxide)	150-320
Paints, Varnishes	Cabinet Paper (Open-coat Garnet)	2½-1½			Wet Paper "A" Weight (Silicon Carbide)	240-400

35-19. *This shows the kind of abrasive paper or cloth to choose for sanding various materials with the finishing sander.*

dle sander, the drum doesn't move up and down as it rotates. However, the drum sander is used for many edge sanding operations similarly to the way a spindle sander is used. Fig. 35-24. When the drum is in the horizontal position, an auxiliary table may be needed to raise the work slightly. Fig. 35-25.

35-21. *Sanding a circle. Use a jig as shown and place the stock on the center pin of the sliding strip. Set the motor to the proper height and lock it in place, directly in front of the jig. Turn on the machine and slowly rotate the stock clockwise on the center pin. After the first sanding, move it slightly closer to the disk and repeat until a smooth circle is obtained.*

35-20. *This multispeed rotary sander has a 6" disk. It operates at 1600, 2700, or 3800 RPM.*

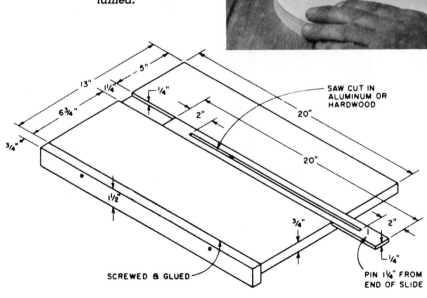

35-22. *Bevel sanding. Place the radial arm in the crosscut position with the motor at the desired angle. Place the stock on an auxiliary table. Pull the disk across the beveled end of the board.*

35-24(α). *Freehand sanding. Place the motor in the vertical position and center the drum over the shaper slot in the table. Tighten the rip clamp and lower the arm so the entire edge can be sanded. Move the work past the drum from left to right.*

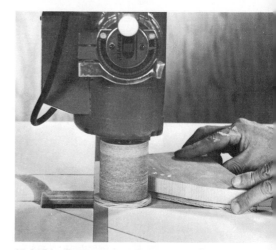

35-24(b). *Pattern sanding can be done by mounting a circular guide under the sanding drum. Make a pattern that will contact this guide. Install three sharp pins in the pattern to hold the work as it is sanded.*

BAND SAW AS A SANDER

The band saw can be used as a thin belt sander by first removing the saw and the guide. A narrow, endless belt is used instead of the saw blade. A support is needed just above the table so that slight pressure can be applied to the belt. A support of wood or metal can be clamped to the table just back of the belt. Fig. 35-26.

DRILL PRESS AS A SANDER

A wide variety of sanding jobs can be done on the drill press by using sanding disks and drums. For spindle and drum sanding, replace the chuck with a sanding drum attachment. Lock the quill and adjust the machine to a speed of about 1800 RPM. The work can be held against the drum freehand, or it can rest on an auxiliary wood table. Fig. 35-27.

JIGSAW WITH SANDING ATTACHMENT

The sanding attachment for the jigsaw is designed to finish concave, convex, or flat surfaces. It replaces the blade in the lower chuck of the jigsaw. Before attaching it, remove the table insert. A knurled knob ex-

35-25. *Surface sanding narrow boards. Place the shaft in a horizontal position. Use the tabletop and the fence as guides. Place the stock tight against the fence. Lower the radial arm until the abrasive touches the stock. Remove the stock and turn on the power. Then feed the work against the rotation of the drum.*

35-23. *Surface sanding. Place the motor in a vertical position. Move it along until the disk is directly over the path of the stock. Lock the unit in place; then push the board from right to left along the fence.*

35-26. *Sanding the edge of an irregular shape on the band saw.*

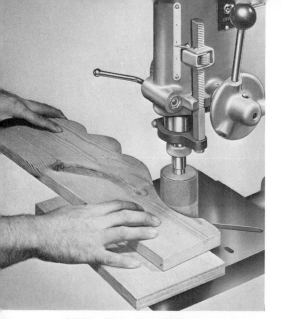

35-27. *Here the workpiece rests on an auxiliary wood table so that the entire edge can be sanded at the same time.*

pands the body of the attachment, thus holding the abrasive paper securely in place. Fig. 35-28. Sleeves are changed simply by loosening the knob. Sanding should be done at slow speed—the finer the abrasive, the slower the speed.

35-28. *Sanding attachment on a jig or scroll saw.*

LATHE AS A SANDER

A drum sanding attachment can be mounted between centers on the lathe. A wood fixture is clamped to the bed of the lathe as a guide when sanding. Fig. 35-29. A disk sanding attachment can also be used on a lathe or combination machine. Fig. 35-30.

ROTARY SANDING ATTACHMENT

The rotary sanding attachment is designed for use on rounded and intricate surfaces. The attachment can be used on a grinder, buffing head, drill press, or portable electric drill. The brushes force abrasive strips over and around contours and into surfaces and small openings where other abrasive tools can't reach. Fig. 35-31.

HAND SANDING

Even though most sanding can be done with machines, there are places a machine can't reach. This is true even in high-production furniture factories, where skilled cabinetmakers must do such sanding by hand.

These are the basic rules for hand sanding. Fig. 35-32.

● Select the correct kind and grade of abrasive for the job to be

35-29. *Sanding the edge of a leg on a sanding drum mounted in a lathe.*

35-30. *Using a disk sanding attachment.*

done. Garnet paper is generally used for hand sanding.

● Make sure all cutting operations are completed before sanding. Except for abrasive machining, sanding is designed to smooth and finish the surface after cutting and shaping have been done with other tools.

● For flat surfaces and edges, use a sanding block so that the sur-

35-31. *The rotary sanding attachment has brushes and abrasive strips.*

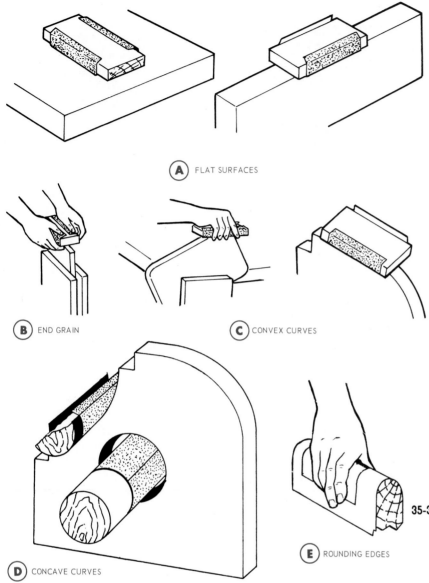

(A) FLAT SURFACES

(B) END GRAIN

(C) CONVEX CURVES

(D) CONCAVE CURVES

(E) ROUNDING EDGES

35-32. *Hand sanding methods.*

faces will be square. There is a tendency in sanding to round all edges and surfaces. Never ruin the accuracy of your work with poor sanding.

● Always sand with the grain of the wood. Apply just enough pressure to make the abrasive cut the surface.

● Clean off the abrasive paper or cloth frequently with a brush.

● Never attempt to sand off glue or pencil marks. These should be scraped off with a sharp tool.

● Many curved and irregular surfaces which must be hand sanded are quite smooth and require only a light sanding with finer grades of paper.

● Break all edges slightly to prevent splintering. Round the corners just enough to give them a smooth "feel" when you run your hand across them.

● After all sanding operations have been completed, use a tack cloth to remove dust before finishing.

36 Wood Lathe

Early American and Traditional furniture often includes turned parts. Fig. 36-1. These parts are produced on a lathe. The wood is rotated about a horizontal axis while being shaped by a fixed tool.

The hand wood lathe combines the skill of hand-tool work with the power of a machine. Some woodworkers use a hand lathe for hobby purposes. In production work, its value is limited. The primary occupational value of this machine is for the modelmaker, the patternmaker, and those who restore and rebuild antique furniture. A few cabinetmakers who are employed by furniture manufacturers must hand turn original patterns that are used to set the knives for the automatic lathe.

The automatic lathe used in industry is a high-production machine that will do all types of turning and many other special kinds of cutting for furniture parts.

PARTS AND SIZES

Lathe size is designated by the *swing* (the largest diameter that can be turned), by the bed length, the distance between centers, and the overall length. The swing is twice the distance from the center of the spindle to the bed. A typical swing is 12". A gap-bed lathe may have a swing over the bed of 12" and a swing over the gap of 15½", with 4" thick stock. Fig. 36-2. This feature makes it possible to do larger faceplate turning on the inside of the lathe.

A lathe may be belt-driven (using step pulleys), it may have a variable-speed pulley, or it may have a direct-drive motor. The speed ranges depend on the drive arrangement. For example, the gap-bed lathe in Fig. 36-2 has a variable-speed control drive which allows it to turn at any speed from 340 RPM (for turning rough wood) up to 3200 RPM.

WOOD LATHE

MAINTENANCE
- Keep all lathe tools properly ground.
- Check the condition of the lathe centers. Grind or replace as necessary.
- Keep headstock and tailstock spindles wiped clean of sawdust and dirt.
- Make sure all adjustments on the tool rest and tailstock operate freely.
- Always remove the live center to drive it into the stock, and always use a mallet.

LUBRICATION
- On variable-speed lathes, use S.A.E. No. 20 oil on counter shaft, bracket screw, variable-speed drive screw, dovetail ways, variable-speed pulley shaft, and tailstock quill adjusting screw.
- On belt-driven lathes, use S.A.E. No. 20 oil on beds, ways, tailstock, quill, and adjusting screws.
- Motors usually have sealed bearings that require no lubrication.

SAFETY
- Never wear loose clothing, a tie, scarf, or jewelry.
- Wear goggles or a face shield.
- Check the wood to make sure it has no defects that would cause it to break when turning.
- Check all glue joints before mounting the stock. A weak joint may come apart when revolving at high speeds. Make sure glued-up stock is completely dry before turning.
- Fasten stock securely between centers. Make sure the tailstock is locked before turning on the power.
- Adjust the tool rest as close to the stock as possible. Then revolve the stock by hand to make sure it clears the rest.
- Always stop the lathe before making any adjustments such as changing the position of the tool rest.
- Run all stock at the slowest speed until it is rounded.
- For stock over 6" in diameter, maintain slower speed; from 3" to 6", medium speed; under 3", faster speed.
- Hold turning tools firmly in both hands.
- Keep the tool rest as close to the work as possible. At intervals, stop the lathe and readjust.
- Make sure the stock is firmly fastened to the faceplate before turning.
- Remove the tool rest when sanding or polishing. If you don't, your fingers may get caught between the tool rest and the stock.

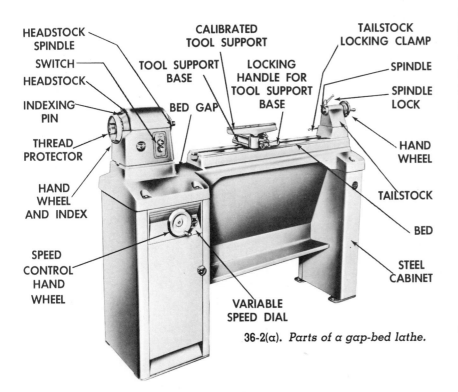

36-1. *This coffee table makes considerable use of turned parts.*

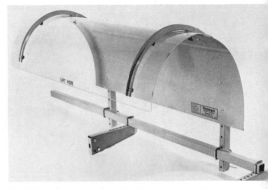

36-2(b). *Safety shield for a wood lathe. Most shields are designed to be used both for turning between centers and for faceplate turning.*

A standard lathe equipped with four-step pulleys has speeds of 915, 1380, 2150, and 3260 RPM. On some lathes, speeds up to 3600 RPM are possible.

The headstock is permanently mounted on the left end of the bed. It has a hollow spindle, threaded on both ends, so that a faceplate can be attached to either end. A spur or drive center can be inserted in the spindle for turning between centers. Fig. 36-3. The tailstock is movable and can be located at many positions along the bed. It also has a hollow spindle in which the cup center is inserted. Sometimes a cone center is used instead of a cup center. Fig. 36-3. In either case it is called the *dead center* because it

doesn't turn with the stock. The tool rest consists of a base which clamps to the bed and the tool rest itself, which clamps to this base.

Many accessories can be used on the lathe, not only for turning but also for buffing, grinding, horizontal boring, disk sanding, and drum sanding.

TOOLS

The six common types of tools for woodturning are: *gouges* for rough cutting stock to round shape, *skews* for smooth cuts to finish a surface, *parting tools* to cut a recess or groove, *spear-point* or *diamond tools* to finish the inside of recesses or corners, *flat tools* for scraping a straight surface, and *round-nose tools* for scraping concave recesses and circular grooves. Fig. 36-4. Measuring tools include a rule, di-

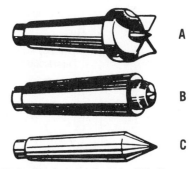

36-2(α). *Parts of a gap-bed lathe.*

36-3. *Kinds of centers: (A) Spur or drive. (B) Cup. (C) Cone.*

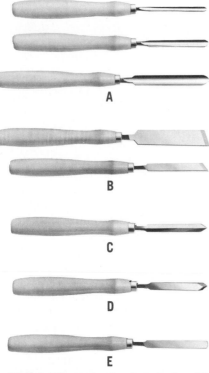

36-4(a). *Common turning tools: (A) Gouges. (B) Skews. (C) Parting tool. (D) Spear-point tool. (E) Round-nose tool. The flat-nose tool is not commonly used except for faceplate scraping and is not shown here.*

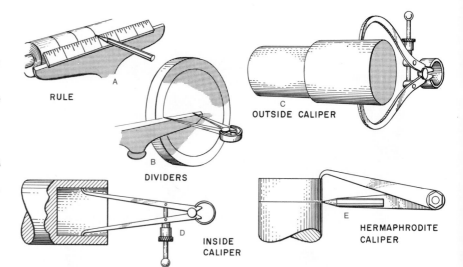

36-5. *Common measuring tools: (A) the rule is needed for making measurements for spindle and faceplate turning and for setting dividers and calipers. (B) The dividers are used for drawing circles and stepping off measurements. (C) The outside caliper is needed for checking the outside diameter of turned work. (D) The inside caliper is used for making measurements of the inside diameter. (E) The hermaprodite caliper is used for laying out distances from the end of stock and for locating the centers for turning.*

viders, outside caliper, inside caliper, and hermaphrodite caliper. Fig. 36-5.

KINDS OF TURNING

The two basic methods of turning are cutting and scraping. Cutting tools include the gouge, skew, and parting tool, while the scraping tools are the flat nose, round nose, and spear point. All of the cutting tools can be used for scraping operations also. In the cutting method, the outer skin of the wood is pierced and a shaving is peeled off. Fig. 36-6. In scraping, the tool is forced into the wood so that particles are scraped away. Fig. 36-7. When only a limited amount of turning is to be done, the scraping method is completely satisfactory.

SPINDLE TURNING

Turning with the stock held between the live (or moving) center and the dead (or stationary) center is called spindle turning.

Turning a Plain Cylinder

A plain cylinder is turned with the work held between the live and dead centers, and a gouge is used. Select a piece of wood of the right kind and size. If the stock is more than 3″ square, first cut it to octagonal shape on the band saw.

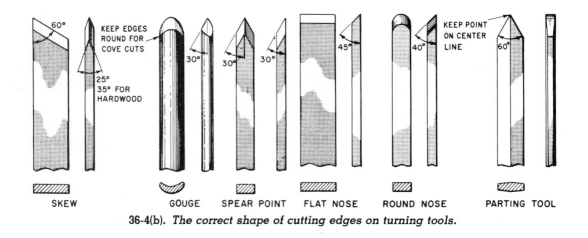

36-4(b). *The correct shape of cutting edges on turning tools.*

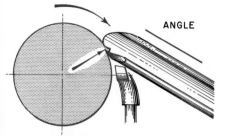

36-6. *The cutting method is faster and results in a smoother surface than does scraping. However, it requires much greater skill and more practice.*

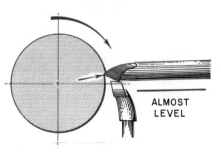

36-7. *The scraping method is easier to do and is accurate but the rougher surface that results requires more sanding. All faceplate turning is done by scraping.*

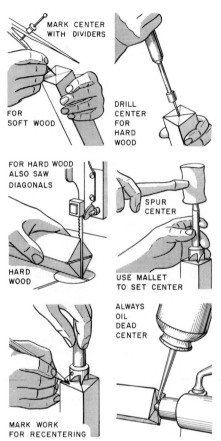

36-8. *Preparing the stock for spindle turning.*

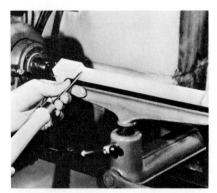

36-10. *The first method of holding a gouge: the thumb is placed over the tool and the fingers under it. Note that the forefinger is used as a guide against the rest. CAUTION: For some photos the safety shield was removed so that details could be seen. The guard symbol in the caption indicates you should use the safety shield when performing this operation.*

Locate the center of the stock on both ends. On the end of the square stock, draw lines across the corners to locate the center. To locate the center of an irregularly shaped piece, use a hermaphrodite caliper adjusted to slightly less than half the thickness. Then mark from each of four sides until the center can be located. Mark the center with a prick punch or scratch awl. If the wood is hard, drill a small hole at the center and cut shallow saw kerfs across the corners. Place a spur center in position and strike it with a mallet to seat it firmly. It is a good idea to mark the end of the work so that, if you take it out of the lathe, it can be put back in the same position. Place the work between centers and turn the tailstock handle until the cup center seats firmly on the wood. Release the pressure slightly and apply a little

oil or graphite. Fig. 36-8. Adjust the tool rest to clear the stock by about ⅛″, with the top of the tool rest about ⅛″ above center.

The speed of the lathe should be adjusted in terms of the diameter, using faster speeds for smaller diameters. Fig. 36-9. Always start turning at low speed until the wood becomes a cylinder. Plant your feet

firmly in front of the lathe and stand erect.

There are two methods of holding the tool. One is to place the thumb over the tool and the fingers under it, using the forefinger as a guide against the tool rest. Fig. 36-10. The second is to place the hand over the tool, with the wrist bent and against the tool rest. Fig. 36-11.

To cut the cylinder to size, begin about one-third of the way in from the tailstock and twist the gouge to the right so that a shearing cut can be taken. Cut towards the tailstock. Fig. 36-12. After each cut, begin about 2″ closer to the live center. To

SPEEDS FOR WOODTURNING

Diameter of Stock	Roughing to Size	General Cutting	Finishing
Under 2″ diameter	900 to 1300 RPM	2400 to 2800	3000 to 4000
2″ to 4″ diameter	600 to 1000 RPM	1800 to 2400	2400 to 3000
4″ to 6″ diameter	600 to 800 RPM	1200 to 1800	1800 to 2400
6″ to 8″ diameter	400 to 600 RPM	800 to 1200	1200 to 1800
8″ to 10″ diameter	300 to 400 RPM	600 to 800	900 to 1200
Over 10″ diameter	200 to 300 RPM	300 to 600	600 to 900

CAUTION: Do not exceed these recommended speeds. Serious injury can result if parts being turned are thrown from the lathe.

36-9. *Recommended lathe speeds for various stock diameters.*

36-11. *The second method of holding a gouge: the hand is placed over the gouge with the wrist bent and against the tool rest. This is not as comfortable as the first method.*

complete the rough turning, tip the cutting tool to the left and work toward the live center. Now adjust the caliper to about ⅛″ oversize and, with the parting tool, make cuts to the correct diameter about every inch or two. The parting tool is held with the narrow edge against the rest and is forced into the wood. At the same time, the diameter is checked with the outside caliper. Fig. 36-13. When using the caliper on revolving stock, be careful not to apply any pressure as this may cause the caliper to spring over the stock, resulting in an accident. Now, continue to rough turn to size with the gouge. The cylinder can also be turned to size by using the gouge as a scraping tool. With this method the point of the gouge is held at right angles to the work,

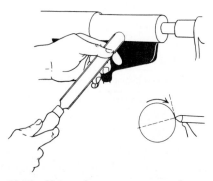

36-12. *Using the gouge to rough cut the cylinder to size. Roll the gouge slightly to help in cutting.*

with the tool in a level position. Force the point into the wood and then move it slowly from side to side. It is important to remove the tool occasionally so that the point will not overheat and burn.

Finish turning on a cylinder is done with a skew. Use either the cutting or scraping method. Place the skew on its side with the cutting edge slightly above and beyond the cylinder. (The uppermost point is called the *toe* and the lower point the *heel*.) Start at a point 2″ or 3″ from the end. Hold the side of the tool firmly against the tool rest. Slowly draw the skew back until the cutting edge is over the cylinder at a point about halfway between the heel and toe. Be careful not to catch the toe of the tool in the revolving cylinder. Tip the skew slightly until the cutting edge can be forced into the wood. Then push the tool along toward the tailstock, taking a shearing cut. Fig. 36-14. Reverse the direction and cut toward the headstock.

A simpler way of doing this is to scrape it to size. You can use either a square-nose (flat) tool or a larger skew. Maintain a high speed. Hold the cutting edge parallel to the cylinder and force it into the work until the scraping begins. Then move it from side to side. Fig. 36-15. Always start the scraping some distance from the end to prevent the tool from catching and splitting the wood. Check with an outside caliper until the finished size is reached.

A block plane can also be used to smooth a cylinder to finish size. Adjust the plane to take a fine shaving. Hold it at an angle of about 45 degrees to the axis of the work. Use a tool rest to support the plane. Start at the center and move it to one end as you would any other cutting tool. Then reverse the tool and cut in the other direction.

To square off the ends, first mark the proper length with a pencil. The ends may be squared by first scrap-

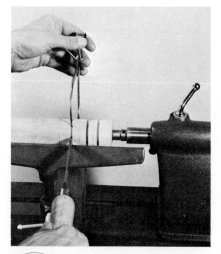

36-13. *Making sizing cuts with a parting tool. Hold the tool in one hand and the caliper in the other. When all of the grooves are cut away along the cylinder, you know the piece will have the same diameter throughout.*

ing with a parting tool and then cutting with a skew. Force a parting tool into the revolving cylinder about ⅛″ beyond the measured length. Always make the groove slightly wider than the width of the tool so that the cutting edge will not burn. As the tool is advanced into the wood, raise the handle slowly to keep producing the scraping action. Reduce the stock at this point to a diameter of about ⅜″.

Now locate the toe of the skew in

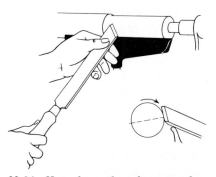

36-14. *Note how the skew touches the cylinder about halfway between the heel and toe of the cutting edge. For heavy cuts, hold the skew by the overhand method shown in 36-11.*

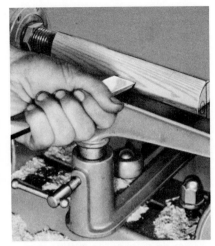

36-15. Using the skew as a scraping tool. Hold the full cutting edge against the work and press lightly. Remove only a little material at a time.

line with the point at which the finish cut must be made. The ground edge of the skew must be parallel with the cut to be made. Tip the heel of the skew slightly to the right or left, away from the cut. Force the

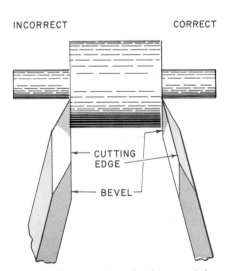

36-16. To cut to length, the toe of the skew is used to remove thin shavings from the side. Hold the skew so that its bottom edge is nearly parallel with the shoulder. Turn the cutting edge away at the top so that only the toe itself does the cutting. Start with the handle low; then raise it slowly to do the cutting.

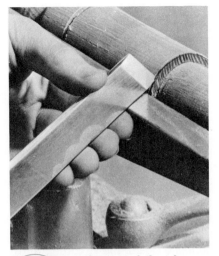

36-17. Using the toe of the skew to make the vertical cut.

toe of the skew into the wood, holding it against the shoulder. Remove a shaving about 1/32" deep with each cut. Fig. 36-16. As the cut becomes deeper, provide clearance for the tool by turning the handle away from the cut, then making some taper cuts to form a half V.

Cutting a shoulder is similar to squaring off an end. Use a parting tool to cut a groove, reducing the diameter at this point to slightly more than the smaller diameter. Then, with a small gouge, remove most of the stock from the smaller

36-18. Using the skew to make the horizontal cut for a shoulder. The heel of the skew must do most of the cutting.

36-19. Forming a shoulder by the scraping method. A skew or a flat-nose tool can be used to do the scraping.

diameter. Cut the vertical part of the shoulder with the toe of the skew. Fig. 36-17. Cut the horizontal part of the shoulder, using the heel of the skew in a manner similar to finish turning. Fig. 36-18. Another way to form a shoulder or square off an end is by the scraping method. Fig. 36-19.

Taper Cuts

Rough turn to the largest diameter. Then use a parting tool to mark the smallest and several intermediate diameters. Rough cut the taper with a gouge by either cutting or scraping. Then finish turn the taper with a skew. Fig. 36-20.

36-20. Finishing a taper with the skew. Always cut from the large to the small diameter.

Cutting Coves

Mark the center and ends of each cove and adjust the caliper to the smallest diameter. To use the scraping method, force a round-nose tool into the center of the cove. Swing the tool from side to side, using the tool rest as a fulcrum point. Fig. 36-21. Continue to measure the center with a caliper until depth is reached.

Coves are scraped to rough shape with a small gouge. Hold the gouge in a vertical position and keep the handle high enough so that the cutting edge is pointed at a line on

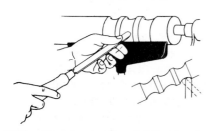

36-21. Cutting a cove with a round-nose chisel. The correct movement of the tool is shown at the lower right.

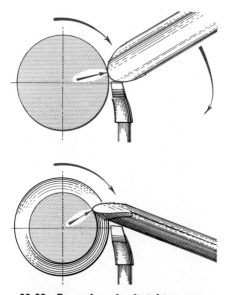

36-22. Procedure for finishing a cove cut. Hold the gouge with the handle high and the tool almost on edge. The blade should be held between the thumb and forefinger. Then roll the tool to complete the cut to the bottom.

center. Begin the cut near the center of the cove. Work toward the finished layout line. In making the cut, roll the gouge to follow the correct shape. Fig. 36-22.

Cutting V's

To scrape a V, use a diamond- or spear-point tool held flat. Force it into the wood.

To cut a V, mark its edges and center. Hold a skew on edge with the heel down. Force it into the stock at the center of the V. Use a slight pump-handle action. Work from one side of the V, cutting with the heel of the skew. Continue to force the tool into the center of the cut and cut one side of the V to correct depth. Then cut the opposite side in a similar manner. Fig. 36-23.

Bead Cuts

Bead cuts are rather difficult and will require some practice. Mark the position of the beads with a line indicating the ends and center of each one. Begin the cut as you

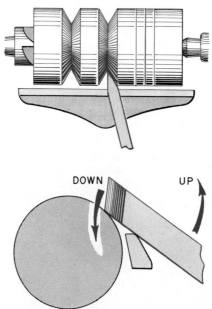

36-23. Cutting V's with a skew. The skew is rotated down into the stock, using the rest as a pivot. Cutting should be done by the heel.

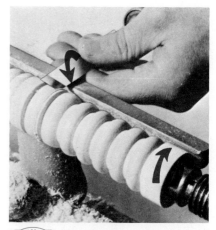

36-24. Cutting beads, using the heel to do most of the cutting.

would for a V, using the toe of the skew to start it. Then hold the skew on its side, with the heel doing most of the cutting. Start quite high on the cylinder, in the center of the bead, and turn the tool in the same arc as the bead. At the same time draw it backward and move it to a vertical position. Fig. 36-24. If the tool is not turned as the cut is made, the heel will dig into the next bead. If separated by sizing cuts, beads are easier to form. Fig. 36-25. They can also be formed by scraping with a spear-point tool. Fig. 36-26.

Turning Complicated Designs

Complicated designs usually consist of a combination of straight turnings, tapers, V's, beads, coves, and long concave or convex surfaces. The first step is to draw a full-size pattern of the part that can be used for taking off measurements. To get a piece of material large enough for the parts, you will sometimes have to glue up pieces to form a laminated structure. When this is necessary, make sure the pieces match and that you have a good glue joint. Then mount the stock in the lathe and rough turn to its maximum size. Use a pencil or pattern to mark important locations

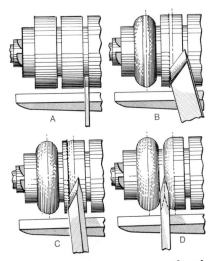

36-25. *Correct steps in cutting beads separated by sizing cuts: (A) Use a parting tool to cut to depth between the beads. (B) Place the skew at right angles with the workpiece, flat against the surface and near the top of the bead. (C) The heel should start the cutting at the top of the bead. Then draw the skew back, slowly raising the handle and turning the blade. (D) As the cutting is done, roll the tool into the groove. The tool must turn 90 degrees in forming the bead.*

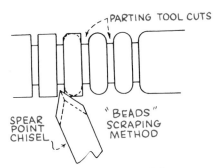

36-26. *Shaping the bead by scraping. Push the spear-point tool straight into the groove and rotate it horizontally to form the bead. The tool must be pulled back slightly as it is rotated so that the point will not cut into the next bead.*

on the cylinder. With a parting tool turn the important diameters at various positions along the cylinder. Use the gouge, skew, and other tools to turn the various parts of the design. Measure the diameters frequently with a caliper.

If more than one complicated design is needed, it is best to follow one of the methods described in the next section. When the design is completed, smooth the surface by sanding. Turnings should be sanded with the machine operating at one of the slower speeds, but not the slowest. For flat cylinders use a sheet of abrasive paper. For complicated designs use narrow strips of abrasive paper from grades 2/0 to 4/0, depending on the roughness of the surface.

Turning Duplicate Parts

Turning identical pieces requires great care and accuracy. There are several ways to make the job simpler. One is to make a thin cardboard or wood pattern, exact and full-size, representing a half section of the turning in reverse. This pattern, or template, can then be held against the turning from time to time to check the design.

Another method is to use a template and diameter board. This method is effective when many turnings of the same design are needed. Turn one piece to the exact shape, then mount it on a board. Place the board behind the lathe on hinges so that it can be moved next to the turnings for comparison. Fig. 36-27. Then cut a diameter board. This is a thin board with semicircular cuts along the edge. These cuts correspond to important diameters along the turning and can be held against the turning instead of using a caliper. Fig. 36-28.

DUPLICATOR ATTACHMENT

If you have tried to turn a complicated design on the lathe, you know that it takes great patience and skill to turn four identical parts — for example, a set of legs for a table. However, with a lathe duplicator or a woodturning duplicator, it is easy to form any number of identical parts automatically. There are sever-

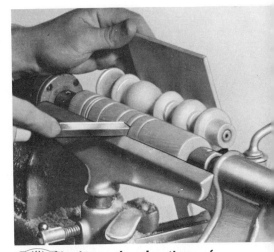

36-27. *Checking the location of major diameters with the original turning.*

al models of duplicators and all are made to fit any model of lathe. With this attachment, the tool holder and tool rest are removed and the duplicator fitted between the headstock and tailstock. The carriage that holds the cutter moves in two directions: back and forth, and in and out. A pattern guide attached to the carriage rides along the pattern (or a turned piece) and guides the cutting edge to assure duplicating accuracy. The pattern or turned piece is clamped to a holder. Fig. 36-29. Regular turning tools are not used. Instead, use a cutter such as a

36-28. *Using a diameter board to check the diameter at important locations.*

36-29(a). *Lathe duplicators make it easy to produce identical parts. Here the turned piece at the bottom is being used as a guide for cutting the duplicate piece at the top.*

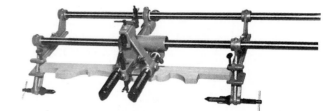

36-29(b). *A pattern (template) can also be used as a guide.*

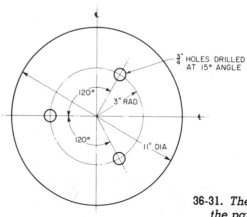

36-30. *This type of lathe attachment is called a woodturning duplicator.*

pointed metal lathe bit that is thin enough to reproduce an intricate design.

A woodturning duplicator is shown in Fig. 36-30. The following instructions explain the setup and operating procedure for using a woodturning duplicator. The steps shown are for turning the legs of a small three-legged stool. Fig. 36-31.

1. Select the wood (a hardwood such as maple is best). Apply three coats of resin sealer, rubbing after each coat with steel wool. Wax the wood.

2. There are several ways of producing the template. One is to turn one leg to the correct shape. Then a thin section of the very center of the turning is cut on the band saw. Another method is to make a full-size drawing of the template on heavy paper. Paste the drawing on hardboard and cut it out on the jigsaw. A third method is to sandwich a piece of ⅛" hardboard between two pieces of wood. The pieces should be ¾" longer than the part to be made so that the sandwich can be held together at the ends with wood screws. Then turn the piece freehand. Disassemble the sandwich, and the template is ready. Be sure the contours have smooth, unbroken lines. Drill two small holes in the template to attach it to the duplicator.

3. Prepare the three pieces for

the legs. The drive center should be driven into the workpiece with a soft hammer or a block of wood. *Never* pound the drive center with a steel hammer. On hard woods, diagonal saw cuts should be made to receive the live center.

4. Turn each piece round to the largest diameter. On only one of the pieces, turn a shoulder on each end, estimating the diameter very accurately with the parting tool and

caliper. The diameter should be the same at each end of the piece. This is very important because you will set the template from these diameters.

5. Place the two clamps on the lathe bed as shown in Fig. 36-32.

6. Place the duplicator on the lathe bed, attaching it to the two clamps, as shown in Fig. 36-33. When using the duplicator on 11"

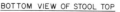

BOTTOM VIEW OF STOOL TOP

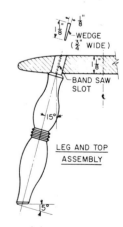

36-31. *The leg of this stool is the part to be turned.*

36-32. *The two clamps (A) have been placed on the lathe bed.*

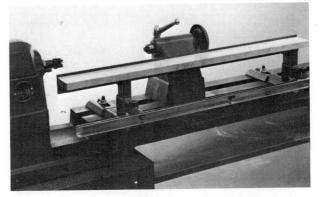

36-33. *Attach the woodturning duplicator to the two clamps.*

36-34. *The guide rail (A) is attached to the duplicator.*

36-35. *Slide the cutting head (A) on the rails.*

36-36. *Adjustment points for positioning the tool bit.*

lathes, the four 1″ riser blocks located between the horizontal and vertical brackets are removed.

7. Attach the guide rail to the duplicator. Fig. 36-34. The long end of the guide rail should be toward the headstock end as shown.

8. Slide the cutting head on the rails as shown in Fig. 36-35.

9. With the duplicator assembled on the lathe bed in about the right position, bring the tool bit (A in Fig. 36-36) near the point of one of the centers. The tool bit should be about ¹⁄₁₆″ above the point of the center. To adjust the tool bit higher or lower, loosen the nut (B) and the setscrew (D), and revolve eccentric (C) until the tool bit is about ¹⁄₁₆″ above center. The tool bit can be moved in or out or turned to the correct position. Tighten setscrew (D) and nut (B).

10. Place the turning (the one with the shoulders) between centers and adjust the duplicator by moving it in or out so that the tool holder overhangs just the minimum amount when the tool bit touches the turning at the largest diameter. Fig. 36-37. Adjust the duplicator parallel with the lathe bed, and tighten the clamp nuts.

11. Bring the tool bit up to one end of the turning. At the same

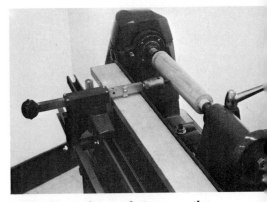

36-37. *Place the workpiece on the lathe and adjust the duplicator.*

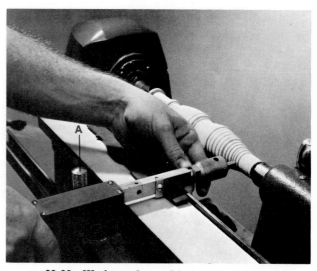

36-38. *Bring the tool bit up to one end of the turning and place the template on the duplicator.*

36-39. *Working the tool holder freehand.*

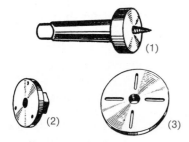

36-40. *Common holding devices for faceplate turning: (1) Screw center. (2) Small 3" diameter faceplate with three screw holes. (3) Larger 6" diameter faceplate with special thread that fits both the right- and left-hand threaded spindles to allow it to be used on either end of the headstock spindle.*

36-41. *Using a wood chuck on a screw center to hold a small object for turning.*

time place the template (A) so that its end touches the corresponding end of the stylus (B) when the tool bit touches the locating point on the workpiece. Hold the template in place with a small C-clamp. Fig. 36-38.

12. Bring the tool bit up to the opposite end and move the template, if necessary, so that it touches the stylus when the tool bit touches the locating point on the workpiece.

13. Double check the position of the template. When it is lined up properly, fasten it in place with two wood screws.

14. With the tool bit clear of the turning, turn on the lathe. Work the tool holder freehand, Fig. 36-39, or use the "fine feed" by turning the knurled feed knob (A).

15. Do not attempt to take too big a cut, but feed the cutting tool gently until you get the feel of the work. The cutting is a scraping action. When turning softer woods, a very light cut should be taken to obtain best possible results.

16. If the turning has very sharp shoulders or grooves, you will not be able to duplicate them exactly because the end of the cutting tool is ground to a small radius. Merely

place the turning between centers as usual and, with the spear-point tool or small skew, clean up the corners.

17. Make the stool top and drill the three holes by following the dimensions shown in Fig. 36-31. Assemble the legs in the stool top.

FACEPLATE TURNING

Bowls, trays, and many other small circular objects are turned on a faceplate. To do the turning, the wood is fastened to a faceplate and shaped by scraping. Faceplates commonly used are the *screw center*, for small objects—no larger than 4" in diameter—and the *standard faceplate*, which has screw holes for fastening the wood in place. Fig. 36-40. For turning extremely small decorative pieces, it may be necessary to make a special holding chuck. Fig. 36-41.

The first step in faceplate turning is to determine the size and kind of material needed. To make a larger bowl or tray it is often necessary to glue up the stock. For a square object, carefully mount the wood on the faceplate. If the object is to be circular, first cut the stock on a band saw to a disk shape, about ¼" larger than the finished diameter and about ⅛″ thick. Then mount it to the faceplate.

If screw holes on the back of the bowl or tray are objectionable, cut a piece of scrap stock at least 1″ thick and about the same size as the base of the project. Glue the two pieces together with a piece of wrapping paper between so that they will separate easily afterwards. Then locate the center of the scrap stock and place the faceplate over it. Mark the hole locations and fasten the faceplate to it with screws about ¾″ long. They should be just long enough to go through the scrap stock without marring the bottom of the workpiece stock.

Remove the live center and fasten the work to the spindle. For extremely large bowls and trays, the faceplate must be attached to the outside end of the spindle. This may require a special stand to hold the tool rest. Another method is to move a second lathe near the outside of the first lathe so that the rest can be used on the end of the bed of the second lathe as the turning is done on the first one. At this point it is often good to make a thin template of the interior and exterior shapes to use as a guide.

Adjust the tool rest across the edge of the stock and set the lathe to a slow speed. Fig. 36-42. Use a flat, round-nose, or spear-point tool to true and dress the outside of the

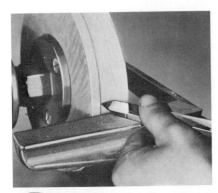
36-42. Adjust the tool rest so that it clears the work by about ⅛″.

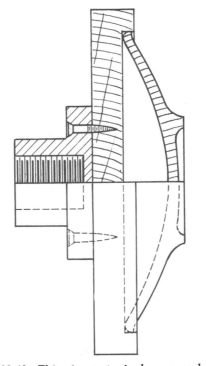
36-43. This is a typical recessed wood chuck.

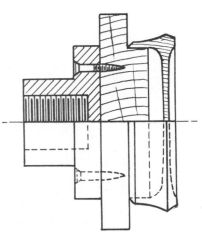
36-44. A spindle chuck for holding work.

disk. Then adjust the tool rest across the face of the disk and trim the face. Start at the center and take scraping cuts toward the outside. Never attempt to cut across the entire diameter since, once you pass the center, the tool will move up and away from the tool holder.

Now you are ready to shape the inside of the bowl. Use various turning tools to remove as much waste material as necessary. Convex curves can be shaped by scraping with a flat-nose or small skew. Sharp corners are formed with a spear-point tool or skew. Concave curves are shaped with a round-nose tool. Remove stock to within ⅛″ of the finished size. Use the template to check the progress of the interior design. On some bowls and trays it is also possible to turn the outside or edge to finished shape with the same setup.

Some faceplate jobs require that both sides of the object be turned. To do this, first turn the front or top and edge of the bowl or tray. When the front is completed, do all the

sanding necessary. Then apply mineral oil or other finish. Separate the scrap stock from the finished piece by driving a sharp chisel between them. Then make a holding chuck. The two common kinds are the recessed and the spindle. The *recessed* chuck is made with a depression in it to hold the face or back of a bowl or tray. Fig. 36-43. The recess cut in the chuck should be just large enough in diameter for the object to go in with a press fit. If the recess is slightly oversize, a piece of paper can be placed between the bowl and the chuck to hold it secure. On a *spindle* chuck the object to be turned fits over the chuck as, for example, a ring design. Figs. 36-44 and 36-45.

FINISHING

There are several ways of applying a finish to a turning. A simple method is to apply paste wax to a cloth and hold it on the revolving stock so that it is completely covered. Then, in about ten minutes, run the lathe at a slow speed and polish the surface with a dry cloth. A second coat of wax can be applied as needed. To apply a French polish, fold a piece of fine cotton or linen cloth into a pad. Then apply about one teaspoon of white shellac to the pad and add several drops of boiled lin-

36-45. *Turning a ring held on a spindle chuck. The spindle chuck is dark wood; the ring is light.*

seed oil. Hold the pad over the work, moving it from one side to the other. Apply even pressure. Add shellac and oil as needed to keep the pad moist. Apply several coats until you get a mirrorlike finish.

Another method is to apply several coats of penetrating finish with a cloth. Sometimes light mineral oil is used for bowls that are to hold food. Vegetable oils are not a good choice since they may become rancid.

37 Combination Machines

Many standard woodworking machines can do several different tasks. For example, the drill press can do not only drilling and boring, but also routing, shaping, sanding, and mortising. While the radial-arm saw was designed primarily for sawing, it can also be used for sanding, routing, and shaping. These, however, are not combination machines.

There are two major kinds of *combination machines*. One type has two different machines permanently connected to a single motor. Both machines operate at the same time. Some examples are a combination saw and jointer, a planer and jointer, and a belt and disk sander. Fig. 37-1. A more common kind of combination machine is the multipurpose type in which many different tools are built into a single machine. Fig. 37-2. For example, one

37-1. *A combination belt and disk sander that operates with a single motor. This machine can be dangerous when two people use it at the same time because only one person controls the switch.*

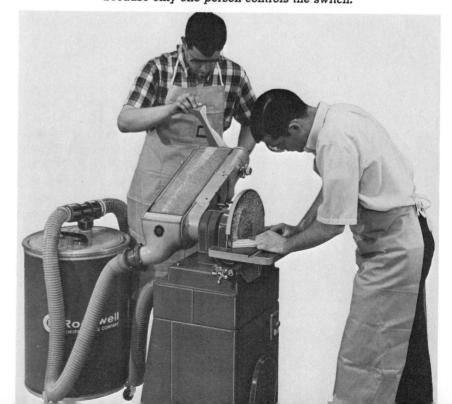

37-2. *A multipurpose machine.*

37-3. *Using the machine as a horizontal boring machine.*

machine can be used as a table saw, lathe, drill press, horizontal boring machine, and disk sander. With special attachments, it can also be used as a band saw, jigsaw, belt sander, router, and jointer.

The major advantage of the multipurpose machine is that it requires much less space in a workshop than individual tools. Also, the cost of the machine is less than the total cost of individual tools. The only disadvantage is that only one type of operation can be performed at a time. Some time is spent changing from one operation to another. While it takes only a very short time to change the machine from a vertical drill press to a horizontal boring machine, more time is involved in changing it from a circular saw to a jointer because an attachment must be added.

While most combination machines are purchased for home workshops, this machine does have a place in the school shop or laboratory that also has standard single-purpose machines. When mass producing products, this machine can be any kind of second machine that may be needed. For example, the machine can serve as an additional drill press, horizontal boring machine, or disk sander. Because this machine is excellent for horizontal boring, it would not be necessary to purchase a separate horizontal boring machine. Fig. 37-3.

Once the setups have been made, the procedures for use are the same as for the individual machines that have been described in earlier chapters.

Section III
QUESTIONS AND DISCUSSION TOPICS

Chapter 20

1. What is a *kerf*?
2. What is the difference between a crosscut saw and a ripsaw? Describe their teeth.
3. Name the handsaws that are used for cutting irregular curves.
4. What is the difference between a back saw and a dovetail saw?

Chapter 21

1. What type of plane is designed to cut end grain?

2. Planing against the grain is a good way to remove stock quickly. True or False.
3. A sharp blade on a plane will be shiny. True or False.
4. What kind of plane is used to clean out the bottoms of grooves and dadoes?

Chapter 22

1. How are chisels and gouges similar? How are they different?
2. When would you use a drawknife and when a spokeshave?

3. Why should you always put a handle on a file or rasp before using it?

Chapter 23
1. What is the difference between drilling and boring?
2. Name the tools used for operating twist drills.
3. Describe three uses for the Foerstner bit.
4. What type of bit has adjustable cutting blades?

Chapter 24
1. What is the difference between grinding and honing?
2. Describe how to check a plane iron for sharpness.
3. What is meant by "hollow-ground"?
4. What is meant by "jointing" a saw?
5. What is the purpose of setting saw teeth?
6. Name and define the four steps for sharpening a circular saw blade by hand.

Chapter 25
1. What is the difference between single and double planers?
2. Will a planer correct or straighten warped stock? Explain.
3. Tell how to square up legs on a planer.
4. If several short pieces of equal thickness are to be surfaced at the same time, what is the best procedure?

Chapter 26
1. Tell why the circular saw is so important in cabinetmaking.
2. Describe four accessories that are available for the circular saw.
3. Name three common types of circular saw blades.
4. Describe four methods of cutting stock to identical length.
5. Is cutting a flat miter a crosscutting or a ripping operation?
6. What is the major hazard in ripping stock?
7. Describe three accessories for ripping that contribute to safety.
8. When should a push stick be used in ripping stock?
9. Define *resawing*.
10. What is the difference between a groove and a dado?
11. Can both the mortise and the tenon be cut on the circular saw? Explain.

Chapter 27
1. What is the chief advantage of the radial-arm saw?
2. In using a radial-arm saw, what operation requires that the stock be moved into the revolving saw blade?
3. Does the work or the saw move for crosscutting operations? Explain.
4. Describe the way mitering is done on the radial-arm saw.
5. How does horizontal cutting differ from vertical cutting on the radial-arm saw?

Chapter 28
1. What is the primary purpose of a band saw?
2. Explain how to replace a band saw blade.
3. Describe how to use a jig for circle cutting on the band saw.
4. Describe three methods for cutting duplicate pieces on the band saw.

Chapter 29
1. What is the primary use for a scroll saw?
2. Name the three main types of blades used on the scroll saw.
3. Describe how to make an internal cut.
4. When sawing metals, how can you prolong the life of the blade?

Chapter 30
1. The portable power saw cuts from the bottom up. True or False.
2. For what is the bayonet saw used?
3. When is an electric plane a valuable tool for the cabinetmaker?

Chapter 31
1. What is the primary use for a jointer?
2. How is the size of a jointer indicated?
3. Describe how to square up stock on a jointer.
4. Explain how to cut a short taper on a jointer.

Chapter 32
1. Why is the shaper a relatively dangerous machine to operate?
2. Name the three basic kinds of cutters used on the shaper.
3. Name the four basic methods of shaping.

Chapter 33
1. How does the router differ from the shaper?

2. Name the five methods of controlling the sidewise movement of a router.

3. Describe how to cut a dovetail dado joint on a router.

4. Describe how the radial-arm saw can be used as a router.

Chapter 34

1. Why are drilling and boring important in woodworking?

2. Can boring be done on a drill press?

3. When is it useful to have a two-speed or variable-speed portable drill?

4. Why would a cabinetmaker need masonry bits?

5. Describe the way a deep hole is drilled on a drill press.

6. Explain how to drill or bore a hole at an angle.

7. What is the purpose of a mortiser?

8. Describe the functions of the bit and the chisel on the mortiser.

Chapter 35

1. Name the four major abrasives used in woodworking.

2. Name four common stationary sanding machines.

3. Name three kinds of portable sanders.

4. How can a lathe be used as a sander?

Chapter 36

1. What is the "swing" of a lathe? How is it determined?

2. What is the difference between cutting and scraping in woodturning?

3. What kinds of objects require faceplate turning?

Chapter 37

1. What is a multipurpose machine?

2. What are the advantages of a multipurpose machine? What are the disadvantages?

PROBLEMS AND ACTIVITIES

1. Trace the history of one hand tool from earliest times to its present design.

2. Trace the history and development of a stationary power tool.

3. Develop a model of the cutting head of a planer.

4. Design and make a tool holder for a hand tool, portable power tool, or an accessory for a stationary power tool.

5. Compare the relative safety of the radial-arm saw and the circular saw.

6. Write a complete set of specifications for ordering a power tool for your own shop.

7. Compare the advantages and disadvantages of blades and knives tipped with high-speed steel or carbide.

8. Trace the history of abrasives.

Section IV

CONSTRUCTION

38 Basic Construction Problems and Procedures

It is important to understand the construction problems involved in using different kinds of lumber and processed materials. Cabinetmakers must thoroughly understand the relationships between materials and machines. They must also cope with the problems and difficulties that result when various species of wood are machined under different conditions.

BUILDING UP LARGE SURFACES

Many furniture designs—tables, for example—have surface areas greater than the standard sizes of boards. There are three common ways to make a large surface for cabinets or furniture: (1) by gluing up solid stock, (2) by using plywood or other large sheet material, and (3) by building a frame and panel. Fig. 38-1. Solid lumber is used for structural parts. Lumber-core plywood or frame and panel construction is generally used for large surfaces. Cabinets and built-ins are usually made of veneer-core plywood or particle board, with some use of solid stock for trim. Frequently, school and small shops use only solid lumber.

If solid, glued-up stock is used for large surfaces, problems of warpage and expansion-contraction must be solved. In gluing up a large surface of solid stock, the standard procedure is to rip the material into widths of 4" to 6" and then to glue the pieces with the growth rings running in opposite directions. This reduces warping but will not completely eliminate the problem. For a tabletop, grooving or slotting the underside to relieve tension also helps prevent warping.

The second problem, expansion and contraction due to changes in humidity, is even more difficult. A wide glued-up surface is constantly changing in size as the moisture content in the air varies. As a matter of fact, a solid, glued-up tabletop may vary as much as ¾" in width. Such a tabletop should be fastened to the base in such a way that this movement will not cause the wood to buckle or crack.

Sometimes a beginner will attempt to glue a band of solid stock to the end of a solid, glued-up tabletop. This is extremely poor practice since wood changes in size much more across the grain (width) than with the grain (length). Much change in humidity is likely to break the glue joint between the band and the end grain. Fig. 38-2.

You may wonder why lumber-core plywood does not cause the same kind of difficulties as solid lumber when it is used for a large surface. Lumber-core plywood has a core of solid strips of lumber glued edge to edge, but this core is covered both with crossbands and with face and back veneer. Also, the edges are usually banded. As a result, there is little chance for moisture to be absorbed by the core itself.

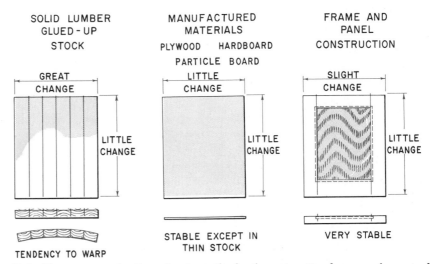

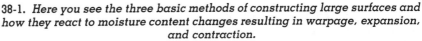

38-1. *Here you see the three basic methods of constructing large surfaces and how they react to moisture content changes resulting in warpage, expansion, and contraction.*

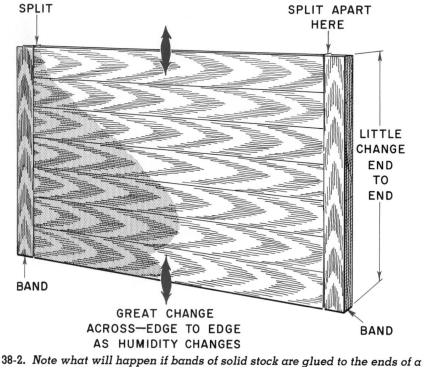

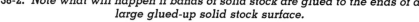

38-2. *Note what will happen if bands of solid stock are glued to the ends of a large glued-up solid stock surface.*

Frame-and-panel construction is commonly used because of its dimensional stability. If plywood is used as the panel center, there is little problem from either warpage or expansion and contraction. However, if solid wood covers the center of the frame, the groove which holds the panel must be deep enough to allow for changes in size. Also, a great deal of stain must be put on the edges of the frame so that when the panel does contract, white wood will not show.

In any solid wood construction, the wood must be free to move without breaking a joint. For example, if the sides of a chest are made of glued-up stock, then the frames should be a little narrower than usual and *should not* be glued into the dadoes. Rather, they should be assembled with screws so that there will be some freedom of movement.

Legs, posts and many other structural parts are usually made of either one-piece solid lumber or laminated materials. The advantage of one-piece material is that there is no chance for a glued joint to show or for breakage at the glue line. Solid lumber also tends to eliminate the wide variations in color from one strip of wood to another, which is often a problem with laminated material. However, laminating does make better use of the material available and is essential in producing many curved parts. Chapter 41 describes laminating and bending.

SELECTION AND HANDLING OF WOODS

It is extremely important to make sure that only kiln-dried lumber is chosen for all cabinetmaking. This lumber should always have less than 10 percent moisture content, preferably in the 7 to 8 percent range. It is best if the lumber is slightly over-dried to about 5 or 6 percent, then stored where the temperature and humidity are correct to bring it up to 7 or 8 percent.

There are two basic ways of determining how much moisture lumber

contains. The more scientific method, called *oven drying,* employs laboratory techniques. In this method, samples of the wood are cut from a green board and baked in an oven at 214-221 degrees Fahrenheit until they stop losing their moisture. The percentage of moisture content equals weight when cut minus oven-dried weight, divided by oven-dried weight, times 100. Written as an equation, this formula is:

$$\text{Pct. moisture content} = \frac{\text{wt. when cut} - \text{oven-dried wt.}}{\text{oven-dried wt.}} \times 100$$

In schools and cabinet shops a *moisture meter* (detector) is used. There are two types. One is supplied with needles that pierce the wood and measure the electrical resistance to current flow through the wood. Fig. 38-3. The other type measures the relationship between moisture content and a constant setting. This type can be recognized by the metal plate or shoe which is applied to the lumber surface.

38-3(a). *This moisture meter shows the moisture content of Douglas fir directly on the meter scale when the temperature of the wood is at 70°F. When the temperature is higher or lower than 70°, the reading should be corrected as shown in the table, Fig. 38-3(b). If the wood being tested is not Douglas fir, add or subtract the species correction shown in Fig. 38-3(c).*

ACTUAL MOISTURE CONTENT FOR VARIOUS WOOD TEMPERATURES (°F)

Meter Reading	−20°F	0°	20°	40°	60°	80°	100°	120°	140°	160°
6	11.5	9.8	8.3	7.2	6.3	5.6	5.2	4.5	4.2	3.8
7	13.5	12.3	9.7	8.4	7.4	6.6	6.0	5.3	4.9	4.5
8	15.2	13.0	11.0	9.6	8.6	7.5	6.7	6.1	5.6	5.1
9	17.0	14.3	12.3	10.8	9.6	8.5	7.6	7.0	6.3	5.8
10	18.5	15.8	13.6	11.8	10.7	9.4	8.5	7.8	7.1	6.5
11	20.5	17.3	15.0	13.1	11.7	10.3	9.4	8.6	7.8	7.2
12	22.5	18.8	16.2	14.3	12.8	11.3	10.3	9.3	8.6	8.0
13	24.0	20.2	17.6	15.5	13.8	12.2	11.2	10.1	9.2	8.6
14	25.8	21.8	18.8	16.6	14.8	13.2	12.0	11.0	10.0	9.2
15	27.5	23.3	20.2	17.7	15.8	14.2	12.7	11.7	10.7	10.0
16	29.0	24.8	21.4	19.0	16.8	15.1	13.7	12.6	11.6	10.7
17		26.3	22.7	20.1	17.9	16.1	14.5	13.3	12.3	11.3
18		28.0	24.4	21.2	19.0	17.0	15.3	14.2	13.0	12.1
19		29.3	25.5	22.3	20.0	18.0	16.3	15.0	13.8	12.8
20			26.8	23.5	21.0	19.0	17.2	15.8	14.5	13.5
21			28.2	24.7	22.1	20.0	18.0	16.7	15.3	14.2
22			29.3	26.0	23.1	21.0	19.0	17.3	16.1	15.0
23				27.0	24.2	22.0	20.0	18.2	16.7	15.6
24				28.2	25.2	22.9	20.7	19.0	17.5	16.2
25				29.3	26.3	23.8	21.7	19.8	18.2	17.0

Example: If meter reads 7 and temperature is 160°F, actual moisture content is 4.5%.

38-3(b). *Temperature corrections for measuring moisture content with a meter. Note that the correction is small at low moisture content. For temperatures within 20° of 70°F, the corrections can be disregarded unless highly accurate measurements are necessary.*

These moisture meters are accurate to within plus or minus one percent of the true figure.

Even if the lumber has been properly kiln-dried, there can still be moisture problems. A piece of wood will take on or give off moisture until it reaches a balance with the surrounding air. The amount of moisture in a piece of wood when it reaches a balance with the air at a certain temperature and humidity is called the *equilibrium moisture content*, or EMC. This is the moisture content at which the wood neither gains nor loses moisture from the surrounding air. However, as the humidity changes, the moisture content of the wood will change.

Air can hold only a certain amount of moisture, and this maximum amount varies as the temperature changes. *Relative humidity* expresses the percentage of this maximum which is actually being held by the air. For example, at 75

CORRECTION TABLE FOR VARIOUS SPECIES OF WOOD

Species	Moisture Detector Readings										
	7	8	9	10	12	14	16	18	20	22	24
Birch	0.9	1.0	0.8	0.7	0.7	1.0	1.0	1.3	1.4	1.6	1.6
Douglas Fir	0.0	0.0	0.0	0.0	0.0	0.0	0.0	0.0	0.0	0.0	0.0
Mahogany, African	0.7	1.4	1.6	2.0	2.8	3.2	3.6	3.8	3.8	3.8	3.8
Mahogany, Honduras	0.3	0.3	0.3	0.4	0.6	0.5	0.2	0.0	−0.5	−1.0	−1.5
Mahogany, Philippine	−1.2	−1.2	−1.5	−1.9	−2.4	−2.8	−3.3	−3.7	−4.5	−5.2	−5.8
Maple, hard	0.7	0.7	0.4	0.1	−0.2	−0.1	−0.2	0.0	0.2	0.5	1.0
Oak, red	−0.4	0.0	0.0	0.0	0.0	0.0	0.0	0.0	0.0	−0.2	0.0
Oak, white	−0.1	−0.2	−0.4	−0.5	−0.5	−0.5	−0.8	−1.1	−1.5	−1.8	−2.0
Pine, ponderosa	0.4	0.6	0.7	1.0	1.4	1.6	1.6	1.4	1.2	1.2	1.6
Pine, white	0.0	0.1	0.2	0.3	0.7	1.1	1.3	1.3	1.2	1.1	0.4
Poplar, yellow	0.1	0.6	0.7	0.7	1.2	1.6	1.6	1.6	1.7	2.0	1.7
Redwood	0.0	0.0	0.0	0.0	−0.2	−0.5	−0.8	−1.0	−1.0	−0.2	0.0
Walnut, black	0.5	0.6	0.4	0.4	0.4	0.5	0.3	0.2	0.0	−0.2	−0.4

Example: When testing birch and the moisture detector reads "10," look opposite Birch and under the Moisture Detector reading of 10, which gives 0.7 to be added to the reading, for a total of 10.7.

38-3(c). *Species corrections. Note that no correction is needed for Douglas fir.*

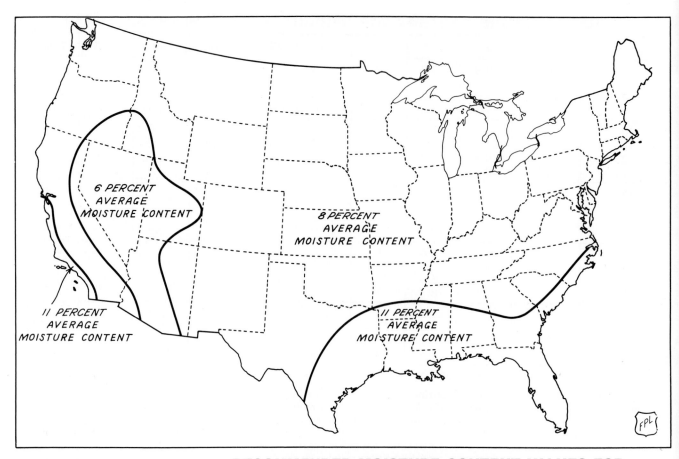

38-4. *Recommended mois-ture content averages for in-terior finishing of woodwork in various parts of the Unit-ed States. Note the differ-ence between the dry de-serts and the wet coastal areas. Of course, humidity can vary a great deal from one season of the year to another.*

RECOMMENDED MOISTURE CONTENT VALUES FOR WOODWORK AT TIME OF INSTALLATION FOR CONTINENTAL UNITED STATES*

Service Condition	Quantity—Entire Lots Are Satisfactory if Individual Pieces Are in Prescribed Range	Dry South-western States	Damp Southern Coastal States	Remainder of the United States
Interior Wood Finish	Average	6	11	7
	Range permitted in individual pieces	4-9	8-13	5-10
Exterior Trim	Average	9	12	12
	Range permitted in individual pieces	7-12	9-14	9-14

*In percentages of oven-dry weight. Modified from "Wood Handbook."

degrees Fahrenheit, air can hold five times as much moisture as it can at 32 degrees. Consider a sample of air at 32 degrees and 100 percent relative humidity. If the sample is heated to 75 degrees and the mois-ture content does not change, the relative humidity will drop to 20 percent; that is, one-fifth of 100.

The woodworker constantly faces this humidity problem. In cold weather, the outside air can hold little moisture. As the air enters the shop and is heated, its relative hu-midity becomes only a fraction of what it was outside. This is why wood in a home or shop tends to dry out excessively in the winter

months. The wood becomes checked or warped and very difficult to machine. Therefore it is desirable to increase the moisture in the air during the winter months and to re-duce it in the summer. In the win-ter, the relative humidity inside many large manufacturing plants is raised and held at the correct point by special equipment. The school or small cabinet shop can apply some limited moisture-control methods, such as a pan of water on the radiator or a small humidifier in the warm air ducts during winter. In the case of steam heat, a valve may be opened to release moisture into the air.

The following points should be considered when selecting and preparing lumber and treating finished products:

● Have the wood at a uniform and proper moisture content before it is put through woodworking machines or applied in use. If the wood is too wet, it will swell. If too dry, it will shrink. This response to changes in atmospheric humidity is more rapid when the wood is cut into smaller pieces.

● If shrinkage across the face of the article is likely to cause a serious problem, use edge-grained softwood and quartersawed hardwood.

● If the product is to be exposed to humidity, the moisture content of the lumber at the time of construction should correspond with the at-mospheric conditions in which the finished article will be placed. Fig. 38-4. Protective coatings on finished articles are helpful because they prevent great differences in moisture distribution, especially between the wood surface and the interior.

● As much as possible, protect the wood against extremes of atmospheric humidity during and after construction.

WORKING WITH HARDWOODS*

To build furniture successfully, you need to know not only how to set up and operate the machines, but also a great deal about the wood you are using. Wood, in general, is relatively easy to cut, shape, and fasten together, but it varies greatly from one species to another. The more you know about the behavior of wood when it is sawed, planed, shaped, turned, and sand-

---

*All tests described in this chapter were performed at the Forest Products Laboratory, Madison, Wisconsin.

ed, the better you will be able to work with it. Since most furniture is made of hardwoods, these will be considered.

Characteristics That Affect Machining

How hardwoods react when they are planed, shaped, turned, and sanded is very important to the furniture and cabinet builder. Unless a wood can be fairly easily machined to produce a smooth surface, it is not suitable for furniture and fixtures, even though it may have many other good characteristics. Fig. 38-5.

Many factors affect the machining properties of wood, making some species better for furniture and fine cabinetmaking than others. Some of the most important include specific gravity, rings per inch, cross grain, shrinkage, and warp. Fig. 38-6.

SPECIFIC GRAVITY

Specific gravity is a measure of the relative density of materials. It is expressed as a ratio of the weight of a substance to the weight of an

MACHINING AND RELATED PROPERTIES OF HARDWOODS

Kind of wood	Planing— perfect pieces	Shaping— good to excellent pieces	Turning— fair to excellent pieces	Boring— good to excellent pieces	Mortising— fair to excellent pieces	Sanding— good to excellent pieces	Steam bending— unbroken pieces	Nail splitting— pieces free from complete splits	Screw splitting— pieces free from complete splits
	Percent	Percent	Percent	Percent	Percent	Percent	Percent	Percent	Percent
Birch[1]	63	57	80	97	97	34	72	32	48
Cherry, black	80	80	88	100	100	. .	. .	. .	. .
Mahogany	80	68	89	100	100	. .	41	68	78
Maple, hard	54	72	82	99	95	38	57	27	52
Maple, soft	41	25	76	80	34	37	59	58	61
Oak, red	91	28	84	99	95	81	86	66	78
Oak, white[2]	87	35	85	95	99	83	91	69	74
Pecan	88	40	89	100	98	. .	78	47	69
Walnut, black	62	34	91	100	98	. .	78	50	59
Yellow poplar	70	13	81	87	63	19	58	77	67

[1]Includes yellow, sweet, and all other commercial birches except white or paper birch.
[2]Includes chestnut oak and other commercial white oaks.

38-5. *This table shows how certain hardwoods react to machining, steam bending, and fastening.*

CHARACTERISTICS OF HARDWOODS THAT AFFECT MACHINING

Kind of wood	Specific gravity average	Rings per inch average	Cross grain		Shrinkage (tangential) from moisture content reduction		Warp (per 7-inch widths)— twist
			Slope— spiral grain	Inter-locked— pieces	Green to 6 percent	12 to 6 per-cent	
		Number	Percent	Percent			Inch
Birch	0.58	21	5.5	0	7.5	2.2	—
Mahogany	0.46	—	6.2	10	3.4	1.3	—
Maple, hard	0.57	17	7.9	0	7.8	2.3	—
Maple, soft	0.45	12	6.5	0	6.1	2.1	0.246
Oak, red	0.55	10	4.4	0	9.0	2.5	0.119
Oak, white	0.56	17	5.3	0	8.8	2.4	0.113
Pecan	0.58	14	4.3	0	6.6	2.2	0.187
Walnut, black	0.51	9	5.7	0	6.7	1.7	—
Yellow poplar	0.41	12	5.2	0	6.2	1.9	0.218

38-6. *These characteristics affect the machining properties of hardwood.*

equal volume of water at 4 degrees Celsius. Different species of wood vary in their average specific gravities largely because of differences in the relative proportion of wood substance and air space. Of course, different pieces of the same kind of wood will also vary considerably in specific gravity. In general, heavier woods give a smoother finish and machine better than lighter pieces. On the other hand, heavy woods are relatively hard to work by hand, require more power, dull tools quickly, and tend to split.

Hardness can be measured numerically. When this is done, a relationship is seen between hardness and specific gravity. As specific gravity increases, hardness increases 2¼ times faster. This hardness is one reason why heavier woods are chosen for structural parts and for the exposed parts of lumber-core plywood, while lighter woods are used for the core of plywood.

RINGS PER INCH

The number of growth rings per inch of trunk radius may affect the appearance, workability, and other properties of wood. Pieces of wood that are to be used together should be similar in appearance. Sometimes this means searching through a pile of lumber for pieces that match. Diffuse-porous woods like the maples are less affected by this problem than are ring-porous woods such as oak and elm. The fastest growing species (cottonwood) has about three times as many rings per inch as the slowest (birch). When ring-porous wood is to be used for fine furniture, slow to medium growth wood should be selected because it machines better.

CROSS GRAIN

Cross grain causes many difficulties in machining. While almost all woods have some cross grain, certain species have more than others. The three kinds of cross grain are *diagonal, spiral,* and *interlocking* or *interlocked.* Diagonal grain is usually the result of sawing the board in a particular way. Spiral grain is caused when fibers run around the trunk of the tree in a spiral rather than in a vertical fashion. Interlocked grain, caused by fiber ends

that slope in opposite directions, causes perhaps the greatest amount of difficulty in machining. For example, in steam bending, woods with the highest percentage of breakage are those that have the most interlocked grain. When planing such a board, the knives must revolve against the grain in certain portions of the board, and this often causes chipping. Also, the woods in which interlocked grain is most common are the ones that twist most when drying. Twist is the most pronounced form of warp.

SHRINKAGE

As you know, wood swells or shrinks as it takes on or loses moisture. Comparative freedom from shrinking and swelling is very important in furniture construction. Before starting to construct a piece, be absolutely certain that the wood has been dried properly to the correct moisture content; that is, less than 10 percent. Remember that shrinkage averages about twice as much across a piece of wood as it does at right angles to the wood. Therefore quartersawed hardwood shrinks about half as much in width as does flat-grained.

Although changes in the dimensions of lumber cannot be avoided entirely, some woods do hold shape better than others. As a general rule, the heavier and harder species shrink more than the lighter and softer ones. Since no hardwood with more than 12 percent moisture content should ever be used, and since most furniture manufacturers use lumber at approximately 6 percent, the change in dimensions from 12 to 6 percent moisture content is most important in slecting woods. On Fig. 38-6, note that mahogany changes the least (1.3 percent) while red oak changes the most (2.5 percent).

WARP

Warp has previously been defined

as the variation from the true or plane surface. While all woods will warp to some extent, proper drying can keep this problem at a minimum. Warp includes bow, cup, crook, and twist. Cup and twist are the most serious. Cup is a curve across the width of the piece. Twist is the turning or winding of the piece so that the four corners are no longer in the same plane.

Cup is so common a problem that it should be compensated for when gluing up for wide surfaces. This is why the pieces for a tabletop or other large surface are cut into narrower boards, usually not over 4" to 6" in width. The amount of cup in any piece determines the amount of waste in planing and jointing.

Twist is an even more serious problem. Twist is often two or three times greater than cup for the same wood. However, woods that have the most twist also tend to have the most cup.

Machining Wood

SAWING

The first step in machining any wood is usually to cut out the stock. This is commonly done with a radial-arm saw or a circular saw. Most saws operate at a speed of about 3450 RPM. A crosscut or combination saw blade is a good choice for sawing to length. For ripping and resawing, a ripsaw should be used. For finish sawing and trimming, the blade should be hollow-ground or carbide-tipped. When hand-feeding lumber, feed as rapidly as the saw will cut without burning the wood or slowing down.

PLANING

Planing is done on both a planer (surfacer) and jointer. All hardwoods used in furniture construction must be surfaced on a planer and/or jointer. You must learn to judge when the machine is producing a good surface.

All machine-planed surfaces consist of a series of waves that are really knife marks made on the lumber as it is fed under or over the revolving cutterhead. These marks are at right angles to the edge of the stock. The number of knife marks per inch is determined by four things: the diameter of the cutterhead, the number of knives on the cutterhead, the speed (the number of revolutions per minute of the cutterhead), and the feed. On most medium- and small-size planers the only factor that can be controlled is the feed.

In general, the feed should be adjusted so that on dry lumber there are about 10 to 12 knife marks per inch. On extremely cross-grained or curly-grained wood, it is better to have 15 or more knife marks per inch.

Best planing results are obtained when knives are of equal diameter and sharpness. In other words, each knife must be ground correctly along its length to the same uniform diameter, so that each knife strikes the wood and does an equal amount of cutting.

Most planers are equipped with

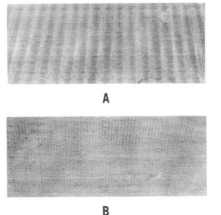

A

B

38-7. *(A) These wide marks resulted when one knife was too high. Only that one knife made a cut on each revolution. (B) After grinding, all the knives began to cut, leaving four knife marks per revolution. Note the improved quality of the surface.*

an attachment for grinding the knives without removing them from the cutterhead. This consists of a small abrasive wheel on a motor that moves along a bar across the cutterhead. Knives can be ground one by one while the cutterhead is stationary. The bevel that is ground is not a straight line but a curve that conforms to the circumference of the grinding wheel. However, even after careful grinding, all knives do not always project equally. It is therefore very important to joint the knives to make them cut equally and produce a smooth surface. Fig. 38-7. In jointing, a carrier that holds an abrasive stone is attached to the grinding and jointing bar, and the cutterhead is set in motion. The stone is lowered until it barely touches a knife edge and then moves across the length of the knife. This will produce a short joint, or *land,* on the full length of each knife. See Chapter 24 for more information on grinding and jointing planer blades.

Some common lumber defects are the result of planing or surfacing. These include:

Raised grain. A roughened surface caused when a growth ring is raised above the general surface but not torn loose. Fig. 38-8. The most

38-8. *Different degrees of raised grain on soft elm. Woods that develop the least raised grain include ash, birch, hickory, and maple.*

38-9. *Different degrees of fuzzy grain in willow.*

common causes of raised grain are dull knives, too much joint on knives, and excessive moisture content. It can also be caused by too low head speed, too high feed, or cutting too light.

Fuzzy grain consists of small particles of fibers that are not cut cleanly. Fig. 38-9. In most cases fuzzy

38-10. *Various degrees of chipped grain in hard maple. Woods such as birch, maple, and hickory tend to have more chipped grain. Jointing or surfacing with the grain tends to eliminate the problem. Also, be sure the chip breaker is working properly.*

grain is due to some unusual wood condition. It can be kept to a minimum by keeping the knives sharp and making sure that the moisture content of the wood is well below 12 percent.

Chipped grain is a surface on which small particles have broken out below the line of cut. Fig. 38-10. Chipped grain is most often the result of machining cross-grain lumber against the grain or having the feed speed too high. The most important step in preventing chipped grain is making sure there are enough knife marks—16 to 20 per inch. This is done by adjusting the cutting feed.

Chip marks are shallow dents in the wood surface caused by shavings that are not taken out by the exhaust system. Fig. 38-11. The chips drop back onto the wood surface and are crushed under the outfeed rolls. Chip marks generally can be prevented if the blower system is working properly, with not too much air leakage. Sometimes feeding too fast will cause chip marks.

Machine burns are black marks across the wood surface. They are caused when lumber sticks in the machine. This often happens when too light a cut is taken and the infeed and outfeed rolls do not keep the lumber moving. Knife marks are much more common than roller burns.

To summarize, the major factors in good planing are to make sure that the moisture content is below 12 percent, that the cutterhead is sharp, that the blades are of equal length, and that the feed is adjusted for at least 10 but preferably 16 to 20 cuts per inch. The quality of the planed surface is also affected by the depth of cut. Forest Products Laboratory conducted a series of tests in which cuts were made at four depths—$\frac{1}{32}''$, $\frac{1}{16}''$, $\frac{3}{32}''$, and $\frac{1}{8}''$. Although a heavy cut may be satisfactory for removing stock, the tests showed that the shallowest cut

38-11. *Different degrees of chip marks in yellow poplar. If you are not certain whether the defect is chip marks or chipped grain, test by placing a few drops of water on each defect and wait a few minutes. Chipped grain (which is actually broken-out particles) will not change. Chip marks (which are dents) will swell as they absorb water.*

is far better for producing a very smooth surface.

SHAPING

Shaping can be done for straight-line cuts such as in making moldings. However, it is more commonly done to form the edge of a curved or irregularly shaped part such as a tabletop. Important factors in good shaping include the kind of wood, the moisture content, the arrangement of the pores, and the specific gravity. Best results are obtained when the shaping operations are done with the grain. When cuts are made at right angles to the grain, surface roughness can result.

Another major factor that affects the quality of work is the peripheral (outside cutter) speed. Higher peripheral speeds generally produce better surfaces. This speed is determined both by the revolutions per minute of the shaper and the diameter of the cutting tool. With a shaper revolving at 3600 RPM, pe-

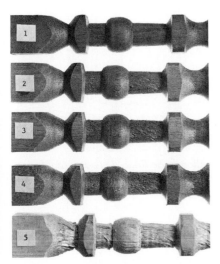

38-12. *These test samples were cut on a hand wood lathe but with a milled-to-pattern knife using the backknife principle. The method of cutting the samples is similar to that used on the lathe duplicator described in Chapter 36. The samples range in quality from No. 1, which represents perfect turning, to No. 5, which is a reject. Differences in the wood resulted in the variations in quality.*

ripheral speed will vary from as little as 470 feet per minute for a ½" router cutter to 9400 feet per minute for a 10" saw.

The best woods for shaping are cherry and the hard maples; the poorest is cottonwood.

WOODTURNING

Woodturning is important in producing tool and implement handles, certain furniture parts, toys, and sporting goods. There is a definite relationship between specific gravity and turning quality. The poorest turning woods are the lightest ones. The best turned parts are made from walnut, oak, mahogany, pecan, and cherry. Moisture content should be from 6 to 12 percent. Fig. 38-12.

BORING

Boring is done extensively in furniture construction when using dowels, spindles, and rungs or when in-

stalling screws. A smoothly cut, accurately sized hole is especially important for a good dowel joint. Fig. 38-13. Woods of higher specific gravity require more power and are more difficult to bore than the softer woods. In general, however, best results are obtained on heavy woods. The medium to heavy species produce 90 percent or more of good to excellent holes, based on smoothness of cut. The same bit, when used in different woods, can produce both oversized and undersized holes. These differences in the way woods react to boring explain why some woods split more than others when doweled.

MORTISING

The mortise-and-tenon joint is not as common as it was in the past but is still used extensively in furniture and cabinet construction. In general, specific gravity is the principal factor in high-quality mortise cutting. Heavier woods produce smoother and more uniform mortis-

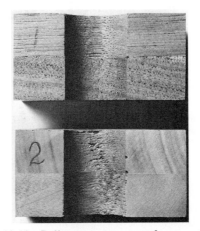

38-13. *Difference in smoothness of bored holes. The top sample shows a smooth-bored hole in pecan. The bottom sample is a rough-bored hole in willow. Holes bored in dry wood increase in size as the moisture content increases. For good dowel construction the wood and the dowel must be at the same moisture content when gluing is done. Plastic dowel pins eliminate part of the problem.*

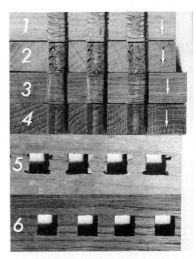

38-14. *Contrast in smoothness of cut in mortising different woods: 1, 2, and 5 are maple; 3, 4, and 6 are red oak. Nos. 1 and 3 show side-grain surfaces; 2 and 4 show end-grain surfaces. Note that the cuts in side grain or those parallel to the grain are much smoother than the cuts across grain. Soft maple is one of the poorest woods for mortising.*

es than do lighter woods. Good results are obtained in cherry, mahogany, oak, and pecan. Fig. 38-14.

SANDING

Sanding is one of the most important steps in the completion of furniture. Small scratches and other imperfections show up more after a finish is applied. Although sometimes done for surfacing and for making slight corrections in the fitting of parts, sanding is usually done to produce a smooth surface for a fine finish and to smooth the finish itself.

A series of sanding tests was conducted with wood at 6 percent moisture content, using both the drum sander and the belt sander. The grit used was garnet of 2/0 coarseness. Results were checked for fuzz-free and scratch-free surfaces. In general, the harder woods sanded better. Also, coarse-textured woods showed less scratching than fine-textured woods, and hard species fuzzed less than soft ones.

COMPATIBILITY OF GRAIN AND COLOR

In constructing objects of wood, it is highly desirable to use individual pieces that are in harmony with one another. This is true for both solid wood and plywood. Harmony of grain is determined by the position in the log from which the boards are sawed. Color compatibility depends largely on the growing conditions under which the tree developed. Since both grain and color harmony are difficult to obtain, the best method is to surface at least three times as much lumber as is needed for a particular product. This provides a good supply of boards for matching. Often the total stock of lumber can be used to make three items, each of which will have above average compatibility of grain and color.

DESIGN AND CONSTRUCTION OF CASEWORK AND FURNITURE

The term *casework* means cabinets and other built-ins normally produced in a shop and installed on a job or built on the job. The cabinet design and joinery details may differ somewhat from one region of the country to the other. Furniture design and construction details also differ somewhat from manufacturer to manufacturer. However, all types can be grouped into one of three categories of construction: exposed-face frame, flush overlay, and reveal overlay.

Exposed-Face Frame

There are two types of exposed-face frame construction: *flush* and *lipped*. Fig. 38-15. In flush case construction (often called *conventional flush*), the drawer and door faces are flush with the face frame. This design allows for different thicknesses of wood on doors and drawer fronts. The exposed-face

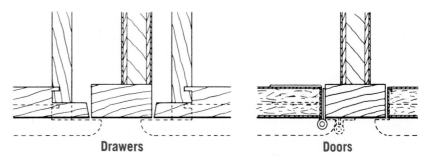

Drawers   **Doors**

38-15. *Exposed-face frame. The solid line shows the flush drawers and doors. The dashed line shows the lipped drawers and doors. For details of cabinet construction, see Chapter 51.*

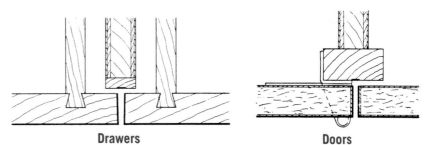

Drawers   **Doors**

38-16. *Flush overlay. Note the small space between the doors and drawers. This design can be built with or without a face frame. For further details, see Chapter 51.*

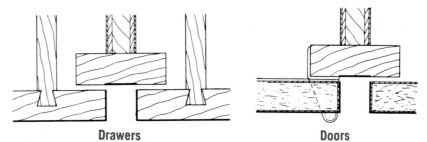
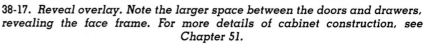

Drawers   **Doors**

38-17. *Reveal overlay. Note the larger space between the doors and drawers, revealing the face frame. For more details of cabinet construction, see Chapter 51.*

frame provides a solid surrounding for operating doors and drawers and also helps them keep in line.

However, flush case construction is more difficult because there must be very careful fitting and aligning of the doors and drawers. Otherwise, they will stick and bind in the frame. This construction is not as desirable when covering surfaces with plastic laminate. Often the edges of the doors and drawers

must be planed and/or sanded slightly during the fitting to make sure that they operate freely.

The second type of exposed-face frame, the *lipped* design, also has a face frame. However, the doors and drawers have a lip that covers part of the frame. As a result, the fitting of these drawers and doors is less critical. Most cabinets of Early American style have frames of lipped design.

Flush Overlay

The flush overlay design, Fig. 38-16, requires no face frame because the door and drawer fronts cover the cabinet edges. This type is commonly used for contemporary designs. A matched grain effect can be achieved by cutting all of the fronts of the doors and drawers from the same panel. This type of construction also is ideal for the application of plastic laminates to exposed surfaces. The design frequently eliminates the need for drawer pulls. However, heavy-duty hardware is needed. For example, the hinges must be attached to the inside of the case, not the edge.

Reveal Overlay

This is a variation of the flush overlay design. Fig. 38-17. This construction gives a raised panel effect. While this type requires a face frame, much of it is concealed by the front of the doors and drawers. Therefore, the fitting is not as critical as in the lipped design.

GETTING OUT STOCK

The first step in the actual building of a piece of furniture or a cabinet is cutting the stock to rough (stock-cutting) size. In getting out the stock, always cut the pieces of like thickness before going on to the next. When making duplicate parts, perform the same operation on all parts before starting a new step.

Regardless of whether the stock is Rgh (rough) or surfaced (S2S or S4S), first examine the end of the board to see if it is split, checked, or otherwise imperfect. If necessary, trim off a small amount to remove any imperfection and to square off the end. Now examine both surfaces of the board for any serious imperfections, such as a knot, split, check, or dry rot. With proper layout, only small areas need to be wasted, even if there is an imperfection.

Most hardwood stock is purchased rough; so first you must get the stock and square it up. The steps needed to bring it to finished size are described here. For most cabinetmaking, stock is brought to correct thickness and width by planing and jointing, and to correct length by sawing. If end grain is exposed, it may be necessary to plane the ends. Before stock is rough cut to length, it should be checked for defects.

Always surface a board *with the grain*. Planing against the grain roughens the surface. It may be difficult to see grain direction on a rough board. However, jointing will make it easier to see.

Squaring Up Stock by Machine

Preparing a face surface (side) that is *flat* in width, *flat* in length, and without wind is the first step in any squaring operation. (*Wind* —rhymes with *kind*—is a defect in which a board rests on two diagonally opposite corners when laid on a flat surface.) The face surface and the face edge must be square with each other. These are the true reference surfaces from which all accurate measurement must be taken.

Rough cut the pieces to length, allowing enough material for squaring up. This can be done on a radial-arm or circular saw. Now check each piece of stock to determine which appears to be the best side. Arrange the lumber so that the best side will appear on the outside of the product you are building. Often, the first side that is surfaced will be the poorer side, but this will always be called the *face surface*. Don't confuse the face surface (side) with the best-looking surface. Often the two will be on opposite sides. A face mark on a board means that face is the reference surface for measurements, not that

it will be on the outside of the product.

The first edge to be surfaced will be called the *face edge*. This must be the most accurate. Therefore, when laying out joints, always mark from the face surface and face edge.

The common procedure for squaring up rough stock is:

1. True up one face. Plane the face surface on the jointer to smooth the stock and remove any defects. Fig. 38-18,A.

2. True up one edge. Joint the first edge by holding the face surface against the fence of the jointer. Fig. 38-18,B. Mark the face surface and edge. Fig. 38-18,C.

3. Plane to thickness. Use a planer (surfacer) if one is available. If not, buy S2S (surfaced on two sides) lumber. Fig. 38-18,D.

4. Cut and plane to finished width. Adjust the fence of the circular saw to cut about $\frac{1}{16}''$ to $\frac{1}{8}''$ over finished width and then rip. Plane to finished width on a jointer. Fig. 38-18, E.

5. Cut and/or plane to finished length. Cut one end square on the circular saw. Lay out the correct length and cut to finished length. Remember to allow enough for joints. If the end grain must be exposed, cut one end square and surface it on the jointer. Then cut the other end $\frac{1}{16}''$ too long and surface to exact length on the jointer. Fig. 38-18, F.

Squaring Up Stock by Hand

The method of squaring stock by hand is determined by the kind of lumber and how the material will be used in the project. If rough lumber is used, a great deal more planing must be done. Most of the wood you use will be S2S. This lumber will have to be planed very little on the two surfaces. Sometimes only two surfaces and one edge need to

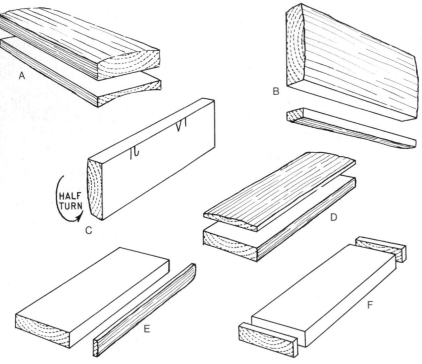

HALF TURN

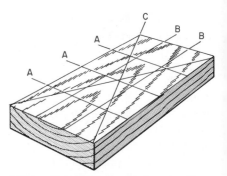

38-19. *Checking the surface for flatness: (A) Check from edge to edge. (B) Check from end to end. (C) Finally, check across the corners.*

38-18. *Steps in squaring up stock by machine.*

be planed, such as when cutting out a design. When the ends don't show —for example, in joint construction —the surfaces and edges are planed and the ends cut to length with a backsaw. However, there will be times when you must completely square up stock by hand. First rough cut the stock to length and width using a handsaw. Then check to see if the board is straight and without defects.

1. Plane the face surface true and smooth with a jointer plane. Check to see that it is flat in all directions. Fig. 38-19.

2. Plane the face edge using a jointer plane or bench plane. If the board is to be used for gluing up stock edge to edge, cut a slightly concave surface.

3. Plane the first end using a block plane.

4. Measure the correct length and mark a line across the face surface and end. Use a backsaw and cut about 1/16″ longer than the finished length. Plane the second end to correct length.

5. Plane to correct width. If the board is rather narrow, adjust the marking gauge to the correct width and mark a line along the face surface and the second surface. If the board is quite wide, mark the width at several points and then use a straightedge to draw a line showing the width. Saw to about 1/8″ of the layout line. Now plane the second edge smooth, straight, and square.

6. Plane the second face. Adjust the marking gauge to correct thickness and mark a line from the face surface along the edges and ends. Plane to correct thickness.

It is easy to remember the steps: face, edge, end; then reverse: end, edge, and face. Fig. 38-20. Some woodworkers like to square the stock in a different order. They plane the face surface, then the face edge, the first end, the second edge, the second face, and finally the second end.

38-20. *Steps in squaring up stock by hand.*

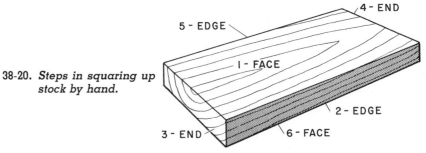

39 Cabinetmaking Joints

The skilled cabinetmaker must have a thorough knowledge of joinery. He or she must know how to select the correct kind of joint for a particular product and how to lay out, cut, fit, and assemble the joint. The construction quality of any cabinetwork or furniture largely depends on the quality of the joints.

The term *joint* is used to describe the close securing or fastening together of two or more smooth, even surfaces. Although there are over 100 kinds of joints in cabinetmaking and furniture construction, they can be grouped into several basic types. You may know other names for some of the joints in this chapter, but the terms used here are commonly accepted. The joint to select for each kind of construction depends to some extent on the need for strength, the desired appearance, and the equipment available. Simple joints can be made by hand or with basic machines. More complicated ones, like the dovetail, require special equipment.

The kind of joint to use will also depend on the materials involved. Solid wood joints rely for their strength on their interlocking features, plus glue and metal fasteners. Particle-board joints must be modified somewhat because of the lower strength of the particle board. Plywood joints, especially veneer core, also must be different from solid wood because of the ply construction. For example, nails and wood screws tend to split plywood when installed in the edges. It is often necessary to join two different materials together in one project, such as when adding a solid wood edge to particle board or plywood. In this case, the joint must be designed so that the solid wood will give protection to the particle board or plywood. Therefore when a tongue-and-groove joint is made, the tongue is made on the solid wood and the groove in the plywood or particle board. Suggestions on the best joint to used for these materials are included in Fig. 39-1.

It is generally best to choose the simplest joints that will do the job satisfactorily. Often the selection of a joint is determined by the cost factor and the amount of material involved. Instead of the mortise-and-tenon joint, many furniture and cabinet manufacturers use dowels and corner blocks to reinforce butt joints where the rails and legs of tables and chairs are joined. Using dowels with a butt joint saves time and materials and is therefore less costly. Strength tests have revealed that this simpler construction is equally as strong as the mortise and tenon.

ELEMENTS OF JOINERY

Follow these basic principles in all joinery:

- Make all measurements from a common starting point. This will eliminate the possibility of error.
- Use the *superimposing method* of laying out a joint as often as you can. In this method, one piece is placed over another to do the marking. A good example of this is laying out the width of a rabbet or dado. Fig. 39-2.
- Mark all duplicate parts at the same time. Often this can be done by clamping the pieces together and then marking across them. Whenever possible, cutting should be done in duplicate.
- Whenever a joint is made of two pieces of solid wood, make sure that there is room for the fitted part of the joint to expand. For example, if a solid shelf is fitted into a plywood case, the shelf should be slightly narrower than the side of the case so that it can shrink and swell without harming the case. Also, the shelf should be fastened with screws rather than glue so that the parts can move.
- Undercut joints wherever a close fit is not required. A good joint requires a close fit for most surfaces. For example, the cheek of a tenon must fit the sides of the mortise snugly. However, the end of a tenon can be undercut so that there is space for glue.
- As mentioned earlier, use the simplest joint that will serve the purpose. The quality of the product should dictate the kind of joinery. Design of the product also has an effect on the kind of joint to select.
- Keep the parts of the joint in correct proportion so that there will not be a weak link in the chain. There is no point, for example, in

making a mortise-and-tenon joint if the tenon is so small that it will break under a reasonable load.

● Use only quality wood, kiln dried, for all parts of the product.

● Remember, quality in cabinet-making means many things: careful work, wood selection, type of construction, and, most important, the *kind of joint.* A piece of furniture is no stronger than its weakest joint.

FASTENING AND STRENGTHENING JOINTS

Most joints are permanently fastened together with glue and sometimes screws. Quality joints are always glued under pressure. Nails and staples are rarely used for exposed surfaces in quality construction. Furniture and cabinet manufacturers do use staples and nails to fasten structural parts together. For example, they are used to fasten glue blocks, drawer guides, and other hidden parts. Exposed nails are used in on-the-job construction of cabinets and built-ins. The following are common methods of strengthening joints:

Dowels

A dowel is a pin or peg of wood, plastic, or metal that fits into two matching holes. Joints which use such pins are called *dowel joints.* Figs. 39-3 and 39-4. Dowel rod can be made from any hardwood, such as maple or birch. It comes in diameters of ⅛″ to 1″ and in lengths of 3′. It is cut to the desired length for dowel pins. Small dowel pins of wood or plastic are available with spiral grooves and pointed ends. The grooves help the glue to flow more freely and allow the air to escape from the bottom of the holes. Fig. 39-5.

It is important to keep the moisture content of wood dowels to 5 percent or less. Actually, a very dry dowel with less than 5 percent moisture is best. If the moisture

JOINTS FOR VARIOUS MATERIALS

	Solid Wood	Plywood	Particle Board
Butt Joints			
on edge	Good	Poor	Poor
flat	Good	Fair	Poor
corner butt with glue block	Excellent	Good	Fair
corner butt with dowels	Excellent	Good	Excellent
butt-frame	Good	Fair	Poor
middle-rail	Good	Good with dowel	Good with dowel
Edge Joints			
plain	Good	Poor	Poor
dowel	Excellent	Fair	Poor
spline	Good	Fair	Poor
tongue-and-groove	Excellent	Fair	Good with solid wood
rabbet	Good	Good	Poor
milled	Excellent	Poor	Poor
Rabbet Joints			
simple	Good	Good	Good with corner block
back-panel	Excellent with hard-board	Good with hardboard	Poor
Dado Joints			
simple	Good	Good	Fair
blind	Excellent	Good	Poor
corner	Excellent	Poor	Poor
rabbet-and-dado	Excellent	Fair	Fair
half-dovetail	Excellent	Poor	Poor
Lap Joints			
cross	Excellent	Poor	Poor
edge	Excellent	Poor	Poor
middle	Excellent	Poor	Poor
dovetail	Excellent	Poor	Poor
end	Excellent	Poor	Poor
Miter Joints			
simple flat	Fair	Poor	Poor
simple edge	Fair	Poor	Poor
flat with dowels	Good	Fair	Good
edge with dowels	Excellent	Good	Good
flat with spline	Excellent	Fair	Fair
edge with spline	Excellent	Fair	Good
flat with key	Excellent	Fair	Poor
polygon	Good	*	*
compound	Good	*	*
with rabbet	Excellent	Good	Good
lock	Excellent	Good	Good

* Not used.

(Continued on next page)

JOINTS FOR VARIOUS MATERIALS (Continued)

	Solid Wood	Plywood	Particle Board
Mortise-and-Tenon Joints			
simple	Excellent	*	*
haunched	Excellent	*	*
open	Good	Fair	*
stub	Excellent	Fair	Good
Dovetail Joints			
lap	Excellent	*	*
stopped-lap	Excellent	*	*
Finger Joint	Excellent	*	*
Lock Joint	Excellent	*	*

* Not used.

39-1. *Selection of joints for solid wood, plywood, and particle board.*

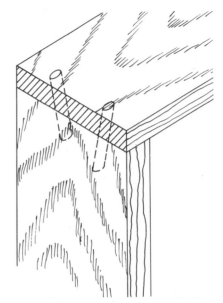

39-4. *Often dowels are installed in butt joints at an angle to increase their holding power.*

content is too high, the dowel will later dry out, reduce in diameter, and cause joint failure. When a dry dowel covered with glue is driven into a hole of correct diameter, the dowel will absorb moisture, swell in diameter, and tighten up. Always store wood dowel in a dry place, next to a heater if possible.

The diameter of the dowel should not be less than one-third nor more than one-half the thickness of the wood. The length of the dowel should be ⅛" to ¼" less than the combined depth of the two holes. Always use two or more.

Good dowel joints depend on the accuracy of hole alignment and also on whether the holes are at right angles to the face surfaces. In other words, if the holes are not correctly bored, the matching surfaces cannot be properly aligned. In cabinet shops, the holes for most dowel work are drilled or bored on a drill press or small horizontal boring machine. Usually some sort of jig or

fixture is used to hold the stock to make sure that all matching holes are aligned properly.

If only a few joints are to be made, it may be faster and easier to use a hand method. One common way is to lay out the location for the dowel holes on one part of the joint and then bore the holes using a doweling jig. Metal dowel centers are then placed in these holes. Fig. 39-6. When the two pieces are held together, the dowel centers mark the hole locations in the second

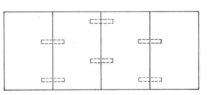

39-2. *Marking the width of the rabbet by superimposing. This insures accuracy.*

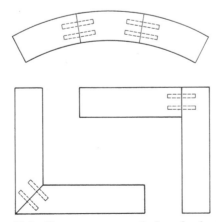

39-3. *Common uses of dowels for joint construction.*

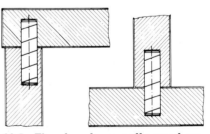

39-5. *The dowel normally used on ¾" particle board stock is the ⅜" diameter spiral groove hardwood dowel. The length of the dowel is 1¾" or less, depending on the type of joint. For greater precision, use a doweling jig when drilling the holes.*

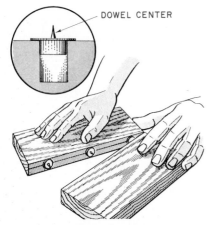

39-6. *Using dowel centers to locate the matching holes for an edge dowel joint.*

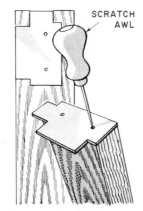

39-7. *Marking dowel locations with a metal template and scratch awl. This method is especially good when the rails are set back from the leg.*

piece. Another good method for boring matching holes for legs and rails is to use a small metal template with corners cut out. When used on both the leg and the rail, the template will insure matching holes. Fig. 39-7.

Plastic dowels are also made in right-angle shapes for strengthening miter joints. With these dowels the holes can be bored at right angles to the face surfaces instead of at right angles to the cut surfaces. Fig. 39-8.

Splines

A spline is a thin piece of wood, plywood, hardboard, or metal (clamp nail) that is inserted in a groove (kerf or slot) between two parts of a joint. Fig. 39-9. It is most common in miter joints. The groove or slot must be cut in both parts of the joint. Then the thin spline is inserted in these grooves to help hold the parts in alignment and to strengthen the joint. A good groove or slot should be about ⅛″ wide and ¼″ deep. On a flat miter, the spline is centered between the face surfaces. On an edge miter, the groove should be closer to the inside corner.

When joining solid woods, the spline should also be of solid wood, with grain direction at right angles to the edge. In other words, the grain direction of the spline should be the same as that of the joint. For plywood construction, ⅛″ three-ply birch plywood or hardboard makes a good spline. For particle board, use a ³⁄₁₆″ plywood spline.

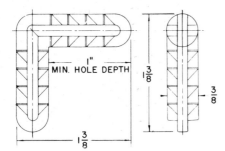

⅜ ″ DIAMETER HOLE   90° Angle

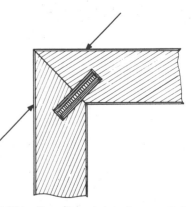

39-8. *Plastic miter dowels can be used for frame construction. The holes should be bored before cutting the miters. Glue is applied to the joint surfaces and the dowel holes.*

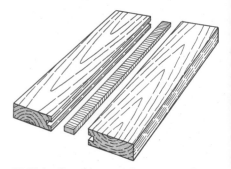

39-9(a). *A spline used to strengthen an edge joint.*

39-9(b). *A miter joint in particle board. The spline is cut from ³⁄₁₆″ 3-ply plywood. Note that the spline is located off-center to allow for greater width.*

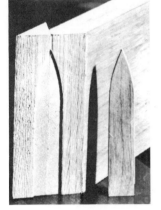

39-10. *A blind spline helps make a strong, neat miter joint.*

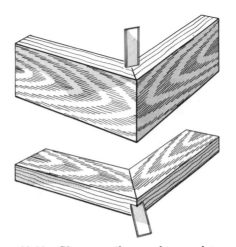

39-11. *Clamp nails can be used to join miters. On wider trim stock that exceeds 3″, nails must be driven from both ends.*

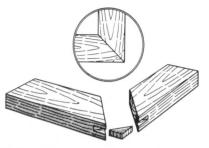

39-12. *A key is another good device for locking two parts of a joint together.*

39-13. *Glue blocks can be square or triangular. They are used to strengthen adjoining surfaces.*

The slot, kerf, or groove for the spline can be cut with a saw blade or dado head on a circular or radial-arm saw. Most splines are made the full length of the joint. Sometimes, however, a blind spline is used. Fig. 39-10. Another kind of blind spline is lemon shaped. Sometimes a wood plug is used as a spline. A hole is bored partway through the joint from the back. Then a cross-grain plug is glued in place to strengthen the miter.

Clamp nails are commonly used instead of wood splines for less expensive construction. The clamp nail is flanged slightly on both ends so that it acts as a wedge to hold the two parts firmly together. The groove or kerf for clamp nails must be cut with an extra-thin, 22-gauge circular-saw blade to a depth from 7/32″ to 3/8″, according to the width of the fastener. Clamp nails for miter corners should be set below the surface of the wood to allow for filling. Fig. 39-11.

Keys

A key is a small piece of wood inserted in a joint to hold it firmly together. Fig. 39-12. The key is sometimes called a *feather*. It is often placed across the corners of miter joints.

Glue Blocks

Glue blocks (sometimes called *rub blocks*) are small triangular or square pieces of wood used to strengthen and support two adjoining surfaces. Fig. 39-13. If you examine the inside of a quality chest or cabinet, you will find many glue blocks installed for strength.

Corner Blocks

A corner block is larger than a glue block and triangular in shape. It is used for added strength at the corners of frames or where legs and rails join. As made in the cabinet shop, it is a simple, triangular piece of wood cut to fit into the corner. It is fastened in place with glue and screws. Many furniture manufacturers install corner blocks that have dovetail-dado joints. Fig. 39-14.

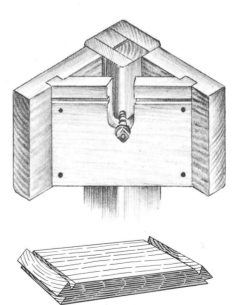

DOVETAIL CORNER BLOCK

39-14. *The dovetail corner block adds rigidity to corner construction.*

There are also many kinds of patented metal corner blocks.

KINDS OF JOINTS

The following are the more common joints used in cabinetmaking. Basically, these same joints are used in all wood construction. Specific directions for cutting them can be found in the chapters on the circular saw, radial-arm saw, etc.

Butt Joints

On the butt joint, sometimes called the *plain* joint, the square end of one piece fits against the flat surface or edge of the second piece. Without reinforcement the butt joint is very weak, since end grain is poor for joining. However,

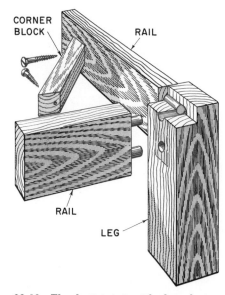

39-16. The butt joint with dowels is given added strength by means of a corner block. Glue and wood screws hold the parts permanently together.

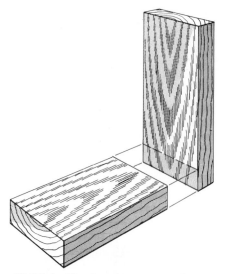

39-15(a). The butt joint on edge is used for box construction.

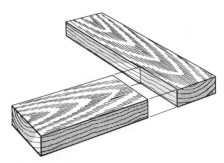

39-15(b). The butt joint flat is used for frame construction.

with dowels it becomes a high-quality joint. The simplest butt joint is one fastened *on edge* or as a flat butt joint. Fig. 39-15. The corner of the butt joint is often reinforced with a glue block, as shown in Fig. 39-13. The *butt joint strengthened with dowels* is used to join the ends of rails (aprons) to the edges of legs for leg-and-rail construction. Fig. 39-16. The *corner butt with dowels* is used for some types of case and box construction. Fig. 39-17. A *frame butt with dowels* is an end-to-edge joint that is often made for a web or skeleton frame. Fig. 39-18. The *middle-rail butt with dowels* is an end-to-face or edge-to-surface joint commonly used when installing dividers in furniture and casework. Fig. 39-19.

Edge Joints

Edge joints are used primarily to build up larger surfaces for such things as the tops of tables and desks, the core of plywood, and for interior paneling and door construction. These joints are made with the grain of the two parts running parallel, but with the growth rings facing

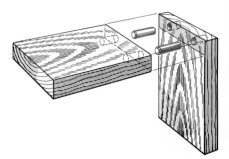

39-17. The corner butt with dowels is sometimes found in case construction.

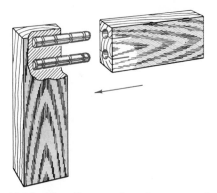

39-18. Usually two dowels are used in each corner of a frame butt joint.

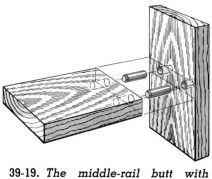

39-19. The middle-rail butt with dowels.

in opposite directions. The simplest edge joint is called the *butt* or *plain edge.* Fig. 39-20. It is cut with a carbide-tipped blade on a circular or radial-arm saw. The edges don't require surfacing. If the blade is a standard one, it is a good idea to surface the edges on the jointer. When the edges are carefully cut or surfaced and glued under pressure, the joint will be as strong as the wood itself.

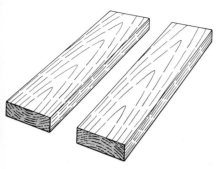

39-20. *Plain or butt edge.*

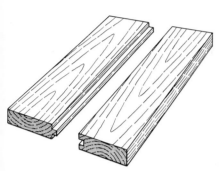

39-21. *Tongue-and-groove joint.*

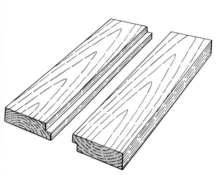

39-22. *Rabbet edge.*

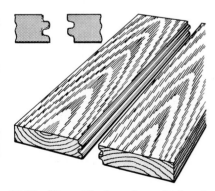

39-23. *The milled or shaped edge is sometimes called a glue joint. Its major advantage over the plain edge is ease of assembly.*

A *dowel edge* strengthens the adjoining edges. It is important to locate and drill matching holes accurately. The outside ones should be about 3" or 4" from the edges and the rest should be about 1" to 18" apart. This is best done on a drill press or a horizontal boring machine.

The *spline edge* is another joint for adding strength. With a dado or molding head, a groove with a width of ⅛", ³⁄₁₆", or ¼" is cut along each of the adjoining edges. Then a spline of solid wood, plywood, or hardboard is fitted into the grooves. Note that if solid wood is used, the grain should run at right angles to the length. Fig. 39-9(a).

The *tongue and groove* is used for paneling, flooring, and other interior construction. Fig. 39-21. This is usually mill-produced and purchased as a stock mill item. Usually a small V is formed at the exposed surface for better appearance. The tongue and groove can be cut with matching sets of cutters or blades using the dado head or molding head of a circular or radial-arm saw or on a shaper.

The *rabbet edge* is made by cutting two rabbets, one on each edge, but from the opposite surfaces. Fig. 39-22. This is best done with a dado head on a circular or radial-arm saw.

The *milled* or *shaped edge* is used in cabinet shops primarily to speed assembly and to add surface for gluing. Fig. 39-23. It doesn't greatly increase the strength of the joint. It is best cut with a molding head on a saw or with a cutter on a shaper or router.

Rabbet Joints

The rabbet joint is found in simple box-and-case construction. A rabbet is an L-shaped groove cut across the edge or end of one piece. The joint is made by fitting the other piece into it. Fig. 39-24. Width of the rabbet should equal

the thickness of the material, and its depth should be one-half to two-thirds the thickness. Fig. 39-25. The rabbet joint conceals one end grain and also reduces the twisting tendency of a joint.

The backs of most cases, cabinets, bookcases, and chests are joined with the end grain facing the back. For this joint, called a *back-panel rabbet joint,* the rabbet is cut to a depth equal to the thickness of the back panel. Fig. 39-26. However, for casework that is to be hung on a wall, the rabbet is cut to a depth from ½" to 1" so that there will be material to trim off to fit the back of the cabinet against the wall.

There are many simple ways of cutting a rabbet joint on circular and radial-arm saws, jointers, shapers, and routers. Perhaps the easiest method is on a circular or radial-arm saw, either by making two cuts or

39-24. *A rabbet joint.*

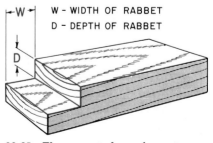

W – WIDTH OF RABBET
D – DEPTH OF RABBET

39-25. *The correct shape for a strong rabbet joint.*

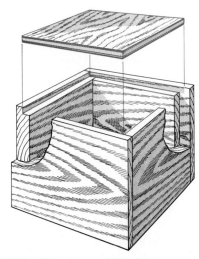

39-26. *A back panel fitted into a case or box with a rabbet joint.*

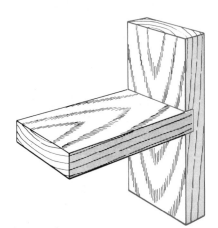

39-27. *A dado joint is used when cross pieces or frames must support weight and give stability to the case.*

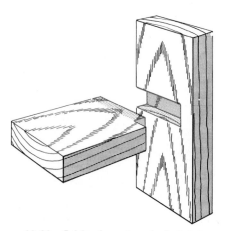

39-28. *A blind or stop dado joint.*

by cutting the rabbet in one pass with a dado head. The rabbet joint is usually fastened with glue and nails or screws.

Dado Joints

Dado joints are found in cabinets, bookcases, chests, or wherever a joint is needed to provide a supporting ledge. The dado is a groove cut across grain. In the *simple dado joint*, the butt end of the second piece fits into this groove. Fig. 39-27. The major objection to the simple dado is that, unless a faceplate trim is added to the front of the case, it has an unattractive appearance.

For better appearance, a *stop* or *blind dado* is used. Fig. 39-28. In this joint, a dado is cut partway across the first piece. Then a corner is notched out of the second piece so that the two pieces fit together. However, when this joint is cut with a dado head, a rounded surface forms at the end of the cut. This must either be cleaned out with a hand chisel, or the notch must be cut to fit into the full depth of the dado.

In the *corner dado joint* a rectangular groove is cut across the edge of one member, and a corner is cut off the second member to fit into the groove. Fig. 39-29. A dowel may be added. This joint is sometimes used for a lower shelf on a table.

The *rabbet and dado,* sometimes called the *dado and tenon* or *dado box corner*, is a combination of a dado on one piece and a rabbet on the other. Fig. 39-30. The rabbet cut forms a tenon that fits into the dado. It is used as a back corner joint in good drawer construction since it holds the two pieces square. The joint is cut with a dado head on a saw.

The *half-dovetail dado joint* is an excellent locking joint that will carry a great deal of weight. Fig. 39-31.

The *full-dovetail dado joint*, sometimes called a *housed dovetail*

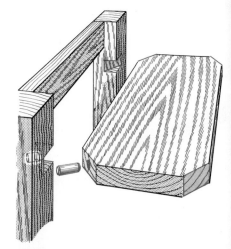

39-29. *The corner dado joint. Note that a dowel can be installed for better support.*

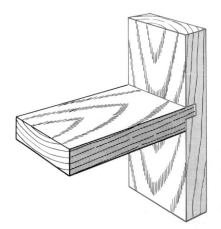

39-30. *The rabbet-and-dado joint gives added strength and rigidity.*

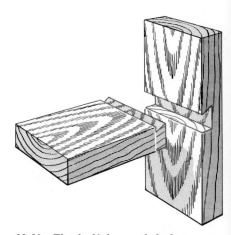

39-31. *The half-dovetail dado is not hard to cut and makes a good lock joint.*

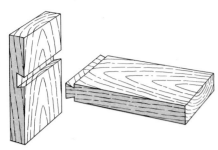

39-32. *The dovetail-dado is used as a shelf, frame, or drawer joint.*

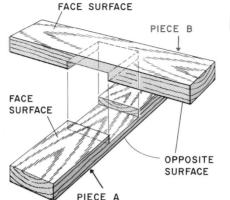

39-33. *Cross-lap joint.*

39-35. *Middle or T lap.*

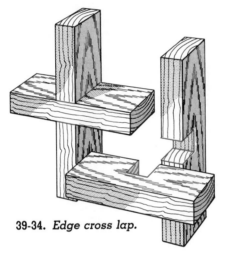

39-34. *Edge cross lap.*

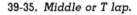

39-36. *Dovetail lap.*

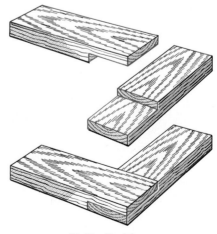

39-37. *End lap.*

or *through dovetail*, is excellent for any type of construction in which a lock joint is required. Fig. 39-32. All dovetail-dado joints can be cut with the router or on a circular or radial-arm saw.

Lap Joints

This is a large group of joints in which one member laps over the other. The *cross lap* joins two pieces with flush faces. Fig. 39-33. The pieces may cross at any angle. The joint is made by cutting dadoes of equal width and depth on the two pieces so that the face surfaces are flush when assembled.

The *edge cross lap* is very similar to the cross lap and is commonly used in making egg-crate or grid designs. Fig. 39-34.

In the *middle lap* or *T lap*, the end of one member joins the middle of the other. Fig. 39-35. In this joint a dado is cut on one piece and a rabbet on the other.

The *dovetail lap* is similar to the middle lap except that it is a lock-type joint. Fig. 39-36.

The *end lap* is made by cutting a rabbet at the ends of both pieces, which usually join at right angles. Fig. 39-37. This joint is used in constructing simple frames. Most lap joints are cut with a dado head on a circular or radial-arm saw.

Miter Joints

A miter joint is an angle joint that hides the end grain of both pieces. Miter joints are commonly used for

frame and case construction and are usually cut to form right-angle joints. The joint is relatively weak unless strengthened with a spline, key, feather, or dowel.

A simple miter can be *flat* or *on edge*. Fig. 39-38. Both types can be strengthened as mentioned above. Usually two or more dowels are placed at each corner.

If a spline is used, it can run either the full length of the groove or only partway across it. The latter is called a *blind-spline* (splined) *miter*. The spline on an edge miter should be placed closer to the inner corner for strength.

Polygon miters are those cut at angles of more or less than 45 degrees to form three- to ten-sided ob-

329

39-38(a). *A flat miter can be held together with nails, corrugated fasteners, or screws.*

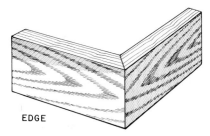

39-38(b). *Edge miter.*

jects. Fig. 39-39. The correct setting for cutting the angles is shown in Fig. 39-40.

The *compound miter* or *hopper joint* is used to make shadow-box picture frames, tapered containers, and similar work. Fig. 39-41. The cut is a combination miter-and-bevel cut. Fig. 39-42.

The *miter-with-rabbet joint* (sometimes called the *offset miter*) combines the best features of both the rabbet and miter joints. It is especially good for plywood casework and corner joints for paneling since

39-40. *These are the gauge settings for common polygons.*

it helps to hold the corner square and also provides plenty of gluing surface. Fig. 39-43. The layout for this joint is shown in Fig. 39-44. Cut the joint on a radial-arm or circular saw or on a shaper.

The *lock miter* is excellent because it combines the appearance of a miter corner with the strength of a dado. Fig. 39-45. The best method of cutting this joint is with a matching pair of lock-miter cutters on a shaper or router.

ANGLES FOR COMMON POLYGONS

Three Sides	=	30.0 Degrees
Five Sides	=	54.0 Degrees
Six Sides	=	60.0 Degrees
Seven Sides	=	64.3 Degrees (Approx.)
Eight Sides	=	67.5 Degrees
Nine Sides	=	70.0 Degrees
Ten Sides	=	72.0 Degrees

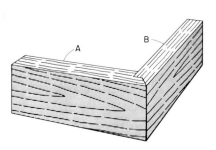

39-43. *Miter-with-rabbet joint, also called offset miter.*

39-41. *A tapered box formed by making compound miter cuts.*

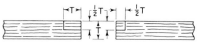

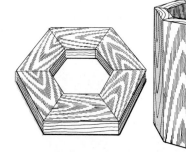

39-39. *Polygon miters. To find the correct gauge setting in degrees, divide 180 by the number of sides and then subtract this amount from 90 degrees.*

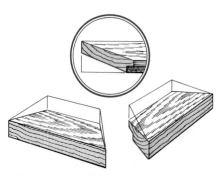

39-42. *Compound miter or hopper joint. See Figs. 26-34 and 27-25(b) for correct saw settings.*

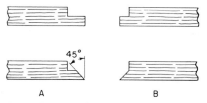

39-44. *Layout for cutting a miter-with-rabbet joint. There are several methods for making the cuts. For example, you could do all the angle cuts first and then the rabbet cuts. Always make the angle cuts with the face side down.*

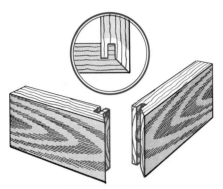

39-45. *Lock miter.*

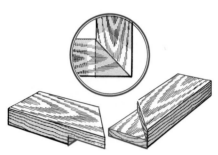

39-46. *Miter with end lap.*

The *miter-with-end-lap joint* combines the strength of a lap joint with the neat appearance of a miter joint. Note that the end grain shows only from one side of the frame. This joint is used in frame construction for cabinet doors. Fig. 39-46.

V-Grooving

V-grooving, sometimes called miter folding or V-folding, is another type of joint construction in common use to produce parts for furniture, cabinets, and other wood products. For most V-grooving, particle board is used as the core with vinyl (a flexible material) for the covering. The simplest method of V-grooving is to cut a 90-degree angle to produce two 45-degree miters on the board without cutting through the vinyl cover. Using the vinyl as a hinge, the material is folded and glued to make a 90-degree joint. Rigid laminates such as wood veneers or decorative plastic laminate can also be V-grooved and folded. However, with these materials, a plastic tape such as Mylar is applied to the face of the laminate along the line the groove will follow. This tape forms the hinge for the folding operation. The grooving cuts must go all the way through the laminate to the tape itself. V-grooving can be done with a router, shaper, or a V-grooving machine. Fig. 39-47.

Mortise-and-Tenon Joints

Many kinds of mortise-and-tenon joints are used in frame, leg-and-rail, and other types of construction. The mortise is cut first because it is easier to make the tenon fit the mortise than vice versa. In making this joint, it is necessary to decide whether the mortise will have square or rounded corners. For square corners the cut is made on a mortiser or mortising attachment. Rounded corners are cut on a router. The mortise should be at least 5/16" from the outside face and at least 1/8" deeper than the tenon for clearance. The tenon should be about one-half the thickness of the stock. If a router-cut mortise is used, then the tenon must be rounded on the edges to fit or it must be cut narrow enough to fit into the straight part of the mortise. Fig. 39-48. The tenon is cut on a saw, shaper, or tenoner.

In the *blind mortise-and-tenon joint*, the mortise does not extend all the way through the stock. This joint is often used in leg-and-rail construction. The mortises are cut in the legs, and the tenons are cut on the rails. A simple base for a table requires eight mortise-and-tenon joints.

The *barefaced mortise-and-tenon joint* is similar to the blind except

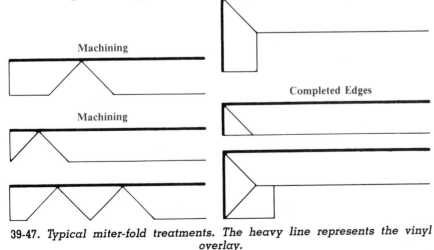

39-47. *Typical miter-fold treatments. The heavy line represents the vinyl overlay.*

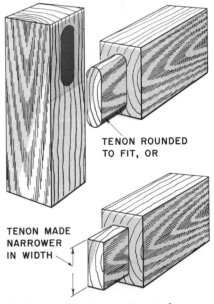

39-48. *A blind mortise-and-tenon joint in which the mortise has been cut on a router. The router is a simpler machine for mortise cutting.*

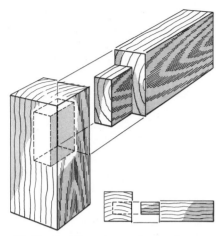

39-49. *Barefaced mortise-and-tenon joint.*

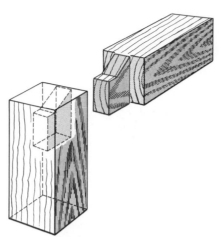

39-51. *Concealed haunched mortise-and-tenon joint.*

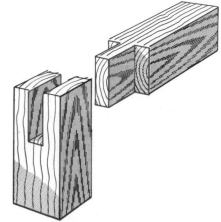

39-52. *An open mortise-and-tenon.*

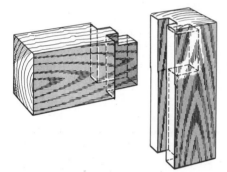

39-50. *Haunched mortise-and-tenon joint.*

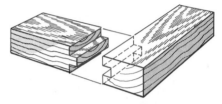

39-53(a). *A stub mortise-and-tenon joint.*

posed tenon end is not objectionable. Fig. 39-52. The advantage of this joint is that both mortise and tenon can be cut with a dado head on the circular or radial-arm saw.

The *stub mortise-and-tenon joint* is sometimes used in frame construction and is made with a short tenon that fits into the groove of the frame. Fig. 39-53.

The *keyed mortise-and-tenon joint* is often used on Early American furniture. Fig. 39-54.

Dovetail Joints

The dovetail joint is found in the finest grades of drawer construction and decorative boxes. Most common are the *lap* or *multiple dovetail* and the *stopped-lap dovetail*. Figs. 39-55 and 39-56. This is a

that the tenon has only one cheek. This joint is used with leg-and-rail construction where the surfaces must be flush. Fig. 39-49.

The *haunched mortise-and-tenon joint* is used in frame construction for added strength. Fig. 39-50. The tenon is made the same thickness as the groove, or plow, in the frame. The mortise is cut deeper than the depth of the groove. The haunch is then cut out from the tenon.

The *concealed haunched mortise-and-tenon joint* is quite similar to the haunched joint except that the groove for the haunch is cut at an angle and the tenon is cut to match. Fig. 39-51.

The *open mortise-and-tenon joint* is most commonly used in simple frame construction where an ex-

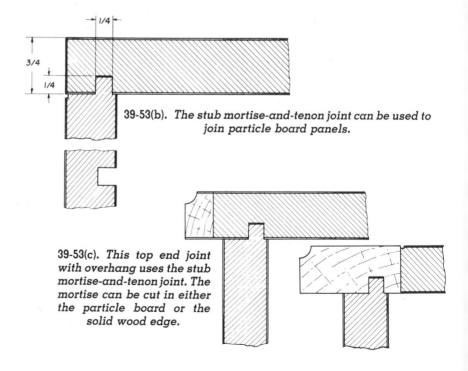

39-53(b). *The stub mortise-and-tenon joint can be used to join particle board panels.*

39-53(c). *This top end joint with overhang uses the stub mortise-and-tenon joint. The mortise can be cut in either the particle board or the solid wood edge.*

39-54. *The stretcher of this table is locked to the uprights by using a key in the tenon.*

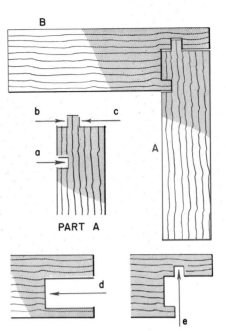

PART A

PART B

39-58. *Lock joint. Follow the lettering to do the cutting.*

difficult joint to make unless the proper equipment is available. In small cabinet and school shops, the joint can be cut with a dovetail attachment on a portable router or with a fixture on the radial-arm saw. In large shops and factories, a dovetailer machine is used which is designed for production work.

Other Joints

The *box* or *finger joint* is a simplified form of dovetail joint. It is made by cutting matching notches and fingers in the two pieces to be joined. Fig. 39-57. This joint can easily be cut on the circular or radial-arm saw without special equipment. It is found in many Scandinavian designs.

The *lock joint* is found in drawer and box construction. This extremely solid joint can be made on the circular or radial-arm saw with a dado head. The correct cutting method is shown in Fig. 39-58. There must be a slight clearance between the parts so that the two pieces can slide together.

The *coped joint* is often used in place of the miter joint for trim work. To make this joint, cut the first piece to exact length and install in place. Then cut a 45-degree angle on the second piece so that the contour of the molding will show on the front edge of the miter cut. Using a coping saw or jigsaw, cut along the profile and remove this piece. It is a good idea to back-cut

this profile so that it fits tightly at the front. The second piece should then fit snugly over the contour of the first piece. Fig. 39-59.

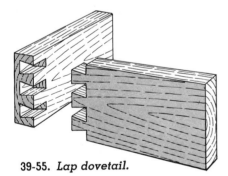

39-55. *Lap dovetail.*

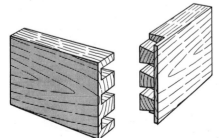

39-56. *Stopped-lap dovetail.*

39-57. *The finger or box joint is easy to make and strong.*

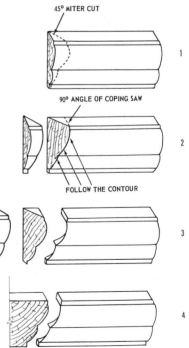

39-59. *Steps in cutting a coped joint.*

333

40 Gluing and Clamping

Gluing and clamping are important cabinetmaking processes at several stages of construction. In the early stages it is necessary to glue up stock to form wide surfaces or large areas for legs, rails, or posts. Later, subassemblies must be glued together. Final assembly of a piece of furniture or cabinetwork again calls for gluing.

There are also many special gluing operations involved in wood lamination, veneering, and installing plastic laminates. Particle board and plywood are good examples of how wood and adhesives can be combined to produce materials that are, in many respects, superior to wood alone. Since there are a great many kinds of adhesives, it is important to know how to select and use the right one for each particular job.

SELECTING ADHESIVES

An *adhesive* is a substance capable of holding other materials together by surface attraction. Glues, cements, pastes, and mucilage are common forms. The use of all adhesives is sometimes loosely called "gluing." The kind of adhesive to select for a particular job depends on many factors.

Nature of Wood

Wood, you recall, is porous, and each kind of wood has different properties. For these reasons, wood is not easy to glue. Further differ-ences arise from the way the pieces are to be fastened together. Gluing edge to edge is simplest. Gluing face to face is more difficult, and gluing end grain is particularly complicated because the many cut-off ends of hollow fibers absorb so much adhesive. Even when end grain is glued to the edge or face of wood, extra adhesive is needed because of this absorption. Fig. 40-1.

Moisture Content of Wood

The amount of moisture in wood affects both the rate at which glue dries and the strength of the finished joint. If wood has too much moisture before it is glued, a weak

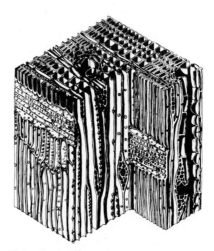

40-1. *An enlarged view of a tiny piece of wood, showing the tubular structure. Can you see why it is more difficult to glue end grain than edge or face grain?*

joint results. If wood takes on too much moisture during gluing, it first swells and then shrinks. This can set up stresses along the glue line which could result in failure of either the wood or the glue.

Fit of Joints

A joint that fits well is important for most gluing. Some adhesives have better gap-filling properties than others. Therefore, if the joint is not accurately made, an adhesive with good gap-filling properties should be selected.

Assembling and Curing

Several factors affect the assembly of parts and the curing. Some adhesives must be mixed just before assembly. Others come ready mixed. Some must be heated and then spread while hot. Others will spoil if not used rapidly. Still others remain usable for long periods. The amount of pressure needed to hold parts together after gluing varies. Some adhesives, such as contact cement, require no clamping, while others require good clamping. Temperature at which gluing is done is also a factor. Many glues must be applied at 70 degrees Fahrenheit or above. The rate at which glues dry also varies greatly. Certain synthetic glues can be dried instantly using high-frequency gluing equipment. Still another factor is the quality of the machined surfaces to be glued. A smooth, unsanded surface is usually required. The use of carbide-tipped blades will eliminate the need for jointing wood before bonding.

Glues should be applied in a clean, dust-free area. Apply just enough adhesive to hold and no more.

KINDS OF ADHESIVES

Only a few of the great variety of adhesives available will be described here. These can all be purchased under trade names that are widely advertised. The description on the label indicates the kind of glue and the procedure for mixing and applying it. Follow the label directions carefully. This is especially true for such adhesives as contact cement, of which there are a great many kinds, each involving different chemical formulas. Figs. 40-2 and 40-3.

Animal Glue

Animal (hide) glue, made from hooves, bones, and hides of animals, is one of the oldest glues of the cabinetmaker. In liquid form it is excellent for all types of interior furniture. It also comes in a flake form which requires careful mixing and heating and is therefore not commonly used except in certain kinds of fine furniture manufacturing. Animal or hide glue is one of the best gap-filling adhesives and is a good choice when joints are not perfect. This glue gives best results with wood that has a moisture content from 4 to 6 percent.

Casein Glue

Casein glue is made from milk curd and is purchased in powder form. It must be mixed with cold water to the consistency of heavy cream. It is extremely important that the glue be neither lumpy nor too thin. Though not 100 percent waterproof like resin glues, casein glue will withstand considerable moisture. This glue will bond at any temperature above freezing, but the

warmer the better. This is a great advantage when gluing out-of-doors in cool weather. This glue has fair gap-filling properties and is best when moisture content of the wood is from 5 to 15 percent.

There are two difficulties in using casein glue. It has an abrasive effect on cutting tools and therefore must sometimes be avoided. Also, it stains some woods, making it necessary to bleach the area around the glue joint before finishing.

Polyvinyl or White Liquid Glue

This is one of the handiest and most common glues for simple cabinetwork. It is available in almost any hardware or supply store in the familiar plastic squeeze bottle. This glue is always ready for use, nonstaining, economical, and odorless. It gives a colorless glue line and cures rapidly at room temperature. It does not cure by chemical action, as some glues do, but sets by losing water to the wood and air. This glue is moderate in cost and has good strength and gap-filling properties. Its disadvantages are that it has relatively poor resistance to moisture and tends to soften at high temperature.

Aliphatic Resin Glue

This cream-colored, ready-mixed glue has an extremely high-strength bond. As a matter of fact, it produces a joint that is stronger than the wood itself. It also has high resistance to heat and solvents and is easy to sand. The major weakness of this glue is that it lacks moisture resistance and therefore is satisfactory only for interior work.

Resorcinol Resin Glue

This bonding material is thermosetting (sets with heat) and is made by mixing liquid resin with a powder catalyst. It comes in a can divided into two compartments and must be

mixed as needed. This glue is excellent for exterior use because it is completely waterproof. The major disadvantage is that it creates a dark glue line.

Contact Cement

Contact cement is a ready-mixed rubber or butane material available in liquid form. It can be used for applying plastic laminates or veneers to wood or plywood. This cement requires no pressure or clamps. A disadvantage is its relatively low resistance to heat, cold, and solvents. Many commercial types of contact cement are available. When using one, it is important to follow the manufacturer's directions.

Urea Formaldehyde Resin

Urea formaldehyde resin has been found the best adhesive to use with electronic gluing equipment. This glue is a thermosetting resin of synthetic origin. Since so many combinations of the adhesive are possible, a glue manufacturer should be contacted to determine the exact content for any application other than those given on the container.

Other Adhesives

Elastomeric construction adhesives are used in building construction to bond plywood to floor joists and wall paneling to studs. They are applied with a caulking gun. They add strength, stiffness, and resiliency to the structure, and they reduce the number of nails required. The adhesive has good gap-filling properties.

The *thermoplastic synthetic resin adhesives*, also known as hot-melts, are used to edge-band panels with lumber, veneer, or plastic laminates. A special gun is used to melt and apply the glue. The adhesives are based upon various plastics.

Generally, the same adhesives that are suitable for wood-to-wood

COMMON ADHESIVES

CHARACTERISTICS

Kind	Animal (Liquid Hide) Glue	Powdered Casein	Polyvinyl "White" Liquid Resin Glue	Aliphatic Resin (Yellow Glue)	Resorcinol	Contact Cement	Urea Formaldehyde Resin or Plastic Resin
Especially good for:	First choice for furniture work and wherever a tough, lasting wood-to-wood bond is needed. A favorite for cabinetwork and general wood gluing.	Will do most woodworking jobs and is especially desirable with oily woods: teak, lemon, yew.	A fine all-around household glue for furniture making and repair. Primarily a wood glue. Makes joints stronger than the wood itself. Excellent for hardboard and particle board.	Good for furniture and case goods assembly. Also, edge and face gluing. Same as polyvinyl but with better results.	This is the glue for any work that may be exposed to soaking: outdoor furniture, boats, wooden sinks.	For bonding veneer, plastic laminates, leather, plastic, or canvas to wood.	Edge gluing with high-frequency and steam-heated pressing. Interior and limited exterior use.
Disadvantages:	Because it is not waterproof, do not use it for outdoor furniture or for boat building.	Not moisture resistant enough for outdoor furniture. Will stain acid woods such as redwood. Must be mixed for each use.	Not sufficiently moisture-resistant for exposure to weather. Softens under heat and solvents.	Lacks moisture resistance. Tends toward separation of glue and thinner during storage.	Not good for work that must be done at temperatures below 70°F. Because of dark color and mixing, not often used unless waterproof quality is needed.	Parts can't be shifted once contact is made. Dangerous without proper ventilation.	Poor gap-filling properties. Limited pot life. Requires careful mixing and handling. Moisture content of wood must be from 7 to 10 percent.
Advantages:	Very strong because it is rawhide-tough and does not become brittle. It is easy to use, light in color, resists heat and mold. It has good filling qualities, so gives strength even in poorly fitted joints.	Strong, fairly water-resistant, works in cool locations, fills poor joints well.	Always ready to use. Nonstaining, clean and white. Fast-set qualities recommend it for work where good clamping is not possible. Suitable for edge or face gluing, mortising, doweling, and veneering.	Compared to polyvinyl, it resists heat better, sands better, spreads easier, and is less affected by lacquers. Not easily rubbed off.	Very strong, as well as waterproof. It works better with poor joints than many glues do.	Adheres immediately on contact. No clamping. Test for dryness by pressing wrapping paper to surface. If paper doesn't stick, surfaces are dry and ready for bonding.	Highly moisture resistant. Ideal for high-frequency bonding. Dries white or nearly colorless.
Source:	From animal hides and bones.	From milk curd.	From chemicals.	From chemicals.	From chemicals.	Synthetic rubber (neoprene, nitrile, or polysulfide).	From chemicals. A thermosetting resin.

Kind	Animal (Liquid Hide) Glue	Powdered Casein	Polyvinyl "White" Liquid Resin Glue	Aliphatic Resin (Yellow Glue)	Resorcinol	Contact Cement	Urea Formaldehyde Resin or Plastic Resin
			USE				
Room Temperature	Sets best above 70°F. Can be used in colder room if glue is warmer.	Any temperature above freezing. But the warmer the better.	Any temperature above 60°F. But the warmer the better.	Any temperature above 45°F.	Must be 70°F or warmer. Will set faster at 90°F.	70°F or warmer.	70°F or warmer.
Preparation	Ready to use.	Stir together equal parts by volume glue and water. Wait 10 minutes and stir again.	Ready to use.	Stir before using. Ready for use.	Mix 3 parts powder to 4 parts liquid catalyst.	Ready to use.	Resin and catalyst must be carefully mixed.
Application	Apply thin coat on both surfaces; let get tacky before joining.	Apply thin coat to both surfaces. Use within 8 hours after mixing.	Spread on and clamp at once.	Spread on and clamp.	Apply thin coat on both surfaces. Use within 8 hours after mixing.	Brush on liberal coat. Dry for 30 minutes. Apply second coat.	Apply with roller.
70°F Clamping Time	Hardwood: 2 hrs. Softwood: 3 hrs.	2 hrs. 3 hrs.	1 hr. 1½ hrs.	1 hr. 1½ hrs.	16 hrs. 16 hrs.	No clamping. Bonds instantly.	A few seconds with high-frequency heat.

40-2. *This table lists the characteristics and uses of common adhesives.*

gluing may also be used for gluing wood-base materials such as particle board or hardboard. The materials may be glued to themselves or to wood.

CLAMPING DEVICES

The following are the more common clamping devices. In the furniture industry many mechanical, hydraulic, and air-operated clamping devices are used in addition to these.

Hand Screws

Hand screws, or wooden parallel clamps, are the best holding devices for wood, plastic, and many other materials. They can be used on finished surfaces without any protective wood strips or cauls. They are made in sizes from 5/0, which has a jaw length of 4″ and a maximum opening between jaws of 2″, to size 7, with a length of 24″ and a maximum opening between jaws of 17″. When using a hand screw, the center spindle is held in the left hand and the end spindle in the right hand. Then the hand screw can be opened or closed by twisting the handles in opposite directions.

Rough adjustment of the hand screw is done rapidly by swinging it. Hold the handles firmly with your arms extended. By moving your wrists only, the jaws can be revolved around the spindle. Fig. 40-4. When the jaws are open about the right amount, place the end spindle in the upper position with the middle spindle as close to the stock as possible. Adjust the spindles so that the jaws will be parallel when the hand screw grips the stock. Turn the end spindle clockwise to close the ends of the jaws on the work. Apply final pressure by turning the end spindle only, using the middle spindle as a fulcrum.

Hand screws can be used not only when gluing stock face to face but also for many other clamping jobs, such as furniture repair.

337

FACTORS TO CONSIDER IN CHOOSING ADHESIVES

Questions	Animal Hide Glue	Casein	Liquid Polyvinyl	Yellow Glue	Resorcinol	Contact Cements	Urea Formaldehyde Resin
Base material	Hides, hoofs, horns	Casein (milk)	Polyvinyl acetate	Aliphatic resins	Resorcinol resin	Neoprene	Urea formaldehyde
Moisture resistance (cold water)	Low	Very high	Medium	Medium	Waterproof	Very high	Excellent
Heat resistance	Good	Good	Adequate	Good	Unaffected	Fair	Unaffected
Solvent resistance	Unaffected	Unaffected	Fair	Good	Unaffected	Poor	Unaffected
Clamp time	30 min.	3 to 6 hrs.	30 min.	30 min.	Several hours	No Clamping	2 to 8 hrs.
Pressure required	Low	Low	Low	Low	Heavy	Momentary	150 lbs. per sq. in.
Maximum assembly time	1½ min.	15 to 20 min.	5 min. open, 10 min. closed	5 min. open, 10 min. closed	10 to 15 min.	1–2 hrs.	15 to 20 min.
Room temperature	Lumber must be warm	33°F or higher	60°– 110°F	60°– 110°F	70°F or higher	60°F or higher	70°F or higher
Thermal setting?	No	No	No	No	Yes	No	Yes
Abrasive to cutting tools?	No	Mild	No	No	Yes	No	Yes
Does it stain?	No	Mild	No	No	Yes	No	No
Self-bonding?*	Yes	Yes	Yes	Yes	No	Yes	No
Suitable for edge gluing?	Yes	Yes	Yes	Yes	Yes	No	Yes
Suitable for joint gluing?	Yes	Yes	Yes	Yes	Fair	No	Fair
Bench life?	Daily mix	8 to 10 hrs.	Indefinite	Indefinite	1 to 2 hrs.	Indefinite	3 to 4 hrs.
Shelf storage life?	1 yr.	1 yr.	6 mo. plus at 60°–90°F	6 mo. plus at 60°–90°F	1 yr.	6 mo. plus at 60°–90°F	1 yr.
Bond imperfect joint?	Yes	Yes	Yes	Yes	No	No	No
Recommended for face veneering?	No	No	No	No	No	Yes	Yes
Gluing plastics to plywood?	No	Yes	Yes	Yes	No	Yes	Press work only
Mixing time	30–45 min.	20 min.	None	None	One min.	None	One min.

*Self-bonding definition: satisfactory joints possible without clamp pressure. Except for contact cements, however, all glue joints will be better if clamped for clamp times shown.

40-3. *When selecting an adhesive, consider the characteristics of the adhesive and how it will be used.*

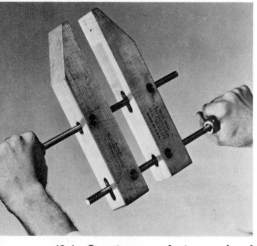

40-4. *Opening or closing a hand screw.*

Metal Bar Clamps

Bar clamps or cabinet clamps of steel or aluminum are used primarily for edge-to-edge gluing, for clamping up large surfaces, and for assembling furniture. Common lengths are from 2′ to 10′. One end is adjusted by a friction clutch or catch while the other end has a screw for applying pressure. Fig. 40-5. When using bar clamps, the screw should be turned out completely. The friction clutch or catch is moved until the clamp is slightly wider than the total width of the stock to be clamped. Fig. 40-6. The clamp is then tightened by turning the screw. When using bar clamps on finished stock, as in assembling furniture, the surface of the wood must be protected. Place clamp pads or pieces of scrap stock between the jaws and the wood.

Wood Bar Cabinet Clamps

These are similar to steel bar clamps except that the bar itself is of wood rather than metal. This kind of clamp is used for the finest cabinetwork, upholstery, and antique repair work. The major advantage is that the wood bar is less likely to cause damage to a finished surface.

40-5. *Using steel bar clamps for edge-to-edge gluing. Notice that the clamps are reversed to equalize the pressure.*

40-7. *Pipe clamps. Any length can be made by mounting the fixtures on threaded pipe. Fixtures are available for ½″ and ¾″ diameter pipe.*

Pipe Clamps

Pipe clamps are similar to bar clamps. Instead of a metal or wooden bar, the screw and the friction clutch are mounted on plumbing pipe that is threaded at the ends. Any length of pipe can be used. Fig. 40-7.

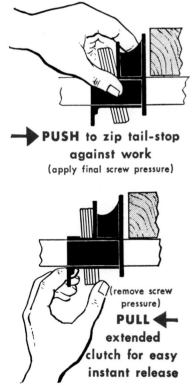

→ **PUSH to zip tail-stop against work**
(apply final screw pressure)

(remove screw pressure)

PULL ◄ **extended clutch for easy instant release**

40-6. *The friction clutch can be moved in or out into any clamping position. The screw pressure must be removed before the clutch will move.*

Spring Clamps

Spring clamps are used for many kinds of clamping. They look like oversize clothespins. Fig. 40-8. They are particularly good when light pressure is all that is needed or when the clamp must be applied and removed quickly. Some have rubber-covered jaws to protect the work. There is a heavy-duty type that has pivoting jaws made of stainless steel with double rows of serrated teeth along the pressure edge. Such jaws can hold parts at any angle so that miter joints and other odd-shaped pieces can be clamped together easily.

C-Clamps

C-clamps, or carriage clamps, are made in a wide variety of sizes and shapes and are commonly used when gluing stock face to face. Fig. 40-9. The maximum-opening sizes vary from 2″ to 12″. Some C-clamps are made with an extra-deep throat which gives maximum working clearance. When clamping a finished surface with C-clamps, always use cauls to protect the surface.

Quick clamps do the work of heavy C-clamps. Actually a short bar clamp, the quick clamp can be ad-

40-8. *A spring clamp.*

40-9. *C-clamps can be used to hold stock face to face and for many other purposes.*

339

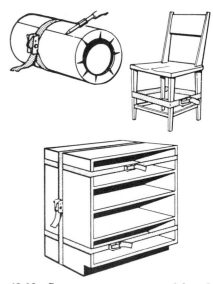

40-10. *The quick clamp can be used for many kinds of small clamping operations in place of a C-clamp.*

40-12. *Some common uses of band clamps.*

justed instantly by sliding the head along the bar. Fig. 40-10. An *edge-clamp fixture* works with a quick clamp to help solve a common and difficult problem: gluing strips of wood to the edges of plywood or solid wood. The quick clamp grasps the work, and the edge clamp applies pressure to the edge material. Fig. 40-11.

Band Clamps

Band clamps are made with a metal clamp and a band of steel or canvas. Fig. 40-12. They are used primarily for clamping round or irregularly shaped sections such as furniture frames. Steel bands are best for round objects, while canvas bands are better for odd shapes.

Hinged Clamps

These clamps fasten to the underside of a bench and are easily swung out of the way when not in use. Fig. 40-13. They can be used for many types of gluing and clamping operations.

The *3-way edging clamp* allows the "right-angle" screw to be centered or positioned above or below the center on various thicknesses of material. Fig. 40-14.

Miter and Frame Clamps

Several different types of clamps and jigs are available for gluing up miter joints and frames:

● The *miter-and-corner clamp* is ideal for assembling frames. Once the two parts are clamped together, the corner can be trued up with a backsaw if it doesn't fit perfectly. Since the corner is open, any kind of metal fastener can be installed easily. Fig. 40-15.

● A *miter clamp* for use with a hand screw is made of pieces of hardwood. This clamping jig is used for assembling many different sizes of frames. The clamp applies uniform pressure to all four joints at the same time. It leaves the joints visible so that you can make sure they are straight and tight. Fig. 40-16. Frame clamps for larger jobs can be purchased.

● A *frame-gluing clamp* is made of four clamp blocks and threaded rods. The blocks should be maple, birch, or oak. For heavy and large frames use 1½" or 2" stock instead of the 1¼" shown on the drawings. The threaded rods can be made in

40-11. *Using an edge-clamp fixture to hold a piece of molding on the edge of a tabletop.*

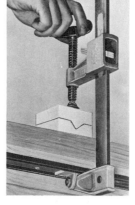

40-13. *Hinged clamps hang free under the bench and out of the way. The work is placed on the bench top and the clamp swings over it. The sliding head is pushed against the work, and pressure is applied by turning the screw.*

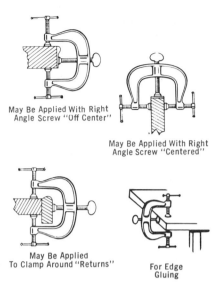

May Be Applied With Right
Angle Screw "Off Center"

May Be Applied With Right
Angle Screw "Centered"

May Be Applied
To Clamp Around "Returns"

For Edge
Gluing

40-14. *Edging clamp.*

40-15. *This miter-and-corner clamp is good for gluing up frames.*

different lengths to handle all sizes of frames. Fig. 40-17.

● A *band clamp* can also be used for gluing up frames. When using this clamp, reinforce the corners of the frame with bent pieces of sheet metal.

MARKING PIECES FOR ASSEMBLY

When getting ready to glue up pieces for subassemblies or a complete project, it is important to clearly mark each part so that no errors are made during assembly. Without proper marking, it is easy to turn one board upside down or to reverse the location of a leg or rail. There are several different marking systems for clear identification of pieces. When gluing up stock, an easy method is to mark a large *X* across the adjoining pieces using a carpenter's crayon or a heavy pencil. Another method is to mark each adjoining board 1-1, 2-2, 3-3, and so forth.

A much better system of marking that can be used for all kinds of assembly is the equilateral triangle. An equilateral triangle has three

40-16(a). *A picture-frame clamp that consists of two halves exactly alike and a single hand screw.*

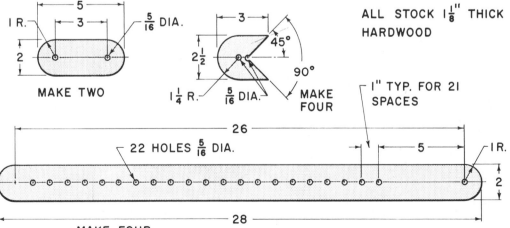

ALL STOCK $1\frac{1}{8}$" THICK
HARDWOOD

5 / 3 / $\frac{5}{16}$ DIA. / 1 R. / 2 / MAKE TWO

3 / 45° / $2\frac{1}{2}$ / 90° / $1\frac{1}{4}$ R. / $\frac{5}{16}$ DIA. / MAKE FOUR

1" TYP. FOR 21 SPACES

26 / 22 HOLES $\frac{5}{16}$ DIA. / 5 / 1 R. / 2 / 28 / MAKE FOUR

40-16(b). *Details for making the parts for a picture-frame clamp. Use a hardwood such as maple. The parts of the clamp are held together with 5/16" bolts. The notched blocks which hold the corners of the frame should be relieved by drilling holes in them.*

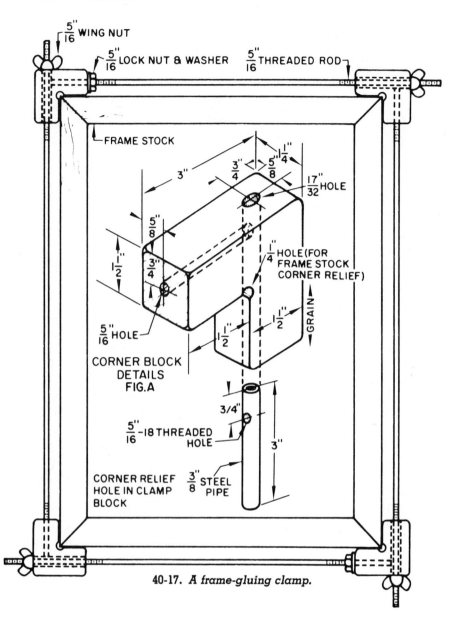

40-17. A frame-gluing clamp.

the second door, a triple line on the third door, etc. When marking rails and legs, the same basic idea can be used. Place the four legs together in correct position, with the outside surfaces exposed. Mark the two adjoining legs with a single triangle, the next with a triangle that has a double line, and so on. Then place the legs and rails adjoining each other and mark a small triangle with a 1-1 on the first joint, 2-2 on the next joint, and so forth.

GLUING PROCEDURE

Make sure the wood is at correct moisture content and that all pieces are as dry as they should be. If the moisture content is too high, the glue that penetrates the cell cavities will be thinned, resulting in a very weak joint. On the other hand, if moisture content is too low, the wood will absorb glue too rapidly. All gluing should be done when the wood is at a moisture content below 10 percent. However, some woods glue better at even lower moisture content. Any glue that contains

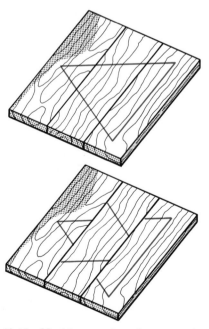

40-18. Marking stock with a triangle will make it easy to reassemble the parts correctly.

equal sides and three equal angles. Here are some examples of how this sytem is used:

1. For gluing up stock, mark an equilateral triangle across the surface of all pieces to be joined, with the base of the triangle towards you and the top away from you. Each piece must have at least two lines of the triangle on it so that the parts cannot be mixed up. With this system, the parts can be moved about and reassembled by completing the triangle. Fig. 40-18. If more than one assembly is to be glued up at the same time, on the second

assembly, use a double line on a side of the triangle that crosses all pieces. On the third assembly, use a triple line, and so forth.

2. Sometimes several parts are involved in the assembly. For a panel door, mark the stiles with one triangle and the rails with another. When the door is to be assembled, each of the two triangles will show up on the door even though parts of the triangle are separated from each other. If two or more panel doors are to be assembled, put a double line on one side of each triangle on

water will raise the moisture content of the wood surrounding the joint, and this causes a raised glue line. If boards are surfaced before the moisture content of the glue line equals that of the remainder of the wood, the glue joint will sink after the surfacing, resulting in what is called a sunken joint. This is especially noticeable on large, finished surfaces.

Some adhesives work well only with carefully fitted joints, while others have better gap-filling properties. *Follow the manufacturer's directions.* Make sure that you use the proper proportions for all mixing and that all lumps have been removed. Also, mix glue only as needed so that each batch is fresh.

Make a trial assembly, making sure that all surfaces are clean and dry and that joints are well fitted. Do this by dry clamping all pieces together. Also, make sure that you have the necessary cauls (protective pieces of wood). Mark the pieces that are to be glued for correct assembly. Make sure that there are enough clamps and that they are adjusted correctly.

Bar clamps should be spaced 10″ to 15″ apart. They should be alternated, one above and the next below. On extremely wide surfaces it is a good idea to put cleats or cauls across the ends to prevent buckling. Put waxed paper underneath to keep the cleats or cauls from sticking. Clamp in place with hand screws or C-clamps. Never glue parts that should be free to move. For example, a drawer bottom should always be assembled without glue.

Edge Gluing

In edge gluing, follow these suggestions:

• The grain of all pieces should run in the same direction. Then, after gluing up, the completed piece will not be difficult to surface.

• Alternate the pieces so that the growth rings run in opposite directions. This helps to prevent cupping.

• Try to match the pieces to form an interesting grain pattern.

• Pieces to be glued should be no wider than 4″ to 6″.

• Check the boards to be glued to make sure the edge is square with the face surface, and that the edge is straight from one end to the other. Some woodworkers plane the edge so that it has a slightly concave surface from end to end. This technique is especially useful when no dowels or splines are used. Then when the boards are glued together, this will put slight pressure on the ends. As the glue dries, the ends give up moisture first, which will release the pressure and keep the joint from splitting.

• Another suggestion for keeping the ends from drying out too fast is to apply masking tape to the end grain when the wood is glued up.

• Make sure that the clamps don't touch the surface of the work, since this will damage or discolor the wood.

Spreading Glue

The common methods of applying glue are with a brush, stick, paddle, or squeeze bottle. A glue roller can also be used. Fig. 40-19. Glues can be applied either to one surface (*single spreading*) or to both surfaces (*double spreading*).

When gluing end grain, apply a thin coat to it first. Then apply a second coat to the end grain and one coat to the other surface. This is done because end grain absorbs more glue. Glue from a squeeze bottle should be applied in a zigzag line. Then the two parts should be pressed together and moved back and forth to produce an even spread.

Generally, tiny beads of glue will appear along a good glue joint at regular intervals of 2″ to 3″. A starved glue joint may result from using too little glue or too much

40-19. *A hand glue spreader has a plastic chamber for holding the glue. A knurled steel roller in the bottom of the chamber dispenses the glue to the rubber roller.*

pressure. It is a good idea to allow the glue to become tacky by letting it set a short time before assembling the parts. Never apply so much glue that squeeze-out is a problem. For example, the mortise-and-tenon joint should not have glue visible around the tenon where it fits against the mortise section.

Applying the Correct Pressure

After gluing, assemble the parts. Some glues, such as hot animal glue, require that this be done very rapidly. With other glues, such as white liquid glue, the assembly time can be longer. At normal room temperature, it is important that the glue is still fluid when the pressure is applied.

Applying excessive pressure after assembly will cause a starved joint; that is, one that is weak because too much glue has been squeezed out. However, there is usually more danger of applying too little pressure than of applying too much. When pressure is correctly applied, a slight amount of glue should be visible along the glue line. This should be allowed to dry, then scraped away.

In edge gluing, the clamps should be alternated, one from one side and one from the other, about every

10" to 15". It is frequently necessary to apply a moderate amount of pressure and then to line up the pieces by striking one or more with a wood mallet before continuing to tighten the clamps.

It is important that correct pressure be allowed to remain on a joint until the pieces are firmly bonded and the glue is dry.

Curing Time

The rate at which glues dry varies greatly with the type of glue and the room temperature. However, with many of the chemical glues, heat is applied to speed the cure. The higher the temperature, the faster the cure. The most common methods of applying heat are with a hot platen and by a high-frequency electrical field.

HIGH-FREQUENCY GLUING EQUIPMENT

A wet glue joint is a good conductor of electricity. When the joint is placed in an electrical field of high frequency, alternating current passes along the glue line and generates heat. This heat dries the glue in a matter of seconds. Animal and casein glues are not suitable for this. It is necessary to use one of the

thermosetting resin glues. The urea resin glues are used for over 90 percent of all high-frequency gluing.

A portable high-frequency electronic gluer or welder is quite easy to use. Fig. 40-20. It comes equipped with a hand gun designed for applying the electricity. The trigger switch turns the electricity on and off. Various styles of electrodes can be attached to the hand gun. Fig. 40-21. Different woods, different glues, the amount of glue, and the thickness of the material create a change of load in the hand gun. A tuning knob on the hand gun can be turned to allow for this change of load. Another knob on the hand gun must be adjusted so that the meter on the electronic welder will always read in the medium-to-high range.

To edge glue, apply glue to one or both edges of the wood and use bar clamps as you would for other gluing. If the joint is not brought firmly together, the glue will be cured but the joint will be weak. Apply the flat electrodes across the glue line and pull the trigger switch. Move the tuning knob to the maximum heat. Keep the hand gun in place until the glue dries enough to stop boiling. This usually takes from two to five seconds for softwoods and a

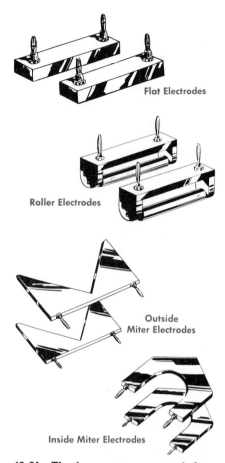

Flat Electrodes

Roller Electrodes

Outside Miter Electrodes

Inside Miter Electrodes

40-21. *The four common sets of electrodes include flat electrodes that are used for edge gluing; roller electrodes for paneling, banding, moldings, and other edges; outside miter electrodes for any square or miter corner; and inside miter electrodes for gluing inside corners.*

40-20. *A portable electronic gluer or welder consists of a high-frequency electric generator, an electronic hand gun, the conductors to the hand gun, and the various styles of electrodes.*

little longer for hardwoods. In edge gluing, apply the electrodes about every 8" and near the ends. When you are finished, release the bar clamps. The glued-up stock has sufficient strength to be worked immediately. The full strength of the bond develops in 8 to 24 hours, depending on the adhesive used.

ASSEMBLING CABINETS AND FURNITURE

Before assembling cabinets and furniture, it must be decided whether the product can be assembled all at one time or whether it is necessary to glue up subassemblies. Generally, tables and chairs consisting of legs and rails are glued up in two steps. The legs and rails on each end are glued up first, and then the entire product is assembled. After the dust panels are assembled, most casework is glued up in one step except for the application of molding and edging. Follow these general steps:

1. Have the correct number of clamps, and make sure they are adjusted to the right openings.

2. Have enough cauls ready so that they can be placed under the clamps to protect the finished surfaces. A mallet is needed for striking the parts to make sure they fit together firmly. A straightedge and square are needed for checking the assembly.

3. Mix the right amount and kind of glue to proper consistency.

4. Apply glue to the joints. Generally, both parts of the joint should be covered. However, in mortise-and-tenon construction, it is better to apply most of the glue to the mortise since the glue will scrape off the tenon as it is pushed in place. Never apply so much glue that it will squeeze out where it is difficult to remove, as around a leg or rail.

5. After the parts are assembled and clamped, make these three checks:

 a. With a square, make sure that the parts are at right angles to one another.

40-22. Checking for levelness.

 b. Use a straightedge to make sure the pieces are all in one plane and are not warped. Fig. 40-22.

 c. Place a stick across the corners to make sure that the diagonal distance is the same both ways. Fig. 40-23.

6. Allow the glue to dry thoroughly before removing the clamps. The clamps can be removed immediately after high-frequency gluing.

7. Prepare the surfaces for finishing. Remove excess glue with a sharp chisel. Sand the joints thoroughly; bleach if necessary.

GLUING PROBLEMS

If the correct kind of glue has been used and the joint properly made, it should be stronger than the wood itself. A test glue joint can be checked by placing a blunt chisel at

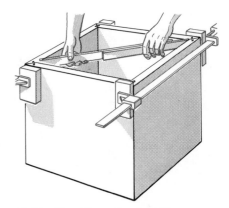

40-23. Checking the length across corners to make sure the distances from corner to corner are equal.

the glue line and striking it with a hammer. A good joint will not split along the glue line.

A weak glue joint may have many causes, such as poor fit, inadequate pressure, too short a pressure time, or a fuzzy glue line. A fuzzy glue line results when very dry lumber is surfaced and then allowed to absorb moisture. This causes fuzzy grain on the surface of the wood. Other conditions that may cause a weak joint are: a *starved joint*, in which there is too little glue; a *chilled joint*, in which the glue became jelly before or immediately after applying pressure; or a *dried joint*, in which the glue dried without bonding. Another problem that sometimes develops is discoloration due to iron in the glue. This particularly affects such woods as oak, walnut, cedar, maple, redwood, and cherry.

41 Bending and Laminating

Many styles of furniture and cabi-network require curved parts such as a drawer front or the rail of a table. Bentwood and molded-plywood chairs are an example of extreme bends in furniture. Fig. 41-1.

Often combined with bending is laminating; that is, the process of building up the thickness or width of material by gluing several thinner pieces together, all with the grain *running in the same direction*. Fig. 41-2. Making *molded plywood* is very similar except that the layers are *at right angles to each other*. Laminating is also done without bending for many straight parts.

Whether to use solid or laminated construction for curved parts depends primarily on how accurate the curved pieces must be. A laminated part holds its shape after removal from the form, but a steam-bent part springs back a little. Also, breakage and rejected parts are more frequent in steam bending.

PRODUCING CURVED PARTS

Following are common methods of producing curved parts for furniture pieces.

Cutting from Solid Stock

The simplest way is to cut the curved part from solid stock on the band saw. However, this is satisfactory only for cutting a relatively limited number of pieces that have slight curvatures. On a sharp curve there is so much short grain at the end that the piece is very weak.

Brick or Segment Method

Circular parts can be built up of rows of solid wood pieces called segments or bricks. Fig. 41-3. The joints are staggered so that there is no weakness. Since all of the pieces are fairly short, there is no extensive end grain on the surface. The pieces are cut to shape, fitted together, then glued into one piece. In constructing a curved piece of segments or bricks, always make sure that there are at least three layers to equalize the stresses. After the pieces are glued together and shaped, the segmented structure is often covered with a face and back veneer.

41-2. *This award-winning glass-topped end table, built by a student, is laminated in layers about one inch thick and joined with finger joints.*

Cross Kerfing Solid Lumber or Plywood

In this method a series of short kerfs is cut to within $\frac{1}{16}''$ of the outside surface so that the material will be more flexible for bending. These deep cuts are made side-by-side in the surface that will form the back (underside) of the circular part. The cutting is done with a radial-arm saw. Fig. 41-4.

To determine the correct spacing for the saw kerfs, first decide on the radius of the curve or circle to be formed. Measure this distance (the radius) from the end of the stock and make a saw kerf at this point. Fasten the stock to the tabletop

41-1. *Bentwood chairs illustrate the highest art of wood bending.*

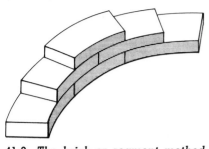

41-3. *The brick or segment method of making curved parts uses solid stock that has been cut to shape on the band saw. The width is built up using several pieces of material, with the end joints staggered. The pieces should be glued together with a water-resistant adhesive.*

with a clamp. Raise the end of the stock until the kerf closes. Fig. 41-5. The distance the end of the stock is raised above the table is the distance needed between kerfs. (Note that in Fig. 41-5, a mark indicates one end of the radius. Therefore the height is measured at that mark, not at the end.)

After the first kerf, mark the space for the second kerf and make the cut. Before moving the stock, mark a pencil line on the guide fence of the radial-arm saw. Make the remaining cuts by locating each new saw kerf at the guide mark.

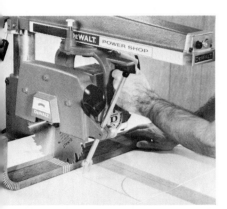

41-4. *Cross kerfing is a practical method of bending wood. This method can be used to round off the corners of paneled walls, to shape rails or aprons, and for similar jobs. The kerfed side forms the back or underside of the bend.*

41-5. *The correct method of determining the distance between saw kerfs. The distance between the kerfs determines the flexibility of the material.*

41-6. *Cut equally spaced kerfs at an angle to produce a spiral curve.*

41-7. *Apply adhesive to the veneer and slip it into the saw kerfs.*

A spiral curve can be produced by cutting kerfs at an angle. Fig. 41-6. When the cuts are complete, the stock is bent slowly until the right curve is obtained. Soaking the wood in warm water will help the bending. Compound curves can be formed in this way by kerfing both sides of the stock. Once the piece is bent, the saw kerfs are filled with sawdust and glue to form a solid, curved piece. The exposed surface can be covered with veneer.

Kerfing Parallel with the Face

Sometimes a piece is needed that is straight for most of its length but curved at the end. The easiest method of producing this kind of bend is to make a series of saw kerfs from the end grain, parallel with the face surface. Usually at

least two or three kerfs should be made. Then cut sheets of ⅛" veneer slightly wider and longer than the kerfs. Apply a good grade of waterproof glue to both surfaces and slip the veneer in place. Fig. 41-7. Fasten the end in a form and use clamps to hold it to shape. Fig. 41-8. Allow the piece to remain in the form until the glue is thoroughly dry. Then trim the extra veneer away from the sides and ends. If extremely thick material is to be bent, it may be necessary to steam the ends to make the wood more plastic (flexible) before the veneer is inserted.

Bending Solid Wood to a Form

Solid wood can be bent to shape by first softening (plasticizing) it with steam or hot water and then placing it in a form until it dries out. Certain chemicals can also be used to make solid wood pliable.

As a piece of wood is bent, it is stretched on the outer (convex) side and compressed on the inner (concave) side. The convex side is longer than the concave side. For this reason the wood must first be softened with moisture and then heated before it is bent.

In general, the moisture content for bending should be between 12 and 20 percent, although it can be as high as 30 percent. The higher moisture content is necessary for sharper bends. The best moisture *at the time of bending* is about 25

347

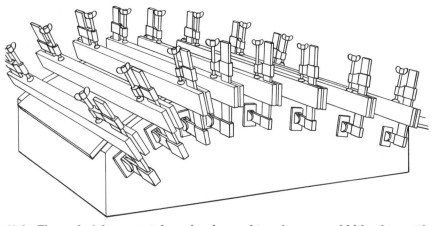

41-8. *The end of the material can be clamped in a form or mold like this until dry.*

SUCCESS RATES OF BENDING DOMESTIC HARDWOODS

	% Unbroken Pieces
Ash	67
Beech	75
Birch	72
Elm, soft	74
Hackberry	94
Hickory	76
Magnolia	85
Maple, hard	57
Oak, red	86
Oak, white	91
Pecan	78
Sweet gum	67
Sycamore	29
Tupelo	42
Walnut, black	78

U.S. Forest Products Laboratory, *Wood Handbook: Wood as an Engineering Material,* 1974.

41-10. *This table shows the percentage of unbroken pieces that results when various hardwoods are steam-bent.*

percent. Slight bends can be made at a lower moisture level—as low as 15 percent. Since wood begins to lose moisture immediately after it is removed from the steam tube or box, it is better to have the wood at a moisture content above 25 percent for very severe bends. Never use overdried lumber for bending stock. Overdried lumber is difficult to steam to a moisture content of 25 percent without weakening the wood.

Steaming wood—having it hot and wet—is the key to good bending. Wood can also be plasticized with a great variety of chemicals, but these are not practical for most woodworking. Many of the chemicals are dangerous to use, involving great safety risks.

BENDABILITY OF DOMESTIC HARDWOODS

1. Hackberry	9. Beech
2. White oak	10. Elm
3. Red oak	11. Willow
4. Chestnut	12. Birch
5. Magnolia	13. Ash
6. Pecan	14. Sweet gum
7. Black walnut	15. Soft maple
8. Hickory	16. Yellow poplar

Compiled by U.S. Forest Products Laboratory

41-9. *The bending ability of common U.S. domestic hardwoods, listed in order from best to least.*

STEAM BENDING

Some kinds of wood steam better than others. The bending qualities of wood vary widely, not only among different kinds but also within the same kind. The bending abilities of common hardwoods are shown in Fig. 41-9. There will be some breakage even among the best of wood. Fig. 41-10. When bending solid wood, remember that the face or exterior surface cannot be stretched more than 1 to 2 percent, while the back surface can be compressed as much as 20 percent.

To produce bent parts from solid wood, it is necessary to have a method of soaking or steaming and also a form or mold in which to clamp the wood until it is dry. If the shop is in a steam-heated building, it may be possible to run the steam by a hose into a retort for softening the wood. Fig. 41-11. However, in most situations it is simpler to soak the wood in boiling water. This requires a metal container such as an old hot-water tank, a large milk tank, or a large-diameter pipe with a welded bottom. The top of the container should be partly covered with a rubber tube or a metal cover with small holes. Heat should be applied until the water boils. The material to be bent is placed in the boiling water. Usually a half hour of soaking is needed for

each inch of thickness, although more time may be required. Fig. 41-12.

You may wish to build a steam tube or steam box. These can be made of many materials. A good tube can be made from 4″ to 5″ diameter aluminum tubing about 5′ to 7′ long. Sometimes a discarded hollow lamppost of aluminum is available for this purpose. Close one

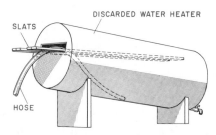

41-11. *A method of softening wood with hot steam. An old hot-water tank acts as a retort (a container for steam). The steam comes from the shop's heating plant.*

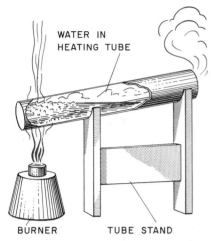

WATER IN
HEATING TUBE

BURNER   TUBE STAND

41-12. *Using hot water to soften wood. An old hot-water heater or a large metal pipe with one closed end can be used. Place some kind of burner under the closed end to heat the water. Place a rubber sleeve over the other end to keep the steam in; this will also act as a safety valve.*

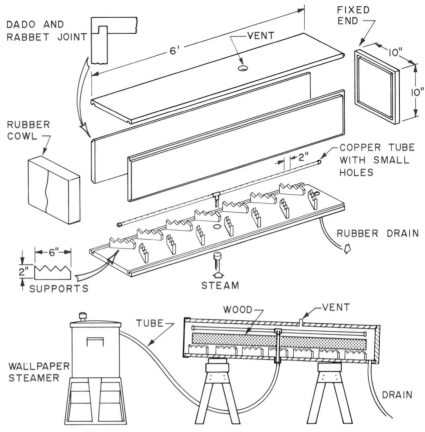

DADO AND
RABBET JOINT

6'

VENT

FIXED END

10"

10"

RUBBER COWL

COPPER TUBE WITH SMALL HOLES

2"

RUBBER DRAIN

6"

2"

SUPPORTS

STEAM

WALLPAPER STEAMER

TUBE

WOOD

VENT

DRAIN

41-13. *A steam box for bending wood.*

end by welding a plate onto it. A steam box can be made of exterior plywood of either C-C or A-C grade. For an even better box, use marine plywood. Make the box large enough to hold the material to be steamed. Add blocks of wood to the inside bottom so that the pieces will not lie directly on the bottom of the box. Assemble the box with tongue-and-groove joints. Permanently close one end and attach a door with a gasket seal to the other, or cover the end with heavy rubber. A drain hole is always needed near the closed

end of any box. Also there must be a hole near the center of the box for a steam tube that extends the length of the box on the inside. For a source of steam, you can buy or rent a wallpaper steamer. Fig. 41-13.

The form or mold for bending can be made of either wood or metal. Generally, for a simple drawer front, a mold cut from a piece of hardwood is satisfactory. Fig. 41-14. In

bending over a mold, a piece of sheet metal, preferably stainless steel, should be placed over the exterior of the stock and the clamps tightened a little at a time as the material is forced around the mold. Drying should be done in as hot a room as possible (up to 140 degrees F). Keep the bent pieces in the form until dry.

LAMINATING AND BENDING

Equipment and Materials

Curved laminated parts are made by gluing together several pieces of thin veneer with the grain running in the same direction. These are then clamped in a form (sometimes called shaped molds or cauls) until dry. In industry, an electronic laminating press is used to produce laminated pieces for furniture parts. In a small cabinet or school shop, lam-

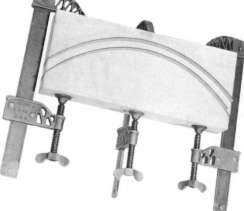

41-14. *A simple wood form or mold such as this can be used to bend small pieces, as for a wood drawer front.*

349

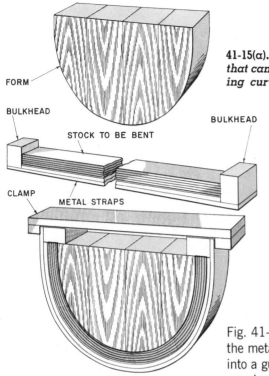

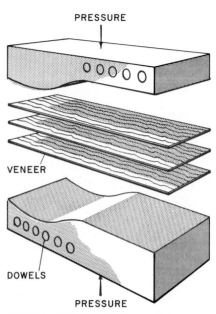

FORM

BULKHEAD

STOCK TO BE BENT

BULKHEAD

CLAMP

METAL STRAPS

41-15(a). *One type of mold that can be used for producing curved or semicircular parts.*

PRESSURE

VENEER

DOWELS

PRESSURE

41-15(b). *This mold is used to produce the rough blanks for a salad server. Note that the hardwood forms are reinforced with several dowels.*

inating and bending call for the following equipment:

● *A form or mold of the correct shape.* The form can be made of glued-up plywood or thick, solid stock such as birch or maple. Fig. 41-15. It can be cut to shape on the band saw. It is a good idea to line the form with rubber (cut from an inner tube) or cork to make the pressure more even. Apply a sealer finish like shellac to wood forms. Forms can also be built of metal.

For production jobs, a special form or mold with built-in V-bolt clamps can be constructed. An adjustable form that can be used for many different shapes is shown in Fig. 41-16. This, however, is satisfactory for only rather narrow parts. First lay out the curvature of the piece on ¾" plywood. The same sheet of plywood can be used for several different shapes merely by changing the location of the wood clamps. Fasten metal pins or nails on the curved lines at intervals of 4" or 5". Make a series of wood clamps similar to those shown in

Fig. 41-17. Place the clamps over the metal pins so that each drops into a guide hole. After the veneers are glued and assembled, C-clamps can be put between the wood clamps for more even pressure.

● *Veneer stock, of the same or contrasting woods, to build up the piece to thickness.* The standard thickness of commercial veneer is ½₈", although veneer can be purchased in thicknesses of ½₀" and ⅟₁₆" also. Thin stock can be cut on the band saw and then surfaced on a planer, although this is a rather difficult job that involves a great deal of waste.

Some of the better woods for furniture and accessory laminating are hardwoods such as birch, maple, walnut, mahogany, cherry, and teak. The thickness is usually built up with an odd number of plies—for example, three, five or seven. However, many furniture manufacturers prefer four layers of veneer for curved laminations. This makes it possible to use two good-quality veneers for the face and back surfaces and two less-expensive layers for the inside. Sometimes woods of contrasting colors are used to form parts for accessories.

● *An adhesive to bind the materials together permanently.* The best

adhesive is one of the synthetic-resin glues such as urea resin (plastic resin) or polyvinyl (white) glue. In commercial fabrication of laminated beams, casein glue is the most commonly used adhesive.

● *Clamping devices to hold the veneers together.* Any of the standard clamps for gluing can be used

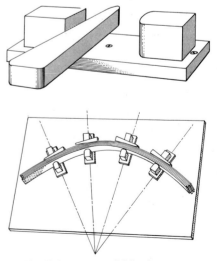

41-16. *A form or mold for laminating simple curved materials.*

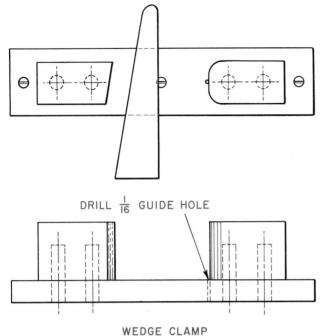

DRILL $\frac{1}{16}$ GUIDE HOLE

WEDGE CLAMP

41-17. *Wood clamps such as these can be made to hold the materials.*

41-18. *A small veneer press can be used to form curved panels. A two-part form or mold is necessary.*

to apply the needed pressure. An old metal wheel can be used as the form and a band clamp as the pressure device for forming circular shapes. A veneer press can also be used to apply needed pressure to the form. Fig. 41-18.

Steps in Laminating and Bending

1. Cut several pieces of veneer slightly larger than the finished size of the part. Usually the pieces should be about ½″ wider and about 1″ to 2″ longer than the completed part to allow for the bend and for slippage.

2. Clamp the pieces together without glue to check the assembly and to make sure enough clamping devices are available. As the pieces are removed, stack them in the exact order in which they must be glued.

3. Apply glue with a brush or roller to both sides of the inside

pieces and one side of the outside pieces. Stack the pieces together after each is glued so that you can place the whole stack in the form at the same time. Stacking will keep the glue from setting too rapidly before pressure is applied.

4. Place a piece of waxed paper or thin plastic in the lower part of the form, then the stack of veneers, and finally another sheet of waxed paper or plastic. Several thicknesses of old newspaper can be placed above and below the stack. It is very important to keep the glue off the form and the rubber or cork liner.

5. Apply pressure by tightening each clamp a little at a time so that the pieces will bend slowly all along the form. When the final tightening is done, apply pressure first at the points of greater curvature and then toward the open ends.

6. Allow the part to dry thoroughly; then remove it from the

form. Usually the paper or plastic will have stuck to the edges of the rough laminate. These should be removed.

7. Trace the final shape on the rough laminate, using a template. Cut to shape on a band saw and round the edges. Then sand the entire piece. Fig. 41-19.

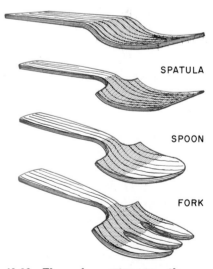

SPATULA

SPOON

FORK

41-19. *These decorative utensils are typical of the many laminated products that can be made.*

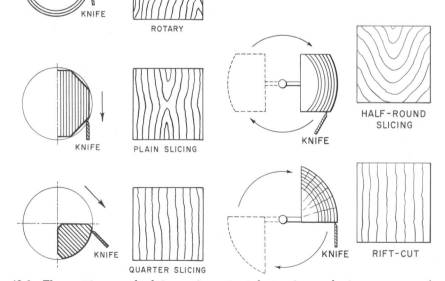

42 Veneering and Inlaying

Veneering is one of the oldest woodworking arts, one that has been practiced for centuries. Through modern techniques, veneers are available in standard-sized panels. Such panels are produced in plywood plants and are used for most paneling, built-ins, kitchen cabinets, and on-the-job construction.

However, standard panels are not well suited for every purpose. For instance, cabinetmakers often make their own plywood to the specific sizes they need, or when banded plywood is required. (Banded plywood is lumber-core plywood with a band or frame of solid stock of the same species as the face veneer.) Some custom woodworking plants also make their own plywood, especially when casework and interiors call for an exotic wood such as rosewood or limba. Fancy veneers are purchased from an importer who specializes in these fine, expensive woods.

At times you will want to produce your own flat or curved veneer panels. For example, when building a table of expensive wood such as teak, you may want to make the top of inexpensive core stock such as fir plywood or particle board, then cover it with teak veneer. Another time to do this would be when you want to make a veneered part with special matching.

The veneering process requires careful work, but it is not too complicated if a few precautions are taken.

METHODS OF CUTTING

Veneer is a thin layer or sheet of wood that is sliced or cut from a log or part of a log called a *flitch*. The way in which veneers are cut greatly affects their final appearance. There are five principal ways of slicing or cutting veneers. The first three are the most common in plywood production. Fig. 42-1.

Rotary

In rotary cutting, the log is mounted centrally in a lathe and turned against a razor-sharp blade. The veneer is cut off much like the way a roll of paper would unwind. Since this cut follows the log's annual growth rings, a bold grain marking is produced. Almost all construction and industrial plywood is produced in this manner. Rotary-cut veneer results in very wide sheeting. In hardwood, the length of rotary-cut veneer is usually not more than 8'.

Flat or Plain Slicing

Half the log or flitch is mounted with the heart side flat against the guide plate of the slicer. The slicing is done parallel with the center of the log. This produces a most inter-

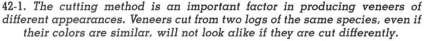

42-1. The cutting method is an important factor in producing veneers of different appearances. Veneers cut from two logs of the same species, even if their colors are similar, will not look alike if they are cut differently.

42-2. *These round tables are distinctive because of the burl veneers which cover their surfaces.*

esting grain pattern, like that of plain sawed lumber.

Quarter Slicing
One-fourth of the log (flitch) is mounted on a guide plate so that the growth rings of the log strike the knives at approximately right angles. This produces a series of stripes or straight lines in some woods and varied figures in others.

Half-Round Slicing
This is a type of rotary cutting in which the log segments or flitches are mounted off-center in the lathe. The result is a cut slightly across the growth rings. This is done most often for cutting veneers from red oak.

Rift Cut
The rift cut is done to various kinds of oak. Oak has ray cells which radiate out from the center of the log like the curved spokes of a wheel. The rift-grain effect is obtained by cutting perpendicular to these rays, either on a lathe or a slicer. Most veneer is sliced off the log with a sharp knife. Some veneer is cut with a saw, but since this

technique is rather wasteful, it is usually limited to the red and white oaks.

KINDS OF VENEERS
All standard veneers are cut $\frac{1}{28}''$ thick, although in a few cases veneers are available in $\frac{1}{16}''$ thickness. Veneer imported from many foreign countries is $\frac{1}{60}''$ thick. These are so thin that it is very easy to damage or sand through them.

Extra-fancy veneers are produced from certain unusual parts of the tree. These include the burl, butt or stumpwood, and the crotch.

Burl
Burls are large, wartlike, deformed growths on the trunk of a tree. Usually these are caused by an injury to the tree just under the bark which makes the cells divide and grow excessively. Additional growth follows the contour of the original deformity, producing little swirls or knots. The twisted, thickened wood fibers have a very beautiful, curling pattern. Fig. 42-2.

Butt or Stumpwood
Butts are obtained from the base or stump of the tree where wood fibers are compressed and tend to wrinkle or twist. This produces an unusual figure in the wood. Butt or stumpwood figures usually have a wavy, rippled marking.

Crotch
The crotch is the part of a tree just under a fork where a main branch joins the trunk. Here the fibers are twisted, creating various figures and grains that are very beautiful. The front and back of the crotch have distinctive figures that gradually fade into a swirling pattern. Veneers from these portions are known as *swirls*.

MATCHING VENEERS
A veneer surface of any size is made by gluing together two or

more pieces of veneer. Because veneers are thin, the sheets that are joined must have similar grain or figure marks. By utilizing this duplication of pattern, all sorts of designs are possible. The following are the most common methods of matching veneers. Fig. 42-3.

● *Slip match.* In slip matching, veneer sheets are joined side by side to make them look as if the pattern is repeated. All types of veneer may be used, but this kind of matching is most common with quarter-sliced veneers.

● *Book match.* All types of veneers are used. Adjacent pieces of veneer from the flitch are fastened side by side. Every other sheet is turned over so that the back of one veneer joins the front of the next.

● *Diamond match.* This is made up of four pieces of veneer that are cut diagonally from the same piece of material. They are fitted together to form a diamond pattern. Veneers

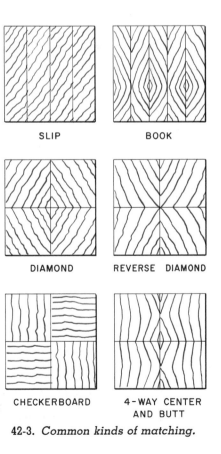

42-3. *Common kinds of matching.*

42-4. These tables have veneers with reverse diamond matching. Some of the tables have been turned to show the tops.

with striped grains are particularly attractive in diamond match.

• *Reverse diamond.* The pieces are fitted exactly opposite to the way they are in a diamond match. Fig. 42-4.

• *Checkerboard match.* Each piece is rotated one-quarter turn to give a checkerboard effect.

• *Four-way center and butt.* This match is usually applied to butt, crotch, or stump veneers since it effectively shows the beauty of the surfaces. Four pieces are joined side to side and end to end.

• *Other matches.* Some other common matching patterns are *vertical-butt and horizontal-bookleaf match, random match,* and *herringbone match.* Fig. 42-5. For the tops of tables and other furniture pieces, special matching effects are obtained by combining veneers from different species.

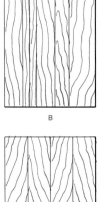

42-5. Other kinds of matching: (A) Vertical-butt and horizontal-bookleaf match is used when the height of the flitch is not enough to produce a panel of the desired height. The match may be vertical as well as horizontal. (B) In random match the veneers are joined with the intention of creating a casual, unmatched effect. Veneers from several logs may be used. (C) The pattern in herringbone match is formed by lines intersecting at acute angles.

TOOLS AND MATERIALS FOR VENEERING

The tools and materials that are necessary depend on the veneering to be done. Usually, however, only a few simple hand tools are needed. These include a fine saw or slicing shears, a knife, veneer pins (plastic-headed pins with very hard, sharp steel points), veneer or masking tape, white glue, contact cement, and a ruler or straightedge. Small brads can be used in place of veneer pins. A veneer press is needed for making lumber-core plywood.

CUTTING VENEERS

Veneer that has been sliced from a log or flitch must be cut into smaller pieces. There are several common ways to do this. A veneer saw will do an excellent job; but, if veneering is done only occasionally, a dovetail saw is satisfactory.

Fig. 42-6. The best method for cutting veneer is to clamp a guide board over the line at which the veneer is to be cut and then saw with a dovetail or veneer saw. A sharp veneer knife can also be used. Fig. 42-7. Veneers can also be cut successfully on a metal squaring shears or with a hand sheet-metal shears.

APPLYING FINE VENEER TO A PANEL CORE

The simplest method of making a fancy veneer is to use fir plywood, particle board, or hardboard as the core. Fir plywood is best since it has smooth, even, sanded surfaces. It is important, of course, to select plywood that has good face veneer on both surfaces. Particle board can also be used; but, unless a crossband is applied, a sliver of the particle board may force its way through the face veneer. Hardboard is also a satisfactory material for core stock. Many commercial veneer panels have a core of particle board, crossbands of hardboard, and face and back veneers of wood.

To produce veneer plywood, follow these steps:

1. Determine the total thickness of stock needed. Since veneers are

42-6. Dovetail saw for cutting veneers.

42-7. A sharp knife with a guide is excellent for cutting veneers.

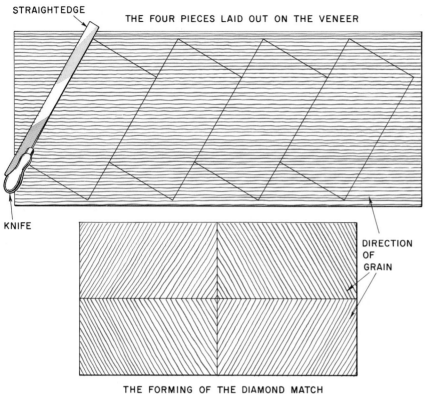

STRAIGHTEDGE

THE FOUR PIECES LAID OUT ON THE VENEER

KNIFE

DIRECTION
OF
GRAIN

THE FORMING OF THE DIAMOND MATCH

42-8. *Layout of pieces for a diamond match.*

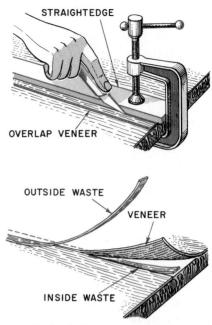

STRAIGHTEDGE

OVERLAP VENEER

OUTSIDE WASTE

VENEER

INSIDE WASTE

42-10. *Cutting a veneer joint.*

only ⅛₈″ thick, for most work the core will make up nearly the total thickness of the material required. Fine veneers are expensive and are sold by the square foot. It is important therefore to pick a fancy veneer for the face surface and less expensive veneer (preferably of the same species) for the back. It is essential that the veneer layer for the back

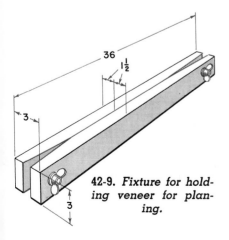

42-9. *Fixture for holding veneer for planing.*

36

1½

3

3

surface have the same thickness as that applied to the face, for balanced construction and to prevent warping.

2. Match the face veneers, using as many pieces as needed. Remember, extra material is needed to allow for trimming the veneer after it is applied. The most common methods of matching are random match, slip match, and book match. However, if diamond match is needed, the pieces must be cut from a veneer of striped grain. The best way to do this is to lay out rectangular pieces with a steel square. Four will be needed. Fig. 42-8. It is a good idea to make the pattern full-size on a piece of paper and then to cut one piece of material from the veneer. Use a straightedge to guide the knife. Next, turn the sheet over and cut the second piece. Reverse the material again for the third, and again for the fourth.

3. The edges of adjoining pieces must fit accurately. To make sure of this, clamp the adjoining pieces of veneer between two hardwood boards with their edges just protruding (⅛₆″ or less). Plane the edges true. Fig. 42-9. The planing can be done with a hand plane or on a jointer. If a jointer is used, clamp the veneers between two pieces of scrap lumber and pass over the jointer. Repeat this step on the other edge of the veneers. Another method of making a veneer joint is to overlap one sheet of veneer with the adjoining piece by about 1″. Then clamp a straightedge along the middle of the overlap. Fig. 42-10. With a very sharp knife or chisel, cut along the straightedge, making sure that both thicknesses are cut at the same time. *Never make more than one cut.* Remove the straightedge and take away both pieces of waste veneer. The edges should then fit accurately without planing. Repeat for each of the adjoining pieces of veneer. Before taping the veneers together, place the two pieces on a cutting board with the edges together to make sure the

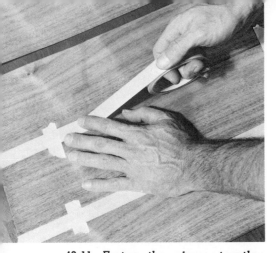

42-11. *Fasten the pieces together with masking tape. Turn the sheet over and inspect the joints. Any cracks showing at this time will appear in the finished panel. Therefore it is important to get a perfect joint.*

joint is very tight. Veneer pins or brads are pressed into both pieces about an inch away from the joint, at the extreme edges, to hold them in place. Slant the veneer pins towards the joint to hold the edges firmly together.

4. Use gummed veneer tape or masking tape to join the pieces temporarily on the face side. Fig. 42-11. Remove the veneer pins and reverse the sheet to check for any cracks. If there are any imperfections, take the joint apart and replane it until it is perfect. Repeat this process for each joint necessary

42-12. *Edge gluing the sections together. Turn the panel over and fold back the sections. Apply white glue to the edges. Lay the panel flat and wipe off any excess glue.*

to produce the face and back veneers.

5. Turn the sheet over on the bench. Open the joints and apply a good grade of white glue to the edges of the adjoining pieces. Fig. 42-12. Wipe off any excess glue and straighten out the veneer sheet. Then tape the back sides of the joint together. Do this for all pieces. Now allow the total sheet to dry overnight. Remember that you must also have the same size sheet of less expensive veneer for the back surface.

6. After the glue is dry, remove the tape from the back or poor side of the veneer, keeping the other tape in place.

7. Cut the core material, usually fir plywood, to the size you want. Use contact cement to fasten the veneer in place. This adhesive can be applied with a brush, roller, or spreader. Two coats must be applied to the core material and one to the veneer. Allow both to dry at least 15 minutes. Dull spots that appear after drying indicate that additional cement must be applied. After the cement is dry, there should be a high gloss over the entire surface. Test for dryness by tamping a piece of brown wrapping paper on the cemented surface. When the paper won't stick, the cement is ready. Remember that when two surfaces covered with contact cement touch, there is an immediate bond and the materials cannot be moved again.

8. Place the veneer carefully over the core stock. Keep in mind that the face and back veneers must be applied at right angles to the face ply of the core. Otherwise there is a tendency for cracks to develop. After the veneer is in place over the core stock, remove the tape. Use a veneer roller on the surfaces, both with and across grain, to make sure the veneer is fastened securely to the core stock. Fig. 42-13. After the face veneer

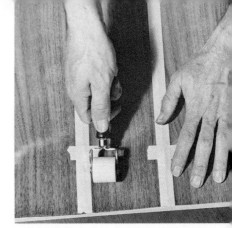

42-13. *Place the veneer on the core stock and roll firmly both with the grain and across it. Remove the masking tape and roll each side again. Allow the panel to dry 24 hours before further handling.*

has been applied, reverse the stock and follow the same procedure to apply back veneer.

VENEERING SMALL PROJECTS

For small projects such as boxes and chessboards, veneering can be done in a much simpler way. Fig. 42-14. The project is built of some fairly inexpensive material such as softwood (construction and industrial) plywood, particle board, or pine. The project, including the edges, is then covered with veneer. Veneer edging is available as follows:

• Plain edging that must be attached with adhesive.

• Edging coated with pressure-sensitive adhesive covered with paper. To glue this edging the paper cover is stripped away and the edging fastened in place.

• Edging coated with adhesive that must be heated with an electric iron to make it stick.

A sharp cutting tool such as a carving knife, paper cutter, or heavy-duty shears can be used for cutting the veneer to size. If veneer adhesive is to be used, a household iron is needed for heating the veneer to set the adhesive.

Applying Veneer with Adhesives

Two adhesives can be used to attach veneer: contact cement and ve-

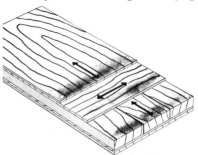

42-14(a). *A chess- or check-erboard can be made with veneers of contrasting colors forming the squares.*

Veneer

Cross-banding

Gauge lines

42-15. *The core of lumber-core plywood is made of narrow, solid wood strips (arranged to equalize stress) which are edge glued together. The core is covered on both sides with crossbands and a face and back veneer.*

neer adhesive. With contact cement, there is an instant bond, and the material cannot be moved once contact is made. Veneer adhesive is almost like contact cement, except that the permanent bond does not occur until heat is applied.

USING CONTACT CEMENT

Cut sheets of veneer for each surface of the project. Put two coats of contact cement on one surface of the project and one coat on the veneer, brushing thoroughly. Allow to dry about 30 minutes. To check if the adhesive is dry, lightly press a piece of kraft paper onto the surface. If the paper does not stick,

42-14(b). *The board can be used as an inlay on a game table.*

the adhesive is ready to receive the veneer.

Hold the veneer over the surface and align it. Then lower it in place. Remember that it cannot be moved once it touches the surface. *Roll the surface with a small roller.* You can also place a block of softwood over the veneer and strike the surface until the veneer is in complete contact with it. Trim excess material off the surface with a knife. Sand lightly for a square edge. Make sure all sawdust is removed from the edge before applying contact cement for the edging.

USING VENEER (THERMOSET) ADHESIVE

One advantage of using veneer adhesive instead of contact cement in making small projects is that the veneer design can be assembled on the project's surface and moved around until heat is applied. Also, a design can be built up piece by piece since the veneer will not adhere until heat is applied.

To use veneer adhesive, brush it on the surface of the project and on the back of the veneer. The adhesive is white in its liquid state. Allow it to dry to a clear gloss. Now place the veneer over the surface and align it properly. Set a regular household iron to about 60 percent of full heat. Once the iron has reached the proper heat, place it on the veneer. Start at one corner, moving the iron slowly. This is im-

portant because heat must penetrate the veneer to liquefy the two adhesive coatings so that they will fuse. As the veneer cools, the bond becomes permanent. It is good practice to follow the iron with a very smooth block of wood, since this will hold the veneer in contact while the adhesive fuses. Trim any excess veneer at sharp right angles to the edges. Make sure that the edges are square, relatively smooth, and free of all sawdust.

If heat-sensitive edging is used, remove the paper liner and apply the edging with hand pressure. Apply an iron to the edging until the heat penetrates the veneer, activating the adhesive. Follow directly behind the iron with a block of wood to hold the adhesive until it cools.

MAKING LUMBER-CORE PLYWOOD

Lumber-core plywood is built of a core of solid, glued-up stock, with crossbands on each side and veneer on face and back. Fig. 42-15.

Make lumber-core plywood as follows:

1. Determine the total thickness of the finished panel. Standard American veneer is 1/28" thick, and crossbanding stock is available in thicknesses of 1/20", 1/10", and 1/8". If, for example, you use two thicknesses of 1/28" veneer and two thick-

nesses of ⅒″ crossband stock and you wish to produce a ¾″ panel, the core must be approximately ¹⁷⁄₃₂″ thick.

2. Select, match, and join the face and back veneers, as previously described.

3. Construct the core. Saw pieces of softwood lumber, such as poplar or basswood, into pieces 2″ to 4″ wide and slightly longer than needed for the furniture piece. Reverse every other board so that the heart side is up for half the boards and down for the other half. This will help reduce the tendency to warp. If the edges of a piece are to be machined, such as the edge of a tabletop, it will be necessary to band a piece of solid wood of the same material as the face veneer to the edges and ends of the core. For example, if the face veneer is mahogany, then a band of mahogany should be added to the sides and ends of the core stock. The more common commercial method is to build a frame of the solid material and fit the plywood into it. Chapter 50 describes this process. Glue the core material together and, after it is dry, plane both surfaces to thickness.

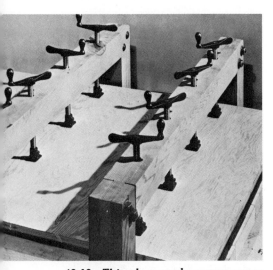

42-16. *This shop-made veneer press can be used to construct small veneer panels.*

4. Cut the crossbanding material slightly larger than the overall size of the core. Whenever possible, the crossbanding material should have no joints.

5. Prepare the veneer press for the gluing operation. Fig. 42-16. Place a thick piece of plywood at the base of the press and then place a piece of waxed paper over this. Also have a second piece of waxed paper and heavy plywood for the top of the "sandwich."

6. Assemble and glue the lumber-core plywood sandwich. Apply a good grade of any type of glue (white is best) to the poor side of the face veneer. Place the veneer with the tape side down in the bottom of the veneer press and over the waxed paper. Now apply glue to both sides of the first piece of crossbanding material and put this in place with the grain running at right angles to the face veneer. Do the same for the core stock and the second piece of crossbanding material. Then apply glue to the inner surface of the back veneer. When arranging the materials, remember that alternate layers of veneers, crossbands, and core should have the grain running at right angles to each other. Veneer pins or brads can be placed in the waste stock to keep the pieces from slipping. Now cover the sandwich with another piece of waxed paper and then a plywood pressure pad. Apply even pressure with the veneer press and allow to dry overnight. In assembling the sandwich, it is important to work as quickly as possible so that the veneers will not absorb too much moisture from the glue. Since veneers are thin, they tend to expand very rapidly from any moisture that is applied.

7. Lumber-core plywood can also be laid up (made) by the following process: First, glue the crossbands to the core. After this sandwich is dried in the press, remove and check to make sure there are

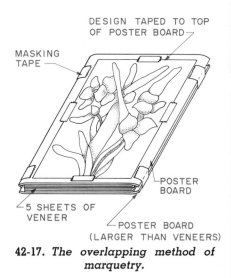

42-17. *The overlapping method of marquetry.*

no loose areas in the crossbands. If there are, cut with a sharp knife and force glue under such areas. Put back into the press and allow to dry. Next glue the face and back veneers over the crossbands. Replace in the press and allow to dry.

8. After the unit has dried thoroughly, trim and sand the edges.

MARQUETRY AND BUILT-UP PATTERNS

Marquetry is fitting pieces of different veneer together to form a picture or design. Sometimes a cabinetmaker will cut and fit the pieces to form such a design. However, if many small pieces are needed, it is more common to purchase the materials already cut.

Overlapping Method

The simplest way of doing marquetry is by the *overlapping method*. Select a relatively simple design and choose wood veneers of contrasting colors to make up the design. The veneers will be wrinkled slightly. You may have to wet the thin wood with a damp cloth and press it between plywood overnight to flatten it out.

Cut two squares of poster board slightly larger than the marquetry design. Tape the first piece of veneer to one piece of the poster board. Then add the next layer of veneer and tape it in place. Add the next and the next until all of the veneers are stacked. Place another piece of poster board over the stack and tape the whole unit together. The poster board serves to keep the stack flat and keeps the top and bottom veneers from tearing when the stack is being cut. When the sandwich is complete, trace or glue your design on the top of the poster board. Fig. 42-17.

Drill a small hole near a corner towards the interior of the design (where it will show the least). The hole should be about 1/16", just large enough for a small jeweler's blade to fit through. Cut the interior of the design first and then work toward the exterior. Use a very slow speed when doing the cutting. Arrange each cut part on a bench, being careful not to mix them up.

Once all the cutting is completed, you will have enough material to make as many designs as you have layers of veneer. Cut the poster board apart to expose the remains of the veneer sandwich. The largest piece of veneer will have a large opening in it where you cut out the design. Stretch pieces of masking tape across this opening, completely

covering it. Then turn this sheet of veneer over and begin assembling the various parts of the marquetry. There will be small cracks between the parts from the saw kerf. However, these will fill in with glue and a finish. After the design is assembled, spread a thin veneer glue or contact cement on the untaped side of the design and apply it to the plywood, hardboard, or other surface. When the total design is dry, remove the masking tape. Fig. 42-18.

Another method of combining several different-colored veneers to form a design is with templates. It is first necessary to make a full-size pattern of the design on paper. Then a template, preferably of metal, should be cut for each different part. Place this template over the veneer and cut around the edge with a small sharp knife. Use the same template to cut the opening in the background veneer. This is a very exacting job and must be done with great care. It is important that the template does not move when the inner and outer shapes are being cut. After all the pieces are cut, place the fitted parts on a flat surface. Apply tape to the face surface to hold all the parts in place. Use contact cement to fasten the design permanently to a core stock.

INLAY

Inlay is a process whereby strips of rare woods are set into the surface of solid wood or other veneers. With a router it is a relatively simple job. First select the inlay banding (material) to determine the width of groove needed. Usually the banding is 1/20" thick. Put a left-hand spiral bit in the router. This cuts clean and doesn't leave any fuzz on the top of the cut. Adjust the depth of cut to slightly less than the thickness of the inlay. Use a straight guide to control the location of the groove. Make one pass to cut a groove equal in width to the band-

42-19. *Here you see two table legs with inlay banding. The one on the right has the groove cut and ready for the multicolored inlay banding. The one on the left has the banding glued in place.*

ing. After the groove is machined, it has rounded corners. These have to be squared up with a small chisel. When the groove has been cut, miter the corners of the inlay strip and then make a trial assembly to be sure the pieces fit. Remove the inlay and apply a small amount of white glue to the groove. Replace the inlay and cover with waxed paper. Clamp a strip of wood over the top until dry. Fig. 42-19.

You can purchase rare-wood block inlays of contrasting or blending colors for mounting in the tops of tables, buffets, fancy boxes, and similar items. Block inlays are usually made to a thickness of 1/20". To apply, first mark the location on the tabletop or other wood product, then cut around the design with a sharp knife. Use a router and a guide to remove as much of the material as possible where the inlay is to go. Adjust for a depth of cut slightly less than the thickness of the inlay. Then remove the rest of the wood within this area by freehand routing or with a chisel. Fig. 42-20. The inlays come with paper on one side. Apply glue to the opposite side and insert in the recess. Clamp until the glue is dry. After the work has dried sufficiently, remove the paper backing by wetting it with water and then sanding

42-18. *The completed picture.*

42-20. *An artistic inlay. The opening into which the inlay will go is already routed out. The bit and knife for cutting the opening are also shown.*

42-21. *A template and ring guide for cutting an inlay and routing out a recess.*

it off. Before finishing with stain or filler, seal the inlay with a coat of shellac so that it won't absorb any of the dye coat.

A special recess and insert guide with ring is available so that the same template can be used to cut the inlay and rout out the recess. The ring controls depth of cut. First, from ⅛″ hardboard make a template of the same shape as the inlay. Fasten the template in position over the material into which the inlay is to fit. Rout out the recess with the ring attached to the guide. Then remove the ring and cut out the inlay, using the same template. Fig. 42-21.

43 Plastic Laminates

Because high-pressure plastic laminates are widely used in furniture, cabinets, and interiors, the cabinetmaker or finish carpenter should thoroughly understand them and their use. Plastic laminates are known by such common trade names as Formica and Micarta.

High-pressure plastic laminates are surfacing materials that combine beautiful colors and designs with exceptional durability. These materials are composed of the following: layers of kraft paper impregnated with specially formulated phenolic resins and covered by a melamine resin; a pattern sheet saturated with plastic and topped by a

protective wear sheet; and, finally, a coat of additional melamine resins. These built-up materials are placed in a large hydraulic press between stainless steel plates and subjected to very high heat and pressure to form a hard-surface sheet. Plastic laminates are popular for cabinet and table tops, walls, and built-ins because they resist wear, burns, stains, and soil. They can be cleaned with soap and water.

Plastic laminates are available in several different surface finishes such as gloss, satin, textured or brushed, and furniture. The textured or brushed finish is an excellent wall covering because it is nonglare. In

addition to plain colors and various designs, plastic laminates can also be made to imitate wood grain. Fig. 43-1. Textured and furniture finishes in wood-grain patterns look and feel like natural woods or veneers, yet they have the same excellent wear resistance as conventional satin-finish laminates.

GRADES OF LAMINATES

General-purpose or *standard grade* is ¹⁄₁₆″ thick. It is used for a wide variety of indoor surfaces such as table, kitchen counter, or desk tops, vanities, walls, fixtures, case goods, and furniture. It can be applied to both vertical and horizontal

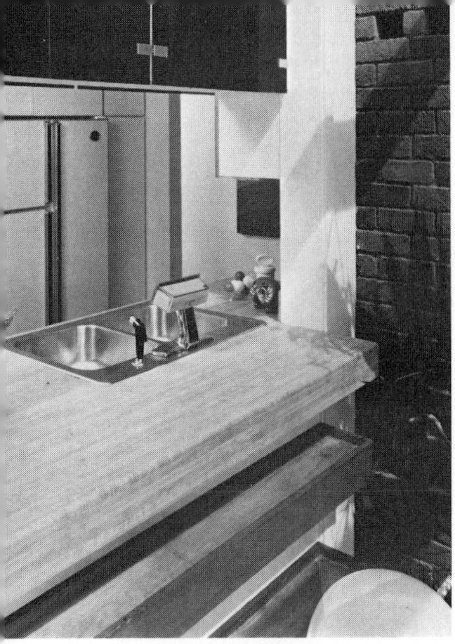

43-1. ***This kitchen counter is covered with wood-grain plastic laminate.***

surfaces and is used where good appearance, durability, and resistance to stain and heat are necessary. The standard grade can be used for edging. It will bend to a 9″ radius without heating and to a 2½″ radius when heated.

The *postforming grade* is about 1/20″ thick. It is designed to permit heating and forming into short radii for use around doors and sill ledges, rolled or covered counter tops, and on small-radius tabletops. An example can be seen in Fig. 43-1.

The *vertical grade* is about 1/32″ thick. It is used only on vertical surfaces such as cabinet fronts and the sides of fixtures and furniture. This same grade is cut into narrower bands 1⅝″ wide and called *edge banding* or *trim.* It can be curved to a 3″ radius at room temperature. By heating it to about 325 to 360 degrees F, it can be bent to a ¾″ radius.

Backer sheets of about 1/32″, 1/20″, or 1/16″ thickness are placed on the underside or back of free-standing tables for dimensional stability. These are low-cost materials which will provide balanced construction when core material is used. Backer sheets are not needed if the underside of the top is well fastened to the base. For example, no backer sheet is needed for a standard coffee table or a kitchen cabinet. Backer sheets should be used when a top has an unsupported area of more than four square feet.

Flame-retardant grade, 1/16″ thick, is designed for wall paneling, doors, and other vertical surfaces which require such protective treatment, as in hotels or dormitories.

SHEET SIZES

Widths commonly available are 24″, 30″, 36″, 48″, and 60″. Most manufacturers add ¼″ to the width so that two 12″ widths can be cut from a 24″ width. The most common lengths are 60″, 72″, 84″, 96″, 120″, and 144″. Since plastic laminates are relatively expensive, it is important to keep these sizes in mind when designing tables and cabinets. For example, it would be poor design to specify a 19″ width since only one such piece could be cut from a 36″ width. Plastic laminates are sold by the square foot with the 1/16″ standard grade as the base.

CORE MATERIALS

Since plastic laminates are quite thin and brittle, they must be attached to a core. The most common core materials are plywood, particle board, and hardboard. Plywood for horizontal surfaces should be at least ¾″ thick. Lumber-core plywood should have at least five plies and veneer-core plywood, seven. Lumber-core and veneer-core plywood for wall and other vertical surfaces should be not less than ½″ thick and have at least five plies. Normally, interior plywood can be used; but if plastic laminate is to be used in bathrooms or other humid places, it is better to choose exterior grade. Some manufacturers recommend Philippine mahogany plywood because it is smoother than softwood plywood. Plastic laminates can also be bonded to particle board or flakeboard that is ½″ or ¾″ thick. Hardboard at least 3/16″ thick can also be used, but not tempered hardboard. In furniture and architectural woodworking plants, high-pressure plastic laminates are bonded to a core of ¾″ particle board or closed-grain hardwood veneer-core plywood. A water-resistant glue is used, and the materials are clamped in a laminating cold press until dry.

ADHESIVES

Many kinds of adhesives can be used to bond plastic laminates to core materials. However, casein, polyvinyl, resin and other slow-setting glues can be used only when the materials are clamped together under pressure long enough to cure the adhesive. For this reason, contact cement is used for most on-the-job applications. Since there are a great many kinds of contact adhesives, it is important to follow the manufacturer's recommendations for each one.

Contact cement is applied to the surface by brushing, rolling, or with a notched spreader. Figs. 43-2 and 43-3. The brushing method is usually best for edge gluing, while the roller is best for flat surfaces. A sol-

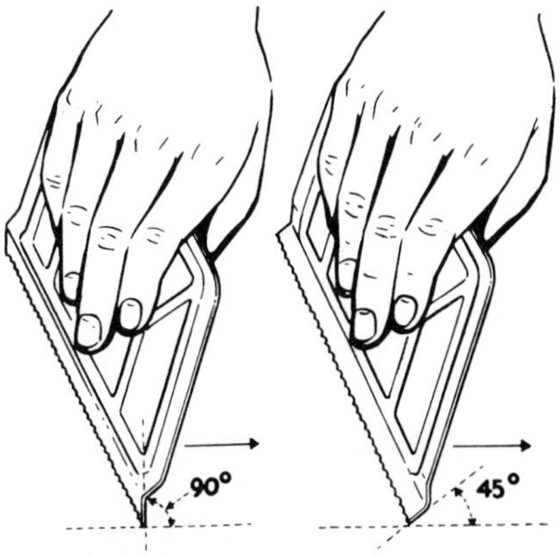

43-2. ***Hold the metal spreader teeth at 90 degrees to the horizontal when applying contact cement to a soft, low-density, or uneven material such as fir or Philippine mahogany plywood. Hold the teeth at 45 degrees when applying cement to hard, high-density, smooth surfaces such as hardboard.***

43-3. *Applying contact cement with a roller to a honeycomb core. Cabinet doors are often made in this way. The rails and stiles are hardwood and the center is filled with impregnated paper honeycomb. Then the surfaces and edges are covered with plastic laminate.*

vent should be available for cleaning off excess cement. There are two basic types of solvents for this. One is a flammable mixture that must be kept away from heat and open flame. The other has a water base.

CLAMPING AND PRESSURE FOR BONDING

For all adhesives except the contact type it is necessary to apply

43-4. *A sheet can be cut into smaller pieces by scoring the face with a sharp-pointed tool. Cut back and forth in the scored groove until the plastic is almost cut in two.*

even pressure to the plastic laminate until the adhesive is dry. If, for example, you wish to fasten a piece of plastic laminate to a core for a tabletop, place a pressure pad of plywood over the laminate and apply clamps or weights such as sand bags until the adhesive is dry. However, for most on-the-job construction, a contact cement should be used.

METHODS OF CUTTING

Sheets of plastic laminate usually have to be cut to a smaller size. Since the material is hard, thin, and rather brittle, it is important to support it as it is cut. The layout line can be marked with a grease pencil. While standard woodworking and metalworking tools can be used, they become dull rather rapidly. For this reason, carbide-tipped cutting tools are recommended. Some final trimming is usually necessary; so it is suggested that the rough-cut pieces be about ½″ wider and longer than the piece to which they will be glued.

Here are the ways plastic laminate can be cut:

● If little or no equipment is available, the sheets can be cut to smaller sizes by scoring the face with a file ground to a sharp point or with an ice pick or an awl. Fig. 43-4. By cutting back and forth in a scored groove, the plastic can be cut almost in two and then broken the rest of the way. This method is good for scoring to a template or cutting irregular shapes. Always break upward with the face *up*. Fig. 43-5.

● A crosscut handsaw with 12 points per inch can be used, provided the angle of cut is kept very low, almost flat against the sheet. The finish side should be *up*.

● A metal hacksaw with a blade that has 32 teeth per inch can be used for short cuts where the frame of the saw will not interfere. The finish side should be *up*.

43-5. *Place a straightedge over the scored line and apply pressure as you pull up on the sheet to break it.*

● Several different portable power tools can be used, including the cutoff saw and the saber saw. With both of these tools, the decorative side should be *down* as this will confine any chipping to the back surface of the material. To cut plastic laminate to size, it is a good idea to clamp it to a bench top, using a piece of wood as a straightedge guide for cutting. Fig. 43-6.

● A portable router can also be used to cut sheets to size. Fig. 43-7. This machine is used also to trim the edge of plastic laminate after it is installed. The finish side should be *up*.

43-6. *Cutting with a saber saw. This is a very practical power tool for on-the-job installations since it can also be used to make the cutout for a sink or other opening. A straightedge is being used to guide the saw.*

43-7. *The router can be used to cut sheets to size if no other power tool is available. The small-diameter, straight carbide cutter bit should be used. Never attempt to use a regular cutter bit since the speed of the router and the amount of the material to be cut will dull the standard bit too quickly for practical use.*

● A circular saw can be used. The best blade is one that is hollow-ground or carbide-tipped. Cutting should be done with the finish side *up*. Keep the saw cutting into the surface at a very sharp angle, as close to straight up and down as possible. This means that great care must be taken, especially when the guard must be removed to accommodate a large sheet. Fig. 43-8.

43-8. *Cutting plastic laminate on the circular saw. Note that the blade must be set very high. Otherwise the blade will overheat and also dull very quickly. However, such a blade setting makes the operation dangerous. Great caution must be exercised. The standard basket guard doesn't function well for this but the guards described in Chapter 26 are very satisfactory.*

● The band saw can be used to cut plastic laminate with the decorative side *up*. The band saw, with a buttress-type tooth, is normally used only when cutting plastic laminates that have already been bonded to the core material.

DRILLING AND BORING

For hand work, a brace and bit with regular boring bits or a bit-stock drill can be used. A standard metal twist drill is also good. For production work, carbide-tipped drills are best. All material to be drilled should be backed with wood to prevent break-out at the bottom of the hole. Start the hole on the finish side.

EDGE TREATMENT

There are many kinds of edge treatment for a plastic-laminate top. Fig. 43-9. The laminate should be applied to the top and trimmed before adding any edges except the self edge or edge banding type. For example, for a metal edge with a T molding, the plastic laminate is applied, then a slot is cut in the edge of the core to receive the molding. If an auxiliary wood fence is not used in cutting the slot, strips of masking tape should be applied to the saw fence to protect the polished surface of the laminate. For self edge or edge banding, the best practice is to apply the edge *before* applying the top surface whenever possible. If the tabletop or counter top has rounded corners, the postforming grade of laminate should be used. A plastic-laminate top has a more pleasing appearance if the edge is built up by adding a strip of wood or plywood of equal thickness directly under and flush with the front edge. This is shown in the edge banding drawing in Fig. 43-9.

Edge Banding

After the edge is smooth, apply one or more coats of contact cement to it and one coat to the back

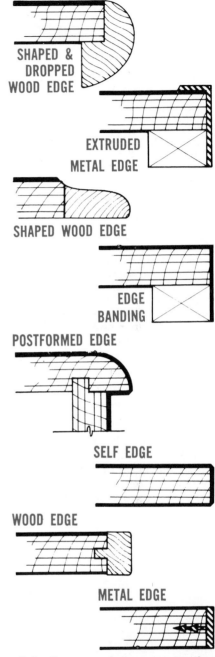

43-9. *Common edge treatments that can be used with plastic laminates. The most popular is the edge banding treatment.*

of the edge strip. Allow the adhesive to set until it is dry to the touch but still a little soft. Another test of dryness is to tamp a small piece of brown paper on the cemented surfaces. When the paper will not stick, the adhesive is ready for

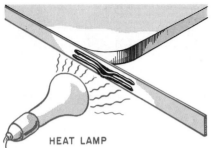

43-10. *Apply heat until the crayon melts.*

43-11. *Curve the strip manually around the corner as shown.*

bonding. Now carefully align the strip and bring it in contact with the edge. *Remember: Once the two surfaces touch, there is an immediate bond. No further positioning is possible.* Roll the strip to make sure it is firmly in place.

43-12. *A small wood block can be used as a guide for the saw in removing excess strip material at the butt joint.*

On rounded corners that have a small radius, the strip must be heated to a temperature of about 300 degrees F. The best way to do this is with a heat lamp. With special crayon or marking material draw two short lines on the material where the curve is to be. Apply heat from the lamp. When the lines melt, the strip is ready to be bent. Fig. 43-10. Put on heat-resistant gloves. Wrap the strip around the corner by pulling it manually. Fig. 43-11. Then roll it until a good bond is obtained.

The butt joint between the ends of two strips is made by cutting away the excess with a hacksaw and then rolling the joint. Fig. 43-12.

After the edge banding is dry, trim the excess away until it is flush with the top to be surfaced. A router with a straight bit is the best tool for doing this. Remember: Don't bevel the upper edge of the banding. Any variation in this edge will cause a poor glue line. Fig. 43-13. The bottom edge can be trimmed with a bevel cut. When applying the top, be sure to cover the top of the edging with adhesive, as well as the rest of the core.

In edge banding a table or counter, a good method is to cover all front-to-back vertical surfaces first, then cover all side-to-side vertical surfaces. Finally, cover all horizontal surfaces.

APPLYING LAMINATE TO A TABLETOP

Plastic laminates can be applied to a tabletop with simple hand tools. Tools and materials needed include a 2" bristle brush, small hand roller, block plane, flat mill file, hammer, two pieces of heavy wrapping paper (each piece slightly larger than half the top to be installed), a block of soft wood, contact cement, and abrasive cloth. Steps in applying the material are as follows:

1. Cut the plastic laminate to

43-13. *Trimming the excess material from the upper edge. Keep this edge smooth and free from nicks.*

size, about ⅛" to ¼" larger in both directions than the top.

2. Make sure the plywood or core material is smooth and has no imperfections in its surface. Fill any holes in the surface and then sand it smooth.

3. Decide on the kind of edge treatment you want. The most common treatment is edge banding. The edge is built up with an extra piece of plywood along the underside of the table. Then a band of plastic laminate is glued to the edge before applying the top.

4. Apply a heavy coat of contact cement to the tabletop and the back of the plastic laminate. Make sure, after the cement dries about 15 minutes, that there is a glossy film over the entire surface. If dull spots appear, it means that additional contact cement must be applied. If a second coat is needed on the core material, make sure the first coat is dry before applying the second.

5. Check to see that the adhesive is dry. This can be done by lightly pressing a piece of wrapping paper on the surface. When the paper will not stick, the cement is ready for bonding.

6. Remember that *a permanent bond is formed the moment the two surfaces touch.* Place the two piec-

es of wrapping paper lightly on top of the core material. Another method is to place strips of laminate (without adhesive) on the surface. Place the plastic laminate over these. Now move the laminate until it is aligned correctly. Gently slip one piece of paper or strip of laminate from under the plastic laminate. The two adhesive surfaces will bond immediately. Take care not to jar the work as the paper is removed. When the first half is in contact, carefully remove the second half.

7. Roll the surface from the center to the outside edges with a small roller. Work towards the edges in all directions. A piece of soft wood can be used in place of the roller. Put the wood over the plastic laminate and tap it with a hammer, covering the entire surface so that there is a complete bond.

8. Remove the excess plastic laminate with a hand plane. Then file the edges smooth. If the edging has already been applied, file at an angle of 20 to 30 degrees. Use long

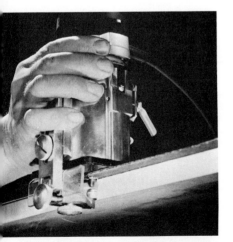

43-14. *Using a plastic-laminate trimmer to remove the excess material and to bevel the edge. This is a simple one-step job if the tool is properly set. With a standard router it is usually necessary to trim the excess material away first with a straight router bit. Then a bevel bit is used to finish off the edge at an angle.*

downward strokes. If the edging has not already been installed, file the edge flush with the core materials so that a good joint can be made when the edging is applied. If a router or laminate trimmer is available, this can be used to trim the edge and bevel it at the same time. Fig. 43-14.

9. Clean the adhesive from the surface by scraping with a scrap piece of plastic laminate. Use soap and water or alcohol to clean the surface and bring back its original luster.

APPLYING LAMINATE TO COUNTER TOPS

One of the most common uses of plastic laminates is for counter tops in kitchens and bathrooms. The procedure for such installations is as follows:

1. Make sure that the wood counter top is in good condition. If it is old, remove all paint, varnish, cement, and dirt. Sand until clean, bare wood is exposed. Fill all holes with plastic wood. Sand again.

2. Cut the plastic laminate by one of the methods described earlier.

3. Fit the plastic laminate to the top of the wood surface as accurately as possible before any adhesive is applied. If a seam or butt joint is required near a sink, try to locate it at the center of the sink. This makes fitting easier.

4. If a self edge or edge banding is used, apply this first. If a metal edge is used, apply this after the top is in place.

5. Apply the contact cement. Follow the manufacturer's instructions as to application, use, and drying. To test for dryness, press a small piece of brown paper on the cement surface. When the paper will not stick, the cement is ready. Again, remember *the bond is immediate and permanent.* Therefore, to align the plastic laminate properly, place several pieces of heavy brown

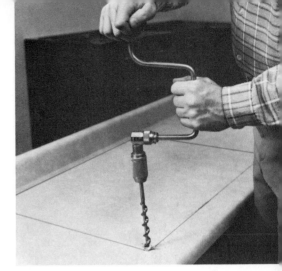

43-15. *Boring holes in each corner of the sink cutout.*

wrapping paper on the wood surface. Overlap them for easy removal. Position the laminate and move the first piece of paper a few inches at a time, pressing the laminate by hand as you go. Remove the remainder of the paper. Roll the laminate using a two-inch roller. Work from the center towards the edges to finish the bonding operation. For places that are hard to reach, use a piece of scrap wood and tap with a hammer to assure a complete bond.

6. Trim the edges. Trim off any excess overhang or rough edge with a portable electric router or trimmer, or with a flat cabinet rasp. Carefully file with downward strokes at an angle.

7. To make a cutout for a sink, follow instructions provided with the sink or rim to mark the position of the cutout. Accurate measurements are important to transfer the cutout's shape to the plastic laminate. Be sure the position will allow for the sink bowl, holding clamps, or plumbing connections to clear the cabinet framing or other obstructions below. Also be sure the rim or flange is well clear (forward) of the backsplash cove. Mark or trace the outline carefully and cover with a strip of cellophane tape. Bore pilot holes (tap a starter point with a sharp punch or nail so the drill won't jump and scar the laminate) in each corner inside and tangent to the marked line. Fig. 43-15. Use a

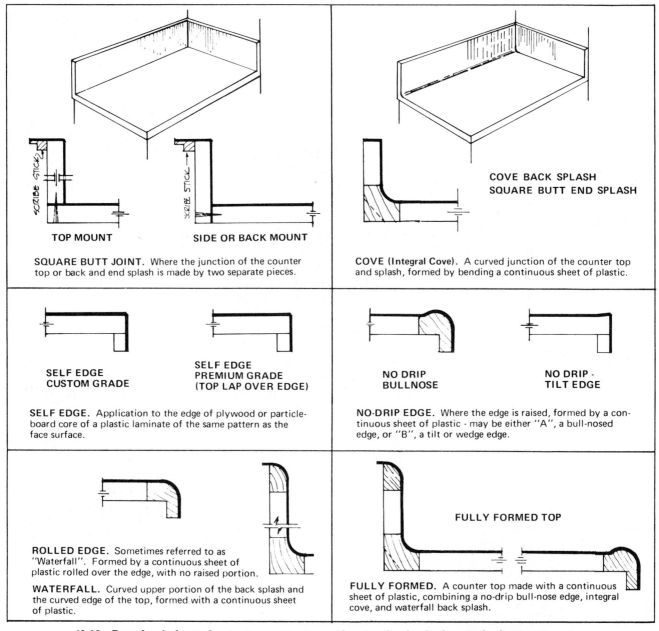

SQUARE BUTT JOINT. Where the junction of the counter top or back and end splash is made by two separate pieces.

COVE BACK SPLASH
SQUARE BUTT END SPLASH

COVE (Integral Cove). A curved junction of the counter top and splash, formed by bending a continuous sheet of plastic.

SELF EDGE
CUSTOM GRADE

SELF EDGE
PREMIUM GRADE
(TOP LAP OVER EDGE)

SELF EDGE. Application to the edge of plywood or particleboard core of a plastic laminate of the same pattern as the face surface.

NO DRIP
BULLNOSE

NO DRIP -
TILT EDGE

NO-DRIP EDGE. Where the edge is raised, formed by a continuous sheet of plastic - may be either "A", a bull-nosed edge, or "B", a tilt or wedge edge.

ROLLED EDGE. Sometimes referred to as "Waterfall". Formed by a continuous sheet of plastic rolled over the edge, with no raised portion.

WATERFALL. Curved upper portion of the back splash and the curved edge of the top, formed with a continuous sheet of plastic.

FULLY FORMED TOP

FULLY FORMED. A counter top made with a continuous sheet of plastic, combining a no-drip bull-nose edge, integral cove, and waterfall back splash.

43-16. *Details of plastic laminate counter tops, showing backsplashes and edge treatments.*

fine-toothed keyhole saw, keeping the blade at a convenient low angle on straight cuts. Elevate the blade for short strokes around curves. Apply pressure *only* on the downstroke to avoid chipping the laminate. Use a wood rasp, fine file, and sandpaper to smooth any high points for a better rim fit. File the edges of all rounded inside corners so that they are smooth and free of cracks and crazes.

8. If a backsplash is needed, it can be applied in several ways. Fig. 43-16.

9. Fit the sink. Set the frame or rim in position and secure it in place according to the instructions supplied with the rim. For a good watertight seal, apply caulking compound before fastening the sink in place. Remove the excess adhesive with the cleaner recommended for the adhesive you are using.

43-17. *All exposed surfaces of these cabinets have been covered with plastic laminate.*

APPLYING LAMINATE TO KITCHEN CABINET FRONTS

Plastic laminates can be installed on either new or old kitchen cabinet fronts to improve their appearance and utility. Fig. 43-17.

RESTORING FURNITURE USING PLASTIC LAMINATES

A good way of restoring or modernizing old furniture is to cover all exposed surfaces with plastic laminates as shown in Fig. 43-18.

43-18(e). *Pull other strips out one at a time in sequence so that the sheet falls exactly into place.*

43-18(a). *An old chest of drawers that will be covered with plastic laminate. The first step is to remove the old finish. Sand down to the bare wood. Fill any cracks or holes with plastic wood. Sand smooth.*

43-18(c). *Saw the plastic laminate about ⅛″ oversized, using one of the methods described earlier in the chapter. After making sure the pieces fit, apply contact cement to the back as shown here. Also coat the surfaces of the chest of drawers. Allow the contact cement to dry.*

43-18(f). *Use a block and hammer to make sure the entire surface is bonded. Then trim off the overhang with a file or router until all edges are smooth and flush.*

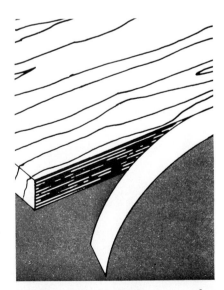

43-18(b). *Cut laminate into edge banding strips, about ¹⁄₁₆″ oversized to allow for file finishing. Using contact cement, apply edge banding to all exposed edges. This must be done before you do the top surface.*

43-18(d). *Place several laminate strips across the surface to be covered. Lay the laminate sheet on the strips and align carefully. Pull out the end strip so that contact is made.*

43-18(g). *The finished product.*

44 Frame-and-Panel Construction

Frame-and-panel construction is widely used in cabinetmaking for doors and windows, sides and fronts of cabinets, and for interior casework. Fig. 44-1. While manufactured materials such as plywood and particle board have become increasingly popular for built-ins and on-the-job cabinets, the frame and panel is still a favorite construction method in millrooms and furniture-manufacturing plants. The following are its distinct advantages:

• The unit has good dimensional stability and will change little in width or height with changes in humidity.

• The unit does not warp. (A large area of glued-up solid stock will warp and, to a more limited extent, so will plywood and other manufactured materials.)

• The unit adds design qualities to furniture. Fig. 44-2. A frame-and-panel door on a fine piece of furniture is much more interesting than a simple flat surface. It can also be made in any style from the simple rectangles of Contemporary furniture to the graceful curves of Traditional.

• By using frame construction, glass or a metal grille can be set into the opening instead of a wood panel. An example is shown in Fig. 44-2.

INTERIOR CABINET PARTS

An *open* or *skeleton* frame (sometimes called a web frame) consists of two vertical members called *stiles* and two horizontal members called *rails*. The parts usually are joined with dowels, a haunched mortise-and-tenon joint, or a stub-tenon joint. These frames are installed on the inside of a chest, desk, or cabinet to add stability to the unit and to provide horizontal support for the drawers. Fig. 44-3. While an open frame is adequate for many uses, better-quality furniture makes use of a *dust panel*, which is a simple frame with a center of plywood or hardboard. Such a panel is installed in chests to keep the dust from seeping down from one drawer to the next. For this kind of construction a groove must be cut around the inside edges of the rails and stiles to receive the panel, which usually is ¼" hardboard or plywood. Fig. 44-4.

EXTERIOR FURNITURE PARTS AND ARCHITECTURAL WOODWORK

Frame-and-panel surfaces for exterior furniture parts vary greatly in design and construction. Some of these differences are as follows:

Frame

The frame is usually made of solid wood and requires four or

44-1. *Frame-and-panel construction is used for all kinds of cabinet doors. The doors shown here have a panel that is bevel raised on one side.*

44-2. *Frame-and-panel construction was used for the doors of this handsome buffet. Note the arched panels at the center and the glass panels at each side.*

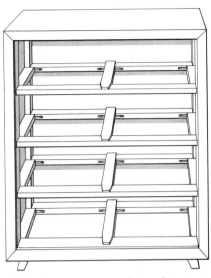

44-3. *Frames are used in cabinets to strengthen the unit and also to serve as drawer supports.*

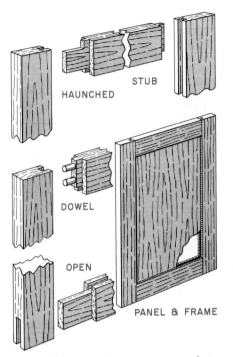

44-4. *The common joints used in making dust panels. A groove (plow) is cut around the inside edges of the rails and stiles to receive the panel of plywood or hardboard.*

more pieces: two pieces for the vertical stiles and two pieces for the horizontal rails. If an intermediate horizontal divider is used, this is called a *cross rail*. An intermediate vertical divider called a *mullion* may also be used. For most furniture and cabinet doors, the thickness of the frame is 11/16″ surfaced stock (¾″ minimum thickness is allowed).

Sticking

Sticking is the term used to de-scribe the shape of the inside edge of the frame. The sticking may be square or molded. Some of the standard molded stickings are the ovolo, the bead and cove, and the ogee. Fig. 44-5.

A panel groove, or plow, is cut around the inside edge to receive the panel. Usually the groove is cut

to a depth of ⅜″. However, if a solid wood panel is used, the groove should be ⅜″ deep in the rails and 1″ deep in the stiles. The extra depth in the stiles takes care of the cross-grain expansion of the solid panel. Solid panels are usually limited to not more than 10″, which means that they are installed only on small cupboard doors for furniture and cabinets.

Corner Joints

Many kinds of corner joints can be used. The normal practice in good construction is to use either a haunched mortise-and-tenon joint or a dowel joint with a stub tenon for all work that has square sticking on the inside edge. Fig. 44-6. Stiles and rails that have molded edges have a mortise-and-tenon joint with the tenon shoulder coped to fit the molded edge of the stile. Fig. 44-7.

Panel

The panel can be made of either plywood (which is the usual practice) or solid glued-up stock. There are many kinds of panel surfaces. Some of them are described here and shown in Fig. 44-8.

● The *flush panel* is often used for the sides of furniture cases and cabinets. A groove, or plow, is cut in the frame and a rabbet is cut

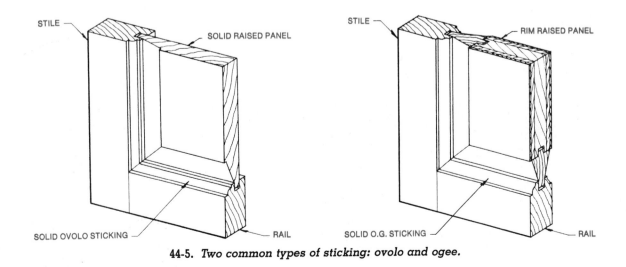

44-5. *Two common types of sticking: ovolo and ogee.*

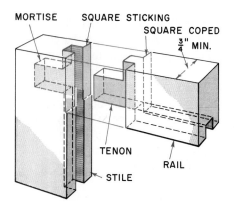

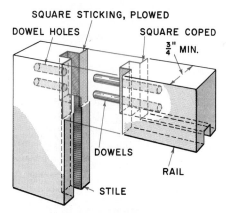

44-6. *The two common methods of stile-and-rail construction when square sticking is used and there is a square coped shoulder on the tenon.*

around the panel so that the outside surface is flush, or level. This construction makes use of a square edge on the frame.

● The *elevated* or *raised panel* is sometimes used for furniture doors.

A groove is cut in the frame and the edges of the panel are cut to fit so that the panel is elevated above the frame itself. The edges of the panel are usually rounded for better appearance.

● The *straight* or *plane panel* is the simplest, especially when used with a square-edge frame. (Note that Fig. 44-8 shows an ovolo rather than a square edge.)

● The *shoulder raised-one-side panel* adds a design characteristic that is especially attractive on Modern or Contemporary furniture.

● The *beveled raised-one-side panel* is the most common one for furniture doors. The inside of the door has a flat panel appearance, while its outside shows a raised panel. Fig. 44-1. In the cabinet shop the raised panel is cut on a circular saw, radial-arm saw, or shaper. If veneer-core plywood panels are used, the plies are exposed on the beveled surfaces. These show up very distinctly when a finish is applied. Therefore furniture and cabinet manufacturers construct lumber-core plywood panels so that the plies won't show. This is done in various ways. If three-ply construction is used, extra-heavy veneers are chosen for the face and back so that they can be cut at an angle without exposing the core. Fig. 44-9. For five-ply construction, the crossbands are made of thick,

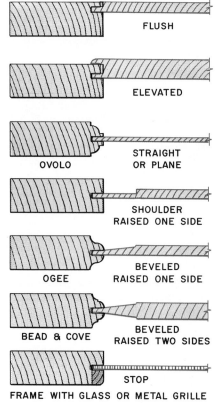

44-8. *Common kinds of panels.*

good-quality wood and the face and back veneers are of very thin material. Then the cutting is done through the crossbands as shown in Fig. 44-10. Note that the face veneer starts at the upper edge of the

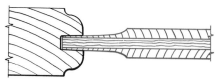

44-9. *Notice how the three-ply panel is made with the face veneer thick enough to allow for the raise.*

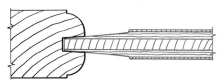

44-10. *This five-ply panel has a thick crossband, so the bevel is cut in this.*

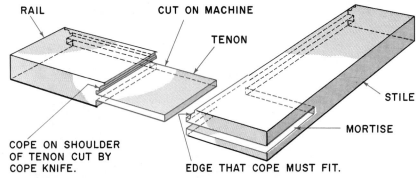

44-7. *Stile-and-rail work with a molded edge. The edge on the stiles is cut on a shaper, sticker, or molding machine. The cope on the shoulder of the tenon is cut on a shaper or tenoner.*

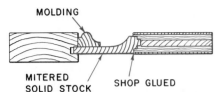

44-11. *This raised panel is made with a mitered rim of solid stock that is grooved into and glued to the edge of the plywood. Notice also the use of molding with a square sticking to give it the appearance of a molded sticking.*

raised panel. Still another method is to cut a mitered rim of solid stock. This rim is grooved and glued into the edge of the plywood panel. Fig. 44-11. The bevel is actually cut in the solid wood rim. This rim can be reinforced with splines, dowels, or clamp nails.

• The *beveled raised-two-sides panel* is used primarily in larger doors where the door is normally seen from both sides.

• A *frame for glass or a metal grille* is made by cutting a rabbet around the inside edge. The glass or grille is usually held in place with a wood stop nailed or stapled to the frame. There are also metal or plastic holders that can be used. See Chapter 14.

CUTTING THE MOLDED EDGES (STICKING)

Simple frame-and-panel construction has square-edge stiles and rails

with grooves for the panels. The panel groove can be cut with a dado head on a circular or radial-arm saw or with cutters on a shaper or router. On quality furniture and cabinets, the inside edges of the stiles and rails have a molded edge. In a small shop these decorative edges are cut to shape on a shaper or router. Furniture and cabinet manufacturers use a molding machine (sticker) and tenoner for these operations.

When molded sticking is used in frame-and-panel construction, it is necessary to have a matched set of *sticking and coping cutters* for the thickness of the frame stock being used. Fig. 44-12. The set of sticking cutters is fastened to the spindle of the shaper, and the inside edges of the stiles and rails are cut to shape. Fig. 44-13. Then a set of coping cutters is fastened to the spindle of the shaper and the ends of the rails (rail shoulders) are coped to fit over the molding on the stiles. Fig. 44-14. If there is a miter joint at the corners, only the sticking cutters are needed.

You will remember that a coped joint is one between two molded pieces in which the end grain of one piece (the rail) is shaped to fit the molded edge of the other (the stile). Fig. 44-15. The usual method of assembly is to use a mortise and tenon or one or two dowels at each

joint. If you carefully study the frame-and-panel construction of quality furniture, you will see that the rails appear to butt against the stiles. This is done by making a coping cut on the ends of the rails to fit the sticking on the edges of the stiles. Very decorative and unusually shaped panel doors are produced in furniture factories on the automatic shaper and double-end tenoning machine. Simpler designs can be made in the school or cabinet shop.

Cutting decorative edges on the

44-13. *Setup for cutting sticking on a shaper.*

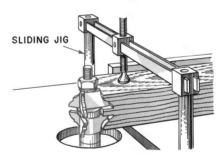

44-14. *Setup for cope cutting on the ends of the rails.*

COVE & BEAD DOOR COPING

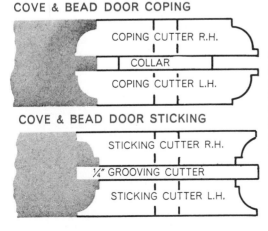

COPING CUTTER R.H.

COLLAR

COPING CUTTER L.H.

COVE & BEAD DOOR STICKING

STICKING CUTTER R.H.

¼" GROOVING CUTTER

STICKING CUTTER L.H.

44-12. *A matched set of coping and sticking cutters for making a cove-and-bead on the inside edge of stiles and rails and for coping the rails. The cutters must be selected for a specific frame thickness and for the correct panel groove.*

44-15. *A coped joint.*

inside of frames is a time-consuming operation unless it is done on a production basis. It is necessary to have the correct set of coping and sticking cutters for the thickness of frame stock being used. Also, a great deal of setup time is required. For this reason it is usually not done for only one or two doors.

However, the decorative effect of sticking can be achieved by applying moldings to the door. One way of doing this is to cut a stub tenon on the inside edges of the frame. The tenon should be of the same width as the thickness of the panel. Then decorative molding is nailed to both edges to hold the panel in

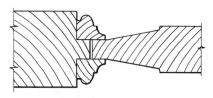

44-16. *Decorative molding installed on both sides of the frame to hold the panel in place.*

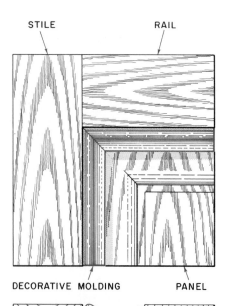

44-17. *Decorative molding installed in the corner along the edge of the frame.*

place. Fig. 44-16. Another way is to use square sticking on the stiles and rails and then nail or staple the molding in the corner between the edge and the panel. Fig. 44-17. When moldings are applied to the frames or surfaces of flush panels, they should be spot glued to the frames, not to the panels, before they are nailed or stapled.

CUTTING A RAISED PANEL

There are three common ways of cutting a raised panel: with the circular saw, the radial-arm saw, and the shaper. In furniture plants an automatic shaper or tenoner sometimes is used.

On the Circular Saw

Tilt the saw blade to 15 degrees from the vertical. On most saws this will be 75 degrees. Adjust the fence to within 3/16" of the saw blade at the table. The blade must tilt away from the fence. Raise the blade to about 1½" above the table. When you are certain the saw is set properly, place the panel on edge with the back surface against the fence and make a cut on each of the four edges. Fig. 44-18.

For a rectangular panel, cut all four bevels. Then set the table saw to cut a shallow shoulder on the bevels. Fig. 44-19. If the top is to be arched, cut to shape on the band saw. Then cut this bevel three times: first with the piece resting on the top of the arch; second, resting on the top and one corner; and third, resting on the top and the other corner. Fig. 44-20. Make the shoulder cuts with a backsaw. Use a sharp, wide chisel to carve the rest of the bevel. Make a neat, sharp intersection at the 30-degree line.

On the Radial-Arm Saw

To cut a raised panel on a radial-arm saw, the machine must be set up for bevel ripping. Use an 8"-diameter blade in place of the stan-

44-18. *Cutting bevels for a raised panel.*

dard 10" one. The 10" blade may strike the column base. Place the saw in the outward position and tilt it to a 90-degree bevel position. Then raise it 5 to 10 degrees (indicated as 80 to 85 on the bevel scale). Place the blade so that it overhangs the guide fence, either on the stationary or auxiliary table, depending on the thickness of the material or the width of cut. To do this, move the saw the correct dis-

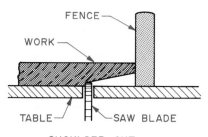

44-19. *Making the shoulder cut.*

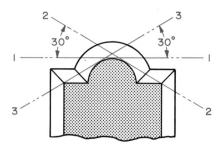

44-20. *The layout for cutting an arched panel.*

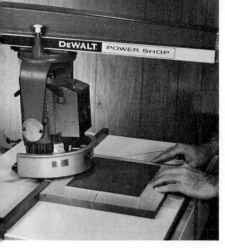

44-21. Cutting a raised panel on the radial-arm saw.

tance from the column and lock it in position with the rip clamp. Before turning on the machine, make sure that the blade moves freely. Then place the stock on the table with the back against the tabletop and the edge against the fence. Feed from right to left. Remember to cut the end grain first and then the edge grain. Fig. 44-21.

On the Shaper

It is necessary to have a panel-raiser cutter mounted on the spindle so that the cutting is done on the upper surface of the panel. The tool can be used to cut a bevel-raised panel on one or two sides. It is ground with proper clearance to make clean cuts with no feather.

A small saw can also be used for cutting a raised panel. The disadvantage of the saw is that the work must be tilted. Usually one or more cuts must be made to produce the beveled edge. Generally one or more heavy roughing cuts followed by a light finishing cut will produce the best surface.

MAKING A FRAME AND PANEL

1. Determine the overall size of the frame. For example, you must decide whether a door is to be the flush, lip, or overlapping type. Then cut the stiles to length. Cut the rails to the correct length, making sure to provide for the correct joint. Fig. 44-22.

2. Square up the stock.

3. If the frame is to have a square inside edge, lay out and cut a groove on all edges into which the panel is to fit. The groove should be as deep as or slightly deeper than it is wide. Usually a groove that is ¼" wide is cut ⅜" deep. If the inside edge is to have molded sticking, both the groove and molded edge are cut on the shaper at the same time. Then another set of matching cutters must be used on the shaper to do the coping on the ends of the rails to match the sticking and to form the tenon.

4. Lay out and cut the panel to the correct size. If necessary, cut the raised panel on one or both sides. The panel should be slightly less in overall dimensions than the distances to the bottom of the frame grooves. The edges of the panel should be about ³⁄₁₆" thick to fit a ¼" groove. If the panel has an irregular shape, first cut to outside size on a band saw and then cut the raised panel.

5. Join the rails to the stiles. In making a stub mortise and tenon, the thickness of the tenon is the same as the width of the groove, and the length of the tenon is the same as the depth of the groove. In

making a haunched mortise-and-tenon joint, the width of the mortise should be the same as the width of the groove. The mortise should be started far enough away from the ends of the stiles to prevent breaking out. The height and depth of the mortise should be about two-thirds the height of the rail. The length of the tenon should be equal to the depth of the mortise plus the depth of the groove. Cut a notch in the tenon so that the long part will fit into the mortise and the short part into the groove. If a molded edge is used, install one or two dowels at each joint. The diameter of the dowels should be equal to half the thickness of the frame.

6. Make a dry assembly of the panel in the frame to see that all parts fit. The panel should be loose enough to provide for expansion and contraction. Then take the unit apart. Reassemble without the panel to shape the inside edge with a router. Give the panel a final sanding. Wax the edges of the panel. Apply glue to the frame joints and assemble. *Never apply glue to the groove or panel.* Clamp securely and allow the unit to dry thoroughly. Then remove any excess glue and sand the frame.

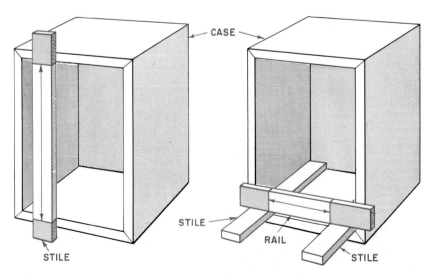

44-22. Marking the lengths of stiles and rails for a flush door. Remember to allow additional length on the rails for the joints.

Doors for furniture and cabinets must be both functional and attractive. Usually designed to close off open shelves or trays, doors also should add interest to the exterior design. Glass, a metal grille, or mesh is often used when silverware and china are to be displayed. Fig. 45-1.

Doors are made from many materials and are hung (fitted into an opening) in various ways. Doors can be divided into two major groups, depending primarily on their size and use. Smaller doors for furniture and casework including built-ins are called *cupboard* or *case* doors. Larger doors for homes and commercial buildings are designated as *exterior* or *interior* doors of a particular type,

45-1. *The glass doors on this china cabinet keep out dust but allow the cabinet's contents to be seen.*

such as panel, solid, flush, hollow-core, louver, or French.

MATERIAL FOR FURNITURE AND CASEWORK DOORS

● *Solid, glued-up stock* is used primarily for small furniture doors made in school and cabinet shops. These doors have the disadvantage of being subject to warpage, expansion, and contraction.

● For cabinets, doors of *tongue-and-groove paneling* can be constructed to any width and length. Fig. 45-2. Lay the pieces to be fabricated flat on the table or floor, with the tongues fitted snugly into the grooves. Cut a piece of $1'' \times 2''$ material for crosspieces at least 2″ narrower than the width. Center this on the paneling for the door. Screw the crosspieces to the paneling at both the upper and lower ends. A long door may also need a crosspiece in the middle. After the door has been fabricated, trim off the exposed tongue and groove with a saw or plane.

● For most built-ins and kitchen cabinets constructed on the job, *veneer-core plywood* is used for the doors because it is easy to cut and fit. It is important to select the correct hinges for veneer-core plywood. They must be the kind that screw into the back surface of the door—not into the edge—since the edges of veneer-core plywood have poor holding power.

● Many furniture factories make

45-2. *The doors of this armoire are made of tongued-and-grooved panels.*

their own *lumber-core plywood* doors. This makes it possible to edge band the doors with the same hardwood lumber as the face veneer. A decorative edge can be machined on the door.

● *Particle board* is frequently used as a base for doors made of plastic laminate. When cupboard doors are made of this, a backing grade of laminate should be added for balanced construction. For storage cabinets, painted particle board doors are excellent.

● *Hardboard* is often used for small sliding doors for cabinets and built-ins. Perforated hardboard is a good choice when ventilation is needed.

● *Frame-and-panel* doors are commonly found on fine furniture

45-3. *The doors of this buffet are of frame-and-panel construction.*

and high-quality kitchen cabinets. Fig. 45-3. Frame-and-panel doors are built as described in Chapter 44. Sometimes a frame with glass, a metal grille, or mesh is installed, especially on china cabinets. A door of glass set in a wood frame is called a *glazed* door. Fig. 45-1.

• *All glass* is often installed in sections of cabinets. Glass requires a special metal or plastic track.

• *Honeycomb-core* doors, very light in weight, are made by building a frame of solid wood and then using a honeycomb filler made of kraft paper and plastic. Fig. 45-4. The surfaces are covered with veneer or plastic laminate. In building

45-4. *Cutout showing a honeycomb door covered with plastic laminate. This makes a very light cabinet door. A simple wood frame is the basic support of the door.*

45-5. *A tambour door has been installed in the top of this lingerie chest.*

these doors it is important to remember that there must be solid wood wherever the hinges or locks are to fit.

• *Flexible* or *tambour* doors are made of narrow pieces of wood fitted together with a flexible wood or plastic joint. Fig. 45-5. They may also be constructed of wood slats mounted on a heavy canvas back. They are made to slide in a track around a corner so that the full width of the cabinet is exposed when the doors are open. They have the advantages of sliding doors without the disadvantages. They operate like an old-fashioned rolltop desk.

• *Folding* or *accordion* doors are made of vertical sections of wood that fold against one another into a compact unit. The sections of a wood folding door are usually fitted together with plastic hinges. Fig. 45-6.

45-6(a). *The wood folding or accordion door is popular for cabinets, interior doors, and many special uses.*

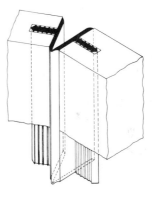

Saw-Kerf Hinge

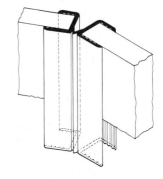

Slip-Over Hinge

45-6(b). *Plastic hinges that mount in a slot or over the edge of a door are usually used with a wood folding door.*

DOOR CONSTRUCTION

Doors must be constructed to fit the three basic types of cabinet construction: *exposed-face frame* (flush and lipped), *flush overlay*, and *reveal overlay*.

● *Exposed-face frame* doors are of two types: the flush door and the lipped door. The *flush* door fits into the frame so that the face of the door is flush with the frame. Fig. 45-7. This type is the most difficult to complete since careful fitting is needed to make the door operate freely. It is also the most time-consuming to install, particularly if butt hinges are used. The *lipped* door, in an exposed-face frame, has a lip that covers part of the frame. The door is made larger than the opening, usually ¾" in both directions. Then a rabbet, usually ⅜" in depth and width, is cut around the back face. The front edge is rounded or shaped with a router or shaper. This style of door is used on

45-7. *This corner cabinet has flush doors with surface hinges.*

45-8. *This cabinet has flush overlay doors.*

Provincial furniture (usually Early American or Colonial). Fig. 45-3. Because the lip covers part of the frame, the door does not have to be as carefully fitted as a flush door.

● The *flush overlay* door covers the edges of the case or carcass. The door does not require that the case have a face frame. Fig. 45-8. The door is made as wide as the total width of the case or carcass. Its height must cover the case from top to bottom, excluding the recess for a kick strip or plinth.

● The *reveal overlay* door is made so that the door covers only part of the face frame. It is similar to a lipped door except that there is no rabbet cut around the inside surface. Fig. 45-9. The front edge is either rounded or shaped. This door is easy to construct and fit.

HINGES

Cabinet hinges are available in an almost endless variety of types, styles, materials, and finishes. To select the correct hinges, the cabinetmaker must know:

● The type of door to be installed.

● The types of hinges that can be used on each type of door. Fig. 45-10.

45-9. *This small bathroom cabinet has reveal overlay doors. Note that there is no rabbet cut on the back of the doors. Self-closing hinges eliminate the need for a door catch.*

● The style of the cabinet or furniture.

● Material and finish of hinges.

Types of Hinges

There are three basic types of hinges: *butt*, *semi-concealed*, and *surface*. In addition there is a great variety of *specialty* hinges.

● *Butt* hinges are made with either fixed or loose pins. Fig. 45-11. The ends of the pins are often very decorative. The leaves of the hinge may be either straight or swaged (shaped). Regular hinges have straight leaves, but they can be ordered with both leaves straight (flat back), one leaf swaged (half swaged), or both leaves swaged. For a very tight fit on the hinge side, use a hinge with both leaves swaged. Fig. 45-12.

The *continuous* butt hinge comes in lengths up to 72" and is usually supplied without holes. Fig. 45-13. *Piano* hinges come in three widths and two finishes and are predrilled, ready for screws to be installed. Both are used on long or heavy doors. The piano hinge is available either as a nickel-plated or brass-plated hinge. Plastic continuous hinges are made of tough polypro-

HINGES FOR DOORS

Type of Door	Type of Hinge
Exposed-Face Frame a. Flush	Butt Surface Continuous Piano Concealed Invisible Wrap-around
b. Lipped	Semi-concealed with ⅜″ inset Surface with ⅜″ offset Wrap-around with ⅜″ inset
Flush Overlay	Butt Continuous Piano Pivot Knife Invisible
Reveal Overlay	Semi-concealed with no inset Semi-concealed with over the door offset Semi-concealed wrap-around with no offset Surface with offset Invisible

45-10. *What kind of hinges to use depends on the door construction.*

FLAT BACK HINGE

HALF SWAGED HINGE

FULLY SWAGED HINGE

45-12. *Methods of swaging hinges.*

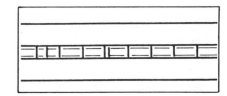

45-13. *Continuous hinges are usually made without holes.*

pylene. These can be used for folding doors and for cabinets. Fig. 45-14.

Another type of butt hinge is the *lift-off* hinge, which is used for doors that must be removed on occasion. *Double-action* hinges are ideal for shutters, screens, and folding doors. Fig. 45-15.

● *Semi-concealed* hinges are used for all types of cabinet doors and built-ins. For lipped doors the semi-concealed hinge is made with a ⅜″ inset (a sharp bend in one of the leaves which fits the rabbet edge). Fig. 45-16. For reveal overlay doors, the leaf is straight. Fig. 45-17. Many semi-concealed hinges are made to be automatic closing; that is, they have a spring action that eliminates the need for a catch. Fig. 45-9.

● *Surface* hinges may be flat for flush doors, or they may be offset to go over the outside of a lipped or reveal overlay door. Fig. 45-7.

● There is a variety of *specialty*

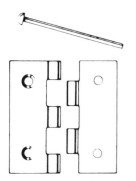

45-11(a). *Loose-pin butt hinge.*

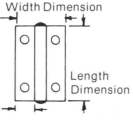

Width Dimension

Length Dimension

Effective Leaf Width

45-11(b). *Hinge measurements.*

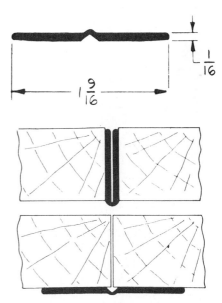

45-14. *Plastic hinges have many uses. They can be attached with screws, nails, or staples.*

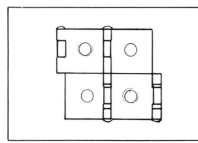

45-15. *Double-action hinges are used on shutters, screens, folding doors, and some kinds of swinging doors.*

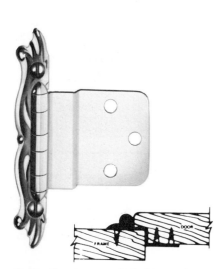

45-16. *Semi-concealed hinge for a lipped door. Note the offset to fit the rabbet.*

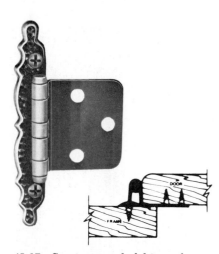

45-17. *Semi-concealed hinge for reveal overlay door. The leaf or pad that is attached to the door is straight. This hinge is designed for a ¼″ overlap of the door over the frame.*

45-18(a). *A concealed wrap-around hinge with a loose pin for ¾″ flush doors.*

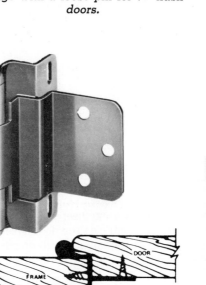

45-18(b). *Wrap-around hinge for a lipped door.*

45-18(c). *Wrap-around hinge for a reveal overlay door.*

hinges. *Wrap-around* hinges are designed for use with a flush, lipped, or reveal overlay door. Fig. 45-18. They are called wrap-around because one leaf wraps around the frame and the other wraps around the door. When used with a lipped door, there must be a ⅜″ inset. When used with a reveal overlay door, half of the hinge is straight. These hinges are designed primarily for doors made of plywood and particle board. *Pivot* hinges are used

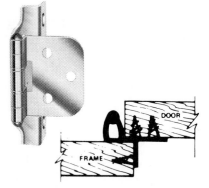

45-18(d). *A semi-concealed wrap-around hinge for a reveal overlay door.*

45-19(a). *Pivot hinges are very similar to knife hinges except that there is a large metal surface for mounting. Pivot hinges are mounted directly on the cabinet side and on the back of the door. A small angle cut must be made at the top and bottom of the door.*

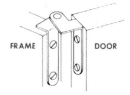

45-19(b). *Pivot hinge installed vertically.*

primarily for the flush overlay door. They are made to be installed either on a vertical or horizontal surface of the door and case. Fig. 45-19. Often a middle pivot hinge is installed in the middle of the door. *Knife* hinges are similar to pivot

45-20(α). *One type of knife hinge used on cabinet doors.*

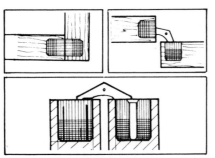

45-21. *A no-gain concealed hinge that requires only a hole in the frame and door to install.*

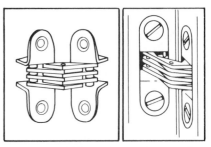

45-22. *Invisible link stop hinge designed for doors and table leaves. When in a closed position, the hinge is invisible.*

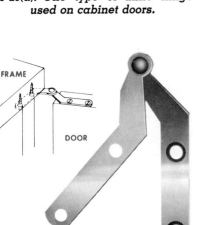

45-20(b). *Another type of knife hinge. It is installed on the top and bottom edge of the door.*

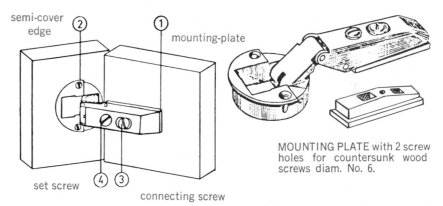

MOUNTING PLATE with 2 screw holes for countersunk wood screws diam. No. 6.

45-23. *A type of invisible hinge that can be used on any kind of door. A shallow hole must be bored in the door to install the hinge.*

hinges and are used primarily for flush overlay doors. Fig. 45-20. *Concealed* hinges are installed by boring a hole in the edges of the door and frame. Fig. 45-21. *Invisible* hinges are similar to concealed hinges, but they require a recess cut in the door and frame. Fig. 45-22. Another type of invisible hinge mounts on the frame and the back of the door and can be used on all types of doors. Fig. 45-23.

Styles

Hinges, handles, and knobs are made in sets for the appropriate furniture styles. For example, they may be Traditional, Provincial, or Modern in style. Often hinges and other hardware are made for a specific style, such as Contemporary or Traditional. For example, compare the hardware on the cabinets in Figs. 45-1, 45-3, and 45-7.

Materials and Finishes

Most hinges are made of steel, but many hinges for fine furniture are brass. Plastic is used for many types of specialty hinges, such as those for folding doors.

Steel hinges come in a wide variety of finishes, such as chrome, brass, copper, bronze, black, hammered black, and with a prime coat for future painting.

Drop-Door and Drop-Leaf Hardware (Lid Supports)

A wide variety of supports can be used for drop doors and leaves. Fig. 45-24. Some are folding-type door supports that will open exactly 90 degrees. On others the amount of opening can be controlled. Fig. 45-25. There are also telescoping supports and an automatic drop-front support which has a braking

45-24(α). *A standard lid support was installed on this drop door. Note that another lid support is used to hold up the mirror at the top.*

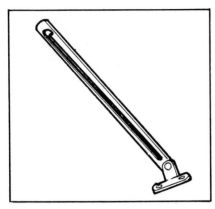

45-24(b). *Drawing of a standard lid support.*

45-25. *With a straight friction lid support like this one, the amount of opening can be controlled.*

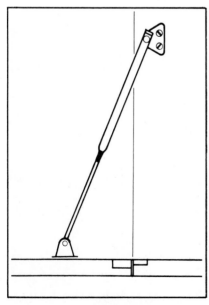

45-26. *A telescoping drop-leaf support.*

action as the door or leaf drops. Fig. 45-26. Fall flap hinges can be used on small doors to control door opening. Fig. 45-27.

HANGING DOORS

Flush Door in Frame

The flush door fits into the faceplate or frame of a case or carcass so that all surfaces are level. Fig. 45-7. For many furniture pieces the flush door must fit into a four-sided frame or faceplate. To get an accurate fit, special care is required. For most kitchen cabinet installations, the flush door is fitted into a frame or faceplate on only three sides. The lower part of the door just covers the lower shelf. Remember that the flush door is always made about $\frac{1}{16}''$ thinner than the frame to allow for slight clearance behind the door.

For a pair of flush doors in a frame, one of several methods can be followed to prevent a crack from appearing between the doors.

• Cut a small chamfer on each door at the point where they meet

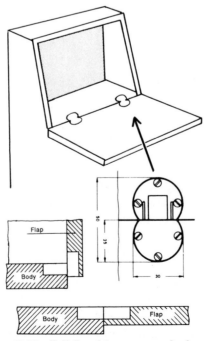

45-27. *Fall flap hinges on a desk.*

so that there appears to be a V groove at the center. Then put a wood or metal stop behind the doors.

• Cut a rabbet on the front of the left-hand door and on the back of the right-hand door. The right door will overlap the left one when they are closed. Remember that extra width is needed for the rabbets.

• Add a raised edge or molding to the right-hand door.

• Cut a rounded edge on the left door and a matching concave recess on the right-hand door. Then both doors will open at the same time.

HINGES FOR FLUSH DOORS

While many types of hinges can be used for flush doors, the most common are the butt, pivot, or decorative surface hinge. To install, follow this procedure:

• Determine the size and number of hinges. For doors up to 3' high and 2' wide, two hinges are enough. Larger doors should have three hinges. Use 2" hinges for smaller doors and 2½" or 3" hinges for larger ones.

• With a square, check the frame of the opening. If the opening is slightly out of square, the door must be carefully trimmed to fit. Also decide in what direction the door will swing. In some cases, hinges may be placed on either side. However, on kitchen cabinets and built-ins, the door is usually hinged so that it will swing against the wall. If the doors are to fit into a four-sided opening, measure the inside height of the door at several points. Cut off the top and bottom of the door so that it will slip into the frame. Plane the top and bottom edges. If there is no lower rail, measure the vertical distance in the opening to the bottom of the shelf so that the door will just cover the lower shelf.

• Measure the width of the opening at several places and transfer these measurements to the door.

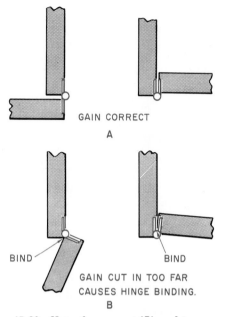

GAIN CORRECT
A

BIND   BIND

GAIN CUT IN TOO FAR
CAUSES HINGE BINDING.
B

45-28. *Note the correct (A) and incorrect (B) ways of mounting a door. If the hinges are mounted too close, the door will strike the sides of the case.*

The opening edge needs to be under-beveled a little so that the door will swing out easily. Generally, a frame door should have about 1/16" clearance all around if it is to be painted. Less clearance is necessary on a fine piece of furniture. Place the door in the frame opening and check it carefully.

● If decorative surface hinges are to be used, fit them first to the door and then install one screw each in the frame. Try the door. If it works properly, install the other screws. Make sure the knuckles of the two hinges are in line. If not, make the necessary adjustments.

● Butt hinges are installed as follows:

1. With the door wedged in place, measure up from the bottom and down from the top, and mark a line on the door and on the frame to indicate the tops and bottoms of the two hinges. Remove the door from the opening. With the try square, continue the line across the edge of the frame and the door to indicate the position of the hinge.

2. Place the hinge over the edge of the door. Determine how far the hinge is to extend beyond the door. A point to remember in installing butt hinges is that the motion of the hinge is in a circle whose center is the pin of the hinge. Therefore make sure that the pin of the hinge is far enough outside the case so that the door will swing properly. If the gain is cut too far, the hinge will bind. Fig. 45-28. Draw a line to indicate the depth of the hinge. Do this on both the door and frame.

3. Measure the thickness of the hinge from one side to the center of the knuckle. Mark a line on the door and frame to indicate this depth.

4. Cut the gains by hand or with a router. Fig. 45-29.

5. Place the hinge in the door edge. Drill the pilot holes for the screws and attach the hinge.

6. Hold the door against the frame and mark the position of one hole on each hinge. Drill a pilot

hole. Insert one screw in each hinge. Now check to see whether the door opens properly. If the door stands away too much from the frame side, it may be necessary to do more trimming. This should be done towards the front edge of the frame. If the door binds on the hinge side, cut a little piece of cardboard to go under the hinge. When the door opens properly, install the other screws.

● The following simplified method of installing butt hinges is commonly used for good furniture. Cut a recess (shallow dado) across the entire edge of the door. The depth of the recess should equal the thickness of the barrel or knuckle. Then one leaf of the hinge is attached to the door and the other leaf to the faceplate. The leaf on the case side is actually surface mounted. Fig. 45-30.

● Use a concealed loose-pin hinge for doors of veneer-core plywood. The concealed loose-pin hinge looks like an ordinary butt

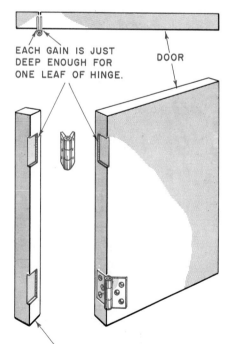

EACH GAIN IS JUST
DEEP ENOUGH FOR
ONE LEAF OF HINGE.

DOOR

FRAME OR FACEPLATE

45-29. *A gain is cut in the door and the frame or faceplate to receive the butt hinge.*

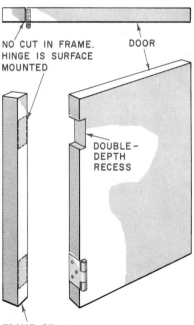

NO CUT IN FRAME.
HINGE IS SURFACE
MOUNTED

DOOR

DOUBLE-
DEPTH
RECESS

FRAME OR
FACEPLATE

45-30. *A recess (shallow dado) is cut in the door. Both leaves fit into this recess.*

hinge when the door is closed, since only the barrel shows. However, the hinge is made so that the screws go into the back face of the plywood instead of the edge grain.

Fig. 45-31. It is necessary to cut a recess into the door equal to the thickness of the barrel. The alternative method is to cut the recess in the frame slightly deeper than twice the thickness of the two leaves.

Lipped Doors

The lipped door is easier to fit because it covers part of the face frame or plate. Therefore no crack shows. A rabbet is cut around three or four edges (three if there is no frame at the bottom) so that part of the door fits inside the frame and the rest covers the frame. The outer edge of the door is usually rounded on simpler kitchen cabinets or built-ins. When a lipped door is installed on fine furniture, a decorative edge is cut on the exposed surface. A simple lipped door can be made in two stages. The rabbet is cut on a circular saw, jointer, or router. The front edge is rounded with a router. The complete edge can be cut in one operation by using the correct cutter on a shaper.

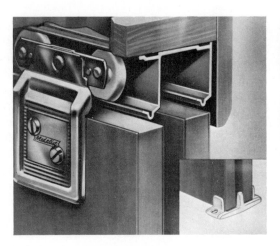

45-32. This is the kind of hardware needed to mount rolling doors. The insert shows how the bottom of the door is held in a vertical position.

45-31. Installing a concealed wraparound hinge in a plywood case. Note that the short leaf is surface mounted and that a recess with a depth equal to the diameter of the barrel is cut in the door.

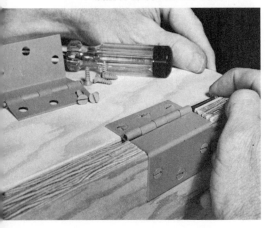

Decide on the kind of hinges. A lipped door is usually fitted with semi-concealed hinges, although other types can be used. Semi-concealed hinges are made in many styles and finishes to match Modern, Traditional, and other styles of furniture. It is important to buy the hinges before the door is cut, to be sure that the correct size rabbet is cut. There are hinges for different thicknesses of doors. Most are made for ¾″ doors with a ⅜″ rabbet. The depth of the rabbet cut determines the hinge dimension. Butt hinges are also used on commercial furniture but should not be selected if the door is made of veneer-core plywood.

If a lipped door is to cover all four edges of the frame, measure the width of the opening and add twice the amount of the lip or overhang to the width. Also, measure the height of the opening. If the lip is to be on only the upper edge, add an amount equal to the lip. If it is to be on both upper and lower edges, add twice the amount of the lip. Cut a rabbet equal to half the amount of the lip around all four sides of the door, or only around three sides if the fourth will not have a lip. Round off the front edge of the door on all sides. Check the door in the opening. Install the hinges on the door itself and then fasten them to the frame.

Flush Overlay Doors

Many modern cabinets and cases are designed so that the doors cover two, three, or four edges of the case or carcass. The doors may cover only the sides, with the top and bottom of the case protruding. The edges may be flush with the face surface of the door, or the door may cover all four sides of the case. Fig. 45-8. With this construction, knife and pivot hinges are used. The pivot hinges are particularly useful for plywood and particle-board doors. Fig. 45-19(a). Only the pivot shows from the front when the door is closed. These units come in pairs for small doors. For larger doors they are in sets of three, called a pair and a half. A slight angular cut must be made at the top and bottom of the door to receive the hinge. When the door is closed, all you can see of the hinge is a small ball or knuckle at each corner. If the door is fairly high, a third hinge of slightly different design is installed in the center of the door.

Reveal Overlay Doors

Reveal overlay doors are cut ½″ larger in width and height than the opening. The doors fit over the opening with exactly ¼″ overlap on all sides. Use semi-concealed hinges with straight leaves or pads for most installations. Other types of hinges can also be used.

45-33. *Rolling and sliding doors are equipped with finger cups. A small handle, round or rectangular, can be mounted when clearance between the doors is adequate or when the doors don't have to pass one another.*

Rolling Doors

A track for rollers is mounted above a rolling door. Fig. 45-32. The bottom of the door is kept from moving in and out by a plastic guide. One type of guide encloses the lower edge. Another fits into a groove cut in the lower edge. These doors are usually equipped with finger cups. Fig. 45-33.

Sliding Doors

Sliding doors are useful when space is limited or when a hinged door would take up too much room. Sliding doors are also used for safety when the doors are all glass. The

major disadvantage of a sliding door is that only half of the cabinet interior is accessible at a time. Sliding doors are made of hardboard, plywood, or glass. There are several ways of installing them, and it is important to determine the method to follow before starting to cut and fit them. In the simplest shop construction, a square piece of stock and two pieces of quarter-round mill stock form the track on the inside of the case. Fig. 45-34. Rectangular pieces can be used in place of the quarter-round. The second method is to cut two grooves in the top and two in the bottom near the front edge of the case for each door. Then a rabbet is cut on the back of the front door and the front of the back door. This allows the doors to meet with only a little gap between, and it also increases the effective depth of the cabinet. For doors of ⅜" plywood, rabbet half the thickness. Always seal the edges and backs of the doors with the same material as the front so that the doors will not warp. To make the doors removable, cut the bottom grooves ³⁄₁₆" deep and the top grooves ⅜" deep. After the doors

45-34. *The simplest track for sliding doors is three pieces of wood mounted as shown here.*

45-35. *Grooves cut into the case for the sliding doors. Note that the top grooves are deeper than the bottom ones so that the doors can be removed when necessary.*

45-36. *A magnetic catch.*

are finished, they can be inserted by slipping them into the excess space in the top grooves. Fig. 45-35. Then they are dropped into the bottom grooves.

The best method of mounting sliding doors is with some kind of plastic or metal track. One kind of metal track has ball bearings on which glass doors can roll to open and close. Glass doors should be at least ¼" thick and should have ground and polished edges with finger cups ground into the glass. Other sliding doors should be equipped with finger cups or handles for opening them.

CATCHES

There are many kinds of catches for holding doors in position. Most popular is the magnetic catch. Fig. 45-36. This is made to fit various positions inside a case. The metal plate is attached, usually to the door, and the magnetic catch is attached to the inside of the case. These types of catches are commonly found on fine furniture cabinets and, when the doors are not too large, on kitchen cabinets. Two other common catches are shown in Fig. 45-37.

PULLS AND KNOBS

Door and drawer pulls and knobs are made in a wide variety of sizes, styles, and designs. On a door, such hardware is usually located quite close to the opening edge and at a convenient position. However, knobs and pulls are sometimes fitted to the exact center of a door, for design reasons. The design of the pulls and knobs should match the furniture style.

45-37(b). *Roller catch.*

45-37(a). *Friction catch.*

46 Drawers and Drawer Guides

Drawers cause some of the hardest problems in furniture construction. Because of the frequent pushing and pulling they receive, drawers must be soundly built. Still, within the limits of good workmanship there is a wide range of quality, from simple cigar-box construction to the finest dovetail joint of production furniture.

Generally speaking, there are three levels of quality in drawer construction. The most elementary is the one which is built on the job. Such a drawer is built by a cabinetmaker or finish carpenter as he or she builds a kitchen cabinet or built-in. Usually he or she has only hand tools, several portable power tools, and perhaps a circular or radial-arm saw. The second quality level is the cabinet-shop drawer, made by a cabinetmaker who has

fairly extensive equipment such as saws, routers, and shapers. Top-quality drawers are made in fine-furniture factories in which the most modern production equipment, including a dovetailer, is available. More detail about these three quality levels is given later in this chapter.

Remember, saying that a drawer is of lower quality does not mean that it is poorly constructed.

Drawers make excellent storage space for the following reasons:

● It is easy to arrange the contents of a drawer since dividers can be installed for keeping various items in separate compartments.

● Drawers are relatively clean and keep their contents dust free.

● Drawers hide items until needed.

The disadvantages of drawers are

that they are expensive to construct and can be frustrating if improperly made.

Drawer construction is often a good indication of overall furniture quality. If the drawer joinery in a certain piece is good and if the drawers slide easily when pulled by their corners, then the furniture is usually of good quality throughout. Other signs of a good drawer are that it does not stick and will pull out far enough for convenient use without tipping or falling to the floor. A well-designed drawer must stay "in square" even after hard use.

Because there are so many ways to build and install drawer guides, the cabinetmaker or finish carpenter usually follows the specifications and information shown in the prints. Only seldom will you be without directions about the kind of construction to follow.

TYPES OF DRAWERS

There are four basic types of drawers:

• The *flush drawer*. The front of this drawer fits flush with the face plate or frame of the cabinet or chest. It is the most difficult to make since precise clearances are necessary. Fig. 46-1.

• The front of a *lipped drawer* covers part of the face plate or frame on three or four sides. On such drawers a rabbet is cut around three or four sides of the drawer front so that part of the drawer front fits over the face of the frame. Fig. 46-2.

• The *flush overlay drawer* front overlaps the sides of the case or cabinet. This type doesn't need a face frame. Fig. 46-3.

• The *reveal overlay drawer* front covers part of the face frame. When closed, this drawer looks like a lipped drawer. Fig. 46-4.

PARTS OF A DRAWER

All drawers consist of five basic parts: one front, two sides, one

46-1. *This night table has a flush drawer, which requires very careful fitting.*

46-2. *This Early American chest has lipped drawers.*

back, and one bottom. Before constructing a drawer you must know what is required for each of these parts since design and quality vary greatly.

Front

Drawer fronts normally are made of either solid stock or of lumber-core plywood and are usually not less than ¾″ nor more than 1⅛″ thick. Some fancy drawer fronts are made of lumber-core plywood with an overlay of solid wood so that the surface can be carved for decoration. Sometimes the drawer front is made of plywood to which molding is attached for design purposes. In most cases the drawer front must match the case or cabinet as to kind of wood, design, and general appearance. Sometimes the drawer front is covered with veneer or plastic laminate to match the rest of the structure. Fine furniture drawer fronts are sometimes of frame-and-panel construction.

Sides

A pair of matching sides is required for each drawer. One-half

inch thick material is usually used for the sides. It can be less expensive than the front. For extremely small drawers, ⅜″ material is satisfactory. Thicker material, often ¾″, is better if a side guide is to be used (for which a groove is cut in each side). The material may be either solid stock or plywood. For less expensive drawers, pine, poplar, or willow are good choices. For quality, oak, maple, mahogany, or other hardwood is preferred since these woods will stand up to hard wear.

Sides of less expensive drawers are usually rectangular. In quality construction, the upper edge is machined (shaper rounded) and there is a relieved section toward the center.

46-3. *This Contemporary six-drawer chest has flush overlay drawers.*

46-4. *A reveal overlay drawer.*

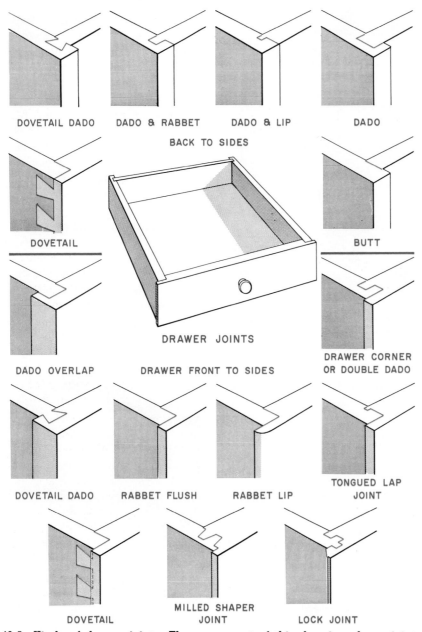

DOVETAIL DADO   DADO & RABBET   DADO & LIP   DADO

BACK TO SIDES

DOVETAIL

BUTT

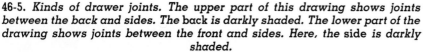

DRAWER JOINTS

DADO OVERLAP   DRAWER FRONT TO SIDES   DRAWER CORNER OR DOUBLE DADO

DOVETAIL DADO   RABBET FLUSH   RABBET LIP   TONGUED LAP JOINT

DOVETAIL   MILLED SHAPER JOINT   LOCK JOINT

46-5. *Kinds of drawer joints. The upper part of this drawing shows joints between the back and sides. The back is darkly shaded. The lower part of the drawing shows joints between the front and sides. Here, the side is darkly shaded.*

Drawer sides are sometimes made much longer than the interior dimensions of the drawer itself. This is particularly true of drawers for an extremely deep case. The ends, which extend to the rear, can act as a stop in closing the drawer. They are also useful in preventing the drawer from tipping or falling out when it is pulled open to the maximum. Most drawer sides have a groove cut towards the bottom on the inside, to receive the drawer bottom.

Back

The back is usually made of ¼" to ½" thick material of the same kind as the drawer sides. In medium- and lower-quality drawers, the back sits over the bottom and, therefore, has no groove in it. On high-quality drawers the back is grooved to receive the bottom, the same as the front and sides, and a notch is cut in the back to provide for the center guide and runner.

Bottom

The bottom normally is made of ¼" plywood or hardboard since these materials do not expand or contract with changes in humidity. For medium- and lower-quality drawers, the bottom fits into a groove cut in the sides and front. It is sometimes nailed or stapled from the underside into the back. On higher-quality drawers, the bottom fits into a groove on all four sides. For very simple on-the-job construction, when power tools are not available, the bottom is sometimes nailed directly to the lower parts of the front, sides, and back. In simple case construction, the drawer bottom is sometimes allowed to extend beyond the drawer sides to act as a drawer guide.

DRAWER JOINERY

Joints for fastening drawer parts together are chosen primarily with regard to the quality of the drawers, the equipment and the time available, and the number of drawers needed. Figure 46-5 shows the basic joints used in drawer construction.

Joining the Front to the Sides

The *rabbet joint* can be used for either a flush or lipped drawer. For both of these the depth of the rabbet should equal two-thirds the thickness of the front. The width of a rabbet for flush drawers should be about ¹⁄₁₆" more than the thickness of the sides. In this way the exposed edge of the rabbet on the drawer front can be tapered slightly for better clearance. For lipped drawers the width of the rabbet

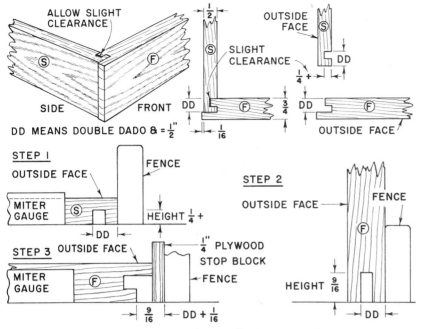

46-6(α). *Steps in making a drawer corner joint.*

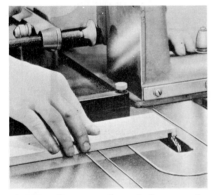

46-6(b). *Cutting the dado in the sides.*

46-6(c). *Cutting the dado in the front.*

46-6(d). *Joint ready except for cutting off the tenon.*

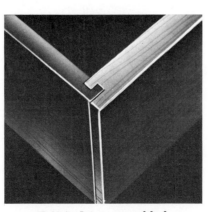

46-6(e). *Joint assembled.*

must be equal to the amount of the lip, plus the thickness of the drawer sides, plus $\frac{1}{16}''$.

The *drawer corner joint* is often used to fasten sides to front because it is strong and easy to make on the circular saw. Figure 46-6(a) to (e) shows this joint made with a $\frac{3}{4}''$ *drawer front and* $\frac{1}{2}''$ *sides*. A clearance of $\frac{1}{16}''$ is allowed for the front to extend beyond the sides. The steps in making this joint are as follows:

1. Use a dado head that is $\frac{1}{4}''$ wide. Adjust the dado head to a height of slightly more than $\frac{1}{4}''$. Set the ripping fence to a distance of twice the width of the dado head measured from the left edge of the blade (double dado), or $\frac{1}{2}''$. Cut dadoes on the inside face of the sides at the front end.

2. Set the height of the dado head to an amount equal to the thickness of the sides plus $\frac{1}{16}''$ (for front overlap), or $\frac{9}{16}''$. With the inside face of the front held against the fence, cut a dado across both ends of the front.

3. Set the dado head to a height of slightly more than $\frac{1}{2}''$. Adjust the fence to a distance of $\frac{9}{16}''$ from the left edge of the dado head. Use a piece of $\frac{1}{4}''$ plywood for a stop block. Place the inside face of the drawer front against the table and trim off $\frac{5}{16}''$ from the inside tenon. The joint should slide together easily.

This joint can also be used for box construction when all parts are of equal thickness.

Figure 46-7 shows another method of cutting drawer joints in which the parts may be any combination of thicknesses. All joints and cuts are made with a single saw blade.

1. Cut a groove in the center of each end of the drawer front. The width of the groove is equal to one-half the thickness of the front. The depth is equal to the thickness of the sides plus a clearance of $\frac{1}{16}''$. Position the blade so that it will cut

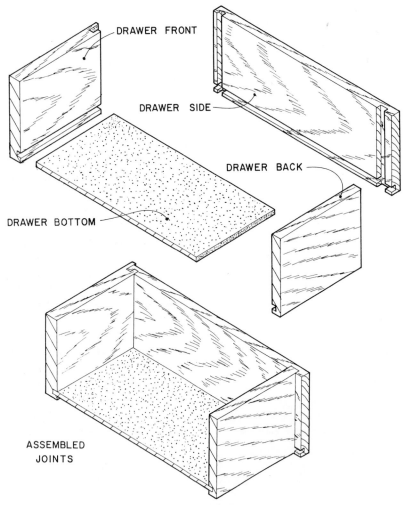

DRAWER FRONT

DRAWER SIDE

DRAWER BACK

DRAWER BOTTOM

ASSEMBLED JOINTS

46-7(a). *Exploded and assembled views of drawer joints.*

the left side of the groove—away from the fence. Make the cuts by holding first one side of the front and then the other side against the fence.

2. Cut the dado for the drawer front in the drawer sides. *Do not move the fence.* Lower the blade to a depth of one-half the thickness of the drawer sides. Make the first cut on both drawer sides. Then move the fence just enough closer to the blade so that the dado in the drawer sides will fit the tongue (inside projection) on the end of the drawer front. Make the additional cuts in the drawer sides.

3. Cut the dado for the drawer back in the drawer sides. *Do not change the height of the blade.* Set the fence so that the first cut in the drawer sides is at least ½″ from the back end of the sides. Make the first cuts on both pieces. Then continue to move the fence away from the blade a little at a time, making additional cuts until the dado is equal to the thickness of the drawer back.

4. Cut the groove for the drawer bottom in the drawer sides. The

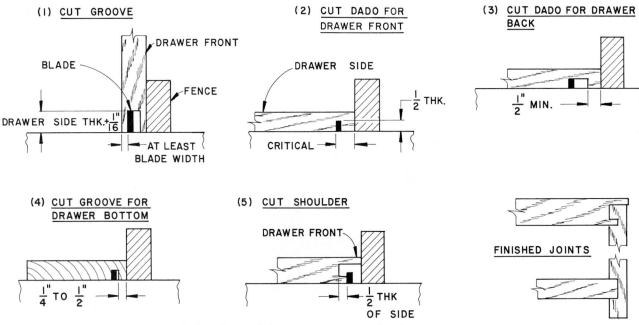

(1) CUT GROOVE

DRAWER FRONT

BLADE

FENCE

DRAWER SIDE THK.+$\frac{1}{16}$″

AT LEAST BLADE WIDTH

(2) CUT DADO FOR DRAWER FRONT

DRAWER SIDE

$\frac{1}{2}$ THK.

CRITICAL

(3) CUT DADO FOR DRAWER BACK

$\frac{1}{2}$″ MIN.

(4) CUT GROOVE FOR DRAWER BOTTOM

$\frac{1}{4}$″ TO $\frac{1}{2}$″

(5) CUT SHOULDER

DRAWER FRONT

$\frac{1}{2}$ THK OF SIDE

FINISHED JOINTS

46-7(b). *Some of the steps in cutting the drawer joints.*

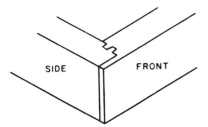

46-8. *Milled shaper joint.*

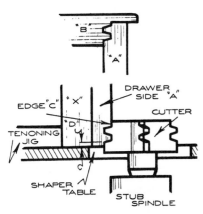

46-9. *Cutting the side of the drawer for the milled shaper joint.*

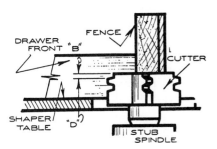

46-10. *Cutting the front of the drawer for the joint.*

drawer bottom is usually ⅛" to ¼" hardboard or plywood. *Do not change the height of the blade.* Adjust the fence so that the groove is either ¼" or ½" from the bottom edges of the sides. This distance is determined by the kind of center drawer guide to be used. A wood center guide and runner usually require more clearance than a commercial metal or plastic guide. Cut the groove in the drawer back at the same distance. Then move the fence slightly closer to the blade so that the groove in the drawer front is ¹⁄₁₆" closer to the bottom edge

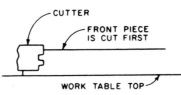

46-11(a). *Cutting the front.*

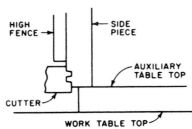

46-11(b). *Cutting the sides.*

than the grooves in the sides and back. This technique will hold the drawer front up slightly from the sides to provide clearance between the drawer front and the cabinet opening.

5. Cut the shoulders. Shoulders are cut on each end of the drawer front to form the tongue that fits into the dado on the drawer sides. Adjust the blade height to cut off stock to form a tongue on the inside of both ends of the drawer front. Locate the fence so that the length of the tongue will be equal to one-half the thickness of the drawer sides. Note in the drawing of the finished joints, Fig. 46-7(b), that the tongue on the drawer front rests at the bottom of the dado on the drawer side. This allows the front to overlap the sides slightly so that the sides will not bind on the cabinet opening.

6. Cut the drawer back to the finished length. This length should be equal to the distance between the ends of the tongues on the inside of the drawer front. Some cabinetmakers recommend that the back be slightly less than this distance to help the drawer slide in and out easily. Also, the bottom edge may be trimmed slightly to make the back narrower than the sides.

7. Cut the bottom. The width of

the bottom is the same as the length of the drawer back minus ¹⁄₁₆" for clearance in the grooves of the drawer sides. The length (from front to back) is ¹⁄₁₆" less than the distance from the bottom of the groove in the drawer front to the bottom of the groove in the drawer back.

The *tongued lap joint* is similar to the drawer corner joint except that the dimensions are different. It has a better appearance.

The *milled shaper joint*, Fig. 46-8, is excellent when cutters are available for the shaper or the radial-arm saw. This matched joint is made on the shaper by following these steps:

1. Adjust the spindle, Fig. 46-9, so that the distance *D* to the tabletop is exactly the same length as edge *C*. This is very important; otherwise the joint will not fit.

2. Adjust the tenoning jig so that the smallest diameter of the cutter, edge *C*, Fig. 46-9, is exactly in line with the drawer's inside face. The cutter must not cut into it, just tangent to it.

3. Cut drawer sides as required and stack.

4. Assemble the cutter on the stub spindle of the shaper.

5. Adjust spindle height so that the lip of the drawer just passes over the top of the cutter. Fig. 46-10.

6. Adjust the stop for depth of cut in the ends of the drawer front.

7. Cut the drawer fronts and stack.

To cut this joint on a radial-arm saw, use a glue-joint cutter. It is symmetrical and cuts both parts of the front-to-side joint. The front of the drawer is cut first with a depth of cut equal to the thickness of stock used for the sides. Fig. 46-11(a). It is possible to cut to within ⅛" of the front surface. The side of the drawer is cut with the work flat on the table. Fig. 46-11(b). Make test cuts on scrap

46-12. *The multiple dovetail joint is found in the finest drawer construction.*

stock to see that the joint fits perfectly.

The *multiple dovetail joint* is found on all high-quality furniture. Fig. 46-12. Furniture manufacturers use a special-purpose machine called a dovetailer to make this joint. In the cabinet shop, a dovetailing attachment can be used with the portable router or radial-arm saw to cut the joint. See Chapters 27 and 33.

The *lock joint* can be cut on a shaper or circular saw using a dado head. Figs. 46-5 and 46-13.

Two joints commonly used when drawer fronts are to extend beyond and cover the sides of the case are the *plain dado* (*dado overlap*) *joint* and the *dovetail dado* (*French dado*) *joint*. The dado is found only on lower-quality construction because it requires that the front be nailed or screwed to the sides. Fig. 46-14. Otherwise there is a tendency for the parts to pull apart. The dovetail dado or through-dovetail joint is excellent for this kind of construction since it is a good lock-type joint. Fig. 46-15(a). The dovetail dado joint can be produced with the circular saw or router or with a combination of these machines.

A well-proportioned dovetail dado joint is one in which the front is

made of ¾" stock and the sides of ½". Always cut the mortise first. Follow these steps for cutting the joint on a circular saw:

1. Cut the mortise [Piece *B* of Fig. 46-15(a)]. To do this, first cut a dado ⅜" wide and ⁵⁄₁₆" deep. Fig. 46-15(b). Replace the dado head with a cross-cut blade. Adjust the blade to an angle of 15 degrees and make the angle cut on both sides to clear out the mortise. A blade with the teeth ground off at 15 degrees can be used for this. Place the ripping fence first to the right and then to the left to do the cutting.

2. Cut the tenon [Piece *A* of Fig. 46-15(a)]. Set the blade to a height of ¹⁄₁₆", with ⁵⁄₁₆" between the fence and the left side of the blade. Make the two shoulder cuts. Adjust the blade to an angle of 15 degrees and set it at a distance of ½" to the

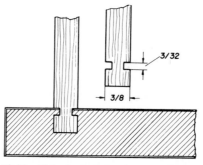

46-13. *This lock joint is routed into the drawer front. The joint is cut so that it is slightly narrower towards the top. Saw cuts are made in the side. The side is inserted into the bottom edge of the front and then forced into place.*

46-14. *Basic steps in constructing a simple drawer with overlap or overlay front. Dado depth should not exceed half the thickness of the front.*

left of the fence. Fig. 46-15(c). Hold one face against the fence and make the first cut; then reverse the stock and make the second.

While most of the traditional drawer joints can be used with particle board, the simpler joints are preferred. Fig. 46-16.

Joining the Back to the Sides

There are six basic joints for fastening the back to the sides:

1. The *butt joint*, the simplest, is found on some on-the-job con-

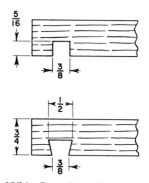

46-15(a). *Dovetail dado joint on a drawer.*

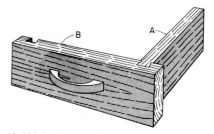

46-15(b). *Details of the mortise.*

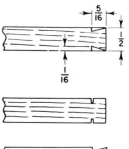

46-15(c). *Details of the tenon.*

46-16. *The box to form this drawer is made with a simple dado-and-rabbet joint. A false front has been added for appearance. This is a good type of drawer for reveal overlay construction.*

struction. It is usually made in combination with a rabbet joint on the front of the drawer. The length of the back piece should be slightly less than the distance to the rabbet on the front of the drawer. This way there is a slight taper to the drawer sides.

2. The *dado joint* is much better for this purpose. With this joint the dado should be located not less than ½" from the back end of the sides.

3. The *dado-and-rabbet joint* is slightly better still, because it tends to hold the drawer "in square."

4. The *dado-and-lip joint* is similar to the dado-and-rabbet joint except for the dimensions.

5. The *dovetail dado joint* is made on good-quality drawers.

6. The *dovetail joint* is found in the best furniture construction.

Cutting the Bottom

The bottom is installed in the drawer in a groove cut on the inside of the front and both sides. The back rests on the drawer bottom. This is not true of high-quality work. For this, a groove is cut in the back also so that the bottom fits into the front, back, and sides of the drawer. The ¼" dado attachment should be used to cut the groove to a depth of at least 5⁄16". There should be 1⁄16" clearance for the drawer bottom in the groove. The location of the drawer bottom in relation to the lower edge of the sides and front is

determined by the drawer guides used. With a side guide, the bottom can be lower than if a center guide is installed.

DRAWER SUPPORTS

Most furniture and better-quality cabinets have a web (skeleton) frame or dust panel to support the drawer and drawer guide. In the finest furniture the dust panel may be either exposed or invisible, depending on the furniture design. Figs. 46-17 and 46-18. However, in much construction of kitchen cabinets, particularly the plywood box (nonframe), there are no horizontal supports or web frames in the drawer section. The drawers operate on metal guides and plastic rollers and bearings. This greatly lowers the cost of construction because of reduced labor. All that is needed is the front opening for the drawer and a vertical strip at the center back to which the back mounting can be nailed or stapled.

DRAWER GUIDES

Drawer guides are needed to keep the drawer in line and to make opening and closing easier. Usually

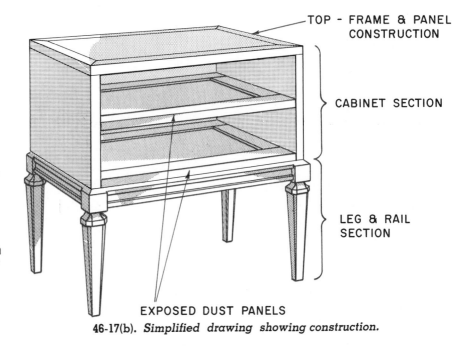

46-17(a). *This beautiful nightstand has flush drawers with exposed dust panels. With this construction, the front edge of the frame must be of the same wood as the exterior of the cabinet.*

the drawer guides are all wood, made either on the job or in the cabinet shop. However, there is increasing use of commercial guides made of metal, metal and plastic, or metal, plastic, and wood. Such guides should be purchased before the drawer is constructed because it is important to know how much

TOP - FRAME & PANEL
CONSTRUCTION

CABINET SECTION

LEG & RAIL
SECTION

EXPOSED DUST PANELS
46-17(b). *Simplified drawing showing construction.*

46-18(a). *This sleek chest of drawers has invisible dust panels.*

times an extra piece with a rabbet cut out of it is fastened between the front and back of a table or desk. Fig. 46-19. This type requires a *kicker*, a piece mounted above the sides of the drawer to keep it from tipping when it is pulled out of the case. The operation of this drawer can be improved by placing nylon-headed tacks on the frame under the drawer sides or by installing small fiber or plastic rollers in the face frame and on the drawer. Fig. 46-20.

Side Guides and Runners

These are commonly used in case and cabinet construction. There are two methods of making this kind of drawer guide. The simplest is to cut grooves (plows) on or slightly above center along the outer face of the drawer side. Then a strip or cleat of hardwood is fastened to the inside of the case on which the drawer slides. Fig. 46-21. This procedure can be reversed and a groove or dado cut in the case. Then a cleat or guide is fastened to the side of the drawer.

clearance to allow. The following are the basic kinds of drawer guides.

Runner for Drawer Sides

The simplest guide is one in which the sides of the drawer fit into the corner formed by the frame and sides or by the frame and wood side guides of the cabinet. Some-

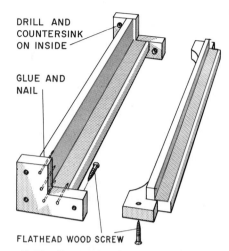

46-19. *A simple drawer guide that can be used on tables and desks. A pair of these is needed for each drawer. This kind works well when fitting a drawer between rails.*

46-20. *A plastic roller eliminates friction between wood parts.*

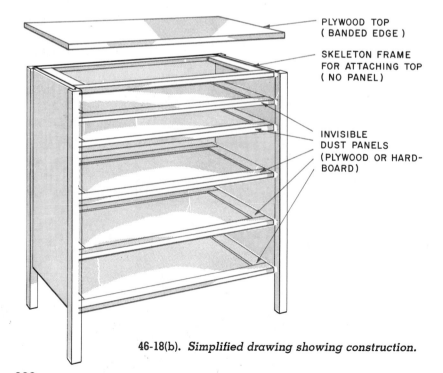

46-18(b). *Simplified drawing showing construction.*

46-21. *Side guide and runner with the groove cut in the drawer sides.*

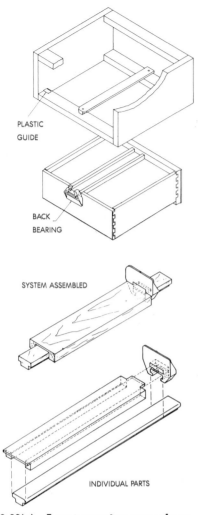

PLASTIC GUIDE

BACK BEARING

SYSTEM ASSEMBLED

INDIVIDUAL PARTS

46-22(a). *A system using a wood center guide and runner. The center guide is fastened to the frame. The runner is fastened to the bottom of the drawer. The plastic bearing on the back of the drawer is not necessary, but it greatly improves drawer action. The plastic guide also helps the drawer slide more easily.*

Center Guide and Runner

The best-quality drawer (rail guides) construction features hardwood center guides and runners. This kind of drawer guide system can be made in many ways. The most common method is to cut a groove in a piece of stock to serve as a runner. This is fastened to the drawer bottom. The runner is usually glued and nailed or stapled in place. Sometimes glue blocks are fastened in the sides between the

46-22(b). *Inside view of a cabinet. The drawer operates quietly and smoothly on plastic guides. There is no wood-to-wood contact with these guides. The center guide of hardwood keeps the drawer from pulling to either side.*

runner and the drawer bottom. Also, a plastic bearing can be used to improve the drawer action. A wood guide is fastened between the front and back of the frame. Fig. 46-22. The front end of the guide is often rounded slightly. In chest construction, this type of guide is fastened by cutting a rabbet on each end so that it fits flush against the dust panel itself, between the front and back of the frame. Fig. 46-23. The procedure can be reversed with the runner fastened to the case or chest, and the guide fastened to the bottom of the drawer.

Commercial Drawer Slides

These can be either side or bottom guides. Side guides come as a matching pair that fits against the inside of the case and along the outside of the drawer sides. The amount of clearance needed between the drawer sides and case varies with the size and kind of slides. Therefore it is important to buy the slides before building the drawers. Some side guides will allow the drawer to be pulled out well beyond the front of the case or cabinet.

46-23. *Center guide installed in a chest.*

A single bottom drawer slide may be placed along the center of the bottom, or a pair may be installed, one towards each side.

DRAWER OPENING DEVICES

There are many devices for opening a drawer. Usually some kind of metal or plastic hardware is attached to the outside of the drawer front. In selecting this hardware make sure it matches the furniture style. Sometimes the drawer pulls are made of matching wood.

Many styles of drawers are made without hardware. A recess is cut under or above the front so that the drawer is easy to pull out. Fig. 46-24. In other cases an opening is cut out at the center of the top edge. Fig. 46-25.

DRAWER DIVIDERS

For greater convenience, a drawer is often divided into sections. There are several ways of doing this. One is to cut dadoes in the sides or between the front and back so that dividers will slip into place. There are also many small plastic and metal channels or drawer-divider supports that can be nailed inside the sides or inside the front and back and into which ¼" stock will fit. If the drawer is to be divided

393

46-24. *This shows how space can be provided for drawer pulls so that there is no need for exposed hardware.*

into four parts, an edge-lap joint can be used on the drawer dividers. Sometimes a small tray is installed inside a drawer. Fig. 46-26. This is actually a small box that fits the drawer from side to side but is shorter from front to back. Usually extra strips for the tray to slide on are fastened inside the drawer sides.

PLANNING FOR DRAWER CONSTRUCTION

Before starting to design and build a drawer, several things must be considered. These are as follows:

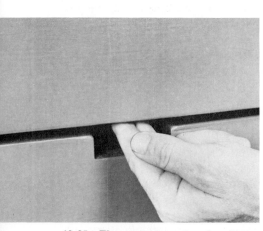

46-25. *The opening in the lower drawer is used for pulling out the upper drawer.*

46-26. *This compartmented drawer has a sliding tray on top.*

● The *drawer guide*. Is it to be a side or center guide and runner? Will it be shop-made or commercial?

● The *drawer front*. Will the drawer fit flush into the frame, will it be a lipped drawer, or will it be a flush overlay or reveal overlay drawer?

● The *joinery*. The kind of joints will affect the dimensions of the parts.

● The *web frame or dust panel*. This is extremely important in chest construction. Some chests are made with the front of the web frame or dust panel exposed. In such instances the same wood is used as for the front of the chest frame. Others have a skeleton or web frame that is set back from the chest and is covered by the drawers. Sometimes the drawer front covers the next lower frame. In other cases the drawer front covers the next higher frame.

● The *dimensions of the parts*. All the above points must be considered when measuring for the dimensions of the parts.

CONSTRUCTING A DRAWER

1. Determine the size of the drawer parts. Measure the opening for height, width, and depth (or run). Fig. 46-27. If it is a flush drawer that will be painted later, there must be about 1/16" clearance all the way around the drawer front on the top and sides. In other words, a dime should slip into the crack easily. For higher-quality drawers the fit should be closer.

2. Select the material for the drawer (size and kind) and rough cut it.

3. Cut a flush drawer front slightly larger than the opening with a slight bevel on all four sides. Try the front in the opening and refit to exact size. A lipped or a reveal overlay front must be at least 3/4" larger than the opening in both directions. For the lipped door a rabbet must be cut around the front before checking it. A flush overlay front must be cut large enough to cover the total width of the casework.

4. Cut the joints that will fasten the sides to the front. Also cut a groove on the inside of the drawer front and sides at least 1/4" up from the bottom. The drawer bottom will fit into this groove.

5. If it will be a flush drawer front, bevel or recess the ends

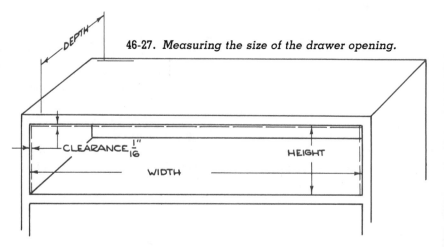

46-27. *Measuring the size of the drawer opening.*

slightly (about ⅟₁₆"). Sometimes the top edge is also beveled slightly.

6. Cut the joints to join the back to the sides. The overall length of the back should be such that, when the drawer is assembled, the completed drawer is slightly narrower in back than in front. If the back of the drawer is to fit over the bottom, then it must be equal in height to the distance from the top of the bottom groove to the top of the sides. If the bottom is to fit into a groove in the back, then the back must have the same dimensions as the sides and must have a groove in it to receive the bottom.

7. Assemble the drawer. For less expensive drawer construction, glue, nails, or screws are used. For medium- or high-quality drawer construction, only glue is used. If the bottom slips under the back, assemble the sides to the front and the back to the sides. Then wax the edges of the bottom and slide it into place. Never apply glue to the drawer bottom itself. It can be nailed to the back with No. 3 box nails.

For finer drawer construction, assemble the front to the sides, then wax the edges of the bottom and slip it in place. Next install the back. Install glue blocks between the bottom and sides of the drawer on the underside. For a center guide, glue and nail or staple the runner to the bottom, making sure that it is square with the front. For commercial slides follow the manufacturer's directions.

8. Check the drawer for squareness before the glue dries. When necessary use a clamp to correct any "out of square." After the glue is dry, try the drawer in the case. Chalk marks on the sides and edges as well as on the runner will tell you where the drawer binds. Often the runner is not fastened at the back of the frame until the drawer operates freely. Some chisel work and sanding may be necessary

to make sure the drawer operates smoothly.

9. For a flush drawer it may be necessary to install drawer stops. These are small blocks of wood that are fastened to the back of the drawer guides so that the drawer will not push in too far. Drawer stops are not necessary for a lipped or overlay drawer front.

QUALITY OF DRAWER CONSTRUCTION

Drawer construction methods vary in cost and complexity. There are three general levels of quality.

On-the-Job Construction

The least expensive and simplest is on-the-job drawer construction. Usually only hand tools are available or, at best, a circular or radial-arm saw and a jointer. The drawers may be all plywood or a combination of solid stock and plywood. The drawers are usually made of ¾" stock for the front and ½" to ¾" stock for the sides. The stock can be purchased with a groove already cut to receive the drawer bottom. Usual construction consists of a rabbet joint on the front and sides and a butt or dado joint on the sides and back. In most cases the bottom fits into a groove in the sides and front although, in some cases, the bottom may be nailed directly to the sides, front, and back. If it is an overlap drawer front, then a simple dado joins the front to the sides. A kicker will be needed over the sides of the drawer.

Cabinet-Shop Drawer Construction

A cabinet shop has need for all the standard machine tools. Therefore drawers constructed in such a shop can be of much better quality than those built on a construction site. Cabinet-shop drawers should have some type of lock joint between the sides and front. They should have either a dado and rabbet or a dado and lip between the

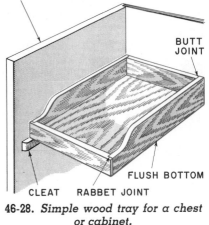

46-28. *Simple wood tray for a chest or cabinet.*

sides and the back. This will keep the drawer "in square" and will prevent the drawer front from being pulled away from the sides. If an overlap drawer front is used, a dovetail dado should be cut.

Factory Construction

The finest quality drawers are made in factories where furniture parts are mass produced. The very finest drawers always have multiple dovetail joints both front and back. The ends and top of the drawer front are machined to a slight bevel. The upper edges of the drawer sides are machined to a slight recess to provide extra clearance, and the edges are rounded. The drawer bottom always fits into all four sides of the drawer, and glue blocks are installed on the underside of the drawer for better and stronger construction. There is always some kind of center guide, with the back of the drawer notched at the bottom to receive the runner of the guide.

TRAYS

Trays are drawers that are fitted to the inside of a case or cabinet. Usually they are hidden from sight by doors. Trays might be found, for example, in a bedroom cabinet for storing clothing. It is quite simple to build the tray and the drawer slide. Fig. 46-28.

A most important factor in designing a storage unit, whether it is a bookcase, kitchen cabinet, room divider, desk, cupboard, or closet, is the interior arrangement. Every possible convenience should be provided. Size and arrangement of shelves must be well planned. A bookcase that is not wide and deep enough is useless. Kitchen cabinets with fixed shelves that are spaced too far apart or too high to reach are equally poor. Interiors should be planned to eliminate waste space.

DESIGNING THE SHELVING

Three things must be considered:

• *Material.*Shelves can be made of solid wood, plywood, or one of the manufactured wood products. Glass shelves are frequently found in china and display cabinets. In built-ins of better quality, shelves are made of particle board or plywood with a band of solid wood glued to the front edges. The shelf material should be thick enough to keep from bending under weight. Shelving that is unsupported for more than 42″ must be at least 1″ thick.

• *Stationary or adjustable construction.* Decide which type serves your purpose best. Most adjustable shelving requires some kind of metal or plastic hardware.

• *Depth and spacing.* Shelf depth should be determined by the overall dimensions of the cabinet. Standard book shelves are usually at least 8″ deep, while those for over-size books are a minimum of 10″. Upper kitchen cabinets should be 12″ to 14″ deep and lower cabinets 24″. Spacing between stationary shelves is particularly important since they cannot be moved. In bookcases, upper shelves should be no less than 9½″ apart, and the lower shelving should have a spacing of not less than 12½″. Correct spacing for kitchen cabinet shelving is discussed in detail in Chapter 53. If the upper half of a china cabinet has wood shelves, cut a shallow groove at a distance of 1½″ to 2″ from the back edge for displaying plates on edge.

INSTALLING STATIONARY SHELVING

The common methods for installing stationary, or fixed, shelving in cabinets and furniture are:

• *A butt joint reinforced with quarter rounds, wood cleats, or metal shelf brackets.* Fig. 47-1. The cleats or quarter rounds can be screwed or nailed into the sides and the shelves. If a molding strip or faceplate is attached to the front of the case, the cleats will not show. On an extremely long shelf where there is danger of bowing in the center, a cleat or batten can be fastened along the back of the shelf

47-1. *Metal shelf brackets and wood cleats (battens) are two simple ways of installing fixed shelving.*

47-2. *A series of dadoes cut in the uprights is a good way of installing fixed shelves.*

47-3. *The stop or blind dado provides excellent support and looks neat from the exposed edge.*

for added support. Another method of handling long shelving is to fasten an upright support about midway between the sides.

● *Shelves fastened to the sides with a dado joint.* This provides great rigidity to the case and also helps to hold the shelves in place. Fig. 47-2. The disadvantage of the plain dado is that the exposed edge is not attractive. However, this is not important if a faceplate molding is put around the case. A better arrangement is a stop-dado joint which has a neat appearance at the front edge. Fig. 47-3. A lock joint such as a dovetail dado or a half-dovetail dado is also a good choice.

INSTALLING ADJUSTABLE SHELVING

The trend in most furniture and cabinetwork is to install adjustable shelving since it will take care of changing needs and increase efficiency. In designing adjustable shelving, it is important to consider the items that will be stored on the shelves. This affects the placement of the hardware and the drilling of holes in the sides. The following are common ways of handling adjustable shelving.

● Cut slightly oversize dadoes in the sides, spaced equally apart. Cut a rabbet (tenon) on the ends of the shelves. The shelves can then be slipped in wherever needed. The equally spaced dadoes in the sides are also a clever design feature. Fig. 47-4.

● Bore holes for dowel pins. Drill a parallel series of equally spaced holes on each side of the vertical supports. Simple wood dowel pins can be installed in these holes to support the shelves. Fig. 47-5. Make sure that the holes are fairly close to the front and back edges of the sides so that the shelf will not wobble or tilt.

● Use plastic or metal shelf pins. A double row of equally spaced, ¼″ holes should be drilled on the inside surface of the cabinet or case sides. The holes should be drilled about 1″ to 2″ from the front and back edges. Their depth should be slightly more than the length of the pin shank. Four pins fit into the holes at each shelf location. Plastic pins will not scratch glass or wood finish and will not rust, corrode, or tarnish. They are made in several different shapes and styles. Fig. 47-6. Such commercial shelf holders are found on much high-quality furniture and cabinets.

● Install adjustable shelf standards and supports for side mounting. This hardware consists of perforated metal strips that can be flush or surface-mounted along the sides of a cabinet or case. Fig. 47-7. When the standards are flush mounted, the shelves can be cut the full width of the cabinet interior. For flush mounting, two parallel vertical grooves must be cut on the insides of the case or cabinet. The standards are attached with threaded nails or drive screws. Support clips can be located at any position

along the standards. Hold-down clips are also available to keep shelves from tipping. Fig. 47-8. While only one standard need be put on each side of the case, the usual practice is to use a pair. Any material can be used for the shelf itself. For glass, supports with rubber cushions are available.

● Install adjustable shelf standards and brackets for back wall mounting. Metal hardware that consists of slotted metal standards and brackets can be fastened against any wall to serve as flexible, open shelving. Fig. 47-9. Both the standards and brackets are made in light- and heavy-duty weights. The brackets are made in sizes (for width of shelves) from 4″ to 20″, in 2″ intervals. The shelving can be glass, wood, or any of the manufactured materials.

● Another way to mount shelves is to cut two pieces of 1″ × 4″ stock and drill a series of 1¾″ holes at equal distance in the two pieces.

47-4(a). *This storage wall, designed as a room divider, has many interesting features. Grooved plywood supports the shelves. The shelves and small storage units can slide into the grooves at varying heights.*

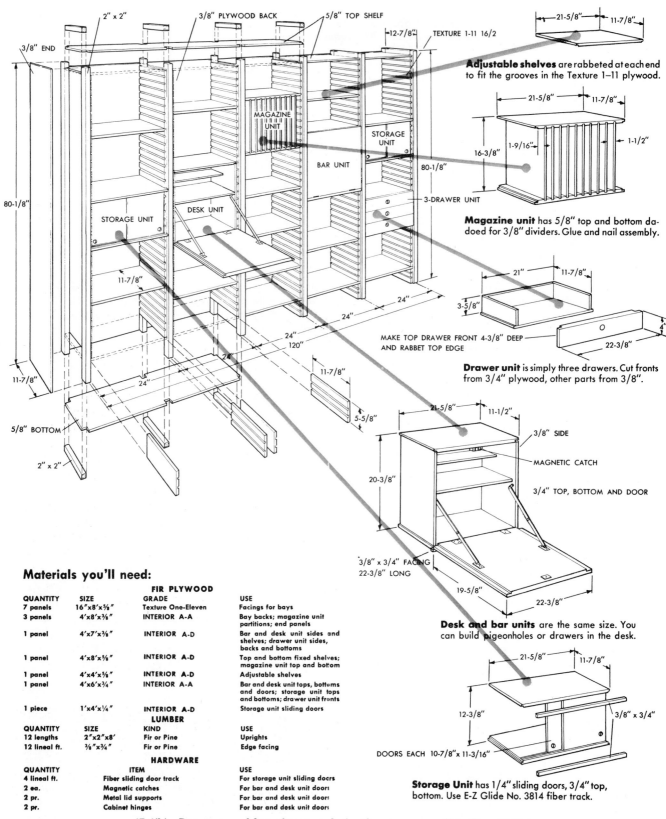

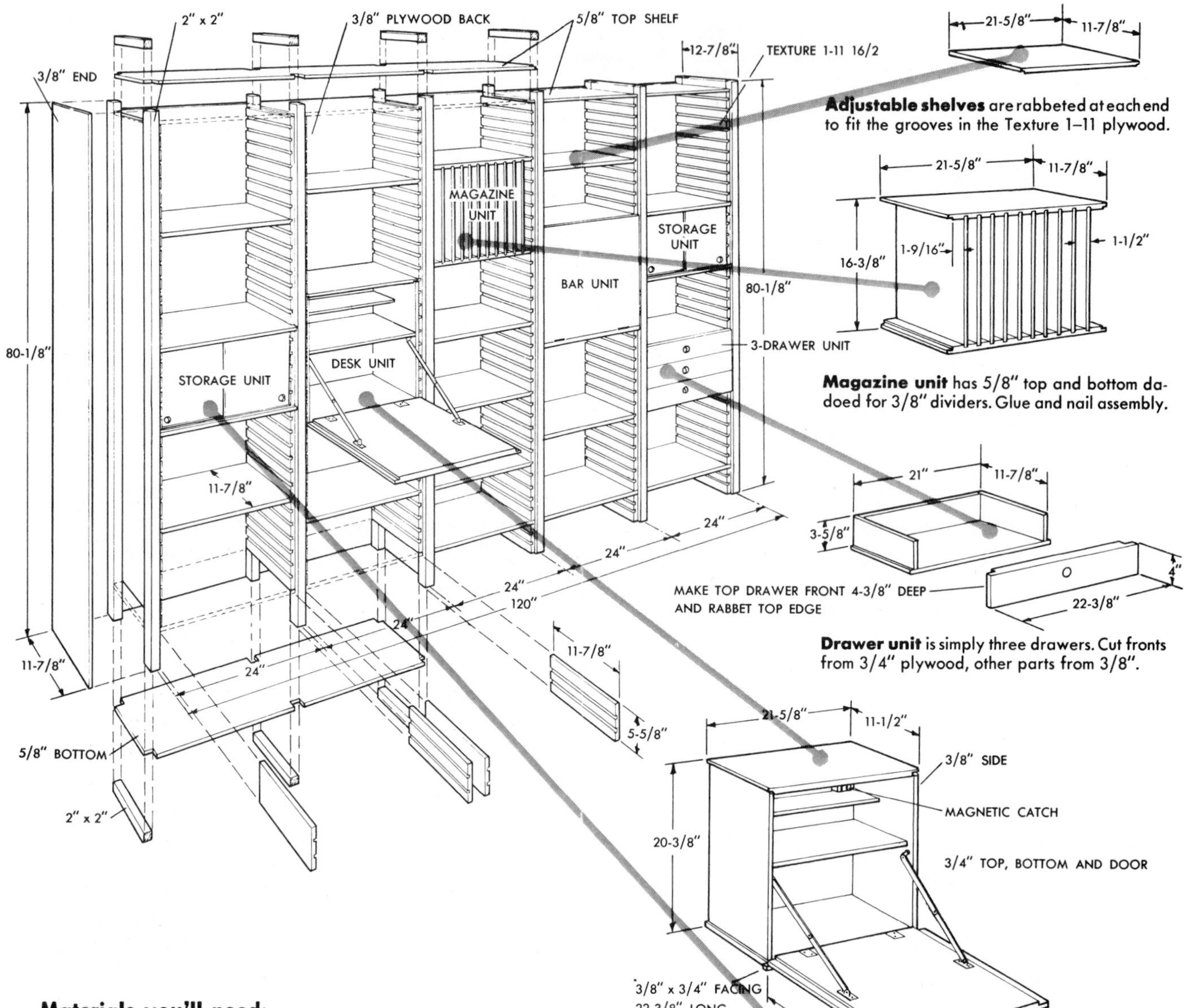
2" x 2"
3/8" PLYWOOD BACK
5/8" TOP SHELF
12-7/8"
TEXTURE 1-11 16/2
3/8" END
MAGAZINE UNIT
STORAGE UNIT
BAR UNIT
80-1/8"
80-1/8"
3-DRAWER UNIT
STORAGE UNIT
DESK UNIT
11-7/8"
24"
24"
24"
120"
24"
24"
11-7/8"
11-7/8"
5-5/8"
5/8" BOTTOM
2" x 2"
21-5/8"
11-7/8"
Adjustable shelves are rabbeted at each end to fit the grooves in the Texture 1–11 plywood.
21-5/8"
11-7/8"
16-3/8"
1-9/16"
1-1/2"
Magazine unit has 5/8" top and bottom dadoed for 3/8" dividers. Glue and nail assembly.
21"
11-7/8"
3-5/8"
4"
22-3/8"
MAKE TOP DRAWER FRONT 4-3/8" DEEP AND RABBET TOP EDGE
Drawer unit is simply three drawers. Cut fronts from 3/4" plywood, other parts from 3/8".
21-5/8"
11-1/2"
3/8" SIDE
MAGNETIC CATCH
20-3/8"
3/4" TOP, BOTTOM AND DOOR
3/8" x 3/4" FACING 22-3/8" LONG

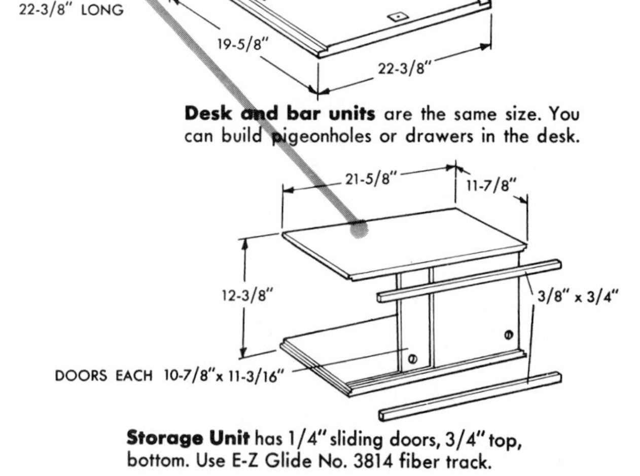
19-5/8"
22-3/8"
Desk and bar units are the same size. You can build pigeonholes or drawers in the desk.
21-5/8"
11-7/8"
12-3/8"
3/8" x 3/4"
DOORS EACH 10-7/8"x 11-3/16"
Storage Unit has 1/4" sliding doors, 3/4" top, bottom. Use E-Z Glide No. 3814 fiber track.

Materials you'll need:

FIR PLYWOOD

QUANTITY	SIZE	GRADE	USE
7 panels	16"x8'x5/8"	Texture One-Eleven	Facings for bays
3 panels	4'x8'x3/8"	INTERIOR A-A	Bay backs; magazine unit partitions; end panels
1 panel	4'x7'x3/8"	INTERIOR A-D	Bar and desk unit sides and shelves; drawer unit sides, backs and bottoms
1 panel	4'x8'x5/8"	INTERIOR A-D	Top and bottom fixed shelves; magazine unit top and bottom
1 panel	4'x4'x5/8"	INTERIOR A-D	Adjustable shelves
1 panel	4'x6'x3/4"	INTERIOR A-A	Bar and desk unit tops, bottoms and doors; storage unit tops and bottoms; drawer unit fronts
1 piece	1'x4'x1/4"	INTERIOR A-D	Storage unit sliding doors

LUMBER

QUANTITY	SIZE	KIND	USE
12 lengths	2"x2"x8'	Fir or Pine	Uprights
12 lineal ft.	3/8"x3/4"	Fir or Pine	Edge facing

HARDWARE

QUANTITY	ITEM	USE
4 lineal ft.	Fiber sliding door track	For storage unit sliding doors
2 ea.	Magnetic catches	For bar and desk unit doors
2 pr.	Metal lid supports	For bar and desk unit doors
2 pr.	Cabinet hinges	For bar and desk unit doors

47-4(b). *Drawing and list of materials for the storage wall in Fig. 47-4(a).*

47-5. *Cut short wood dowel pins to support the shelves.*

47-6(a). *A smooth-shank plastic pin.*

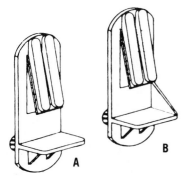

47-6(b). *Plastic shelf pins are made which (A) keep the shelf from tipping or (B) lock the shelf and prevent it from sliding back and forth.*

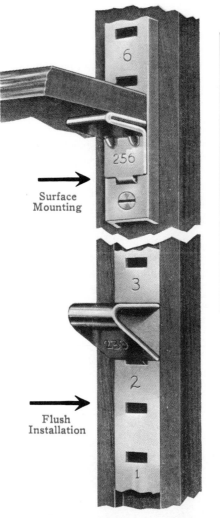

47-7. *Most shelf standards can be either surface mounted or flush mounted. The flush mounting is neater since the shelves can be cut the full width of the cabinet. If the standards are surface mounted, then the shelves must be shortened slightly or notched.*

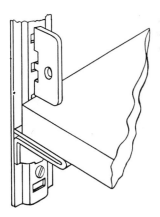

47-8. *The hold-down clips are installed against the top of the shelves. The support clips are installed below to hold the shelf up and to help prevent it from warping.*

47-9. *Wall standards and brackets come in many lengths and finishes.*

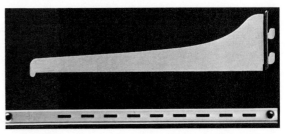

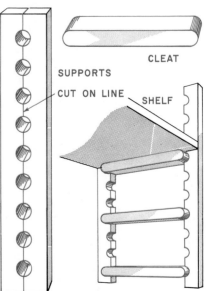

47-10. *Adjustable shelving of all-wood construction.*

Then saw the two pieces in half lengthwise and mount a pair on each side of the cabinet. Now cut 1″ × 2″ stock with rounded ends to fit between the two uprights. The shelves should be notched at all four corners to fit and rest on the 1″ × 2″ supports. Fig. 47-10.

• Still another custom method of making adjustable shelves is to cut a series of equally spaced angles on the inside face surfaces of the vertical supports. Fig. 47-11. Then cut the ends of the shelves at a slight bevel to match the angle of the supports. For adjustable drawer or storage units, cut grooves (plows) on or slightly above the center along the outer faces of the unit. Then cut strips (cleats) of hardwood and fast-

47-11. *The equally spaced angles can support shelves or storage units.*

en them permanently to the sides of the unit. The outer edges of the cleats should be cut at an angle to match the angle of the supports. These will provide excellent support for the unit when it is slipped into place.

• For thin shelves such as in a desk, a series of dadoes is cut in both sides. Hardboard or thin Plexiglas acrylic is used for the shelves.

• Besides those already described, there are many other kinds of commercial shelf holders. One has a spring-wire clip that fits into two small holes on each side of the case. A small groove is cut partway along the end grain on both ends of

each shelf. The shelf then slips over the spring clip so that the front appears to have a butt joint. The small holes on the cabinet interior are hardly noticeable.

CLOSET SHELVING AND FIXTURES

Closet shelving is usually made of ¾" particle board or plywood and supported on the ends with wood battens fastened to the walls. The front or exposed edge should be banded with solid strips of wood. Many types of metal closet fixtures are available for storing all kinds of clothing conveniently.

Legs, Posts, and Feet

48

Legs, posts, and feet are among the most distinguishing features of furniture. Fig. 48-1. They provide one of the quickest ways to identify furniture styles. *Legs* are the basic vertical structure of most tables and chairs. *Posts* are similar to legs but longer. In chair construction, for example, the front supports are usually called legs and the back supports posts. Sometimes these terms are used interchangeably. The term *post* is always used to describe the vertical supports for beds. Fig. 48-2. *Feet* are the supports under chests, cabinets, and some desks. Fig.

48-3. Legs, posts, and feet can be made of solid lumber or laminated materials. These items can also be purchased in matched sets of wood, metal, or plastic for many different styles, finishes, and lengths.

COMMON LEG AND FOOT SHAPES

Common shapes of legs and feet for cabinet construction include the following:

Square, Straight Legs

The square, straight leg is the simplest to make and is commonly

48-1(a). *The bench in this picture and those in (b) through (f) are similar in size and function but not in appearance. Leg shape is the major design feature of each. The French Provincial bench shown here has graceful cabriole legs.*

48-1(b). *The Queen Anne style bench also has cabriole legs, but the curves are more pronounced.*

48-1(e). *Early American furniture also has turned legs.*

48-3. *The feet are made separately and attached to this chest-on-chest.*

48-1(c). *This Italian Provincial bench features tapered, fluted legs.*

48-1(f). *The straight, square legs of this bench identify it as Contemporary.*

on only the two inside surfaces are also popular. The inside taper gives a feeling of lightness to the total design. Fig. 48-4. Square legs tapered on all four sides are found on many Traditional and Provincial fur-

48-1(d). *The traditional English style features turned legs.*

found on Contemporary furniture. Fig. 48-1(f). The leg is made of either solid or laminated stock, by the method described in Chapter 25.

Square, Tapered Legs

The square, tapered leg is made in several designs. Legs with tapers

48-2. *This solid walnut acorn bed won honors for the student who built it. It is called an acorn bed because the finials at the tops of the turned posts resemble real acorns.*

48-4. *This table has square legs tapered on the two inside surfaces. The taper makes legs appear to be at a slight angle.*

niture pieces. The square Italian Provincial leg, for example, has a taper on four sides with a graceful recess or molding just below the rail or apron. Fig. 48-5. Reeding or fluting often is a part of the design.

To make tapered legs, first square up the legs. Lay the four legs side

by side and mark the position at which the taper is to start. Then square a line around all four sides of each leg. Next determine the amount of stock to be removed at the foot of the taper. Set a gauge to this amount and mark a line across the lower end of the leg on the two opposite sides, if all four sides are to be tapered, or on one side, if only two sides are to be tapered. Draw a line along each side to indicate where the taper is to be cut. If tapers are to be cut on adjoining surfaces, the first cut would remove the layout lines on the adjacent side. Therefore make the first cut *before* laying out the taper on the adjacent side. Fig. 48-6.

Cut the taper with a radial-arm or circular saw. Plane the tapered surface smooth and true. After the one or two sides have been cut, do the other one or two the same way.

Round, Tapered Legs

The round, tapered leg is often a commercial product of wood, plastic, or metal. The legs usually have

48-6(a). *Laying out a taper.*

FIRST TAPER MARKED

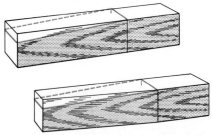

FIRST TAPER CUT, SECOND TAPER MARKED

48-6(b). *When the taper is to be cut on two adjoining surfaces, one side should be laid out and cut before the second layout is made. In the lower drawing, the first taper has been cut. The piece has been turned on its side and the second taper marked.*

brass ferrules with a self-leveling base and come with metal brackets for attaching them.

Turned Legs and Posts

The turned leg or post is characteristic of Early American and Colonial furniture and also of many Traditional pieces. Fig. 48-1(d & e).

Turned legs and posts made on a lathe can vary from relatively simple to very ornate shapes. The turned leg is a combination of many shapes. The concave curve is called a *cove* and the convex curve a *bead*. There are also many combinations of these curves. Short, straight lines called *fillets* separate different parts of the turned leg. Tapered surfaces may be short or long. All of these elements may be combined with a short section of a square leg.

If two or more identical turned legs are needed for a custom-made chair or table, the best method is to use some kind of template or, bet-

48-5. *This Italian Provincial desk has the graceful tapered legs characteristic of this furniture style.*

ter still, a woodturning duplicator on a hand wood lathe. See Chapter 36.

A compression joint can be used for installation of turned legs and rungs in Early American furniture. The end of the spindle is turned a few thousandths of an inch larger than the hole size. Then the dowels or ends of the spindles are slightly reduced in diameter by running the wood through rollers which actually compress the wood fibers. The wood remains compressed as long as it doesn't take on moisture. After glue is applied and the dowel or end inserted in the hole, the moisture in the glue causes the wood to expand back to its original size, making an extremely strong bond.

Another method of fastening a turned leg to a chair seat is to cut wedge slots in the end of the leg. Fig. 48-7. Then cut a wedge equal to the width of the slot. If the hole in the chair seat goes all the way through, place the dowel end of the leg in the hole and then drive the wedge in from the top to expand the dowel. If it is a blind hole, place the wedge in the slot and drive the dowel in from the bottom of the seat. As the wedge comes in contact with the bottom, it will expand the dowel, making a tight fit.

Cabriole Legs

The cabriole leg is characteristic of eighteenth-century furniture. It was originated by French designers who liked its *S* shape, and it is still found in much of the furniture

48-7. You can use a jig like the one shown here to cut slots in the ends of turned legs.

made today, particularly Queen Anne and French Provincial.

Cabriole legs can vary greatly in shape. English designs emphasize the knee, as shown in Queen Anne, while the French call attention to the graceful foot and ankle. Fig. 48-1(a & b). The leg is made with a square top if it is to be attached to a rectangular or square table or chair. It is made with a cat face top if it is to be used on a circular or oval chair. A *cat face* is a large rabbet cut out of the top of the leg to fit against the inside of the rail.

At first glance, the cabriole leg appears quite difficult to produce in the shop. However, this is not so if an accurate pattern is made and the correct steps are followed.

CABRIOLE LEG—FRENCH STYLE

The best way to make the French-style cabriole leg is first to develop an accurate pattern on a piece of heavy cardboard. Then select a piece of stock thick enough for the leg design. If the leg has a rather pronounced S, it may be necessary to glue up pieces to provide the added stock needed at the curves. In this case it is important to match the grain at the protruding sections.

When the stock is ready, trace the design on the two adjoining surfac-

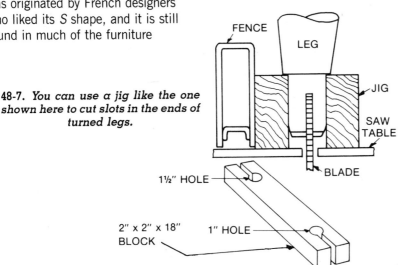

es. On the band saw make two cuts to form one side of the profile. Save these pieces of waste stock and nail them back on in such a way that they will not interfere with the cutting and also will not be a part of the finished leg. Then cut from the other layout line to complete the leg. Fig. 48-8.

A second method of doing the cutting is to make the first two cuts almost up to the end of the stock, leaving about ¼" of unfinished cut. This will support the waste stock when it is turned over to make the second two cuts. Then the waste material is cut off by hand.

After the leg is rough cut to size, it must be smoothed and sanded.

CABRIOLE LEG—QUEEN ANNE STYLE

The Queen Anne leg has a very pronounced knee which requires a rectangular piece large enough for the heavy curved section. Fig. 48-9. While it is possible to begin with solid stock, it is better to produce the rough material for each leg from three pieces of stock of the correct length. Fig. 48-10. Additional material may be needed to add ears (wings) to the upper part of each leg.

Design the pattern for the leg. Trace it on hardboard or heavy cardboard. Cut the pattern, or template, to shape and sand the edges. Place the template on the adjacent sides of each leg so that the curve is away from the corner posts. Fig. 48-11.

Make two cuts on the band saw from one side of the material. Save the waste pieces and tape them back together. Fig. 48-12. Turn the leg a quarter of a turn to the adjacent side and make the next two cuts to complete the rough shape of the leg. Fig. 48-13. Now use rasps, files, and other forming tools to shape the leg completely.

On many Queen Anne legs, an ear must be added to the sides of the

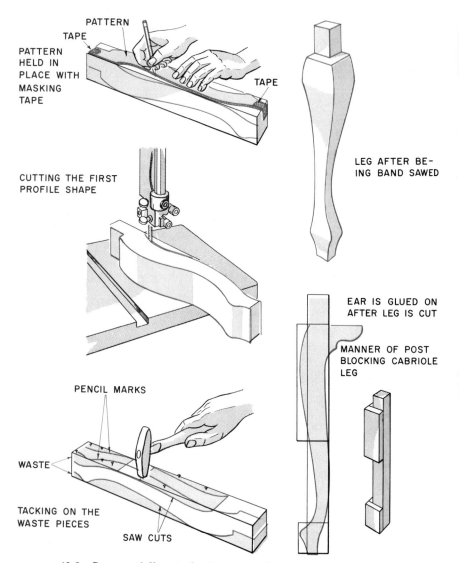

PATTERN

TAPE

PATTERN HELD IN PLACE WITH MASKING TAPE

TAPE

LEG AFTER BEING BAND SAWED

CUTTING THE FIRST PROFILE SHAPE

EAR IS GLUED ON AFTER LEG IS CUT

MANNER OF POST BLOCKING CABRIOLE LEG

PENCIL MARKS

WASTE

TACKING ON THE WASTE PIECES

SAW CUTS

48-8. Steps to follow in laying out and cutting a cabriole leg.

48-10. Glue up three pieces for each of the four legs. Here the longest piece (the corner post) is 1½″ × 1½″ × 12″. One of the shorter pieces is 1½″ × 1½″ stock, and the other is 1½″ × 3″ stock.

48-11. Tracing the design on the adjacent surfaces. Note that the template is larger than the stock at the top. Two ears will be added to each leg, and extra material will be needed for these.

48-12. The first two cuts have been made and the parts taped together with masking tape.

48-9. The Queen Anne legs on this chest are similar to those described in this section.

legs. Cut the material large enough for each ear and then dowel the ears to the legs, but do not glue them in place. Fig. 48-14. Shape the ears using a band saw and forming tools. Then glue the ears to the legs. Shape the legs to complete the finished profile. Fig. 48-15. As a final step, hand sand.

Some cabriole legs have carved feet. To insure uniformity, these can be made with a carving attachment on the router. Fig. 48-16.

Flat Bracket Feet

Flat bracket feet are used on many pieces of Traditional furniture.

The feet can be four separate units or a single base, or plinth. Fig. 48-17.

First, design the shape of the feet. Select the correct kind of wood of the right thickness and width. If the feet are made as a

48-13. The second two cuts have been made. The rough shape of the leg can now be seen.

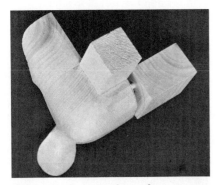

48-14. This shows how the ears are attached to the leg. On the right side, you can see the rectangular ear and the dowels used to join it to the leg. The ear on the left has already been cut, shaped, and glued in place.

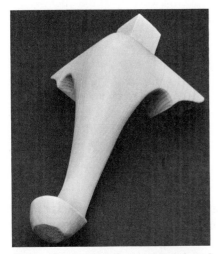

48-15. The leg has been shaped and sanded. It is ready for attaching and finishing.

single base, the length must equal the perimeter of the unit. Rough cut the material into four parts—two for the front and back and two for the sides. Use the design to make a

pattern of cardboard or hardboard. Trace the pattern on the material and cut to shape on a band saw or jigsaw. Cut each part to exact length. Then miter the corners and strengthen with splines. Add corner blocks to attach the base to the cabinet.

Ogee Bracket Feet

Ogee bracket feet with double curves, or two S-shaped curves, are widely used on Traditional furniture, particularly of late eighteenth-century design. Fig. 48-18. There are two methods of constructing these feet. The easier method is with a circular saw. This method is described in the following:

Lay out the design of the feet on a piece of squared paper. Fig. 48-19. Select stock that is thick enough to provide for the double curve. Usually a minimum of 1¾" stock is needed. The stock must be from 4" to 6" in width and long enough to produce the four feet. For the feet shown in this series, a piece 1¾" × 5⅝" × 60" is needed to produce two front feet and two simpler back feet. The front feet are designed with the double curve on both parts. The back feet (where the furniture will stand against the wall) do not need the curved shape on the back portion.

Clamp a wood fence to the table of the saw at an angle of 30 degrees. Adjust the fence so that there

48-18. Nightstand with ogee bracket feet.

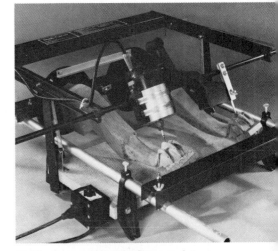

48-16. Some cabriole legs end in a carved animal foot, such as that of a lion or an eagle. This can best be done with a carving attachment for a router.

48-17. Flat bracket feet are used as a plinth for this small chest.

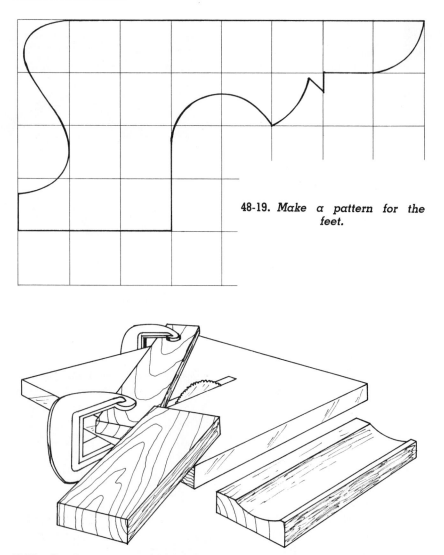

48-19. *Make a pattern for the feet.*

will be a ¾″ flat near one edge and a wider flat near the other. The wider flat must later be shaped with a small plane or other edge-cutting tool to form the second curve. Cut the first curve by making several passes, as described in Chapter 26. The saw blade should be raised about ¹⁄₁₆″ to ⅛″ after each pass until the right depth is reached. Fig. 48-20.

Now cut the stock into six equal lengths, each slightly longer than needed for the finished feet. Four pieces are needed for the two front feet and two pieces for the two back feet.

Rough out the double curved shape of each foot using a small plane or other forming tool. Carefully sand the double *S* curve until it is smooth and even. Fig. 48-21. Make sure that all parts are identical in shape. Cut miters on each of the four parts for the front feet. Do not cut miters on the back feet.

Use the paper pattern to make a template of cardboard or hardboard. Trace the pattern on the *back* surface of each part for the two front feet. Cut the designs with a sharp ¼″ blade on the band saw. Fig. 48-22. Shape and sand the surfaces until smooth.

Cut gains for a spline on the lower portion of each miter, making sure that the saw cut does not go through to the concave curved portion of the feet. Insert hardwood

48-20. *Cut the concave curve for the ogee foot by raising the saw blade about ¹⁄₁₆″ to ⅛″ for each cut until the desired shape is reached.*

48-21. *From left to right: concave curve rough cut on the saw; convex curve rough shaped with edge-cutting tools; wood sanded to final shape with machines or with shaped sanding blocks and abrasive paper.*

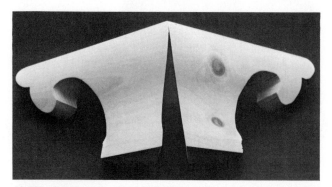

48-22. *Parts of the front foot cut to final shape. Note the mitered corners.*

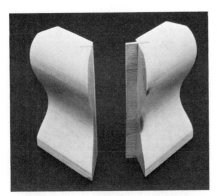

48-23. *An example of a spline in a miter joint.*

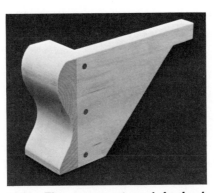

48-25. *This is a section of the back foot showing how the flat bracket is attached.*

48-26. *The legs on this table are a good example of reeding.*

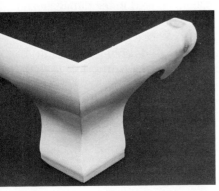

48-24. *Finished ogee bracket front foot.*

splines. Glue up the front feet, making sure the miter is tight. Fig. 48-23.

Finally, sand the feet using power or hand sanding equipment. Fig. 48-24. Make sure the two front feet are identical in shape and appearance.

The back feet do not need the curved shape on their back portion because that piece will stand against the wall. Instead a flat bracket is attached to the side piece of each back foot. Cut a rabbet in the side piece to receive the bracket. The bracket is attached with glue and wood screws. The screw heads are countersunk and covered with plugs. Fig. 48-25.

REEDING AND FLUTING

Reeding and fluting are decorative cuts on legs and posts. *Reeding* is a series of equally spaced convex (curved out) divisions on a leg or post. Fig. 48-26. *Fluting* is exactly the reverse of reeding; namely, a series of equally spaced concave (curved in) divisions. Fig. 48-1(c). Both processes are done in the same general way except that a differently shaped cutting tool is used.

Turned Legs

If the reeding or fluting is done on a turned leg, it is necessary to have a fluting jig or wood lathe to hold the leg and to divide the circumference into an equal number of parts. The fluting jig is really a small lathe in which the work is held. The cutting is done on a shaper, drill press, or portable router. A drawing of the fluting jig is shown in Fig. 48-27. This jig has an indexing head with 24 holes which allows 4, 6, 8, 12, or 24 divisions around a leg. Note that the indexing head is held in place with a nail.

Stops are used to control the length of the cut. These may be pieces clamped to the straightedge, as shown in Fig. 48-28, or pins located in the jig and on a temporary wood table.

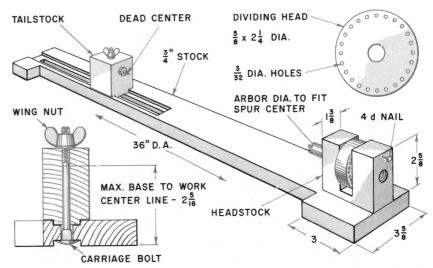

48-27. *This fluting jig can be used for many cutting operations that require the dividing of a leg or post into equal parts.*

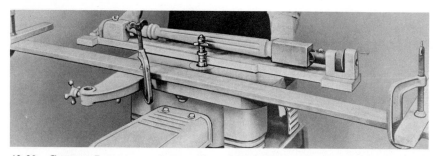

48-28. *Cutting flutes on a shaper. Note the stops used to control the length of cut.*

If the jig is to be used on the shaper, a form board with the same contour as the leg is fastened to the base of the jig. The form then rides along a depth collar the same as for other shaping operations. Fig. 48-29. Figure 48-28 shows the flutes being cut on a tapered leg in

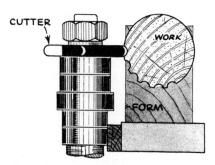

48-29. *This shows how the flutes are cut with the form board at the base of the jig following the depth collar.*

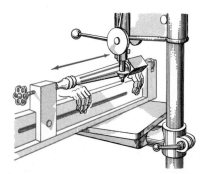

48-30. *Cutting flutes on a drill press. An auxiliary wood table fastened to the table of the drill press is a good idea. Then two nails in this fence and two more in the base of the jig will control the length of cut.*

which case the form is a simple, straight, tapered piece of wood.

If the cutting is to be done on a drill press, a depth collar is placed just below the shaping cutter. Fig. 48-30. A ball-bearing collar is best for this work so that it will turn easily and not burn the wood as may happen with a solid depth collar.

Another method of doing the reeding and fluting is on the wood lathe using a portable router. Most lathes are equipped with an indexing head. The tool holder must be removed from the lathe bed and a plywood base fastened in place. The number and spacing of the cuts around the turning can be arranged with the indexing head. The portable router is used in an attachment which consists of a motor holder mounted to a wood sub-base. This sub-base slides along the plywood base attached to the bed of the lathe. There are two methods for controlling the depth of cut. A

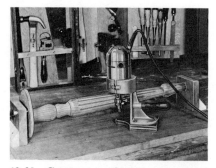

48-31. *Cutting reeds on a tapered leg with a portable router.*

depth collar can be held directly against the work so that it follows the contour. The second method is to fasten a form board to the plywood on the lathe bed at the correct location. Then the rounded end of the wood router base rides against the form board. A fluting jig attached to a bench top can also be used with a router. Fig. 48-31.

Square Legs and Flat Surfaces

If reeding or fluting is to be done on a square leg or post, the work should be held in the fluting jig and the cutting done on the shaper or router. Mark the location of the flutes or reeds on one surface of the leg. Adjust the cutting tool to the correct position for one groove on one side of the leg. Then make this and the matching cuts on all four sides. Readjust the cutter to the next location and make the next four cuts.

Fluting that consists of a series of parallel V grooves on a flat surface can also be done on the radial-arm saw using a dado head. Turn the motor to the bevel-ripping position. Adjust for correct position and depth of cut. The rip scale on the

48-32. *Cutting V-shaped flutes on the radial-arm saw. This method can be followed for square legs and posts and other flat surfaces. Note: Use guard when doing this operation.*

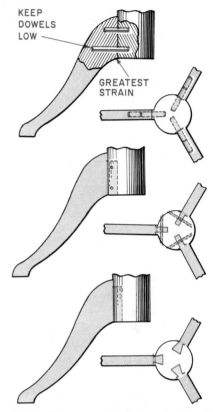

48-33. *This small tilt-top table of mahogany has a pedestal stem with three legs.*

pedestal can easily be divided into three equal parts, 120 degrees apart.

If dowels are used, the holes should first be located and drilled in the pedestal. Notice that the dowels should be kept low since the greatest strain is near the bottom of the pedestal. After the holes in the pedestal are drilled, use dowel pins to locate the holes in each of the three legs. After the holes in the legs have been drilled, it is necessary either to shape the upper end of each leg to fit the curve of the pedestal or to cut a flat surface on the pedestal at each of the three leg positions. This is necessary for a tight joint between the parts.

If a mortise-and-tenon or dovetail dado joint is used, the mortise or dovetail slot in the pedestal can best be cut with a portable router and a cutter of the correct shape. Hold the pedestal in a lathe and use a jig to guide the router. Fig. 48-35. The tenon or tongue on

48-34. *Three common methods of joining a leg to a pedestal.*

radial arm makes it possible to position the grooves an equal distance apart. Fig. 48-32. Finish cuts can be applied to the front of posts or stiles to simulate pillars or columns.

JOINING TRIPOD TABLE LEGS

The tripod or stem-leg assembly has three or more legs which are joined to a central pedestal. (Three legs would be a tripod.) This construction is common in certain Traditional, Duncan Phyfe, and Early American furniture. Fig. 48-33. The legs should be cut with the grain direction approximately in line with the angle of the leg from the foot to the place where it joins the pedestal. A major problem is to join the legs accurately so that they are equally spaced around the bottom. The three common joints are the dowel, blind mortise-and-tenon, and the dovetail dado. Fig. 48-34. The best method of constructing the joints is to hold the pedestal in a lathe and use a fluting jig. Then the

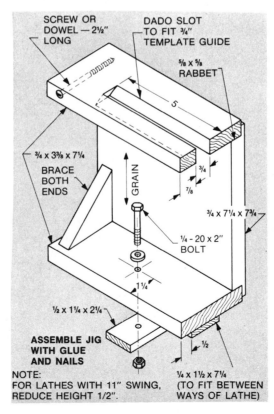

48-35. *Make this jig and clamp it to the lathe bed directly over the section of the pedestal on which the mortises are to be cut. Use a router to cut the mortises.*

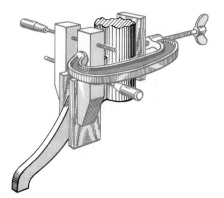

48-36. *Clamping a leg to a pedestal while the glue dries.*

each leg can be cut by hand or on the circular saw. If a flat surface is not provided at each joint location on the pedestal, then the cheek cuts on each leg must be made at an angle of 20 degrees so that the leg will fit tightly around the pedestal. After the joints have been cut, apply glue to the joining surfaces and clamp the legs in place. One of the best methods of applying the necessary clamping pressure is to fasten a hand screw to the leg, parallel with the pedestal, and then to fasten another clamp from the hand screw to the pedestal. Fig. 48-36.

Commercial fasteners can also be used to attach the legs. Fig. 48-37.

COMMERCIAL LEGS

For most construction of tables and chests, it is best to purchase commercial legs in the style of the furniture piece. Most turned wood legs and posts are mass produced on an automatic lathe. Once the knives are ground and set for a particular design, large numbers can be turned out in a very short time.

Cabriole legs are produced in quantity on a profile shaper. However, even with the most modern production techniques, some skilled hand carving and sanding are often necessary.

Most table legs come with bracket attachments so that the legs can be attached in either vertical or slightly slanted position. The brass ferrules have a self-leveling base. For chests, beds, and other pieces of furniture that may be subject to a great deal of weight or side movement, it is better to attach a leg that has a flange permanently mounted to the leg itself.

Legs are available in matched sets of wood, metal, and plastic with many different finishes. The important items to specify in ordering furniture legs include: correct size (length), shape, material, finish, and method of attaching.

BEDS

Most beds are relatively standard structures which involve no new construction problems. Beds normally consist of a headboard, a footboard, and a pair of side rails. Bed posts for Traditional furniture are often turned. Fig. 48-2.

For small beds, the rails and the headboard and footboard can be permanently assembled with mortise-and-tenon or dowel joints. However, for most full-size beds, bed rail fasteners are used. These are made of heavy-duty wrought steel and are available in several different sizes. Fig. 48-38. A slot must be machined in the bed posts to receive half of the fastener. The hook half of the fastener is at-

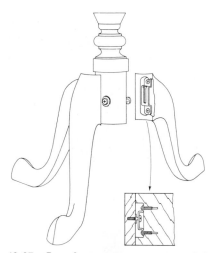

48-37. *A clamp-type commercial fastening system can be used to hold the legs to the pedestal. This method allows the table to be shipped "knocked down."*

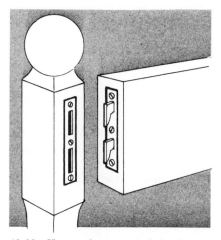

48-38. *Heavy-duty metal bed rail fasteners are available in lengths of 4" and 6".*

tached to the end of the bed rail. When ready to assemble, the rail hook is inserted into the slot in the post and pushed down.

Leg-and-Rail Construction

Most tables and chairs and the stands for many chests and cabinets feature leg-and-rail construction (sometimes called *frame construction*). Fig. 49-1. The simple table base consists of four legs and four rails (aprons) with the rails normally joined to the legs just under the tabletop. Sometimes lower rails, called stretchers, are added for extra strength. In small tables, a drawer is often added directly under the top or under a lower shelf, or a shelf-and-drawer are installed between the table legs.

KINDS OF LEG-AND-RAIL JOINERY

The traditional method of joining a leg to a rail is with a blind mortise-and-tenon joint. Fig. 49-2. With this method the mortises are

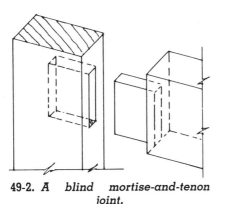

49-2. *A blind mortise-and-tenon joint.*

cut from the two interior, adjoining surfaces of the legs so that the mortises meet. Then the tenons are cut and mitered at the end to make maximum use of the mortise opening. There must be slight clearance between the ends of the tenons so that they will not bind. Fig. 49-3.

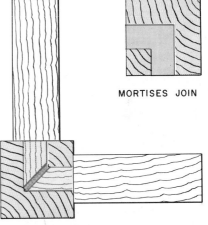

MORTISES JOIN

TENONS HAVE CLEARANCE AT ENDS

49-3. *The mortises are cut from the adjoining surfaces so that they meet. The tenon is mitered on the end for a glue pocket and to keep the tenon from binding and causing a crack between the shoulder of the tenon and the face of the leg.*

49-1. *This table is a good example of leg-and-rail construction.*

Another mortise-and-tenon joint that may be used is the open mortise with a stub tenon. The advantage of this construction is that the mortise can be cut on a circular saw and the tenon can be cut on the same saw or with a router or shaper. Fig. 49-4. An adaptation of this joint is the open or slotted mortise and tenon with edge-lap rails. Figs. 49-5 and 49-6.

Still another possible construction is the dovetail dado joint. Fig. 49-7. This is a good lock joint. It can be used with a metal corner brace for simple furniture that can be "knocked down" for storage or shipping.

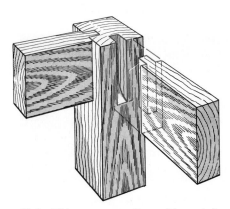

49-4. *This open mortise with a stub tenon is satisfactory only for light construction.*

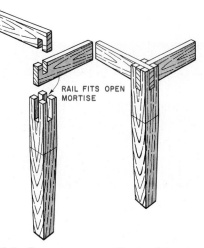

RAIL FITS OPEN MORTISE

49-6. *An open mortise-and-tenon joint with edge-lap rails.*

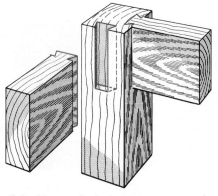

49-7. *Dovetail dado joint for legs and rails.*

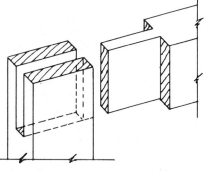

49-5. *An open mortise-and-tenon joint.*

Not many years ago it would have been considered poor construction if legs and rails were not fastened together with mortise-and-tenon joints. Today, however, many makers of fine custom furniture no longer use this joint for leg-and-rail construction. Instead, a butt joint strengthened with two or three dowels is common. A strong wood corner block installed with screws, or a metal corner block, is used for strength. The whole unit is held together with a good adhesive. Fig. 49-8.

There are several good reasons for the change. First, with improved adhesives and good corner blocks, the dowel corner is just as strong as the mortise-and-tenon corner. Second, the dowel corner is much quicker and less expensive to produce. This can easily be seen if we compare the time required to make a layout

and cut a mortise and tenon with the time required to cut a butt joint and install two or three dowels. The difference in labor costs is tremendous. Third, reinforced dowel leg-and-rail construction saves material since the extra length needed for tenons is eliminated. Finally, leg-and-rail construction in which the leg and rail are not at right angles to each other makes construction extremely difficult with the mortise-and-tenon joint. In contrast, with dowels the problem is far simpler.

The important point in doweled

leg-and-rail construction is to make sure that the holes are spaced accurately and that they are bored exactly at right angles to the edge of the leg and into the end grain of the rail.

INSTALLING A DRAWER

On many smaller tables made by leg-and-rail construction, a drawer is installed directly under the top as an added storage convenience. Fig. 49-9. This requires a modification of the rail construction. Sometimes the front of the drawer completely replaces one of the rails. Then an interior web frame, with an

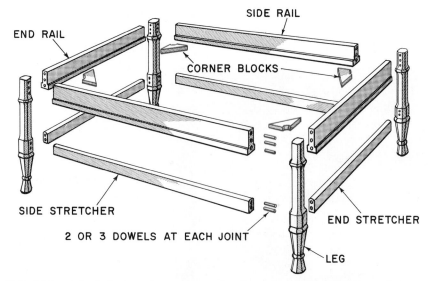

SIDE RAIL

END RAIL

CORNER BLOCKS

SIDE STRETCHER

2 OR 3 DOWELS AT EACH JOINT

END STRETCHER

LEG

49-8. *This exploded view shows leg-and-rail construction (table frame) using dowels and corner blocks. Note how much simpler this is than using mortise-and-tenon joints. The finished table can be seen in Fig. 49-1.*

412

49-9. *A drawer front replaces one of the rails in this end table. A study of its construction would reveal a web frame just below the drawer.*

49-10. *The bottom shelf of this table is installed with corner dadoes.*

exposed front edge of the same material as the drawer front and rails, is installed. This frame supports the drawer and also is used to install the drawer guides. For smaller drawers, an opening is cut in one of the rails into which the drawer fits. Then some type of drawer guide is fitted between the two rails.

INSTALLING A LOWER SHELF

If a lower shelf is to be installed in a table, one of several methods can be followed. The simplest way is to fit the shelf between the legs and then to install a dowel at each corner. Another method especially successful on square, straight, and tapered legs is to cut a corner dado on the legs and then cut off the corners of the shelf to fit into this corner dado. Fig. 49-10.

CHAIR CONSTRUCTION

Most wood chairs are made with leg-and-rail construction. Chair construction is the most difficult job in furniture work. There are several reasons for this. Rarely is any part of the chair at a right angle to the next. The front of the chair is wider

than the back. The back legs are arched or angular. The distance across the top of the back legs is greater than the distance across the bottom. The wood seat is contoured or upholstered. The back rungs or cross supports are frequently made in a slight arc shape for comfort. Fig. 49-11. Because of these difficult construction problems, it is said that a cabinetmaker who can build a chair well can build any other product with ease. Fig. 49-12.

Joints

Most chairs and some tables with leg-and-rail construction are designed with the front wider than the

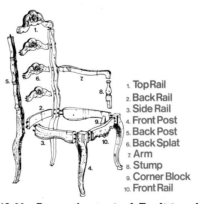

1. Top Rail
2. Back Rail
3. Side Rail
4. Front Post
5. Back Post
6. Back Splat
7. Arm
8. Stump
9. Corner Block
10. Front Rail

49-11. *Parts of a typical Traditional chair.*

back. The back of the typical chair is from 1½″ to 3″ narrower than the front. If a dowel joint is used, the ends of the side rails must be cut at an angle. The dowels are installed in the rails at the same angle.

For a mortise-and-tenon joint, the tenons for the side rails must be cut at the proper angle. Fig. 49-13. The best way to do this is to first make a layout of the rail with the correct angle for the shoulder and cheek cuts. To do this, adjust a sliding T bevel to this angle. Then transfer the angle to the blade of the table saw. Adjust the fence so that the distance from the left edge of the blade to the fence is equal to the length of the tenon. Hold the piece against the miter gauge with the end of the rail against the fence and make the first shoulder cut. Then transfer the miter gauge to the other side of the saw blade and reverse the position of the fence. Adjust for correct length of tenon and make the second cut. The cheek cuts are made with the blade at the same angle. Adjust the fence so

49-12(a). *After studying this chapter, you will see why chairs are so complicated to make.*

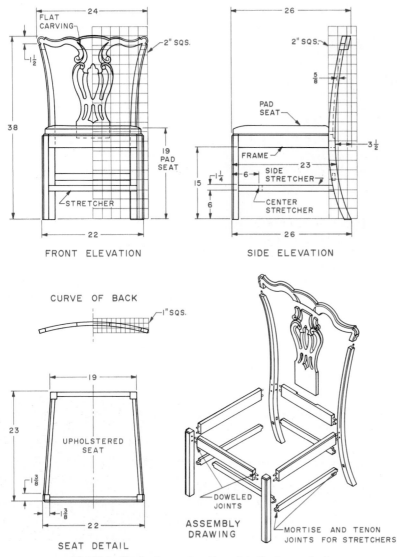

FRONT ELEVATION

SIDE ELEVATION

CURVE OF BACK

SEAT DETAIL

ASSEMBLY DRAWING

MORTISE AND TENON JOINTS FOR STRETCHERS

49-12(b). *Typical construction details for a chair.*

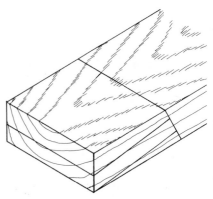

49-14(a). *Layout of a tenon at an angle.*

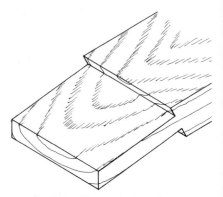

49-14(b). *The completed tenon.*

49-15. *The table and chairs shown here have sculptured joints.*

49-13(a). *The side rails for this wedge-shaped table must have tenons cut at an angle.*

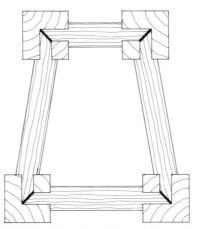

49-13(b). *This drawing shows the leg-and-rail construction for the wedge-shaped table.*

that the distance from the right side of the blade to the fence will remove the correct amount of material from one side of the tenon. Adjust the blade height so that it equals the length of the tenon on one side.

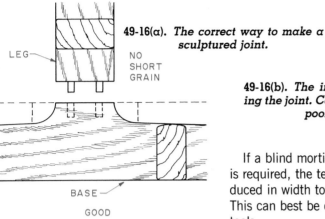

49-16(a). *The correct way to make a sculptured joint.*

LEG

NO SHORT GRAIN

BASE

GOOD

49-16(b). *The incorrect way of making the joint. Can you see why this is poor practice?*

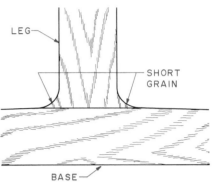

LEG

SHORT GRAIN

BASE

POOR

Make the first cheek cut. Then readjust the fence and the height of the blade slightly before making the second cut. Use a guard or tenoning jig for this procedure. (See Chapter 26.) Fig. 49-14.

If a blind mortise-and-tenon joint is required, the tenon must be reduced in width to fit the mortise. This can best be done with hand tools.

Some Contemporary tables and chairs have sculptured leg-base or leg-rail assemblies. Fig. 49-15. This design has a smooth curve between the two adjoining parts. In planning this type of joint, make sure that there is not a short-grained area that

can easily be damaged. For example, in Fig. 49-16, note that the radius is on the base rather than on the leg. Some extra material should be left on both pieces so that the final shaping can be done after assembly.

50 Tabletops

The tops for most tables, desks, and many chests are made as a removable part that is installed after the other construction is completed. There are many different methods of constructing such tops. The method to choose depends to a large degree on the kind of part, the quality of construction, and the design. Some methods of construction are suitable for cabinets built on the job, while others require equipment usually found only in cabinet shops.

KINDS OF TABLETOPS

Softwood Plywood

The simplest way to build a table-

top is with plywood. Be sure to choose plywood of an adequate thickness, usually ¾″. The major problem in using plywood is that the exposed edges must be treated. Fig. 50-1.

Core Stock Covered with Plastic Laminate

The most popular top construction for many tables and for built-ins is core stock of particle board covered with plastic laminate. Laminates are discussed in Chapter 43.

Hardwood Plywood

Many fine tables are made of veneer-core or lumber-core hard-

wood plywood. For veneer-core plywood, the simplest edge treatment is to add another thickness of material along the underside and then to apply a thin veneer to cover the edge grain. In furniture production, the manufacturer usually makes tops of lumber-core plywood and includes edge banding of the same hardwood as the surface veneer. Then many kinds of edge moldings can be cut. Other methods of treating the edges are shown in Fig. 50-2.

Plywood Center with a Band or Frame

Many small- to medium-size fur-

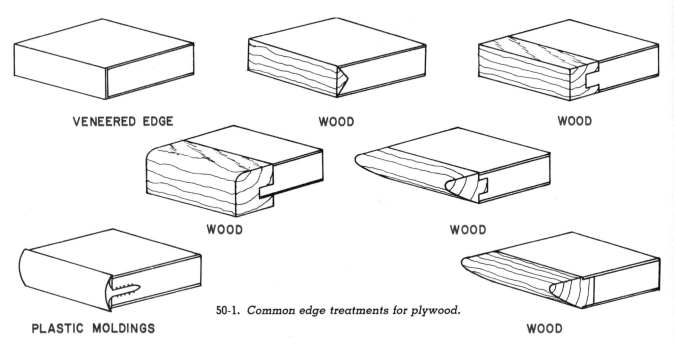

VENEERED EDGE   WOOD   WOOD

WOOD   WOOD

PLASTIC MOLDINGS

50-1. *Common edge treatments for plywood.*

WOOD

niture pieces have tops that consist of a hardwood plywood center with a wide band of solid wood. These tops can easily be made in school and cabinet shops. The band may have mitered or other corner construction. This band, or frame, construction has several distinct advantages. It will not warp and there is little or no expansion and contraction. Because there is a solid wood band, any kind of edge treatment is possible. The band is joined to the plywood with dowels, a spline, or a tongue-and-groove joint. Fig. 50-3. Usually a slight saw kerf is cut where the solid wood joins the plywood. In this way, the solid wood does not have to match the plywood exactly.

In some cases, fir plywood is used for the center and covered with a plastic laminate. When this is done, the band should be 1/16" thicker than the plywood to allow for the thickness of the plastic laminate.

For an unusual tabletop made of an exotic wood or a matching pattern, softwood plywood or particle board can be used for core stock and then covered with a fancy veneer. The back of the sheet material is also covered, but with an inexpensive veneer, to maintain balanced construction.

Solid Glued-Up Stock
Solid glued-up lumber is sometimes used for hand-crafted furniture products made in small cabinet shops and in schools. The two major problems of working with solid glued-up lumber for wide surfaces are warpage and the change in size caused by expansion and contraction. Wide boards tend to cup as the wood takes on moisture or dries out. Therefore when gluing large surfaces together it is a good

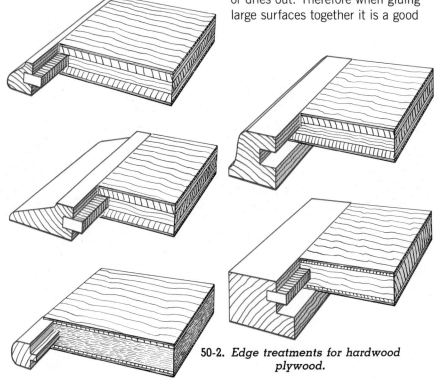

50-2. *Edge treatments for hardwood plywood.*

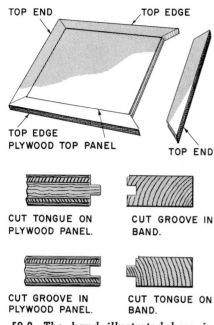

CUT TONGUE ON PLYWOOD PANEL.

CUT GROOVE IN BAND.

CUT GROOVE IN PLYWOOD PANEL.

CUT TONGUE ON BAND.

50-3. *The band illustrated here is joined to the plywood center by a tongue-and-groove joint which can be cut in one of two ways.*

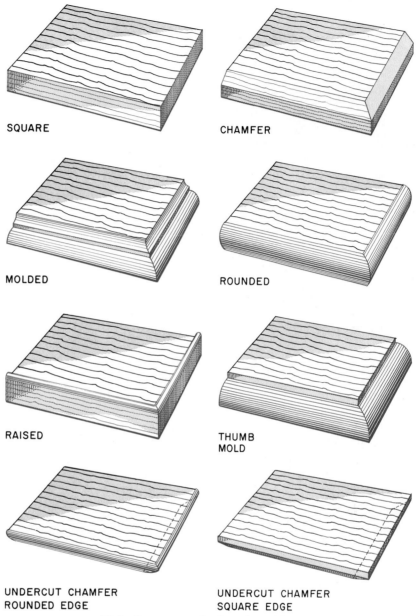

SQUARE

CHAMFER

MOLDED

ROUNDED

RAISED

THUMB MOLD

UNDERCUT CHAMFER ROUNDED EDGE

UNDERCUT CHAMFER SQUARE EDGE

50-4. *Some typical edges for tabletops.*

idea to cut the pieces into small strips not over 4″ to 6″ wide. Then alternate the pieces so that the heart side is up on every other board. This tends to minimize warpage. Another help is to cut small router grooves across grain on the underside of the top before the top is fastened to the legs and rails.

The biggest problem is the expansion and contraction of a large solid surface. Since lumber expands more across than with grain, it is important that the top be fastened to the base in such a way that it can move without buckling or cracking the joints.

EDGE TREATMENT

The edge treatment for tables, chests, and desks depends on whether plywood or solid wood is used, and on the furniture styles. Fig. 50-4. Simple edge treatments such as the square edge are used on many Modern or Contemporary pieces. Some Early American and Colonial designs have rounded edges. Other furniture styles feature

a wide variety of molded edges. The illustrations in this book will give you some idea of the wide variety of edge designs that are possible. Most of the more intricate edge designs must be cut on a shaper or router.

DROP-LEAF TABLES

To design a table with drop leaves, you must decide on the kind of joint, the place where the leaves will attach, and the method of supporting the leaves. The common

joints are the square, 45°, and rule joint. Figs. 50-5 and 50-6. If a joint with square edges is chosen for the tabletop and leaf, several different kinds of hinges can be used. The simplest are two or three butt hinges installed between the top and the leaf. Fig. 50-7. When closed, the leaves drop down but extend beyond the top. When open, some kind of drop-leaf support is needed. Another hinge that can be used is a flap or drop-leaf table

50-5(a). *The leaves of this table have square joints.*

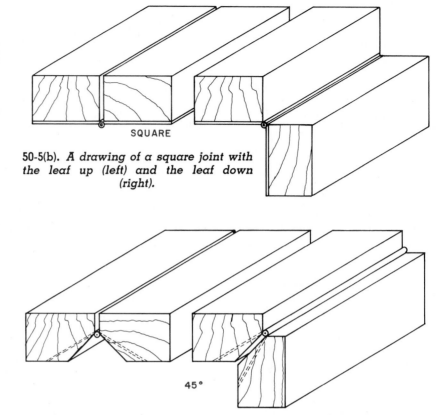

50-5(b). *A drawing of a square joint with the leaf up (left) and the leaf down (right).*

45°

50-6. *Part of the table edge and leaf can be cut at a 45-degree angle so that the leaf will drop partway under the tabletop.*

hinge. This combines the function of both the hinge and the support. When it is closed, the leaf drops below and in line with the edge of the top. Fig. 50-8.

The rule joint is best for certain styles of furniture since it is neater in appearance. It is characteristic of Traditional furniture. Fig. 50-9. This joint has a cove molding on the leaf that slides over the "thumbnail" molding on the top. The rule joint can be cut on a shaper or router or with the molding head on a circular or radial-arm saw. It is extremely important to lay out the joint carefully and to select the correct kind of cutters. *It is always wise to cut a test joint on two scrap pieces of wood of the same thickness as the finished tabletop, and to mount the hinges to make sure that adjustments are correct.* To lay out a rule joint proceed as follows:

1. Measure half the thickness of the knuckle of the hinge, and gauge a line (*X*) from the underside on both the tabletop and the drop leaves. The center of both the concave and convex cuts lies in this gauge line. Fig. 50-10.

2. Set a marking gauge to a distance that is ⅛" less than the thick-

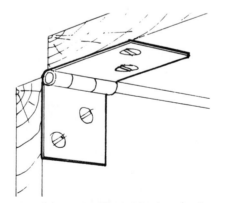

50-7. *Plain steel butt hinges can be used with a square-edge tabletop.*

ness of the table and draw a line (*Y*). Set dividers equal to the distance between lines *X* and *Y*. On Fig. 50-10 this is distance *A*. Scribe an arc on the tabletop from the outer edge to a point on line *Y*.

3. Draw a vertical line from the top of the arc to the top of the table to complete the layout.

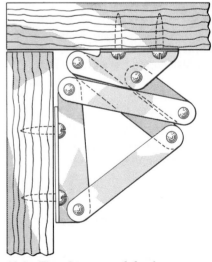

50-8. *This hinge and leaf support, sometimes called a flap table hinge, increases the beauty of Contemporary furniture by eliminating the unsightly gap formed by butt hinges. It provides a flush, clean-cut appearance. When installing the hinge, fasten its smaller leaf to the tabletop. This hinge is designed for ¾" tops only.*

50-9. The rule joint is often used on drop-leaf tables of Traditional design.

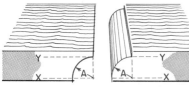

DROP LEAF   TABLETOP

50-10(a). Layout of a rule joint.

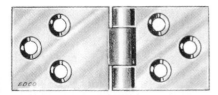

TABLE TOP — A, B, C — TABLE LEAF

50-10(b). Notice that the distance from A to B and from B to C must be the same. Point B is the center of the hinge barrel.

50-11. A hinge for a rule joint.

4. Using the same setting, scribe another arc on the drop leaves, as shown in Fig. 50-10. Frequently the radius is ⅟₃₂″ larger on the drop leaves for clearance between the two moving wood parts.

5. A matched set of cutters for the shaper or bits for the router can be purchased to cut the rule joint on ¾″ thick material. If these are not available, use matching router bits or a shaper cutter to make the joint. For the *router*, select a rounding over/beading bit to cut a convex curve on both edges of the center section. Select a cove bit to cut the concave shape on each leaf. (Router bits are illustrated in Fig. 33-3.) If the edge is to be cut on a *shaper*, the required cutter is mounted on a spindle and the height of the cutter adjusted to the layout lines. The cut on the leaves requires only that the cutter be reversed, with the spindle height and pin setting exactly the same. Remember, it is a good idea to make trial cuts on scrap wood of the correct thickness to check the joint for proper action.

6. After the cuts have been made, turn the table and leaves upside down and place them flat on a bench.

7. Hinges for rule joints must have one long and one short leaf. Fig. 50-11. These are called *back flaps*. It is necessary to cut a shallow groove so that the knuckle fits into the wood with the center of the knuckle exactly on the center of the radius used for cutting the joint. Rout out this groove with a core box bit using the router guide against the edge of the table. A hinge with a slightly bent leaf is available. It does not require a hinge gain.

8. The short leaf is fastened to the underside of the top. The longer half of the hinge must reach across the joint, with the screws set in the drop leaf. The center pin must be in line with the center of the radius used to lay out the joint. If it is impossible to obtain the correct drop-leaf hinges, ordinary hasp hinges can be used.

Supporting the Leaves

There are many ways of supporting drop leaves, including the following:

• *Butterfly drop leaf*. This method is used in Provincial furniture, especially Early American and Colonial. A *wood wing* swings out to support the leaves. Fig. 50-12. In

50-12. This butterfly drop-leaf table has two wood wings that turn on dowel pins to support the leaves.

50-13. *The legs of a gateleg table swing out to support the leaves.*

50-14(a). *The leaves of this server base are held up with slide supports.*

this construction a wing is cut to fit between the rail and stretcher. A wood or metal dowel is fastened permanently in each end of the wing. A hole slightly larger than the dowel is bored in the rail and stretcher. This enables the wing to swing out.

• *Gateleg table.* The gateleg table is one of the oldest and most commonly used extension tables. Fig. 50-13. Each leaf is supported on a swinging leg joined to a movable rail called a *fly rail*. The fly rail is fastened between the table rail and stretcher in a manner similar to the butterfly. The advantages of this design are that the middle section can be much narrower than most drop-leaf tables and swinging legs give excellent support to the leaves.

• *Slide support.* A slide support consists of three narrow boards about 1½″ × 1¾″. The length will depend on the size of the table and leaves. A tongue is cut on both edges of the center board. This tongue slides in the grooves cut into the two fixed boards, called *bearers*. Fig. 50-14. The tongue must fit firmly but slide easily. A notch must be cut in the table rails for the slide and bearers. The bearers are fastened to the rails on the underside of

the top. Usually a stop is placed on the slide and on the leaves so that the slide can't be pulled out too far. A knob is added to the front of the slide so that it can easily be pulled.

• *Pivot rail.* The simplest and easiest method of supporting a drop leaf is with a pivot rail. This is not suitable, however, when heavy loads will be applied to the leaf or for larger leaves. Cut out a section of the rail on each side. The ends of the opening should be at an angle. Then make a support with a bevel on each end that fits the area that has been removed. Drill a hole in the exact center of the support and rail and install a brass pin that

will allow the support to swing. Fig. 50-15.

• *Finger joint.* The finger joint is a flexible, interlocking joint. It has two parts, one movable and one fixed. The joint is divided into five equal fingers, three on the fixed part and two on the movable part. There are two ways in which the joint can be made so that the movable part will swing 90 degrees. One way is to cut the fingers at an angle of 60 degrees as shown in Fig. 50-16. The other method is to shape the fingers on the fixed part with rounded ends and on the movable part with rounded ends and hollows at the bottom of the fingers. Fig. 50-17. After the joint is complete, drill a hole in both parts and

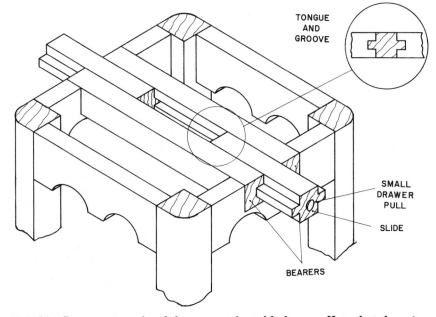

50-14(b). *Construction of a slide support for table leaves. Note that there is a slide at each end.*

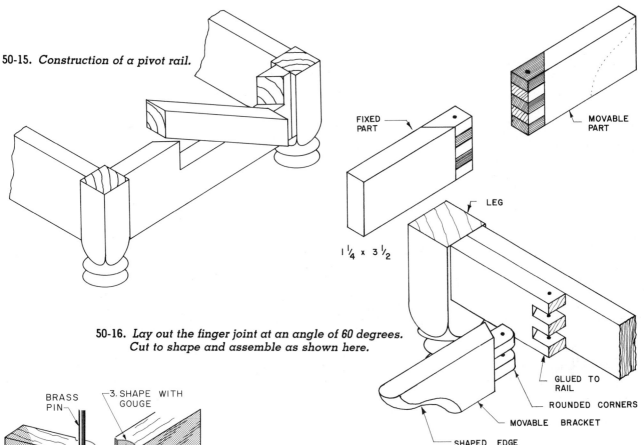

50-15. *Construction of a pivot rail.*

FIXED PART

MOVABLE PART

LEG

$1\frac{1}{4} \times 3\frac{1}{2}$

GLUED TO RAIL

ROUNDED CORNERS

MOVABLE BRACKET

SHAPED EDGE

50-16. *Lay out the finger joint at an angle of 60 degrees. Cut to shape and assemble as shown here.*

BRASS PIN

3. SHAPE WITH GOUGE

FIXED PIECE

1. SHAPE BEFORE CUTTING FINGERS

2. CUT FINGERS

50-17. *Here is another way of making a finger joint for a leaf support.*

install a metal pin, preferably brass. The fixed part is then attached to the rail.

● *Metal table-leaf supports.* A simple method is to use one or two metal supports for each leaf. The size of the supports will depend on the size of the leaf. The most common sizes available are 6″, 8″, 10″, and 12″. They are mounted between the rail or apron and the drop leaf as shown in Fig. 50-18.

Removable Leaves

There are eight basic designs of tables that use removable leaves. Fig. 50-19. To obtain the correct kind of extension table slides and hardware, you must have detailed information about the table on which the slides are to be used. When extension leaves are used, wood or plastic pins are installed along the opening edge of one half of the tabletop and on each extra leaf. These pins keep the leaves in line. Several types of commercial fittings are available for locking the sections of the tabletop together.

FASTENING TOPS TO FURNITURE

There are many common ways of fastening a top to rails (apron) and legs. The most important point to

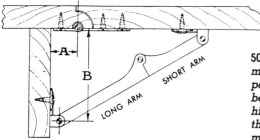

SHORT ARM

LONG ARM

50-18. *The dimensions for mounting a table-leaf support. Measure the distance between the rail and the hinge center ("A"). Look on the chart to find the "B" dimension which corresponds to it. The swivel on the long arm should be placed on the rail so that the distance from the underside of the table to the swivel rivet equals dimension "B" from the chart.*

Dimension A (inches)	Dimension B (inches)		
	6″ Size	8″ Size	10″ Size
$\frac{1}{2}$	$3\frac{1}{2}$	$3\frac{1}{2}$	5
1	$3\frac{1}{4}$	$3\frac{3}{16}$	$4\frac{11}{16}$
$1\frac{1}{2}$	$2\frac{13}{16}$	$2\frac{7}{8}$	$4\frac{7}{16}$
2	$2\frac{1}{2}$	$2\frac{1}{2}$	4
$2\frac{1}{2}$	$2\frac{1}{8}$	$2\frac{1}{8}$	$3\frac{9}{16}$

Dividing Leg. Legs and rim extend with top.

Dividing Base Duncan Phyfe. Pedestals extend with top.

Nondividing Four Leg. Top and rim extend; legs remain stationary.

Nondividing Single Pedestal. Top and rim extend. Single pedestal remains stationary.

Nondividing Pedestal. Top and rim extend. Double pedestals remain stationary.

Drop-Leaf Extension. Legs or pedestals extend with top and rim.

Console Extension.

Drop-Leaf Table. Leaves remain attached to table. Can be supported various ways. May also have removable center leaves.

50-19. *These are the kinds of tables that use removable leaves.*

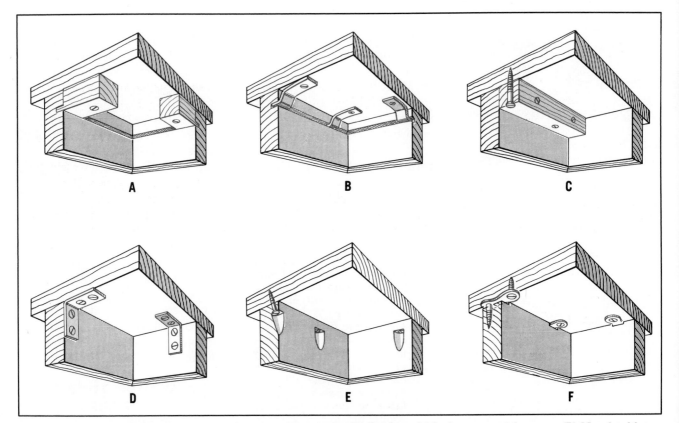

50-20. *Common methods of fastening the tops of furniture. (A) Rabbeted blocks or wood buttons. (B) Metal tabletop fasteners. (C) Wood screws through web or skeleton frame. (D) Angle irons. (E) Wood screws through pocket holes in the rails. (F) Desk-top clips.*

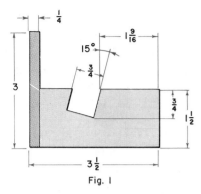

Fig. 1

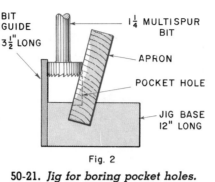

Fig. 2

50-21. *Jig for boring pocket holes.*

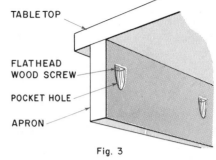

Fig. 3

remember is this: If the top is made of solid lumber, there must be some provision for it to expand and contract without buckling or cracking a joint. For this reason, only methods (A) and (B) shown in Fig. 50-20 should be followed if the top is of solid lumber. Metal tabletop fasteners or clips (method B) are the best. A groove is cut around the rail and

the fasteners are installed at about 12″ intervals. Method (A) has a rabbeted block and requires a slightly wider groove cut in the rail. The blocks or wood buttons are screwed to the top. They can be made with square ends, as shown, or with an arc projection that enables the buttons to be turned and the top removed without unscrewing the

buttons. Methods (C) to (F) in Fig. 50-20 can be followed wherever sheet material such as plywood or particle board has been used or when a banded top is to be fastened in place. The jig for boring the pocket holes at an angle in the rail for method (E) is shown in Fig. 50-21.

51 Casework

Casework basically consists of a box turned on its end or edge and then fitted with dividers, shelves, web frames, faceplates (sometimes called face frames), and drawers or doors to make the enclosure for a particular kind of storage. Such construction is used for kitchen cabinets, cases, counters, desks, and similar items. Casework varies in quality from the most elementary box construction of softwood plywood with butt-joint corners and

painted surfaces to premium cabinets of hardwood plywood with lock-miter corner joints, web frames for rigidity, and a fine transparent finish. Fig. 51-1. The materials, machining techniques, and joinery are less complicated than those employed for fine furniture cabinetwork, described in the next chapter.

MATERIALS

Most casework is constructed of softwood or hardwood veneer-core

plywood, particle board covered with plastic laminate, or solid and glued-up lumber. When using solid lumber it is necessary to allow for parts to swell or shrink. For example, if a web or skeleton frame is fitted into glued-up lumber, the frame must be fastened so that the width of the case can change without bowing or cracking when the humidity changes. The average movement due to humidity change is about plus or minus ⅛″ per 12″ of

423

51-1(a). *This casework of softwood plywood was made by the simplest construction methods and finished by painting.*

width. Skeleton frames must therefore always be slightly narrower than the sides and fastened with screws (not glue). Slightly elongated screw holes should be used in the frame

51-1(b). *These wall units of hardwood plywood illustrate a finer quality of casework.*

itself. For certain kinds of cabinets, a light framework is built and then covered with thin plywood or hardboard.

INTERIOR CONSTRUCTION

The interior construction in lower- to moderate-quality casework consists of solid wood or vertical dividers and horizontal shelves of plywood. These dividers and shelves can be fitted into the case with a simple butt joint, a better dado joint, or the finest rabbet-and-dado or dovetail dado joint. In best-quality casework, skeleton or web frames support the drawers. These frames are set into the sides with a through or plain dado, a stop dado, or a dovetail dado. If a stop dado is used, it must end about ½″ from the front edge of the case. Stop dadoes are not necessary if the front edge is to be covered with a faceplate.

BASE OR LEGS

The base of casework can be constructed in several ways. Fig. 51-2. On many cabinets (particularly kitchen cabinets), the sides are notched at the front bottom edge so that there is a recess about 4″ high and 3″ deep. A solid bottom fits into a dado joint just above this notch. Usually the face frame or plate only fits around three sides of the case. There is no frame at all across the bottom edge. The door covers this edge. The opening below the bottom is set back from the case front and covered with a *toe strip* that is rabbeted on both ends to fasten over the case sides. Heavy wood pieces called *sleepers* are placed on edge from front to back under the case to give extra support. For some casework an extra base frame (sometimes called a plinth) is built to provide toe clearance on two, three, or four sides. A *plinth* is the lowest square or rectangular shape of a cabinet or furniture piece. The

plinth is fastened to the case with glue blocks and cleat strips. There are also many types of shop-made or commercial legs that can be attached to casework.

CONSTRUCTION OF CORNERS AND BACKS

Many types of joints can be used for exterior corner construction. Fig. 51-3. The simplest is the butt joint, but the rabbet joint is found on slightly better construction. The finest corner joints, especially for plywood, are the spline miter, the miter with rabbet (offset miter), and the lock miter. The lock miter is usually made only when the cabinet shop has shaper equipment and cutters.

If the case is to have a back, a rabbet should be cut around the inside of its back edges. This cut usually should be just deep enough to take the plywood or hardboard panel. If the unit is to fit against a wall, the rabbet should be cut as deep as ½″ to ¾″ so that the remaining lip can be trimmed to get a good fit against the wall.

If an extra top is to be applied to the casework, the top of the box itself may be either a web or skeleton frame or a false top (solid plywood or some other solid material over which another top is fitted).

INSTALLING DRAWERS AND DOORS

Drawers are installed in casework following any of the procedures described in Chapter 46. For the very simplest box construction, dadoes can be cut in the sides. Then the bottom of the drawer can be built to extend beyond the sides to act as the drawer guide. Fig. 51-4. A better method for softwood plywood cases is to install a side guide and runner. Fig. 51-5. Fasten cleats to the inside of the case to serve as the guides. The finest casework has a web or skeleton frame to support the drawer. A guide is fastened to

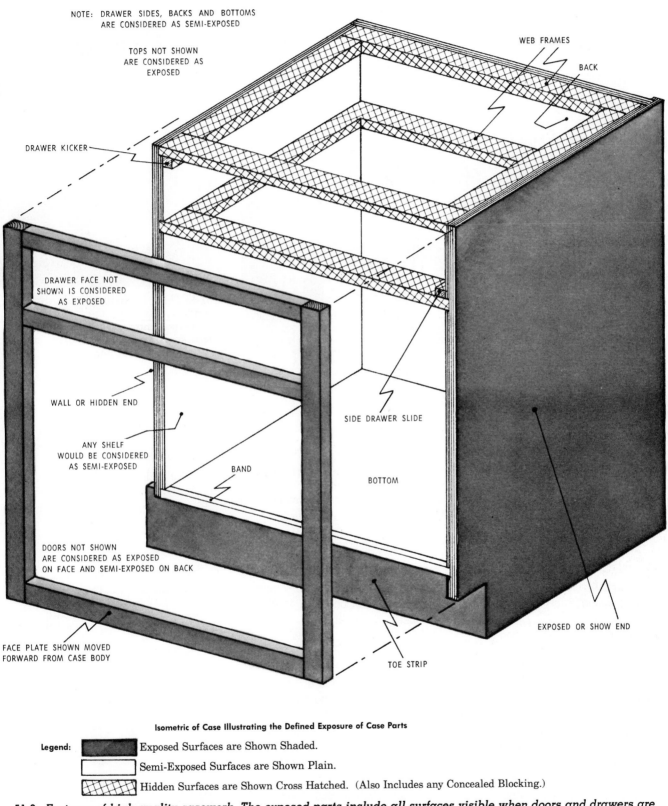

NOTE: DRAWER SIDES, BACKS AND BOTTOMS
ARE CONSIDERED AS SEMI-EXPOSED

TOPS NOT SHOWN
ARE CONSIDERED AS
EXPOSED

WEB FRAMES

BACK

DRAWER KICKER

DRAWER FACE NOT
SHOWN IS CONSIDERED
AS EXPOSED

WALL OR HIDDEN END

ANY SHELF
WOULD BE CONSIDERED
AS SEMI-EXPOSED

SIDE DRAWER SLIDE

BAND

BOTTOM

DOORS NOT SHOWN
ARE CONSIDERED AS EXPOSED
ON FACE AND SEMI-EXPOSED ON BACK

EXPOSED OR SHOW END

FACE PLATE SHOWN MOVED
FORWARD FROM CASE BODY

TOE STRIP

Isometric of Case Illustrating the Defined Exposure of Case Parts

Legend: Exposed Surfaces are Shown Shaded.

Semi-Exposed Surfaces are Shown Plain.

Hidden Surfaces are Shown Cross Hatched. (Also Includes any Concealed Blocking.)

51-2. Features of high-quality casework. *The exposed parts include all surfaces visible when doors and drawers are closed. The semi-exposed parts include those pieces behind opaque doors such as shelves, dividers, interior faces of ends, case backs, drawer sides, backs and bottoms, and the back face of doors. The concealed parts include sleepers (front-to-back base supports), web frames, dust panels, and other parts not usually seen after installation of the casework.*

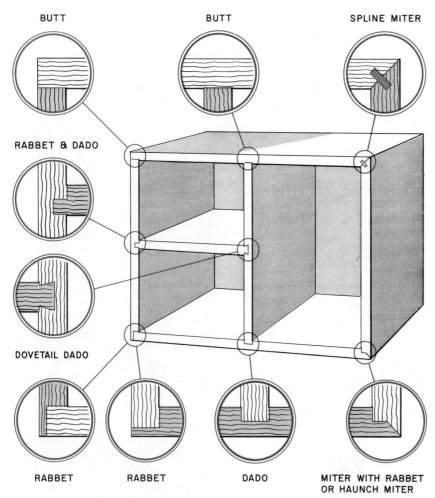

51-4. *This inexpensive drawer is made by fastening the bottom to the sides with nails. The extended bottom serves as a guide in the dado runner.*

51-3. *The most common joints made in casework are shown here with the exception of the lock miter.*

with a stub mortise-and-tenon, dowel, or haunched mortise-and-tenon joint. The faceplate is then fastened to the case with nails alone or nails and glue. On the very best quality casework built in the shop, the faceplate is fastened to

this frame. Dust panels are not normally installed in simple casework but are included in fine furniture cabinetwork.

Any kind of door described in Chapter 45 can be used. Doors for the finest casework should be made of lumber-core plywood or particle board covered with veneer or plastic laminate. On casework of lower quality, veneer-core plywood can be used. The thickness of material limits the size of flush doors that can be used. The following standards should be applied for best-quality construction: For ¾" material, the doors should not be wider than 26" nor higher than 28"; for 1" to 1¼" doors, the maximum size can be

36" wide and 66" high; small sliding doors not exceeding 6 square feet in area can be made of ¼" tempered hardboard.

FACEPLATE

Only the lowest-quality casework of plywood or particle board has exposed edges filled and painted. On medium-quality casework the shelves, dividers, and edges have bands of veneer or solid wood glued and nailed in place. In finest-quality casework all edges are banded with material that has been glued in place under pressure. The front of best-quality casework has a faceplate (sometimes called stiles and rails). This is joined at the corner

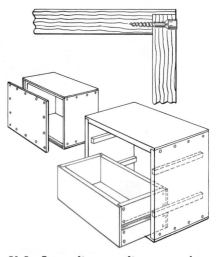

51-5. *A medium-quality case has side guides and runners. The corners are assembled with glue and screws.*

the case with glue under pressure. Only a few nails or staples may be used to position it. Sometimes the exposed end of highest-quality casework is joined to the faceplate with a spline-miter or a lock-miter joint.

ASSEMBLY

Simplest casework is assembled with nails and glue. On better-quality pieces the fastening is done with glue and screws. Finest-quality casework is assembled with glue only, using pressure clamps until the unit is dry.

FINISH

The exterior of casework (those surfaces that can be seen when all doors and drawers are closed) should be carefully sanded before finishing. For a painted or opaque finish, the sanding can be done by machine with medium-grade, 60-grit (½) sandpaper. For a fine, transparent finish, both machine and hand sanding must be done on exposed surfaces. Final sanding requires 100- or 120-grit sandpaper. All cross scratches must be avoided when a transparent finish is to be applied. Apply the finish to the casework as described in Section V.

Since most of the simple casework is constructed of softwood plywood, a painted or opaque finish is usually applied. Some casework may be constructed from prefinished plywood.

CASEWORK STANDARDS

Casework for residential use is made in three different grades. *Premium* grade, which is the highest in both material and workmanship, is used for the finest kinds of installation. *Custom* grade is the middle or normal grade. *Economy* grade is the lowest and is intended for use where costs must be kept to a minimum. All grades have common elements, but they differ in the kind of materials used, joints, assembly methods, and finishes.

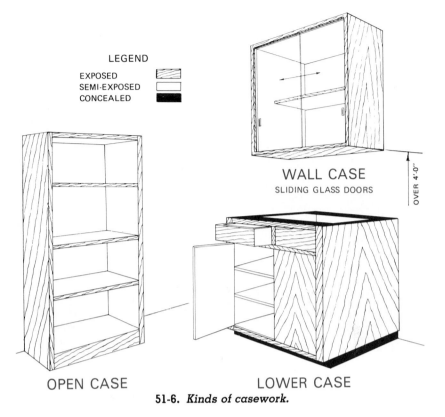

LEGEND
EXPOSED
SEMI-EXPOSED
CONCEALED

WALL CASE
SLIDING GLASS DOORS

OVER 4'-0"

OPEN CASE

LOWER CASE

51-6. *Kinds of casework.*

Kinds of Casework

There are three basic kinds of casework: *lower*, *wall*, and *open*. Fig. 51-6. The *exposed* parts of casework include all surfaces that are visible when the doors and drawers are closed. The undersides of wall cases that are 4' or more above the floor are considered to be exposed. The *semi-exposed* parts include shelves, dividers, drawer sides, backs and bottoms, as well as interior faces of doors, ends, and backs. *Concealed* parts include sleepers, web frames, and other surfaces not normally seen. The undersides of wall cabinets less than 2' from the floor are considered to be concealed.

Materials

Materials used include lumber, hardwood plywood, softwood plywood, covered particle board, and hardboard. For premium grade, the best-quality lumber is used along with hardwood plywood for exposed, transparent finishes. The custom grade may use a lower quality of hardwood plywood or particle board covered with plastic laminate. Normally the economy grade uses a less expensive lumber, the lowest grades of hardwood plywood, and softwood plywood and particle board.

Case Body Construction

All cases use the same basic construction shown in Fig. 51-2. For premium grades, the dado or concealed dado joint is used in construction. Stop dadoes are always required for the exposed edges. For custom grade, the same kind of joint construction is used except that stop dadoes are required only for a transparent finish. In the economy grade either the open or through dado or the concealed dado joint can be used. Fig. 51-7.

When constructing the faceplates and the web frames of stile-and-rail joinery, various types of joints are used. All faceplates must use either mortise-and-tenon or dowel construction glued under pressure. All

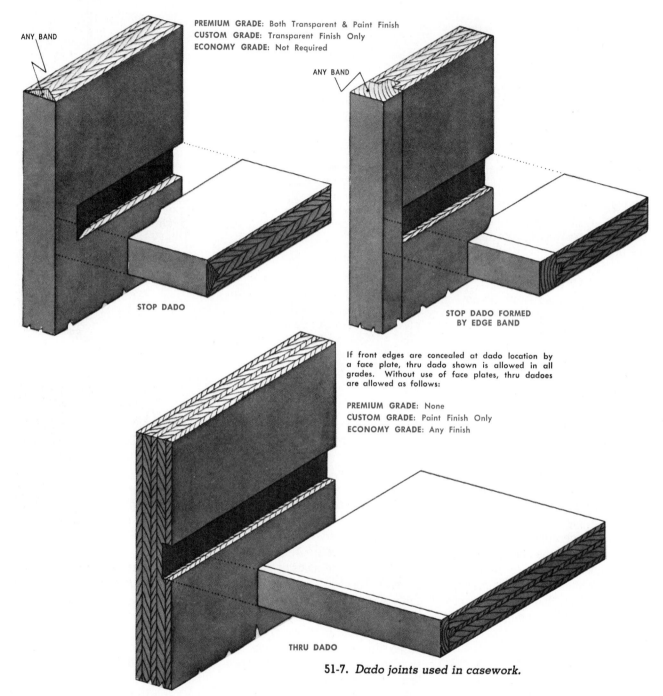

ANY BAND

PREMIUM GRADE: Both Transparent & Paint Finish
CUSTOM GRADE: Transparent Finish Only
ECONOMY GRADE: Not Required

ANY BAND

STOP DADO

STOP DADO FORMED
BY EDGE BAND

If front edges are concealed at dado location by
a face plate, thru dado shown is allowed in all
grades. Without use of face plates, thru dadoes
are allowed as follows:

PREMIUM GRADE: None
CUSTOM GRADE: Paint Finish Only
ECONOMY GRADE: Any Finish

THRU DADO

51-7. *Dado joints used in casework.*

web frames can use stub tenon construction. Fig. 51-8. Dust panels are not normally included in the web frames unless specified.

Assembly of the Case

There are important differences in the corner joints and the way in which the faceplate is attached to the body of the case. For premium-grade casework, the lock miter, offset miter, or splined miter must be used with glue blocks on the corners. Fig. 51-9. Custom cases have the same kinds of joints, but without glue blocks. For the economy case, either a butt or miter joint can be used.

The faceplate is attached to the body of the case in different ways.

For the premium grade the exposed ends must be lock mitered and glued to the faceplate using either a lock-miter joint or a miter joint with a spline. Fig. 51-10. For the custom grade, the faceplate is pressure glued to the case body. Nails are used only for positioning the faceplate. For the economy grade, the faceplate is glued to the case using

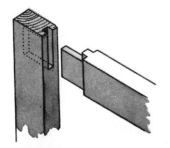

MORTISE-AND-TENON JOINT

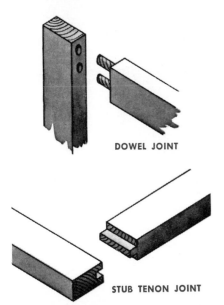

DOWEL JOINT

STUB TENON JOINT

51-8. *Cabinetmaking joints used for faceplates and web frames.*

only nails for pressure. No clamps are used.

Drawer Construction

Drawer construction quality varies

widely from the premium to the economy grade. Fig. 51-11. (You will find Figs. 51-11 through 51-15 on pages 430 through 433.)

Cabinet Tops

Most cabinet tops are made of plywood or particle board with plastic laminate exteriors. Fig. 51-12. The method by which the top is attached to the case differs for each grade. In the premium grade, tops are fastened to the web frame with screws, glue blocks, and other hidden fasteners. Fig. 51-13. For the custom grade, the method for attaching depends on whether the top is made with plastic laminate or will be painted. Fig 51-14. If the case is to have a transparent finish, hidden fasteners must be used, as for the premium grade. For the economy grade, the tops are fastened with nails only, except for high-pressure plastic laminates. These are fastened as required for custom grade. Fig. 51-15.

Finishes

Finishes used on cabinets depend on the kind of materials and whether the exterior shows open-grain or closed-grain woods. Both the premium and custom grades require a series of quality finishes similar to those described in Section V. Most economy grades are painted.

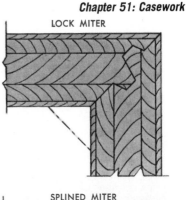

LOCK MITER

SPLINED MITER

GLUE BLOCK BACK OF MITERS

OFFSET MITER

51-9. *Typical corner joints for premium casework. The joints are fastened by gluing, and additional strength is provided by adding glue blocks.*

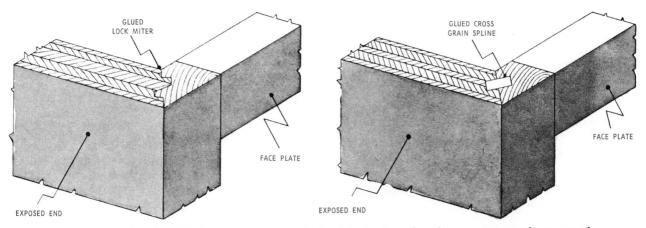

GLUED LOCK MITER

FACE PLATE

EXPOSED END

GLUED CROSS GRAIN SPLINE

FACE PLATE

EXPOSED END

51-10. *Exposed ends must be lock mitered and glued to the faceplate for premium-grade casework.*

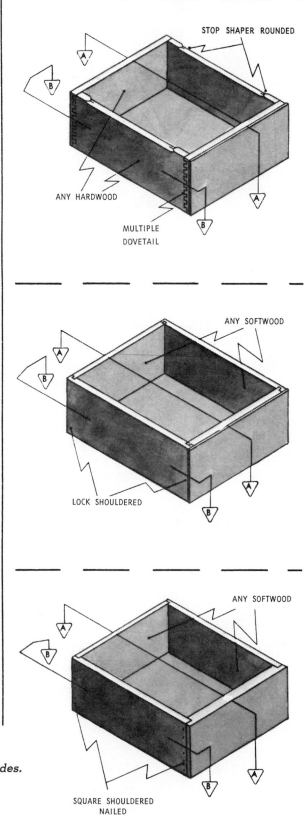

ISOMETRIC OF DRAWER

STOP SHAPER ROUNDED

PREMIUM GRADE

Connections between fronts, backs and sides shall be regular multiple drawer dovetails with joints glued, except that through top-to-bottom dovetail shall be used when drawer fronts must extend beyond drawer side, as would be done to hide the ends of metal drawer slides. Top edge of drawer sides shall be stop shaper-rounded. Two hardwood side guides and one hardwood kicker-strip shall be used. Drawer sides and backs may be any hardwood. As an alternative a center T guide with nylon tracer guide fastened to back of drawer may be used. Drawers shall rest upon web-body frame, unless hardwood plowed-in side slides or metal drawer slides are used.

ANY HARDWOOD

MULTIPLE
DOVETAIL

ANY SOFTWOOD

CUSTOM GRADE

Connections between fronts, backs, and sides of drawers shall be lock-shoulder, glued and nailed. Two softwood side guides and one kicker-strip, or hardwood center guides may be used. Drawer sides and backs may be any softwood. Drawers shall rest upon web-body frame, unless plowed-in side slides or metal drawer slides are used.

LOCK SHOULDERED

ANY SOFTWOOD

ECONOMY GRADE

Connections between fronts, backs, and sides shall be square shouldered and nailed. No web frame is required as side guides may form same. One softwood kicker-strip shall be required.

51-11. *Drawer construction for the three different grades.*

SQUARE SHOULDERED
NAILED

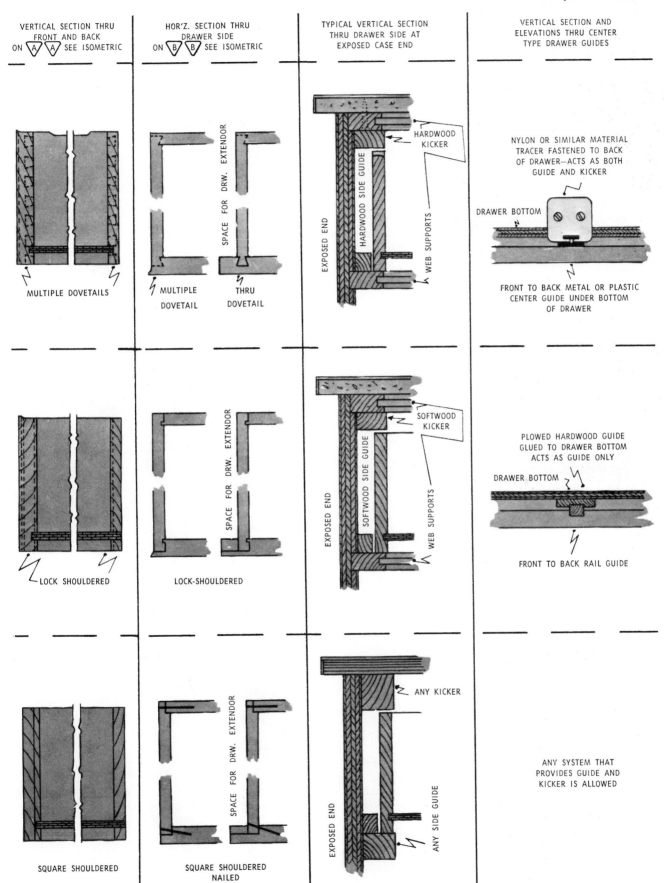

VERTICAL SECTION THRU
FRONT AND BACK
ON A—A SEE ISOMETRIC

HOR'Z. SECTION THRU
DRAWER SIDE
ON B—B SEE ISOMETRIC

TYPICAL VERTICAL SECTION
THRU DRAWER SIDE AT
EXPOSED CASE END

VERTICAL SECTION AND
ELEVATIONS THRU CENTER
TYPE DRAWER GUIDES

MULTIPLE DOVETAILS

MULTIPLE DOVETAIL

THRU DOVETAIL

SPACE FOR DRW. EXTENDOR

HARDWOOD KICKER

EXPOSED END

HARDWOOD SIDE GUIDE

WEB SUPPORTS

NYLON OR SIMILAR MATERIAL
TRACER FASTENED TO BACK
OF DRAWER—ACTS AS BOTH
GUIDE AND KICKER

DRAWER BOTTOM

FRONT TO BACK METAL OR PLASTIC
CENTER GUIDE UNDER BOTTOM
OF DRAWER

LOCK SHOULDERED

LOCK-SHOULDERED

SPACE FOR DRW. EXTENDOR

SOFTWOOD KICKER

EXPOSED END

SOFTWOOD SIDE GUIDE

WEB SUPPORTS

PLOWED HARDWOOD GUIDE
GLUED TO DRAWER BOTTOM
ACTS AS GUIDE ONLY

DRAWER BOTTOM

FRONT TO BACK RAIL GUIDE

SQUARE SHOULDERED

SQUARE SHOULDERED
NAILED

SPACE FOR DRW. EXTENDOR

ANY KICKER

EXPOSED END

ANY SIDE GUIDE

ANY SYSTEM THAT
PROVIDES GUIDE AND
KICKER IS ALLOWED

431

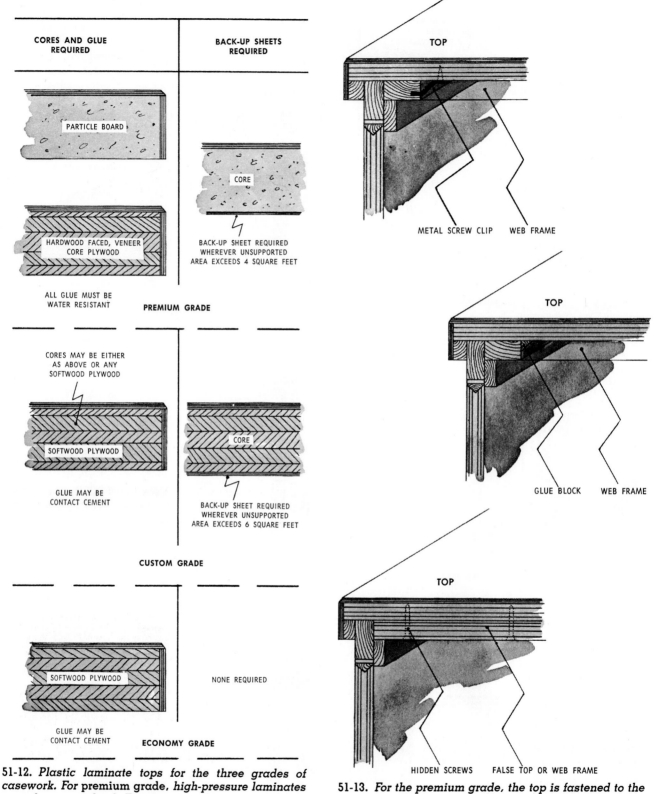

CORES AND GLUE REQUIRED	BACK-UP SHEETS REQUIRED

PARTICLE BOARD

CORE

HARDWOOD FACED, VENEER CORE PLYWOOD

BACK-UP SHEET REQUIRED WHEREVER UNSUPPORTED AREA EXCEEDS 4 SQUARE FEET

ALL GLUE MUST BE WATER RESISTANT

PREMIUM GRADE

CORES MAY BE EITHER AS ABOVE OR ANY SOFTWOOD PLYWOOD

SOFTWOOD PLYWOOD

CORE

GLUE MAY BE CONTACT CEMENT

BACK-UP SHEET REQUIRED WHEREVER UNSUPPORTED AREA EXCEEDS 6 SQUARE FEET

CUSTOM GRADE

SOFTWOOD PLYWOOD

NONE REQUIRED

GLUE MAY BE CONTACT CEMENT

ECONOMY GRADE

51-12. *Plastic laminate tops for the three grades of casework. For premium grade, high-pressure laminates must be press glued. For custom and economy grades, contact cement may be used.*

TOP

METAL SCREW CLIP   WEB FRAME

TOP

GLUE BLOCK   WEB FRAME

TOP

HIDDEN SCREWS   FALSE TOP OR WEB FRAME

51-13. *For the premium grade, the top is fastened to the web frame with screws, glue blocks, and other hidden fasteners.*

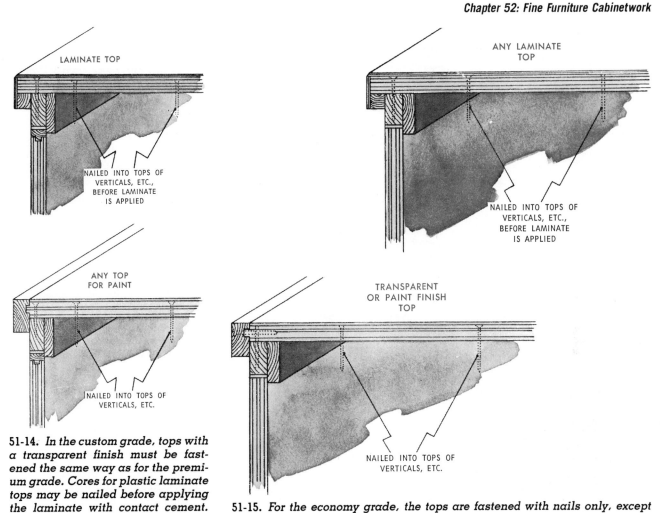

51-14. *In the custom grade, tops with a transparent finish must be fastened the same way as for the premium grade. Cores for plastic laminate tops may be nailed before applying the laminate with contact cement. All tops for a paint finish may be nailed.*

51-15. *For the economy grade, the tops are fastened with nails only, except when plastic laminates are used. Then the same standards as for the custom grade must be followed.*

52 Fine Furniture Cabinetwork

Fine furniture cabinetwork includes chests, desks, china and other storage cabinets, stereo cabinets, and similar furniture pieces. Most fine furniture cabinets (carcass construction) include drawer and door construction, shelves, and other internal cabinet details. It is difficult to describe in specific detail the construction of such pieces since each cabinet shop has its own distinct methods. Fig. 52-1. It is true, however, that there is a wide range of quality both in materials and construction. The

TOP, END, & SKELETON
FRAME ATTACHMENT

CORNER BLOCKS AT THE
CENTER UPRIGHT

CORNER BLOCKS AT THE
REAR CORNERS OF THE
DUST PANELS

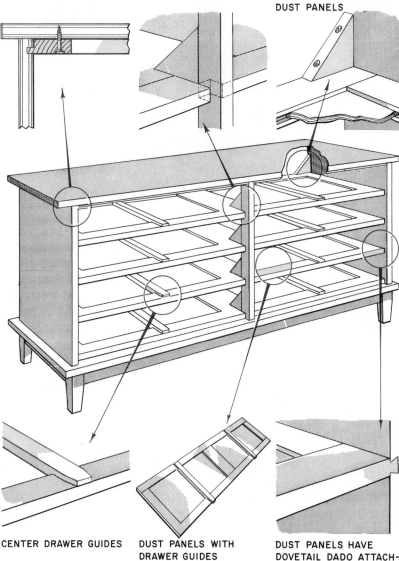

CENTER DRAWER GUIDES

DUST PANELS WITH
DRAWER GUIDES

DUST PANELS HAVE
DOVETAIL DADO ATTACH-
MENTS TO ENDS

52-1. *This drawing shows some of the structural features and construction methods that may be used in fine cabinetwork.*

els with some type of dado joint or with a tongue-and-groove joint. Dust bottoms fit into these frames. Vertical and horizontal parting rails use an edge cross lap (notched) joint. Fig. 52-4.

● *Lay-on top construction* uses a case assembly with interior frame construction. The top is attached to the top frame. Fig. 52-5.

Basic casework and fine furniture cabinetwork have much in common. Both require the construction of a box or carcass that is fitted with shelves, drawers, or doors. Fine furniture cabinetwork differs from basic casework in the following ways:

● A greater variety of fine woods and plywoods is used in furniture cabinetwork. These include not only the fine native hardwoods but also exotic imported woods. Fig. 52-6.

● Many different materials, including wood, glass, ceramics, metal, cane, and fabric, are part of fine furniture cabinetwork.

● Frame-and-panel construction is more commonly used for sides, fronts, doors, and drawers of cabinetwork.

● Greater use is made of solid wood for legs, posts, rails, and other exposed structural parts. Legs and posts are frequently an integral part of a fine piece of furniture cabinetwork.

● Fancy, machined surfaces, including turned and carved legs and posts, are part of many designs. The exposed surfaces, including doors and drawers, often have fancy moldings, inlays, overlay, and carving. Fig. 52-7.

● All quality furniture has mortised joints on the fronts and backs of drawers. The faceplates are often made with a miter joint strengthened with a spline.

● More complicated joinery is used for fine cabinetwork.

● The corners may be square or coved (rounded) solid lumber joined to plywood or to solid lumber with a tongue-and-groove joint. Fig. 52-8.

experienced cabinetmaker recognizes this immediately when studying the interior construction, doors, and drawers of a cabinet.

Many methods of construction are shown in this and other chapters of this book. Sometimes a piece of furniture shown with a drawing of a construction method was not made by that precise method. The drawing only suggests how the product *could be* built. Figs. 52-2 and 52-3.

There are two basic types of casework construction used in building furniture:

● *Flush top construction* uses top, end, and base panels that are all the same thickness. The top and sides (ends) are usually assembled with a lock-miter joint or other kinds of corner joints. A rabbet joint is often used to attach the base panel to the end panels. Interior dust frames are attached to the end pan-

52-2. *This refreshment bar has a plastic-laminate top and rosewood-veneer exterior. The finest methods of construction are represented.*

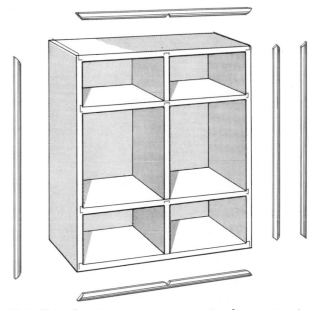

52-3. *This drawing suggests very simple construction techniques for the carcass of the refreshment bar. More complicated joinery techniques were used in the unit shown in Fig. 52-2.*

• Fine furniture finishes of a transparent type are typical.

• Fancy hardware, much of it designed specifically for a certain style of cabinetwork, is used to enhance the beauty of the furniture.

• Plastic laminates of matching woodgrain are usually used only for the tops of tables, chests, or cabinets. They are rarely used on the other exposed surfaces.

• Tables, chairs, beds, and other open-frame units are not considered cabinetwork even though much of the construction is the same.

CABINET CORNER CONSTRUCTION

Many high-quality pieces of cabinetwork have fine hardwood plywood

52-4(a). *A dresser with flush-top construction.*

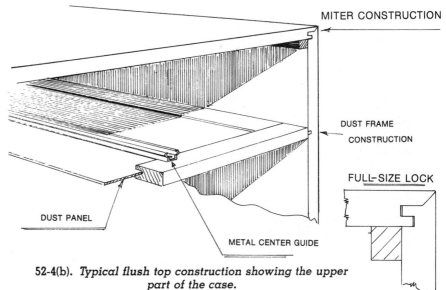

FLUSH TOP CONSTRUCTION

MITER CONSTRUCTION

DUST FRAME CONSTRUCTION

FULL-SIZE LOCK

DUST PANEL

METAL CENTER GUIDE

52-4(b). *Typical flush top construction showing the upper part of the case.*

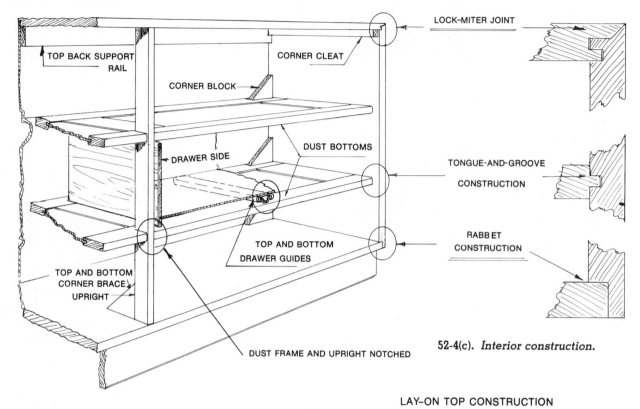

LOCK-MITER JOINT

TOP BACK SUPPORT RAIL

CORNER CLEAT

CORNER BLOCK

DRAWER SIDE

DUST BOTTOMS

TONGUE-AND-GROOVE CONSTRUCTION

RABBET CONSTRUCTION

TOP AND BOTTOM DRAWER GUIDES

TOP AND BOTTOM CORNER BRACE UPRIGHT

DUST FRAME AND UPRIGHT NOTCHED

52-4(c). *Interior construction.*

for the casework, with the sides, top, and bottom joined at the corners with a lock-miter joint (or other joint of equal quality) to form a sharp right angle. This is done for flush top construction. Fig. 52-9. Other cabinets are constructed so that the sides overlap the top and bottom. On this construction, the

LAY-ON TOP CONSTRUCTION

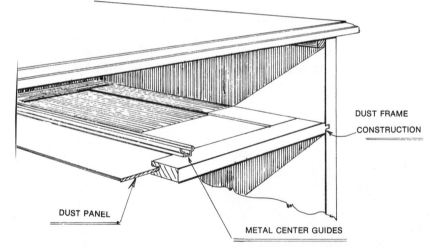

DUST FRAME CONSTRUCTION

DUST PANEL

METAL CENTER GUIDES

52-5(b). *Typical lay-on top construction showing the upper part of the case.*

52-5(a). *A chest that uses lay-on top construction.*

52-6. *This cabinet in a modern design is made of oak frames with rosewood veneer inserts on the top and door fronts.*

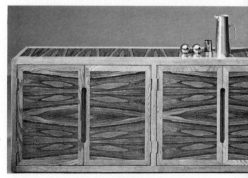

52-7. *Many pieces of Traditional furniture are decorated with shell carvings.*

top and bottom may fit into the sides with some kind of dado joint or with dowel construction. Other fine cabinets have exactly the reverse arrangement, with the top and bottom overlapping the sides. With such overlapping it is common to use a web or skeleton frame to complete the inner rectangular box. Then the exposed top and bottom are fitted to the frame. This is lay-on top construction.

CHEST CONSTRUCTION

The typical chest of drawers consists of a case which is divided and held together by framed dust panels. Such panels may be either invisible or exposed, with the front of the frame made of the same wood as the exterior of the chest. Drawers are usually fitted into the case with center guides and runners. Drawer fronts may be flush, lipped, flush overlay, or reveal overlay.

LARGER CABINET PIECES

Larger pieces of furniture, particularly cases, chests, china cabinets, and buffets, consist of two, three, or four separate and distinct structural parts. These parts are constructed separately and then fastened together with cleats, glue blocks, corner blocks, and screws. Fig. 52-10. These structural parts include the following:

Base Unit

The base unit, which is the lowest part of cabinetwork, may be one of the following:

52-9. *The case of this storage cabinet is made of lumber-core plywood with sharp right-angle corners.*

- *Legs* attached directly to the lower casework or carcass. These may be shop-made or commercial. The style must match the cabinetwork.
- *Leg-and-rail construction*, similar to the bottom of a table or chair.

52-8. *Two methods of constructing the corners for cabinet (carcass) construction.*

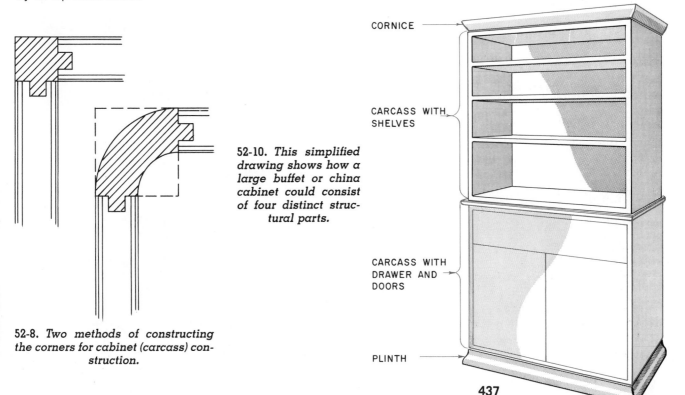

52-10. *This simplified drawing shows how a large buffet or china cabinet could consist of four distinct structural parts.*

CORNICE

CARCASS WITH SHELVES

CARCASS WITH DRAWER AND DOORS

PLINTH

52-11. *The plinth under this display cabinet is recessed on all sides.*

CORNER BLOCK

MITER JOINT WITH SPLINE

PLINTH

52-12. *Typical plinth construction. Many other kinds of corner joints could be used.*

Upper Case or Cabinet Unit

This case or cabinet usually consists of shelves, doors, and sometimes one or more drawers. Glass doors, in wood frames or of the sliding type, are often installed.

• A *plinth (enclosed base)*. The plinth should be from 2″ to 4″ high, depending on the size of the furniture piece. Sometimes the front is set back a few inches from the lower case to protect against shoe marks. Some plinths are recessed on all sides. Fig. 52-11. There are many ways to make a plinth but the common one is to build a simple, hollow, rectangular frame. Usually a spline-miter corner joint is used and a corner block added for greater strength. Fig. 52-12. The plinth is usually attached to the lower casework or cabinet, with cleats on all four interior surfaces.

Lower Case or Cabinet Unit

This case or cabinet usually consists of a carcass fitted with doors, drawers, shelves, or other interior details.

52-13. *This china cabinet illustrates many of the features that can be built into furniture: (A) The finial is a decorative terminal piece installed vertically to accent a point or the ending of a structure. (B) The broken pediment is borrowed from classical architecture. Its sloping lines stop short of the peak, leaving a gap for the ornamental finial. (C) A cornice is a projecting molding used to give an architectural finish to the top edge. (D) A row of dentils (small rectangular blocks) projects under the cornice. (E) The frame-and-panel doors have leaded glass panels. (F) Fittings are metal mounts, handles, etc., applied to the completed piece of furniture. (G) The cabinet rests on a rectangular plinth.*

Cornice

The uppermost part of the unit is called the *cornice*. This may be anything from a simple molding to an extremely complicated rectangular unit consisting of several highly decorated parts. Fig. 52-13.

PRIZE-WINNING FURNITURE

Here are some examples of fine furniture built by student woodworkers. Fig. 52-14.

A - FINIAL

B - BROKEN PEDIMENT

C - CORNICE

D - DENTIL

E - FRAME-AND-PANEL DOOR

F - FITTING

G - PLINTH

52-14. *These award-winning projects were built by students.*

53 Cabinets

Cabinets for the kitchen, bathroom, laundry room, and other parts of the home make up one of the major areas of cabinetmaking. The chief purpose of cabinetry is to provide functional storage and work convenience. It is for this reason that cabinets must be carefully planned and well built. Functional cabinets must be adaptable to changing conditions. They must be suitable for storing various sizes and shapes of items. All cabinetmakers and finish carpenters need to have a thorough understanding of every aspect of cabinetry. Fig. 53-1.

METHODS OF PRODUCING CABINETRY

There are three basic ways in which cabinets are produced.

● Many are built on the construction site piece by piece from the detail elevations and floor plans supplied by the architect. The design of the home, whether it is Contemporary, Provincial, or Traditional, may influence to some extent the design of the cabinets. In general, however, their construction is relatively simple, and the assembly is with glue and nails. Primarily, cabinetmakers use softwood or hardwood plywood, with solid wood for facings and perhaps for drawer fronts and sides. Usually the cabinets have either flush or lipped doors and drawers. Such on-the-job construction is on the decline because shop- or

53-1. *An adaptable, functional, energy-saving kitchen is essential to the well-designed home. This kitchen has drawers and cabinets of various sizes, open shelving, a wine rack, plus additional storage in the drop ceiling above the cabinets.*

factory-built units are usually of better quality and often less expensive.

● The second method is to purchase mill-made cabinets in a knockdown condition. The cabinet-maker then assembles the parts and installs the cabinets. These usually have medium-quality joinery with perhaps a lock joint on the drawers. Most parts are nailed or stapled together.

● The third basic method is to purchase cabinets that are mass produced. The quality of such cabinets varies widely. The least expensive are only slightly better than those built on the job, but the best are of a quality equal to the finest furniture. Highest-grade cabinets for kitchens, baths, etc., have exactly the same standards of construction, materials, and workmanship as do top-quality furniture cabinets or chests of drawers. The use of production equipment makes it possible for manufactured cabinets to have such features as all lumber-core plywood construction, complicated joinery such as multiple dove-tail joints on fronts and backs of drawers, commercial drawer guides, and the finest finishes. Such cabinets come in a wide range of designs similar to those found in other fine furniture. Some manufacturers use the same basic cabinets for all designs. They use various moldings, trim, hardware, and finish to achieve styling. Fig. 53-2.

KINDS OF CABINETS

In the kitchen, five basic kinds of cabinets are used: base unit, range or sink unit, wall unit, tall unit, and special-purpose unit. Some of these units are also used in other areas of the home. For example, they might be used in a laundry room.

The **base cabinet** is the basic storage section of every kitchen. Fig. 53-3. It is designed with drawers, doors, shelves, and pullouts for a wide variety of storage. Pots and pans, serving dishes, food staples, and cleaning supplies are usually kept on its shelves. The drawers hold silverware, utensils, and linen. The top of the base cabinet is usually covered with plastic laminate and is used for a work surface. Base cabinets made to fit into corners are available. Often these are fitted with revolving "lazy Susan" shelves. Fig. 53-4.

A good base unit must be extremely sturdy, with no sticking doors or drawers, loose hardware, or sagging doors. It should always be designed with a recessed toe board.

The widths of factory-built cabinets are based on a 3″ module from 12″ to 48″ and on a 1′ module for widths up to 8′. The 12″ width, when available, is usually designed for special purposes, such as stor-

53-2. *This illustration shows how moldings and hardware can change the appearance of a door.*

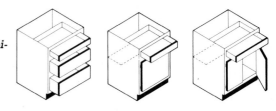

53-3. *Typical base cabinets.*

53-4. *Lazy Susan shelving makes maximum use of a corner cabinet.*

53-5. *This narrow base cabinet has dividers for tray storage.*

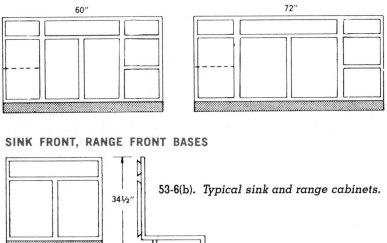

53-6(a). *This cooking top is built into a cabinet designed for that purpose.*

age for trays or soiled towels. Fig. 53-5. Cabinets up to 21″ wide have a single door. Those 24″ in width might have one or two doors. Cabinets wider than 24″ have two doors. Most base cabinets are about 24″ in depth, as measured from the face of the cabinet to the wall. The FHA (Federal Housing Administration) specifies that the depth of shelving in base cabinets shall range from a minimum of 12″ to a maximum of 24″. The height of the base cabinet, measured from the floor to the top of the counter, is about 36″. Some manufacturers offer cabinets 30″ high. These lower cabinets are convenient for the mixing counter. However, the variation in height can cause problems. For example, a continuous counter top cannot be used when the base cabinets are of different heights. The FHA restricts the height of the counter top to a maximum of 38″, and any counter top below 30″ is excluded when determining counter top area. FHA further requires that shelving in base cabinets be spaced at least 7″ for depths up to 15″, and 10″ for depths from 15″ to 24″.

Range and sink cabinets are designed in various widths for a built-in cooking top or sink. When there are other cabinets on each side of the cooking top or sink area, it is possible to use a front only instead of a complete cabinet. Fig. 53-6.

Wall cabinets are hung above the counter top and are used for storage of dishes and food. Fig. 53-7. The well-designed wall unit has adjustable shelving to accommodate items of various sizes and shapes.

Wall cabinets are about 12″ to 15″ deep and 30″ high when hung above a standard base cabinet. To take advantage of space over the refrigerator, cooking surface, or other areas, wall cabinets of less height are available. Angular and lazy Susan cabinets fit into corners.

The standard clearance between the top of a base cabinet and the bottom of a wall cabinet is 18″. Wall cabinets installed over refrigerators should have a clearance of 4″. The FHA requires a 24″ mini-

UNDER SINK BASES

60″   72″

SINK FRONT, RANGE FRONT BASES

34½″

53-6(b). *Typical sink and range cabinets.*

441

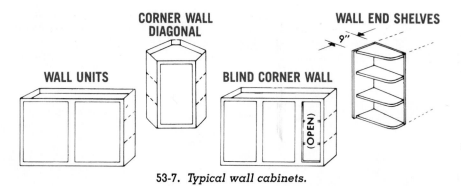

53-7. *Typical wall cabinets.*

mum clearance over the range and sink and 15" over other base cabinets.

Most kitchens are designed with a drop ceiling (also called a soffit or bulkhead) above the wall cabinets. Fig. 53-1. The reasons for lowering the ceiling 12" to 18" for the cabinets are:

• If cabinets were built to the ceiling, the last shelves could not be

53-8. *This tall cabinet features pull-out trays. Adjustable shelves on the doors provide additional storage.*

reached without a stool or stepladder.

• By dropping the ceiling 12" to 18", a standard 30" wall cabinet can be used for all kitchens even though the ceiling height may vary.

• If a drop ceiling is not used, the cabinets are attached to the wall at the proper height above the base cabinets. Then the tops of the cabinets can be used as shelves for decorative items or for additional storage. Sometimes this space is filled in with small cabinets that have separate doors. These cabinets are used for dead storage.

Tall cabinets are designed for many purposes. Fig. 53-8. Oven units are often fitted into these full-

53-9. *This is a small bathroom cabinet for towel storage.*

height cabinets. The utility unit usually has shelves for dishes, linens, packaged goods, and cleaning supplies. Some tall units also have cabinet drawers at top or bottom.

Tall cabinets are aligned with the base and wall cabinets. The height is usually 81", the width 20" to 24", and the depth 14" to 24".

In addition to these basic cabinets, there are many **special designs**, such as the desk unit, pull-out table, hamper base, medicine cabinet, and many others. Fig. 53-9. Various doors are available for these units. For example, most medicine cabinets have mirrored sliding doors.

PLANNING THE KITCHEN LAYOUT

It is usually the responsibility of the architect to plan the kitchen layout and to design the general appearance of the kitchen cabinets for a new home. The specifications will indicate whether the cabinets are to be built on the home site or purchased as manufactured units and then installed. The responsibility of the finish carpenter or cabinetmaker is much greater if the kitchen cabinets are to be built on the site since even the detail elevation of the kitchen cabinets does not indicate specific construction details for the cabinet interiors. Results can be poor if the cabinetmaker does not know what is needed for an efficient kitchen.

The finish carpenter or cabinetmaker has even greater responsibility when it comes to remodeling a kitchen. Frequently no architect is involved and the woodworker must measure the kitchen carefully and make the new layout for it. He or she must decide whether the cabinets should be built on the job, purchased knocked down, or purchased already assembled.

To plan a remodeled kitchen, first make a careful layout of the existing area, as follows: Starting at the cor-

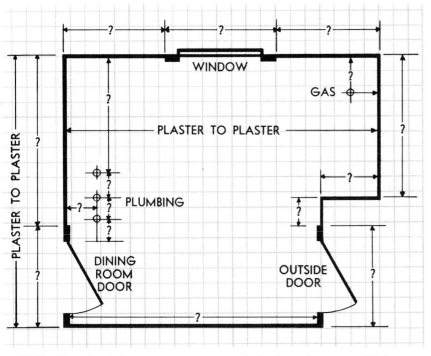

53-10. *Sample of the measurements needed when planning a kitchen.*

ner of the room, measure the kitchen carefully, taking the measurements 36″ from the floor. This is the line of the counter tops which must fit snugly to the wall. Draw the old kitchen layout to scale on ¼″ squared paper. Start from any corner and continue around the entire room using the sample layout in Fig. 53-10 as a guide. Be sure to show location and measurements of windows and doors (including trim) as well as obstructions such as pipes, radiators, chimneys, flues, and stairways. Indicate where doors lead. Show the location of plumbing. If the new kitchen is to be enlarged to include a second room, such as a pantry or breakfast nook, show this area on the floor plan. Indicate any partitions, windows, or other features that can be eliminated or moved. Show all present appliances and built-ins that will continue to be in use. Number the windows and doors shown on the floor plan and give their dimensions. Fig. 53-11. *Measurements must be correct to ⅛″.* To check the accuracy of individual measurements, measure the total length of each wall, plaster to plaster. Don't forget to measure ceiling height. Fig. 53-12.

Once the layout is complete, standard units from a particular line of manufacturer's cabinets can be fitted into the available space. Several arrangements can be suggested. If cabinets are to be built in, a detail floor plan and elevations should be drawn.

KITCHEN ARRANGEMENTS

Although the ways to arrange a kitchen may seem countless, there are four basic arrangements from which most kitchens are adapted. The advantages and disadvantages of each arrangement, as well as the space available, largely determine the choice of plan.

A well-planned kitchen includes three basic work areas: the food storage/refrigerator center, the food preparation/range center, and the cleanup/sink center. The placement

of these areas should form a "work triangle." The perimeter of this triangle should be not less than 12′ or more than 22′. It is usually broken down into 4′ to 9′ between the range and refrigerator, 4′ to 7′ between the refrigerator and sink, and 4′ to 6′ between the sink and range (center to center measurement).

These work centers are arranged in one of four basic layouts: straight wall, or in-line; corridor, or two-wall; L-shaped; and U-shaped. Each work center should have adequate cabinet and counter space for the activity in that area. Peninsulas or islands may add storage and counter space. The choice of kitchen plan will depend on floor space, location of doors and windows, access to other rooms, and the needs of the people who will be using the kitchen.

Straight Wall Kitchen

The straight wall or in-line kitchen may be used in smaller houses or

windows

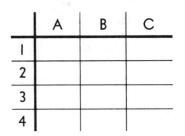

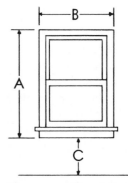

53-11. *Measure all windows and doors and record the information about them. For the doors, measure the height and width and make another list like this one.*

HOW TO MEASURE YOUR KITCHEN

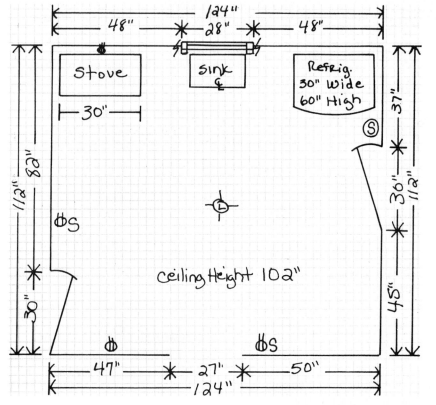

- Draw a free hand sketch of the entire room.
- Measure everything in inches.
- Start measuring from a corner and work in sequence around the room until you have returned to starting point.
- Measure major appliances and their location against the wall.
- Measure at approximately countertop height.
- Always measure outside of window and door casings. Be sure to make note of casing width.
- Note ceiling height.

NOTE: HEAT REGISTERS RADIATORS - AIR CONDITIONING VENTS - COLD AIR RETURN AND ELECT. OUTLETS AND SWITCHES

TYPICAL CONSTRUCTION SYMBOLS

OUTSIDE WINDOW WITH CASING		220V RANGE OUTLET
SINK WASTE CENTER LINE		OUTLET-SWITCH COMB.
CONVENIENCE OUTLET		CEILING LIGHT
SWITCH		GAS RANGE

53-12. *Completed sketch of a kitchen.*

apartments where space is very limited. The entire kitchen is along one wall. The work triangle cannot be used in this plan, and care should be taken to include adequate space (at least 4') between work centers. Fig. 53-13. The arrangement allows for a dining or living area in the rest of the room.

Corridor Kitchen

The corridor or two-wall kitchen is also found in small homes. The eating area may be at one end of the kitchen, or it may be a separate room. Fig. 53-14. At least 4'6" to 5'4" is needed between the facing equipment for two people to work and pass by each other. The doors

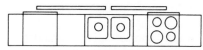

53-13. *In the straight wall or in-line kitchen there is no work triangle. The work path is a straight line between the work centers.*

are located in such a way that a major traffic lane does not go through the working area. Whenever possible, the refrigerator and oven are placed so that they do not open across a doorway.

L-Shaped Kitchen

A third popular design is the L-shaped kitchen. In this design the work centers are arranged along two adjacent walls. This arrangement creates an eating area without sacrificing space from the work areas.

53-14(a). *A two-wall or corridor kitchen with a dining area at one end.*

cleanup center is placed along the window wall. Sometimes the short leg of the L can be widened to create a peninsula between the eating space and the work area, with the cooking area placed on the kitchen side of the peninsula and an eating bar on the other side.

U-Shaped Kitchen

The fourth basic arrangement is the U-shaped kitchen. Fig. 53-16. Generally considered the most efficient arrangement, the U-shaped

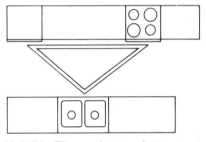

53-14(b). *The work triangle in a typical corridor kitchen.*

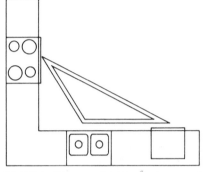

53-15(b). *The work triangle in a typical L-shaped kitchen.*

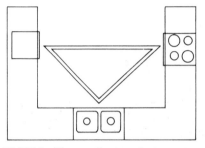

53-16(b). *The work triangle in a typical U-shaped kitchen.*

445

Fig. 53-15. The work triangle is also kept free of through traffic.

In an L-shaped kitchen, the best sequence of work centers provides a work flow from refrigerator to sink to range. Other arrangements can be awkward and difficult to work with. In most L-shaped kitchens, the sink/

53-16(a). *A U-shaped kitchen. The cabinets on the right can be opened from either side.*

53-15(a). *An L-shaped kitchen arrangement.*

kitchen's greatest advantage is the short distance between work centers. The U-shaped plan is also adaptable to both large and small kitchens. However, if the distance across the U is less than 6′ between base cabinets, the work area gets too cramped. More than 9′ results in too many steps between work centers. The U shape also prevents any traffic through the work triangle. Minor disadvantages are the extensive counter tops and the need for special cabinets to fit the corners.

STANDARDS

Clearances and Counter Widths

In designing all types of kitchens, specific clearances and counter widths must be taken into consideration. It must be remembered that counter areas between equipment can often serve two purposes. For instance, a counter mixing center next to a sink can also be used for stacking dishes. These are the standards that should be followed:

● When the mixing center extends into the corner, the arm of the counter next to the sink should provide 24″ to 36″ of flat surface.

● When the cabinet is between two pieces of equipment, provide 36″ to 42″ for the mixing surface.

● Provide 12″ to 24″ on both sides of the surface cooking area.

● Provide 18″ to 36″ of counter to the left and 24″ to 36″ to the right of the sink. If there is a dishwasher, allow 24″ for it, either to the left or right of the sink.

● Provide at least 16″ of clearance between the latch side of the refrigerator and the turn of the counter. Provide counter space near the refrigerator for foods taken from it.

● Provide at least 14″ of clearance between the center of the sink bowl and the turn of the counter for standing.

● Provide at least 14″ of clear-

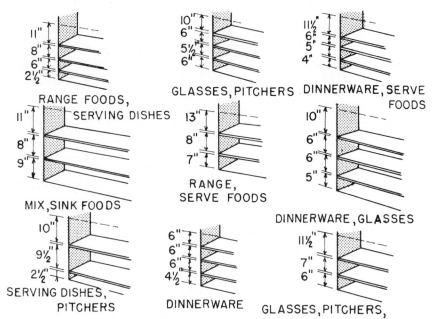

53-17. *Shelf spacing for wall cabinets.*

ance between the center of the front unit or burner and the turn of the counter for standing.

● Provide at least 16″ of clearance between the center of the front unit or burner and a wall or high equipment unit, and between the center front of a wall oven and the adjoining wall.

Shelf Spacing and Drawer Depth

Wall cabinets are usually built from 12″ to 15″ deep, although 12″ is considered standard. It is recommended that all shelves be adjustable to the heights shown in Fig. 53-17. For base cabinets, the shelf spacing and drawer depths shown in Fig. 53-18 will accommodate most of the items needed in a kitchen. Remember, shelves that slide out increase the usability of base cabinets.

The FHA requires the following minimum kitchen storage capacities:

1. Total shelving in wall and base cabinets shall be at least 50 square feet, with not less than 20 square feet in either wall or base cabinets.

2. The minimum drawer area shall be 11 square feet.

3. Usable storage area in cooking ranges when provided in the form of drawers or shelving may be included in the minimum shelf area.

4. Shelf area of revolving base shelves (lazy Susan) may be considered as twice its actual area in determining required shelf area, provided clear width of opening is at least 8½ inches.

5. Drawer area may be substituted for not more than 25 percent of required base shelf area.

6. If a range at least 39″ in width or a 40″ space for a range is provided, the following may be counted toward required areas: base cabinet shelving, 4 square feet.

7. If a range is not provided, leave at least a 40″ space for a range.

POINTS TO CONSIDER WHEN INSTALLING CABINETS

1. Cabinets must be attached to studs for full support. Studs are usually located 16″ on center. Locate them with a stud finder, by

tapping the wall with a hammer, or by driving a nail through the plaster at a height that will be hidden by the cabinet. Cabinets must always be attached to walls with screws. *Never use nails.*

2. Cabinets must be installed perfectly level—for function as well as appearance. Use a level to find the highest point of the floor.

3. Using a level or straightedge, find the high spots on the wall where the cabinets will hang. Some high spots can be removed by sanding. In other cases, it will be necessary to "shim" to provide a level and plumb installation.

4. From the highest point on the floor, measure up the wall to a height of 84". This is the top height of wall cabinets, oven cabinets, and broom closets. An 84" cabinet can be cut down to 81", if necessary.

5. Remove the baseboard and chair rail on the walls where cabinets are to be installed. This is required for a flush fit.

6. Start your installation in one corner. First assemble the base corner cabinet, then add one unit on each side of it. This assembly can then be installed in position as one unit. Additional cabinets are then added to each side as required.

7. To ensure proper alignment, use C-clamps to hold cabinets securely in position while you are connecting them together. Drill 2 or 3 holes through the ½" end panels, into the adjoining cabinet. Insert T-nut and secure with 1½" bolt. Draw up snugly. If you prefer, you may drill through the side of the front frame as well as "lead hole" into the abutting cabinet, insert screws, and draw up snugly.

8. Check each cabinet with a level as it is installed on the wall. Check front to back, and also across the front edge. Be certain that the front frame is plumb. If necessary, use shims to level the cabinets. Attach the base cabinets to wall studs with screws. For additional support and to prevent back rail from "bowing," insert a block between cabinet back and wall. After bases are installed, cover the toe kick area with the material provided.

9. Attach the counter top to the base cabinets. After installation, cover counter tops with cardboard. This will help prevent accidental damage while you are completing the installation.

10. Wall cabinets may then be installed, beginning with a corner unit as described in Step 6. Screw through the hanging strips built into the backs of the cabinets at both top and bottom. Place the screws ¾" below the top and ¾" above the bottom shelf, from the inside of the cabinet. Attach only loosely at first, so that final adjustments can be made.

11. Be sure that wall cabinets are plumb and level. Check them with a level on cabinet fronts, sides, and bottom. It might be necessary to shim at the wall and between the cabinets to correct for uneven walls or floors. After cabinets and doors are perfectly aligned, tighten all screws.

Do's and Don'ts of Cabinet Installation

• **Do** use screws or T-nuts to fasten cabinets together.

• **Do** install all base units before installing wall cabinets.

• **Do** fasten bases, fillers, and wall cabinets together with screws through the front frame.

• **Do** start setting base units from the highest point on the floor.

• **Do** check that each unit is plumb and level before securing.

• **Do** cut off shims at the floor even with the toe space.

• **Do** attach cabinets to the wall and to each other so that they can be removed if necessary.

• **Do** use molding for a neater, more attractive installation.

• **Do** putty and touch up nail holes in molding.

• **Do** align all doors.

• **Don't** use nails other than for attaching molding.

• **Don't** unpack the units from cartons until you're ready to install them.

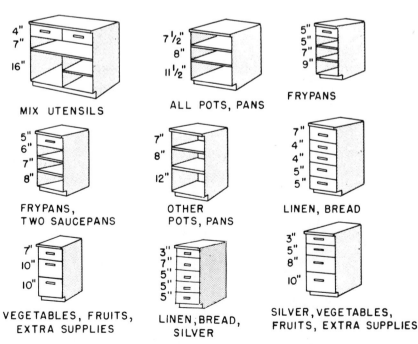

MIX UTENSILS
4"
7"
16"

ALL POTS, PANS
7½"
8"
11½"

FRYPANS
5"
5"
7"
9"

FRYPANS, TWO SAUCEPANS
5"
6"
7"
8"

OTHER POTS, PANS
7"
8"
12"

LINEN, BREAD
7"
4"
4"
5"
5"

VEGETABLES, FRUITS, EXTRA SUPPLIES
7"
10"
10"

LINEN, BREAD, SILVER
3"
7"
5"
5"
5"

SILVER, VEGETABLES, FRUITS, EXTRA SUPPLIES
3"
5"
8"
10"

53-18. *Shelf and drawer spacing for base cabinets.*

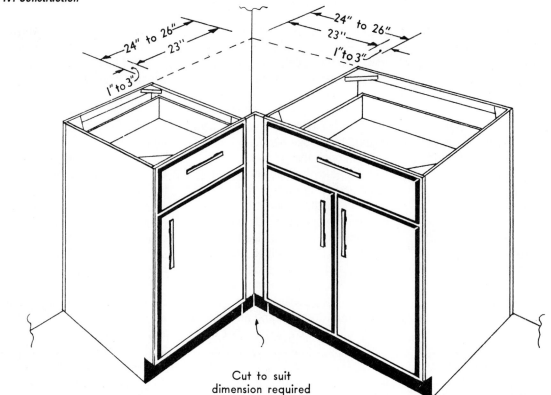

53-19. *Two standard base cabinets can be placed so that the face frames almost meet. Then a filler strip can be added.*

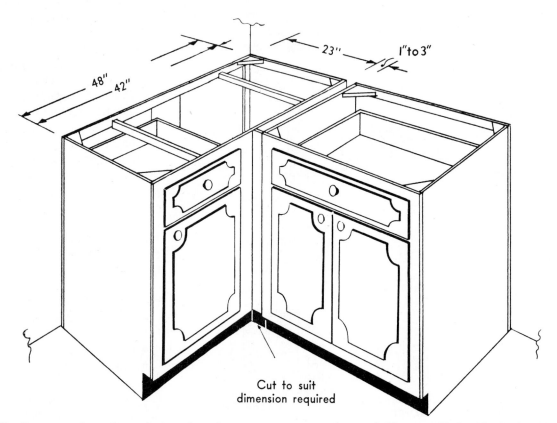

53-20. *A rectangular cabinet designed so that corner space can be used. This is called a blind-island base.*

- **Don't** use the counter top as a workbench.
- **Lazy Susan base cabinet**. Attach both adjacent units to lazy Susan before securing to wall. This provides better positioning and alignment of the completed unit.
- **Dead corner**. In order to provide proper clearance for door and drawer openings, insert 1″ corner filler.
- **Sink front**. Sink front should be attached to adjacent cabinets with screws. Sink fronts can be cut down as much as 3″ on each side rail.

INSTALLING MILL- OR FACTORY-BUILT CABINETS

Most kitchen cabinets are built in a mill cabinet shop or in kitchen-cabinet manufacturing plants. They are installed by a finish carpenter following plans supplied by an architect or kitchen planning specialist. Since many kitchen cabinets are of extremely fine construction, materials, and finish, the carpenter must be very careful not to harm them during installation.

To install base cabinets, first place the cabinet in its approximate location. Then remove the skids, braces, or other protective devices. Make sure there is no quarter round, baseboard, or other protrusion behind the cabinet. If there are any defects in the cabinet, these should be repaired before installation.

Always fit corner cabinets first since a corner is a special problem. There are three basic ways of handling a corner installation. One is to have two standard cabinets so that there is blank space in the corner. Usually a filler strip is cut to fit the space between. A filler strip is necessary to provide enough clearance for opening doors and for pulling out drawers and trays. Fig. 53-19.

The second method is to use a rectangular cabinet designed for corner storage. Though a bit hard to reach, such space is usable for

many purposes. Fig. 53-20. On such installations some kind of filler strip must be placed between the cabinets.

The third and best solution to the corner problem is to install a corner cabinet that is fitted with either fixed shelves or with revolving (lazy Susan) shelving. Fig. 53-21.

Figure 53-22 shows how to install cabinets. Further information is given here. Move all cabinets, one at a time, as close to the wall as possible. Use a level to make sure each cabinet is plumb (vertical) and level (horizontal). Commercial cabinets provide for a good wall fit in two ways. The most common way is to have the back set in from the sides and the bottom open. Then either the cabinet ends or the bottom can be trimmed off. A floor or wall can be uneven in two ways. Usually a floor slopes away from the wall. In this case, open a pair of dividers to the widest space between the bottom of the cabinet and the floor, and scribe a line along the bottom edge of the base. Then trim the base ends with a saw. Fig. 53-23. If the floor is level and the wall slopes away, the backsplash (part of the top) will be away from the wall. This can be corrected with wooden strips of proper thickness placed on the wall from the bottom of the wall cabinet to below the splash line. These strips can be covered with plywood or hardboard. Fig. 53-24.

A second method of fitting cabinets is first to place them as close

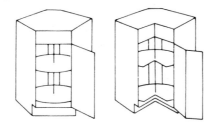

53-21. *Base corner units for revolving shelves.*

as possible to the wall and block them up so that they are plumb and level. Then cut the spacer strips that come with the cabinets to fit between the cabinets and the wall.

Once the base cabinets are properly fitted, they are fastened to the wall with wood screws through the back frames or nailing strips and into the studs. Screws must always go into the studs so that the cabinet will be solidly attached. Cabinets should be bolted together side to side just back of the front facing or faceplate.

While some cabinets come with counter tops already covered with plastic laminate, this is usually not a part of the cabinetry. The usual practice is to fit the ¾″ plywood or particle board on the cabinet tops with the proper backsplash. Then plastic laminate is installed as described in Chapter 43.

To install wall cabinets, first build a simple brace or support of scrap material on which the cabinets can rest while they are being installed. Fig. 53-25. Place the cabinets in position, starting with the corner ones. Check to make sure they are plumb and level. If the wall is uneven and out of plumb, place wood shims behind the cabinets. Then fasten the cabinets to the wall with long wood screws or toggle bolts. These should go through the back rail. Screws must be fastened into the wall studs. Fig. 53-26.

Quarter round or trim can be put on the exposed corners between the cabinets and the wall. This is always necessary when much shimming was done.

BUILDING KITCHEN CABINETS ON THE JOB

Building cabinets on the job requires a thorough knowledge of cabinetmaking and also the ability to read and carry out the house plans prepared by the architect. The first step is to check the plans and specifications for the location of all ap-

53-22. *Steps in installing factory-built cabinets.*

1

Locate the position of all wall studs where cabinets are to hang by tapping with a hammer. Mark their position where the marks can easily be seen when the cabinets are in position.

2

Find the highest point on the floor with a level. This is important for both base and wall cabinet installation later.

3

Remove the baseboard from all walls where cabinets are to be installed. This will allow them to go flush against the walls.

4

Start the installation with a corner or end unit. Slide it into place, then continue to slide the other base cabinets into the proper position.

5

When all base cabinets are in position, fasten the cabinets together. This is done by drilling a ¼" diameter hole through the face frames and using the 3" screws and T-nuts provided. To get maximum holding power from the screw, one hole should be close to the top of the end stile and one should be close to the bottom.

6

Check the position of each cabinet with a spirit level, going from the front of the cabinet to the back of the cabinet. Next shim between the cabinet and the wall for a perfect base cabinet installation.

7

Starting at the high point in the floor, level the leading edges of the cabinets. Continue to shim between the cabinets and the floor until all the base cabinets have been brought to level.

8

After the cabinets have been leveled, both front to back and across the front, fasten the cabinets to the wall at the stud locations. This is done by drilling a 3/32" diameter hole 2¼" deep through both the hanging strips for the 2½" x 8 screws that are provided.

9

Fit the counter top into position and attach it to the base cabinets by predrilling and screwing through the front corner blocks into the top. Use caution not to drill through the top. Cover the counter top for protection while the wall cabinets are being installed.

10

Position the bottom of the 30" wall cabinets 19" from the top of the base cabinet, unless the cabinets are to be installed against a soffit. A brace can be made to help hold the wall cabinets in place while they are being fastened. Start the wall cabinets installation with a corner or end cabinet. Use care in getting this cabinet installed plumb and level, since this is the key for the entire installation.

11

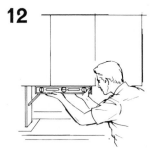

Temporarily secure the adjoining wall cabinets so that leveling may be done without removing them. Drill through the end stiles of the cabinets and fasten them together as was done with the base cabinets.

12

Use a spirit level to check the horizontal surfaces. Shim between the cabinet and the wall until the cabinet is level. This is necessary if doors are to fit properly.

13

Check the perpendicular surface of each frame at the front. When the cabinets are level, both front to back and across the front, permanently attach the cabinets to the wall. This is done by predrilling a 3/32" diameter hole 2¼" deep through the hanging strip into the top and below the bottom of the cabinets at the stud location. Enough number 8 screws should be used to fasten the cabinets securely to the wall.

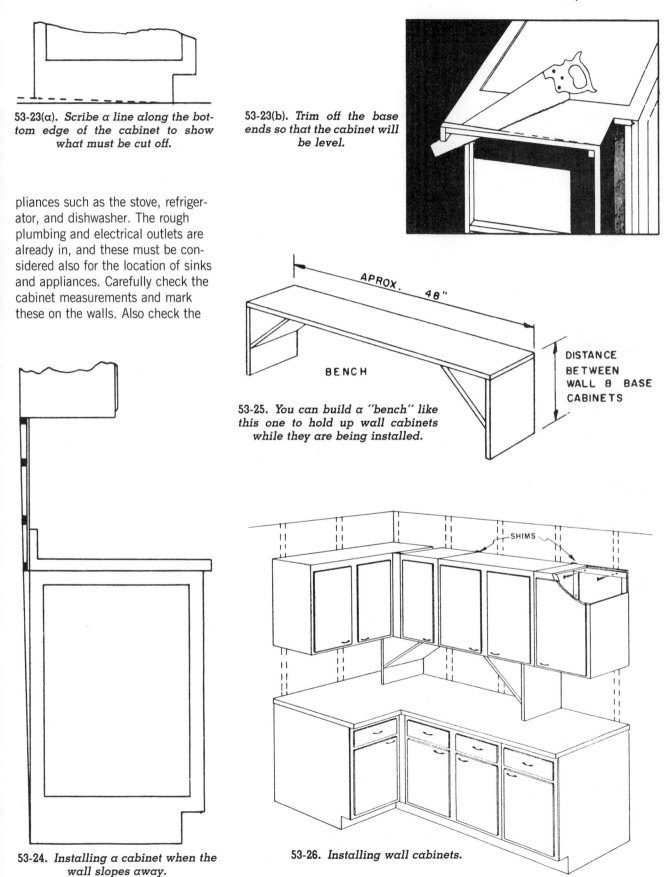

53-23(a). *Scribe a line along the bottom edge of the cabinet to show what must be cut off.*

53-23(b). *Trim off the base ends so that the cabinet will be level.*

pliances such as the stove, refrigerator, and dishwasher. The rough plumbing and electrical outlets are already in, and these must be considered also for the location of sinks and appliances. Carefully check the cabinet measurements and mark these on the walls. Also check the

53-25. *You can build a "bench" like this one to hold up wall cabinets while they are being installed.*

53-24. *Installing a cabinet when the wall slopes away.*

53-26. *Installing wall cabinets.*

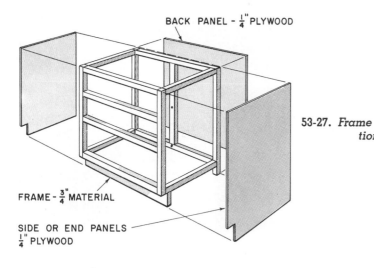

BACK PANEL - $\frac{1}{4}$" PLYWOOD

FRAME - $\frac{3}{4}$" MATERIAL

SIDE OR END PANELS $\frac{1}{4}$" PLYWOOD

53-27. *Frame construction.*

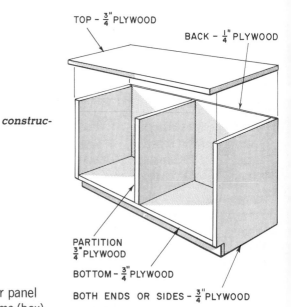

TOP - $\frac{3}{4}$" PLYWOOD

BACK - $\frac{1}{4}$" PLYWOOD

PARTITION $\frac{3}{4}$" PLYWOOD

BOTTOM - $\frac{3}{4}$" PLYWOOD

BOTH ENDS OR SIDES - $\frac{3}{4}$" PLYWOOD

53-28. *Non-frame or box construction.*

walls and floor to make sure they are plumb and level.

The height of the wall cabinet will depend on its location: whether it is over the sink or range or above the base cabinets, and whether or not there is a drop ceiling. In most kitchen construction a drop ceiling over the cabinets is roughed in so that the cabinets do not have to go all the way up to the ceiling. Usually the upper shelves are unused if they are too high. If there is no drop ceiling, it is better to have two sets of cabinets: small ones towards the ceiling for dead storage and larger ones below for more useful storage.

The cabinetmaker has a choice of two methods of building on-the-job cabinets. The first and more common is to build the cabinets *piece by piece as built-ins.* This is usually much simpler since no backs are required. The cabinets are built against a plastered wall or finished dry wall. Also, the interior construction can be kept very simple by using center drawer guides of metal. The other choice is to build the cabinets as *separate units* (like factory-built cabinets) and then fit them in place.

The cabinetmaker also has a choice of two kinds of cabinet construction. *Frame* construction makes use of solid wood framing material (about ¾" × 1½") that is covered

with thin plywood and other panel stock. Fig. 53-27. *Non-frame* (box) or all-panel construction makes use of plywood, hardboard, and particle board for both the exterior of the case and the structural support. Fig. 53-28. The only solid wood used in this second method is for drawer guides and runners and face framing (or faceplate).

All base cabinets are built with a toe strip. This can be done in one of two ways. A *base frame* (plinth) can be built on which the cabinet rests.

The more common method is to have the cabinet sides go completely to the floor. Then these sides are notched out at the bottom front to provide toe space. The toe strip is fitted against the cabinet ends.

For a flush or lipped door and drawer, the front of the cabinet

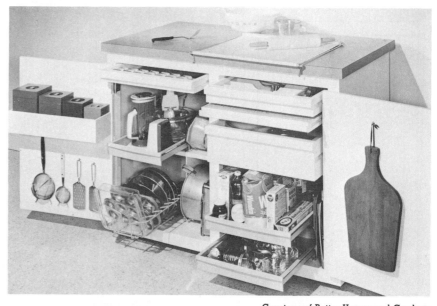

Courtesy of Better Homes and Gardens

53-29(a). *Mobile mixing center.*

MATERIALS LIST FOR MOBILE MIXING CENTER

(All pieces plywood unless otherwise specified.)

A	—	26 × 50 × ¾	1 pc.	N —	2¾ × 19¼ × ½	2 pcs.
B	—	23¼ × 33 × ¾	2 pcs.	O —	20½ × 19 × ⅛ hardboard	1 pc.
C	—	23¼ × 46½ × ¾	1 pc.	**Drawer 3**		
D	—	32⅝ × 47¼ × ⅜	1 pc.	L —	6 × 21⅝ × ¾	1 pc.
E	—	22⅞ × 31½ × ¾	1 pc.	M —	6 × 19¾ × ½	2 pcs.
F	—	22⅞ × 20 × ¾	1 pc.	N —	6 × 19¼ × ½	2 pcs.
G	—	3¾ × 22⅞ × ¾	2 pcs.	O —	20½ × 19 × ⅛ hardboard	1 pc.

A — 26 × 50 × ¾ — 1 pc.
B — 23¼ × 33 × ¾ — 2 pcs.
C — 23¼ × 46½ × ¾ — 1 pc.
D — 32⅝ × 47¼ × ⅜ — 1 pc.
E — 22⅞ × 31½ × ¾ — 1 pc.
F — 22⅞ × 20 × ¾ — 1 pc.
G — 3¾ × 22⅞ × ¾ — 2 pcs.
H — 8 × 22⅞ × ¾ — 2 pcs.
I — 8 × 22⅞ × ⅜ — 2 pcs.
J — 12½ × 22⅞ × ⅛ hardboard — 2 pcs.
K — 21¾ × 30 × ¾ — 2 pcs.

Drawer 1
L — 2¼ × 21⅝ × ¾ — 1 pc.
M — 2¼ × 19¾ × ½ — 2 pcs.
N — 2¼ × 19¼ × ½ — 2 pcs.
O — 20½ × 19 × ⅛ hardboard — 1 pc.
P — 1½ × 21⅝ × 1½ — 1 pc.

Drawer 2
L — 2¾ × 21⅝ × ¾ — 1 pc.
M — 2¾ × 19¾ × ½ — 2 pcs.

N — 2¾ × 19¼ × ½ — 2 pcs.
O — 20½ × 19 × ⅛ hardboard — 1 pc.

Drawer 3
L — 6 × 21⅝ × ¾ — 1 pc.
M — 6 × 19¾ × ½ — 2 pcs.
N — 6 × 19¼ × ½ — 2 pcs.
O — 20½ × 19 × ⅛ hardboard — 1 pc.

Facing—1½ × ¾ pine—approx.
Frame for top—2 × ¾ pine—approx.
Cutting board—as shown on drawing
Pullout plastic drawers
Wire lid rack
Flush door hinges
Metal drawer slides
Casters
Knob
Catches
Door pulls
Plastic laminate for top—to fit

53-29(b). *These are the materials you will need to build the mobile mixing center.*

should have a face frame or plate attached to it. This is usually made of solid wood 1″ thick and 1½″ to 2¾″ wide. On cabinets with flush overlay doors and drawers, the face frame is not needed. The top of all base cabinets generally extends 1½″ beyond the top of the case.

SAMPLE KITCHEN CABINETS

The following are some of the kitchen cabinets that can be built with hand and machine tools. They are typical of on-the-job construction. All of these cabinets are built with non-frame (box) construction.

Mobile Mixing Center

This is shown in Fig. 53-29. Begin by assembling the basic plywood box as shown in Fig. 53-29(c). Be sure to cut the grooves for dividers (*I*) and (*J*) in bottom piece (*C*) before assembly. Note that the bottom (*C*) is set up ¾″ from the bottom of the side

pieces (*B*). Set the back piece (*D*) in ⅜″ × ⅜″ rabbets in pieces (*B*) and (*C*) as shown. Nail in divider (*E*) and shelf (*F*). Be sure to cut grooves in shelf (*F*) before fastening in. Put in dividers (*I*) and (*J*) and nail on spacers (*G*) and (*H*). These

spacers compensate for the thickness of the facing to allow the drawers to clear. Nail on the facing as shown. Note that the top of the bottom facing piece is flush with the top of piece (*C*). Assemble the top piece (*A*) and its frame; then nail it

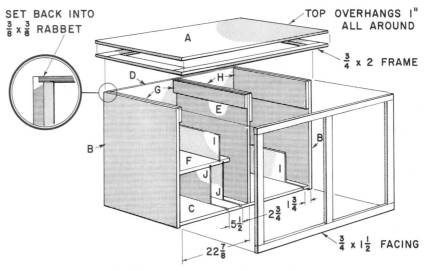

53-29(c). *Basic construction details.*

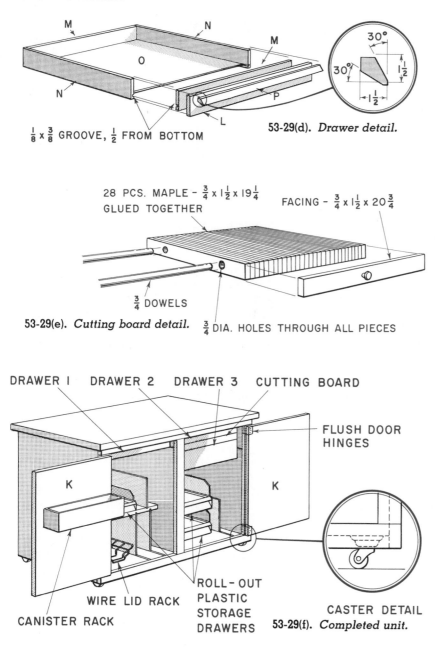

$\frac{1}{8}$ x $\frac{3}{8}$ GROOVE, $\frac{1}{2}$ FROM BOTTOM

53-29(d). *Drawer detail.*

28 PCS. MAPLE – $\frac{3}{4}$ x $1\frac{1}{2}$ x $19\frac{1}{4}$ GLUED TOGETHER

FACING – $\frac{3}{4}$ x $1\frac{1}{2}$ x $20\frac{3}{4}$

$\frac{3}{4}$ DOWELS

53-29(e). *Cutting board detail.* $\frac{3}{4}$ DIA. HOLES THROUGH ALL PIECES

DRAWER 1   DRAWER 2   DRAWER 3   CUTTING BOARD

FLUSH DOOR HINGES

K   K

WIRE LID RACK

CANISTER RACK

ROLL-OUT PLASTIC STORAGE DRAWERS

CASTER DETAIL

53-29(f). *Completed unit.*

on. Note that the top overlaps the basic cabinet by 1″ all around. Apply plastic laminate to the top and edges.

Hang doors (*K*) with flush door hinges. Fig. 53-29(f). Apply pulls and catches at convenient locations. Screw casters to the underside of the unit as shown. Build the canister rack from scrap $\frac{3}{8}$″ plywood. This is simply a small plywood box which you fasten to the door. Be sure to make it short enough to

clear as you open and close the door.

Build the drawers as shown. Fig. 53-29(d). They are simple plywood boxes with hardboard bottoms. You install them with metal drawer slides. They have been dimensioned for $\frac{1}{2}$″ clearance on each side for the slides. Apply the fronts and handle (*L* and *P*) after the basic drawers have been installed to make fitting easier. Make the cutting board as shown in Fig. 53-29(e)

from strips of maple glued together with waterproof glue. Cut to exact width (20¾″) and apply drawer slides to the sides. The plastic storage drawers are commercial units which you simply buy and install according to directions.

Set all nailheads, fill over them, and sand the whole unit as necessary. Finish it with one coat of enamel undercoat, plus two coats of semigloss enamel, sanding between coats.

Overhead Storage Unit

This unit is simply a large plywood box with sliding doors on the front. It provides storage space in kitchens with high ceilings. Fig. 53-30. Since it must be built to fit existing space, no exact dimensions or materials list can be given. However, you should plan to make the shelves no deeper than 18″, and the bottom of the cabinet should be about 6′8″ from the floor. You build the basic box as shown, then fasten it in place with screws through the back, sides, and top into the wall studs and ceiling beams. Install the aluminum dual sliding door track and fit in the ¼″ hardboard sliding doors. Now nail

53-30(a). *Overhead storage units.*
Courtesy of Better Homes and Gardens

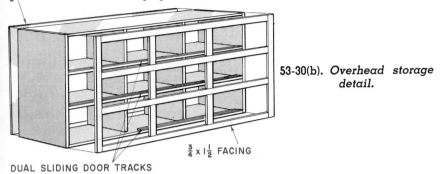

⅜ PLYWOOD BACK SET IN ⅜ x ⅜ RABBETS

53-30(b). *Overhead storage detail.*

¾ x 1½ FACING

DUAL SLIDING DOOR TRACKS

on the 1½″ × ¾″ facing. Notice that the vertical facing pieces are toenailed to the horizontal facing only. The sliding doors bypass each other behind these facing pieces.

Oven and Storage Unit

Built-in ovens are practical and easy to install even in kitchens not designed for them. Space is also provided for bulky utensils often awkward to store. Fig. 53-31.

Carefully measure the space for the cabinet. Determine the final dimensions according to the kitchen and the particular oven unit you are to install. Cut all structural parts to size. For a natural finish, cut matching doors and faces from the same panel so that the grain pattern will be uniform. Sand all edges and

check all parts for proper fit before assembly. Assemble the cabinet face down on the floor. Attach the ends and back to the bottom, top, and shelves with glue and finishing nails. Stand the unit in place on the base and level up if necessary to compensate for an uneven floor. Fit and install the face panels and doors. Make certain all door edges are carefully primed and finish both faces of the doors with an equal number of coats. Install the shelf supports and pan dividers after finishing.

Range Counter Cabinet

This unit is shown in Fig. 53-32.

Determine the exact final dimension to suit the range unit and the space the cabinet will occupy. Cut all structural parts and framing members to size. Sand the edges and check for correct fit. Assemble

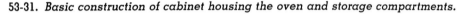

53-31. *Basic construction of cabinet housing the oven and storage compartments.*

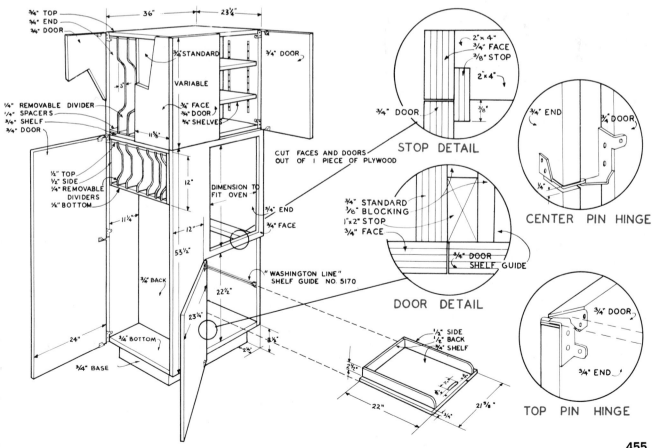

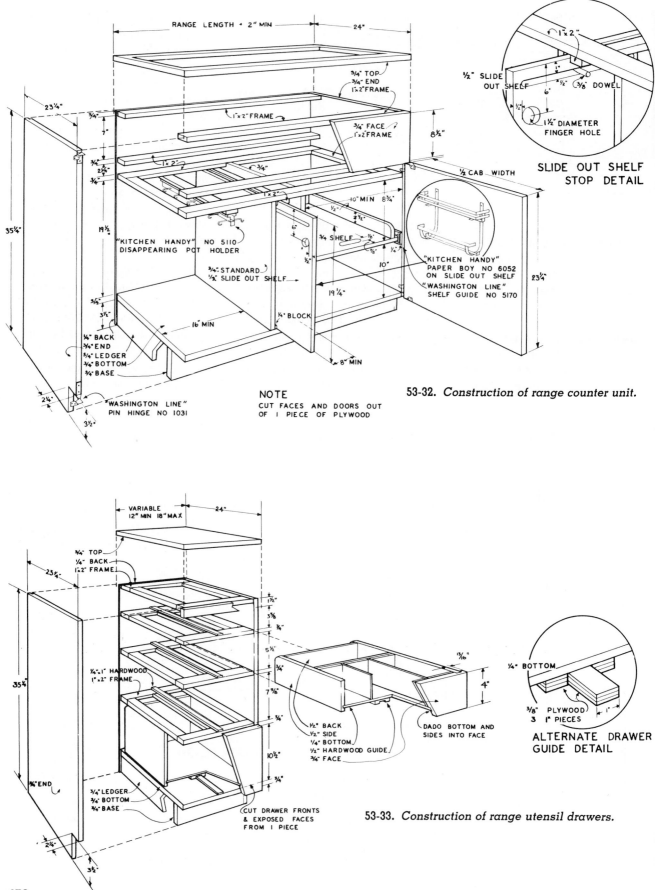

SLIDE OUT SHELF STOP DETAIL

NOTE
CUT FACES AND DOORS OUT
OF 1 PIECE OF PLYWOOD

53-32. *Construction of range counter unit.*

ALTERNATE DRAWER GUIDE DETAIL

53-33. *Construction of range utensil drawers.*

53-34(a). *This laundry cart is on casters, so it can be moved easily.*

by attaching the base and ledge to the bottom shelf. Then install the ends, back, intermediate standards and frame. Join with glue and nails.

Install the face panel and counter top. Hang the doors and do the finishing. Fit sliding shelves in place after finishing. Attach accessories.

Range Utensil Drawers

Variable dimensions on this plan make it easy to fit nearly any space with the drawer cabinets. Fig. 53-33. Cut all structural parts and framing members to size, sand edges, and fit in place. Start the assembly by attaching the bottom shelf to the base and ledge strips, then assemble ends, back and frames. Use glue and finishing nails. Level the cabinet as required. Cut drawer parts, sand edges, fit into openings, and assemble with glue and nails. The facing strip and all drawer fronts should be cut from one panel if the wood grain pattern is to match. Attach the top, applying plastic laminate.

Laundry Cart and Sink Cabinet

This handy cart is divided into separate compartments for white and colored clothes. Fig. 53-34. When empty, it fits out of the way under the sink counter. You can decide on the dimensions to suit the space and the sink to be installed.

Cut all structural panels and frames to size. For any sink cabinet, use only fir plywood made with waterproof glue. Make all joints with glue and finishing nails. Sand all edges and check for fit. Then fasten the bottom shelf to the base and ledger strips. Attach ends, back, face, and framing members next. Then attach the top. Apply counter surfacing material, band the edges, and install the sink. Move the unit into place, leveling the base if the floor is uneven. Cut, fit, and hang

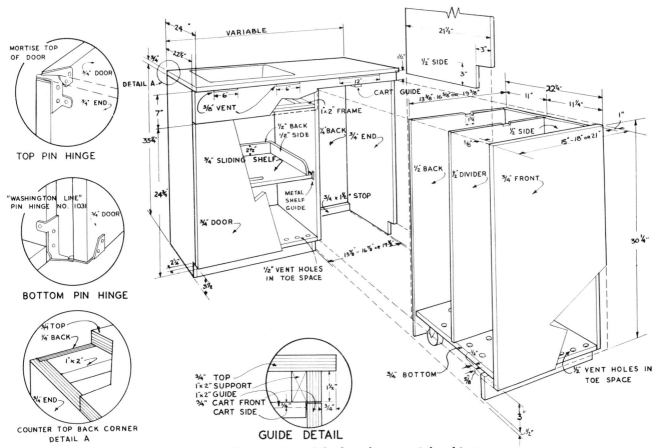

53-34(b). *Construction of the laundry cart-sink cabinet.*

53-35(a). Sliding spice rack.

the door. Sand and prime all door edges thoroughly. Finish both inner and outer door faces alike.

Cut the parts for the laundry cart. Sand the edges and check how it fits in place. Dado the side panels, or form slots with ½" wood strips for removable ½" divider. Glue and nail bottom to toe piece. Apply sides and ends. Attach casters. Cut the sliding shelf to size. Assemble and install the shelf after finishing the cabinet and cart.

Sliding Spice Rack

This sliding spice rack and tuckaway shelf puts space to maximum use and provides for tall bottles as well as small cans and boxes. Fig. 53-35. It can easily be added to the shelves in an existing cabinet or built into a new wall cabinet. Its size is determined by the dimensions of the cabinet. Cut all parts to size. Sand the edges and check for proper fit. All joints should be glued and nailed. Fasten the tuckaway shelf to the cabinet shelves and back with finishing nails. Also use finishing nails and glue to assemble the sliding spice rack. Install track and hang doors on cabinet. Finish as desired. Be

53-35(b). Construction of sliding spice rack.

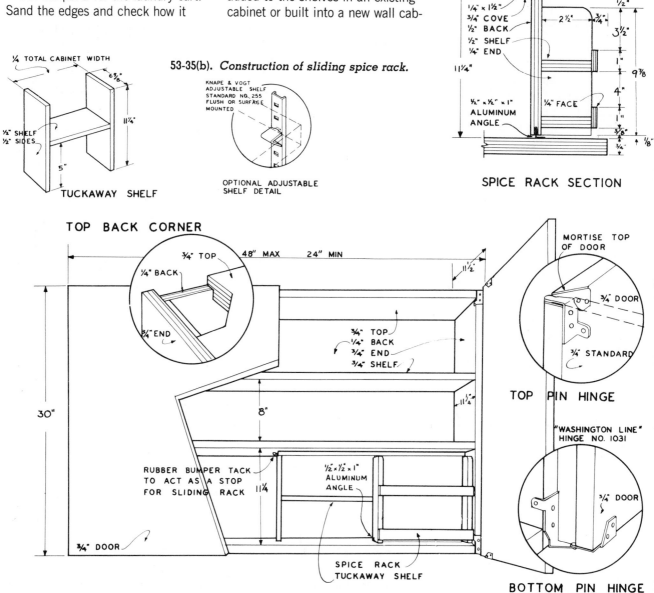

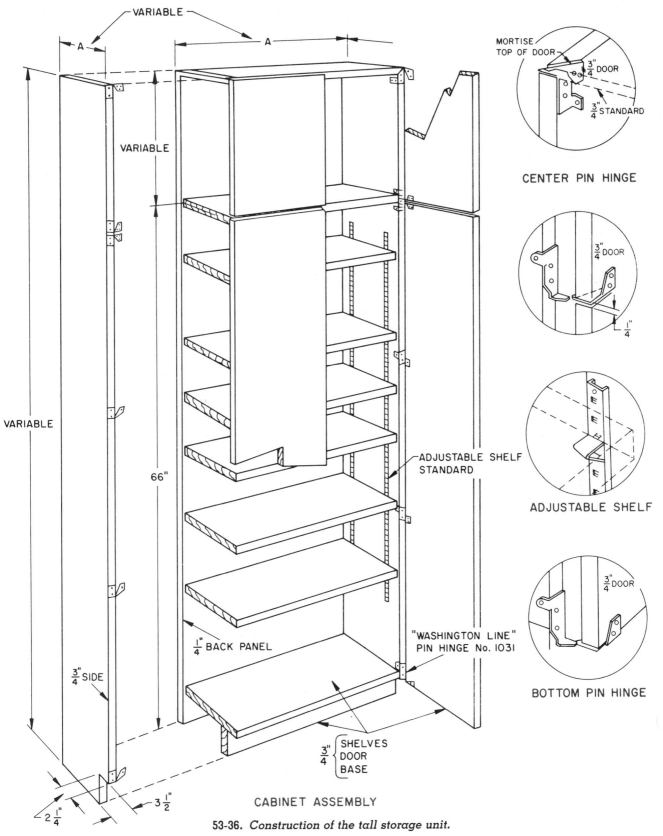

TOP PIN HINGE

MORTISE
TOP OF DOOR
MORTISE
$\frac{3}{4}$" DOOR
$\frac{3}{4}$" STANDARD

CENTER PIN HINGE

$\frac{3}{4}$" DOOR

$\frac{1}{4}$"

ADJUSTABLE SHELF

BOTTOM PIN HINGE

$\frac{3}{4}$" DOOR

VARIABLE

VARIABLE

VARIABLE

66"

$\frac{3}{4}$" SIDE

$2\frac{1}{4}$"

$3\frac{1}{2}$"

$\frac{1}{4}$" BACK PANEL

ADJUSTABLE SHELF
STANDARD

"WASHINGTON LINE"
PIN HINGE No. 1031

$\frac{3}{4}$ { SHELVES
DOOR
BASE

CABINET ASSEMBLY

53-36. *Construction of the tall storage unit.*

53-37(a). *A vanity cabinet.*

very careful to prime edges of doors and finish both faces alike.

Tall Storage Unit

Canned goods can be orderly and easy to find when you build storage shelves like these. Fig. 53-36 (Page 459). Cabinet height is variable, so the piece may even be built for use above a base cabinet. Decide on the dimensions, then cut sides, top, bottom, back, and shelves to size. Sand all edges and check for fit.

You can assemble this cabinet in place or flat on the floor. If you put it together on the floor, be sure the diagonal of the sides does not exceed the ceiling height.

Glue and nail all joints with finishing nails. After nailing the bottom shelf to its base, fasten the sides, top, back, and upper shelf in place. Slide or tip the cabinet into position and level the base if necessary.

For matching grain pattern, cut all doors from a single panel. Sand the edges, fit, and hang the doors. All door edges should be well primed, and both faces should have the same number of finishing coats. Finish the complete unit, including movable shelves, and install shelf supports.

BATHROOM CABINETS

Bathroom cabinets involve many of the same elements of planning as for the kitchen. Most bathroom cabinets are base units, sink units, or special units such as a medicine cabinet or a storage unit for towels. Base and sink units for a bathroom are about 30″ in height (without top) and about 16″ to 21″ in depth. They are shorter and narrower than those used in the kitchen. Fig. 53-37. Planning for bathrooms is simpler than for kitchens because fewer units are involved and there are usually no corner cabinets.

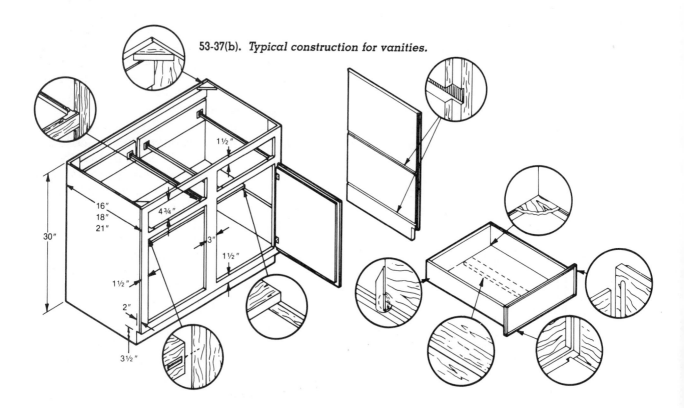

53-37(b). *Typical construction for vanities.*

Built-Ins, Including Room Dividers

There are two major ways of building and installing cabinets and other interior units. One is to purchase factory- or cabinet-shop casework built to an architect's plans and specifications. Such pieces are then brought to the site and installed. The second method is to build the cabinets on the job, adding one piece of material to another in its permanent location. These are called built-ins. Fig. 54-1.

There are several important differences between a piece of casework built in the shop and a completely built-in cabinet piece that fits into a house. With shop-built cabinets, the work is done with the square. Each part is checked to make sure it is

54-1. *The built-in shelves and cabinets next to the fireplace add useful storage space as well as architectural interest.*

square with the other pieces. Also, larger equipment is available, so complicated joinery is possible. Sometimes, shop-built cabinets also are made of panel construction, and this technique is rarely used for built-ins.

For the built-in, a good deal of the preliminary work is done with a level. The reason for this is that no wall or floor is exactly plumb (vertical) or level (horizontal). The built-in must be made to fit these irregular surfaces. Generally, the architectural plans give the overall dimensions for the built-ins as well as a front elevation detail that shows the general appearance and dimensions. However, it is the responsibility of the cabinetmaker or finish carpenter to determine the dimensions for such items as drawer or door parts, interior construction, and other measurements not given on the prints. Built-ins often must be planned for such equipment as a sink, a sewing machine, or a stereo system. Sometimes only a sketch with a very few dimensions is available. In this case, a more complete drawing and a materials list must be made by the cabinetmaker.

KINDS OF BUILT-INS

Built-ins may be used in any part of a home. They can provide essential drawers and closet space as well as special storage for hobbies and other activities. A custom-built appearance is one advantage of built-ins. They also make many movable pieces of furniture unnecessary, which simplifies housecleaning and eliminates many dust-catching areas.

Living Room

A living room may have a built-in book cabinet with areas for stereo equipment, television, and hobby or entertainment items. Many homes have built-in units around the fireplace which include shelving. Fig. 54-1. The living room may be set off from the front hallway or other parts of the house by a built-in divider wall.

Bedroom

Many bedroom plans illustrate built-ins for nearly all furniture—beds, dressing tables, storage drawers, desks, counters, and other items. Fig. 54-2.

Kitchen

While most kitchen cabinets are factory- or mill-built and then installed, some carpenters and cabinetmakers like to build their own. This may be necessary if the house has an unusual design. Sometimes, standard mill-built cabinets just cannot be used. The walls of the kitchen may be at an angle or curved so that the cabinets must be built on the job in order to fit.

Family Room

In family rooms, built-ins are usually designed to hold items for recreation and housework. Sewing,

461

54-2. *Rugged, built-in furniture is especially popular for children's bedrooms.*

ironing, photography, sports, games —equipment for all these and many other activities is often stored in built-ins. Separate storage may be provided for each activity.

Bathroom

Probably no other room of the home except the kitchen makes as much use of built-ins as does the present-day bathroom. At one time this was not possible. Use of lumber products in the bathroom was limited because of the moisture problem. Today, however, modern sealers and paints make it possible to build cabinets under the sink, in the walls, even around the bathtub, without fear that they will buckle or

54-3. *Wood built-ins are often used in bathrooms.*

that the finish will come off. Fig. 54-3.

GENERAL PROCEDURE FOR CONSTRUCTING BUILT-INS

Since every built-in is different, it is impossible to give specific directions for completion. However, the first step should be to check the space available along the wall and floor with the architectural plans.

Make sure there is enough space for the built-in you are going to make. Check the wall with a level to see whether it is exactly perpendicular. Check the floor to see whether it is out-of-level and, if so, how much. Check the corners to see how much out-of-square they are. All of these must be taken into consideration in cutting pieces that will fit. Also check and mark the wall studs and floor joists where major parts of the built-in can be permanently attached with nails or screws. Check the sizes of any equipment to be included, such as a refrigerator, washing machine, television set, or stereo system. Verify all the dimensions that are necessary to fit the built-in into the area.

A materials list must be made and the necessary lumber, plywood, and other materials ordered and delivered before work can go ahead. Usually the major vertical pieces must be adjusted to the overall ceiling height and the major horizontal

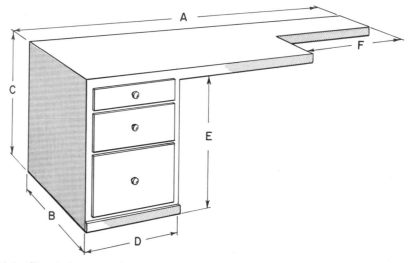

54-4. *Check the exact dimensions from the plans and then measure the actual space available. A is the distance between the left and right wall of the recess into which this unit must fit. B will be determined by the depth of the recess. C is very important since the person who will use the desk may want this much lower than the standard 30" usually specified for a desk. The height might need to be a compromise between present and future needs. D could vary in size depending on the space needed between the bed and the drawers for a chair. E is important especially on a lower counter so there will be adequate leg room. F should be about equal to the width of a bed pillow because the bed will fit under this shelf.*

462

pieces adjusted to the distance from side to side. Cut and install the major horizontal and vertical pieces and shim them up as necessary so that they are plumb and level. Then fit the intermediate pieces in between these major units. After this, the necessary face frame can be installed and the necessary interior work done for shelves, drawer guides, dividers, and other parts. The final step is usually to build the doors and drawers for the built-in and fit them in place.

Figure 54-4 shows a typical dressing table and desk for a child's bedroom. To build this unit, you would need to check the plans and measure the room to determine the best dimensions for *A, B, C, D, E,* and *F.* You would then follow these steps:

1. Prepare the major vertical and horizontal members.

2. Cut to size and install the drawer ends.

3. Install the necessary wall cleats to which the top will be attached.

4. Cut the top to shape and install it.

5. Fit the frames or dividers for drawers.

6. Cut and install the face-frame baseboard and the trim on the unit.

7. Build the drawers and install them.

8. Finish as desired.

BUILT-IN STORAGE UNIT

Here's a built-in storage cabinet that will transform unused space under a sloping ceiling into one of the most useful areas in a home. Fig. 54-5. By cutting the sides to the proper angle, it can be made to fit any ceiling slope.

Lay out all plywood parts carefully on the large panels and cut to size, making sure to allow for saw kerfs. Also make sure the top edges of the side pieces and partitions are cut to the proper angle to fit the

54-5(a). *This storage unit is built under a sloping ceiling. It includes closet space, drawers, and shelves as well as a drop-lid desk.*

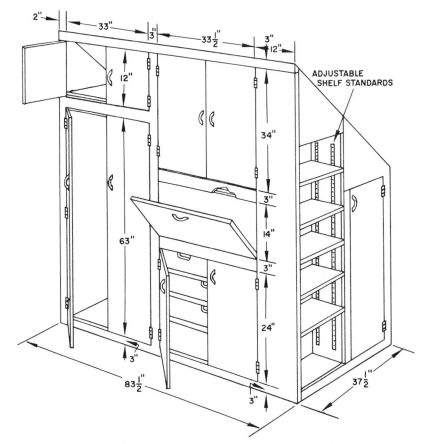

54-5(b). *Major dimensions of the storage unit.*

54-5(c). *Bill of materials for the storage unit.*

No. of Pieces	Where Used	Size
Panels		
7 Panels (Interior Grade) APA-A-A	Partitions, doors, front, sides, floor, shelves, drawer fronts and desk front	¾ × 48 × 96
2 Panels (Interior Grade) APA-A-D	Interior partitions, back, drawer sides	½ × 48 × 96
1 Panel (Interior Grade) APA-A-D	Drawer Bottoms	¼ × 48 × 48
Lumber		
3 ft.	Dowel (Clothes Pole)	1¼″ Diam.
12 ft.	Framing, door stop, miscellaneous	1 × 2
12 ft.	Drawer Guides	¾ × 1⅛
44 ft.	Shelf Cleats	1 × 1
Hardware		
12 pairs	Cabinet Hinges (Door)	
10	Friction Catches (Doors)	
10	Pulls (Door)	
2	Metal Chains (Drop Shelf)	
18 ft.	Adjustable Standards (Shelves)	

slope of the ceiling. Fig. 54-6. The center partition is notched as shown for beveled 1″ × 2″ frame stock. Fig. 54-6, Perspective 2.

Attach the 3″ plywood base strips to the bottom with 6d finishing nails and glue. Before applying the sides and partitions, cut the shelf cleats to length and fasten them in position with countersunk screws. Turn the bottom so that its front edge rests on the floor. Then you can work from the underside of the bottom to fasten the sides and partitions in place. Mark the location of the sides and the two forward partitions on the floor of the unit. Fasten

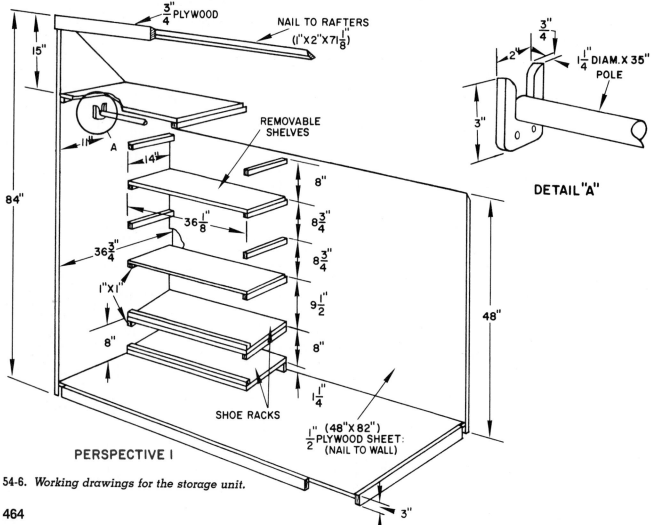

54-6. *Working drawings for the storage unit.*

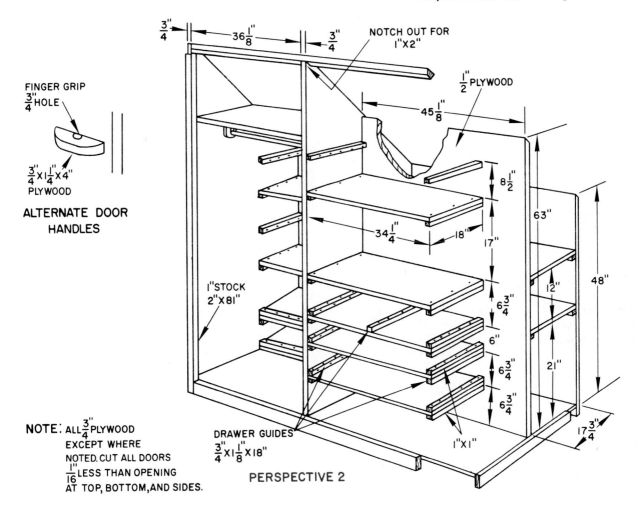

FINGER GRIP
$\frac{3}{4}$" HOLE

$\frac{3}{4}$" x $1\frac{1}{4}$" x 4"
PLYWOOD

ALTERNATE DOOR
HANDLES

NOTCH OUT FOR
1" x 2"

$\frac{3}{4}$"

$36\frac{1}{8}$"

$\frac{3}{4}$"

$\frac{1}{2}$" PLYWOOD

$45\frac{1}{8}$"

$8\frac{1}{2}$"

63"

48"

$34\frac{1}{4}$"

18"

17"

12"

$6\frac{3}{4}$"

6"

21"

$6\frac{3}{4}$"

1" STOCK
2" x 81"

$6\frac{3}{4}$"

1" x 1"

$17\frac{3}{4}$"

NOTE: ALL $\frac{3}{4}$" PLYWOOD
EXCEPT WHERE
NOTED. CUT ALL DOORS
$\frac{1}{16}$" LESS THAN OPENING
AT TOP, BOTTOM, AND SIDES.

DRAWER GUIDES
$\frac{3}{4}$" x $1\frac{1}{8}$" x 18"

PERSPECTIVE 2

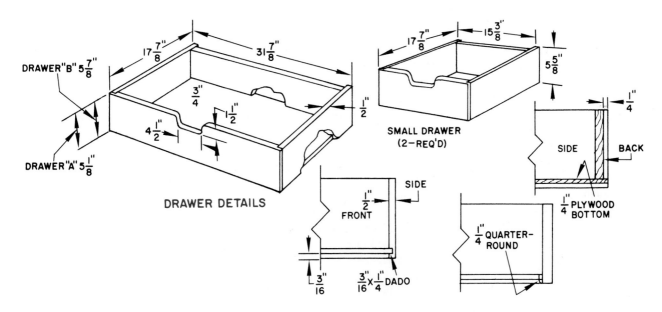

DRAWER "B" $5\frac{7}{8}$"

$17\frac{7}{8}$"

$31\frac{7}{8}$"

$\frac{3}{4}$"

$1\frac{1}{2}$"

$\frac{1}{2}$"

$4\frac{1}{2}$"

$1\frac{1}{2}$"

DRAWER "A" $5\frac{1}{8}$"

DRAWER DETAILS

$17\frac{7}{8}$"

$15\frac{3}{8}$"

$5\frac{5}{8}$"

SMALL DRAWER
(2-REQ'D)

$\frac{1}{4}$"

SIDE

BACK

$\frac{1}{4}$" PLYWOOD
BOTTOM

$\frac{1}{2}$"

SIDE

FRONT

$\frac{3}{16}$"

$\frac{3}{16}$" x $\frac{1}{4}$" DADO

$\frac{1}{4}$" QUARTER-
ROUND

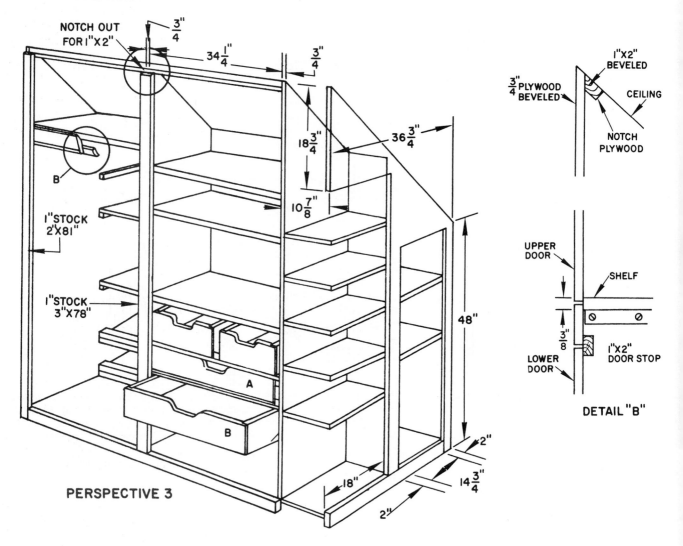

NOTCH OUT FOR 1"X 2"

$\frac{3}{4}$"

$34\frac{1}{4}$"

$\frac{3}{4}$"

$18\frac{3}{4}$"

$36\frac{3}{4}$"

$10\frac{7}{8}$"

B

1"STOCK 2"X 81"

1"STOCK 3"X 78"

48"

A

B

PERSPECTIVE 3

18"

2"

$14\frac{3}{4}$"

2"

1"X2" BEVELED

$\frac{3}{4}$"PLYWOOD BEVELED

CEILING

NOTCH PLYWOOD

UPPER DOOR

SHELF

LOWER DOOR

$\frac{3}{8}$"

1"X2" DOOR STOP

DETAIL "B"

them with glue and also by nailing through the bottom of the unit. Next add the partition behind the drawer section.

Turn the unit up so that you can complete the frame around the front. Before adding the frame across the top, be sure the top edge is at the same angle as the sides and partitions so that the total unit will fit snugly against the walls and ceiling. Make sure the assembly is in perfect square before fastening the 1" × 2" frame around the front. Use 6d finishing nails and glue. Add the back so that the lower edge overlaps the bottom. The total unit should be square and plumb.

Slide the assembly into position, using wedges where necessary to level the unit if the floor is uneven. Nail it into place with 8d finishing nails through the ½" plywood back into the roof rafters.

Cut out two plywood supports for the clothes pole and fasten them in the wardrobe compartment as shown in detail "A," Perspective 1. Standard wood escutcheons can be used if desired. Install the shelf above and those below as well as the shoe racks towards the bottom as indicated in Perspective 1.

Drawer guides are next cut to length and applied to the shelves with flathead wood screws. Back

shelves are fastened in position behind the ½" plywood partition.

Install the 12" face panel on the front and the triangular panels above the shelves and door on the right side.

Dado and rabbet the drawer parts. Assemble and fit them as shown in the drawer details.

Doors are hung with semi-concealed cabinet hinges. Install friction catches, metal chains for the drop shelf, and door pulls. Be sure to use 1" × 1" door stop where required. See detail "B," Perspective 3.

Break all sharp corners and sand all edges with 2/0 garnet paper. Re-

54-7(a). *This redwood grillwork is used as a room divider.*

move door pulls and fill nail holes with wood paste. Prepare for finishing by sanding with 3/0 garnet paper.

Paint or stain as desired.

ROOM DIVIDERS

Room dividers are built-ins that are used to separate two parts of a room. They are popular for living rooms in homes that do not have a separate entrance hallway. These di-

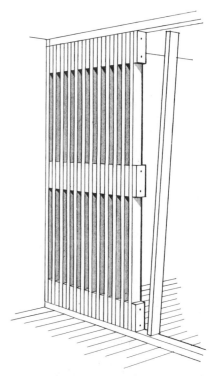

54-7(b). *This room divider is easy to build and has the general appearance of the one shown in Fig. 54-7(a). A 2″ × 4″ is nailed to the floor and the ceiling. Then 1″ × 4″ pieces with blocking between are installed to give an open look.*

viders are semiwalls of either closed or open construction. The solid screen is usually built partway to the ceiling with standard lumber and paneling. The open room dividers may be built on the job, or commercial architectural grillwork can be installed for part or all of the divider wall. Fig. 54-7. Frequently, storage units are combined with room dividers for greater utility. Fig. 54-8.

54-8. *The kitchen and family room are separated by a built-in bookcase and folding louvered doors.*

Section IV
QUESTIONS AND DISCUSSION TOPICS

Chapter 38

1. What are the three basic ways of building up large surfaces for furniture and cabinets? Discuss the advantages and disadvantages of each.

2. Describe two methods for determining the moisture content of lumber.

3. Define *equilibrium moisture content.*

4. How are hardness and specific gravity of wood related?

5. Name the three kinds of cross grain and tell how they affect the machining of wood.

6. How do you decide when a surface is properly planed?

7. Name five common defects that may result when lumber is incorrectly planed or surfaced.

8. What is the relationship between specific gravity and the turning qualities of wood? Between specific gravity and ease of boring? Specific gravity and mortising?

9. Name and briefly describe the three kinds of casework construction.

10. Describe the procedure for squaring up rough stock by machine.

Chapter 39

1. Name four factors that determine joint selection.

2. Describe the *superimposing* method of laying out a joint.

3. Describe four methods of strengthening a joint.

4. What is the primary use of edge joints?

5. Describe the blind dado joint.

6. How can a miter joint be strengthened?

7. Describe V-grooving.

8. In a mortise-and-tenon joint, which part is cut first? Why?

9. Compare the dovetail joint with the finger joint.

10. Describe how to cut a coped joint.

Chapter 40

1. Why is it difficult to glue end grain?

2. How does the moisture content of wood affect its gluing properties?

3. Name five types of adhesives that can be used for woods.

4. List four kinds of clamping devices used in cabinetmaking.

5. What is a "starved" joint?

6. Describe the operation of portable high-frequency gluing equipment.

Chapter 41

1. What is the difference between wood lamination and molded plywood?

2. What are some advantages of using laminated construction for curved parts?

3. Describe three common ways of producing curved parts for furniture.

4. What is the best moisture content for wood at the time of bending?

5. What are the best adhesives to use when making laminated parts in the shop?

Chapter 42

1. What is veneer?

2. Describe the three most common ways of cutting veneer.

3. Name four methods of matching veneer.

4. Tell how to apply a fine veneer to a core of plywood.

Chapter 43

1. Of what are plastic laminates made?

2. Name four common grades of plastic laminate.

3. What are the three most common core materials for plastic laminates?

4. What kind of adhesive is used for on-the-job installation of plastic laminate?

5. Describe the steps for applying plastic laminate to a counter top.

Chapter 44

1. What are the advantages of frame-and-panel construction?

2. What is *sticking?*

3. What is the usual size limit on solid wood panels?

4. Name three types of panels that can be used in frame-and-panel construction.

Chapter 45

1. Name five materials commonly used for furniture and casework doors.

2. What are the three methods of fitting a door to a case?

3. Name the three basic types of hinges.

4. Which hinges are most commonly used for flush doors? For lipped doors?

5. What are the advantages and disadvantages of sliding doors?

Chapter 46

1. Name the four basic kinds of drawers.
2. What are the five basic parts of a drawer?
3. Describe two kinds of drawer guides.
4. List the points to consider when planning to build a drawer.
5. Describe the various levels of quality in drawer construction.

Chapter 47

1. What three factors must be considered when designing shelves for cabinets?
2. Name two methods of installing stationary shelving.
3. Name three of the ways to install adjustable shelving.
4. When designing adjustable shelving, why must you still consider the items to be stored on the shelves?

Chapter 48

1. Can the design of furniture be determined by the appearance of the leg? Discuss.
2. Tell how to cut a tapered leg.
3. What is a cabriole leg? On what furniture styles is it found?
4. What is the difference between reeding and fluting?
5. Explain how to attach the legs for a tripod table.

Chapter 49

1. What are *stretchers*? Why are they used?
2. Name three of the joints that may be used in the leg-and-rail construction.
3. Why have dowel joints become more common for leg-and-rail construction?
4. Why is chair construction the most difficult job in furniture work?

Chapter 50

1. Name five kinds of tabletops.
2. What is a rule joint and how is it constructed?
3. List three methods of supporting a drop leaf.
4. What methods should be followed for attaching a tabletop if the top is made of glued-up solid wood? Explain.

5. Describe four methods for attaching tabletops made of plywood.

Chapter 51

1. Name three of the materials most often used in constructing simple casework.
2. What is a *plinth*?
3. Describe how to install a back in a piece of casework.
4. What is meant by the *exposed parts* of casework?
5. What are the three grades of residential casework?

Chapter 52

1. Describe the two basic types of casework construction used in building furniture.
2. How does fine furniture cabinetwork differ from basic casework?
3. Name the four structural parts found in larger pieces of furniture.
4. What are *dentils*?

Chapter 53

1. Name three ways of producing cabinets.
2. What are the five basic kinds of cabinets?
3. Why do most kitchens have a drop ceiling for the wall cabinets?
4. Tell how to plan a kitchen layout.
5. What are the four basic kitchen arrangements? Which is considered the most efficient?
6. Even if cabinets are very well made, you must check for level and plumb as you install them. Why?
7. How do you install factory-made wall cabinets?
8. Describe the two basic methods of building on-the-job cabinets.

Chapter 54

1. Discuss the differences between built-ins and casework built in a shop.
2. What are the uses of built-ins in a home?
3. Why must kitchen cabinets sometimes be built in rather than purchased from a mill or factory?
4. Describe the general procedure for constructing built-ins.

PROBLEMS AND ACTIVITIES

1. Design an experimental joint of *all-wood construction* that is different from any shown in this book.

2. Design a joint, making use of some plastic or metal reinforcement. Test the strength of this joint.

3. Design an assembly method for cabinets that does not make use of adhesives, nails, or screws.

4. Develop plans for an item to be mass-produced, including the drawings, jigs, fixtures, route sheets, and work stations.

5. Compare the strength of various common corner joints.

6. Compare the machining qualities of two common cabinet woods.

7. Study the holding power of some common adhesives.

8. Study the use of plastic laminates in commercial construction and compare their advantages and disadvantages with those of solid wood or plywood.

9. Develop a form or mold for laminating a wood product.

10. Visit some houses being built and inspect the kitchen-cabinet construction.

Section V

FINISHING

Preparation for Finishing

Before actually finishing a product, it is essential to complete all of the prefinishing operations. Fig. 55-1. These include removing mill marks and any exterior surface glue, repairing imperfections, and final sanding. For some finishes, bleaching must also be done. Remember that any imperfections or scratches left after the final sanding will show up more when the final finish is applied.

REMOVING MILL MARKS

If you look closely at stock that has been surfaced, you will see small "waves." These are knife marks left by the rotating cutter of the planer or jointer. These mill marks must be removed with a hand plane before final sanding. Fig. 55-2.

REMOVING EXCESS GLUE

When you assemble products, it is important to apply the right amount of glue. If too much is applied, some will have to be removed, which is a problem. Also, your fingers should not be covered with glue or oil during assembly since these materials will seal wood pores and prevent stains and other finishing materials from going on the wood evenly.

When the product is ready for finishing, check it carefully for excess

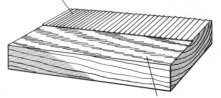

MILL MARKS FROM SURFACER OR PLANER

SMOOTH HAND PLANED SURFACE

55-2. *Remove all jointer and planer mill marks with a sharp, finely set jack plane.*

glue on the surface, particularly around the joints. Remove any such glue with a sharp chisel. Glue spilled on the surface should always be removed by scraping. Never attempt to sand it off since this forces the glue into the wood, and glue will not take stain. Make sure every bit of glue is removed.

REPAIRING WOOD SURFACES

In the process of building any wood product there is always the chance of small damage. There are four common ways to repair a wood surface.

• It is possible to raise a shallow dent with a wet cloth and a hot iron. Place the cloth over the dent and the iron over the cloth. Fig. 55-3. This will usually raise the grain enough so that it can be sanded to an even surface.

• A good way to fill small cracks is by the burn-in method. Shellac or lacquer sticks are used. These are hard pieces of material that become

55-1. *A beautiful finish cannot be achieved unless the surface first is properly prepared.*

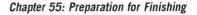

55-3. *Swelling a dent in wood with a damp cloth and a hot iron. Don't wet the wood too much, especially when working with plywood.*

soft when heated. They come in many different colors such as light oak, dark oak, light and dark walnut, and mahogany of various colors. When heated, the patching material will blend with the wood surface, just like paint, to match any color.

Clean out the crack or hole carefully, making sure that it is completely dirt free. Heat one or two knives, either with a special electric furnace or over an alcohol torch.

55-4(a). *An electric furnace with a pair of burn-in knives.*

Fig. 55-4. A special electric knife can also be used. Pick up the patching material on the tip of the hot knife. Fig. 55-5. Roll the knife over and drop the material onto the defect. Fig. 55-6. While it is still in a semiliquid condition, pull the burn-in material into the depression with the return stroke. Fig. 55-7. Never stop the motion, or the hot knife may mar the wood surface. Continue the movement to wipe the excess into a thin film and lift it away with the knife. Fig. 55-8. This method requires considerable practice and should not be done the first time on the product itself. It should be practiced on scrap stock.

• A third method of filling cracks and holes is to use a filler material such as wood dough or plastic wood. Plastic wood comes in various colors, including natural, light mahogany, oak, walnut, maple, and many others. Wood dough is a synthetic wood that comes in many colors. In using both plastic wood and wood dough, make sure that the color is correct before applying. Then add enough material to make a slight hump on the surface. Allow it to dry; then sand off smooth and level.

• A good way to cover nail or screw holes is with wood pegs or plugs. For small nail holes, pegs of the same wood as the product can be made from 1/32" stock. Point the end in a pencil sharpener. Apply glue to the point and insert in the hole. Then cut off and sand smooth.

55-5. *Picking up the material with the knife.*

55-6. *Roll the knife over and drop the material onto the defect on the back stroke.*

55-7. *Now pull the knife forward over the defect. Never allow the hot knife to come to a stop.*

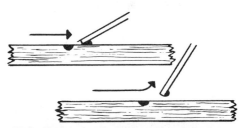

55-8. *Pick up the excess material with the end of the knife. Notice how the knife is brought up to a vertical position at the end of the stroke.*

55-4(b). *An ordinary knife and an alcohol torch can also be used.*

Wood plugs for screw holes can be cut with a plug cutter, or fancy wood plugs can be purchased. These are glued in the counterbored holes.

BLEACHING

Bleaching is done to lighten a wood surface. This step is done for many of the honey-toned, colored finishes and for applying medium-tone finishes to such woods as walnut, mahogany, and pecan. Bleaching removes color by oxidation.

Kinds of Bleaches

The simplest kind of bleach is made by mixing oxalic acid crystals in hot water. This relatively mild solution is satisfactory only for small furniture pieces. The most common commercial bleach consists of two solutions. Solution No. 1 is normally a caustic soda (bleach activator). Solution No. 2 is hydrogen peroxide in a concentrated form, with approximately 35 percent peroxide. This commercial bleach is a powerful oxidizing agent that removes wood colors by oxidizing them into colorless forms. While these two solutions can be applied one after the other, usually they are mixed together and applied at the same time. The strongest bleach is obtained when equal parts of both solutions are used. A weaker bleach can be made by using twice as much of No. 2 as No. 1 and then adding a small amount of water.

A bleach leaves a thin residue that must be washed off and then sanded before the finishing can proceed. A major disadvantage of

bleaching is that moisture is added to the wood when the residue is washed off. *It is absolutely necessary that the wood be properly dried before proceeding with the finishing.* Usually a piece must dry overnight at 70 degrees if heating ovens are not available.

Another problem that can develop, particularly when applying bleach to solid glued-up stock, is that the water applied to the face surface during bleaching will cause the wood to cup. Therefore, when washing off the bleached surface, it is often a good idea to apply plain water to the opposite face also so that the moisture content of the wood will be equalized.

Safety

Wood bleaches are powerful substances that can injure the person applying them. They are also flammable due to their high oxygen content. Follow these safety suggestions:

• Wear eye goggles or a face mask, rubber gloves, and a rubber apron.

• Mix the bleach in a glass, ceramic, or stainless steel container.

• Do the bleaching where there is good ventilation. Stay away from any open flame or spark.

• If bleach comes in contact with the skin, wash it off immediately with soap and water.

• Apply bleach with a rope brush or cellulose sponge. Never use rags.

• Never allow mixed bleach to stand around for any length of time. Always clean out the container and mix a fresh batch when needed.

Application

Bleach is applied by spraying or with a rope brush or sponge. The following is the correct procedure:

1. Mix the bleach to the correct proportion.

2. Apply the bleach, working from the top down. Fig. 55-9.

3. Allow the bleach to remain about 30 minutes. If necessary, apply a second coat.

4. Wash down the bleach with a 50-50 solution of clear water and white vinegar, using a sponge to wipe it off.

5. Allow the surface to dry at least 12 hours at 70 degrees F. Make sure there is good air circulation around it.

6. Carefully sand the bleached surface with 6/0 (220) garnet paper and wipe it clean before finishing.

REMOVING HARDWARE

The preliminary fitting of hardware is usually done while the product is in the white wood (unfinished) stage. Holes and openings are drilled for handles, catches, locks, or other hardware. Most of these items, except certain hinges, are removed before bleaching, final sanding, and finishing.

FINAL SANDING OF CASEWORK AND BUILT-INS

The final sanding of casework and built-ins depends on the kind of finish to be applied and the quality of construction. If paint or some other opaque finish is used, final sanding with 1 (50) or 1/2 (60) garnet paper is satisfactory. However, if a trans-

55-9. *Applying bleach with a synthetic sponge.*

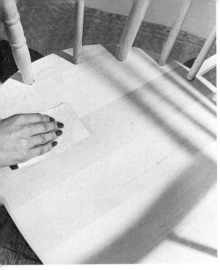

55-10(a). *Hand sanding a chair seat. Remember to sand in the same direction as the grain.*

55-10(b). *Use a strip of sandpaper to get into crevices.*

parent finish is to be applied, the surfaces should be given a final sanding with 2/0 (100) garnet paper. Care should be taken so that there are no cross scratches, especially where there is a solid wood frame around a plywood center.

FINAL SANDING OF FURNITURE

Final sanding is usually done after the product has been assembled. The exterior surfaces are sanded with portable belt and fin-ishing sanders. Sides and fronts of drawers are sanded as they are fitted into the case or cabinet. Hand sanding must also be done. Fig. 55-10.

There is no complete agreement among finishers as to what constitutes suitable sanding before finishing. The final sanding recommendation of a leading abrasives manufacturer is shown in Fig. 55-11. Other finishers recommend that the final sanding be done with garnet paper at least as fine as 6/0 (220) for dense woods like oak or maple and 7/0 (240) for low-density woods.

Some finishers recommend that, before final sanding, a glue size be applied to the exterior surface to hold the wood fibers firmly in place during finishing. This glue size is made by mixing one-fourth pound of liquid animal glue for every gallon of warm water. This is applied with a brush and allowed to dry thoroughly. Then the final sanding is done. This procedure is particularly recommended for the fibrous woods. However, care must be taken in the final sanding since, if too much of the size is left on the surface, it will interfere with the finishing process. On the other hand, if too much sanding is done, all of the size will be sanded away.

Generally the surface should be hand sanded with 3/0 (120) to 5/0 (180) garnet paper. Remember that sanding must always be done with the grain. Care must also be exercised when sanding 1/28" veneer surfaces with a portable sander so that

FINAL SANDING

Type of Operation	Type Mineral and Technical Grades	Product Form (Rolls, Discs, etc.)	Special Remarks Concerning Usage
Drawer Sanding	40-X (1½) or 50-X (1) or 60-X (½) GARNET Cloth	Drawer Sanding Belts	Sanding dovetails—on lip-type machine. Usually oak sides most severe test for belt joint.
Portable Belt Sander	80-X (0) or 100-X (2/0) ALUMINUM OXIDE Cloth	Belts	Portable belt machine—take sander to assembled case to flush—square backs, tops of drawer fronts—general touch-up fitting.
Hand Sanding	100-C (2/0) or 120-C (3/0) or 150-C (4/0) GARNET Cabinet Paper	Sheets	Breaking edges using sheets and felt blocks—touch-up.
Vibrator Sanding or (Oscillating) Finishing Sander	120-A (3/0) or 150-A (4/0) GARNET Finishing Paper	Sheets	Final inspection station—white wood sanding. Tops—final touch-up before top coat.

55-11. *Recommendations for final sanding.*

the surface is not sanded too thin. After final sanding, all dust must be removed. This can be done first with a brush or vacuum cleaner (use a brush attachment). Then wipe the surface with a *tack rag*. A tack rag is a piece of cheesecloth or cotton rag moistened with thinned varnish or similar liquid. (The varnish is thinned with turpentine.) Such a rag will pick up small particles of dust from a wood surface.

Another method of preparing wood for finishing is to:

1. Sponge the surface with warm water to raise the grain.

2. Sand with the grain, using 3/0 (120) grit abrasive paper.

3. Apply a light sealer to the surface. The sealer should be one part final finishing material, such as varnish or lacquer, and five parts thinner. Use turpentine or mineral spirits to thin varnish; use lacquer thinner for lacquer. This application will hold any loose fibers in place.

4. When dry, sand again with the grain (very lightly) using a piece of *worn* 3/0 (120) grit abrasive paper.

56 Finishing Equipment and Supplies

The kind of finish applied to cabinets and furniture is determined to a large degree by the equipment available. Some finishes can be applied with a rag, brush, or roller. In industry, however, most are applied by spraying with either lacquer or some synthetic finish.

SPRAYING EQUIPMENT

There are many different kinds of spraying equipment. Typical equipment used in a cabinet shop or well-equipped school workshop consists of the following:

● An *air compressor* takes the air at atmospheric pressure and delivers it at a higher pressure through pipe and hose to operate a spray gun. Fig. 56-1. The high air pressure breaks up the finishing material into a fine spray. The capacity of a compressor is determined by the cubic feet of air delivered per minute (cfm). Compressors with a high cfm force more air through the hose to the spray gun.

● A *metal pipe* or an *air hose* connects the compressor to the transformer.

● An *air transformer* removes all of the oil, dirt, and moisture from the compressed air. It also filters and regulates the air. A gauge on the transformer indicates the air pressure in pounds. There are at least two outlets on the transformer, one for the spray-gun hose and another for other air tools. The air regulator, which is part of the transformer, maintains the correct air pressure with a minimum of change.

● A *hose* carries the air from the transformer to the spray gun. In some types of machines hoses also carry the paint or finishing material from the paint or fluid container to the gun. Some systems have pressure-feed tanks that hold the finishing fluid. Air pressure forces the fluid up from the container to the gun. Fig. 56-2.

● The finishing material is fed through a *spray gun* either by means of a suction cup attached directly to the gun or by a hose from the pressure-feed tank. A *suction-* or

56-1(a). *This compressor and storage tank is the stationary type, commonly found in school and industrial shops.*

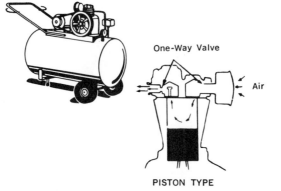

56-1(b). *This portable compressor and tank can be used at any common electrical outlet. The tank assures constant pressure at the spray nozzle. All large compressors have a piston action that compresses air in a cylinder. The air then enters a pulsation chamber where the strokes are smoothed into a steady flow before traveling through the hose to the gun.*

56-3. *With a suction- or siphon-fed gun, the compressed air passes over the fluid tube inside the nozzle, creating a vacuum which draws the finishing material up from the container. A suction-fed gun always has an air hole in the paint container cover. This type is recommended for finer atomization where an extra-fine finish is required.*

siphon-fed gun, on which a container is directly mounted, uses a stream of compressed air to create a vacuum. This allows the atmospheric pressure to force the material from the attached container to the spray head. Fig. 56-3. The *pressure-fed* gun has an air cap that does not necessarily cause a vacuum. The air is forced through the gun by air pressure from the tank or cup. Fig. 56-4. In both pressure-fed and suction-fed guns, the mixing of the air and fluid usually takes place outside the gun. This is called *external mix.* This is the only type suitable for lacquer and other fast-

drying materials. In an *internal mix* spray gun, the mixing takes place inside the cap. Fig. 56-5.

Spray guns may also be classified in two ways according to air control. In the *bleeder* gun there is no air valve; so a certain amount of air is constantly going through the gun. The *non-bleeder* type is more common. It does have a valve which shuts off the air when the trigger is released. Fig. 56-6.

● Spraying should be done in a *spray booth* whenever possible. There are two common types: *dry* and *water-wash.* The dry one is mainly found in smaller shops where quick-drying material like lacquer is used and spraying is not done continuously. Fig. 56-7. In the dry booth, the contaminated air is

drawn through baffles and expelled. The booth may be anything from a small bench type to a large floor model. The water-wash booth makes use of a curtain of water to trap the overspray and to cool the air as it

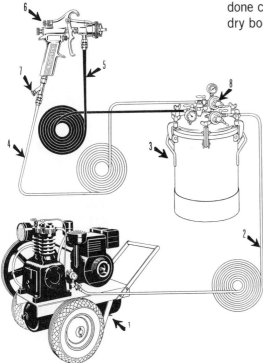

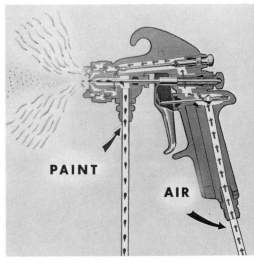

56-2. *Typical heavy-duty portable spraying equipment includes a portable air compressor (1), a hose to convey air from the compressor to the material tanks (2), a pressure-feed tank (3), a hose to convey air to the spray gun (4), a hose to convey finishing material to the gun (5), a pressure-fed spray gun (6), and an air controlling device, such as an air adjusting valve attached to the spray gun (7) or an extra air regulator and gauge installed at the tank (8).*

56-4. *In a pressure-fed system, air forces the paint or finishing material into the gun and then breaks up (atomizes) the fluid into a fine mist. Pressure-fed guns are usually used for fastest spraying and for heavier materials.*

EXTERNAL

INTERNAL

56-5. *Spray guns have two types of nozzles: external mix and internal mix. The external mix can be used with either pressure- or suction-fed guns and is better for fast-drying material such as lacquer. The internal mix is best for heavy-bodied paints and can be used only with a pressure-fed gun.*

is drawn through to the outside. Fig. 56-8.

• A *respirator* or *mask* is worn over the nose and mouth to prevent inhaling finishing materials. The organic vapor mask that covers only the nose and mouth is the most common. It comes with replaceable cartridges which remove the organic vapors.

The simplest spraying equipment consists of a small portable compressor, a length of air hose, and a suction-fed spray gun. Most compressors are of the piston type in which the air is drawn through an intake valve, compressed, and then expelled through the exhaust valve to the air line to provide the air pressure. Only the very simplest portable units have a diaphragm compressor in which the pressure is developed by the reciprocating action of a flexible disk. Fig. 56-9.

Red is the standard color for air hoses that connect the compressor to the spray gun on portable or low-pressure units. However, some units have black and orange, braid-covered hose. The spray gun of a portable unit is usually of the bleeder type, with external mix and suction feed. Such guns are designed for use on small air compressor outfits that do not have an air valve. They can be used inside in a spray

Trigger controls only paint

BLEEDER   Air

Trigger controls air and paint

NON-BLEEDER   Air

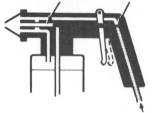

56-6. *The bleeder gun has air flowing from the nozzle all the time, but material flows only when the trigger is pulled. This gun must be used only with a compressor that runs all the time. The nonbleeder gun has a trigger that controls the flow of both air and finishing material. Nonbleeder guns are used only with spraying outfits that have an air storage tank.*

booth. When there is no spray booth, the spraying must be done out of doors on a very quiet day. It is necessary for the operator to wear a respirator.

USING A SPRAY GUN IN A BOOTH

Connect the air hose leading from the transformer to the air inlet of the spray gun. If a small portable unit is being used, lacquer is usually thinned half and half with lacquer thinner. For spray outfits that have greater air pressure, lacquer can be used just as it comes from the can. Some lacquer may have to be strained through fine cheesecloth or fine window screening to remove any impurities, but normally this is not needed.

There are two common adjustments on the suction-fed spray gun.

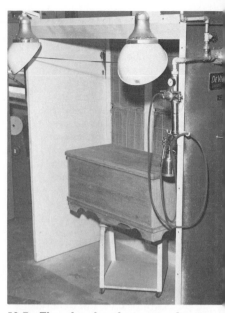

56-7. *The dry booth is simpler to install and is most common in school shops. The booth is used when it isn't necessary to prevent overspray from being discharged to the outside.*

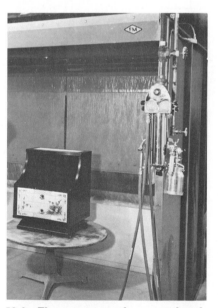

56-8. *The water-wash spray booth reduces fire hazard and is used where the exhausted air must be clean as it leaves the stack.*

The *fluid needle adjustment screw* controls the amount of fluid flow. Fig. 56-10. Flow can also be controlled by limiting the amount the

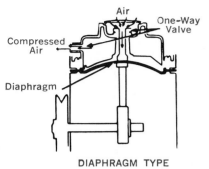

56-9. *The diaphragm-type compressor compresses air by the flexing of a plastic diaphragm.*

trigger is pulled. The *spreader adjustment valve* changes the spray pattern. Fig. 56-11. The patterns may be round, flat, or fan-shaped. When a transformer and pressure-

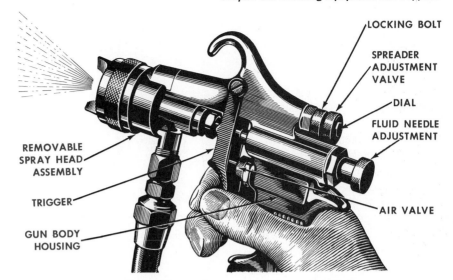

56-10. *Parts of a suction-fed spray gun.*

PATTERN	CAUSE	CORRECTION
	Dried material in side-port "A" restricts passage of air through it. Result: Full pressure of air from clean side-port forces fan pattern in direction of clogged side.	Dissolve material in side-port with *thinner*. Do not poke in any of the openings with metal instruments.
	Dried material around the outside of the fluid nozzle tip at position "B" restricts the passage of atomizing air at one point through the center opening of air nozzle and results in pattern shown. This pattern can also be caused by loose air nozzle.	If dried material is causing the trouble, remove air nozzle and wipe off fluid tip, using rag wet with thinner. Tighten air nozzle.
	A split spray or one that is heavy on each end of a fan pattern and weak in the middle is usually caused by (1) too high an atomization air pressure, or (2) by attempting to get too wide a spray with thin material.	Reducing air pressure will correct cause (1). To correct cause (2) open material control to full position by turning to left. At the same time turn spray width adjustment to right. This will reduce width of spray but will correct split spray pattern.
SPITTING	(1) Dried out packing around material needle valve permits air to get into fluid passageway. This results in spitting. (2) Dirt between fluid nozzle seat and body or a loosely installed fluid nozzle will make gun spit. (3) A loose or defective swivel nut on siphon cup or material hose can cause spitting.	To correct cause (1) back up knurled nut (E), place two drops of machine oil on packing, replace nut and tighten with fingers only. In aggravated cases, replace packing. To correct cause (2), remove fluid nozzle (F), clean back of nozzle and nozzle seat in gun body using rag wet with thinner, replace nozzle and draw up tightly against body. To correct cause (3) tighten or replace swivel nut (G).

56-11. *Faulty spray patterns and how to correct them.*

feed tank are used, start the fluid pressure at 15 pounds and the air pressure at 75 pounds. This should be changed as necessary until the best spray is obtained. First test the action of the gun. If the spray patterns seem starved for material, open the fluid needle adjustment screw. If necessary, thin the material. If the spray is too fast, reduce the flow by turning in the screw or lowering the air pressure. If the spray is too fine, reduce the pressure, making sure the fluid adjustment is wide open. If the spray is too coarse, increase the air pressure or reduce the amount of fluid flow.

Following are some common difficulties that must be corrected if the spraying is jerky or fluttering:

● The container is at too sharp an angle. Straighten it.

● There isn't enough fluid in the container.

● Dirt or other impurity is in the fluid passageway.

● The fluid tip is damaged.

56-12. *Keep the gun the correct distance away from the surface.*

● There is a crack in the fluid tube. When this happens on a suction-fed gun, it is usually because the material is too thick. It must be thinned. It may also be caused by a clogged air vent in the cup lid.

SPRAYING TECHNIQUES

The only way to learn to spray correctly is to get plenty of practice. The following are some helpful suggestions:

1. Hold the gun about 6″ to 8″ from the surface being sprayed. This distance can be determined by following the technique shown in Fig. 56-12.

2. Move your arm, not your wrist, when spraying. Keep the gun at right angles to the surface at all points along the stroke. Fig. 56-13.

3. The ends of the stroke should be feathered out by triggering the gun. To trigger correctly, begin the stroke before pulling the trigger and release it before ending the stroke. Never move the gun in

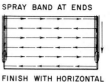
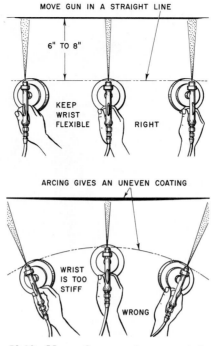

56-13. *Move the gun in a straight line, never in an arcing motion.*

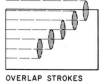
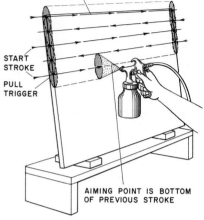

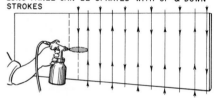

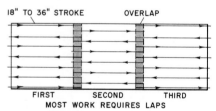

56-14. *Banding. Vertical bands sprayed at the ends of a panel prevent wasted spray from the horizontal strokes. When spraying a panel, use alternate right and left strokes, releasing the trigger before the end of each stroke. Long work is sprayed in sections of convenient length, each section overlapping the previous one by 4″.*

an arc since this will make the spray uneven.

4. Spray corners by holding the gun so that these surfaces will be sprayed equally and at the same time.

SOME SPRAY PAINTING TROUBLES AND REMEDIES

56-15. *Possible causes of spray painting troubles and their remedies.*

Trouble	Possible Causes	Suggested Remedies
Sags	1. Dirty air cap and fluid tip. 2. Gun stroked too close to surface. 3. Trigger not released at end of stroke. 4. Gun stroked at wrong angle to surface. 5. Paint too cold. 6. Paint applied too heavy.	1. Remove and clean cap and tip. 2. Stroke 6–10 inches from surface. 3. Release trigger after every stroke. 4. Gun should be stroked at right angles to surface. 5. Use an approved paint heater. 6. Calculate depth of wet film.
Streaks	1. Dirty air cap and fluid tip. 2. Insufficient or incorrect overlapping of strokes. 3. Gun stroked too rapidly. 4. Gun stroked at wrong angle to surface. 5. Stroking too far from surface. 6. Too much air pressure. 7. Split spray. 8. Paint too cold.	1. Remove and clean cap and tip. 2. Follow the previous stroke accurately. Deposit a wet coat. 3. Take deliberate slow stroke. 4. Gun should be stroked at right angles to surface. 5. Stroke 6–10 inches from surface. 6. Use minimum air pressure needed. 7. Clean fluid tip and air cap. 8. Heat paint to get good flowout.
Orange-Peel	1. Paint not thinned out sufficiently. 2. Paint too cold. 3. Not depositing a wet coat. 4. Gun stroked too rapidly. 5. Insufficient air pressure. 6. Using wrong air cap or nozzle. 7. Gun stroked too far from surface. 8. Overspray striking a previously sprayed surface.	1. Add correct amount of solvent by measure. 2. Heat to get good flowout. 3. Check solvent. Use correct speed and overlap of stroke. 4. Take deliberate slow stroke. 5. Increase air pressure or reduce fluid pressure. 6. Select correct air and nozzle for material and feed. 7. Stroke 6–10 inches from surface. 8. Spray detail parts first. End with a wet coat.
Excessive Paint Loss	1. Not triggering at each stroke. 2. Stroking at wrong angle. 3. Stroking too far from surface. 4. Wrong air cap or fluid tip. 5. Depositing paint film of irregular thickness. 6. Fluid pressure too high. 7. Air pressure too high.	1. Release trigger after stroke. 2. Stroke at right angle to surface. 3. Stroke 6–10 inches from surface. 4. Use correct setup. 5. Make it a practice to calculate the depth of wet film. 6. Reduce pressure. If pressure keeps climbing, clean regulator on pressure tank. 7. Use minimum air needed.

5. Overlap strokes about 50 percent as the gun is moved back and forth across the surface. This will eliminate the need for double or cross coats. Fig. 56-14.

6. When spraying curved surfaces, hold the gun at the normal distance but use a curved stroke.

COMMON SPRAYING PROBLEMS

A troubleshooting chart for some spray painting problems can be found in Fig. 56-15. Two other common problems are mist and starving the spray gun.

• Mist or fog is caused by having the material too thin or the air pressure too high.

• Starving the spray gun means that insufficient air or fluid reaches the gun itself. This is often due to dirt in the hoses.

CLEANING A SUCTION-FED GUN

1. Loosen the air cap two or three turns and remove the fluid container. Hold a cloth over the air cap and pull the trigger. This will force the fluid that remains in the gun back into the container.

2. Empty the container and clean it thoroughly with lacquer thinner.

3. Fill the container about half full of lacquer thinner and reassemble the gun. Spray the thinner to flush out the fluid passages.

4. Remove the air cap and clean it. Soak it in the thinner to remove all traces of the finishing material. Then brush or scrape until it is perfectly clean.

5. Clean out any clogged holes with a toothpick or match stick. Never use a sharp wire or nail. Wipe off the gun with a solvent-soaked rag. Reassemble the gun so that it is ready for the next use.

FINISHING SUPPLIES

The following supplies are needed for the various finishing processes:

• *Turpentine*, made from the resin of pine trees, is used as a solvent for paint and enamel.

• *Linseed oil*, made from flaxseed, is used in paints, fillers, and stains.

• *Alcohol*, a colorless liquid made from wood drippings or chemicals, is used as a thinner and solvent for shellac. The U.S. government has established a standard alcohol mix called Formula Special No. 1 denatured alcohol, which contains ethyl alcohol and wood alcohol.

• *Benzene*, a solvent and cleaning fluid, is made from coal tar.

• *Mineral spirits* is a pure distillation of petroleum that will do everything that turpentine will do. It can be used as a thinner or solvent.

• *Waxes* can be either liquid or paste. Both types are made from a base of beeswax, paraffin, carnauba wax, and turpentine. Wax provides a water-resistant surface that can be renewed often.

• *Steel wool* is made of thin metal shavings. It comes in pads or rolls and can be purchased in grades from 0000 (very fine) to 3 (coarse).

• *Pumice* is a white powder made from lava. It is available in several grades. The most common grades for wood finishing are FF and FFF. It is combined with water or oil to rub down the finish.

• *Rottenstone* is a reddish brown or grayish black iron oxide that comes from shale. Much finer than pumice, it is used with water or oil to produce a smoother finish after the surface has been rubbed with pumice.

• *Rubbing oil* should be either petroleum or paraffin oil. If oil refined from petroleum is used, be sure it is a thin grade.

• *Abrasive papers* needed are garnet or aluminum oxide finishing papers in grades No. 4/0 (150) and No. 6/0 (220). No. 4/0 (150) is used for sanding after staining, after applying the first coat of shellac, and before applying the filler coat. No. 6/0 (220) is used for final

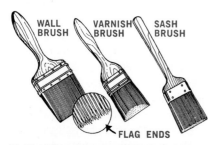

56-16. *Three common kinds of brushes. The split (flagged) ends make the brush work better.*

smoothing after shellac coats or other finish. These may be used dry or with oil.

• *Waterproof (wet-or-dry) abrasive papers* in grades from 240 to 400 grit are used with water for hand sanding between lacquer coats or for rubbing enamel or lacquer.

• A *tack rag* is a piece of cheesecloth or cotton rag moistened with thinned varnish. It is used to pick up tiny particles of dust from the wood surface before applying finish.

BRUSHES

Many kinds and sizes of brushes can be used to apply finishing materials. Most are made with Chinese or Russian boar or nylon bristles. Nylon bristles are most common for varnish and enamel. Bristle length determines the flexibility of the brush and its quality. When the ends of the bristles are bent over, they should spring back in place without any loose ends. In a good-quality brush the bristles should be set in rubber and there should be enough of them to give a full feeling when they are squeezed between the fingers. On animal-hair brushes the bristle ends should be split for better performance. Fig. 56-16.

A *varnish* or *enamel brush* is sturdy. It is used for applying heavier paints as well as varnish and enamel. It has a chisel edge. Nylon-bristle brushes 2″ to 4″ wide and ⅜″ to ¹¹⁄₁₆″ thick are best for most surfaces.

A *wall brush* is more flexible than a varnish brush and it has longer bristles. It is usually 4″ to 5″ wide with a straight-cut edge for use with sweeping strokes on large, flat surfaces.

A *utility brush* is a small brush for painting trim of window frames. It should be about 1″ to 1½″ wide.

Sash brushes are used for fine work in painting around windows and doors. These brushes have long handles and oval, round, or flat bris-

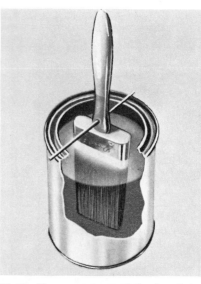

56-17. *You can suspend the brush in solvent like this.*

tle heads. They come in various bristle lengths, either straight-cut or chisel-cut.

Good Use of Brushes

The following are some general suggestions for using brushes:

• Revolve a new brush rapidly by the handle to dislodge loose bristles. Remember that all new brushes have them.

• To break in a brush, soak it in a solvent up to the metal cap for about one hour. Then wrap the brush in a heavy piece of paper for some time before using it.

• Dip the brush into the finishing material about one-third the bristle length. Tap the excess against the side of the can. Never scrape against the rim of the can because this loosens the bristles.

• When using a brush, always hold it at a slight angle to the work surface.

• Never paint with the side of the brush. This is one of the main causes of "fingering."

• Never use a wide brush to paint small, round surfaces such as dowel rods. Your brush will "fishtail."

• Never let the brush stand on its

bristle end. Its own weight bends and curls the bristles. This will make it hard to use the brush.

Cleaning a Brush

1. Work the proper solvent or a commercial brush cleaner into the heel of the brush. Turpentine is the correct solvent for cleaning brushes used in oil paints and varnishes. Alcohol should be used to clean shellac brushes, and lacquer thinner is used to clean brushes used in lacquer. Brushes used in latex paints and stains are cleaned with soap and water.

2. Surplus solvent is removed by squeezing the bristles between the thumb and fingers. Continue working clean solvent into the bristles until the solvent that is worked out appears clean.

3. Wash the brush in a mild soap and warm water until the lather is white and free of all traces of the finishing material.

4. Rinse the brush and shape the bristles with a stiff brush or with your thumb and fingers.

5. Either suspend the brush in the correct solvent or wrap the bristles with paper and fold the end up. Fig. 56-17. Be careful not to bend the ends of the bristles when folding up the end of the paper wrapper. Place a rubber band or tie a string around the paper, over the metal ferrule of the brush, to hold the paper wrapper in place.

ROLLERS

Rollers can be used for some painting of large, flat surfaces and for applying some oil finishes. They cannot be used for finishes that dry rapidly. The simple roller is dipped into the paint. A self-feeding roller is sometimes used by commercial painters. Various roller covers are available which make it possible to achieve different textures.

57 Finishing Procedures

Good design and a fine finish are two important characteristics of quality furniture. A fine finish, one which truly enhances the beauty and utility of the furniture piece, can be difficult and time-consuming to achieve. This is largely because wood is a variable material, with light and dark areas, natural colors and dyes, and soft and hard spots.

Today woodworkers have a wide choice of materials for finishing. Besides the traditional varnish and lacquer, there are polyurethane finishes for durability, wipe-on finishes for ease, and oil finishes for the natural look. No one type of finish will serve all purposes. Every type has differ-

ent advantages and disadvantages. Try several finishes on scrap material and choose the one that best suits your project.

Several steps may be necessary to obtain a final finish. However, the steps are not the same for every kind of finish. As a matter of fact, some good finishes can be obtained through processes involving just three, two, or even one step. Fig. 57-1.

The finishing process to choose depends partly on the type of wood and the appearance wanted. Also it is important to consider what finishing facilities and equipment are available. If your shop is equipped

with a spray booth and good drying facilities, then a lacquer finish may be applied. Otherwise a simple finish that can be applied with a rag or brush is better.

A STANDARD FINISHING SYSTEM

The following are some of the basic steps necessary for a fine wood finish. Fig. 57-2. Covering capacities and drying times are shown in Fig. 57-3.

Bleaching

Bleaching removes color from wood. It is necessary for very light and for medium-light or honey-

57-1(α). *This Contemporary table has a standard surface finish. Ten separate and distinct finishing procedures were followed to complete its fine finish.*

57-1(b). *In contrast, this table was given a simple penetrating "oil-rubbed" finish.*

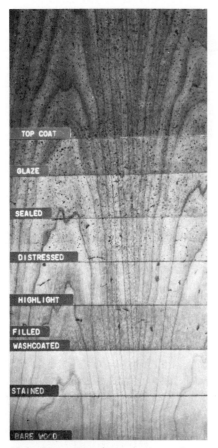

57-2. *Many finishes require a large number of materials and operations to achieve the beautiful effects seen on fine furniture.*

colored finishes. Many of the natural and darker finishes require no bleaching.

Bleaching is also done when the natural color of the wood is to be changed. For example, when finishing mahogany, it may be desirable to achieve a light honey color rather than red. This can be done by bleaching the red from the mahogany, then staining to the desired tone.

Prestaining

This is sometimes called *sap staining* because it is necessary when starting with natural woods in which color variation is great. A good example of this is walnut, in which the sapwood is very light and the heartwood is quite dark. Sap staining is also done when different kinds of wood, such as gum and mahogany, are combined in the same product and a uniform color is desired for the final finish.

Staining and Coloring

Staining adds color to the wood and emphasizes the grain. It is also done to change the tone or shade of

a wood surface. Many kinds of stains or toners can be used.

Wash Coating

Wash coating is done to keep the stain from bleeding into the filler and to provide a hard surface for

COVERING CAPACITIES

Material	Sq. Ft. Per Gal.
Bleaching Solutions	250–300
Lacquer	200–300
Lacquer Sealer	250–300
Liquid Filler	250–400
Water Stain	350–400
Oil Stain	300–350
Pigment Oil Stain	350–400
Non-Grain-Raising Stain	275–325
Paint	400–500
Spirit Stain	250–300
Shellac	300–350
Rubbing Varnish	450–500
Flat Varnish	300–350
Liquid Wax	600–700

57-3(α). *Covering capacities of common finishing materials. These are general averages. The actual coverage will vary considerably, depending on such things as thickness of coat and application to porous or nonporous surfaces.*

applying the filler. The wash coating is a very thin coating of shellac or lacquer sealer that leaves the pores open so that filler can be added. A good sealer for many stains is a wash coat of white shellac that is a mixture of seven parts alcohol to one part of four-pound-cut shellac. Lacquer sealers are frequently used for wash coating when the final finish is to be spray lacquer.

Filling

Fillers add color and close the pores of wood. Closed-grained woods with very small pores such as pine, cherry, poplar, fir, and cedar require no filler. Others such as birch, gum, and maple may take a liquid filler. Open-grained woods, particularly oak, mahogany, and walnut, require a paste filler. With these woods, the filler is sometimes eliminated to give the wood an open-pore appearance. For blond finishes, the filler can be zinc oxide or a natural paste that is a light color in oil.

Sealing or Wash Coating

A sealer or wash coat is applied over the filler to prevent color from bleeding into the finish. A good sealer for most finishes is a shellac

wash coat. If a lacquer finish is to be applied, a lacquer sealer can be used in place of the wash coat of shellac.

Glazing

Glazing is the application of a coat of thin, transparent finishing material over filler or sealer to give a highlighted, shaded, or antique effect. This is used most frequently in the finer finishes. To antique by glazing, thoroughly wipe off the glaze from the flat surfaces and edges that should appear worn, and leave the glaze in the recessed areas.

Topcoating

A varnish, synthetic, or lacquer finish can be applied as topcoat after all coloring and filling have been completed.

Rubbing, Polishing, and Cleaning

After the topcoat is on, the surface is rubbed, polished, and waxed to a high sheen.

FINISHING OPEN-GRAINED WOOD

The following are the usual steps in producing a fine finish on mahog-

any, walnut, oak, and other open-grained woods. For a lighter or honey-toned finish, it is necessary to bleach the wood before starting the finishing process. For medium to darker finishes, this procedure should be followed:

1. Apply a thin glue size mixed in water (one part hide glue to five parts water). Allow to dry. The purpose of the glue size is to make sure the thin, hairlike wood fibers are held down or held up so that they will be removed when sanded. Sand the surface well with 3/0 (120) garnet paper. Clean thoroughly with a tack rag.

2. Apply water stain and allow it to dry thoroughly. Sand lightly with 3/0 (120) garnet paper.

3. Apply a wash coat of shellac or lacquer sealer. Allow it to dry three to four hours. Then sand the surface with 5/0 (180) garnet paper.

4. Apply a colored filler with a brush. Rub across grain with a circular motion, forcing the filler into the pores. Then wipe across grain with burlap to remove excess filler. Next wipe along the grain with a fine cloth, using a light stroke to even up the surface. Allow it to dry overnight.

5. Apply a sealer coat of shellac or lacquer, allow to dry, and sand with 6/0 (220) or 7/0 (240) garnet paper.

6. A glaze can be applied over the sealer to give a highlighted, shaded, or antique effect. This step is not necessary for Contemporary or Modern finishes.

7. Apply three coats of lacquer with sufficient drying time between each coat. Sand lightly.

8. Rub to a light sheen with pumice stone and water or paraffin oil.

9. Rub with a good paste wax and polish.

COMMERICAL SYNTHETIC FINISHES

Many commerical finishes can be

DRYING TIMES

Material	Touch	Recoat
Lacquer	1–10 min.	1½–3 hrs.
Lacquer Sealer	1–10 min.	30–45 min.
Paste Wood Filler	. . .	24–48 hrs.
Water Stain	1 hr.	12 hrs.
Oil Stain	1 hr.	24 hrs.
Spirit Stain	Zero	10 min.
Shading Stain	Zero	Zero
Non-Grain-Raising Stain	15 min.	3 hrs.
NGR Stain (Quick Dry)[1]	2 min.	15 min.
Pigment Oil Stain	1 hr.	12 hrs.
Pigment Oil Stain (Q.D.)[2]	1 hr.	3 hrs.
Shellac	15 min.	2 hrs.
Shellac (Wash Coat)	2 min.	30 min.
Varnish	1½ hrs.	18–24 hrs.
Varnish (Q.D. Synthetic)	½ hr.	4 hrs.

[1]NGR = non-grain-raising.
[2]Q.D. = quick dry.

Courtesy of Practical Builder

57-3(b). *Average drying times for finishing materials. Different products vary somewhat from these figures.*

57-4. *Here you see the difference between a penetrating finish and a surface finish. Most simplified finishes are penetrating, while standard finishes are of the surface type.*

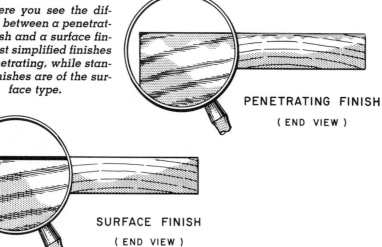

PENETRATING FINISH

(END VIEW)

SURFACE FINISH

(END VIEW)

used in the shop with little difficulty. Most of these soak into the wood. Fig. 57-4. Such finishes do away with the dust problem that is so bothersome when using varnish.

Sealacell

This three-step process involves three different materials, each of which can be applied with a rag or cloth. The materials include the following:

• *Sealacell*, a moisture-repellent, penetrating wood sealer, is applied over the raw wood. (Ground-in-oil pigments can be mixed with the Sealacell to serve as a stain). Stain and filler can be applied in one step by mixing paste filler in the Sealacell and then adding ground-in-oil pigment to get the right color. Apply very liberally with a cloth, as the depth of penetration depends on the amount applied. Let dry overnight. Buff lightly with fine steel wool.

• *Varno wax* is a blend of gums and waxes. To apply, make a small cloth pad about 1″ × 2″. Coat with wax and rub with a circular motion first, then wipe out with the grain. Buff lightly with 3/0 steel wool.

• *Royal Finish* is the final coat. It is applied in the same manner as the Varno wax. Two or more applica-tions of Royal Finish increase the depth of luster. A soft eggshell (slightly glossy) finish can be obtained by buffing with fine steel wool.

Minwax

Minwax is a penetrating wood seal and wax that is applied directly to raw wood. Two coats will complete the job. The natural beauty of the wood is preserved because this finish penetrates and seals, leaving the finish in the wood, with very little on the surface. Minwax is available natural as well as colored. It dries rapidly, and more than one coat can be applied in one day. Although it isn't necessary to rub between coats, it is a good idea to use 4/0 steel wool to obtain a very fine finish.

Deft

Deft is a semigloss, clear, interior wood finish. It is easy to use, requires no thinning, will not show brush marks, and will not darken. This material seals, primes, and finishes the wood, and it dries in 30 minutes. Three coats are recommended. The first coat seals the wood, the second adds depth, and the third results in a mirror-smooth, fine furniture finish. The third coat can be sanded with 6/0 wet-dry sandpaper or rubbed mirror-smooth with pumice and rottenstone. All three coats can be applied in a few hours. Deft can also be applied from an aerosol spray can.

Watco Danish Oil Finish

This super-penetrating oil finish consists of oils and resins which are used for natural wood furniture and interiors. It seals, primes, finishes, and preserves wood in a single application. After penetrating the wood surface, it actually combines with it chemically. Fig. 57-5. Ideal for fast simple finishes, Watco oil finish dries to a flat, natural appearance. The finish is particularly recommended for walnut, teak, and rosewood. The process is relatively simple:

1. Finish sand the wood surface with 6/0 (220) garnet paper. Make sure the surface is clean and dry. If necessary, stain and fill the wood surface, using oil-paste fillers mixed with the oil-finishing material. A ready-mix wood stain can also be applied under the oil finish.

2. Apply the wood oil liberally, flooding and saturating the surface. This can be done with a brush or by

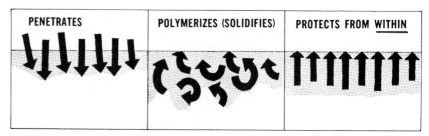

PENETRATES	POLYMERIZES (SOLIDIFIES)	PROTECTS FROM WITHIN

57-5. *A chemical action takes place when the material is applied.*

spraying. Keep the surface wet for 15 to 30 minutes to assure penetration and saturation.

3. While the surface is wet, scuff-sand with 6/0 wet-dry, silicon-carbide paper, keeping it well lubricated with the oil. One or two minutes of wet sanding is usually enough.

4. Remove all surplus oil with a soft, lint-free cloth. Allow to dry about 12 hours or overnight.

5. Wipe lightly with an oil-dampened rag. Wipe dry and buff with a soft cloth. If desired, a liquid carnauba satin wax may be applied and buffed to a soft luster.

One major advantage of these finishes is that they can easily be repaired. Simply rub the damaged area with fine steel wool and apply the oil finish.

SYNTHETIC SEALER FINISHES

Many different companies make a penetrating sealer finish that can be used for the entire finishing system. These materials are used only on new or unfinished wood or wood from which the old finish has been completely removed. The sealer finish can be applied with a lint-free cloth or a brush. The final finish gives a "close-to-the-grain" appearance. The sealers are often made in two basic types: light and dark. The color is achieved by adding a tube or package of tinting color. The sealer is then applied with a brush or cloth. Fig. 57-6. Allow a short time for penetration, less than 20 minutes for most woods. If the penetration does not appear uniform before wiping, apply a second coat after the first one dries. Then wipe

off the excess with a clean cloth. As the protective topcoat, the same sealer, without the color, or a clear finish is usually used. When the finish is thoroughly dry, a rich polish can be obtained by buffing with extra-fine steel wool. Wax may be applied.

SIMPLIFIED SHOP FINISHES

There are several fine finishes that do not require special equipment or many commercial materials. Two of these are shellac and natural oil. However, the shellac finish is not a good choice if the wood is to be exposed to moisture because shellac turns cloudy in dampness.

Shellac Finish

White shellac is a clear finish that adds no tone at all. It is particularly good for light, closed-grained woods such as pine, birch, and maple.

1. Go over the surface for final sanding with 5/0 (180) garnet paper.

2. Mix an equal amount of four-pound-cut shellac and alcohol in a glass or procelain container.

3. Apply the shellac evenly with a good-quality 1½" to 2" brush.

4. Allow to dry four hours, and smooth evenly with 4/0 steel wool.

5. Apply three or four thin coats this way, rubbing down between coats.

6. After the final coat, rub down with 4/0 steel wool and apply paste wax. The time needed for shellac to dry depends to some degree on weather conditions.

Oil Finish

Contemporary furniture of walnut or teak is frequently given an oil or

57-6. *Applying the finish with a brush. Allow time for penetration.*

oil-varnish finish to emphasize the beauty of the grain and to preserve the wood. This finish is especially attractive when several coats are applied and rubbed thoroughly. The finish grows slightly darker and richer with time, and additional coats of the same oil can be applied as needed, usually once a year.

1. Use a mixture of two parts boiled linseed oil and one part turpentine *or* equal parts of spar varnish, boiled linseed oil, and turpentine.

2. Place the container with the mixture in boiling water for 10 to 15 minutes to thin the oil properly.

3. Apply the finish by saturating a cloth with the oil and rubbing the entire surface until a uniform color is obtained.

4. Rub small sections of the surface for 10 to 25 minutes at a time. Wipe off the excess with a lint-free cloth.

5. Allow 24 hours between coats. A week to a month later, additional coats can be applied.

58 Staining

Stains provide a rich undertone and bring out the beauty of wood grain. Staining is the first step in the standard finishing process, provided the wood is not bleached.

Changing the kind and color of stain will make the same wood appear entirely different. For example, dark red stain has been widely used in Traditional mahogany furniture. Many people even today think of mahogany as a dark-colored wood. Actually, much Contemporary mahogany furniture is light, honey-toned brown.

Stains can also be used to make a less expensive wood look like a costly one. Gum, for example, is often stained to imitate mahogany.

Stains help to make the color of wood more uniform. Many pieces of furniture have parts made from different kinds of wood, or one species of wood may have variations in color. Because woods do vary, test the stain you want to use on an inconspicuous spot. Then you can make sure you get the color and effect you want. Fig. 58-1.

SAP STAINING

When there is wide variation in wood color, especially between sapwood and heartwood, sap staining should precede regular staining. Use either an alcohol-base sap stain or a water-soluble stain. Apply to the light areas by brushing or spraying. By continuing to apply the stain, you can make the light areas as dark as the rest of the wood. Then standard staining procedures can be followed.

INGREDIENTS IN STAINS

Stain consists of two materials: coloring and vehicle. The coloring matter is either soluble color (aniline dye) or pigment color.

Soluble colors actually dissolve into the solution. When they are applied to wood, they penetrate the pores. Some aniline dyes are made from natural substances such as certain plant and animal extracts. The great majority, however, are modern industrial chemicals obtained from coal tar. Many of these dyes are very similar to fabric dyes used in the textile industry.

Aniline dye stains are usually available in powder form and are soluble in different vehicles: water, alcohol, or lacquer solvents or oil. They are also available premixed in alcohol.

An outstanding feature of dye stains is their clarity. They are more transparent than pigment base stains and will show a better grain pattern.

Pigment colors are finely ground color particles that disperse in the vehicle but do not dissolve. When pigment colors are used as stain, the particles of color remain on the wood surface, giving it a uniform appearance. Pigment colors may also be made from natural materials or have a chemical base. The natural color pigments include iron oxide, yellow oxide, burnt sienna, raw sienna, burnt umber, raw umber, ochre organic pigment, titanium oxide, zinc sulfate, cadmium sulfate yellow, cadmium sulfate orange, lead chromate yellow, and orange chromate.

KINDS OF STAINS

Water Stains

Water stains come in powder form. They are mixed in hot water. From one to eight ounces of powder per gallon of water is used, depend-

58-1. *Differences in color and other irregularities can be eliminated with stains. (A) Pith flecks in basswood are narrow streaks resembling pith. (B) Streaks of different degrees of darkness in oak.*

58-2. *Sanding the surface after sponging. A sanding block is being used to obtain even pressure.*

ing on the color wanted. Generally, the mixture is about four ounces of powder per gallon. Water stains are available in common colors such as brown mahogany, mahogany, orange, green, yellow, golden oak, fumed oak, and red mahogany. Water stains have several important advantages:

• The stain is absorbed by the wood and therefore shows a greater contrast in figure than is possible with other kinds of stains.

• Water stains are easily applied with a brush and do not require expensive equipment.

• Water stains are cheaper than most other stains because they are purchased as dry powder and mixed in water.

• Water stains do not bleach when exposed to light as much as pigment oil stains will.

• Water stains can be darkened by applying a second or third coat if the first is not suitable.

• Water stains dry quickly. Some disadvantages are:

• Water stains swell the wood fibers and raise the grain.

• If several coats must be applied, water stains may have an adverse effect on glue joints.

APPLYING WATER STAINS

Mix a small amount of powder in a gallon of boiling water and test the stain on a piece of scrap wood of the same kind as the product. The color of water stains will appear somewhat darker on larger surfaces than on the small test piece. Therefore it is a good idea to apply a slightly lighter coat than seems necessary.

Before applying the water stain, sponge the surface lightly with water. It may help to add just a little hide glue to the water to hold the surface fibers in place. This should dry four to five hours and then be sanded with 5/0 sandpaper. Fig. 58-2. Always sponge end grain with water before applying the stain to keep it from absorbing too much stain and darkening too much.

Apply the stain evenly with a brush or sponge. Then wipe off the excess with a rag or sponge. Allow to dry overnight. Sand lightly.

Oil Stains

There are two common kinds of oil stain: pigment and penetrating.

PIGMENT-OIL STAINS

Pigment-oil stains are made by adding pigment color to boiled linseed oil and turpentine. Fig. 58-3.

Such stains are usually purchased ready-mixed in a wide variety of colors. These stains are often used in school shops. Advantages of pigment-oil stains are:

• They are available ready-mixed.

• They are easy to apply.

• They do not raise the grain.

• They can be mixed with wood filler to make a combination stain and filler.

Disadvantages:

• Pigment-oil stains are more expensive than water stains.

• They do not penetrate deeply, and therefore they sand off easily.

• They are slow to dry. Pigment-oil stains are best used on wood with small pores, such as birch, gum, beech, and maple. They are also good when the surface has an uneven color.

COMMON COLORS IN OIL (TINTING COLORS)

Lt. Yellow	Light Green
Medium Yellow	Medium Green
Raw Sienna	Dark Green
Burnt Sienna	Blue
White	Toluidine Red
Raw Umber	Deep Red
Burnt Umber	Chrome Orange
Ochre	Lampblack
Orange	

58-3(a). *Common colors that can be used to tint oil stains.*

USING COLORS IN OIL FOR FINISHING

White	Use zinc oxide ground in oil.
Golden Oak	Use white zinc tinted with yellow ochre and raw sienna.
Light Brown	Use Vandyke brown.
Medium Oak	Use raw sienna and burnt sienna.
Dark Brown	Use Vandyke brown and drop black.
Walnut	Use half Vandyke brown and half burnt umber.
Black	Use drop black.

58-3(b). *Sample colors that can be shop-made for finishing.*

To apply pigment-oil stains, sand the surface smooth and wipe free of any dust. Always wipe the surface with a tack rag before applying the stain. Make sure the stain is of the right color and is well stirred so that there is an even distribution of pigment. Brush an even coat of linseed oil onto the end grain to keep it from absorbing too much of the color.

Apply the stain with a soft, clean brush or lint-free cloth. Dip the brush in the stain about one-third its length. Apply even pressure, working with the grain of the wood. Avoid skips or pile-up of stain along the edges.

After the stain has been applied, allow it to dry for a few minutes. Then use a soft, lint-free rag to wipe the stain to "blend" or even up the color and to pick up any excess. Wipe with the grain. If the wood varies greatly in color between sapwood and heartwood, wipe the darker areas more quickly and allow the stain to remain on the lighter areas for a longer time. The longer the pigment-oil stain remains on the wood without wiping, the more it darkens the surface. After the stain has been wiped, allow it to dry overnight before proceeding with the remaining finishing steps.

PENETRATING-OIL STAINS

Penetrating-oil stains are made by mixing soluble dyes in oil. While these stains can be purchased as dry material and then mixed in oil, they are more commonly used in ready-mixed form. Penetrating-oil stains are relatively easy to apply and do not show streaks. They can also be mixed with wood filler to make a combination stain-filler. Penetrating-oil stains are not commonly used with lacquer finish because they tend to bleed through the sealer. Also, they fade in sunlight.

Spirit Stains

Spirit stains are made by dissolving soluble dyes in alcohol. They dry very rapidly but do not penetrate deeply into the wood. Because of their fast-drying action, the second coat needed to produce the darker shades can be applied almost immediately. A difficulty is that spirit stains tend to bleed.

Non-Grain-Raising Stains (NGR)

Non-grain-raising stains, made by mixing aniline dyes in a solution of glycol and alcohol, have all the advantages of water stains without the disadvantages. They are so named because they tend not to raise wood grain. They can be purchased in ready-mixed colors or as a concentrated base color that can be mixed to different shades. These stains have bright, transparent colors and are excellent in sunlight since they do not fade. Another advantage is that they are nonbleeding, especially when lacquer or varnish is used as the top coat. Because it is necessary to apply these stains by spraying, they are used primarily in industrial finishing.

Sealer Stains

Sealer stains, commonly called commercial stains, are really synthetic sealers that can be used both as stains and sealers. Fig. 58-4. They give a "close to the grain" appearance that is partly penetrating and partly surface in nature. Color can be added by mixing in tinting colors from a tube.

TRANSPARENT LACQUER TONERS

Made from dyes and lacquer, these give a combined staining and sealing effect. However, their staining properties are not especially good. They are sometimes used over another stain or a filler to add color.

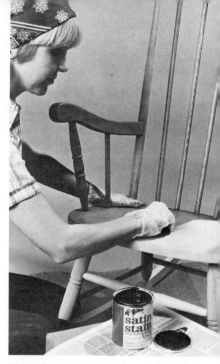

58-4. *Applying a sealer stain with a rag.*

To start, mix enough stain for the entire job. Test for color on scrap wood of the kind to be stained. It is better to apply two light coats of stain than one heavy one. It is much easier to darken the wood than it is to lighten it.

WASH COAT

Wash coating (sealing) is done to keep stain from bleeding, to provide a hard surface for applying filler, and to improve the toughness of the finish. Good sealer for many stains is a wash coat of shellac. This is a mixture of seven parts alcohol to one part of four-pound-cut shellac. In furniture production in which lacquer is used as the final finish, lacquer sealers are used.

A wash coat must be applied very thin so that it doesn't completely fill the pores and prevent the use of fillers. If shellac is used, brush on a light coat and allow it to dry about one hour. If lacquer sealer is sprayed on, it will dry in about half an hour. Next sand lightly with 6/0 or 7/0 sandpaper. Wipe clean. The surface is then ready for filling.

59 Filling and Sealing

FILLING

All woods may be classified as either porous (open-grained) or nonporous (closed-grained). Pine, birch, cherry, and maple are examples of nonporous or semi-porous woods,

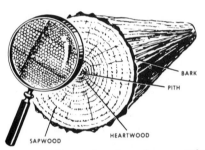

59-1(a). *Many hardwoods contain large vessels and are very porous. When this lumber is surfaced, the tubular cells are ruptured, leaving tiny troughs that run lengthwise.*

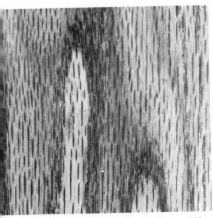

59-1(b). *Unfilled pores make a filler necessary for certain hardwoods. This sample is red oak.*

and they do not require a filler. Oak, ash, walnut, and mahogany are examples of porous woods that do require a filler with a built-up finish. Fig. 59-1. No filler is used with an oil finish since the oil must penetrate the wood surface.

Wood fillers are used in the finishing process for two purposes. They fill and level the pores of the wood, and they add color to the final finish. The filler may be about the same color as the stain; or a lighter filler can be used with a darker stain to achieve a two-toned effect. Fig. 59-2. While application of the filler may seem simple, it can ruin the complete finish if done incorrectly.

Kinds of Fillers

Woods with large pores, such as walnut, mahogany, oak, chestnut, hickory, and ash, require a paste filler. These fillers consist of about 75 percent pigment and 25 percent liquid. The pigment is primarily ground silica and color. The liquid is usually oil. Paste fillers can be purchased in the natural color and then tinted by adding stains or such pigment colors as burnt sienna or raw umber. White and off-white fillers are usually made from titanium oxide mixed with oil and resin.

A liquid filler may be used on birch, maple, gum, or cherry. Liquid fillers can be purchased from commercial sources or made by thinning paste filler with turpentine. While no filler is needed for closed-grained woods such as poplar, fir, pine, and

basswood, it is a good idea to apply a sealer.

Applying Paste Fillers

Add turpentine, benzene, or naphtha to paste filler until it has the consistency of heavy cream. Mix oil color with a little turpentine and then add this to the filler until you

59-2. *A pickled finish is one in which the wood filler contrasts sharply with the basic finish of the wood. For example, an ebony-stained wood might be filled with white paste filler. Can you see the results of pickling in this clock?*

491

59-3(a). *Applying filler with a brush. Brush first with the grain.*

get the color you want. Test on a sample piece that has been stained. Apply the filler with a stiff brush, rubbing it into the pores. Brush both across and with the grain. Fig. 59-3. Rub the filler in with the palm of your hand or with a piece of burlap or a heavy rag. Always add extra filler to end grain.

In applying filler, the idea is to work the paste well into the pores. After it has dried about 30 minutes (until the gloss disappears), rub across the grain with burlap or coarse cloth to remove most of the excess filler. Then, with a fine cloth, wipe very lightly with the grain to make sure the filler is evenly applied.

Remember that the filler must be packed firmly into the pores. Otherwise it may come loose after the topcoat has been applied and ruin the finish. However, do not rub too hard as this would remove some of the filler from the pores. To obtain the best results, the cleaning must be done while the excess is still

soft. To remove extra filler from sharp corners, use a sharpened wood stick covered with a rag. This job must be carefully done so that there is no residue to become hard and dry. Such residue would have to be removed with a rag moistened with turpentine.

Applying Liquid Fillers

Liquid fillers are sometimes used on woods such as birch, beech, cherry, and redwood. If the filler is made from paste, add turpentine until it is very thin. Apply with a brush and follow the same general process as for a paste filler.

Defects in Filling

Several common defects can occur when filler is not applied properly, rubbed in well, and the excess removed. *Pinholing* occurs when air is tamped into an improperly filled pore. After the topcoat has been applied, a bubble of air will show on the surface. *Flow-out* results when a good wash coat has not been applied between the stain and the filler coats. The filler appears to squeeze out of the pores. *Graying* is a condition that often develops after filler has dried for several hours. The surface appears to have a grayish cast. This is usually because the binder has been absorbed by the wood or because the wrong kind of filler has been used. *Bleeding* results when a good sealer coat is not applied over the filler or when the filler is not dry before sealing. It is caused by a mixing of the filler and the sealer.

APPLYING A SEALER

Before the top or finish coats are applied, it is necessary to seal the surface to form a barrier coat over the filler and to provide a good

59-3(b). *Brush across grain, over the first filler coat. Rub into the pores.*

foundation for the topcoats. Even when woods have not been stained and filled (sometimes this is the case with plywood), it is important to have a good sealer on the surface. There are three common kinds of sealers; shellac, lacquer, and synthetic resin. White shellac is an excellent sealer but is not used when lacquer is the finish coat. Shellac sealer is made by mixing one part of four-pound-cut white shellac with seven parts of alcohol. Shellac sealer is applied with a brush. A lacquer sanding sealer is available. It is sprayed on as an undercoat for a lacquer finish. A penetrating resin sealer is a ready-mixed material commonly used on closed-grain and small-pored woods to seal the surface and prevent the wood from absorbing moisture. There are also glazing sealers applied over the filler and before glaze is put on the surface. After a sealer is applied, it should be sanded lightly and then wiped with a tack rag.

There are several overtone treatments that add interest to the finish on a furniture piece or give it an antique appearance. Most of these are done after the filler and sealer are applied and before the final topcoats.

HIGHLIGHTING

To highlight means to purposely make the finish uneven in color. This is done to simulate worn spots caused by frequent use over a period of years. Highlighting is done by wiping off a portion of the stain and/or filler while it is still wet or by using steel wool or sandpaper after it is dry. Fig. 60-1.

DISTRESSING

Provincial furniture is often given a distressed treatment to imitate the appearance of age and wear. Fig.

60-1. *Highlighting gives this washstand an antique look.*

60-2. *The distressed finish of this chest adds to its rustic look.*

60-2. This can be done either mechanically or with a finishing material. In mechanical distressing, coral rock, a chain, a hammer, and many other items can be used to put small gouges, scratches, and dents in the wood surface. These are frequently filled with black glaze or dark stain to imitate wear marks on a genuine antique. Many types of finishing materials such as heavy wax crayons, black paint, or dark stains can be applied or brushed on to add this worn look.

GLAZING

After the filler or sealer is applied, glazing may be done to give a furniture piece a highlighted, shaded, or antique appearance. Glaze can also be applied over a painted or enameled surface. Fig. 60-3. Traditionally, antique glaze was applied over white or ivory enamel. However, the trend is toward a base color coupled with a tinted glaze. There are many

60-3. *This bench-chest illustrates the use of glazing over an undercoat of paint. The colors range from rich terra cotta to light apricot on the raised and smooth surfaces. The full beauty of carved panels can be brought out by glazing.*

60-4. *The antique appearance of this lamp table is due to its finish. Note the imitation wormholes on the drawer and other parts.*

commercial glazing materials. Some are already colored. Others must be tinted with lamp black or other pigments. A simple antique glaze can be made by mixing a tablespoon of burnt umber in one-half pint of pure turpentine, then adding one teaspoon of drop black.

Glazing over a Stain and Filler

The traditional method of glazing furniture that has a transparent finish is to use a light color for the stain and filler. Next a darker glaze is added. This is wiped off except around the edges and in the corners

so that they appear to be worn. A thin glaze coat is sometimes applied over the entire piece to even up the color.

Glazing over a Painted or Enameled Surface

Glazing over a painted or enameled surface gives an antique finish that is two-toned, blended, or shaded. It is achieved by applying a tinted glazing liquid over an enameled base. This finish can be applied to either new or old furniture. The procedure is as follows:

1. Apply an undercoat of either "flat" paint or enamel of the color you want. Two coats are needed for new wood, while one may be enough for a surface already finished. Apply the undercoat generously, but make sure there are no drips or sags. Always brush with the grain. Allow the undercoat to dry thoroughly, at least 24 hours.

2. Mix the glaze thoroughly and tint if necessary. The glaze has a gelatin-like consistency. It will not drip, sag, or run. Brush a thin coat of glaze on the entire surface, making sure indentations and low places are coated. If the furniture piece is large, it is better to apply the glaze in sections and then wipe it off. Allow the glazed surface to "set up" (become slightly tacky). This may take as much as 15 minutes.

3. Wipe off the glazing liquid in several places. Then use a piece of cheesecloth to blend unwiped areas into the wiped ones. Wipe lightly at first, then more heavily in those places where more highlights are wanted (usually the high points of carvings or the center of door pan-

els). Wipe in long, straight lines in the direction of the grain. Paper towels, rags, burlap, and similar materials can be used. Each texture contributes a slightly different effect. Every effort should be made to create the illusion of wear by blending; that is, having one coat of finish show through another.

4. After the glaze is completely dry (allow at least 24 hours) additional highlighting can be done mechanically. Fine sandpaper (No. 280) can be used to highlight certain areas, such as the centers of panels. Always leave a heavy glaze near the edges. Gently "feather" the edges of highlight so that there won't be an abrupt or obvious line between the highlighting and shading. Steel wool can also be used to highlight rounded or carved surfaces. For a heavy, durable finish, a topcoat must be applied over the glazed surface.

OTHER TREATMENTS

Shading is done by adding a darker stain, sealer, or glaze around the edges and in corners. *Spattering* is a method of adding a speckled texture to the surface by flipping a glaze or other finishing material off the end of a stiff brush. This process also imparts an antique appearance. When applying this, bend the bristles with your fingers or a stick to get the spring action that throws the spray. To avoid blobs of finishing material, do not overload the brush. To be effective, spattering must not be overdone. *Imitation wormholes*, to give the impression of antique furniture, can be made by spattering. Fig. 60-4.

61 Protective Coatings

To protect a fine wood product, it must be given a good finish. Fig. 61-1. The two principal types of finishing systems in use today are the oil type and the built-up type. The oil type is a penetrating finish that is very popular on today's Contemporary furniture, shelving units, and stereo systems. With this kind of material, the result is a smooth, satin finish. It is very easy to apply and pleasing in appearance and touch. There are many oil finishes available. Chapter 57 discusses several of these penetrating finishes.

A built-up finish leaves a film of material on the surface of the wood. Built-up finishes include such popular topcoats as lacquer, varnish, and polyurethane.

One of the main advantages of using a built-up finish is that it will afford more protection than an oil finish. If a piece that has been finished with oil is scratched, the wood itself will also be scratched. With a built-up surface finish, the damage will be to the surface film, not the wood. On the other hand, oil finishes are usually easier to repair than varnish or polyurethane.

LACQUER

Lacquer is commonly defined as any finishing material that dries quickly by evaporation to form a protective film on a wood surface. Because they are fast-drying, lacquers are used primarily for high production. Usually they have fewer solids than varnishes do, and they require more coats to achieve a sufficient buildup. Lacquers are usually applied by spraying.

Production of Lacquer

In industry, about 80 percent of all laquers are of the nitrocellulose type. Cellulose can be obtained from wood. However, most of the cellulose used in making lacquers comes from cotton. Cellulose must be made soluble by various acid treatments. The resulting substance, nitrocellulose, will dissolve in various chemical solvents. When lacquer is sprayed on a surface, the solvents evaporate, leaving a thin film of nitrocellulose and other additives.

By itself, nitrocellulose is rather hard and tough but not very elastic. For this reason, other things are added, such as plasticizers, resins, and oil. Plasticizers increase the elasticity of nitrocellulose. Resins and oils give more body.

By using different additives and solvents, many kinds of lacquers are produced. Lacquer should be carefully selected by studying the description supplied by the manufacturer. It should be used just as it comes from the container. The only thing that may be added is lacquer thinner *made by the same manufacturer.* Don't mix lacquers or use a different brand of thinner.

The most common lacquer top-

61-1. *While good materials, attractive design, and quality work are important, they are not enough. A fine product, such as this cabinet, must be given a good protective finish.*

coat for the school or cabinet shop is a cold-spraying variety made with 20 to 30 percent solids. It is water-white and semigloss. Clear lacquers that have more than about 25 percent solids tend not to spray easily. If the lacquer contains too many solids and is sprayed cold, it may not atomize (break up into fine particles) properly, resulting in orange-peel defect. The best spraying lacquer is one that contains a proper balance of solids for good coverage and liquids for free flow-out.

Advantages and Disadvantages

Some common advantages of lacquer finishes are:

• Lacquers are fast-drying. Therefore several coats can be applied in a short time. It is not necessary to have special drying equipment.

• A lacquer coating is thin and clear. This is well suited to Contemporary styles that require a close-to-the-wood appearance. Fig. 61-2.

• Damage in lacquer finishes is easy to repair.

• Lacquer finishes have good durability. They are relatively high in resistance to damage by water, beverages, and food.

• They do not get soft and tacky

61-2. *This mahogany end table with inlay top has a lacquer finish.*

when exposed to extreme temperatures.

• They are easy to rub, polish, and wax.

Some common disadvantages of lacquer finishes are:

• Lacquers are not highly resistant to such substances as nail polish and perfume.

• Excessive moisture (such as in a bathroom) may cause the lacquer to peel off the wood. Also, white water spots may develop.

• Lacquers dry so rapidly that it is very difficult to apply them with a brush.

• Lacquers are not as tough as some of the newer synthetic finishes.

Kinds of Lacquers

Since lacquers are made from such a wide variety of formulas, it is important to be very specific when ordering the kind needed for each furniture finish. Some lacquers are primarily for use on metals, while others are for wood only. Never apply a metal lacquer over wood since it may check badly. Also, some lacquers are meant for brushing; others for spraying.

Wood spraying lacquers are sold in a variety of sheens ranging from full gloss to flat. The three usually kept in stock are gloss, semigloss, and flat. However, the final sheen of a lacquer coat can be changed greatly by the amount of rubbing and polishing done after application. There is a lacquer wood sealer made especially for applying a sealer coat over filler before spraying on the lacquer. Most lacquers are clear, although there are also colored lacquers.

Applying a Spray Lacquer Finish

Spraying is the most common industrial method of applying a lacquer finish. It is best to do this in a spray booth. Spraying can be done out of doors on a calm day, but a

mask must be worn. For more thorough discussions of spraying equipment, see Chapter 56.

1. Clean the surface first with a tack rag.

2. Check the spray gun to make sure it is clean.

3. Use enough lacquer to make the spray container about half full. If the spraying equipment is of small capacity and low pressure, the lacquer must be thinned with about 50 percent lacquer thinner. With larger capacity equipment, the lacquer can be used just as it comes from the container.

4. Try the spray gun on a piece of scrap stock. It should spray with a fine, even mist. Hold the gun about 6" to 8" from the work and move back and forth with straight, uniform strokes. Always keep the gun perpendicular to the surface. Start the stroke off the work and pull the trigger when the gun is just opposite the edge. Release the trigger at the other end. Spray on four or five thin coats of lacquer. Sand lightly between coats. Usually the first coats are gloss or bright and the last coats are made dull or semigloss by rubbing. After you have finished spraying, clean all equipment with lacquer thinner.

Applying a Clear, Brushing Lacquer Finish

1. Apply the stain and filler coats the same as you would for shellac and varnish finishes. It is better to use a water stain than an oil stain because it won't bleed so much. Apply a thin coat of lacquer sealer before using the lacquer.

2. Open a can of clear, brushing lacquer and stir it well. Lacquer usually does not have to be thinned. If it does, use lacquer thinner of the same brand. Select a brush with soft bristles such as a camel's-hair brush. Dip it about one-third of the way into the lacquer, but do not wipe it on the side of the container. Load the brush heavily. Apply with

long, rapid strokes. Lap the sides of each stroke. Do not attempt to brush the lacquer in as you would paint or varnish. Remember that lacquer dries very quickly and gives a smooth, tough surface.

3. Allow the lacquer to dry about two hours. Then go over the surface lightly with No. 6/0 sandpaper.

4. Apply second and third coats in the same way. After the third coat is dry, rub and polish the surface.

VARNISH

Varnishes were at one time the mainstay of furniture finishing. However, because most of them are slow-drying and their color retention is not good, varnishes have been largely replaced by lacquer. They are still used to some extent in school and small cabinet shops, and they are often used in home workshops. Their slow drying makes it extremely important to apply them in a very clean, dust-free place.

Oleoresinous varnishes are made from vegetable drying oils such as linseed or tung oils combined with resins. (*Oleoresinous* means a combination of oil and resin.) The original resins used in these varnishes were natural, but today most of them are synthetic. Tung oil (wipe-on) varnishes are a combination of tung oil and various other materials. Tung oil comes from the nut of the tung tree, which grows in China and neighboring countries. Tung oil varnish is quick-drying and water-resistant. It is available under many brand names.

The great advantage of varnish is that it is relatively low in cost. It contains from 45 to 50 percent solids and can be reduced with an inexpensive thinner. Varnishes are easy to apply and have good coverage. When dry, they are tough and quite durable. They are high in water resistance, and some are excellent for exterior uses.

Applying Varnish

Varnishing should be done in a well-ventilated room and at a temperature of 65°F or more. When using a brush, make sure it is clean and of good quality. Some wood finishers prefer a foam polybrush since it reduces the chance of bubbling. The result is a thin, smooth coat of varnish. Some varnishes are wiped on with a clean, lint-free cloth.

Stir the varnish before using, but do not shake it. Apply the varnish evenly and liberally, stroking across the grain first. Follow immediately with light strokes *with the grain* and always in the same direction. Finish a small area at a time and proceed quickly before the edges have a chance to set. Go from the drier area into the wet area. Do not try to touch up spots that may be partially dry.

On wood that has been stained, filled, and coated, or previously varnished, apply one or two coats of selected varnish without thinning. On new or unfinished wood, thin the first coat of varnish with mineral spirits or turpentine, one pint spirits or turpentine to one gallon of varnish. The second coat should not be thinned. Allow each coat to harden thoroughly, normally from six to eight hours. Sand lightly with very fine sandpaper before recoating.

SYNTHETICS

In a sense, almost all finishing materials can be considered synthetics, since they are made in whole or in part from manufactured chemicals. However, the term *synthetic* is especially applied to some of the newer finishes, such as epoxies, polyurethanes, and polyesters.

You may have noticed that some of these finishes have the same names as adhesives mentioned in Chapter 40. As a matter of fact, these basic chemical substances (which are really a part of the plastics industry) are used as adhesives, finishes, structural materials, and

61-3. *Applying a wipe-on polyurethane topcoat.*

for still other purposes. For example, various forms of epoxy are used for adhesives, furniture-protective coatings, production tools in furniture manufacture, and plastic laminate construction.

The most popular of the synthetic finishes is polyurethane. Liquid polyurethane is closer to being a true plastic than any other synthetic finish. Polyurethane is extremely durable. It is the hardest and toughest finish available. However, some brands are harder than others. The finish is also quite brittle. These characteristics make it difficult to sand. Polyurethane is not as flexible as conventional varnishes. Flexibility would be a factor where there might be frequent changes in humidity, resulting in contraction and expansion of the wood.

Polyurethane can be applied with a brush or a lint-free cloth. Fig. 61-3. It dries quickly to a clear finish. Here are some hints for applying this material:

● Most finishes don't require shaking or stirring. Doing so produces air bubbles that can affect the finish. Satin finishes, however, usually require a gentle stirring. Check the label to be sure.

• If you are using a brush, make sure it is perfectly clean and of good quality. Nylon or natural bristles are preferable. If you are using a cloth, select clean, lint-free material such as an old T-shirt.

• Always "flow on" the finish. Dip the brush into the can, but do not wipe it off on the side. Let the excess drip off. Then brush it on the wood. This method prevents air bubbles from forming, both in the can and on the surface.

• After applying the finish, make the final brush strokes long, even, and with the grain across the entire surface.

• When you are through, leave the room and close the door. Foot traffic and air circulation stir up the dust in the room.

RUBBING, POLISHING, AND CLEANING

After the topcoat is dry, the surface should be rubbed, polished, and cleaned to provide a sheen and additional protective coating. These steps are done only for varnish or lacquer finishes, not for polyurethane. The time between the application of the last topcoat and these final operations depends on the finishing materials used. If a lacquer finish is applied, the final rubbing and polishing can be done almost immediately, although it is best to allow the lacquer to dry from one to four hours. If the surface has been varnished, at least a week should be allowed for it to dry thoroughly.

Equipment needed for rubbing, polishing, and cleaning includes wet-dry abrasive paper, pumice, rottenstone, and waxes. Abrasive manufacturers make various commercial rubbing and polishing compounds for these operations. They also make many different cleaners and polishes for final work.

Rubbing is done to smooth the surface and to remove irregularities that may have developed during finishing. It is done with abrasive paper and lubricant. The lubricant is important because it keeps the paper from filling up with material rubbed off the surface.

Polishing is a burnishing action that removes or blends together fine scratch patterns. Polishing requires extremely fine abrasives such as pumice or rottenstone and some kind of lubricant such as oil or water. A felt pad is attached to a machine or to a wood block to do the polishing.

Cleaning removes from the surface all foreign matter that resulted from rubbing and polishing. This is usually done with a detergent-moistened cloth. Cleaning is usually followed by waxing and/or polishing. Many waxes and polishes contain water-repellent silicones which provide excellent protection for a fine finish. They give a clean, dry surface when wiped with a dry, lint-free cloth.

Finishing Methods

Topcoats are sanded to remove "orange peel" and any foreign matter from a surface before producing a satin or luster finish. It is common practice to do this sanding with wet-dry sandpaper, a straight-line or reciprocating sander, and lubricant or rubbing oil. It can also be done with an air-operated, reciprocating machine or by hand. Whether the rubbing operations should be done with only a single grade of abrasive paper or a sequence of grades depends on such factors as the hardness of the surface, the speed with which the operation must be completed, and the desired quality of finish. If several grades of paper are to be used, grade 280 should be used first. Then use progressively finer papers including grades 300, 400, and 500. Grades 360 to 500 should be used for the final rubbing.

Dull satin finish. To obtain a dull satin finish, first rub by hand with grade 360 to 400 wet-dry sandpaper. Then apply a good coat of furniture cleaner and polish.

Period satin finish. To produce a satin finish for period furniture, first rub with grade 360 to 400 wet-dry sandpaper. Follow this by polishing with a slurry (mixture) of pumice and oil. As a final step, apply a furniture cleaner and polish or wax.

High-sheen satin finish. To obtain a high-sheen satin finish, rub with grade 500 wet-dry sandpaper. Follow by polishing with a slurry of rubbing oil and fine pumice (FF or FFF) and then rottenstone and rubbing oil.

Deep-luster finish. To obtain a deep-luster finish, do the final rubbing with grade 500 wet-dry sandpaper. Then use a deep-pile buffer to remove all scratches and bring the surface to a mirrorlike finish. Clean with lamb's wool. As the final step, polish with furniture cleaner.

Here are two other simple methods of rubbing, polishing, and cleaning a surface after topcoats have been applied.

• Make a paste consisting of FFF pumice and rubbing oil or water. Rub with the grain, applying medium pressure. Fig. 61-4. A felt pad

61-4. *Rubbing down a surface by hand with pumice and water, using a felt pad.*

is best for this. Continue to rub until the surface is very smooth. Then wipe the surface clean with a dry cloth. Make another slurry of powdered rottenstone and rubbing oil, and repeat the rubbing process.

Wipe dry with a cloth and then apply a wax coat.
● Rub the surface with water and grade 400 wet-dry sandpaper, sanding with the grain and applying medium pressure. Then wipe the sur-

face clean. Rub the surface with a commercial polishing compound or with rottenstone or oil mixture. Finally, apply paste or liquid furniture wax.

Section V
QUESTIONS AND DISCUSSION TOPICS

Chapter 55
1. What are mill marks?
2. Should excess glue be sanded off? Why or why not?
3. Describe three methods of repairing a dent or crack in wood.
4. What is the purpose of bleaching wood?
5. Describe one method of sanding wood to prepare it for finishing.

Chapter 56
1. What is the purpose of an air compressor?
2. What does an air transformer do?
3. For spraying lacquer, should you use an internal or an external mix gun?
4. Describe two kinds of spray booths.
5. What is "orange peel" and what causes it?

Chapter 57
1. List the steps in a standard finishing system.
2. What is the purpose of a wash coat?
3. List the steps in applying a shellac finish.
4. Describe how to mix a simple oil finish.

Chapter 58
1. What is the purpose of staining?
2. Why is sap staining sometimes necessary?
3. What is the difference between soluble color and pigment color?
4. Name four advantages of water stains.

5. Compare the advantages and disadvantages of oil stains and water stains.
6. What are sealer stains?

Chapter 59
1. What types of wood require a filler?
2. What is the purpose of wood filler?
3. Describe how to apply paste filler.
4. Describe four common defects that can result when filler is applied incorrectly.
5. What is the purpose of a sealer?

Chapter 60
1. What is highlighting?
2. How is furniture given a distressed finish?
3. What is a glaze and why is it used?
4. How is spattering done?

Chapter 61
1. Name the two principal types of finishing systems.
2. What is lacquer and how is it made?
3. What are the advantages and disadvantages of lacquer?
4. What are the advantages and disadvantages of varnish?
5. What is the difference between rubbing and polishing? Name some of the materials used for rubbing and polishing.

PROBLEMS AND ACTIVITIES

1. Cut test panels from one kind of wood and apply several different finishes. Compare the results.
2. Study the use of chemicals for bleaches on wood and write a report.
3. Compare the advantages and disadvantages of varnish and lacquer when used for topcoating.

4. Investigate the chemical composition of a finishing material used by one of the large furniture manufacturers.

Index